ENCYCLOPEDIA OF AMERICAN MILITARY HISTORY

ENCYCLOPEDIA OF AMERICAN MILITARY HISTORY

VOLUME III
P TO Z

Spencer C. Tucker, General Editor

ASSOCIATE EDITORS
David Coffey
John C. Fredriksen
Justin D. Murphy

Facts On File, Inc.

Encyclopedia of American Military History

Facts On File, Inc.
132 West 31st Street
New York NY 10001

Library of Congress Cataloging-in-Publication Data

Encyclopedia of American military history / Spencer C. Tucker, general editor ;
associate editors David Coffey, John C. Fredriksen, Justin D. Murphy.
    p. cm.
    Includes bibliographical references and index.
    ISBN 0-8160-4355-8 (set)—ISBN 0-8160-4352-3 (vol. 1) —
    ISBN 0-8160-4353-1 (vol. 2) — ISBN 0-8160-4354-X (vol. 3)
    1. United States—History, Military—Encyclopedias. I. Tucker, Spencer, 1937–

E181 .E63 2003
355′.00973′03—dc21   2002029658

Facts On File books are available at special discounts when purchased in bulk
quantities for businesses, associations, institutions or sales promotions. Please call our
Special Sales Department in New York at (212) 967-8800 or (800) 322-8755.

You can find Facts On File on the World Wide Web at http://www.factsonfile.com

Text design by Joan M. Toro
Cover illustration by Nora Wertz
Cover design by Cathy Rincon
Maps by Dale Williams and Jeremy Eagle

Printed in the United States of America

VB TB 10 9 8 7 6 5 4 3 2 1

This book is printed on acid-free paper.

Contents

List of Entries

ENTRIES
P TO Z

P

pacifism/war resistance *Opposition to warfare and the military*

Since colonial times many Americans have adhered to pacifism—a refusal to bear arms based on moral or religious considerations. In addition, most conflicts in American history have encountered political opposition, and widespread public fears that a "standing army" threatened liberty created a deep suspicion of the military.

During the colonial and revolutionary periods war resistance came primarily from Christian pacifists who were attracted to America by religious freedom. Most prominent was the Society of Friends, commonly known as the Quakers, who founded Pennsylvania in 1680. In contrast to other colonies, Pennsylvania sought amicable relations with neighboring Indians and steadfastly refused to create a militia until the FRENCH AND INDIAN WAR (1754–63).

In other colonies, pacifists typically refused to participate in militia musters, pay taxes for war, or maintain fortifications. As early as 1673, Rhode Island passed a law that exempted conscientious objectors from military service; by the time of independence, all the states had enacted similar provisions. Pacifists on occasion, however, incurred the ire of their fellow citizens. In some cases pacifists were beaten and jailed for refusing to bear arms or were forced into military service against their will.

The emergence of America's first national peace organizations was closely linked to social reform crusades of the early 19th century, most notably the antislavery movement. Pacifists, both religious and secular, developed an ethic of direct action and nonviolent opposition to war. Philosopher Henry David Thoreau's essay *On Civil Disobedience,* written during the MEXICAN-AMERICAN WAR, became a classic of antiwar and protest literature. The 19th-century peace movement had but limited success. Although activists resisted and protested the war with Mexico, they failed to significantly influence American war policy.

During the Civil War many pacifists abandoned their views and backed the war to end slavery. Initial draft laws during that conflict did not exempt members of peace churches from military service. Not until 1864 did the federal government allow conscientious objectors to perform alternative service. Confederate draft laws later exempted members of peace churches, but the desperate need for troops often led to an erosion of such provisions.

Seldom have Americans gone to war united, and most conflicts have generated concerted political resistance. During the War of 1812 Federalists in the Northeast opposed America's war effort so strenuously that some called for the dissolution and reformation of the Union to exclude the western states. During the Mexican-American War, antislavery politicians in the Whig and the Democratic parties spoke out fervently against a conflict they believed was being waged to gain new territories for slaveholders. The Civil War spawned political opposition in both the Union and the Confederate states. Most notable among Civil War protests were the draft riots that broke out in the North in 1863. New York City experienced the most destructive of these, in which more than 100 people died.

America's rise to world power at the dawn of the 20th century led to protest against military involvement overseas. The Anti-Imperialist League, founded in 1898, spearheaded a powerful political movement against expansionism that included such notables as William Jennings Bryan, Andrew Carnegie, and Carl Schurz.

American entry into World War I sparked both pacifistic and political opposition, resulting in vigorous government efforts to suppress dissent. Many pacifists were inducted forcibly into the military; those who refused to cooperate frequently were harassed, beaten, court-martialed, and jailed. The Espionage and Sedition Acts curbed freedom of speech and the press. The government spied upon and often jailed socialists and other left-wing war opponents. To enforce support for the war, the federal government embarked on a massive propaganda campaign spearheaded by the Committee on Public

Information. So-called superpatriots staged vigilante attacks against people suspected of disloyalty. Antiwar sentiment during World War I was kept in check, but largely through coercion.

World War II was remarkably different. Because the nation had been attacked, political opposition to the war was minimal. Harassment of conscientious objectors was much less common, and most found opportunities to perform noncombat service.

Expanded U.S. military commitments during the COLD WAR led to a corresponding increase in peace activities. Although the anticommunist hysteria of the 1950s minimized overt opposition to the KOREAN WAR, the VIETNAM WAR of the 1960s and 1970s saw an explosion of antiwar protest. Millions of Americans viewed the war as unjust and morally wrong because they believed that the United States was endeavoring to put down a peasant nationalist movement. The brutal realities of the war, broadcast nightly on American television, further inflamed public sentiments. Religious pacifists, most notably Dr. Martin Luther King, Jr., spoke out against the Vietnam War. College campuses experienced countless antiwar protests, which by 1968 had grown violent. By the 1970s, Vietnam War soldiers and veterans had become prominent in the peace movement, and the lack of public support for the war limited U.S. military options in Vietnam.

The peace movement saw mixed results in the last quarter of the 20th century. The largest peace protest in American history occurred in New York City in 1982, when 800,000 people marched to oppose President Ronald Reagan's expansion of America's nuclear arsenal. However, during the 1991 Gulf War the movement was divided, dispirited, and ineffective in influencing public opinion toward the war.

Pacifism and war resistance have had a varied impact on American history. Never have peace movements been responsible for ending U.S. involvement in a war. However, in some cases the peace movement has affected public opinion, limited the options of political and military leaders, and impacted military policy.

Further reading: Curti, Merle. *The American Peace Crusade, 1815–1860.* New York: Octagon Books, 1973; Kohn, Stephen Martin. *Jailed For Peace: The History of American Draft Law Violators.* Westport, Conn.: Greenwood Press, 1986; Morison, Samuel Eliot, Frederick Merk, and Frank Friedel. *Dissent in Three American Wars.* Cambridge, Mass.: Harvard University Press, 1970; Wittner, Lawrence S. *Rebels Against War: The American Peace Movement, 1933–1983.* Philadelphia: Temple University Press, 1984.

— Mark D. Van Ells

Palmer, John M. (1870–1944) *U.S. Army general, longtime advocate of universal military training*
Born on 23 April 1870 at Carlinville, Illinois, John McAuley Palmer graduated from the U.S. Military Academy, WEST POINT, in 1892. His early military career included riot control duty associated with the 1894 Chicago PULLMAN STRIKE, Indian frontier service, occupation duty in Cuba, participation in the 1900 BOXER UPRISING relief expedition, teaching at West Point, and two years (1906–08) as civil governor of the Philippine Lanao District in Mindanao. While studying at the Command and General Staff College, Fort Leavenworth, Palmer became firm friends with rising young military officer George C. MARSHALL. Assigned to the General Staff under chief of staff Major General Leonard WOOD and Secretary of War Henry L. STIMSON, Palmer suggested a reorganization of the army on the basis of tactical units rather than company-sized frontier posts. In 1911 Palmer rejoined his unit, the 15th Infantry Regiment, then serving in Tianjin, China, as part of a post–Boxer Uprising international peacekeeping garrison. Promoted to major, he transferred to the 24th Infantry Regiment in Manila, and in 1916 returned to the General Staff.

As American intervention in WORLD WAR I seemed increasingly likely, Palmer formulated plans for potential American mobilization while advising the civilian PLATTSBURG MOVEMENT, which sought to introduce universal military training. He contributed to its journal, *National Service.* After America entered the war, Palmer helped to write the 1917 Draft Act.

Accompanying General John J. PERSHING, commander of the AMERICAN EXPEDITIONARY FORCES (AEF), to France as assistant chief of staff for operations, Palmer was responsible for formulating overall strategy for victory over Germany. He suffered a brief breakdown from overwork; after recovery, Palmer, now a colonel, commanded the 58th Infantry Brigade of the 29th Division in its successful late 1918 attack on the Hindenburg line at Verdun, an experience that, together with his work for Pershing on staff officer training schools, convinced him that National Guard citizen-soldiers could fight effectively.

After the armistice Pershing sent Palmer to Washington to give Congress his views on army organization, which he did clearly, rationally, and comprehensively, subsequently drafting much of the 1920 National Defense Act. Palmer proposed universal military training, which Congress and army chief of staff General Peyton C. MARCH rejected, and other measures that overall allowed civilian elements, including the National Guard, to constitute significant components of the American military. When Pershing became chief of staff in 1921, Palmer became his personal assistant, spending his final four years in Panama before retiring in 1926 as a brigadier general.

In retirement, Palmer wrote prolifically on civilian military training and service, and after the start of World War II, he helped to draft and lobbied for the SELECTIVE SERVICE Act of 1940. Shortly before the Japanese attack on PEARL HARBOR, Marshall, now chief of staff, recalled Palmer to active duty to advise on reserve forces. His advocacy of a strong, highly trained, and well-organized reserve was ultimately successful, although Congress refused to endorse the proposals for universal military training that Palmer incorporated into Marshall's final report. The U.S. Army's oldest serving officer, Palmer finally retired in September 1946. He died at Washington, D.C., on 26 October 1955.

See also MILITARY TRAINING CAMPS ASSOCIATION.

Further reading: Clifford, J. Garry. *The Citizen Soldiers: The Plattsburg Training Camp Movement, 1913–1920.* Lexington: University Press of Kentucky, 1972; Clifford, J. Garry, and Samuel R. Spencer. *The First Peacetime Draft.* Lawrence: University Press of Kansas, 1986; Holley, I. B., Jr. *General John M. Palmer: Citizen Soldiers and the Army of a Democracy.* Westport, Conn.: Greenwood Press, 1982; Palmer, John McAuley. *America in Arms: The Experience of the United States with Military Organization.* New Haven: Yale University Press, 1941.

— Priscilla Roberts

Palo Alto, Battle of (8 May 1846) *First battle of the 1846–48 Mexican-American War*
In January 1846 President James K. Polk ordered Brigadier General Zachary TAYLOR, in command of the U.S. Army of Occupation at Corpus Christi, Texas, to advance his force to the Rio Grande. Relations between the United States and Mexico had soured after Texas was annexed to the United States, and Taylor had been ordered to the region the previous year to deter a Mexican invasion. After Polk learned that his latest diplomatic effort to solve the crisis had failed, he ordered Taylor forward, perhaps to pressure Mexico into negotiations.

Taylor had 4,300 men at Corpus Christi, and they departed for the Rio Grande on 8 March 1846. Once he reached the Rio Grande, Taylor established a supply depot at Point Isabel on the Gulf of Mexico and began to construct a stronghold, which he named Fort Texas, opposite Matamoros. The Mexican government ordered Division General Mariano Arista to take command of the Army of the North and attack Taylor's force.

Arista took up a blocking position near the Point Isabel–Matamoros road and sent a portion of his force to lay siege to Fort Texas. The two armies met on 8 May at Palo Alto, a prairie dotted with tall mesquite, high, stiff grass, and marshy depressions. Although outnumbered,

Taylor planned to assault Arista's force, which was deployed in a line astride the road. At 2:30 P.M. Mexican artillery opened fire on the U.S. force, and batteries under the command of Brevet Major Samuel Ringgold and Captain James Duncan dashed forward and engaged the Mexican line. Oxen hauled two 18-pounder cannon into place to join the light batteries. U.S. artillery savaged the Mexican troops, who were forced to stand and endure the punishment. Mexican attempts to take the offensive with cavalry and infantry assaults were hampered by the terrain and effective American artillery fire and defensive tactics. Late in the afternoon, Duncan was able to place his battery in position to enfilade the Mexican right, causing the Mexican troops briefly to break line, although Arista and other officers were able to stop the exodus and restore order. At 7:00 P.M. Arista was out of artillery ammunition and withdrew his forces from the field.

This tactical American victory was a triumph for WEST POINT–educated officers such as Samuel Ringgold and for military reforms that had created the highly mobile light artillery. Ringgold was killed in the engagement and became a national martyr.

See also MEXICAN-AMERICAN WAR, CAUSES OF.

Further reading: Bauer, K. Jack. *Zachary Taylor: Soldier, Planter, Statesman of the Old South.* Baton Rouge: Louisiana State University Press, 1985; Haecker, Charles M., and Jeffrey G. Mauck. *On the Prairie of Palo Alto: Historical Archaeology of the U.S.-Mexican War Battlefield.* College Station: Texas A&M University Press, 1997.

— Dan Monroe

Palo Duro Canyon, Battle of   See RED RIVER WAR.

Panama invasion (20 December 1989–3 January 1990) *U.S. invasion of Panama to remove General Manuel Noriega from power*
Panama's history is distinct in Latin America in that after independence from Colombia in 1903, secured in large part with U.S. assistance, Panama had a strong American military presence. The purpose of this presence was to protect the new Panama Canal and the zone around it, ceded by Panama to the United States.

Panama's own security forces never played a large role in its national political life, at least until the 1940s. When José Antonio Remón took over the National Police, he changed its name to the National Guard and reorganized it along the lines of a regular military establishment. Remón, who later became president, followed policies that were both nationalistic and anti-American, as did subsequent Panamanian strongmen such as Arnulfo Arias and Omar

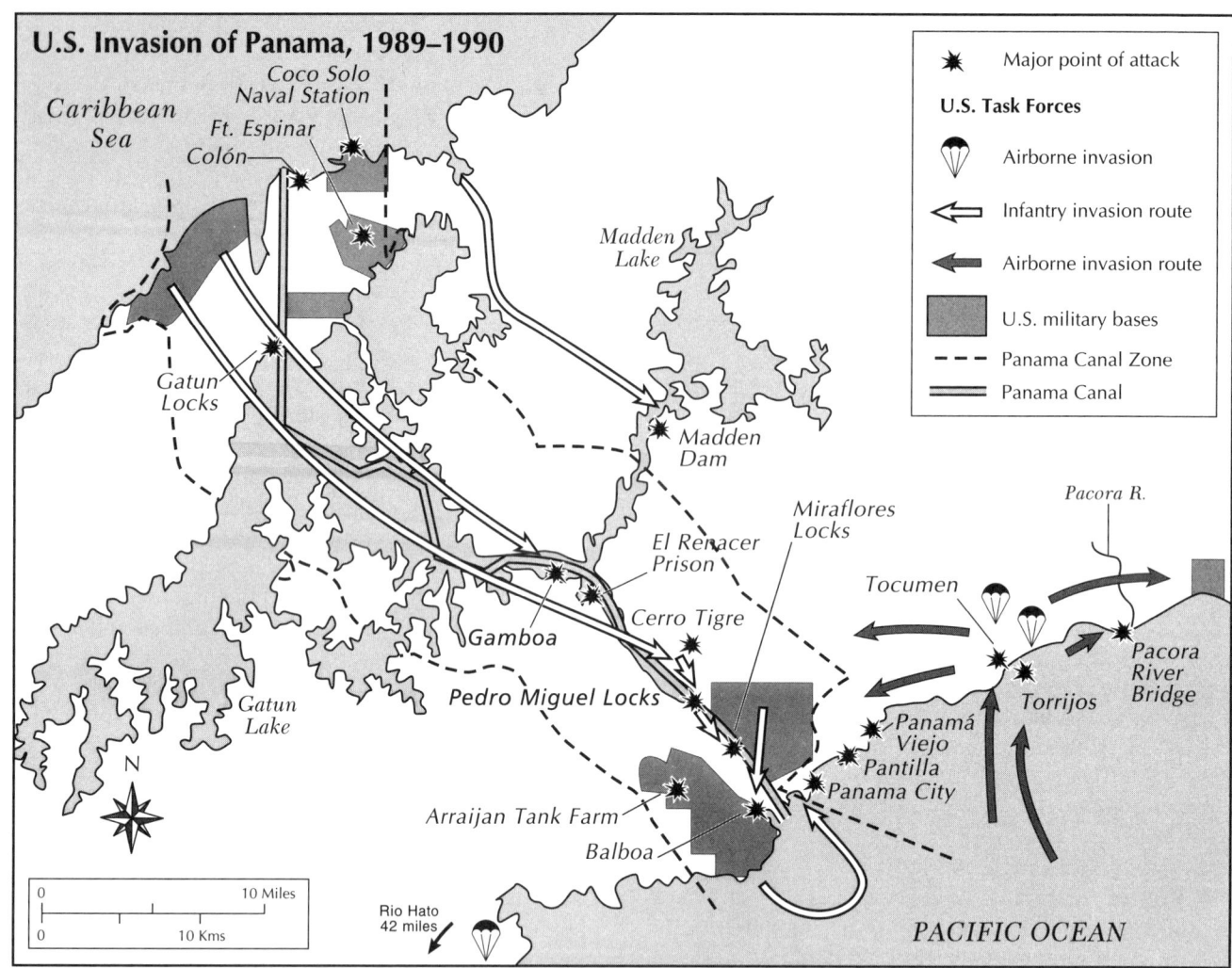

U.S. Invasion of Panama, 1989–1990

Torrijos. These leaders continually called for Panamanian sovereignty over the canal. Over the years, they were successful in negotiating canal treaties more favorable to Panamanian interests, but the canal continued under U.S. control. While their rhetoric was anti-American, none of these Panamanian leaders used the National Guard to threaten U.S. military or civilians in Panama.

In 1977 Torrijos, at the time head of the National Guard, and the power behind Panama's government, signed a treaty with President Jimmy Carter's administration that called for the United States to turn over the canal to Panama at the end of 1999. Two years after Torrijos's death in 1981, Colonel Manuel Antonio Noriega emerged as Panama's strongman. His regime became increasingly dictatorial and corrupt, and Noriega renamed the National Guard the Panamanian Defense Force (PDF) and used it to intimidate the Panamanian people and, eventually, to threaten U.S. citizens. The regime was involved in assassination and drug and arms trafficking.

Noriega, who earlier had been an intelligence asset for the United States, also began to confront Washington, especially after his 1988 indictment in Florida for drug trafficking. The following year Noriega overturned the results of a democratic election and allowed the PDF to harass U.S. military personnel stationed in Panama. This antagonism resulted in a U.S. embargo and diplomatic pressure from Washington to force Noriega from power. The failure of these efforts, the killing of a Marine officer in Panama City, and the beating of a U.S. Navy officer by the PDF finally led to President George H. W. BUSH's decision to invade Panama and remove the Noriega regime.

The military name for the Panama invasion was Operation Just Cause. Its objectives were to protect American lives and property, to capture Noriega and turn him over to U.S. authorities, and to bring down the PDF. Washington also planned to replace Noriega with the democratically elected government of Guillermo Endara and to build a new Panamanian security force.

Bush gave overall operational command of Just Cause to General Maxwell Thurman, commander in chief of the U.S. Southern Command. Lieutenant General Carl Stiner commanded the task force that carried out the operation. The task force consisted of more than 26,000 soldiers, airmen, sailors, and marines deployed from multiple locations in the United States and Panama. Launched on the early morning of 20 December 1989, attacks were directed against 27 separate targets in Panama.

Just Cause was an operational and tactical success. It also saw the first use of the F-117 Stealth fighters. Within days, all ground objectives were secured; on 24 December, Noriega surrendered to the Papal Nunciature, and on 3 January he turned himself in to U.S. authorities. By this time, the PDF was virtually eliminated as a serious threat. Early in the operation, the Endara government was sworn in at a U.S. military base in Panama. The goal of establishing a civilian police force—a more difficult task—was accomplished several months later under the supervision of civilian advisers contracted for by the U.S. Department of Justice. Twenty-three U.S. servicemen were killed in action during Operation Just Cause. Panamanian losses were much heavier.

Operation Just Cause answered skeptics who had criticized the U.S. military after the 1983 invasion of GRENADA (Operation Urgent Fury) for the failure of the services to work together in joint operations. Just Cause was a vast improvement over Urgent Fury. It demonstrated that the 1986 Goldwater-Nichols Act had been a success. Under this act, Congress gave more authority to the chairman of the Joint Chiefs of Staff and to the warfighting, or "unified," commanders in the conduct of effective joint operations.

Nonetheless, events over the next decade led to continuing estrangement between the United States and Panama. Despite attempts by Washington to negotiate an agreement with Panama to retain military bases from which to conduct counterdrug operations, no agreement could be reached. One reason cited for this was that after 1994 Noriega's political party gained control of the government and a vocal minority of its members remained strongly anti-U.S. and fought any attempt to allow a U.S. presence in the country. Also, by most accounts Panama continued in the 1990s as a transshipment country for cocaine and other illegal drugs moving from South America to the United States, and as a drug-money laundering center.

Further reading: Baker, Caleb, Thomas Donnelly, and Margaret Roth. *Operation Just Cause: The Storming of Panama.* New York: Lexington Books, 1991; McConnell, Malcolm. *Just Cause: The Real Story of America's High-Tech Invasion of Panama.* New York: St. Martin's Press, 1991; Tsouras, Peter G., and Bruce W. Watson, eds. *Operation Just Cause: The U.S. Intervention in Panama.* Boulder, Colo.: Westview Press, 1991.

— Paul Coe Clark, Jr.

Panay incident (12 December 1937) *Incident in which the U.S. Navy patrol river gunboat* Panay *was sunk by Japanese aircraft*

The *Panay,* a flat-bottom craft built in Shanghai, China, specifically for river duty, was launched in November 1927. Named for an island in the Philippines, *Panay* (PR-5) was commissioned in September 1928 and served as part of the navy's Yangtze Patrol in the Asiatic Fleet, responsible for patrolling the river and protecting American lives and property.

Following the start of the Second Sino-Japanese War in the summer of 1937, Japanese forces moved on the city of Nanjing (Nanking) in December. The *Panay* evacuated remaining Americans from the city on 11 December 1937, bringing the number of people on board to 5 officers, 54 seamen, 4 embassy staff, and 10 civilians. The following day, while upstream from Nanjing, the *Panay* and three Standard Oil tankers—*Mei Ping, Mei An, and Mei Hsia*—came under attack from Japanese aircraft ordered to strike all ships on the Yangtze above Nanking. Although the *Panay* was flying flags that clearly identified it as a U.S. Navy vessel, Japanese naval planes attacked at 1:27 P.M., causing it to sink at 3:54 P.M. The attacks left three dead, and 43 sailors and five civilians wounded. The survivors were later taken aboard the USS *Oahu* and HMS *Ladybird.*

Washington formally protested the attack, and the Japanese later made a formal apology. Tokyo continued to maintain, however, that the attacks were unintentional. U.S. radio intercepts indicated otherwise. Tokyo subsequently paid an indemnity of $2,214,007.36 to the United States on 22 April 1938, officially settling the *Panay* incident.

See also WORLD WAR II, CAUSES OF U.S. ENTRY.

Further reading: Perry, Hamilton Darby. *The Panay Incident: Prelude to Pearl Harbor.* New York: Macmillan, 1969; Tolley, Kemp. *Yangtze Patrol: The U.S. Navy in China.* Annapolis, Md.: Naval Institute Press, 1971; U.S. Navy Department, Navy History Division. *Dictionary of American Naval Fighting Ships.* Vol. 5. Washington, D.C.: Government Printing Office, 1970.

— Trevor K. Plante

Panmunjom armistice negotiations (1951–1953)
Armistice negotiations to end the Korean War

In early July 1951 a series of meetings began between the principal belligerents of the KOREAN WAR that would last two years. Delegations from the People's Republic of China

(Communist China), Democratic People's Republic of Korea (DPRK, North Korea), Republic of Korea (ROK, South Korea) and the United States and its United Nations Command (UNC) coalition allies met initially in the village of Kaesong, a former Korean capital. In October the talks moved to the nearby village of Panmunjom, located near the 38th parallel, six miles from Kaesong and about 30 miles northwest of Seoul.

UNC commander Lieutenant General Matthew B. RIDGWAY selected Commander, Naval Forces, Far East, Vice Admiral C. Turner JOY to head the United Nations military delegation to the talks. DPRK president Kim Il Sung and senior Chinese military commander Marshal Peng Dehuai (Peng Teh-huai) were the key decision makers on the Communist side, although they were not part of the negotiating delegation at the talks.

The major areas of contention were the exact locations of the military demarcation line and demilitarized zone, the return and exchange of prisoners, and the removal of foreign troops from Korea. In addition, ROK president Syngman Rhee disapproved of any solution that divided the country. At Kaesong a workable agenda was agreed on in late July, but military operations, troop deployments, training activities, and logistical preparations continued on both sides. Major fighting resumed in August 1951, but in late October a second round of talks began at the new site of Panmunjom.

War and talk continued over the next two years, with neither side gaining any significant advantage on the battlefield or at the conference table. UNC forces held a significant advantage in air power and controlled the seas, inflicting a heavy price on the North Koreans and the Chinese for their continued intransigence at the conference table. Both sides reached agreement on the other issues, including establishment of a demilitarized zone to separate the two sides. The sticking point in the talks centered on prisoner repatriation. The Communist side insisted on involuntary repatriation. Many Chinese and North Koreans did not wish to return home, and the problem was complicated by the forced incorporation into Communist forces of many South Koreans. The UNC position embraced voluntary repatriation.

Finally, on 27 July 1953, following trying and frustrating negotiations and very bitter and costly offensives and counteroffensives by both sides, an armistice to end the first major conflict of the COLD WAR was signed by Chinese, American, and North Korean representatives. The thorny issue of prisoner repatriation was solved with the establishment of a neutral commission to interview the prisoners individually and allow them to choose. This Committee for Reparation of Prisoners of War worked directly for the Military Armistice Commission (MAC), established by the armistice agreement. In addition, a Neutral Nations Supervisory Commission (Sweden, Switzerland, Poland, and Czechoslovakia) and subsequent inspection teams were established to supervise, observe, inspect, and investigate and report activities and violations to the MAC. The armistice called for a military demarcation line and demilitarized zone, and it outlined arrangements to carry out the complex cessation of hostilities and redeployment of forces. The MAC included Joint Observer Teams to "supervise implementation" and "settle through negotiations any violations." Article IV of the agreement called for a future "political conference" to discuss the withdrawal of foreign forces and, ultimately, a peace accord.

No final peace treaty to end the war in Korea has been signed, and major U.S. forces continue to be stationed in Korea. Panmunjom, located in the Demilitarized Zone, continues as the site of Military Armistice Commission meetings.

Further reading: Hermes, Walter G. *U.S. Army in the Korean War: Truce Tent and Fighting Front.* Washington, D.C.: U.S. Government Printing Office, 1966.

— J. G. D. Babb

Paoli, Battle of (21 September 1777) *Battle of the American Revolutionary War, near Paoli Tavern, northwest of Philadelphia*

Following his defeat at the Battle of BRANDYWINE on 11 September, Continental army commander General George WASHINGTON withdrew in order to recover before again attempting to halt the British march on Philadelphia. As Washington moved the main army to counter Major General William Howe's feints toward the capital, he ordered Brigadier General Anthony WAYNE with 1,500 men and four cannon to remain behind and attack the British rearguard and baggage train. Believing his presence a secret, Wayne quartered his troops near Paoli Tavern, only four miles from British lines, and planned to attack on 21 September. Apprised of Wayne's position by Tory sympathizers, however, Howe ordered Major General Charles Grey to attack the exposed Continentals.

As darkness fell on the night of 20 September, Grey's column, comprising the 2d Battalion Light Infantry, the 42d and 44th Regiments of Foot, and 13 troopers of the 16th Dragoons, supported by Lieutenant Colonel Thomas Musgrave's 40th and 55th Regiments, secretly marched toward Wayne's encampment. To prevent accidental discharge and premature discovery, Grey ordered all muskets unloaded and the attack conducted by bayonet only. Those soldiers unable to draw their charges from their muskets struck the flints from them instead, earning the British general the nickname of "No Flint" Grey.

Wayne was not ignorant of a potential attack. Around 9:00 P.M. Morgan Jones, the father of Wayne's chaplain and a local resident, brought secondhand intelligence of the impending British assault. Wayne immediately increased his picket force of four men by two and posted mounted vedettes (mounted sentinels) to watch local roads. At 11:00 P.M. Grey's screen of riflemen and light infantry encountered a vedette nearly a mile from Wayne's position.

Warned by his sentry's shot, Wayne formed his men. Lacking information on the British position, he ordered his left flank to withdraw as he assembled a covering force on his right. Grey's redcoats quickly overwhelmed the American pickets and discovered Wayne's soldiers, silhouetted by their campfires, attempting to form a defense. After delivering a single volley, the American covering force was swept into a confused retreat by Grey's vigorous bayonet charge, which ended only when the British general thought it prudent to consolidate his force and withdraw.

The disparity in casualties attests to Grey's success. While the British suffered only three dead and seven wounded, Wayne lost 150–200 dead (all by bayonet) and another 71 captured. Although Wayne managed to bring off his artillery, he did lose from eight to 10 loaded wagons, their teams, and 1,000 muskets.

"Wayne's Affair" quickly became an issue of personal honor and propaganda. Seething at challenges to his honor, Wayne demanded a court martial, which exonerated him of all wrongdoing but left him with a desperate need to prove his courage and prowess. In rebel eyes, the action at Paoli became a massacre, serving as both anti-British propaganda and a rallying cry at the Battle of GERMANTOWN two weeks later.

See also AMERICAN REVOLUTIONARY WAR, LAND OVERVIEW.

Further reading: McGuire, Thomas J. *Battle of Paoli.* Mechanicsburg, Pa.: Stackpole Books, 2000; Nelson, Paul David. *Anthony Wayne: Soldier of the Early Republic.* Bloomington: Indiana University Press, 1985; Rankin, Hugh F. "Anthony Wayne: Military Romanticist," in *George Washington's Generals.* Edited by George Athan Billias. New York: William Morrow, 1964, 260–90.

— David M. Corlett

Papua New Guinea (November 1942–January 1943)

World War II Pacific campaign

The arrival of General Douglas MACARTHUR in Australia on 17 March 1942 marked a new phase of war in the Pacific: the deployment of U.S. troops to halt the Japanese advance. MacArthur envisaged Papua New Guinea as the best site from which to defend Australia.

The May 1942 Battle of the CORAL SEA thwarted a planned Japanese amphibious assault against Port Moresby on the Papua New Guinea southeast coast. Following their June defeat in the Battle of MIDWAY, the Japanese landed

troops under Major General Tomitaro Horii at Basabua, on the northeast coast, on 22 July. The Japanese hoped to take Port Moresby by an overland crossing of the rugged Owen Stanley Mountains. At the end of August 1942 another Japanese force, which had landed at Milne Bay, was evacuated after an unsuccessful attack on the Australian and American defenders of Milne Force. The main Japanese force then withdrew over the infamous Kokoda trail toward BUNA for possible redeployment on Guadalcanal.

MacArthur then seized the initiative and launched a three-pronged attack on 1 October, involving Major General Edwin Harding's 32d Division and the Australian 7th Division. A lack of jungle experience, the tropical climate, disease, and the difficult terrain all seriously hindered the Allied offensive. By November the Japanese had retreated into a beachhead along the northern coast, encompassing the villages of Buna and Gona. The 6,500 defenders utilized the jungle to conceal numerous bunkers.

An Allied attack on 16 November failed to dislodge the Japanese. The 32d struggled on without armor or air support, while exhaustion, malnutrition, and disease all took an alarming toll. A further push on 5 December also failed, although the 126th Infantry Regiment and Australian troops managed to occupy Gona village at the western end of the beachhead. Meanwhile, the Japanese landed reinforcements and supplies at their remaining foothold at Sanananda and Buna Mission. The 128th Infantry Regiment, assisted by M-3 light tanks of two fresh Australian battalions, again assaulted these areas on 18 December. Advancing along two fronts, desperate fighting ensued, and by 28 December only Sanananda remained in Japanese hands.

Remaining pockets of Japanese resistance were eliminated by 22 January 1943, thanks to assistance provided by the newly arrived 162d Infantry Regiment of the 41st Division. The Papua campaign had cost the two U.S. divisions 671 men killed and an additional 10,879 casualties.

The Japanese had not abandoned New Guinea, and supplies from Rabual still reached positions west of Buna. In September 1943 the Allies launched an offensive to remove the Japanese from the northwestern part of the country. A combined U.S.-Australian force landed near Lae on 4 September, while U.S. Army paratroops captured Nadzab the following day in the first American airborne operation in the Pacific theater. Salamua fell on 11 September and Finschhafen on 2 October. Allied troops continued to fight in the jungle along the Huon Peninsula before it was declared secure in February 1944.

See also WORLD WAR II, COURSE OF U.S. INVOLVEMENT: PACIFIC.

Further reading: Mayo, Lida. *Bloody Buna.* New York: Doubleday, 1974; Milnes, Samuel. *Victory in Papua.*

Washington, D.C.: Department of the Army, 1957; U.S. War Department, General Staff. *Papuan Campaign. The Buna-Sanananda Operation: 16 November 1942–23 January 1943.* Washington, D.C.: Historical Division, War Department, 1945.

— David M. Green

Paris, Treaty of (10 February 1763) *Peace treaty that concluded the 1754–63 French and Indian War (and the 1756–63 Seven Years' War in Europe), removing France from North America*

The Treaty of Paris brought fundamental changes to the imperial balance in North America as well as territorial changes in Africa, Asia, and South America. By far the most significant change was France's cession of Acadia, Cape Breton Island, Canada, and all territory east of the Mississippi River (except New Orleans) to Great Britain. In return, the French retained their fishing rights off Newfoundland and received the small islands of St. Pierre and Miquelon off Canada. In the West Indies, France retained Guadeloupe and Martinique and acquired St. Lucia. France restored Minorca in the Mediterranean and St. Vincent, Dominica, and Tobago in the Caribbean to Great Britain, agreed to evacuate Hanover, and ceded Senegal to Great Britain. Great Britain restored Belle Isle and Gorée to France, both of which were vital for the French slave trade, and returned French trade stations, which had to remain unfortified, in Bengal and on the Malabar and Coromandel coasts of India. Great Britain agreed to return Cuba to Spain in exchange for both East and West Florida (excluding New Orleans).

In order to gain Spain's acceptance of the loss of Florida, France had granted Spain the Louisiana Territory and New Orleans in the 3 November 1762 Treaty of San Ildefonso. In addition, Spain surrendered its claims to fishing rights off Newfoundland, granted England logging rights in Honduras, and renewed all commercial treaties with Great Britain, included the *asiento* (the right to supply African slaves to the Spanish colonies).

See also FRENCH AND INDIAN WAR.

Further reading: Anderson, Fred. *Crucible of War: The Seven Years' War and the Fate of Empire in British North America, 1754–1766.* New York: Knopf, 2000; Dorn, Walter L. *Competition for Empire, 1740–1763.* New York: Harper & Row, 1963.

— Justin D. Murphy

Paris, Treaty of (30 November 1782) *Peace treaty that concluded the American Revolutionary War*

In the aftermath of the American victory at YORKTOWN in October 1781, Lord North was forced to resign as prime minister (20 March 1782), clearing the way for a new "peace" ministry headed by Lord Rockingham and including Charles James Fox and the earl of Shelburne. The new British ministry immediately dispatched Richard Oswald to Paris to begin negotiations with Benjamin Franklin. Although the Franco-American Alliance prohibited separate negotiations, Franklin and his associates John Jay, Henry Laurens, and John Adams feared that the French and their Spanish ally were prepared to allow the war to drag on in order to gain British territory.

After Rockingham's death and Shelburne's appointment as prime minister, the British cabinet empowered Oswald to negotiate terms with the Americans. The preliminary articles signed on 30 November 1782 recognized the independence of the United States and defined its borders to the territory south of the Great Lakes, east of the Mississippi River, and north of the 31st parallel. The British also recognized American fishing rights off the Grand Banks of Newfoundland. Other provisions were less clear. Both sides validated the debts owed to creditors, but provided no means to enforce payment. The United States promised to "recommend" that states restore Loyalist lands. The British vowed to evacuate the northwestern forts "with all convenient speed." Failure to implement these latter provisions hampered relations between the two nations and ultimately were not resolved until Jay's Treaty in 1795.

Confronted with a fait accompli in the preliminary articles, the French and Spanish eventually agreed to the terms in the final articles signed on 3 September 1783. Spain regained Florida and France secured Senegal and Tobago.

See also AMERICAN REVOLUTIONARY WAR, CAUSES OF; AMERICAN REVOLUTIONARY WAR: LAND OVERVIEW; AMERICAN REVOLUTIONARY WAR: NAVAL OVERVIEW; FRANCE AND THE AMERICAN REVOLUTION.

Further reading: Alden, John Richard. *The American Revolution, 1775–1783.* New York: Harper & Row, 1954; Black, Jeremy. *War for America: The Fight for Independence, 1775–1783.* Stroud, England: Alan Sutton, 1991.

— Justin D. Murphy

Paris, Treaty of (10 December 1898) *Peace treaty that concluded the Spanish-American War*

Following its defeat at SANTIAGO, the Spanish government requested (through the French ambassador to the United States, Jules Cambon) that Washington provide its terms for peace. Preliminary discussions produced a protocol on 12 August by which the United States and Spain agreed to hold negotiations in Paris on the following terms: Cuban independence; U.S. acquisition of Puerto Rico and one of the Ladrone Islands; and U.S. occupation of MANILA, pending a final settlement. President William McKinley then appointed a peace commission consisting of Senators William P. Frye, Cushman K. Davis, and George Gray, *New York Tribune* publisher Whitelaw Reid, and former secretary of state William R. Day. Although the United States had previously declared that it was fighting solely for the liberation of Cuba, McKinley and all of the commissioners except Gray firmly supported annexation of the Philippines. McKinley was motivated by fears that Germany, Great Britain, or France would annex the Philippines if the United States left them alone, and by the belief that the Filipinos were unready for self-government.

On 1 November the American delegation formally presented its demand for all of the Philippines, and after one month of deliberations Spain reluctantly agreed to the terms of the treaty, which was signed on 10 December. Under its provisions, Spain ceded the Philippines to the United States in exchange for $10 million. Spain relinquished control of Cuba and assumed $400 million in Cuban debt, and it ceded Puerto Rico and Guam to the United States as an indemnity.

Even before the terms of the treaty were known in the United States, critics had formed the Anti-Imperialist League, denouncing the annexation of the Philippines as a violation of American democratic values. Its membership included such luminaries as former president Grover Cleveland, labor leader Samuel Gompers, and steel magnate Andrew Carnegie. After intense debate, the Senate ratified the treaty on 6 February 1899, by a vote of 57 to 27 (one vote more than the necessary two-thirds). Senator August O. Bacon's amendment to guarantee Philippine independence as soon as a stable government was formed failed after Vice President Garret A. Hobart cast a tie-breaking vote. As a result of the treaty, the United States became a world power with overseas territories. The treaty terms also set up the subsequent confrontation with Japan.

See also SPANISH-AMERICAN WAR.

Further reading: Faulkner, Harold U. *Politics, Reform, and Expansion, 1890–1900.* New York: Harper & Row, 1959; O'Toole, G. J. A. *The Spanish War: An American Epic, 1898.* New York: W. W. Norton, 1984.

— Justin D. Murphy

Paris accords (27 January 1973) *Agreement signed by the United States, the Republic of Vietnam (South Vietnam), the Democratic Republic of Vietnam (North Vietnam), and the Provisional Revolutionary Government (Communist front organization in South Vietnam) nominally ending the Vietnam War*

Four years of negotiations in both open and secret sessions had produced nothing of substance, agreement always foundering on Hanoi's insistence that the United States withdraw support from the government in South Vietnam as a condition of any pact. This the United States steadfastly refused to do.

Washington, for its part, had long sought to include mutual withdrawal of U.S. and North Vietnamese forces from South Vietnam in any agreement. The North Vietnamese rejected this, disingenuously maintaining against all evidence that they had no forces in the South to begin with.

In the autumn of 1972 both sides modified their demands, North Vietnam accepting continued existence of the South Vietnamese government and the United States tacitly agreeing to the continued presence of North Vietnamese troops in the South. The resulting agreement called for a cease-fire in place throughout South Vietnam, withdrawal of all remaining U.S. troops, and the release of prisoners of war throughout Indochina. North Vietnam was prohibited from infiltrating additional troops and matériel into the South, and it agreed to withdraw its forces from Laos and Cambodia and to refrain from using the territory of those countries for military action against South Vietnam. Military movement across the 17th parallel was banned, and international supervisory elements were prescribed to monitor compliance with terms of the agreement.

The Republic of Vietnam had viewed the December agreement with apprehension, particularly as the agreement was silent on the large number of Communist forces within South Vietnam's borders while requiring all U.S. and other allies to withdraw completely. President Nguyen Van Thieu ultimately refused to sign it, and Hanoi then promptly published its terms. President Richard M. NIXON sought some modifications to placate Thieu, but the North refused, claiming with some justification that an agreement had already been reached. Nixon then initiated a massive bombing of North Vietnam. The so-called Christmas bombing of December 1972 brought Hanoi back to the negotiating table in Paris and led to a few cosmetic changes in the agreement. To induce Thieu's acquiescence, Nixon made repeated pledges of continued American support and of military retaliation should Hanoi violate the agreement.

The Paris accords, formally designated the Agreement on Ending the War and Restoring Peace in Vietnam, were signed in Paris on 27 January 1973. All U.S. personnel held as prisoners of war were released by 27 March and the last U.S. forces departed South Vietnam a day later.

Within days of its signing the North Vietnamese began systematic violations of the agreement. Embroiled in the Watergate scandal, the Nixon administration failed to respond as it had promised the South Vietnamese it would. When the U.S. Congress scaled back dramatically the promised logistical and financial support, while North Vietnam's patrons substantially increased support to their client, the war's eventual outcome was no longer in doubt. The Paris accords, achieved after so much military and diplomatic effort, were ultimately revealed as unenforceable and irrelevant.

See also KISSINGER, HENRY; LINEBACKER II; VIETNAM WAR.

Further reading: Kissinger, Henry. *Years of Upheaval.* Boston: Little, Brown, 1982; Nixon, Richard M. *RN: The Memoirs of Richard Nixon.* New York: Grosset & Dunlap, 1973.

— Lewis Sorley

Paris peace settlement (1919) *Peace settlement following World War I*

In January 1919 representatives of the Allied governments met at Paris to hammer out peace treaties with the Central Powers. Eventually there were five treaties, all named for Paris suburbs: Versailles (with Germany); St. Germain-en-Laye (with Austria); Trianon (with Hungary); Neuilly (with Bulgaria); and Sèvres (with Turkey).

Many Germans claimed that an armistice implied a negotiated settlement between equals, but the Allies did not intend this any more than had the Germans with Russia at Brest-Litovsk in March 1918. Twenty-seven countries—Russia was a notable absentee—sent delegations to Paris. Most important decisions of the conference were reached by the Big Three: U.S. President Woodrow WILSON, British Prime Minister David Lloyd George, and French Premier Georges Clemenceau. The British and Americans stood together on most major issues, and Wilson was the key figure of the conference.

Although Wilson sought to recast Europe's boundaries along "clearly recognizable lines of nationality," his chief interest at Paris was establishing an international organization to promote peaceful settlement of future disputes. On his insistence, it was taken up first. France wanted a league with mandatory membership and its own independent military force, but the Anglo-Saxon powers got their way; the League of Nations was entirely voluntary and emphasized the rule of law and peaceful settlement of disputes. Its strongest enforcement weapon was economic sanctions. One problem with the League, as Clemenceau pointed out, was that many people assumed it was a cure for the world's security problems.

Clemenceau's chief concern was French security. While Wilson and Lloyd George agreed to the restoration of Alsace and Lorraine to France and compensation of coal production of the Saar basin to France for 15 years because of deliberate German destruction of French mines, they balked at Clemenceau's demand for a separate Rhineland state or states under permanent Allied military occupation. In March 1919 they pledged to guarantee France's eastern border if Clemenceau would drop his demand for an independent Rhineland. Thereafter the Rhineland was to be permanently demilitarized, along with the right (east) bank of the Rhine to a depth of 50 kilometers (about 30 miles). The British would occupy for five years a northern zone around the Rhine bridgehead at Köln (Cologne), the Americans a center zone at Koblenz (Coblenz) for 10 years, and the French a southern zone with its Rhine crossing at Mainz for 15 years. Belgium received two small border enclaves.

Italy's northern frontier was another difficult problem. Italy received the Austrian Tyrol and territory along the Adriatic, but Italians were unhappy with what they believed were meager gains. In eastern Europe, Estonia, Latvia, and Lithuania became independent, the result of the desire of the West to contain the spread of Russian communism. Poland was a difficult problem to resolve. Prompted by the large number of Polish voters in the United States, Wilson had made "a free and independent Poland with access to the sea" one of his Fourteen Points. France also sought a strong Poland to help contain Germany. The "Polish Corridor," however, cut off East Prussia from the remainder of Germany, and the matter of Poland's eastern border led to war with Russia.

Two other new states also appeared in central Europe: Czechoslovakia and Yugoslavia. Romania, an Allied power, was greatly enlarged, in part to block communism. Austria shrank to a small homogeneous state and Hungary lost two-thirds of its prewar territory. Bulgaria also had to give up territory. Turkey lost its non-Turkish populations, with France receiving a mandate over Syria (and Lebanon) and Britain obtaining Iraq and Palestine.

One of the bitterest controversies of the peace settlement concerned the reparations issue. Article 231 of the Treaty of Versailles, which blamed the war on Germany and its allies, was its justification. British election politics, meanwhile, drove up the amount by adding pensions. In 1921 reparations were finally set at $33 billion.

Another controversy concerned the size and nature of the German military. Germany emerged with a 100,000-man all-volunteer force serving 12-year enlistments. Germany could have no air force, no tanks, and no heavy artillery, and its navy was sharply limited, with no submarines.

The ink was barely dry on the signatures to the treaties when the wartime alliance of France, Britain, and the United States collapsed. The U.S. Senate rejected the settlement and retreated into isolation. Britain then declared itself no longer bound by the Anglo-American Treaty of Guarantee and returned to a policy of noninterference in Continental matters. This left France alone to enforce the Treaty of Versailles. But with Germany half again as populous as France, and much stronger economically, enforcement was really up to the Germans themselves. The Versailles treaty was badly flawed, but in the end it was not a matter of whether the Treaty of Versailles was too harsh or too lenient. The settlement failed because it was not enforced.

See also WASHINGTON AND LONDON NAVAL AGREEMENTS.

Further reading: Czernin, Ferdinand. *Versailles 1919. The Forces, Events and Personalities that Shaped the Treaty.* New York: Putnam, 1964; Mee, Charles L., Jr. *The End of Order: Versailles 1919.* New York: Dutton, 1980; Mayer, Arno J. *Politics and Diplomacy of Peacemaking: Containment and Counterrevolution at Versailles, 1918–1919.* New York: Random House, 1967.

— Spencer C. Tucker

Parrott, Robert Parker (1804–1877) *U.S. Army officer and ordnance pioneer*

Born on 5 October 1804 at Lee, New Hampshire, Robert Parker Parrott graduated from the U.S. Military Academy, WEST POINT, in 1824. He remained at West Point as an instructor from 1824 to 1829, then served as a second lieutenant in the 3d U.S. Artillery during operations against the Creeks in the Southeast and later as assistant to the chief of the Ordnance Bureau. Promoted to captain, Parrott became ordnance inspector at the privately owned West Point Foundry at Cold Spring, New York, one of the primary suppliers of artillery to the army. In October 1836 Parrott resigned his commission to become superintendent of the foundry.

Parrott is best known for his development of the muzzle-loading Parrott rifled cannon, which he patented in 1861

Union troops man a Parrott gun at Fort Totten on the defensive ring of Washington, D.C. *(Hulton/Archive)*

and which was one of the most widely used types of artillery during the Civil War. Parrott's chief contribution to cannon design lay in heat-shrinking a wrought-iron reinforcing band around the weapon's breech, the point of greatest strain. Parrott thus produced a stronger, more reliable weapon.

West Point Foundry manufactured the model 1861 and the more simplified 1863 Parrott designs in a wide variety of calibers. The 1.9-inch (10-pounder) field gun was quickly superseded by a three-inch version, so that its ammunition would be interchangeable with the other widely used field gun, the three-inch Ordnance Rifle. The West Point Foundry also produced the heavier 3.67-inch (20-pounder) and 4.2-inch (30-pounder) guns, as well as massive 10-inch (300-pounder) siege and naval pieces. Although popular with gunners for their superior range and accuracy in all calibers, the larger model Parrotts earned a rather disturbing reputation for exploding during service. Despite such drawbacks, the Parrott remained popular among field gunners. Southern foundries copied it for Confederate service.

Parrott also designed cylindro-conical projectiles primarily for his rifled guns. From 1856 to 1859 Parrott collaborated with Dr. John Brahan Reed of Tuscaloosa, Alabama, in a number of government experiments. Parrott and Reed conducted their tests at Fort Monroe and West Point, and their first projectiles were initially manufactured at the Washington Navy Yard. The partnership between Parrott and Reed eventually fell victim to the impending war as Reed's loyalty lay with his home state. Parrott purchased an interest in Reed's patents upon the latter's return to the South in 1859. During the succeeding years, Parrott focused primarily on perfecting his projectiles' sabots and fuses; he also developed sighting instruments for his various guns.

Parrott's contemporaries commended him for his selfless patriotism. During a time of rampant war profiteering, the West Point Foundry supplied the federal government with weapons at the cost of their manufacture rather than the typical inflated costs. Parrott remained superintendent to the West Point Foundry until his retirement in 1867. He died at Cold Spring, New York, on 24 December 1877.

See also ARTILLERY, LAND.

Further reading: Dickey, Thomas S., and Peter C. George. *Field Artillery Projectiles of the American Civil War.* Mechanicsville, Va.: Arsenal Publications II, 1993; Melton, Jack W., Jr., and Lawrence E. Paul. *Introduction to Field Artillery Ordnance, 1861–1865.* Kennesaw, Ga.: Kennesaw Mountain Press, 1994; Hazlett, James C., Edwin Olmstead, and M. Hume Parks. *Field Artillery Weapons of the Civil War.* Newark: University of Delaware Press, 1983; Olmstead, Edwin, Wayne E. Stark, and Spencer C. Tucker. *The Big Guns: Civil War Siege, Seacoast, and Naval Cannon.* Alexandria Bay, N.Y.: Museum Restoration Service, 1997.

— Jeff Kinard

Partridge, Alden (1785–1854) *Pioneer in military education*

Born on 12 February 1785 at Norwich, Vermont, Alden Partridge attended Dartmouth College from 1802 to 1805, when he entered the U.S. Military Academy, WEST POINT. Graduating from West Point in October 1806, Partridge was commissioned a first lieutenant of engineers.

Partridge spent the next 12 years, his entire military career, stationed at West Point. Named assistant professor of mathematics on graduation, he was promoted to captain in July 1810. In April 1813 he was advanced to professor of mathematics and head of the mathematics department. He became the first full professor of engineering in September 1813.

In January 1815, Partridge replaced Colonel Jonathan WILLIAMS as superintendent of West Point. His tenure was brief. Partridge sought to promote his own vision of the academy, but he was a poor administrator who soon alienated most of the faculty.

While Partridge was on leave in July 1817, Major Sylvanus THAYER was appointed superintendent in his stead. When Partridge refused to relinquish his post, he was tried by court-martial on charges of neglect of duty and insubordination. Convicted in November 1817, he was sentenced to be cashiered, but President James Monroe remitted the punishment and allowed him to resign from the army in April 1818.

Upon his resignation, Partridge participated in a survey of the northeastern boundary of the United States, but his first interest was military and technical education. He believed that a professional standing army was a threat to the Republic and urged that the nation train a "citizen soldiery" to be available in time of war.

In September 1820, at Norwich, Vermont, Partridge founded the American Literary, Scientific and Military Academy—the world's first purely technical and military school for the training of citizen soldiers and the first U.S. private military school. Norwich, as the academy was known colloquially, developed a reputation for an excellent academic program, embodied in a tough, disciplined military environment. The curriculum included classes in political science, foreign languages, history, engineering, agriculture, and physical education. Partridge emphasized interactive learning as a complement to passive lectures, and he encouraged field trips to sites of interest to connect classroom theory to the realities of the day.

Partridge believed that the ideal solution for the nation's military lay in the creation of institutions that combined military discipline and civilian education. In times of crisis their graduates would form a trained MILITIA. Partridge and graduates of Norwich in the 1840s and 1850s founded literally dozens of private military schools, particularly in the South.

Partridge also became a politician and author. He was surveyor-general of Vermont during 1822–23, and he served in the Vermont state legislature in 1833, 1834, and 1839. Three times he ran unsuccessfully for Congress. Partridge was also one of the most prolific military writers of his day, and he lectured widely on military science and historical and scientific topics across the country. Partridge died at Norwich on 17 January 1854.

See also EDUCATION: HIGHER MILITARY SCHOOLS; MILITARY ACADEMIES.

Further reading: Baker, Dean Paul. *The Partridge Connection: Alden Partridge and the Southern Military Education.* Ann Arbor, Mich.: University Microfilms International, 1990; Harmon, Ernest N. *Norwich University, Its Founder and His Ideals.* New York: Newcomen Society in North America, 1951; Webb, Lester A. *Captain Alden Partridge and the United States Military Academy, 1806–1833.* Northport, Ala.: American Southern, 1965.

— John J. Dempsey and Tracy M. Shilcutt

Patriot War (1812–1813) *Attempted American annexation of Spanish territory in northeast Florida (present-day Nassau County), in which former Georgia governor George Mathews led an effort by Warhawks and Georgians to secure land south of the U.S. border*

U.S. Senator William Harris Crawford of Georgia urged President James Madison to annex Florida, even as war loomed with Great Britain in 1812. Crawford recommended that George Mathews lead the effort.

The United States had coveted Florida for some time, but U.S. attempts to purchase it from Spain in 1803 and 1805 had failed. The United States claimed West Florida as far as the Perdido River as the eastern boundary of Louisiana. During the Napoleonic Wars, rebels in Florida proclaimed the Republic of West Florida and sought U.S. annexation. In 1811, Congress allowed Madison to take all of West Florida to the Perdido River. Madison, meanwhile, encouraged a revolt by a small number of insurrectionists ("Patriots") in East Florida in what was called the Patriot War.

In March 1812, Mathews moved into East Florida with some 70 or 80 men to stimulate a rebellion against Spanish rule, hoping to secure support from American farmers in the area. Mathews helped to organize a provincial government that drafted a constitution and chose John H. McIntosh as governor. Mathews believed he had the support of President Madison.

The Madison administration had ordered navy captain Hugh Campbell to patrol the coast off of the Georgia-Florida border with sloops *Wasp* and *Nautilus* and five gunboats. Although Campbell was not ordered to assist the insurgents, Mathews persuaded him to sail two gunboats off the coast of Amelia Island. This was to pressure Spanish authorities at Fernandina into surrendering the town. The gunboats arrived there on 11 March 1812; and on 14 May, Campbell conveyed some 200 Patriots on his vessels from their camp opposite the Saint Mary's River (at Rose's Bluff) inside East Florida to Amelia Island.

These insurgents, commanded by Colonel Lodowick Ashley, demanded Fernandina's surrender; but the Spanish commander, Justo López, refused. Although López had land forces that could oppose Mathews's army, he feared that Campbell's gunboats with their guns aimed on the town would open fire. On 18 May, López surrendered Amelia Island to Colonel Ashley and a Patriot force of 800 men who were reinforced from Georgia. The Patriots raised their own flag, and soon afterward the U.S. flag flew over the fort at Fernandina.

Regular U.S. Army forces of 120 men commanded by Colonel Thomas Adams Smith then crossed the Saint Mary's River, supposedly to protect the Patriots from Spanish forces, and held the territory south of the Saint Mary's River to Saint Augustine. The troops next laid siege to the Castillo de San Marcos, the Spanish fort at Saint Augustine. But the Spanish governor refused to surrender to Mathews. Unable to take the fort with his limited men and supplies, Mathews withdrew north of the Saint John's River, under pressure from Spanish troops and Seminoles, who opposed his invasion and U.S. annexation.

Meanwhile, relations with England had deteriorated, and orders eventually were given for Mathews to withdraw from Spanish territory. Madison did not admit knowledge of the invasion and subsequently dismissed Mathews for attempting to attack Saint Augustine. Mathews intended to go to Washington to reveal the extent of his mission and culpability of the Madison administration, but before he could do so he died of fever in Augusta, Georgia.

See also WAR OF 1812.

Further reading: Owsley, Frank L., and Gene A. Smith. *Filibusters and Expansionists: Jeffersonian Manifest Destiny, 1800–1821.* Tuscaloosa: University of Alabama Press, 1997; Patrick, Rembert W. *Florida Under Five Flags.* Gainesville: University Press of Florida, 1945; Tucker, Spencer C. *The Jeffersonian Gunboat Navy.* Columbia: University of South Carolina Press, 1993.

— Kenneth Cavanagh Stein

Patterson, Robert P. (1891–1952) *Secretary of war*

Born on 12 February 1891 at Glen Falls, New York, Robert Patterson attended Union College in Schenectady,

New York, and Harvard Law School. He then practiced law in the firm of Elihu ROOT. His legal career was interrupted by military service in the PUNITIVE EXPEDITION INTO MEXICO in 1916 and in France during World War I. He served with the 306th Infantry Regiment of the AMERICAN EXPEDITIONARY FORCES (AEF), earning the Distinguished Service Cross. In 1930, Patterson became a judge of the United States District Court, Southern New York District; he became noted for the record number of verdicts not reversed by higher courts.

In the summer of 1940, President Franklin D. ROOSEVELT appointed Patterson assistant secretary of war under Henry L. STIMSON, a prominent but elderly Republican and former secretary of state. Patterson's mandate was to facilitate industrial procurement, manpower, and training as the United States military, much neglected during the 1930s, readied itself for a potential major war. Patterson worked indefatigably, showing a mastery of logistics, and in December 1940 earned promotion to undersecretary. Throughout his tenure he made winning the war as swiftly and expeditiously as possible his overriding goal, demanding that American industrialists and workers alike devote all their energies to this end. He made a particularly effective team with his naval counterpart, Undersecretary James V. FORRESTAL.

When the war ended, President Harry S. TRUMAN appointed Patterson secretary of war, replacing Stimson. Convinced that the developing COLD WAR demanded substantial increases in U.S. military commitments and budgets, Patterson took the politically unpopular course of deferring draftees' demobilization. In 1947 he strongly supported military aid to Greece and Turkey and to other countries threatened by Communist insurgencies. Patterson also forcefully advocated unification of the three armed services under a single secretary of defense; when the National Security Act of 1947 accomplished this, he finally returned to his law practice.

In private life Patterson was prominent in organizations lobbying for the Marshall Plan and Western European unity. In 1950 he was a founder of the Committee on the Present Danger, which demanded major increases in American defense expenditures. Patterson died in an air crash in Elizabeth, New Jersey, on 22 January 1952.

Further reading: Eiler, Keith E. *Mobilizing America: Robert P. Patterson and the War Effort, 1940–1945.* Ithaca, N.Y.: Cornell University Press, 1997; Hogan, Michael J. *A Cross of Iron: Harry S. Truman and the Origins of the National Security State, 1945–1954.* Cambridge: Cambridge University Press, 1998; Hooks, Gregory. *Forging the Military-Industrial Complex: World War II's Battle of the Potomac.* Urbana: University of Illinois Press, 1991; Sanders, Gerry W. *Peddlers of Crisis: The Committee on*

the Present Danger and the Politics of Containment. Boston: South End Press, 1983.

— Priscilla Roberts

Patton, George S., Jr. (1885–1945) *U.S. Army general*

Born on 11 November 1885 at San Gabriel, California, George Smith Patton, Jr., did not begin his formal education until he was 12. He loved to read, especially military history. He spent one year at the Virginia Military Institute before entering the U.S. Military Academy, WEST POINT, in 1904. Because of difficulty with mathematics, Patton did not graduate until 1909. An accomplished equestrian, in 1912 he represented the United States at the Olympic Games in Stockholm, Sweden, placing fifth in the military pentathlon.

Patton served as an aide to Brigadier General John J. PERSHING during the PUNITIVE EXPEDITION INTO MEXICO, 1916–17. Promoted to captain, Patton traveled with Pershing to Europe in May 1917. He transferred to the new Tank Corps and observed tank schools in England and France. Promoted to major, Patton organized the American Tank Center at Langres, France. Promoted to lieutenant colonel, he assumed command of the 304th Tank Brigade in March

Lieutenant General George S. Patton, Jr., in 1944   *(Library of Congress)*

1918. Wounded in the SAINT-MIHIEL OFFENSIVE, he rose to colonel and fought in the MEUSE-ARGONNE OFFENSIVE.

After the war, Patton reverted to the rank of captain. A champion of armored warfare, he graduated from the Cavalry School (1923), the Command and General Staff School (1924), and the Army War College (1931). In 1932 Patton commanded cavalry during the BONUS ARMY INCIDENT, carrying out General Douglas MACARTHUR's orders to disperse World War I veterans who encamped in Washington, D.C.

As the country rearmed on the eve of World War II, Patton returned to armor and was promoted to brigadier general in October 1940 and major general in April 1941. Patton assumed command of the 2d Armored Division in April 1941, the I Armored Corps in January 1942, and then the Desert Training Center.

Patton commanded the Western Task Force in the 8 November invasion of northwest Africa, Operation TORCH, leading the landing at Casablanca, Morocco. In March 1943 General Dwight D. EISENHOWER assigned Patton, promoted to lieutenant general, to rebuild II Corps after the U.S. defeat at the KASSERINE PASS.

Patton commanded Seventh Army in the invasion of SICILY in July 1943. Following an incident at a military hospital in which he slapped a soldier suffering from shell shock for being a coward, Patton was relieved of his command. Returned to duty, Patton commanded Third Army in Britain in the months leading up to the NORMANDY INVASION, but served as a decoy in a successful Allied effort to convince the Germans that the major landing in France would occur in the Pas de Calais area.

At last unleashed, the Third Army was activated in France on 1 August 1944. Breaking out from Saint Lô in a brilliant campaign, Patton's tanks moved rapidly across France until they literally outran their supply lines. During the December 1944–January 1945 Battle of the BULGE, Patton changed fronts and relieved Bastogne. In March 1945, the Third Army crossed the Rhine and moved into Czechoslovakia from Germany. In April, Patton was promoted to general. By the end of the war, his forces had covered more ground and taken more prisoners than any other Allied force.

At the end of the war, Patton became military governor in Bavaria but was soon removed from this post after public comments caused controversy; he subsequently assumed command of Fifteenth Army. Slated to write the army's official history of the war, in December 1945 Patton suffered a broken neck in an automobile accident. He died from its complications at a military hospital in Heidelberg, Germany, on 21 December 1945. One of America's most famous warriors, Patton was a skilled and inspirational field commander. His failure to appreciate the delicacies of coalition warfare and the political considerations it involved no doubt kept him from an even greater role in the war.

See also FALAISE-ARGENTAN POCKET; COBRA, OPERATION; RHINE CROSSINGS; TANKS.

Further reading: Blumenson, Martin. *Patton: The Man Behind the Legend, 1885–1945.* New York: Morrow, 1985; D'Este, Carlo. *Patton: A Genius for War.* New York: HarperCollins, 1995; Patton, George S. *War as I Knew It.* New York: Bantam, 1980.

— John David Rausch, Jr.

Peacemaker explosion (28 February 1844) *Explosion of a heavy gun aboard a U.S. Navy ship*

The U.S. steam sloop *Princeton* was an innovative vessel and the world's first designed and built screw propeller warship. It mounted two 12-inch wrought-iron guns and two 42-pound carronades. The 12-inch guns were among the largest on any ship in the world and fired 225-pound shot. One, designed by John ERICSSON and manufactured in Britain, was named the Orator. The second, named Peacemaker, had been ordered in the United States by Captain Robert F. Stockton, commander of the *Princeton*. Weighing about 10 tons, it was manufactured—too quickly, it turned out—by Ward & Co. of New York.

Stockton had the Peacemaker mounted in the place of honor in the bow of his ship, where the gun was fired for demonstration purposes. On 28 February 1844 the *Princeton* took aboard somewhere from 250 to 400 people, including President John Tyler, at Alexandria, Virginia, for a cruise down the Potomac River. The "Peacemaker" was fired twice with success, but blew up on its third firing. The blast killed eight people, including Secretary of State Abel Upshur and Secretary of the Navy Thomas Gilmer, and injured nine others. Tyler, below at the time, was unhurt.

The inquiry into the explosion exonerated Stockton but found fault with the quality of the iron in the gun's construction. The explosion led to the Bureau of Ordnance and Hydrography's assumption of sole responsibility for the proof of naval ordnance and brought experiments in metallurgical techniques that resulted in higher-quality guns. But it also obstructed the introduction of heavy guns aboard ship, and it produced a regulation that sharply reduced the powder charges in U.S. Navy guns. The latter may have enabled the CSS *Virginia* to escape destruction at the hands of the USS *Monitor* during their battle on 9 March 1862.

See also NAVAL ORDNANCE.

Further reading: Tucker, Spencer C. "The Explosion of the 'Peacemaker' aboard Sloop Princeton," in *New Interpretations in Naval History: Selected Papers from the Eighth Naval History Symposium.* Annapolis, Md.: Naval

Awful explosion of the 'Peace-Maker' on board the U.S. Steam Frigate *Princeton.* Currier & Ives lithograph   *(Naval Historical Foundation)*

Institute Press, 1989, 175–89; ———. *Arming the Fleet: U.S. Navy Ordnance in the Muzzle-Loading Era.* Annapolis, Md.: Naval Institute Press, 1989.

— Spencer C. Tucker

Pea Ridge, Battle of (Elkhorn Tavern) (6–8 March 1862) *Civil War battle that ensured Union retention of Missouri*

For four months following the Battle of WILSON'S CREEK, exhausted Union and Confederate forces faced off in a stalemate over the control of Missouri. On 2 March 1862, Commander of the Confederate Trans-Mississippi Military District Major General Earl Van Dorn arrived in the Boston Mountains in northwest Arkansas to take personal control of the Army of the West. Two days later Van Dorn marched north to destroy the Union Army of the Southwest under Brigadier General Samuel R. Curtis and clear the way for a subsequent advance across Missouri to St. Louis.

Detecting Van Dorn's approach on 5 March, Curtis concentrated his 10,500 Federals and 49 guns on the high bluffs overlooking Little Sugar Creek by late afternoon on the 6th. The attrition of a hard march drastically reduced Van Dorn's original strength of 16,500 men, but he still outnumbered Curtis with 13,000 men and 65 guns.

Rather than squander this rare Confederate numerical supremacy by attacking head-on against an enemy entrenched on high ground, Van Dorn decided on an enveloping movement. He ordered a night march past the Union right flank along the Bentonville Detour, which curved around Big Mountain to connect with the Telegraph Road, Curtis's lifeline to Missouri. Van Dorn hoped to reach Pea Ridge, a broad plateau south of Big Mountain, by daylight, and to deploy his army two miles behind the surprised Yankees.

Fatigue, darkness, natural obstacles, and roadblocks placed by vigilant Federals subjected Van Dorn's night march to repeated delays. Dawn found his column spread out between the Telegraph Road and Little Sugar Creek. Desperate to reach the other side of Big Mountain, Van Dorn split his forces. His vanguard, the Missouri State Guard under Major General Sterling Price, proceeded south past the east end of Big Mountain, straining to seize the Union supply depot at Elkhorn Tavern. At the same time, Brigadier General Ben McCulloch's mixed division of infantry and cavalry from Arkansas, Louisiana, Texas, and Indian Territory moved around the west end of Big Mountain.

By 8:00 A.M. on 7 March, Curtis learned that the Confederates were in his rear, but he did not panic. Instead, he did something unprecedented and never repeated in the Civil War. He had the Army of the Southwest execute a 180-degree change of front and seek out the enemy.

On the Union left, Curtis's subordinates fought McCulloch's division to a standstill. Federal infantry threw the Confederates into confusion by killing General McCulloch and his second in command, Brigadier General James M. McIntosh. On the right, Price's Missourians captured Elkhorn Tavern after several hours of savage fighting, but Curtis managed to form a new line 800 yards to the south.

When the battle resumed on 8 March, Van Dorn's artillery soon ran short of ammunition. Sensing his advantage, Curtis ordered a grand attack by his entire army and swept the Confederates from the field.

Pea Ridge cost Curtis 203 killed, 980 wounded, and 201 missing. Van Dorn sustained at least 2,000 casualties and suffered additional attrition during his retreat. His impetuous handling of the battle wrecked the Confederacy's last chance to regain Missouri. McCulloch's death was considered a major blow to the Confederacy's efforts in the West.

See also CIVIL WAR, LAND OVERVIEW.

Further reading: Christ, Mark K. *Rugged and Sublime: The Civil War in Arkansas.* Fayetteville: University of Arkansas Press, 1994; Cutrer, Thomas W. *Ben McCulloch and the Frontier Military Tradition.* Chapel Hill: University of North Carolina Press, 1993; Hartje, Robert G. *Van Dorn: The Life and Times of a Confederate General.* Nashville, Tenn.: Vanderbilt University Press, 1994; Shea, William L., and Earl J. Hess. *Pea Ridge: Civil War Campaign in the West.* Chapel Hill: University of North Carolina Press, 1992.

— Gregory J. W. Urwin and Derek W. Frisby

Pearl Harbor, attack on (7 December 1941)

Surprise attack on the U.S. Pacific Fleet at Hawaii that inaugurated open warfare between the United States and Japan and American intervention in World War II

The Pearl Harbor attack marked the culmination of a decade of deteriorating Japanese-American relations. After Japan's 1931 annexation of Manchuria from China as the puppet state of Manchukuo, which the United States refused to recognize, American officials imposed economic embargoes on exports of war materials. With these they hoped to deter further Japanese expansionist moves within Asia, which included an invasion of China in 1937 and efforts to establish a "Greater East Asian Co-Prosperity

Sphere" of influence, whereby Japan would dominate Asia. The absorption of the European imperial powers of Britain, France, and the Netherlands in war with Germany encouraged Japan to consider the annexation of their Asian colonial possessions. A year after general European war began in September 1939, Japan signed the Tripartite Pact with Germany and Italy, under which each signatory committed itself to join any new war with a currently nonbelligerent state in which any other Axis power might become involved.

In January 1941, Admiral Isoroku Yamamoto, commander in chief of the Japanese Combined Fleet, drew up plans for an attack on the United States Pacific Fleet, the region's only navy capable of thwarting Japan's objectives. Yamamoto's proposal was predicated on the miscalculation that the fleet's destruction would give Japan a year's breathing space to annex French Indochina, the Dutch East Indies, Malaya, and the Philippines, and that, faced with this fait accompli, the United States eventually would negotiate peace.

In summer 1941, the American extension of its embargo to include all petroleum exports to Japan, leaving Japan fuel stocks sufficient only for two years of military operations unless it took over the oil-rich Dutch East Indies, intensified the crisis, as did the existing Japanese government's ouster in October 1941 by a more bellicose cabinet headed by General Hideki Tojo as prime minister. Discussions between American and Japanese negotiators, supposedly intended to resolve the crisis and reach a settlement acceptable to both nations, continued until 7 December, but with increasingly scant chance of success. Although Japanese leaders initially intended to hand American officials in Washington a declaration of war approximately an hour before the attack, slowness in transcribing the message meant that it was delivered 30 minutes after the raid began. Popular resentment of what generally was considered an unheralded sneak raid contributed to American determination to fight Japan to the finish. Pearl Harbor was also an important step in American progress toward activist internationalism, marking a decisive break with the limited overseas involvement and efforts to avoid war that characterized interwar American foreign policy.

As early as January 1941, reports suggested that Japan might attack Pearl Harbor; but civilian and military officials in Washington and Hawaii largely discounted these reports, considering an assault on the Philippines or European colonial possessions more likely, and underestimating Japan's ability to conceal preparations for such an operation. By summer 1941 American leaders knew, thanks to the success of the magic cryptanalysis operation in breaking Japanese military operational codes, that in the relatively near future Japan was likely to take military action of some kind, but they underestimated Japanese capabilities,

Rescuing a survivor near the USS *West Virginia* during the Japanese attack on Pearl Harbor, 7 December 1941   *(Naval Historical Foundation)*

particularly the capability of the fleet to maintain radio silence while covertly moving close to Pearl Harbor.

On 7 December 1941, a Japanese naval task force under Admiral Chuichi Nagumo dispatched 352 aircraft toward Pearl Harbor. Beginning at 7:55 A.M., Hawaiian time, the Japanese launched a two-wave air attack on shore installations and the U.S. Pacific Fleet commanded by Admiral Husband E. KIMMEL at Pearl Harbor in Hawaii. Within two hours, Japanese aircraft had destroyed or seriously damaged 18 American vessels, including eight battleships, three light cruisers, three destroyers, and four auxiliary craft. Some 73 aircraft were destroyed and 120 damaged, most of them on the ground at Hickham Field. The raid killed 2,403 Americans and wounded 1,178. Japanese losses were 29 planes, one large and five midget submarines, and 64 men. The Japanese failed, however, to

eliminate two carriers, then at sea, and also left unscathed the machine shops and oil storage tanks with 4,500,000 barrels of fuel oil, all vitally important to the Pacific Fleet's subsequent ability to recover.

On 8 December 1941 the U.S. Congress declared war on Japan. Three days later Germany and Italy, Japan's Tripartite Pact allies, likewise declared war on the United States, effectively bringing the United States into the European war.

The failure of United States intelligence to identify Pearl Harbor as Japan's eventual target later generated accusations that President Franklin D. ROOSEVELT and his pro-Allied advisers, eager to overcome public opposition to American intervention in World War II, had deliberately left Pearl Harbor exposed to Japan and suppressed reports that would have permitted American forces to anticipate the raid and take advance precautionary measures. Some historians have claimed, without substantiation to date, that the Soviet Union and Britain possessed this information but, desiring full-scale American involvement in the war, concealed it from Washington. Evidence suggests that bureaucratic failures within the State, War, and Navy Departments and the U.S. military in coordinating and interpreting intelligence intercepts were largely responsible, compounded by a last-minute communications blunder that delayed the transmission to Hawaii of warning of the raid. Repeated congressional investigations placed much of the blame for American unpreparedness upon Admiral Kimmel and Lieutenant General Walter Campbell

SHORT, the army commander in Hawaii. Both of them were demoted a rank in consequence. The investigations also found Roosevelt, Chief of Staff General George C. MARSHALL, Secretary of War Henry L. STIMSON, and Secretary of the Navy William Franklin KNOX at fault. The failure to predict the Pearl Harbor attack generated substantial pressure to establish an intelligence agency to coordinate classified information and prevent future such disasters.

See also WORLD WAR II, COURSE OF U.S. INVOLVEMENT: PACIFIC THEATER.

Further reading: Borg, Dorothy, and Shumpei Okamoto, eds. *Pearl Harbor as History: Japanese-American Relations,*

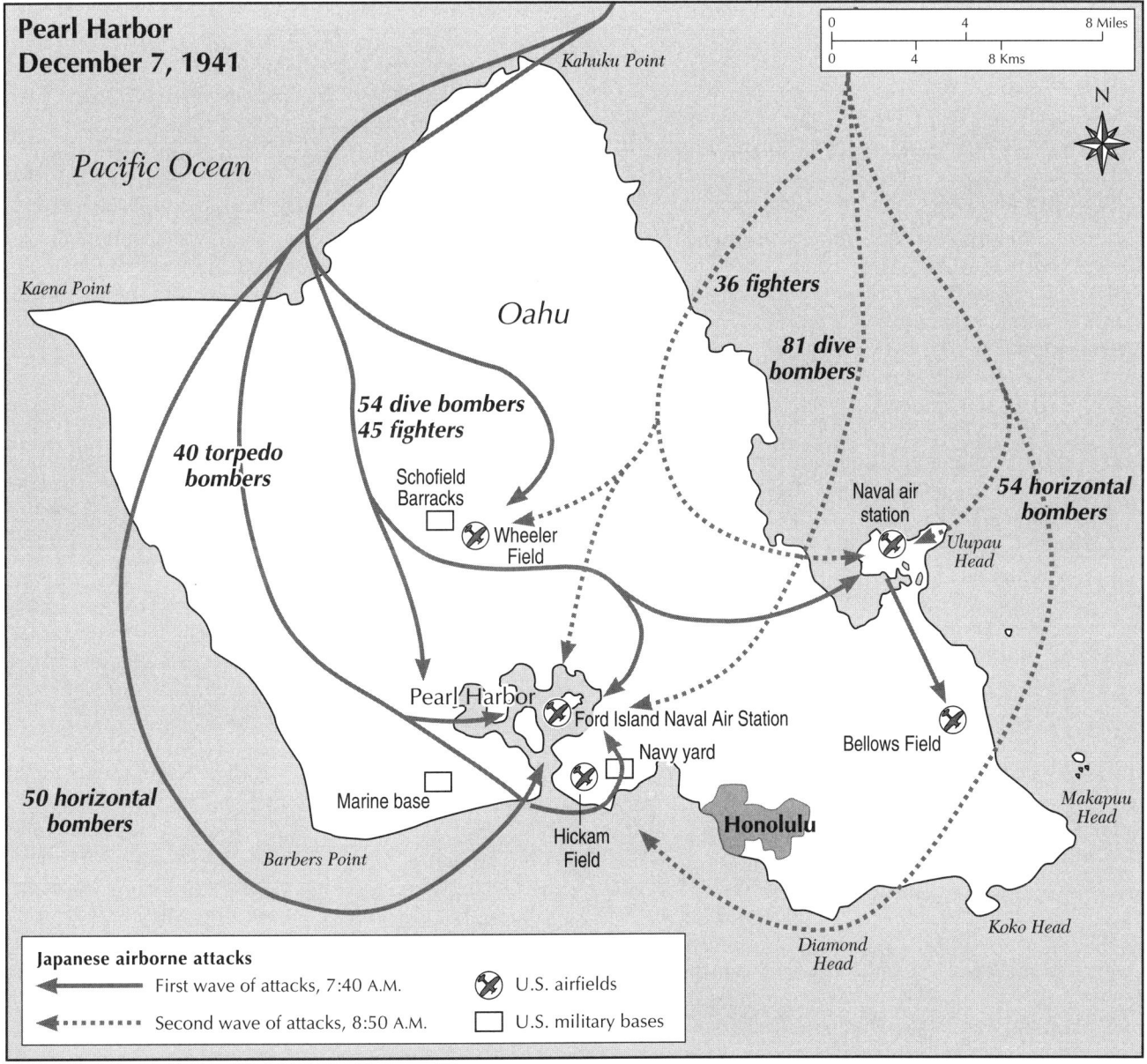

Pearl Harbor
December 7, 1941

0   4   8 Miles
0   4   8 Kms

N

Pacific Ocean

Kahuku Point

Kaena Point

Oahu

36 fighters

81 dive bombers

54 dive bombers
45 fighters

40 torpedo bombers

Schofield Barracks

Wheeler Field

Naval air station

Ulupau Head

54 horizontal bombers

Pearl Harbor

Ford Island Naval Air Station

Navy yard

Bellows Field

50 horizontal bombers

Marine base

Barbers Point

Hickam Field

Honolulu

Makapuu Head

Koko Head

Diamond Head

Japanese airborne attacks

⟵————— First wave of attacks, 7:40 A.M.

⟵·········· Second wave of attacks, 8:50 A.M.

⊗ U.S. airfields

☐ U.S. military bases

1931–1941. New York: Columbia University Press, 1973; Conroy, Hilary, and Harry Wray, eds. *Pearl Harbor Reexamined: Prologue to the Pacific War.* Honolulu: University of Hawaii Press, 1990; Goldstein, Donald M., and Katherine V. Dillon, eds. *Pearl Harbor: Inside the Japanese Plans.* Washington, D.C.: Brassey's, 1993; Iriye, Akira. *Pearl Harbor and the Coming of the Pacific War: A Brief History with Documents and Essays.* New York: St. Martin's Press, 1999; Love, Robert W., Jr., ed. *Pearl Harbor Revisited.* New York: St. Martin's Press, 1995; Prange, Gordon William, with Donald M. Goldstein, and Katherine V. Dillon. *Pearl Harbor: The Verdict of History.* New York: McGraw-Hill, 1986; Weintraub, Stanley. *Long Day's Journey Into War: December 7, 1941.* New York: Dutton, 1991; Wohlstetter, Roberta. *Pearl Harbor: Warning and Decision.* Stanford, Calif.: Stanford University Press, 1982.

— Priscilla Roberts

Peary, Robert E. (**"Bertie"**) (1856–1920) *American explorer generally credited with leading the first successful expedition to reach the North Pole*
Born on 6 May 1856 at Cresson, Pennsylvania, Robert Edwin Peary graduated from Bowdoin College in 1877. In 1881 he entered the U.S. Navy after becoming a civil engineer. As a naval engineer, Peary gained experience on the Nicaragua Canal Survey in 1884 and 1885. In 1886, he and his African-American companion Matthew Henson traveled more than 100 miles inland from Disko Bay, Greenland, arriving at an elevation of almost 7,500 feet above sea level. This was to be only the first of several exploratory trips by Peary to Greenland and the Arctic.

Over the next 25 years, Peary, through the help of sponsors such as the Academy of Natural Sciences in Philadelphia and the American Geological Society of New York, undertook expeditions to Greenland and the Arctic. On a voyage in 1891 he was accompanied by Frederick Cook, who later would claim his arrival at the North Pole five days before Peary. The study during this expedition of Inuit ethnology and culture contributed to the survival skills of the arctic explorers. Also, information on geological and glacial formations recorded during this and other trips to Greenland helped in the planning of Arctic exploration. Peary's system of advanced supply stations was first used during the 1891 Greenland expedition.

After attempts in 1902 and again in 1905–06, Peary made a final effort to reach the North Pole during 1908–09. Accompanied by Henson and four Inuit companions, he reportedly succeeded in his quest on 6 April 1909. In September 1909, Peary returned within telegraph communication and learned that Frederick Cook, five days previously, claimed to have reached the North Pole in April

1908. While Cook later was discredited by some scientists and geographers, the celebrations for Cook upset Peary.

In 1911, Peary retired from the U.S. Navy as a rear admiral. Although Peary's claim to have reached the North Pole first was generally accepted by the time of his death on 20 February 1920, at Washington, D.C., the claim remains controversial.

See also BYRD, RICHARD E.

Further reading: Bryce, Robert M. *Cook and Peary: The Polar Controversy, Resolved.* Mechanicsburg, Pa.: Stackpole Books, 1997; Weems, John Edward. *Peary: The Explorer and the Man, Based on His Personal Papers.* Boston: Houghton Mifflin, 1967.

— Jonathan Breyfogle

Peleliu, capture of (15 September–27 November 1944) *World War II Pacific theater amphibious Marine-Army operation*
To protect General Douglas MACARTHUR's right flank in his return to the Philippines, Admiral Chester NIMITZ was ordered to seize the Palau Islands group. While naval leaders believed an anchorage at Ulithi was essential for its future operations, they also favored bypassing the Japanese garrisons on the Palaus. The Joint Chiefs of Staff agreed to bypass the main island of Babelthaup but required the seizure of the two southernmost Palau Islands, Peleliu and Anguar, along with Ulithi.

On 15 September 1944, after an intensive air and naval bombardment, Major General William Rupertus's 1st Marine Division landed on Peleliu. This began an intense and costly two-month battle for control of the island. Two days later, Major General Paul Mueller's 81st Infantry Division landed on Angaur Island. With Angaur secured on 20 September, Mueller committed his 321st Regimental Combat Team to reinforce the marines on Peleliu.

Japanese resistance on Peleliu seemed pointless after the successful marine landings, which put the island effectively in American hands. But rather than surrender or launch a campaign-ending banzai attack, the Japanese defended the inner island in formidable defensive positions along the Umurbrogol Ridge. The 300-foot-high Umurbrogol, known as "Bloody Nose" to the marines, was a complex pocket of ridges, draws, valleys, caves, and tunnels. The lack of vegetation—most had been destroyed by the U.S. naval bombardment—exposed many Japanese positions but also left the invaders to withering Japanese fire.

The fanatical Japanese defense made their inevitable defeat a slow and painful process. Small teams of marines and soldiers systematically eliminated Japanese positions at considerable expense in such infamous places as Wildcat

Bowl, Five Sisters, and the Horseshoe. By mid-October, the navy declared the assault phase over and withdrew the 1st Marine Division. Elimination of the remaining defenses was turned over to the 81st Infantry Division, which spent another six weeks securing the island. The costly campaign finally ended on 27 November. U.S. casualties totaled approximately 1,650 dead and 9,100 wounded, while the Japanese suffered estimated casualties of 11,000, most of them dead.

Even with a large Japanese force annihilated, the overall value of the campaign seems questionable. Considering the inability of the Japanese to conduct any offensive against MacArthur, the force on Peleliu could have been bypassed. Only the capture of Ulithi for a naval anchorage and resupply operations seemed essential to the overall Pacific campaign. While the American high command did not plan to take any risks in jeopardizing MacArthur's attack against the Philippines, no one could have anticipated that Peleliu would become the scene of some of the most savage and intense individual combat of the war.

See also GEIGER, ROY S.; PULLER, LEWIS B.; WORLD WAR II, COURSE OF U.S. INVOLVEMENT: PACIFIC THEATER.

Further reading: Falk, Stanley. *Bloodiest Victory: Palaus.* New York: Ballantine Books, 1974; Gayle, Gordon D. *Bloody Beaches: The Marines at Peleliu.* Washington, D.C.: History and Museums Division, Headquarters, U.S. Marine Corps, 1996; Hallas, James H. *The Devil's Anvil: The Assault on Peleliu.* Westport, Conn.: Greenwood Press, 1994; Sledge, E. B. *With the Old Breed at Peleliu and Okinawa.* Annapolis, Md.: Naval Institute Press, 1981.

— Thomas D. Veve

Pemberton, John C. (1814–1881) *Confederate Army general*
Born on 10 August 1814 at Philadelphia, Pennsylvania, John Clifford Pemberton graduated from the U.S. Military Academy, WEST POINT, in 1837. Commissioned a second lieutenant in the 4th Artillery Regiment, he served in the Second SEMINOLE WAR in Florida and received promotion to first lieutenant in 1842. He was then posted at Fortress Monroe at Norfolk. Wounded twice during the MEXICAN-AMERICAN WAR, he earned brevets to captain and major. Promoted to captain in 1850, he served on the frontier and during the UTAH WAR.

Although a Northerner by birth, Pemberton had married into a prominent Virginia family and, with the outbreak of the Civil War, he declined a colonelcy in the U.S. forces to offer his services to Virginia. Appointed a lieutenant colonel in Virginia's state forces, Pemberton was soon elevated to colonel responsible for training new artillery and cavalry units. He transferred to Confederate

service as major of artillery, but in June 1861 he was appointed a brigadier general. He headed a brigade at Norfolk before assuming a district command in the Department of South Carolina, Georgia, and Florida. Promoted to major general to rank from January 1862, he commanded the department from March to September.

Having never led a large field force, in October 1862 Pemberton was promoted to lieutenant general and given command of the Department of Mississippi and East Louisiana. Charged primarily with holding the Mississippi River bastions of VICKSBURG and PORT HUDSON, he soon was confronted by Major General Ulysses S. GRANT's relentless efforts to capture Vicksburg. Ordered by President Jefferson DAVIS to hold the city at all costs, Pemberton found himself overmatched. After a series of battles east of Vicksburg, notably CHAMPION'S HILL, his forces fell back into the city's extensive defenses. Surrounded and isolated by Grant's forces, Pemberton, his men, and hundreds of civilians endured a siege of almost 50 days. But with no relief forthcoming and starvation mounting, on 4 July 1863 Pemberton surrendered the city and almost 30,000 soldiers to Grant.

Paroled and eventually exchanged, Pemberton the Northerner became a convenient scapegoat, enduring hateful criticism and unfounded charges of treason in the South. Although he had followed orders and likely did as much as he could do under the circumstances, he was finished as a Confederate general. With no position commensurate with his rank in the offing, he resigned his commission and offered to serve as a private. But a sympathetic Davis appointed him a lieutenant colonel of artillery and he served for the balance of the war, mostly in the Richmond defenses. After the war, he farmed in Virginia before settling in Philadelphia, where he died on 13 July 1881.

See also JOHNSTON, JOSEPH E.; CIVIL WAR, LAND OVERVIEW.

Further reading: Ballard, Michael B. *Pemberton: The General Who Lost Vicksburg.* Oxford: University Press of Mississippi, 1999; Winschel, Terrence J. *Vicksburg: Fall of the Confederate Gibraltar.* Abilene, Tex.: McWhiney Foundation Press, 1999.

— David Coffey

Penobscot expedition (25 July–14 August 1779) *Dismal amphibious operation of the American Revolutionary War*
In 1779 the British constructed a fort on Bagaduce Peninsula (now Castine, Maine) in Penobscot Bay. This was to obtain a site from which warships could attack New England privateers, to secure timber from Maine's great forests

and deny it to Americans, and to provide protection for Loyalists. When news arrived that 700 British regulars had been transported to Bagaduce on 17 June, the Massachusetts State Board of War immediately began to collect ships, men, and supplies with which to oust the British before their fort became too formidable. State and Continental warships and privateers numbered 18, but the 900 men gave the attackers a mere two-to-one superiority. The Board of War directed land commander Brigadier General Solomon Lovell and naval commander Captain Dudley Saltonstall to cooperate.

By 19 July, the expedition had sailed, and its leaders held a council of war that concluded that the 104 guns on the ships would suffice against the 56 the British had on three ships commanded by Captain Henry Mowat. On 24 July, British pickets reported the arrival of "40 sail" to men in the unfinished fort, named Fort George. The next morning, the American warships remained out of range and the troop transports anchored while American leaders conferred on their flagship, the 32-gun frigate *Warren*.

The nine American ships then proceeded toward Mowat's ships and exchanged desultory fire, but they failed to land troops on Bagaduce. Similar exchanges the following morning produced only damaged rigging. A council of war then decided to capture and site guns on Banks Island, which dominated Mowat's ships. With artillery leader Lieutenant Colonel Paul Revere in charge, marines landed three guns and a howitzer and on the following day so damaged Mowat's ships that they withdrew farther into the harbor.

The moment to assault Bagaduce had arrived. Two divisions of marines and one of militia, covered by ship cannon fire, began to land at midnight on the 28th. British fire on Americans struggling to climb up the face of the bluff on which the fort sat prevented the Americans from gaining a toehold until morning, when they consolidated rather than attacked, and the attack by the three heaviest-gunned American ships on Mowat proved ineffectual. During the next week, American raids on British defenders accomplished little. Morale on board the American ships plummeted when Saltonstall would not allow his vessels to continue operations until the fort was destroyed. He was supported by privateer and militia leaders. A directive from the Massachusetts war board delivered to Saltonstall on 12 August ordered him to press on against Mowat. Preparations for this action were made the next day, involving General Lovell with 400 men ashore and Saltonstall with his five strongest ships. That afternoon, the Americans sighted seven ships entering the bay and realized that they had acted too late. Leading the British ships was the 64-gun *Redoutable*. Aided by rain, the Americans ashore returned to their ships.

In the morning, the tide against them, most of the slower ships and transports sailed up the Penobscot River.

The fighting ships formed a line of battle but then scattered when formidable British ships advanced. All the American ships were either run ashore, burned by their crews, blown up to escape capture, or seized by the British. Survivors marched back to Boston. Saltonstall was court-martialed and cashiered, and Massachusetts was out $8.5 million.

The American failure in the Penobscot expedition had several causes. The detailed planning required for an amphibious operation had not been made; two heads rather than one had held command; leadership had been passive rather than aggressive; and insufficient troops had been used, and most of these were green. Following the war, Fort George was the last fort to be handed over by the British—and not until January 1784.

See also AMERICAN REVOLUTIONARY WAR: NAVAL OVERVIEW.

Further reading: Allen, Gardner W. *A Naval History of the American Revolution*, 2 vols. Boston: Houghton Mifflin, 1913. Reprint. Williamstown, Mass.: Corner House, 1970; Fowler, William M., Jr. *The American Navy During the Revolution*. New York: Charles Scribner's Sons, 1976; ———. "Disaster in Penobscot Bay," *Naval War College Review*, Vol. 31 (Winter 1978): 75–80; Shaw, Henry I. "Penobscot Assault," *Military Affairs*, Vol. 17 (Summer 1953): 83–94.

— Paolo E. Coletta

Pensacola, Florida, seizure of (7 November 1814)

Military action during the War of 1812

Seventh Military District commander Major General Andrew JACKSON decided to invade Florida in order to protect his eastern flank, even though this action did not have government approval. On 6 November 1814, Jackson arrived at Pensacola with 4,000 troops and several hundred allied Choctaw and Chickasaw Indian warriors. His appeal to Governor Don Matteo González Manrique to surrender was rebuffed.

In the early hours of 7 November Jackson led the main body of his army around Pensacola to the east. After dawn, the remaining detachment of 500 men staged a noisy demonstration with artillery, creating the impression the attack would occur from Jackson's camp on the west. Achieving complete surprise, Jackson's men swiftly overran Pensacola from the east.

In 1814 Pensacola was a small village built around a square. Two forts, Santa Rosa and San Miguel, were located on opposite sides of the square and garrisoned by 500 Spanish troops. With the town in Jackson's possession, their commanders delayed surrender, hoping the British at Fort Barrancas on Pensacola Bay would mount a counterattack. The delay kept Jackson from attacking Fort Barrancas before dark.

Early on 8 November, however, after destroying as much as they could, the British abandoned Fort Barrancas and sailed away. On 9 November, Jackson restored Pensacola to Spanish control and returned to Mobile. The capture of Pensacola had cost Jackson 5 dead and 11 wounded; the Spanish lost 14 dead and six wounded. The operation, while successful, almost cost Jackson the time he needed to organize the defenses of NEW ORLEANS against British attack.

See also CREEK WAR; WAR OF 1812: LAND OVERVIEW.

Further reading: McGovern, James R., ed. *Andrew Jackson and Pensacola.* Pensacola, Fla.: Tom White, 1974; Owsley, Frank Lawrence, Jr. *Struggle for the Gulf Borderlands: The Creek War and the Battle of New Orleans, 1812–1815.* Gainesville: University Presses of Florida, 1981.

— A. J. L. Waskey

Pepperrell, William, Jr. (1696–1759) *Colonial merchant and military and political leader*
Born on 27 June 1696 to a prosperous mercantile family at Kittery Point, Maine (then a section of Massachusetts), William Pepperrell entered the family business at an early age. By 1724 his business successes in the Atlantic trade gained him sufficient status to be elected to the Massachusetts General Court. His marriage in 1723 to the daughter of a leading mercantile family further strengthened his social and political connections. In 1727 Pepperrell was appointed to the colony's council, in which he served 31 years. He also held various judicial posts and was named colonel of the Maine militia.

Pepperrell's trading empire was threatened by the outbreak of KING GEORGE'S WAR in 1744, and he quickly sided with Governor William SHIRLEY's plan to capture the French stronghold of LOUISBOURG. Extremely popular in New England, Pepperrell was made a general and given command of the 1745 expedition. Britain, at Shirley's request, agreed to provide a large fleet, siege guns, and logistical support.

The French had designed the fortress of Louisbourg to withstand naval attack. Pepperrell, commanding 4,000 colonial troops (mostly paid New England volunteers), instead attacked the fort from the land side. The colonials quickly captured the isolated French Grand Battery and turned its guns on the fort itself. The siege ended quickly; the French surrender there was their most humbling defeat of the war.

All of New England celebrated the victory, and Pepperrell became an instant hero. Knighted by King George

II (he was the first native-born American to be given the title of baron), he also received a commission as a colonel in the regular British Army. Pepperrell was slated for further commands in 1746 and 1747, but the British cancelled these expeditions before they started. In 1749 he was promoted to lieutenant general.

Severe family problems and a falling out with Governor Shirley troubled Pepperrell for the next few years and he showed little interest in the preparations for the FRENCH AND INDIAN WAR. He came out of semiretirement to lead colonial troops for a short time only after the French attack on FORT WILLIAM HENRY in 1757. His health was failing, however, and he soon gave up his command. Pepperrell remained active in business and was a member of the council until his death at Kittery, Maine, on 6 July 1759.

Further reading: Fairchild, Byron. *Messrs. William Pepperrell: Merchants at Piscataqua.* Ithaca, N.Y.: Cornell University Press, 1954; Rolde, Neil. *Sir William Pepperrell of Colonial New England.* Brunswick, Maine: Harpswell Press, 1982; Pepperrell, William, Sir. *The Pepperrell Papers/Sir William Pepperrell.* Boston: Massachusetts Historical Society, 1899.

— Kyle F. Zelner

Pequot War (30 July 1636–28 July 1637) *Colonial War in New England between the Puritans and the Pequot Indians*
Arriving only a few years before the English, the Pequot had settled in the area between the Thames River (in what is now Connecticut) and Narragansett Bay (in Rhode Island) and on eastern Long Island. Having defeated the Narragansett and forced them to pay tribute, the Pequot were feared and hated by their Indian neighbors. Indeed, "Pequot" is Algonquin for "destroyers of men." For this reason, the Narragansett viewed the technologically superior English Puritans as useful allies against them.

As Puritans pushed into the Connecticut River Valley in 1636, conflict with the Pequot became inevitable. Two years earlier, in 1634, Captain John Stone, leader of an English trading party, had been murdered, possibly by Pequot but most likely by their allies the Western Niantics. Regardless of who was responsible, Puritans blamed the Pequot, in part because other "friendly" tribes had fed Puritan suspicions against them. Thus, when Captain John Oldham, a Puritan trader who had settled near Wethersfeld, was murdered on 30 July 1636 (most likely by Narragansett), soon to be followed by the deaths of three women and six men also from Wethersfeld, Governor John Winthrop and other leaders of the Massachusetts Bay Colony immediately blamed the Pequot.

In late August 1636, Winthrop authorized Captain John Endicott and Lieutenant Lion Gardiner to lead retaliatory raids against Pequot villages in eastern Connecticut. Although several villages were burned, the raids served only to irritate the Pequot, whose chief, Sassacus, sought to persuade other tribes, including the Narragansett, to join them in a war against the Puritans. Roger Williams succeeded in convincing the Narragansett to reject Sassacus's overtures, leaving the Pequot to fight the English alone.

In early spring 1637 the Pequot struck at the Puritan settlement at Wethersfield, Connecticut, killing 30 settlers in retaliation for the burning of their villages the previous year. Puritan leaders from Massachusetts and Connecticut hastily dispatched some 90 militiamen under Captain John Mason, Captain John Underhill, and Lieutenant Robert Seeley. Joined by several hundred Narragansett and Wampanoag, the Puritans descended upon the Pequot with a fury that shocked their Indian allies. Convinced that they were God's elect, the Puritans saw the Pequot as adversaries on the side of Satan. After catching the Pequot off guard and surrounding their chief village on the Mystic River (near modern Stonington) on 26 May 1637, the Puritans set fire to the village, cutting off every means of escape and killing some 400 to 500 Pequot, most of whom were women and children. The remnants of the tribe were hunted down and slaughtered near New Haven on 28 July, bringing the Pequot War to an end. The Puritans killed almost all adult male Pequot, and the few remaining women and children either were sold off as slaves to the West Indies or taken in by the Mohegan.

See also AMERICAN INDIAN WARS: OVERVIEW.

Further reading: Cave, Alfred A. *The Pequot War.* Amherst: University of Massachusetts Press, 1996; Pomfret, John E., with Floyd M. Shumway. *Founding the American Colonies, 1583–1660.* New York: Harper & Row, 1970; Washburn, Wilcomb E. *The Indian in America.* New York: Harper & Row, 1975.

— Justin D. Murphy

Perry, Matthew Calbraith (1794–1858) *U.S. Navy officer and diplomat*
Born on 10 April 1794 at Newport, Rhode Island, Matthew Perry first went to sea in 1809 as a midshipman in a schooner commanded by his older brother, Oliver Hazard PERRY. He continued at sea until 1833, first as aide to Commodore John RODGERS in the 44-gun frigate *President,* which in 1811 engaged the British schooner *Little Belt,* and in 1812 in the frigate *Belvidera.* Following a cruise to Norway and promotion to lieutenant, he was assigned to Commodore Stephen DECATUR's frigate *United States.* After the War of 1812, he was first lieutenant of a brig in the squadron of Commodore William BAINBRIDGE that secured peace with the Barbary powers.

After commanding merchant ships for his brother-in-law, Perry hunted slave ships off the African coast and helped to establish a residence for free African Americans in Liberia, during 1820–22. He next hunted pirates in the West Indies before serving, sometimes in command, of the flagship of the Mediterranean Squadron, in 1825–26. On shore he led a party that fought a fire in Smyrna and helped draft the first treaty between Turkey and the United States.

During the decade 1833–43, Perry rose to command the New York Navy Yard, sponsored steam propulsion, increased education for service personnel, and established the first naval ordnance testing laboratory. He supervised the building of the steamer *Fulton II* and then designed and supervised construction of steam frigates *Mississippi* and *Missouri.* His system of training apprentices at sea, begun in 1836, was abandoned after the 1842 *Somers* mutiny, but officers could increase their knowledge in his lyceum and from reading his *Naval Magazine,* the first American professional naval journal. In addition, Perry advised the Navy Department on the Charles WILKES exploring expedition (1838–42) and on the curriculum for the U.S. Naval Academy, established at Annapolis in 1845.

In 1847, during the MEXICAN-AMERICAN WAR, Perry assumed command of U.S. naval forces off the east coast of Mexico when Commodore David Connor became ill. Perry quickly organized assets for the capture of VERACRUZ and various other sites.

Perry's greatest fame came from obtaining the first treaty with Japan. In 1853 he entered Edo (Tokyo) Bay with two steam frigates and two sloops and delivered President Millard Fillmore's letter to the Japanese requesting a promise of humane treatment of stranded American sailors, provision of wood, water, and supplies to repair damaged ships, and trade relations. Upon his return in 1854 with seven powerful black-painted steamers, he gave the Japanese many gifts illustrating the industrial capacity of the United States, and secured the Treaty of Kanagawa. This authorized a consul to live in one of two ports opened to trade and promised humane treatment of stranded Americans. Perry obtained a similar treaty with the Kingdom of the Ryukyus and bought a coaling site in the Bonin Islands. His last duties were to serve on the Naval Efficiency Board and prepare a three-volume *Narrative* of his Japan expedition. Perry died in New York City on 4 March 1858, one of the most important naval officers in American history.

See also NAVY, U.S.; *PRESIDENT V. LITTLE BELT.*

Further reading: Barrows, Edward M. *The Great Commodore: The Exploits of Matthew Calbraith Perry.* Indianapolis, Ind.: Bobbs-Merrill, 1935; Morison, Samuel E.

"Old Bruin": Matthew Calbraith Perry, 1794–1858. Boston: Little, Brown, 1967; Pineau, Roger, ed. *The Japan Expedition: The Personal Journal of Commodore Matthew Calbraith Perry.* Washington, D.C.: Smithsonian Institution Press, 1968; Walworth, Arthur C. *Black Ships off Japan: The Story of the Japan Expedition.* New York: Knopf, 1946.

— Paolo E. Coletta

Perry, Oliver Hazard (1785–1819) *U.S. Navy officer, elder brother of Matthew Calbraith Perry*

Born on 20 August 1783 at Rocky Brook, South Kingston, Rhode Island, Oliver Hazard Perry studied navigation at a school in Newport and entered the navy as a midshipman in April 1799. He first saw service during the QUASI-WAR WITH FRANCE on the frigate *General Greene,* commanded by his father, Captain Christopher R. Perry.

After action in the Mediterranean during the TRIPOLITAN WAR, Perry won promotion to lieutenant in 1807. He returned to Rhode Island to oversee construction of gunboats and enforce the Embargo. In 1809 he took command of schooner *Revenge.*

In 1810 Perry recovered the *Diana,* an American ship seized by the British, but early the next year lost the *Revenge* when it ran aground at New London. Acquitted by

Commodore Oliver H. Perry, 1813, in dress uniform. Engraved by Henry Meyer from an original painting by John W. Jarvis.   *(Naval Historical Foundation)*

a court of inquiry, Perry received command of a flotilla of gunboats at Newport.

At the beginning of the WAR OF 1812 Perry requested sea duty. When a billet was not available, he wrote Commodore Issac CHAUNCEY and offered his services on the Great Lakes. In February 1813, Perry took command of naval forces on Lake Erie while still at SACKETS HARBOR. While preparing to transfer, he took part in the 27 May 1813 capture of FORT GEORGE.

That summer Perry ensconced himself at Presque Isle (Erie), Pennsylvania. With 10 ships, the largest being the 493-ton brigs *Lawrance* and *Niagara,* he crossed the Erie bar in August. The water was so shallow that the guns and heavy equipment had to be removed to get the ships over the bar. After several weeks of watching the British fleet at Amherstburg, Perry engaged the enemy in the 10 September 1813 Battle of LAKE ERIE. Although his flagship, the *Lawrence,* was disabled, he decisively defeated the British. Perry reported his victory with the words, "We have met the enemy and they are ours." The capture of the British fleet gave the United States control of Lake Erie, and Perry became a national hero.

After the battle Perry, received promotion to captain and served as aide to Major General William Henry HARRISON at the Battle of the THAMES. In July 1814 he was given the command of the frigate *Java* (44 guns); but because of the British blockade, he was unable to go to sea until the war ended. From 1816 to 1817 Perry commanded the *Java* in the Mediterranean. In 1819 he had charge of the corvette *John Adams* on a successful mission to Venezuela to halt attacks on U.S. commerce. Perry died of yellow fever on the return trip on 23 August 1819 at Port Spain, Trinidad. His body was later removed to Newport, Rhode Island.

See also PERRY, MATTHEW CALBRAITH; WAR OF 1812: NAVAL OVERVIEW.

Further reading: Dillion, Richard. *We Have Met the Enemy: Oliver Hazard Perry, Wilderness Commodore.* New York: McGraw-Hill, 1978; Hickey, Donald R. *The War of 1812: A Forgotten Conflict.* Urbana: University of Illinois Press, 1989; Mahan, Alfred T. *Sea Power in Its Relation to the War of 1812.* 2 vols. Boston: Little, Brown, 1919.

— J. W. Thacker

Perryville, Battle of (8 October 1862) *Civil War battle in Kentucky*

In the summer of 1862, Confederate General Braxton BRAGG resolved to draw the Federal Army of the Ohio out of Tennessee by mounting a major advance into Kentucky. While Bragg's Army of Mississippi moved northward into Kentucky, another Confederate force under Major General

E. Kirby Smith marched from eastern Tennessee to capture Lexington and Frankfort. Bragg meanwhile moved toward Louisville before concentrating, on 30 September, at Bardstown, 30 miles southeast of Louisville. Bragg and Smith hoped to rally Kentucky to the Confederate cause but were disappointed. They did manage to draw Major General Don Carlos BUELL's Army of the Ohio out of Tennessee. Buell, who had followed Bragg's advance, occupied Louisville and there resupplied and reinforced.

Under great pressure from Washington to defeat the Confederates, Buell ordered his army of approximately 54,000 troops to advance on the Confederate position in three columns. Union forces first skirmished with the Confederates west of Perryville, on the Springfield Road, on 7 October. Poor cavalry reconnaissance and faulty intelligence reports led Bragg to believe that his small army of nearly 20,000 men faced a single corps from Buell's army. Convinced he could win a decisive victory, early on the afternoon of 8 October the Confederate commander took the initiative and ordered his forces to advance.

Bragg's troops struck the Union left flank and forced it to retreat approximately half a mile until Federal reinforcements arrived. Union troops then launched a counterattack, but soon fell back when nightfall and stiff Confederate resistance made further fighting hazardous. Despite his tactical success, Bragg then learned that he faced Buell's entire army. Short of supplies and unable to inspire support from the citizens of Kentucky, Bragg decided to withdraw on the night of 8 October. Bragg's forces had suffered more than 3,000 casualties, while Buell's army sustained more than 4,000.

The Confederate army retreated first to Harrodsburg, where it joined Kirby Smith's command, then to Bryantsville, before marching south toward the Cumberland Gap and into Tennessee. Buell's cautious pursuit of Bragg's army convinced his superiors that he had allowed the Confederates to escape. President Abraham LINCOLN soon removed Buell from command and replaced him with Major General William S. ROSECRANS.

The Battle of Perryville was inconsequential strategically. Bragg's bold attempt to invade Kentucky failed, and the Union maintained control of the state.

See also CIVIL WAR: LAND OVERVIEW; STONES RIVER/MURFREESBORO, BATTLE OF.

Further reading: Hafendorfer, Kenneth A. *Perryville: This Grand Havoc of Battle.* Lexington: University Press of Kentucky, 2001; Hess, Earl J. *Banners to the Breeze: The Kentucky Campaign, Corinth, and Stones River.* Lincoln: University of Nebraska Press, 2000; McDonough, James Lee. *War in Kentucky: From Shiloh to Perryville.* Knoxville: University of Tennessee Press, 1994; Noe, Ken-

neth. *Perryville: The Grand Havoc of Battle.* Lexington: University Press of Kentucky, 2001.

— Alexander Mendoza

Pershing, John J. (1860–1948) *U.S. Army general, commander of the American Expeditionary Forces (AEF) in World War I, and chief of staff of the army*
Born on 13 September 1860 at Laclede, Missouri, John Joseph Pershing entered the U.S. Military Academy, WEST POINT, in 1882 and became president of his class and first captain. He served on the Nebraska and New Mexico frontier and taught military science at the University of Nebraska—where he simultaneously earned a law degree. He then taught at West Point.

During the SPANISH-AMERICAN WAR in 1898 Captain Pershing saw combat with the African-American 10th Cavalry Regiment in the Battle of SAN JUAN HEIGHTS. By this time he had an outstanding record as a dedicated, demanding, and efficient officer. As aide to Army General in Chief Major General Nelson A. MILES, Pershing attracted the attention of Secretary of War Elihu ROOT, who decided that

General of the Armies John J. Pershing   *(Library of Congress)*

Pershing's international vision and legal training made him the ideal candidate to create and direct the army's new Bureau of Insular Affairs, charged with making and implementing policy in the new American colonial possessions. Between 1899 and 1913 Pershing spent nine years in the Philippines, fighting in the PHILIPPINE-AMERICAN WAR and then pacifying the Moros in Mindanao and Luzon. He also served as a military observer in the 1904–05 Russo-Japanese War. His 1903 success in efficiently utilizing a small force to subdue rebellious chieftains around Lake Lanao won particular acclaim and brought his promotion to brigadier general. Pershing spent the years 1909 to 1913 as military governor of Moro Province.

In 1913 Pershing returned to the United States, commanding first the Presidio, San Francisco, where his wife and three daughters died in a fire, and then Fort Bliss, Texas. In March 1916 Pershing led 11,000 men into Chihuahua, Mexico, in the PUNITIVE EXPEDITION INTO MEXICO to capture Mexican rebel Pancho Villa in retaliation for Villa's raid on Columbus, New Mexico. This difficult and frustrating assignment lasted until February 1917. Pershing experimented with military aviation and truck transport and trained his men in trench warfare and modern weaponry. In September 1916 he received promotion to major general.

When the United States entered World War I, Secretary of War Newton D. BAKER selected Pershing to command the AMERICAN EXPEDITIONARY FORCES (AEF) in Europe. In May 1917, Pershing sailed for France. With the support of President Woodrow WILSON, Pershing was determined to create a separate American army rather than amalgamate the AEF into experienced British and French units. During the desperate situation in the spring of 1918, Pershing placed American divisions under command of Allied Supreme Commander General Ferdinand Foch.

On 12 September 1918, Pershing commanded the U.S. First Army as it attacked the German SAINT-MIHIEL salient, and later that month he launched a second offensive in the MEUSE-ARGONNE area. Pershing took great pride in the American army's record. He would have preferred to demonstrate Germany's defeat by invading the country and marching to Berlin, and he regretted that the Allies concluded an armistice so expeditiously.

Returning to the United States, Pershing was named general of the Armies of the United States. Appointed army chief of staff in 1921, he warned unsuccessfully against drastic cuts in American military forces. Pershing retired in 1924, dabbled in Republican politics, and wrote his memoirs, *My Experiences in the World War* (1931). He died at Washington, D.C., on 15 July 1948.

See also WORLD WAR I, COURSE OF U.S. INVOLVEMENT.

Further reading: Cooke, James J. *Pershing and His Generals: Command and Staff in the AEF.* Westport, Conn.: Praeger, 1997; Goldhurst, Richard. *Pipe Clay and Drill: John J. Pershing, the Classic American Soldier.* New York: Reader's Digest Press, 1977; Smith, Gene. *Until the Last Trumpet Sounds: The Life of General of the Armies John J. Pershing.* New York: Wiley, 1998; Smythe, Donald. *Guerrilla Warrior: The Early Life of John J. Pershing.* New York: Scribner, 1973; Smythe, Donald. *Pershing: General of the Armies.* Bloomington: Indiana University Press, 1986; Vandiver, Frank Everson. *Black Jack: The Life and Times of John J. Pershing.* 2 vols. College Station: Texas A&M University Press, 1977.

— Priscilla Roberts

Petersburg, siege of (15 June 1864–12 April 1865)
Final stage of Union Commander in Chief Lieutenant General Ulysses S. Grant's Virginia Overland Campaign, which began on 4 May 1864

After a month of nearly continuous fighting and tremendous casualties, General Robert E. LEE's Army of Northern Virginia still held strong defensive positions around Richmond. Instead of attacking Richmond directly from the north, GRANT now decided to shift the Union Army of the Potomac south across the James River to threaten the strategic city of Petersburg, 23 miles south of Richmond. Petersburg was a rail and road hub that connected the Confederate government and Lee's army to its sources of supply in the deep South. Grant hoped to take Petersburg before Lee could react.

On 15 June, Union forces crossed the James River and attacked the Confederate fortifications protecting Petersburg. After four days of heavy fighting, Grant had cut off two of the four rail lines into the city and two major roads. But Lee's entire army numbering about 50,000 men was now entrenched before the Army of the Potomac's 110,000 troops. Unable to capture the city by direct assault, Grant reluctantly settled for a siege.

Over the next nine months, Grant carried out a slow and laborious encirclement of Petersburg to cut off the last few lifelines left to Lee. As Grant extended his lines of entrenchments westward, so too did the Confederates. Grant had the numbers to man these trenches, however, while Lee did not.

The most spectacular event during the siege was the 30 July Battle of the CRATER, in which Union forces exploded a great mine under the Confederate lines, but the attack that followed was a failure. Unlike this engagement, most of the siege warfare involved small, but very brutal, battles for control of the rail lines and roads leading into the city. Grant could afford this battle of attrition, but Lee could not easily replenish his losses.

As the siege wore on into the spring of 1865, desertions, illness, and combat losses depleted the Army of Northern Virginia. Those who remained had little to eat

The siege of Petersburg, June 1864–April 1865. Fortifications here presaged those of World War I. *(Library of Congress)*

and lacked clothing and supplies. Grant's army, well supplied from the massive depot at City Point, was daily growing stronger.

On 25 March Lee directed Major General John B. GORDON to break the Union lines at Fort Stedman, but the Confederates were quickly overwhelmed and driven back with heavy losses. It was Lee's final offensive action. A few days later, on 1 April, Major General Philip SHERIDAN shattered Major General George PICKETT's Confederates on the far right flank of the army at FIVE FORKS. On 2 April, Grant ordered a general assault on the Confederate lines. That night, after a desperate defense, Lee abandoned Petersburg, breaking out westward toward Amelia Courthouse. Union troops entered the city before dawn on the 3rd. Richmond fell a few hours later and Lee surrendered at APPOMATTOX Court House on 9 April.

See also CIVIL WAR, LAND OVERVIEW; MEADE, GEORGE G.; OVERLAND CAMPAIGN.

Further reading: Horn, John. *The Petersburg Campaign: June 1864–April 1865.* Conshohocken, Pa.: Combined Books, 1993; Lykes, Richard. *Campaign for Petersburg.* Washington, D.C.: U.S. National Park Service, 1970; Trudeau, Noah Andre. *The Last Citadel: Petersburg Virginia June 1864–April 1865.* Boston: Little, Brown, 1991; Sommers, Richard J. *Richmond Redeemed: The Siege of Petersburg.* New York: Doubleday, 1981.

— Keith D. Dickson

Philadelphia, burning of the USS (16 February 1804) *One of the most important naval operations of the 1801–05 Tripolitan War*

One of only two frigates operating in Commodore Edward PREBLE's Mediterranean Squadron, the 36-gun *Philadelphia* was commanded by Captain William BAINBRIDGE. On 31 October 1803 it ran aground while conducting blockading operations off the coast of Tripoli, and Bainbridge, his crew of 306, and his ship were captured by the Tripolitans. The Tripolitans then managed to free the *Philadelphia* from the shoals along with much of its armament. It now threatened the security of the remaining U.S. ships.

Determining that it would be impossible to recapture the vessel, Preble organized a mission to destroy the *Philadelphia* at anchor. On 16 February 1804, Lieutenant Stephen DECATUR and 75 men sailed into the harbor on board a captured Tripolitan ketch, renamed the *Intrepid*. They secured the ketch to the *Philadelphia*, boarded it and overpowered the Tripolitan prize crew, and burned the frigate. Miraculously, amidst a crossfire from the shore and from other Tripolitan vessels in the harbor, as well as from the *Philadelphia*'s own guns, which discharged as the vessel burned, Decatur and his entire crew escaped without a single loss of life.

The story of the destruction of the *Philadelphia* was widely recognized as an act of singular daring, even by the vaunted British admiral Horatio Nelson, and it became one of the most celebrated episodes in the U.S. Navy's young history.

See also TRIPOLITAN WAR.

Further reading: McKee, Christopher. *Edward Preble: A Naval Biography, 1761–1807*. Annapolis, Md.: Naval Institute Press, 1972; Whipple, A. B. C. *To the Shores of Tripoli: The Birth of the U.S. Navy and Marines*. New York: William Morrow, 1991.

— Christopher A. Preble

Philippine-American War (Philippine Insurrection)

(1899–1902) *First U.S. colonial war as a world power*
The Philippine-American War, also known as the Philippine Insurrection or the Philippine War of Independence, officially lasted from 4 February 1899 to 4 July 1902.

The war was the result of the Filipino struggle for independence. Filipinos had fought Spanish colonial rule since 1896, with limited success. After the American victory over Spain in the 1898 SPANISH-AMERICAN WAR, the Filipino resistance, led by Emilio AGUINALDO, hoped for the independence of the islands and rejected acquisition by the United States.

By late January 1899, Aguinaldo and other leaders of the independence struggle had written a constitution, organized a government at Malolos, and proclaimed the Philippine Republic. Fighting between the new republic's poorly equipped Philippine Army and the American Expeditionary Force in the islands began in February 1899.

The war occurred in two distinct phases. The first, from February 1899 to November 1899, consisted mostly of a conventional war fought mainly in the northern half of the big island of Luzon. Filipino forces commanded by General Antonio Luna conducted conventional operations, seeking a military decision in open battle. This strategy played into the hands of the much better trained and equipped U.S. troops in VIII Army Corps under the leadership of Major General Elwell S. Otis. Throughout this phase of the war, American troops won numerous victories and inflicted heavy casualties on the Filipino forces.

During the second phase, from November 1899 until the end of the war, the Filipino resistance concentrated mostly on guerrilla attacks by small bands on regular troops. They engaged in hit-and-run operations throughout the islands. Major General Arthur MACARTHUR, who succeeded Otis in spring 1900, responded by concentrating civilians in camps. He devised zones of military operations under martial law to cut off guerrillas from the support of the civilian population. This strategy was carried out with regional variations. Common to all theaters of operations, however, was the brutal form of this warfare, which virtually eliminated any distinction between combatants and noncombatants. Each side committed numerous atrocities.

By the summer of 1901, insurgent operations had been crushed in almost all of Luzon. Major General Adna R. CHAFFEE, who succeeded MacArthur, carried the war to the Visayas, where the Filipino resistance was crushed in 1901. The strongest resistance was on Samar, where Brigadier General Jacob H. Smith practiced a form of total warfare against the insurgents. He eventually was court-martialed and officially admonished for his ruthless measures throughout the campaign.

U.S. military operations ultimately proved successful as they were accompanied by an extensive program of social engineering. The military and civilian administration of the islands carried out public works programs that included the building of schools and hospitals as well as improvements in the transportation infrastructure of the islands. U.S. authorities also placed great emphasis on a substantial program of general education. More than 1,000 teachers sent to the islands introduced Filipinos to an American-style educational system.

In all, some 125,000 U.S. troops took part in the Philippine operations; some 4,500 of these died, and 2,800 were wounded. Estimates of Filipinos killed run from 200,000 to 600,000. The enormous death toll among the civilian population resulted from famine and malnutrition that accompanied warfare as the fighting destroyed livestock and the concentration policy interrupted farming activities. The war cost the United States government at least $160 million.

In the United States the war produced substantial opposition from anti-imperialists, who rejected the drive for colonial possessions. In the Philippines the war was accompanied by a massive assimilation program. The subsequent U.S. occupation and reconstruction was one of imperialism's few success stories, however. Independence for the Philippine Islands was delayed by World War II until 1946.

See also BALANGIGA, BATTLE OF; BASEY, MARCH TO; DEWEY, GEORGE; FUNSTON, FREDERICK; MANILA, SIEGE OF; MANILA BAY, BATTLE OF; MERRITT, WESLEY.

Further reading: Gates, John M. *Schoolbooks and Krags: The United States Army in the Philippines, 1898–1902.* Westport, Conn.: Greenwood Press, 1973; Linn, Brian M. *The Philippine War, 1899–1902.* Lawrence: University Press of Kansas, 2000; ———. *The U.S. Army and Counterinsurgency in the Philippine War, 1899–1902.* Chapel Hill: University of North Carolina Press, 1989; Miller, Stuart C. *"Benevolent Assimilation": The American Conquest of the Philippines, 1899–1902.* New Haven, Conn.: Yale University Press, 1982; Welch, Richard E. *Response to Imperialism: The United States and the Philippine War, 1899–1902.* Chapel Hill: University of North Carolina Press, 1979.

— Frank Schumacher

Philippines, loss of the (1942) *A U.S. possession at the start of World War II, the Philippines were invaded and conquered by the Japanese following the 7 December 1941 Japanese attack at Pearl Harbor*
In December 1941, Allied forces in the Philippines numbered 130,000, but only 20 percent of this force was comprised of U.S. Army troops. The remainder were Filipino, and many of these were composed of untrained levies. The best organized were the Philippine Scouts, crack professional regiments with American officers and Filipino enlisted men. They made up a third of the regular army defense forces and formed the core of the Philippine Division.

The U.S. plan to defend the Philippines was based on the premise that the U.S. Pacific Fleet would soon be able to come to the rescue. It presumed a retreat back into the BATAAN Peninsula and CORREGIDOR until relief could arrive. However, General Douglas MacARTHUR, commander of U.S. forces in the Philippines, scrapped this long-standing plan in favor of trying to hold the entire islands against invasion. Adequate resources were not available to accomplish this, however, and the result was a good deal of confusion that contributed to the American and Filipino defeat.

News of the Japanese attack at PEARL HARBOR reached the Philippines at 2:30 A.M. on 8 December. Morning fog on Formosa, meanwhile, delayed a planned Japanese air strike against the Philippine Islands. On the American side there was confusion, which has been a continuing source of controversy. Major General Lewis H. BRERETON, commander of MacArthur's air force, had the largest concentration of four-engine bombers in the world, 35 B-17s. He wanted to bomb Formosa with his

B-17s once he learned about the Pearl Harbor attack, but MacArthur refused to make the first move. As a result, the big bombers at Clark Field were ordered to fly around Luzon to avoid being caught on the ground. At 11:00 A.M. they landed to prepare for their strike just as the delayed Japanese aircraft arrived overhead. Because of an insufficient American warning system, most U.S. aircraft were destroyed on the first day: 70 fighters and bombers on the ground and 25 fighters in the air. By the end of December, 277 U.S. aircraft, the vast majority of them obsolescent, had been destroyed.

The Japanese landings began on 11 December 1941 at Aparri on northern Luzon and Vigan on western Luzon. MacArthur believed they were diversions and held most of his forces back. On 12 December, Japanese forces landed on southern Luzon at Legaspi. Finally the main force of Lieutenant General Masaharu Homma's Fourteenth Army came ashore beginning on 22 December with the main body in the Lingayen Gulf, meeting little resistance. Altogether, Homma commanded some 65,000 troops.

MacArthur directed his field commander, Major General Jonathan WAINWRIGHT, to fight delaying actions on successive lines as the main body of U.S. and Filipino forces withdrew into the Bataan Peninsula. Because it had no military value, Manila was declared an open city and ceded to the Japanese without a struggle. MacArthur really had no other alternative. He sought to use knowledge of the terrain to counter Japanese superiority in air power, tanks, artillery, and trained manpower.

The retreat into the Bataan Peninsula was a complex operation executed with great skill at considerable loss to the attackers, much to the surprise of the Japanese. Wainwright's pattern of standing, fighting, and then slipping away delayed the Japanese long enough for MacArthur to get all his men and what supplies they could carry into Bataan. Unfortunately nothing had been done to prepare for a defense there. Civilian buses and vehicles helped compensate for the lack of military transportation, but there were civilians who had to be fed, and large stocks of supplies and food could not be transported into the peninsula in time. This doomed the defenders to slow starvation, with rations being cut in half as the defenders entered Bataan. Malarial conditions also weakened the defense.

Corregidor Island, separated from Bataan by two miles of water, served as a supply base and means to deny the Japanese use of Manila Bay.

Sensing the inevitable, on 11 March 1942 President Franklin ROOSEVELT ordered MacArthur to evacuate himself to Australia. Wainwright took over command of the remaining Allied forces in the Philippines. With U.S. and Filipino forces exhausted, morale low, and ammunition stocks dwindling, the American commander on Bataan,

Major General Edward P. KING, surrendered to the Japanese on 9 April after 98 days of fighting. Filipinos and Americans taken prisoner were then subjected to the infamous BATAAN DEATH MARCH.

Following their victory on Bataan, the Japanese attacked Corregidor Island, subjecting it to massive artillery and air attacks. On 5 May 1942 they invaded the island with tanks, and the next day Wainwright surrendered all forces in the Philippines.

Except for the few U.S. and Filipino soldiers who refused to surrender and began guerrilla warfare, all organized resistance ended by June 1942. For six months, however, the "Battling Bastards of Bataan," starving and suffering from malaria and other tropical diseases, had fought the well-trained and equipped Japanese forces to a standstill. Perhaps surprising was the loyalty of the great majority of Filipinos to the United States, even during the Japanese occupation.

See also KELLY, COLIN; WORLD WAR II, COURSE OF U.S. INVOLVEMENT: PACIFIC THEATER.

Further reading: James, D. Clayton. "The Other Pearl Harbor," *Military History Quarterly* 7, No. 2 (winter 1995): 22–29; MacArthur, Douglas. *Reminiscences.* New York: McGraw-Hill, 1964; Morgan, Louis. *The United States Army in World War II: The War in the Pacific. The Fall of the Philippines.* Washington, D.C.: Government Printing Office, 1953.

— John E. Foley

Philippines, retaking of the (20 October 1944–15 August 1945) *Recapture of the strategically located island archipelago and U.S. possession conquered by Imperial Japanese forces in 1942*

On 26–27 July 1944, President Franklin D. ROOSEVELT met with his senior commanders in the Pacific, Admiral Chester NIMITZ and General Douglas MACARTHUR, to determine the next target for U.S. forces. Nimitz and the navy wanted to bypass the Philippine Islands in favor of Okinawa, but MacArthur successfully argued for the reconquest of the Philippines. Roosevelt decided to do both. MacArthur pointed out that the vast majority of Filipinos had remained loyal to the United States and that there were thousands of U.S. women and children as well as prisoners of war held in concentration camps on the islands.

Japanese leaders knew all too well that were the Philippines to fall, their communications with the East Indies and much of Southeast Asia, including vital supplies of oil, would be cut. The Japanese army was determined to hold the Philippines, and the Japanese navy planned an attack to destroy the American beachhead once it had been estab-

lished. The latter resulted in the 23–26 October 1944 Battle of LEYTE GULF.

The American plan for retaking the Philippines had three distinct phases. The first step was to invade and take the island of Leyte. Phase two would be the invasion and taking of the big island of Luzon. In phase three, U.S. forces would clear islands south of Leyte.

The landing on Leyte commenced on 20 October 1944. It involved some 700 ships, landing the 174,000 men of Lieutenant General Walter Krueger's Sixth Army. The Americans had an accurate picture of Japanese strength and dispositions as a consequence of intelligence provided by Filipinos. Cutting Japanese lines of communications and attacking Japanese stragglers, Filipino and U.S. guerrillas conducted several daring raids that rescued thousands of American civilians and prisoners of war. Guerrillas also served as flank security, scouts, and raiding forces. The obvious support of the Filipino people was also a great morale booster for U.S. forces.

Despite this, the advance on Leyte was slowed by heavy rains, well-prepared Japanese defensive positions, and rugged terrain. MacArthur went ashore with the third assault wave, accompanied by members of the Philippine government, and delivered his famous "I have returned" remarks.

MacArthur's opponent, General Tomoyuki Yamashita, the Japanese commander in the Philippines, landed 50,000 fresh troops on Leyte with orders to hold at all costs. To close the back door to Leyte by which the Japanese were landing supplies and reinforcements, the U.S. 77th Division landed on the west coast of Leyte. Japanese defenses wilted under the three-way assault. More than 80,000 Japanese soldiers were killed and only 798 were captured. There were no survivors from the Japanese 16th Division, which had conducted the infamous BATAAN DEATH MARCH.

Before operations on Leyte were completed, deception plans had caused Yamashita to pull most of his 250,000 troops on Luzon south toward Manila. As a consequence, on 9 January 1945 advance elements of the Sixth Army were able to land almost unopposed in northern Luzon and strike south. Then, when Yamashita had committed his forces to the northern threat, the Eighth Army landed in southern Luzon and attacked north. Handicapped by shortages of equipment, transport, and air support, Yamashita organized his forces on Luzon into three main groups and settled in for a static defense.

Rear Admiral Sanji Iwabuchi defied Yamashita's order to withdraw from the city and ordered his 17,000-man Manila Naval Defense Force to hold the capital in a suicidal defense. The subsequent battle, during February and March 1945, resulted in the destruction of much of the city and an estimated 100,000 civilian casualties. Afterward Yamashita would be held responsible for Japanese atrocities committed here and executed as a war criminal. Manila was taken on 3 March 1945, and much of Luzon was secured by July.

With no hope of victory or rescue, some Japanese soldiers fought on in the Philippines until Yamashita surrendered, with 50,000 men remaining, on 15 August 1945. The U.S. campaign for the Philippines was skillfully fought, with proportionately few U.S. casualties. Japan lost its entire 400,000-man garrison, 312,000 of whom were killed in action. U.S. losses were 14,000 killed and 48,000 wounded. The high ratio of losses for the Japanese compared to the lower figure for Americans is an exception to the general rule that attackers suffer heavier casualties in battle, and also a tribute to the skill of the American commanders.

See also EICHELBERGER, ROBERT L.; WORLD WAR II, COURSE OF U.S. INVOLVEMENT: PACIFIC THEATER.

Further reading: MacArthur, Douglas. *Reminiscences.* New York: McGraw-Hill, 1964; Morison, Samuel Eliot. *History of United States Navy Operations in World War II.* Vol. 13: *The Liberation of the Philippines, Luzon, Mindanao, the Visayas, 1944–August 1945.* Boston: Little, Brown, 1963; Smith, Robert Ross. *The United States Army in World War II: The War in the Pacific. Triumph in the Philippines.* Washington, D.C.: U.S. Government Printing Office, 1963.

— John E. Foley

Philippine Sea, Battle of the (19–21 June 1944)

Decisive naval battle in the Central Pacific during World War II

The first major fleet action between the Japanese and the U.S. Navy in two years, it was triggered by U.S. landings on Saipan in the MARIANA ISLANDS. In early June, elements of Vice Admiral Marc MITSCHER's Task Group 58, comprised of seven fleet and eight light carriers with 956 aircraft, seven battleships, 21 light and heavy cruisers, and 69 destroyers, plus supporting elements, hit Saipan with fighter and bomber sweeps that cost the Japanese 200 aircraft and a dozen or more cargo ships. Then came bombardment by naval fire.

Landings on Saipan by Fifth Amphibious Force began on 15 June, prompting Imperial Fleet Headquarters to order Vice Admiral Jisaburo Ozawa to engage the ships supporting the invasion. Ozawa's Mobile Fleet had half the number of ships and aircraft available to Mitscher: five fleet and four light carriers, five battleships, 11 heavy and two light cruisers, and 28 destroyers. The Japanese could launch 473 aircraft from their carriers, and had another 110 positioned on Guam, Rota, and Yap. The Japanese hoped also to catch the Americans off guard, engaging them at longer range and landing planes at Guam in shuttle bombing. Admiral Raymond SPRUANCE, aware of Japanese dispositions, gathered his Fifth Fleet to do battle. Mitscher first removed his carriers, and later all warships, from the waters off Saipan to engage the Japanese.

On 18 June, Mitscher positioned his forces some 160 miles west of Tinian. The resulting Battle of the Philippine Sea over 19–21 June destroyed the Japanese fleet. Things went badly for the Japanese from the beginning. U.S. submarines sank two Japanese carriers very early in the action. Mitscher's aircraft also took a terrible toll on the poorly protected raiding Japanese planes. Most of those that did get through were brought down by antiaircraft fire. The so-called Great Marianas Turkey Shoot cost the Japanese 346 planes in addition to the two fleet carriers. U.S. losses were only 30 planes and some slight damage to a battleship from a Japanese bomb. Mitscher's planes strafed Guam and Rota and neutralized Japanese airfields there. By the evening of the 19th, the battle was over.

The Japanese now departed, but Mitscher pursued. Late on the afternoon of the 20th, U.S. forces again located the Japanese, and Mitscher launched 216 planes. The late launch would mean a night recovery, however. This strike sank another aircraft carrier and two tankers and seriously damaged several other vessels. The U.S. lost 20 planes; the Japanese, 65.

The U.S. planes now had to find their way back to the carriers in the dark, however. Mitscher took the gamble of lighting his ships to guide the planes home. Some 80 planes ran out of gas and either ditched or crash-landed, but they could easily be replaced. Destroyers later picked up 50 flyers in the water. Total U.S. personnel losses that day were 16 pilots and 33 crewmen.

Ozawa's remaining ships now got away, and U.S. naval units returned to Saipan to support the shore battle there. Japanese losses in the Battle of the Philippine Sea were severe, not only in aircraft carriers and aircraft: The more than 460 trained combat pilots killed in the battle would be impossible to replace. In effect, the Battle of the Philippine Sea eliminated Japanese naval aviation as a serious threat.

See also WORLD WAR II, COURSE OF U.S. INVOLVEMENT: PACIFIC THEATER.

Further reading: Grove, Eric. *Big Fleet Actions: Tsushima, Jutland, and Philippine Sea.* London: Arms and Armour, 1995; Morison, Samuel Eliot. *History of United States Naval Operations in World War II.* Vol. 8: *New Guinea and the Marianas, March 1944–August 1944.* Boston: Little, Brown, 1950; Y'Blood, William T. *Red Sun Setting: The Battle of the Philippine Sea.* Annapolis, Md.: Naval Institute Press, 1981.

— Spencer C. Tucker

Phips, Sir William (1651–1695) *Colonial military leader and governor of the Massachusetts Bay colony*

Born on 2 February 1651 to a frontier family near present-day Woolwich, Maine, William Phips was apprenticed to a ship's carpenter in Boston. In 1673, after marrying a prominent merchant's widow, he became a ship captain. In the 1680s, Phips undertook a number of expeditions to find sunken Spanish treasure ships, and in 1686 he located a valuable wreck off the coast of Haiti. The expedition brought him wealth and fame, as well as the attention of King James II, who knighted him in 1687; Phips was the first American so honored.

On a trip to London, Phips worked closely with Increase Mather to restore the Massachusetts charter, which had been revoked in 1684. Their success and Phips's personal religious conversion cemented his alliance with the powerful Mather family. This paid off when Phips was named commander of the Massachusetts expedition against Nova Scotia during KING WILLIAM'S WAR.

In May 1690, Phips set sail with a force of 736 men to capture Port Royal, Nova Scotia, from the French. Landing without opposition, Phips's men soon surrounded the crumbling fortification and forced its surrender. The fort was destroyed; booty and French prisoners were escorted back to Boston.

Phips then received command of the crucial component of an intracolonial invasion of French Canada, the naval expedition to capture the capital of Quebec. The 2,300-man force got off to a slow start from lack of financial backing. Its 32 ships took two months to reach Quebec, and smallpox exacted a devastating toll on the troops. Landing in October, Phips learned that the overland part of the invasion had failed, and he faced a full French garrison. After a poorly planned and ineffectual bombardment of Quebec's formidable defenses, Phips withdrew, barely escaping the St. Lawrence before the ice closed the river. Only 1,300 men made it back to Boston; 1,000 had perished, mostly from disease.

In 1692, Phips was in London when a new political charter was issued for Massachusetts, appointing him the colony's first royal governor. Phips, the first American-born royal governor, arrived in Boston at the height of the Salem witchcraft outbreak and soon helped to end the hysteria. His tenure as governor was not successful, however, and he was ordered back to London in 1694. He died there on 18 February 1695.

Further reading: Baker, Emerson W., and John G. Reid. *The New England Knight: Sir William Phips, 1651–1695.* Toronto, Canada: University of Toronto Press, 1998; Thayer, Henry O. *Sir William Phips, Adventurer and Statesman: A Study in Colonial Biography.* Portland: Maine Historical Society, 1927.

— Kyle F. Zelner

Pickens, Andrew (1739–1817) *U.S. militia general in the Southern campaigns of the American Revolutionary War*

Born on 19 September 1739 in Bucks County, Pennsylvania, Andrew Pickens was educated in local schools. After a series of moves beginning in 1752, his family finally settled in the Long Cane District of South Carolina, where Pickens worked as a farmer and Indian trader. He served with the South Carolina militia in the 1760 CHEROKEE WAR.

When the American Revolution began, Pickens returned to military service as a captain in the Patriot militia. During the first year of the war, he fought the Cherokees on the frontier and campaigned against Loyalists in the Ninety Six District of South Carolina. On 14 February 1779 his 300 militia defeated a force of 700 Loyalists at Kettle Creek, Georgia.

Following the siege of CHARLESTON and the city's capture by the British in May 1780, Pickens accepted a British parole. Soon afterward, Loyalists destroyed some of his property, an act that he believed violated the terms of his parole. He then assembled a force of militia and conducted partisan operations against the British. When Major General Nathaniel GREENE assumed command of the Southern Army, Pickens cooperated effectively with the Continentals. He united his troops with Brigadier General Daniel MORGAN's force and commanded the militia in the Battle of COWPENS on 17 January 1781, leading the counterattack that helped to seal the British defeat. In recognition of this service, Pickens was made a brigadier general.

Pickens operated to the rear of British Lieutenant General Charles, Lord Cornwallis's army as it pursued Greene across North Carolina. He was with Colonel Henry LEE who, posing as British Lieutenant Colonel Banastre Tarleton, lured Loyalists moving to join Cornwallis into an ambush on 25 February. Pickens also cooperated with Lee in the siege of Augusta, Georgia, which ended in a British surrender on 5 June. They then marched to Ninety Six and joined Greene's force in an unsuccessful siege that was lifted on 19 June. Pickens led his militia in the Battle of EUTAW SPRINGS on 8 September; and in 1782 he commanded a force that defeated the Cherokees in a three-week campaign.

After the war Pickens served several terms in the South Carolina legislature and one term in the U.S. Congress. He was appointed major general of the state militia in 1795. He died on 11 August 1817 in Tomassee, South Carolina.

See also AMERICAN REVOLUTIONARY WAR: LAND OVERVIEW; GREENE'S OPERATIONS.

Further reading: Morrill, Dan L. *Southern Campaigns of the American Revolution.* Mount Pleasant, S.C.: The Nautical & Aviation Publishing Company of America, 1993;

Waring, Alice Noble. *The Fighting Elder: Andrew Pickens.* Columbia: University of South Carolina Press, 1962.

— Jim Piecuch

Pickett, George E. (1825–1875) *Confederate Army general*

Born on 28 January 1845 at Richmond, Virginia, George Edward Pickett graduated from the U.S. Military Academy, WEST POINT, last in his class of 1846, and was commissioned a second lieutenant of infantry. He served in Major General Winfield SCOTT's army during the MEXICAN-AMERICAN WAR and saw action at VERACRUZ, CERRO GORDO, and CHAPULTEPEC, and was breveted to first lieutenant and captain for gallantry. Pickett served in several postings in the West after the war. After the outbreak of the Civil War and Virginia's secession, Pickett resigned his commission in June 1861 to join the Confederacy as a colonel.

Pickett was promoted to brigadier general in January 1862 and saw action during the Peninsula campaign actions of WILLIAMSBURG and SEVEN PINES/FAIR OAKS. At Gaines's Mill, during the Battles of the SEVEN DAYS, Pickett was wounded and out of action for several months, which caused him to miss the Battle of ANTIETAM/SHARPSBURG. Promoted to major general in October 1862, he commanded a division under Lieutenant General James LONGSTREET in the Battle of FREDERICKSBURG, but he was absent from CHANCELLORSVILLE, along with the remainder of Longstreet's Corps.

Pickett's division arrived at GETTYSBURG on 2 July 1863 and formed part of General Robert E. LEE's frontal assault the next day against Cemetery Ridge. He acquitted himself well, but the task was impossible. His division was devastated in what became known as Pickett's Charge.

Made commander of the Department of Virginia and North Carolina, Pickett failed to recapture New Bern, North Carolina, but he successfully repulsed the first Union attempt to seize PETERSBURG at Bermuda Hundred in April 1864. Pickett then returned to command his old division and saw action at COLD HARBOR. During the siege of Petersburg he commanded two divisions, which repulsed Major General Philip SHERIDAN's attack at Dinwiddie Court House. Sheridan then overwhelmed Pickett's Division at FIVE FORKS, which forced the Army of Northern Virginia to give up the trench lines around Richmond-Petersburg.

Pickett was never on good terms with Lee after Gettysburg, and Lee relieved him of command after the debacle at Sayler's Creek, but he remained with the Army of Northern Virginia until Lee surrendered at APPOMATTOX on 9 April 1865. Pickett long after blamed Lee for the destruction of his division at Gettysburg. After the war, he entered the insurance business in Virginia. He died at Norfolk on 30 July 1875.

See also CIVIL WAR, LAND OVERVIEW.

Further reading: Freeman, Douglas Southall. *Lee's Lieutenants: A Study in Command.* 3 vols. New York: Charles Scribner's Sons, 1942–44; Longacre, Edward G. *Pickett: Leader of the Charge.* Shippensburg, Pa.: White Mane Publishing, 1995.

— Thomas D. Veve

Pike, Zebulon M. (1779–1813) *U.S. Army general and explorer*

Born on 5 January 1779 at Lamberton, New Jersey, Zebulon Montgomery Pike was the son of an American Revolutionary War veteran. He entered his father's company of the 2d Infantry Regiment at 15, transporting supplies to Major General Anthony WAYNE's garrisons along the Miami River. Commissioned a second lieutenant in March 1799, he served in various garrisons along the frontier.

In 1805 Major General James WILKINSON ordered Lieutenant Pike to lead an expedition to the source of the Mississippi River. He was to gather information on Indian tribes and discourage foreign influence among them, collect scientific and astronomical data, determine Upper Louisiana's boundaries, report on its soil and flora, discover the courses and navigability of its rivers, and choose sites for military posts and factories. Pike and 20 men left St. Louis on 9 August. Although he failed to locate the Mississippi's source, Pike opened U.S. relations with Indian tribes, warned off foreign traders, purchased the site of the future Fort Snelling, and gave the U.S. claim to Minnesota.

Pike returned to St. Louis on 30 April 1806, having covered 5,000 miles. Two months later, Wilkinson ordered him to return Osage prisoners to their people, establish peaceful relations with the Comanche and neighboring tribes, and map the Arkansas and Red Rivers. Moving up the Arkansas, Pike sighted but could not reach the promontory named for him, Pike's Peak, in the Rocky Mountains in what is now Colorado. Upon discovering the source of the Arkansas, the party turned south into the Rio Grande Valley. Captured by the Spanish, Pike was questioned by the governor in Santa Fe and by officials in Chihuahua before being warned and escorted to Natchitoches, Louisiana, in June 1807. There Pike found he was a suspect in Aaron BURR's conspiracy to establish a pro-Spanish republic in the Southwest, but evidence about this was inconclusive. The Spanish had confiscated his journals, but Pike reconstructed his endeavors from memory and in 1810 published *Account of the Expeditions to the Sources of the Mississippi and Through the Western Parts of Louisiana.* Pike's papers provided important information regarding the Spanish Southwest, but his bleak assessment of the region he explored was discouraging.

Promoted to captain while he was on this expedition, Pike rose to major in 1808 and lieutenant colonel in 1809. In June 1812, following the declaration of war against Great Britain, he was promoted to colonel and took command of the 15th Infantry Regiment. In March 1813, Pike was promoted to brigadier general and became inspector general of the Northern Army and commander of Fort Tompkins at Sackets Harbor on Lake Ontario. Commanding the invasion of YORK, Canada, on 27 April Pike led ashore the 6th, 15th, and 60th Regiments and Lieutenant Colonel Benjamin FORSYTH's Rifles. The Americans defeated the British and advanced on York's fort. Just as the Americans reached the fort, the British fired its magazine, raining stone and timber down on the Americans. Pike was among 100 or so American casualties. He died a few hours later aboard the U.S. flagship *Madison.*

See also CLARK, WILLIAM; LEWIS, MERIWETHER; LOUISIANA PURCHASE; WAR OF 1812: LAND OVERVIEW.

Further reading: Hollon, W. Eugene. *The Lost Pathfinder: Zebulon Montgomery Pike.* Norman: University of Oklahoma Press, 1969; Quaife, Milo M. *The Yankees Capture York.* Detroit: Wayne University Press, 1955; Terrell, John Upton. *Zebulon Pike: The Life and Times of an Adventurer.* New York: Weybright & Talley, 1968.

— Michèle T. Butts

Pinkerton, Allan (1819–1884) *Union espionage agent during the Civil War*
Born on 25 July 1819 at Glasgow, Scotland, Allan Pinkerton fled that country in 1842 to escape prosecution stemming

Allan Pinkerton's spies during the 1862 Peninsula Campaign *(Library of Congress)*

from his involvement with the Chartists, a workers' movement in Great Britain. After living briefly in Canada and Chicago, Pinkerton settled in Dundee, Illinois.

Pinkerton's first exposure to detective work came in 1847, when he discovered a group of counterfeiters while searching for wood. He returned with the local sheriff, who arrested them. Moving back to Chicago in 1850, Pinkerton did detective work for local and federal agencies, investigating counterfeiting and kidnapping cases. In February 1855 he formed his own detective firm, the North-West Police Agency. Railroad officials in Illinois employed Pinkerton to help them investigate suspected employee thefts.

In January 1861, while Pinkerton was in Philadelphia investigating threats by Southerners against a Northern railroad company, he heard rumors of a plot to assassinate president-elect Abraham LINCOLN in Baltimore, Maryland. Pinkerton was able to persuade Lincoln's advisers to have the president-elect travel incognito. The existence of the plot was never proven.

Lincoln selected Pinkerton to organize the Federal Secret Service. When his friend Major General George B. MCCLELLAN assumed command of the Army of the Potomac, Pinkerton directed intelligence operations for him. One of Pinkerton's spies, Timothy Walter, was captured and executed by the Confederates, but Pinkerton unmasked Confederate spy Rose Greenhow in Washington. Pinkerton's information gathering was almost as controversial as McClellan's command, and his wildly exaggerated reports of Confederate strength may actually have helped McClellan lose the campaign before Richmond. After Lincoln dismissed McClellan, Pinkerton returned to his detective agency, renamed Pinkerton's National Detective Agency.

After the Civil War, Pinkerton's business grew rapidly. Pinkerton agents were still involved in investigating various crimes against railroads, but they gained notoriety as strikebreakers. In his later years, Pinkerton published several books about his detective experiences. He died in Chicago on 1 July 1884.

See also CIVIL WAR, LAND OVERVIEW; INTELLIGENCE.

Further reading: Mackay, James. *Allan Pinkerton: The First Private Eye.* New York: Wiley, 1996; Morn, Frank. *"The Eye That Never Sleeps": A History of the Pinkerton National Detective Agency.* Bloomington: Indiana University Press, 1982.

— Mary S. Rausch

Plains of Abraham, Battle of the   See QUEBEC
CAMPAIGN.

Plattsburg, Battle of (Plattsburgh) (11 September
1814) *Decisive battle of the War of 1812*

In the fall of 1814 Sir George Prevost, the governor-general of Canada, led an army of 11,000 veteran British troops across the American border and down the Lake Champlain corridor. His immediate objective was the capture of Plattsburg, New York, the American naval base on Lake Champlain, in preparation for future operations against Vermont or Albany. Prevost's task was materially aided by the U.S. Secretary of War John ARMSTRONG, who in the previous month ordered Major General George IZARD to march the bulk of his army to the Niagara frontier. Hence, despite its significance, Plattsburg was defended only by a single brigade of U.S. Army regulars and invalids under Brigadier General Alexander MACOMB. Together with a force of some 800 New York and Vermont militia, Macomb's entire garrison mustered only 3,000 men.

Prevost's columns lumbered irresistibly onward and, following some sharp skirmishing along Beekmantown Road on 6 September 1814, they arrived before Plattsburg. When Prevost failed quickly to secure a convenient ford across the Saranac River to his front, however, he suspended all operations, pending the arrival of a British naval squadron under Captain George Downie. This period of inactivity confounded many senior British officers, accustomed to the duke of Wellington's victorious campaigning in Spain, and Prevost was roundly criticized.

The British remained idle for nearly five days, and Macomb used the impasse to strengthen his position. This consisted only of three wooden forts and two blockhouses on the south bank of the Saranac River astride Lake Champlain. Although his situation was essentially hopeless, Macomb did his best to keep the British occupied and delay their river crossing. On the night of 9 September 1814 he dispatched a force of 50 picked men under Captain George McGlassin, 6th U.S. Infantry, to attack a British rocket battery. McGlassin succeeded and escaped intact. Prevost remained stationary until the morning of 11 September 1814, when the British squadron finally entered the bay at 9:00 A.M.

Downie's appearance was the signal for Prevost to set the army in motion. As his fleet engaged the U.S. Navy squadron under Captain Thomas MACDONOUGH, Major General Frederick Robinson's brigade searched for a ford on the Saranac to turn Macomb's left flank. Simultaneously, another brigade, under Major General Thomas Brisbane, directly engaged American troops drawn up in front of Plattsburg. A third veteran brigade, under Major General Manly Powers, stood in ready reserve.

Robinson's crucial turning movement was hampered by a late start. He lost an additional hour by marching down the wrong road. Brisbane also had a much harder time attempting to cross in the face of determined resistance. However, just as the British columns began to make progress against the defenders, at 10:30 A.M. they incredulously received orders to halt and withdraw immediately. Downie's fleet had been decisively beaten by Macdonough on LAKE CHAMPLAIN. Deprived of naval support, Prevost grew apprehensive about the safety of his position. Mindful of the fate of Major General John Burgoyne in this same region in 1777, he ordered a general withdrawal. To the astonished defenders this was an incredible victory. The British force had withdrawn several miles before Macomb, still firmly ensconced behind his emplacements, realized they were gone.

British casualties in the Battle of Plattsburg numbered around 250, with American losses about half as many. For his stirring stand against impossible odds, Macomb received a gold medal and promotion to major general. Dissatisfaction with Prevost's timid performance was vocal, and he was recalled to England to face an official inquiry. The unexpected American triumph further dampened British claims for territorial concessions during peace negotiations at Ghent.

See also WAR OF 1812: LAND OVERVIEW; WAR OF 1812: NAVAL OVERVIEW.

Further reading: Everest, Allan S. *The War of 1812 in the Champlain Valley.* Syracuse, N.Y.: Syracuse University Press, 1981; Fitz-Enz, David G. *The Final Invasion: Plattsburg, the War of 1812's Most Decisive Battle.* New York: Cooper Square Press, 2001; Stanley, George F. G. *War of 1812: Land Operations.* Ottawa: National Museums of Canada and Macmillan, 1983.

— John C. Fredriksen

Plattsburg movement (1914–1920) *Movement to facilitate civilian military training*
The Plattsburg movement was an offshoot of a program of student military training camps established in 1913 by the then army chief of staff, Major General Leonard WOOD, with support from former President Theodore ROOSEVELT. In 1915 and 1916 similar camps, run by army officers, were organized at Plattsburg in upstate New York, catering largely to well-to-do East Coast professional men, lawyers, and businessmen, and their college-age sons. Skeptics christened the participants, who generally found the experience a strenuous but enjoyable break, "tired businessmen" or "TBMs." The camps' elite supporters, led by Grenville Clark, a New York lawyer, banded together in the MILITARY TRAINING CAMPS ASSOCIATION. Strongly pro-Allied in outlook, they sought to produce potential volunteer officers for the war with Germany that seemed increasingly likely. After American intervention in April 1917, the government established 16 similar camps to train officer candidates.

Plattsburg supporters hoped ultimately to establish a comprehensive system of compulsory military training to provide all young American men a similar elementary instruction in martial skills, thereby inculcating in American youth—recent immigrants in particular—physical hardihood and a sense of the obligations of democratic citizenship. The 20th-century United States military eventually rejected universal military training, during successive conflicts, preferring to institute conscription. The Plattsburg movement did, however, help to build enduring connections between the United States military and elite politicians and businessmen, many of whom traced a heightened consciousness of international issues back to their shared Plattsburg experience and later served in the national security bureaucracy.

See also PATTERSON, ROBERT P.; ROOT, ELIHU; SELECTIVE SERVICE; STIMSON, HENRY L.

Further reading: Clifford, J. Garry. *The Citizen Soldiers: The Plattsburg Training Camp Movement, 1913–1920.* Lexington: University Press of Kentucky, 1972; Finnegan, John Patrick. *Against the Specter of a Dragon: The Campaign for American Military Preparedness, 1914–1917.* Westport, Conn.: Greenwood Press, 1974; Kington, Donald M. *Forgotten Summers: The Story of the Citizens' Military Training Camps, 1921–1940.* San Francisco: Two Decades Publishing, 1995; Pearlman, Michael. *To Make Democracy Safe for America: Patricians and Preparedness in the Progressive Era.* Urbana: University of Illinois Press, 1983.

— Priscilla Roberts

Plei Mei, Battle of (19–29 October 1965) *Vietnam War battle in the Central Highlands, typical of many such engagements*
In the fall of 1965, People's Army of Vietnam (PAVN, North Vietnamese) troops concentrated in the western Central Highlands. Brigadier General Chu Huy Man, commander of PAVN units on the western plateau, planned to lay siege to the Special Forces camp at Plei Mei, then held by 12 Americans and some 400 Montagnards. He believed this attack would attract a road-bound Army of the Republic of Vietnam (ARVN, South Vietnamese) relief force, which could then be ambushed. With the relief column destroyed and the Special Forces camp taken, Man hoped to assault Pleiku City, clearing the way for an advance down Route 19 toward Qui Nhon and the coast, cutting South Vietnam in two.

Man positioned his 32d, 33d, and 66th Regiments around the 2,500-foot-high Chu Pong massif on the Cambodian border. On the evening of 19 October, his troops attacked the 200-yard triangular-shaped Plei Mei camp. At 10:00 P.M., PAVN troops overran the southern outpost; at 12:30 A.M. on the 20th, Man launched the main attack. PAVN sappers with satchel charges and bungalore torpedoes blasted through the barbed wire, followed by infantry with assault rifles. At 2:15 A.M. a flareship arrived, illuminating the battle area as PAVN forces continued to press their attack. Jet aircraft arrived at 3:45 A.M. to assist in the defense. Daylight air attacks drove the PAVN back. On the morning of 21 October, two companies of the ARVN 91st Airborne Ranger Battalion of Major Charles Beckwith's Project Delta were lifted by helicopter to a landing zone near the camp. They reached Plei Mei that night, taking a circuitous route to avoid ambush, and entered the camp on the morning of the 22nd. Beckwith then took command, reorganizing the camp's defenses with his additional personnel. PAVN troops, however, beat back counterattacks on 22 and 25 October to clear the high ground. On the evening of the 25th, an ARVN relief column of an armored cavalry squadron and a battalion of infantry arrived, despite having been badly mauled by PAVN ambushes on 21 and 23 October. The camp received its last PAVN mortar barrage on 29 October.

Air support and 330,000 pounds of air-lifted ammunition, food, medicines, and water were vital in blunting the PAVN assault. Two helicopters and a B-57 Canberra bomber were shot down; another B-57 crash-landed at base. Two A-1E Skyraiders were also lost, and of 19 C-123 cargo aircraft hit by ground fire, seven were shot up so badly that they had to be scrapped.

On 26 October, General William WESTMORELAND, commander of Military Assistance Command, Vietnam, decided to commit the newly arrived 1st Air Cavalry Division to an offensive throughout the area to destroy PAVN forces responsible for the attack. This led directly to the Battle of the IA DRANG VALLEY.

See also VIETNAM WAR.

Further reading: Currey, Cecil B. *Victory at Any Cost: The Genius of Viet Nam's Gen. Vo Nguyen Giap.* Washington, D.C.: Brassey's, 1997; Moore, Harold G., and Joseph L. Galloway. *We Were Soldiers Once . . . and Young: Ia Drang: The Battle That Changed the War.* New York: Random House, 1992; Stanton, Shelby L. *Green Berets at War: U.S. Army Special Forces in Southeast Asia, 1956–1975.* Novato, Calif.: Presidio Press, 1985.

— Spencer C. Tucker

Ploesti, raids on *World War II air raids to destroy the dozen Romanian oil refineries ringing the city of Ploesti that provided Germany with more than a third of its oil*

The first raid, causing little damage, occurred in the predawn hours of 12 June 1942. Carried out by 12 B-24 bombers commanded by Colonel Harry Halverson, the raid stretched the flying range of the planes and was carried out by men who had never before experienced combat or seen an enemy aircraft. They flew at night from Fayid, Egypt, over neutral Turkey (without challenge), struck the target, and returned to their base without loss.

The best-known raid on Ploesti, however, was Operation Tidal Wave on 1 August 1943 by IX Bomber Command, commanded by Brigadier General Uzal G. Ent. Over the objections of Ent and his group leaders, a low-level attack was ordered. Some 178 planes in five bomb groups began the flight from bases in North Africa, but 13 were lost for a variety of reasons before the target was reached.

Allied intelligence credited Ploesti with fewer than 100 antiaircraft guns; in reality there were 237. The Germans and Romanians could also attack withdrawing American bombers with some 300 fighter planes. German lieutenant general Alfred Gerstenberg commanded Ploesti's defenses during the entire aerial siege. Over time Gerstenberg added additional antiaircraft guns, some 2,000 smoke pots (ignited to obscure the refineries from the air), electronic gun tracking devices, and an early warning system that allowed refinery workers 40 minutes to gain bomb shelters.

A Consolidated B-24F Liberator nicknamed the "Sandman," of the 98th Bomb Group, IX Bomber Command, pulls away from the target in the low-level bombing attack against the oil refineries at Ploesti, Romania, on 1 August 1943. *(San Diego Aerospace Museum)*

German agents reported the U.S. air armada taking off from its North African bases, and the Germans then tracked the aircraft all the way to Ploesti. A navigational error caused the lead group to attack from a wrong direction, confusing trailing groups in their bomb runs. Some bombers flew so low that their gunners actually fired up at enemy flack towers. Antiaircraft fire and Axis fighters downed more than 40 bombers. Although the raid temporarily reduced oil output, the refineries were soon back to full production. Five officers were awarded the Medal of Honor for this raid; two others received the award posthumously in subsequent raids.

The U.S. Fifteenth Air Force resumed daylight attacks in 1944. Between 5 April and 19 August 1944, 5,479 American heavy bombers made 19 raids, in which 223 planes were lost. On 10 June 1944, 46 U.S. P-38 fighter-bombers attacked Ploesti in a low-altitude raid; 24 planes were lost. During summer 1944 the British lost 38 planes in a series of night raids by 924 heavy bombers. In a little more than a year, 6,627 Allied planes had raided Ploesti, with a loss of 339 aircraft. When the Russians seized Ploesti on 30 August, 12 days after the last raid, they found five refineries turning out 20 percent of normal production.

See also BRERETON, LEWIS HYDE; EAKER, IRA C.; STRATEGIC BOMBING, WORLD WAR II.

Further reading: Ardery, Philip. *Bomber Pilot: A Memoir of World War II.* Lexington: University Press of Kentucky, 1978; Dugan, James, and Carroll Stewart. *Ploesti.* New York: Random House, 1962; Dmitri, Ivan. *Flight to Everywhere.* New York: Whittlesey House, 1944; Newby, Leroy W. *Target Ploesti: View From a Bombsight.* Novato, Calif.: Presidio Press, 1983; Wolf, Leon. *Low Level Mission.* New York: Doubleday, 1957.

— Uzal W. Ent

Plum Point Bend, Battle of (10 May 1862) *Civil War naval battle and the first real engagement of the war between naval squadrons*
The battle occurred on 10 May 1862, on the Mississippi River just above Confederate Fort Pillow. Although three Confederate rams had sortied upriver from Fort Pillow two days before, no Union lookouts were posted downriver. Commodore Charles H. Davis commanded the U.S. Navy Mississippi Flotilla. He had taken charge only on 9 May from an ailing Commodore Andrew H. FOOTE.

At 6:00 A.M. on 10 May Union mortar boat *No. 16* was just above Craigshead Point, firing into Fort Pillow and protected by the Union gunboat *Cincinnati.* Eight Confederate gunboats, under Senior Captain James Montgomery, then appeared around Craigshead Point. Montgomery hoped to cut out or destroy the mortar boat and its cover-

ing gunboat, which were separated from the rest of the flotilla.

The Confederate gunboats made straight for the *Cincinnati* as its crew sought to get their vessel underway. The Confederate gunboat *General Bragg* rammed *Cincinnati,* opening a large hole in the Union gunboat's starboard quarter. As the *General Bragg* wrenched free, a broadside from the *Cincinnati* disabled it. The Confederate gunboat then drifted downstream out of action. Two other Confederate vessels then also rammed the *Cincinnati,* although its captain got his gunboat to shore before it sank.

At this point four other Union gunboats arrived from upriver. The Confederate gunboat *Van Dorn* rammed the *Mound City,* tearing off part of its bow, but the *Mound City's* captain was able to ground his gunboat before it sank. Montgomery then signaled his vessels to retire. As the Confederate ships fled downriver, three received hits in their boilers and were disabled.

The battle lasted only an hour. Union casualties were four wounded, one mortally. Perhaps 108 Confederates died, many of them scalded by the release of steam from the boilers. Despite its heavier personnel losses, the South had won a tactical victory by temporarily disabling two of the powerful Union gunboats.

See also CIVIL WAR, NAVAL OVERVIEW.

Further reading: Milligan, John D. *Gunboats Down the Mississippi.* Annapolis, Md.: Naval Institute Press, 1965; Musicant, Ivan. *Divided Waters. The Naval History of the Civil War.* New York: HarperCollins, 1995; Slagle, Jay. *Ironclad Captain. Seth Ledyard Phelps and the U.S. Navy, 1841–1864.* Kent, Ohio: Kent State University Press, 1996.

— Spencer C. Tucker

Point Pleasant, Battle of (10 October 1774) *The most significant battle of Dunmore's War*
As English colonial settlements pushed west of the Blue Ridge Mountains and beyond, the Shawnee and their Native American allies launched guerrilla attacks on the new arrivals. John MURRAY, 4th earl of Dunmore, and Virginia's royal governor from 1771 to 1776, decided to take upon himself the mission of eliminating the Shawnee menace from the areas already settled by the English colonists or designated for future expansion of the colony.

Dunmore's primary focus was the upper Ohio River Valley. Dunmore instructed Brigadier General Andrew LEWIS to recruit militiamen from the western Virginia counties for the intended operation. Lewis, with Augusta County militia and units from neighboring counties, was to proceed to the Ohio and rendezvous with units from the Potomac region who were to be led by Lord Dunmore himself.

As the militias moved toward their intended convergence point on the Ohio, the Shawnee chief, Cornstalk, maneuvered to confront the two divisions separately. It was Lewis's contingent that encountered the Shawnee first, on 10 October 1774, and defeated them at Point Pleasant, where the Kanawha River empties into the Ohio. However, it proved a close-fought engagement with heavy casualties to both sides.

As a consequence of this battle, the Shawnee were forced to submit to Dunmore's "terms of reconciliation," which compelled them to vacate all lands south of the Ohio. They were also obliged to return all prisoners and property (including slaves) taken in previous raids.

The terms of the agreement were potentially moot with the outbreak of the American Revolutionary War, and the Shawnee resumed their frontier attacks. In 1777, Cornstalk appeared at Point Pleasant—now a stockaded fort manned by Virginia militia—to explain that, although he personally was opposed to an Indian alliance with the British, since a majority of the Ohio Valley Indians were in favor, the chief felt obligated to side with his fellow Indians. The frontiersmen took Cornstalk hostage to keep him from joining forces with the British and their Indian allies. A group of Rockbridge County militiamen, whose families had been subjected to Shawnee attacks during the FRENCH AND INDIAN WAR, seized the opportunity to murder Cornstalk, his son, and several other Shawnee hostages on 10 November 1777.

See also AMERICAN INDIAN WARS: OVERVIEW; DUNMORE'S WAR; FALLEN TIMBERS, BATTLE OF; WAYNE, ANTHONY.

Further reading: Lewis, Virgil A. *History of the Battle of Point Pleasant. . . .* Charleston, W.Va.: Tribune Printing Co., 1909; Simpson-Poffenbarger, Livla Simpson. *Battle of Point Pleasant: First Battle of the American Revolution, October 10, 1774.* Point Pleasant, W.Va.: Mattox Printing Service, 1963.

— David W. Coffey

Polk, Leonidas (1806–1864) *Confederate general*
Born on 10 April 1806 at Raleigh, North Carolina, Leonidas Polk came from a prominent family. A relative of President James K. Polk, he attended the University of North Carolina prior to his appointment to the U.S. Military Academy, WEST POINT, graduating in the class of 1827. While a student, Polk forged friendships with several people who later influenced his military career, including future Confederates Jefferson DAVIS, Joseph E. JOHNSTON, and his roommate, Albert Sidney JOHNSTON.

Upon graduation, Polk resigned his commission and traded his uniform for clerical vestments. In 1830, after attending the Virginia Theological Seminary, Polk was ordained an Episcopal deacon. Eight years later he was named missionary bishop of the southwest. In 1841 Polk became bishop of Louisiana. He was also instrumental in establishing the University of the South at Sewanee, Tennessee.

With the eruption of the Civil War, Polk's friendship with Davis earned him a commission as major general in the Provisional Confederate Army. He soon was known as the Fighting Bishop. Charged with defending the Mississippi River, Polk violated Kentucky's shaky neutrality when he seized Columbus on 4 September 1861. Replaced by his friend General A. S. Johnston, Polk later bested Brigadier General Ulysses S. GRANT in the Battle of BELMONT on 7 November 1861. He also commanded a corps in the Battle of SHILOH, leading at least four charges against the Federal line.

During the 1862 Kentucky campaign, Polk was second-in-command in the Battle of PERRYVILLE, where he commanded one wing of Braxton BRAGG's Army of Mississippi. Two days later, on 10 October 1862, Polk was promoted to lieutenant general.

Tensions between Bragg and Polk began during the Kentucky campaign, when Polk refused to obey unclear orders and delayed the attack at Perryville. Bragg believed that Polk had been a bishop for too long to be an effective officer, and Polk led the anti-Bragg faction in the army. After the Confederate failure at STONES RIVER/MURFREESBORO, Polk urged Davis to replace Bragg. Following the Battle of CHICKAMAUGA, Bragg had Polk court-martialed for delaying his 20 September 1863 attack, and he was eventually reassigned to command the Department of Alabama, Mississippi, and East Louisiana.

In May 1864, Polk's Army of Mississippi joined General J. E. Johnston's Army of Tennessee in Georgia to help repel Major General William Tecumseh SHERMAN. On 14 June, while Polk and a group of officers watched Federal troops from the top of Pine Mountain, Polk was struck in the chest by an artillery round and died instantly.

See also ATLANTA CAMPAIGN; BEAUREGARD, P. G. T.; CIVIL WAR, LAND OVERVIEW; HOOD, JOHN BELL.

Further reading: Connelly, Thomas L. *Army of the Heartland: The Army of Tennessee, 1861–1862.* Baton Rouge: Louisiana State University Press, 1967; ———. *Autumn of Glory: The Army of Tennessee, 1862–1865.* Baton Rouge: Louisiana State University Press, 1971; Parks, Joseph H. *General Leonidas Polk, CSA.* Baton Rouge: Louisiana State University Press, 1962.

— Stuart W. Sanders

Pontiac (ca. 1720–1769) *Chief of the Ottawa and leader of Pontiac's Rebellion*
Born around 1720 in either northern Ohio or the Detroit region, Pontiac (Obwandiyag) emerged as a war chief of

the Ottawa during the FRENCH AND INDIAN WAR. Angered by British trade policies imposed after France's defeat, and inspired by the teachings of Neolin, the Delaware Prophet, who demanded a rejection of white ways, Pontiac summoned a council of Ottawa, Potawatomie, and Wyandot on 27 April 1763, and incited them to war against the British.

On 9 May Pontiac and some 460 warriors laid siege to Fort Detroit. By July more than 900 warriors had joined him, while other warriors launched attacks on British outposts throughout the Great Lakes region. Although Pontiac defeated a British sortie at Bloody Run on 31 July, he eventually lifted his siege on 15 October because the French had failed to return, his allies were becoming divided, and he lacked supplies to continue the siege through the winter.

Although Pontiac refused to attend a peace conference with Sir William JOHNSON at FORT NIAGARA in the summer of 1764, most of the tribes that had joined in his rebellion agreed to terms. In January 1765 the British offered Pontiac not only peace but also recognition as the chief spokesman for the tribes in the Great Lakes region. Pontiac accepted the British offer at a conference with Johnson on 24 July 1766, but only on the grounds that the British guarantee Indian land rights and occupy their forts as tenants.

Pontiac expected that his new alliance with the British would make him an intertribal leader, but other tribal leaders resented his pretensions, especially after the British did not follow through with their promises of gifts. Discredited, Pontiac fled his own village in 1768 and sought refuge among his wife's relatives at Cahokia. There he was murdered by a Peoria warrior on 20 April 1769.

See also AMERICAN INDIAN WARS: OVERVIEW; PONTIAC'S REBELLION.

Further reading: Anderson, Fred. *Crucible of War: The Seven Years' War and the Fate of Empire in British North America, 1754–1766.* New York: Knopf, 2000.

— Justin D. Murphy

Pontiac's Rebellion (May–November 1763) *Indian uprising against the British in the Old Northwest after the 1754–63 French and Indian War*

Although the British had forced the French to surrender Canada and the eastern half of North America in the 1763 TREATY OF PARIS, the Indians of the Old Northwest (Great Lakes region) did not feel defeated and thus were unwilling to accept British-imposed trade terms. Indeed, the origins of Pontiac's Rebellion can be traced to a tribal conference held on 9 September 1761 at Fort Detroit, where representatives from many of the tribes who would later participate in Pontiac's Rebellion demanded that the British lower the price of trade goods, furnish ammunition, and recognize Indian land rights. When the British refused, the tribes believed they had little choice but war.

At an intertribal council held on 27 April 1763, PONTIAC, an Ottawa war chief, incited tribes to go on the warpath. On 9 May, Pontiac and a war party of some 460 warriors laid siege to Fort Detroit, which was defended by just 125 soldiers and 40 traders under the command of Major Henry Gladwin. Within the first week, the British suffered casualties of 20 dead and 15 captured. By the end of July, Pontiac's forces, which had grown to more than 900 warriors, had defeated repeated British attempts to reinforce Fort Detroit. Meanwhile, Pontiac's allies had captured a series of British forts: Fort Sandusky (on Lake Erie), by Wyandot on 16 May; Fort St. Joseph (near modern Niles, Michigan), by Potawatomie on 25 May; Fort Miami (modern Fort Wayne, Indiana), by Miami on 27 May; Fort Ouiatenon (near modern Lafayette, Indiana), by Miami on 1 June 1763; and Fort Michilimackinac, by Chippewa on 2 June. Although Gladwin continued to hold out at Fort Detroit, every fort west of it had fallen.

In addition, on 28 May the Delaware had placed FORT PITT under siege, wiping out nearby settlements in the process. Fort Pitt's commander, Captain Simeon Ecuyer, who had appealed to Colonel Henry BOUQUET for reinforcements from Philadelphia, refused to surrender at a parley with Delaware leaders on 24 June. Making matters worse for Gladwin and Ecuyer, the Seneca (members of the Iroquois Confederacy) abandoned their traditional alliance with the British and joined the rebellion. The Seneca disrupted British attempts to send supplies around Niagara Falls to Fort Detroit and captured every fort between FORT NIAGARA and Fort Pitt (Fort Venango on 16 June, Fort LeBoeuf on 18 June, and Fort Presque Isle on 21 June).

Surprised by the magnitude of the uprising, Major General Sir Jeffery Amherst, commander in chief of British forces in North America, hurriedly dispatched forces from New York to relieve Fort Detroit and Fort Pitt and even suggested that the British distribute smallpox-infected blankets to the Indians (something that Ecuyer had already done at his parley with Delaware leaders on 24 June). Captain James Dalyell arrived at Fort Detroit on 28 July with a relief party of 260 men, only to march out three days later in hope of forcing Pontiac to lift the siege. Ambushed by Pontiac's warriors on 31 July, the British force suffered 20 dead (including Dalyell), 35 wounded, and 100 captured in the Battle of Bloody Run. One week later, Bouquet, leading a force of 400 British regulars to relieve Fort Pitt, ran into a force of Shawnee, Delaware, Mingo, Wyandot, Ottawa, and Miami approximately 25 miles east of Fort Pitt. Although the Indians were dispersed in the resulting

Battle of BUSHY RUN on 5 August, Bouquet's forces lost 50 dead and 60 wounded before limping into Fort Pitt on 8 August.

In the end, the onset of winter, not British military victory, brought an end to Pontiac's Rebellion in 1763. Agreeing to a truce on 15 October, Pontiac lifted his siege of Fort Detroit, not knowing that the British had only about two weeks worth of supplies remaining. Likewise, the Indian forces besieging Fort Pitt abandoned their campaign by the end of October.

Although Pontiac attempted to resume the offensive the following year, almost all of his allies abandoned the war. In the fall of 1763, Sir William JOHNSON, New York commissary for Indian affairs, negotiated peace with the Seneca, thereby placing pressure on the Shawnee and Delaware and freeing the supply lines around Niagara Falls. Realizing that the French would not return, one tribe after another signed treaties with the British, who now recognized the need to grant more favorable terms to the Indians. Pontiac himself eventually agreed to peace terms with Johnson on 24 July 1766.

Pontiac's Rebellion had important consequences both for Native Americans and the British Empire. On 7 October 1763 George III issued the Proclamation of 1763, which forbade settlement beyond the Appalachian Mountains, securing the tribes approximately 30 years of peace from land-hungry whites. On a more infamous note, anti-Indian vigilantes known as the Paxton Boys massacred Christian Indians at Conestoga, Pennsylvania, on 14 December 1763 in retaliation for the rebellion. Finally, Pontiac's Rebellion contributed directly to the coming of the American Revolution for it led to Prime Minister George Grenville's efforts to raise revenue from the colonies to pay for the stationing of British regulars in North America for defense against the Indians.

See also AMERICAN INDIAN WARS: OVERVIEW; FRENCH AND INDIAN WAR.

Further reading: Anderson, Fred. *Crucible of War: The Seven Years' War and the Fate of Empire in British North America, 1754–1766.* New York: Knopf, 2000.

— Justin D. Murphy

Pope, John (1822–1892) *U.S. Army general*
Born on 16 March 1822 at Louisville, Kentucky, John Pope graduated from the U.S. Military Academy, WEST POINT, in 1842. Commissioned a second lieutenant in the Topographical Engineers, he spent four years on survey duty. During the MEXICAN-AMERICAN WAR, he earned two brevets for gallantry. Promoted to first lieutenant, he performed engineering duties on the frontier and was elevated to captain in 1856. With the outbreak of the Civil War, in June 1861 Pope was appointed a brigadier general of U.S. Volunteers.

Pope held various district and field commands in Missouri, and in February 1862 assumed command of the Army of the Mississippi, with which he captured New Madrid and ISLAND NO. 10 on the Mississippi, opening the northern approaches to Memphis. Promoted to major general of Volunteers in March, Pope led his army under Major General Henry HALLECK in the glacial advance on CORINTH.

In June, President Abraham LINCOLN brought Pope to the East in hope of spreading the lessons of western success to the struggling Federal armies in Virginia, and Pope said as much in addresses to his new command. His vainglorious pronouncements angered the eastern soldiers, while his promise to crack down on Confederate sympathizers in Virginia earned him the wrath of General Robert E. LEE, who termed him a miscreant in his only such reaction to an opposing commander.

In order to facilitate his advance over more senior Volunteer generals, Pope was awarded the Regular Army rank of brigadier general. Various commands were combined to form the Army of Virginia, which he led against Lee's forces. Thoroughly outgeneraled by Lee, Pope and his new command were defeated at CEDAR MOUNTAIN and routed in the Second Battle of BULL RUN/MANASSAS in August. Although he blamed subordinates for the defeat and succeeded in ruining the career of Major General Fitz John Porter, who had not hesitated to criticize him openly, Pope was relieved of command and reassigned to the distant Department of the Northwest.

To his credit, Pope made the most of his situation and succeeded somewhat in resurrecting his reputation. He performed well in his new role, most notably in suppressing the Sioux Uprising in Minnesota, and laid the groundwork for a long and generally successful career. Brevetted major general in the Regular Army, he was mustered out of the Volunteers in September 1866. As a Regular Army brigadier, Pope was among the senior officers in the postwar establishment. He held a series of meaningful departmental commands and proved to be an effective administrator during the AMERICAN INDIAN WARS. Promoted to full-rank major general in 1882, he retired as commander of the Military Division of the Pacific in 1886. Pope died at Sandusky, Ohio, on 23 September 1892.

See also CIVIL WAR, LAND OVERVIEW; RED RIVER WAR; SIOUX WARS.

Further reading: Cozzens, Peter. *General John Pope: A Life for the Nation.* Urbana: University of Illinois Press, 2000; Utley, Robert M. *Frontier Regulars: The United States Army and the Indian, 1866–1891.* New York: Macmillan, 1973.

— David Coffey

Pork Chop Hill, Battle of (23 March–11 July 1953)

Battle of the Korean War

Pork Chop Hill (Hill 234) was so named because it resembled a pork chop in shape. Taken from the Chinese on 6 June 1952, it was made one of a series of defensive outposts scattered across the United Nations Command (UNC) front.

In November 1952, a Thai battalion defeated a Chinese attack on the hill. On 23 March 1953, Chinese forces attacked both Pork Chop and a nearby hill known as Old Baldy. Old Baldy was lost, as was part of Pork Chop. A counterattack drove the Chinese from the hill. A few days later, Eighth Army decided not to try to retake Old Baldy but to keep Pork Chop as an outpost.

On 16 April 1953, two platoons of E Company, 31st Regiment, occupied Pork Chop. Twenty men were on two-man listening posts, five on a patrol, leaving but 51 on the position. Chinese troops, completely investing the hill, overwhelmed all but a few men of the garrison. One platoon-sized American advance on the hill was quickly defeated. All that night, both American and Chinese artillery bombarded Pork Chop. In the predawn hours of the 17th, K and L Companies of the 31st Infantry lost heavily in reinforcing E Company. Shortly after 8:00 A.M., G Company, 17th Infantry Regiment of the 7th Infantry Division began to arrive on the hill. The Chinese, also reinforced, attacked with renewed fury, supported by mortars and artillery. Fighting on Pork Chop was vicious and often hand-to-hand; losses were appalling.

Strangely, commanders and staff officers in the rear believed that only mopping up was in progress on Pork Chop. Messages, expressing the urgency for reinforcement, went unanswered. Carriers bringing flamethrowers, ammunition, and litters stopped short of the hill as a consequence of Communist artillery and mortar fire. Then orders came for the survivors of two companies and all of G Company to withdraw by 3:00 P.M. At 2:45 P.M., the 7th Division's Public Affairs Officer arrived on the hill with two photographers to take pictures of the American success. Instead, he went to the rear with another plea for help.

Although both battalion and regimental headquarters knew that the troops on Pork Chop were exhausted, the commander of the 31st Infantry had not been informed that K and L Companies had taken excessive casualties. Therefore, he stressed troop exhaustion, not terrible casualties, in requesting reinforcement or relief from division headquarters.

At 3:00 P.M. the survivors of G Company left the hill. Twenty-five men remained in a tiny perimeter atop Pork Chop. F Company, 17th Infantry arrived on the hill about 9:30 P.M. E Company followed a few hours later, and then A Company, also of the 17th. The Chinese also reinforced, precipitating another ferocious infantry and artillery fight.

The Americans had committed companies and the Chinese battalions. Ultimately the UNC abandoned Pork Chop on 11 July 1953. Today it is in the Demilitarized Zone between North and South Korea.

See also KOREAN WAR.

Further reading: Hermes, Walter G. *Truce Tent and Fighting Front.* Washington, D.C.: Office of the Chief of Military History, United States Army, 1966; Marshall, S. L. A. *Pork Chop Hill.* New York: Berkley, 1986.

— Uzal W. Ent

Porter, David (1780–1843) *U.S. Navy officer*

Born on 1 February 1780 at Boston, Massachusetts, into a maritime family, David Porter entered the U.S. Navy as a midshipman in 1798. His first assignment was aboard the frigate CONSTELLATION. The ship's captain, Thomas TRUXTON, befriended the young officer and provided a much needed role model. Porter distinguished himself during the capture of the French frigate *L'Insurgente* in February 1799 and was promoted to lieutenant.

During the QUASI-WAR WITH FRANCE, Porter was involved in several exploits that garnered him much attention. In 1803 he served aboard the frigate PHILADELPHIA when Tripolitan forces captured the ship. He remained a prisoner until 1805—the end of the TRIPOLITAN WAR.

Porter rose to master commandant in April 1806 and commanded the New Orleans Station from 1806 to 1810. Assigned as captain of the 32-gun frigate ESSEX in 1811, he was promoted to captain in 1812. After the onset of the WAR OF 1812, the *Essex* captured the first British warship of the conflict. In 1813, still commanding the frigate, Porter made the first voyage by a U.S. Navy ship around Cape Horn and decimated the British whaling fleet operating around the Galapagos Islands. While in the Pacific, he also claimed the Marquesas Islands for the United States, but the government refused to recognize his action.

On 21 March 1814, two British warships defeated the *Essex* in a sanguinary fight off Valparaiso, Chile. Following the war, Porter served as a navy commissioner until 1822, when he assumed command of the West Indies Squadron, charged with suppressing Caribbean piracy. Within that command was the *Sea Gull*, the first steam-powered warship to engage in hostilities. While Commodore Porter was generally successful, his inflated sense of honor brought him before a court of inquiry in 1825 after he landed a force at Fajardo, Puerto Rico, and demanded an apology from the Spanish governor for insulting one of his officers. The court found him guilty not only of the Fajardo landing but also of insubordination to the president—the latter because of offensive correspondence he sent to both President John Quincy Adams and Secretary of the Navy

Samuel Southard. Despite the conviction, the court passed a lenient sentence of only six months suspension with full pay. Nevertheless, Porter resigned his commission.

From 1826 to 1829, Porter commanded the Mexican Navy, creating an effective force, given the country's limited resources. In 1831, President Andrew Jackson's administration appointed Porter chargé d'affaires to the Ottoman Empire. David Porter died in Constantinople on 3 March 1843 but was eventually laid to rest in Philadelphia. His son, David Dixon PORTER, and foster son, David G. FARRAGUT, went on to fame during the Civil War, continuing the family naval tradition.

See also *ESSEX V. PHOEBE AND CHERUB; GAMBLE, JOHN M.*

Further reading: Long, David F. *Nothing Too Daring: A Biography of Commodore David Porter.* Annapolis, Md.: United States Naval Institute, 1970; Turnbull, Archibald Douglas. *Commodore David Porter, 1780–1843.* New York: Century, 1929.

— Rodney Madison

Porter, David Dixon (1813–1891) *U.S. Navy admiral*
Born on 8 July 1813 at Chester, Pennsylvania, David Dixon Porter was the son of Commodore David PORTER and brother of Commodore William D. Porter. His adopted brother was Admiral David F. FARRAGUT. As a child Porter accompanied his father on pirate suppression expeditions in the Gulf of Mexico. Indeed, he spent much of his early life at sea and consequently received little formal education. At 14 he joined the Mexican Navy as a midshipman, and in 1829 he entered the U.S. Navy at the same rank. Promoted to lieutenant in 1841, he saw considerable service during the MEXICAN-AMERICAN WAR but spent the next several years in private merchant enterprises before returning to active duty in 1855.

After 20 years as a lieutenant, with the outbreak of the Civil War, Porter was promoted to commander. He served in the Gulf Coast Blocking Squadron and led the mortar flotilla under now Flag Officer Farragut in the capture of NEW ORLEANS. In October 1862 he assumed command of the Mississippi River Squadron, and he cooperated with Major General Ulysses S. GRANT in the campaign against VICKSBURG. For his excellent service rendered there, Porter was promoted directly to rear admiral, bypassing the ranks of captain and commodore.

In April and May 1864 Porter led a large fleet up the Red River to support Major General Nathaniel P. BANKS's army in Louisiana. In the RED RIVER CAMPAIGN the fleet was harassed by Confederate land forces and slowed by low water levels during its difficult withdrawal. In all, it was a frustrating experience for Porter. Ordered to the East, he

directed the North Atlantic Squadron for the balance of the war. In December 1864 he supported Major General Benjamin BUTLER's failed attempt to capture FORT FISHER, a stronghold that protected the Confederacy's last open port at Wilmington. Porter urged a second effort, and in January his fleet backed the expedition directed by Brigadier General Alfred TERRY that took the bastion. In the closing days of the war, Porter led a flotilla up the James River to support Grant's efforts at Richmond and PETERSBURG.

After the war Porter became superintendent of the U.S. Naval Academy, Annapolis, serving in that post until 1869. In 1866 he was promoted to vice admiral, and in 1870, upon the death of Farragut, he rose to full admiral. He spent his remaining years as head of the navy and wrote numerous books, including *Incidents and Anecdotes of the Civil War* and *The Naval History of the Civil War.* Porter died in Washington, D.C., on 13 February 1891.

See also CIVIL WAR, NAVAL OVERVIEW.

Further reading: Hearn, Chester G. *Admiral David Dixon Porter.* Annapolis, Md.: Naval Institute Press, 1996; Porter, David Dixon. *The Naval History of the Civil War.* Reprint. Secaucus, N.J.: Castle Books, 1984.

— David Coffey

Port Hudson (22 May–9 July 1863) *Last important Confederate bastion on the Mississippi River to fall to the Union during the Civil War*
In accordance with the so-called Union ANACONDA PLAN, the Confederacy would be strangled by blockading its ports and split along the Mississippi. By summer 1862 Union forces were well on their way to achieving that end, having taken FORT HENRY, FORT DONELSON, ISLAND NO. 10, FORT PILLOW, MEMPHIS, and NEW ORLEANS, and threatening VICKSBURG.

To strengthen the Confederate hold on Vicksburg, Trans-Mississippi Department commander Major General Earl Van Dorn ordered Port Hudson fortified. In late 1862, the Confederates began to turn it into a formidable bastion with guns positioned atop an 80-foot bluff that commanded the river. A series of positions allowed the defenders to direct fire on attackers. The Confederates could not receive new shipments of heavy guns by water because the Mississippi was controlled by the ironclad *Essex* and other Union warships, but they obtained them via railroads and road as well as from a Union ship that beached.

The partially successful passage of Port Hudson by forces under Rear Admiral David G. FARRAGUT on 24 March 1863 showed the strength of the Confederate positions and that reduction of their batteries would require land troops. Not until mid-May 1863, however, did Major General Nathaniel BANKS's Army of the Gulf begin an offensive against Port Hudson, where Major General Franklin Gardner commanded some 7,000 Confederates. By 23 May, some 10,000 Union troops had Port Hudson encircled.

Despite the support of gunboats in the river, the Union troops failed in an attempt to take the fortress on 27 May, in part because of Banks's inability to coordinate his superior assets. The assault on Port Hudson marked the first use of African-American troops by the Union as two regiments of Louisiana Native Guards took part in the attack on the Confederate left. In the attack, the Federals sustained nearly 2,000 casualties, while the defenders lost 250–275 men.

Banks then resorted to bombardment and siege and continued to build up his strength, ultimately to 30,000 men. He attempted another assault early on 14 June but again was repulsed. The Confederates, although short of ammunition and food, held out until 8 July, when Gardner decided that, with the recently confirmed fall of Vicksburg, honor had been satisfied. The siege had cost the Confederacy nearly 900 casualties and the remainder of the garrison became prisoners. Union casualties came to 4,500 from battle and almost as many to disease and sunstroke.

See also AFRICAN AMERICANS IN THE MILITARY; CIVIL WAR, LAND OVERVIEW; CIVIL WAR, NAVAL OVERVIEW.

Further reading: Cunningham, Edward. *The Port Hudson Campaign 1862–1863.* Baton Rouge: Louisiana State University Press, 1963; Hewitt, Lawrence Lee. *Port Hudson: Confederate Bastion on the Mississippi.* Baton Rouge: Louisiana State University Press, 1987.

— Paolo E. Coletta

Powder River expedition (November–December 1876) *Campaign of the Sioux Wars, 1876–77*
In the aftermath of the LITTLE BIGHORN disaster, the army rushed troops from across the West to avenge Lieutenant Colonel George Armstrong CUSTER and the more than 250 troopers of the 7th Cavalry who died with him. Throughout the summer of 1876 an unprecedented concentration of frontier military might scoured the Yellowstone watershed with little to show for it. Sioux leaders SITTING BULL, CRAZY HORSE, and Gall, with hundreds of their people, remained free and defiant, as did Dull Knife's Cheyenne and other bands. Although Colonel Nelson MILES and a small force remained in the field, doggedly pursuing Sitting Bull and his followers, most of the army units in the region geared up for a fall campaign.

A second wave of reinforcements, including Colonel Ranald S. MACKENZIE and six troops of his excellent 4th Cavalry, reported to Brigadier General George CROOK at Camp Robinson, Nebraska. In November 1876 Crook pre-

pared to take the field. At Fort Fetterman he assembled a giant force: 11 troops of cavalry from the 2nd, 3rd, 4th, and 5th Regiments under Mackenzie; 15 companies of infantry from the 4th, 9th, 14th, and 25th Regiments and the 4th Artillery under Lieutenant Colonel George P. Buell; 400 INDIAN SCOUTS and auxiliaries and a massive supply train—more than 2,000 men in all. On 14 November the expedition marched up the Bozeman Trail for the Powder River country in search of Crazy Horse's village.

Although hampered by heavy snow, the long column made steady progress. But before the force could reach the area where Crook hoped to find Crazy Horse, his scouts reported a large Cheyenne village on the Red Fork of the Powder River in the Bighorn Mountains of Wyoming. Crook dispatched Mackenzie with most of the cavalry and Indian auxiliaries to strike the village.

On the frozen morning of 25 November, Mackenzie's 1,100 men attacked the village of 200 lodges holding some 400 warriors and their families. This was the village of Cheyenne chiefs Dull Knife and Little Wolf. Flushed from their lodges, warriors rushed their families to safety before fighting back. A fierce battle for the village lasted into the afternoon, with Mackenzie's Indian auxiliaries taking a leading role. The soldiers and their allies finally gained control of the village, in which they found evidence—equipment and a guidon from the 7th Cavalry—of Cheyenne involvement in the Battle of the Little Bighorn. They then burned the lodges and precious food and clothing. Mackenzie's command also took possession of 700 ponies .

Mackenzie lost one officer and five men killed and 26 wounded while killing 40 Cheyenne—a heavy toll for a commander known for taking and inflicting light casualties. But the true measure of devastation came in the destruction of the village and the loss of ponies. Left with the clothes on their backs and what belongings they managed to carry away, the surviving Cheyenne faced a wintry nightmare. The next night the temperature dropped to 30 degrees below zero. Eleven infants froze to death before the Cheyenne found sanctuary in Crazy Horse's village.

The soldiers and their Indian allies suffered too as they continued the march in heavy snow storms and subzero temperatures without locating Crazy Horse's village. Crook suspended the expedition in December. The so-called Dull Knife Fight dealt a crippling blow to the Cheyenne and hastened the capitulation of the Sioux.

See also AMERICAN INDIAN WARS: OVERVIEW; INDIAN WARFARE; SIOUX WARS.

Further reading: Bourke, John G. *On the Border with Crook.* Reprint. Lincoln: University of Nebraska Press, 1971; Utley, Robert M. *Frontier Regulars: The United States Army and the Indian, 1866–1891.* New York: Macmillan, 1973.

— David Coffey

Powell, Colin L. (1937–   ) *U.S. Army general and secretary of state*

Born on 5 April 1937 to an immigrant Jamaican family in the Harlem section of New York City, Colin Luther Powell graduated from City College of New York in 1958 with a B.A. in Geology and was commissioned an infantry second lieutenant through the ROTC.

Following a tour in Germany, Powell served two tours in Vietnam, 1962–63 and 1968–69. During the first tour he was an adviser to an Army of the Republic of Vietnam (ARVN) infantry battalion and was wounded by a booby trap. During his second tour he was injured in a helicopter crash but still helped rescue other troops from the burning wreck. On this tour, Powell served as an assistant operations officer in the 23d (American) Division. He drafted the division's first official response to rumors of the MY LAI MASSACRE. Powell reported that the rumors were unfounded. He continued to maintain that he knew nothing about this massacre of civilians until much later.

Powell attended the Command and General Staff College in 1968 and earned an M.B.A. from George Washington University in 1971. During 1972–73 Powell was a

General Colin L. Powell   *(Library of Congress)*

White House Fellow. He attended the National War College in 1976 and as a colonel commanded a brigade of the 101st Airborne Division (1976–77). He was senior military assistant to the secretary of defense (1983–86) and as a lieutenant general commanded V Corps in Germany (1986–87). He was then assistant to the president and to the national security advisor (1987–89). Promoted general, the first African American to hold that rank, he headed the U.S. Army Forces Command. In October 1989 Powell became chairman of the Joint Chiefs of Staff (JCS), the youngest man and first African American in that position.

As chairman of the JCS, Powell played a major role in the PANAMA INVASION, Operations DESERT SHIELD and DESERT STORM (the Gulf War), and the beginnings of the post–cold war military drawdown. Building on the Vietnam War experience, Powell insisted that once a decision had been made to employ military force, it should be overwhelming and decisive. To employ less would produce a protracted conflict with attendant waste in lives and resources. Nonetheless, Powell was criticized for recommending what many believe was a premature halt in the successful Allied ground offensive in the Gulf War.

Powell retired from the army in September 1993, wrote his memoirs, and became active in promoting volunteerism. He considered but declined runs for the presidency as a Republican. In early 2001, Powell was named secretary of state in the administration of President George W. Bush.

See also AFRICAN AMERICANS IN THE MILITARY; VIETNAM WAR, COURSE OF.

Further reading: Powell, Colin. *My American Journey: An Autobiography.* New York: Random House, 1995; Roth, David. *Sacred Honor: A Biography of Colin Powell.* San Francisco: Harper, 1993.

— Spencer C. Tucker

Powers, Francis Gary (1929–1977) *American pilot and espionage agent whose capture while on a reconnaissance mission over the Soviet Union provoked a major international crisis*

Born on 17 August 1929 at Burdine, Kentucky, Francis Gary Powers joined the U.S. Air Force in 1950. In 1955 the CENTRAL INTELLIGENCE AGENCY (CIA) recruited Powers, who officially resigned his air force commission to work for Lockheed Corporation under the name Francis G. Palmer. Powers agreed to spend three years, supposedly with the 2d Weather Observation Squadron, flying photographic reconnaissance missions over the Soviet Union from bases in Turkey and Pakistan in the newly developed U-2 airplane, after which he could rejoin the military without losing seniority.

On 1 May 1960, in the U-2 INCIDENT, a Soviet missile battery fired at and disabled Powers's plane. He bailed out over Soviet territory and was captured. Although the U.S. government initially claimed that a meteorological observation flight had inadvertently entered Soviet airspace, inspection of the plane's wreckage revealed it to be a military photoreconnaissance espionage flight; President Dwight D. EISENHOWER eventually confirmed this fact. Powers made a full confession and stood trial in Moscow, receiving a 10-year sentence.

In February 1962, the Soviet Union exchanged him for its own agent, Colonel Rudolf Abel, who was then in U.S. custody. Powers returned to the Air Force, subsequently worked for the CIA and Lockheed, publishing his memoirs in 1970. He eventually became an airborne traffic reporter, dying on 1 August 1977 in a helicopter crash.

See also COLD WAR; INTELLIGENCE.

Further reading: Berman, Harold J., ed. *The Trial of the U2.* New York: Notable Trials Library, 1995; Beschloss, Michael R. *MAYDAY: Eisenhower, Khrushchev, and the U-2 Affair.* New York: Harper & Row, 1986; Peebels, Curtis. *Shadow Flights: America's Secret Air War Against the Soviet Union.* Novato, Calif.: Presidio Press, 2000; Powers, Francis Gary, with Curt Gentry. *Operation Overflight: The U-2 Spy Pilot Tells His Story for the First Time.* New York: Holt, Rinehart & Winston, 1970.

— Priscilla Roberts

Powhatan (ca. 1547–1618) *Native North American chief, head of the Powhatan confederacy, and father of Pocahontas*

Powhatan, formally called Wahunsonacock, was the son of an Algonquian chieftain whose people had migrated north to coastal Virginia during the 16th century. Eventually his father subjugated five of the local tribes and established a loosely organized confederacy. Inheriting the confederacy upon his father's death, Powhatan conquered 24 other tribes and absorbed them into the alliance. At the peak of his power he controlled 200 villages, with a population of about 13,000 people.

When the English founded the Jamestown colony in 1607, the Powhatan empire embraced most of tidewater Virginia and the eastern shore of Chesapeake Bay. Each tribe provided military aid and tribute in the form of food, furs, and precious metals to Powhatan. Most of the Indians lived along rivers in fortified villages consisting of long dwellings sheathed with bark. Largely a sedentary people, they focused on cultivating crops, fishing, and hunting.

By all accounts, Powhatan was an intelligent and forceful ruler. Despite several clashes with the colonists, he adopted a policy of cautious assistance and wary suspicion toward the fledgling English settlement. He soon developed a gainful trade with the newcomers, swapping corn, beans, squash, and rice for kettles, traps, fishhooks, needles, hatchets, swords, and guns. To maintain Powhatan's cooperation, in 1609 the English presented him with a royal crown, an elaborate coronation ceremony, and gifts. As more adventurers arrived in Virginia in search of easy riches, rather than wasting time bartering for new land or clearing the forests, they drove or defrauded the Indians off their fields, set their villages on fire, or attempted to enslave them. Fighting worsened when Powhatan's warriors retaliated and almost annihilated the English.

In 1613 the now frantic settlers captured Powhatan's daughter, Pocahontas, and ransomed her for white captives held by the Indians. Although Powhatan released the prisoners, the English refused to free Pocahontas, who claimed she wished to remain with her captors. While in custody, she had converted to Christianity, learned English, and presumably fallen in love with planter John Rolfe. In 1614, tired of incessant warfare and eager to see his daughter again, Powhatan finally agreed to peace terms and permitted Rolfe to marry Pocahontas.

The tranquil relations between the English and the Indians that resulted from the treaty proved short-lived. Following Powhatan's death in 1618, the peace disintegrated when settlers resumed their theft of Indian lands on which to grow tobacco. Although Powhatan's brother and successor, OPECHANCANOUGH, led an uprising in 1622 that killed 347 people, including John Rolfe, the English soon launched a vindictive reprisal that destroyed the Powhatan confederacy. Sporadic warfare continued until 1644, when Opechancanough led one last uprising in which 500 whites died before the English captured and executed him.

See also AMERICAN INDIAN WARS: OVERVIEW; ANGLO-POWHATAN WAR.

Further reading: Craven, Frank Wesley. *White, Red, and Black: The Seventeenth-Century Virginian.* Charlottesville: University Press of Virginia, 1971; Gleach, Frederic W. *Powhatan's World and Colonial Virginia: A Conflict of Cultures.* Lincoln: University of Nebraska Press, 1997; Rountree, Helen C. *The Powhatan Indians of Virginia.* Norman: University of Oklahoma Press, 1989.

— Aldo E. Salerno

Preble, Edward (1761–1807) *U.S. Navy officer and commodore of the U.S. Mediterranean Squadron during the Tripolitan War*

Born on 15 August 1761 at Falmouth (now Portland), Maine, Edward Preble was the son of Jedidiah Preble, who served in the FRENCH AND INDIAN WAR and who became a brigadier general during the American Revolutionary War. He ran away from home at 16 to serve on a privateer during the Revolutionary War. Captured at sea, he was later exchanged and rose to lieutenant in 1782. Afterward he served in the merchant marine.

Granted a commission in the U.S. Navy as a lieutenant in 1798, during the QUASI-WAR WITH FRANCE Preble took several prizes while in command of a revenue cutter. Given command of the new frigate *Essex* in 1799, the next year he sailed around the Cape of Good Hope to Java, the first time a U.S. Navy vessel had done so.

In 1803, as a commodore, Preble led a squadron of vessels against the Barbary states of North Africa that had been seizing U.S. merchant vessels. He swiftly reaffirmed a treaty with Morocco, originally signed in 1786, and then turned his attention to Tripoli, which had declared war on the United States the previous spring in an effort to extract greater concessions. Setting up a base of operations in Syracuse, Sicily, Preble imposed a blockade of Tripoli and conducted shore bombardment operations using gunboats borrowed from Sicily. Preble avenged the capture of frigate *PHILADELPHIA* by successfully organizing its destruction.

Preble was a stern and quick-tempered commander who initially earned the enmity of his young officers. By his example, however, he soon earned their respect. His influence within the fledgling navy was extended through the many junior officers who served with him in the Mediterranean. In addition to Stephen DECATUR, Preble also guided the early careers of Isaac HULL and David PORTER.

Preble is frequently credited with having established some of the earliest traditions of the U.S. Navy, including the principle of an officer caring for his men before attending to his own needs. He also stressed the importance of frequent drill, inspection, and training.

Relieved of his Mediterranean command in 1804, Preble returned to the United States, where he briefly supervised the building of gunboats. He died in Portland, Maine, on 25 August 1807.

See also TRIPOLITAN WAR.

Further reading: McKee, Christopher. *Edward Preble: A Naval Biography, 1761–1807.* Annapolis, Md.: Naval Institute Press, 1972; Pratt, Fletcher. *Preble's Boys: Commodore Preble and the Birth of American Sea Power.* New York: Sloane, 1950.

— Christopher A. Preble

precision-guided munitions (PGMs) *Weapons guided to their target by some mechanism until impact*
As early as 1924, Winston Churchill speculated that in the future explosives might be "guided automatically in flying machines by wireless or other rays, without a human pilot, in ceaseless procession on a hostile city, arsenal, camp, or dockyard." During WORLD WAR II, both Germany and the United States experimented with several early "smart bomb" designs, the most successful of which was the U.S. radio-controlled VB-1 Azon.

During the 1950s and the 1960s both the United States and the Soviet Union fielded a series of revolutionary antiaircraft missiles that relied on radar or heat-seeking technology. During the VIETNAM WAR, U.S. air-to-air missiles proved to be something of a disappointment, hitting their targets only 10-15 percent of the time, while Soviet-designed surface-to-air missiles (SAMs) faired even worse, with a success rate of only about 2 percent. Still, even this was a vast improvement in range and lethality over previous antiaircraft weapons; and, as the Israeli Air Force discovered during the 1973 Arab-Israeli war, SAMs were improving rapidly in effectiveness. In contrast, the approximately 27,000 "smart bombs" used during the Vietnam War achieved some startling successes, in some cases destroying bridges in minutes that had previously withstood attacks for years, and in general achieving a "circular error probable" (CEP) of only about 30 feet. (CEP is the radius within which statistically half of the weapons will hit.)

In the 1980s, attention turned within the U.S. Army to the potential of "emerging technologies" to revolutionize ground warfare in the same way PGMs had already done for air combat. The 1970s had already seen the deployment of a very successful first generation of wire-guided antitank missiles, and it was hoped that advances in electronics would make possible a second generation of weapons that could offset Soviet armored numerical superiority. PGMs with a variety of other missions also grew in importance in the 1980s. These included missiles that homed in on the radar emissions of SAM sites and antiship missiles such as the famous French-built Exocets, used with such effect against the British by the Argentines during the 1982 Falklands War.

Perhaps the most destabilizing development of this period was the application of precision-guidance to the world of NUCLEAR WEAPONS. Ground-, sea-, and air-launched cruise missiles, along with the latest generation of intercontinental BALLISTIC MISSILES (some deploying warheads with CEPs of perhaps 100 meters or fewer), threatened the doctrine of Mutual Assured Destruction (MAD) by providing the capability to destroy even hardened missile silos. The promise of PGMs and other even more exotic technologies was also enough to convince President Ronald Reagan that STRATEGIC DEFENSE against nuclear weapons was now a realistic possibility, resulting in the "Star Wars" program.

It was not until the 1991 Gulf War, however, that many of these technologies faced realistic battle conditions on a large scale. The first blows to land in Operation DESERT

STORM were laser-guided Hellfire missiles fired by helicopters against Iraqi radar sites. These were followed shortly thereafter by laser-guided bombs (LGBs) and Tomahawk cruise missiles, targeting some of the most heavily defended installations in Iraq. Soon even the usually skeptical U.S. press corps openly marveled at the accuracy of these weapons and reinforced their words with video images beamed around the world of smart bombs entering buildings through windows and chimneys. Patriot surface-to-air missiles intercepted incoming Scuds and produced spectacular fireworks displays, literally in front of network cameras. Although later analysis concluded that the Patriots had intercepted far fewer incoming missiles than was originally believed, the fact that a missile designed to intercept aircraft could hit an incoming missile at all was still an impressive omen of things to come. (And given that Scuds were always more of a political and public relations problem than a military threat, in a sense the Patriots accomplished their mission as soon as news organizations reported that they had done so.)

Largely forgotten in all of this was the vastly improved performance of other classes of PGMs, especially antitank, antiradiation, and other categories of air-to-ground missiles. None of this would have been possible also without the many recent improvements in target acquisition and communications technology.

Still, as critics pointed out, even after six weeks of bombardment Iraq had not surrendered, requiring a massive ground invasion to bring victory. Further, only about 10 percent of the bombs dropped during Desert Storm had been "smart," and while in good weather many PGMs could hit their targets 70 percent or more of the time, in bad weather these rates often plummeted, with some weapons becoming ineffective altogether. The desert had also provided an environment unusually well-suited to the use of PGMs, and for the most part the Iraqi military had not proved the most wily of adversaries—two conditions that would not always hold in later conflicts.

Nonetheless, PGMs had proven to be enormously useful in fulfilling a fundamental requirement of most post–cold war military interventions: the reduction of casualties among both attackers and the civilian population. In contrast to the 1991 Gulf War, PGMs accounted for almost 70 percent of the weapons used during the three-week 1995 Deliberate Force NATO air campaign over Bosnia, and by the three-month 1999 Allied Force air campaign over Kosovo and Serbia, this proportion had exceeded 90 percent.

Although weather proved a major impediment in both of these operations, its effects were lessened in the late 1990s by the introduction of weapons that relied in part on Global Positioning System (GPS) receivers. PGMs also were used extensively during numerous post-1991 air strikes on Iraq, including major attacks in January 1993,

September 1996, and the Desert Fox operation of December 1998, not to mention the attacks on air defense sites in Iraqi no-fly zones that had become almost routine by 2000. The demand for reduced civilian casualties became such that in 1999 the U.S. Air Force began sometimes to drop LGBs filled solely with concrete, relying on kinetic energy alone to destroy their targets. For even smaller operations, in which policy makers demanded a virtually zero possibility of friendly casualties, although not necessarily of collateral damage, Tomahawk cruise missiles proved to be the weapon of choice, being the sole weapons used in a strike on the Iraqi intelligence headquarters in June 1993 and on suspected terrorist facilities in Afghanistan and Sudan in August 1998.

In the future, PGMs undoubtedly will play a large role within the U.S. military. It remains to be seen, however, if the short-term gains realized by these politically expedient, small-scale uses of force will outweigh the potential bitterness generated overseas by such "Tomahawk diplomacy." Perhaps the most chilling observation of all relating to PGMs and the future remains the reported comment by India's military chief of staff on what he had learned from watching American military technology at work in the 1991 Gulf War: "Never fight the United States without nuclear weapons."

See also ELECTRONIC WARFARE; NAVAL ORDNANCE.

Further reading: Blackwelder, Donald I. *The Long Road to Desert Storm and Beyond: The Development of Precision Guided Bombs.* Maxwell AFB, Ala.: Air University Press, 1993; Cohen, Eliot A., ed. *Gulf War Air Power Survey.* 5 vols. Washington, D.C.: Office of the Secretary of the Air Force, 1993; Friedman, George, and Meredith Friedman. *The Future of War: Power, Technology and American World Dominance in the 21st Century.* New York: St. Martin's Press, Griffin, 1998; McDaid, Hugh, and David Oliver. *Smart Weapons: Top Secret History of Remote Controlled Airborne Weapons.* New York: Barnes & Noble, 1997.
— David Rezelman

Prescott, William (1726–1795) *Continental Army officer*

Born on 20 February 1726 at Groton, Massachusetts, William Prescott saw military service during both KING GEORGE'S WAR and the FRENCH AND INDIAN WAR. As a lieutenant of provincial troops, Prescott distinguished himself in the 1745 campaign that took Cape Breton Island and the fortress of LOUISBOURG. Because of his leadership during that campaign the British offered the 19-year-old Prescott a commission in the British army. Declining the offer, he returned to his family and farming.

A staunch supporter of the Patriot cause, Prescott was instrumental following closure of the port of Boston in

1774 in sending supplies of food to the city's inhabitants. When the American Revolutionary War began he was a colonel of militia at Pepperell, Massachusetts. He led his men to Concord on 19 April 1775, but the unit arrived too late to take part in the fighting. Later Prescott was a member of the council of war at Cambridge, Massachusetts, which directed the militia units surrounding Boston.

When Brigadier General Artemas Ward learned that the British were preparing to occupy Dorchester and Charlestown Heights, he ordered Prescott to fortify Charlestown Heights first. Arriving in the Charlestown Peninsula, Prescott decided, after consultation with the other officers, to fortify Breed's Hill as opposed to BUNKER HILL, because the former was a more defensible position. The task was only partially accomplished by the time the British were joined in battle on 17 June 1775. Debate continues over whether Prescott or Brigadier General Israel PUTNAM was in command of Patriot forces on the field of battle. Regardless, Prescott had charge of Patriot forces defending a vital point in the line, and he demonstrated both courage and outstanding leadership. He was one of the last to leave the redoubt. After the engagement, Prescott offered, if supplied, to lead three fresh regiments against the hills lost to the British, but this was rejected.

In January 1776 Prescott became colonel of the 7th Continental Army Regiment. He took part in operations connected with the evacuation of New York in 1776. Age and the effects of an injury sustained in agricultural work prevented Prescott from winning further military laurels. He did, however, volunteer to advise Major General Horatio GATES during the Battles of SARATOGA in 1777. Retiring to his farm, he served the community in various civil capacities, including those of selectman and representative in the general court. During SHAYS'S REBELLION in 1787, Prescott was again called upon, and he took part in the suppression of the uprising. Prescott died on his estate at Pepperell, Massachusetts, on 13 October 1795.

See also AMERICAN REVOLUTIONARY WAR: LAND OVERVIEW; MINUTEMEN.

Further reading: Fleming, Thomas J. *Now We Are Enemies: The Story of Bunker Hill.* New York: St. Martin's Press, 1966; Harris, John. *American Rebels.* Boston: Affiliated Publications, 1976; Ward, Christopher. *The War of the Revolution,* vol. 2. New York: Macmillan, 1952.

— Erica Ardolino

President–Little Belt encounter (16 May 1811)

Naval incident that demonstrated the degree of friction between the U.S. and Royal Navies

Officers and men of the U.S. Navy yearned to avenge the insult of the 1807 CHESAPEAKE-LEOPARD AFFAIR, in which a British warship had fired into and disabled an unresisting U.S. Navy vessel. Continued incidents of impressment of American seamen and seizures of merchant vessels by the Royal Navy also rankled, and in June 1810 Secretary of the Navy Paul Hamilton sent a letter to captains, pointing out "injuries and insults" committed by both France and Great Britain against America, especially the attack on the *Chesapeake*. He called on the officers to "be prepared and determined at every hazard, to vindicate the injured honor of our Navy, and revive the drooping Spirit of the Nation."

It fell to Captain John RODGERS to avenge the *Chesapeake*. The issue was again impressment, when the British frigate *Guerrière* (38 guns) halted an American merchant brig off New York and impressed a seaman, a native of Maine. Learning of this on 6 May 1811, Hamilton ordered Rodgers to take the 44-gun frigate *President* to sea. On the afternoon of the 16th, about 45 miles northeast of Cape Henry, a lookout on the American frigate sighted a warship. The unknown ship approached aggressively until its captain realized that the *President* was an American frigate rather than a merchantman, at which point it made all sail south. Probably hoping that this unidentified vessel was the *Guerrière,* Rodgers ordered a pursuit. The wind decreased, so that the *President* was able to overtake it only after nightfall. Rodgers claimed that although he could identify the other ship as a frigate, he was unable to determine its actual force. It was actually HMS *Little Belt* (the former Danish *Lille Belt,* taken by the British in 1807), a ship sloop of 22 guns captained by Commander Arthur B. Bingham.

After several attempts to position his ship close to windward, Rodgers finally was able to hail. British and U.S. accounts differ as to the hails and responses and which side fired first, but both ships were soon trading broadsides. Perceiving that the British ship was smaller than his own and soon much cut up, Rodgers again hailed during a lull in the firing. This time Bingham answered that he commanded a Royal Navy warship, although Rodgers could not catch the name. Rodgers then identified his own vessel and gave orders for the *President* to wear and carry out repairs.

At daybreak, the British warship was several miles off, and Rodgers ordered the *President* to run down to it. He then sent a boat to learn its identity and extent of the damage and to offer assistance. Rated at 22 guns but actually mounting only 18 guns, the *Little Belt* had been badly damaged in the exchange and had 13 dead and 19 wounded. The Americans had only a boy wounded in the arm (although amputation was required). The *President* had sustained minor damage to its masts, mainly from carronade shot.

Bingham declined assistance, replying that he could make all repairs required for the ship to be able to return to

Halifax, and the two ships parted company. The *Little Belt* was sold out of the service later that same year.

Both President James Madison and Secretary Hamilton approved Rodgers's conduct in the affair, as did a naval court of inquiry. The commodore found himself hailed as the man who avenged the *Chesapeake*. In a flurry of diplomatic efforts, London unsuccessfully sought redress.

While the encounter did not lead to war between the two nations, it certainly was a glaring example of the friction and misunderstanding that brought war a year later.

See also WAR OF 1812: CAUSES.

Further reading: Fowler, William M., Jr. *Jack Tars and Commodores. The American Navy, 1783–1815.* Boston: Houghton Mifflin, 1984; Tucker, Spencer C., and Frank T. Reuter. *Injured Honor. The Chesapeake-Leopard Affair, June 22, 1807.* Annapolis, Md.: Naval Institute Press, 1996.

— Spencer C. Tucker

Princeton, Battle of (2–3 January 1777) *Key battle of the American Revolutionary War*

The Battle of Princeton followed Continental Army commander General George WASHINGTON's stunning victory at TRENTON on 26 December 1976. The day after that battle, Washington and his entire army were back across the Delaware River, in Pennsylvania. Despite the victory, he had reason to be dispirited: At the end of the month the majority of his army's enlistments would expire and most of the men would probably return home.

On 27 December, Major General John Cadwalader and 2,100 Pennsylvania militia crossed the Delaware River, capturing an empty Burlington, New Jersey. Cadwalader informed Washington of the situation and urged him to recross the Delaware and join forces; Washington agreed.

On 30 December, Washington recrossed the river and reoccupied Trenton. He then addressed his men, urging them to sign on for an additional six weeks and promising them a bounty of $10 each if they did so (though without authority from Congress). Although about half of Washington's troops agreed, the remainder went home. In the end, Washington had perhaps 1,100 men.

Washington then had his men fortify their positions at Trenton in order to fight a defensive battle. Finally, joined by troops under Colonel Thomas Mifflin and Cadwalader, Washington had some 5,000 men, most of whom were militia, and 40 guns.

British army commander Major General William Howe was determined to redress the loss at Trenton, and he ordered Major General Charles, Lord Cornwallis, to finish off Washington. Cornwallis set out for Trenton with 8,000 men and 28 guns. Washington, meanwhile, placed on the road toward Princeton an advanced force of 1,000 men

and 2 guns under French adventurer Brigadier General Matthias Fernoy, who, however, abandoned his command, leaving it with Colonel Edward Hand. Utilizing hit-and-run tactics, Hand and his men delayed the British advance. It was not until 5:00 P.M. on 2 January that Cornwallis reached the American lines at Assunpink Creek. Repulsed three times, chiefly by the well-handled American artillery, Cornwallis decided to wait for daylight before resuming the attack.

On the night of 2–3 January, Washington carried out a daring flanking move and slipped his entire army around the British flank to attack Princeton, which he had learned was only lightly defended. Washington left at Trenton only 400 New Jersey militia to keep the campfires burning so as to make the British believe the Americans were still there in force. Making certain the British were settled in their camps, Washington and the remainder of his men departed at 1:00 A.M.

Princeton was defended by some 1,700 crack British regulars under Lieutenant Colonel Charles Marwood: three regiments of the 4th Brigade and three troops of light dragoons. Marwood was already on his way to join Cornwallis at Trenton when, at 8:00 A.M., he spotted some 350 of Washington's men under Brigadier General Hugh Mercer and immediately fell back on defensive positions at Princeton. The British had muskets and bayonets; the Americans were armed with slower-firing rifles and had no bayonets. Realizing this, Marwood ordered a bayonet charge, and the Americans broke. Mercer's horse was shot from under him, but Mercer refused to surrender. Bayoneted seven times, he later died of his wounds. Additional American forces then came up, but these militia also were routed, the day being saved by two American 4-pounder guns.

The battle seesawed back and forth, but ended in an American victory. Washington's force suffered 40 killed and wounded; the British lost 28 killed, 58 wounded, and 194 taken prisoner. Washington also took a considerable quantity of British stores, then hastened away to Morristown before Cornwallis could come up.

This time Washington had out-generaled and defeated not Hessians but British regulars. The Battles of Trenton and Princeton fanned hope back into the Patriot cause and established Washington's military reputation. Correspondingly, the two battles greatly embarrassed the English.

See also AMERICAN REVOLUTIONARY WAR: LAND OVERVIEW.

Further reading: Bill, Alfred N. *The Campaign of Princeton, 1776–1777.* Princeton, N.J.: Princeton University Press, 1948; English, Frederick. *General Hugh Mercer: Forgotten Hero of the American Revolution.* New York: Vantage Press, 1975; Smith, Samuel S. *The Battle of*

Princeton. Monmouth Beach, N.J.: Philip Frenchau Press, 1967; Ward, Christopher. *The War of the Revolution*, vol. 1. New York: Macmillan, 1952.

— Stephen J. Kaufman

Printz, Johan B. (1592–1663) *Swedish officer and colonial governor of New Sweden*

Born on 20 July 1592 of noble parentage in Bottnaryd, Smaland, Sweden, Johan Printz left Sweden in 1618 to study theology in Germany at the Universities of Rostock and Greifswald.

Later, on a stipend from King Gustavus Adolphus, he was invited to study at the Universities of Leipzig, Wittenberg, Helmstadt, and Jena. While traveling through northern Europe (ca. 1620), he was captured by, and forced into the ranks of, a roving band of soldiers on their way to Italy. He found, however, that the military lifestyle suited him, and as a mercenary during the 1618–48 Thirty Years' War, Printz served under Leopold of Austria, Duke Christian of Brunswick, and King Christian IV of Denmark.

Printz joined the Swedish army in 1625. In 1639 he was appointed commander of Chemnitz as a lieutenant colonel. That same year he was forced to surrender Chemnitz to a larger Saxon force.

In April 1642, Printz was appointed director (governor) of New Sweden. In February 1643, he arrived with two ships, the *Fama* and *Swan*, at Fort Christina, New Sweden, in North America. Shortly afterward, he began construction of Fort Elfsborg at Varkens Kill. Swedish territory extended from Cape Henlopen to Sankikan (present Trenton, New Jersey), and was bounded to the north by the Dutch New Netherlands and to the south by British colonies.

Printz managed to maintain excellent relations with the Native Americans. The Indians called him "Big Guts," because of his great girth. A stern disciplinarian, he once had the ringleader of a group of disgruntled settlers executed. Problems in New Sweden continued, however; and in September 1653 he turned over his position as director to his deputy and son-in-law John Papegoja. Returning to Sweden, Printz became governor of his native district and built a manor named Gunillaberg. He died there on 3 May 1663.

Further reading: Johnson, Amandus. *The Instruction for Johan Printz, Governor of New Sweden.* Philadelphia: Swedish Colonial Society, 1930; ———. *The Swedes on the Delaware, 1638–1664*, 2nd ed. Philadelphia: Swedish Colonial Society, 1915; Weslager, Clinton A. *New Sweden on the Delaware: 1630–1655.* Wilmington, Del.: Middle Atlantic Press, 1988.

— Sven Jensen

privateers in the American Revolutionary War
(1776–1783) *Private ships and crews fighting under license during the American Revolutionary War*

Privateering provided the only real naval success for the American cause during the American Revolutionary War. The privateers' capture of British merchant shipping affected the resupply of the British army in North America, drove up maritime insurance rates, and increased pressure on the British government to make peace.

The naval situation that confronted the Continental Congress in 1775 was not promising. The British navy was the largest in the world. Although neglect had reduced British strength, the Royal Navy was still larger than the navy of France, its nearest rival. In a war with the colonies, its navy gave Britain a singular advantage, allowing London to shift troops at will along the coast and keep them supplied.

Leaders of the Continental Congress recognized early on that they could not hope to challenge Britain in the number or size of warships. Instead, they adopted a three-prong strategy. The first was to secure an alliance with France, which became a reality in 1778. The French navy then played a decisive role in the war, culminating in the 1781 Battle of the CHESAPEAKE. The second was the construction of a small Continental navy, largely of frigates, chiefly for commerce raiding, but this had a mixed record at best. The third path, privateering, was tremendously successful.

The practice of authorizing private ships to sail out and capture enemy merchant ships was, at the time, a well-recognized part of naval warfare. Privateers were required to follow the laws of war and, when captured, were to be treated as legal combatants and made prisoners of war. This sort of combat fit well with the decentralized character of the colonies and, indeed, colonial inclinations. Americans were fiercely individualistic, and thousands leapt at the chance to engage in a profitable private war with Britain. Privateering also took advantage of the largely seagoing culture of many of the colonies. The New England colonies, especially, and all the other colonies to a lesser degree, depended on the ocean for transportation of people and goods. As a result, there were a large number of ships and sailors available at the beginning of the war. From 1776 to 1783, the Continental Congress authorized 1,697 privateers with 15,000 guns and 55,000 crewmen. State-sanctioned privateers added roughly another 1,000 ships to the total.

The privateering campaign did not start off well. Continental army commander General George WASHINGTON attempted to organize local ships to attack British transports coming into Boston during the siege of 1775. They proved less than effective, with Washington noting that "our rascally privateers" have provided nothing but "plague, trouble and vexation." In March 1776 the Continental Congress sought to regularize this when it authorized both letters of marque (carried by armed cargo ships) and privateering licenses (carried by private warships).

The system was simple. Privateers holding a license from Congress or from a colony would set out to make their fortune. Their ships usually mounted fewer than 20 guns and relied on speed and nimbleness to elude British warships. They would usually be heavily overmanned, so that captured merchant ships could be boarded and then crewed. Prime hunting grounds on the American side of the Atlantic were the Gulf of Saint Lawrence and the Caribbean. The concentration of privateers in those spots was sometimes so heavy that colonial ships found themselves attacking each other by mistake.

Once a merchant ship had been captured, a prize crew would sail the ship into the nearest colonial harbor. This was not always easy. The prize crew was usually heavily outnumbered by the British prisoners, and numerous ships were retaken by their own sailors. Patrolling British warships often recaptured prizes as well. If a prize was successfully brought into port, it would be valued by an admiralty court, auctioned off, and the proceeds of the sale split between the owners of the privateer and its crew.

During the first two years of the war, privateering was moderately successful. British merchant shipping proved rich pickings, but the British navy could still spare the resources to fight privateering, and to attack shipping off the British Isles required a lengthy voyage, both for the privateers and for their prizes.

This situation changed in 1778 when France entered the war, forcing Britain to spread its naval assets thin. American privateers soon took advantage. French ports also provided a convenient base from which privateers could attack shipping off the British coast. The result was a surge in the number of privateers and in their success.

Perhaps the most successful privateer, the Philadelphia-based *Holker,* worked during this period. On its first cruise to the Caribbean in 1779, it took six prizes valued in total at more than £1 million. It managed £1 million captures in 1780, 1781, and 1782, before finally being lost in a storm in 1783.

By the time the war ended in 1783, privateering had inflicted heavy damage on the British shipping industry. Colonial privateers took roughly 2,200 ships worth about £66 million. British insurance rates for shipping increased anywhere from 30 to 50 percent.

The effect of privateering on the British military effort is less clear. Privateers certainly did not and could not defend the colonies from the British navy, but they did harass and harry the marine supply line so crucial to the British war effort in North America. In this sense, privateering should be seen as the naval equivalent of the guerrilla war being fought in the southern colonies, a campaign to break London's will to continue the fight.

The revolutionaries were not the only ones to outfit privateers. The British and American Loyalists both sent them to sea. British privateers tended to work off the coast of France and Spain, while Loyalist privateers concentrated off friendly North American ports such as New York, where prizes would have only a short sail to safety. During 1778–79, Loyalist privateers operating from New York Harbor did such sufficient damage to American shipping that George Washington authorized a naval counterattack specifically against them. During the course of the war, British and Loyalist privateers took some 1,135 American merchant ships.

See also AMERICAN REVOLUTIONARY WAR: NAVAL OVERVIEW; *GUERRE DE COURSE;* NAVY, U.S.

Further reading: Clark, William Bell. *Ben Franklin's Privateers: A Naval Epic of the American Revolution.* Baton Rouge: Louisiana State University Press, 1956; Fowler, William. *Rebels under Sail: The American Navy During the Revolution.* New York: Scribner's, 1976; Miller, Nathan. *Sea of Glory: The Continental Navy Fights for Independence, 1775–1783.* New York: D. McKay, 1974; Tilley, John A. *The British Navy and the American Revolution.* Columbia: University of South Carolina Press, 1987.

— David Silbey

privateers in the War of 1812 *Private American vessels and crews operating under letters of marque—in this case, against British merchant shipping during the War of 1812.*

Privateering has a long and distinguished tradition in U.S. naval history, dating back to the colonial and Revolutionary War periods. As late as 1798, during the QUASI-WAR WITH FRANCE, privateering served as an effective adjunct to regular naval activities, and it also trained a generation of future leaders, including Joshua BARNEY, Stephen DECATUR, David PORTER, and John RODGERS. Its conduct throughout the War of 1812 was even more strikingly successful. In two and a half years of warfare, 517 licensed privateers, with an aggregate of 2,893 guns, captured 1,345 British prizes. This represented the loss of an estimated $45 million in commerce and 30,000 prisoners. Furthermore, because American privateers routinely raided British home waters and the Irish Channel, their activity caused insurance rates to skyrocket. The accomplishments of the U.S. Navy in this conflict, while justly celebrated, paled in comparison.

Immense social implications also arose from privateering. The acquisition of personal fortunes was not uncommon, and for many dispossessed inhabitants living in ports along the east coast, privateering represented an avenue of considerable social mobility. The lure of lucre proved extremely profitable for cities such as Boston, Bristol, Philadelphia, and Charleston, all of which maintained large, viable fleets of privateers. But the most successful exponent of commerce raiding proved to be Baltimore, the notoriety of which by 1814 led the British to launch a major invasion to capture it.

By and large, the Royal Navy was singularly unsuccessful in its attempt to curb losses to privateering. These sleek, speedy raiders could usually outrun lumbering warships, and a convoy system, similar to that which emerged in the two 20th-century world wars, had to be implemented. However, many privateers were unsuccessful in their brushes with the Royal Navy, and their crews constituted the majority of prisoners held at facilities such as Dartmoor.

Many individual ships and seamen stood out for exemplary success in the War of 1812. Foremost among these was the *Yankee* of Bristol, Rhode Island, a 168-ton brig mounting 14 cannon with a crew of 120 men. This vessel completed six cruises under the command of such experienced sailors as Oliver Wilson, Elisha Snow, and Thomas Wilson, who took it from Nova Scotia to the African coast and into the chops of the English Channel. By war's end the *Yankee* accounted for no fewer than 40 prizes, including nine ships, 25 brigs, five schooners, and a sloop, representing around $5 million in seized property. James De Wolfe, the owner, deposited more than $1 million in captured goods at Bristol alone and emerged from the war as one of the richest men in Rhode Island.

Further north, the *America* of Salem, Massachusetts, distinguished itself in the employ of the influential Crowninshield family. This vessel was somewhat large for its class at 350 tons, 20 guns, and a crew of 150 men, but it hoisted an enormous expanse of canvas aloft. Consequently, the *America* was one of the fastest privateers of the day. In the course of four highly successful cruises under Captains Joseph Ropes and James W. Cheever, the *America* netted no fewer than 21 prizes worth in excess of $1 million. Furthermore, because a vast quantity of goods captured at sea could not be brought home and was destroyed at sea, the actual loss to British owners was probably twice that amount. By war's end, the smart-sailing *America* brought the Crowninshields an estimated $600,000 in profit, further cementing their status as among the wealthiest families of Salem.

In the mid-Atlantic region, two of the most notorious privateers were commanded by a single captain, the legendary Thomas Boyle. His first command, the *Comet*, was a 16-gun schooner that took 27 vessels in the course of several cruises. Boyle then transferred to a newer, faster ship, the *Chasseur*, that went on to take a staggering 53 addi-

tional prizes. But Boyle's most audacious feat occurred in August 1814 while cruising the English Channel, when he sent leaflets ashore, declaring the British Isles under a state of blockade. By war's end, Doyle's endeavors had netted him an estimated $1 million in prize money, while his *Chasseur* became publicly toasted as "the Pride of Baltimore." Thereafter, other low-lying, fast vessels with similar lines were generally known as Baltimore clippers.

The privateers' hit-and-run strategy rarely allowed them to make raids of military value, but one vessel waged an impressive battle with considerable strategic implications. On 26 September 1814, the *General Armstrong*, out of New York under Captain Samuel C. Reid, put into the neutral port of Fayal in the Azores. Soon after, it was joined by a British squadron consisting of the ship of the line *Plantagenet*, the frigate *Rota*, and the brig *Carnation*, which anchored nearby. They were conveying 2,000 troops to join an expedition against New Orleans, but their commander, Commodore Edward Lloyd, could not allow so tempting a target as the *General Armstrong* to remain unscathed.

In direct violation of Portuguese neutrality, Lloyd assembled several hundred men in barges and attacked. Reid, who commanded only 90 men, fought back furiously, repulsing two determined attacks to carry his vessel by the sword. When it became apparent that Lloyd was bringing his entire squadron to bear upon the *General Armstrong*, Reid scuttled it at anchor, took his men ashore, and prepared for a final stand. Lloyd spent nearly a week repairing his ships and tending to nearly 300 casualties. Reid's losses were two killed and seven wounded. Meanwhile, Vice Admiral Alexander Cochrane was forced to postpone his attack on New Orleans until the reinforcements arrived, thereby granting General Andrew JACKSON additional time to arrange the city's defenses. Reid also sued the British government for this overt breach of international law, and a celebrated legal case ensued that lasted 70 years. Reid's son finally was awarded damages for the claim in 1882.

Privateering as practiced by the United States—a unique blend of nautical skill, patriotism, and profit seeking—was the most successful naval aspect of the War of 1812. Despite the very effective blockade imposed by the Royal Navy upon American commerce and the U.S. Navy, it ultimately failed to contain the swarms of highly motivated raiders. However, the War of 1812 was the last conflict to witness privateering on such a vast scale. Despite occasional use throughout numerous Spanish-American wars for independence, the practice generally fell into disuse and was outlawed by most nations in 1856. Privateering was briefly revived by the Confederate States of America in 1861, but the victorious United States government finally renounced the practice four years later.

See also *GUERRE DE COURSE;* NAVY, U.S.; WAR OF 1812: NAVAL OVERVIEW.

Further reading: Gillmer, Thomas C. *Pride of Baltimore: The Story of the Baltimore Clippers, 1800–1900.* Camden, Me.: International Marine, 1992; Huntsberry, Thomas V. *Maryland Privateers, War of 1812.* Baltimore: J. Mart, 1983; Kert, Faye M. *Prize and Prejudice: Privateering and Naval Prize in Atlantic Canada in the War of 1812.* St. Johns, Newfoundland: International Maritime Economic History Association, 1997; Winslow, Richard E. *Wealth and Honour: Portsmouth during the Golden Age of Privateering, 1775–1815.* Portsmouth, N.H.: P. E. Randall, 1988.

— John C. Fredriksen

propaganda *Communicated information intended to influence the opinions, attitudes, or behavior of a targeted group in order to provide some gain or benefit to the sponsor*

Propaganda is as old as war itself. It has been used to destroy an enemy's will to resist, but is also directed at one's own population to demonize an enemy and increase popular willingness to fight. The purpose of propaganda is to

"We Can Do It!" Popular poster issued by U.S. Office of War Information in 1943 during World War II   *(National Archives)*

alter behavior and, in turn, alter the strategic or tactical balance in favor of the propagandist.

In warfare, propaganda generally attempts to produce at least one of four behaviors in a target audience: submission, subversion, cooperation, or panic, depending on the vulnerabilities of the audience and the media chosen to convey the message. The target audience may be diverse enough that the propagandist can employ several different messages through a variety of media to produce all four behaviors. The propagandist's message will tell the target audience what it wants to hear in order to get that audience to adopt the propagandist's chosen line of thought and then display attitudes that lead to the desired behavior. This process is carefully monitored in order to evaluate the effect of the propaganda campaign.

Propaganda is classified into two broad categories—white and black. In white propaganda, the source of the information in the message distributed to the target audience is either clearly known or openly stated. In black propaganda, the true source of the information is intentionally hidden from the audience, or a false source is acknowledged. Black propaganda has been used in subversion and deception operations, most often in support of insurgency or counterinsurgency campaigns. The message can be designed to have a personal or impersonal appeal, depending on target audience susceptibility to such an appeal. Propaganda can be conveyed in printed or spoken words, through images or sounds, by physical acts, or even by material objects. Physical destruction or specific acts of violence also can be made to have a propaganda effect.

In the modern era, propaganda is employed to supplement and support the instruments of national power: military, diplomatic, and economic. The rise of mass communications in the 20th century has made propaganda an essential part of a nation's grand strategy because it can be applied in both peace and war to support the nation's interests.

American wartime propaganda themes have been remarkably consistent throughout history, beginning with the American Revolutionary War. Three of the most consistent have been the righteousness of the American cause, usually drawn starkly between the morality of the U.S. effort and the immorality of that of the enemy; the overwhelming strength and capabilities of American combat power, usually shown in terms of weapon effects or numbers of tanks, planes, or ships; and the promise of good treatment for every enemy soldier who surrenders, depicted in terms of physical comfort and security.

Although called *psychological operations* (or PSYOP) today, propaganda remains part of a larger effort called *information operations*, which plays an essential role in U.S. peacetime engagement strategy. Psychological operations are employed in peace to deter potential aggressors and build support for U.S. policies. In wartime, propaganda is a formidable, proven weapon used to attack target audiences at the tactical, operational, and strategic levels. Regardless of new technologies that continually shape warfare, the fundamental purpose of propaganda has not changed: to demoralize an enemy and break its will to fight.

See also COLD WAR; DESERT SHIELD, OPERATION; DESERT STORM, OPERATION; KOREAN WAR, COURSE OF U.S. INVOLVEMENT; SPANISH-AMERICAN WAR, CAUSES OF; WORLD WAR II, COURSE OF U.S. INVOLVEMENT: EUROPEAN THEATER; WORLD WAR II, COURSE OF U.S. INVOLVEMENT: PACIFIC THEATER.

Further reading: Chandler, Robert W. *The War of Ideas: The U.S. Propaganda Campaign in Vietnam.* Boulder, Colo.: Westview Press, 1981; Davidson, Philip G. *Propaganda and the American Revolution, 1763–1783.* Chapel Hill: University of North Carolina Press, 1941; Dyer, Murray. *The Weapon on the Wall: Rethinking Psychological Warfare.* Baltimore: Johns Hopkins University Press, 1959; Rhodes, Anthony. *Propaganda: The Art of Persuasion, World War II.* New York: Chelsea House, 1976.

— Keith D. Dickson

psychological warfare   *Efforts designed to affect adversely the morale and fighting ability of enemy forces*

Contrary to general opinion, the United States has a long and quite successful history of tactical psychological operations (or "psyop") against its enemies. This tradition has not been extensively documented, however.

U.S. military psychological operations go back to the very beginnings of the nation's struggle for independence. The earliest documented example is that of a printed leaflet, encouraging defection of British troops after the Battle of BUNKER HILL. The British were promised not the blessings of liberty, but rather "fresh provisions and in plenty" and "freedom, affluence, and a good farm." The unknown author of this psychological warfare (or "psywar") leaflet employed techniques that would be used later—and with great success—in the two world wars of the 20th century, in Korea and Vietnam, and in the Gulf War. The appeal was concrete and believable. America had abundant land and its harvests were bounteous. To a British soldier living on salt pork and bread, coming from a country where the very term "landowning classes" meant the impossibly wealthy, the promise of "a good farm" could prove irresistible. In fact, thousands of British and Hessian troops defected during the American Revolutionary War—at a time when deserters could be flogged to death. The Bunker Hill leaflet was a harbinger of things to come. Paper was expensive and printing slow in the 18th century.

In fact, the United States did not employ mass psychological operations until World War I.

The G-2 Section of the AMERICAN EXPEDITIONARY FORCE (AEF) drew up only 20 leaflets (several written by the later-eminent columnist Walter Lippman) during its participation in World War I. But these were run off in the millions, and, according to interviews and surveys of German POWs, they had a profound effect on German troops. As in the classic Bunker Hill leaflet, these fliers for the most part avoided any "political" discussion, concentrating rather on conditions in the German army on the Western Front and providing a way out. The most successful was the "rations" leaflet. It simply stated that POWs of the Americans are entitled to the same rations as American soldiers— and listed these U.S. Army rations in what must have seemed mouth-watering detail to troops then living on "Kommisbrodt," which they claimed was made from the sweepings of bakery floors. By all indications, this particular leaflet was instrumental in pushing thousands of discouraged, hungry German soldiers into outright defection.

During World War II, American psywar proved again an effective weapon, although, as in World War I, there were doubters from the high command on down. American battlefield psyop, for the most part, avoided discussion of Nazism or democracy, and once again concentrated on down-to-earth issues ("You are Losing This War—Why Die in a Hopeless Cause?"). Undoubtedly the most successful leaflet in the European theater of operations was the *Passierschein,* a "Surrender and You will be Well-Treated" pass that played to the Germans' innate respect for authority. Signed by General Dwight D. EISENHOWER, bearing the coats of arms of the Western Allies, and bordered by complex "fish net," the leaflet looked like an international treaty. More than one surrendering Wehrmacht trooper, waving the pass, is supposed to have informed his captors that "I have a message here from General Eisenhower!" And, once again, POW questionnaires and interviews gave to American and British battlefield psywar high marks for the hundreds of thousands of captive German troops. For the first time, Allied psywarriors also employed electronic propaganda in broadcasts and loudspeaker operations, although the leaflet, whether air-dropped or artillery-fired, remained the "foot soldier" of psychological warfare. Loudspeaker teams, however, were very successful in talking terrified Allied civilians out of bunkers and cellars and in laying down the law to German civilians.

American psywarriors proved much less successful against their Japanese enemy. One of their first leaflets offered a "Surrender" pass to Japanese soldiers—ignoring the established fact that Japanese troops hardly even knew the word. A later, more successful pass, said rather "I Cease Resistance." In contrast to home front propaganda, which caricatured the Japanese as nearsighted vicious slugs, bats, and vermin, battlefield psywar, understandably, depicted the enemy as a brave fellow misled by his wicked leaders, one who should realize that the war was lost and that he should save himself to build a new and better Japan after the war. Nonetheless, no more than 2,000 Japanese soldiers were captured in World War II, and, of course, not all of these had surrendered. Most of those "Japanese" who did surrender were in fact Taiwanese or Koreans, who were considerably less motivated than their Japanese overlords.

U.S. psywar during World War II was hampered by the division and suspicion between the "conservative" civil-military OFFICE OF STRATEGIC SERVICES (OSS) and the civilian "liberals" of the Office of War information (OWI). The former emphasized straightforward appeals to enemy troops to defect and be well treated; the latter, the "brave new world of tomorrow" strategic propaganda.

The KOREAN WAR may well have seen the peak of American leaflet art. One of the most effective was a strikingly drawn Chinese soldier, his face a skull festooned with icicles. The message was simple: "You're going to Die!"—unless you give up now. For the first time, psychological operations took some public attention, for the Communists were supposedly masters of propaganda. Actually, Communist propaganda in Korea varied from marxist boilerplate (e.g. "Running Dogs of Wall Street") and impossible demands ("End this Unjust War!"), to the thought-provoking ("Leave Korea to the Koreans!"). In the end, however, the United States gained a final propaganda victory when no fewer than 22,000 Communist POWs refused to return to their marxist homelands.

The COLD WAR had highlighted the role and need for American psychological warfare, and in Vietnam, for the first time, this part of "the Other War" came to public attention. A Psychological Warfare Center was established at Fort Riley, Kansas, in 1951; the following year, it moved to Fort Bragg, North Carolina, from which the army's elite GREEN BERETS emerged, also in 1952. Each Special Forces "A" Detachment, in fact, had one NCO who was a specialist in psywar.

The psywar campaign during the VIETNAM WAR was enormous and arguably the most effective in history. Over a period of 10 years, no fewer than 100,000 low-level Vietcong (VC) cadre defected to the Allied side; almost all analysts agreed—and captured VC documents flatly stated—that it was Allied, and particularly American, psyop that pushed them from dissatisfaction to actual disaffection.

In the GULF WAR, American psywar, honed to a fine pitch during President Ronald Reagan's military buildup, finished off an Iraqi army already demoralized by round-the-clock Coalition bombardment. Leaflets showered down on Iraqi troops, emphasizing that this was a war against the evil Saddam Hussein, who had ranged against him many Islamic and Arab nations. An Iraqi general later stated that Coalition psywar was second only to the incessant bombing in destroying his troops' morale. Loudspeaker teams talked out of their bunkers shell-shocked and starving Iraqi troops, while the Voice of the Gulf soothed Arab speakers with straightforward discussions of the goals of the Coalition, as well as with music and other cultural programs. American psywarriors for the first time were even assigned to the Enemy Prisoner of War (EPW) cages, where they picked up intelligence, and calmed the EPWs, improbably, with large-screen television action and adventure films.

Over the decades, several conclusions have informally guided American psywar and have made it generally successful: 1) Tell no outright lies; the first uncovered lie will drain the reservoir of belief that has been built up by honest psywar; 2) Make believable, concrete promises: "I, General Eisenhower, Promise that You Will be Well-Treated"; "Chinese Soldier, No Tobacco? You'll Have Plenty in a UN POW Camp"; 3) Forgo "political" appeals ("End the War"; "Communism Enslaves You!") that tend to go over the heads of most enemy troops; 4) Divide and conquer usually works well ("Stalin will Fight to the Last North Korean!" "Italian Soldiers, Why Do You Fight for Germany?"); 5) Give the enemy straight news. Soldiers of totalitarian regimes are so starved for objective information and news that they will read almost anything. Newsletters and information sheets, even though the enemy knows where they come from, will be read eagerly, and the soldier will then be "softened" for the subtle "slant" of the news toward American goals ("Nazi Party chiefs denied recently that Party cadres received extra rations of soap, food, or transportation coupons"; "British Troops Land at Pusan"); and 6) Enemy currency, their flag, or famous leaders of the past will get enemy troops' attention. The appeal of money lying about is obvious, but flags or such icons as Hammurabi, Bismarck, or Sun Yat Sen can also draw attention, and allow the reader some protection from retribution if discovered. ("Sir, I had no idea that the Americans had befouled our flag with their lying propaganda. I am shocked!").

Finally, it should be noted that few American troops have defected to the enemy in time of war. It may be that soldiers of the nation that invented Madison Avenue and Hollywood are uniquely immune to their own or anyone else's propaganda.

See also PROPAGANDA.

Further reading: Chandler, Robert. *War of Ideas: The U.S. Propaganda Campaign in Vietnam.* Boulder, Colo.: Westview Press, 1981; Laurie, Clayton. *The Propaganda Warriors: America's Crusade Against Nazi Germany.* Lawrence: University Press of Kansas, 1996; Linebarger, Paul A. M. *Psychological Warfare.* Washington, D.C.: Infantry Journal Press, 1954; Pease, Stephen E. *Psychological*

Warfare in Korea, 1950–1953. Harrisburg, Pa.: Stackpole Books, 1992; Sandler, Stanley. *Cease Resistance, It's Good for You: A History of U.S. Army Combat Psychological Operations.* Fort Bragg, N.C.: U.S. Army Special Operations Command, 1994, 1998.

— Stanley Sandler

PT boats *Patrol torpedo boats*

Known as PT or Mosquito boats, these swift, agile, heavily armed craft provided a fast attack capability in WORLD WAR II naval operations, particularly in the South and Southwest Pacific and Mediterranean theaters. Made possible by interwar torpedo and propulsion improvements, American boat types evolved from European designs. Based on the threat of Japanese aggression, in 1938 the U.S. Navy funded experimental 20-ton boats mounting two torpedoes, .50 caliber machine guns, and a smoke generator.

In 1939, Hubert Scott-Paine of the British Power Boat Company produced a highly maneuverable, 45-knot-per-hour craft. The Elco Company of Bayonne, New Jersey, purchased manufacturing rights to the 70-foot Scott-Paine design and, replacing the Rolls-Royce engines with Packard models, easily outclassed all competitors. However, the sacrifice of weight for speed made the boats' seaworthiness questionable. Elco responded with a 77-foot, heavier design. Constructed almost entirely out of plywood, mahogany, and cedar, with only the aluminum pilothouse and turrets made of metal, the 77 footer retained the speed and handling characteristics of its forerunner. Armed with four 21-inch torpedoes and machine guns in turrets and powered by three 1200-hp Packard engines, the Elco boats represented the entire PT force in December 1941.

Elco improved the design with the 80 footer, which proved to be the most successful PT model, and which was manufactured in the greatest number. The new design had a higher freeboard and greater carrying capacity than the previous 77 footer. Additionally, a 20mm Oerlikon cannon provided improved antiaircraft defense. Powered by upgraded 1350-hp Packard engines, the boat reached top speeds of 43 knots despite a weight of 51 tons. With a crew of two officers and nine enlisted men (torpedoman, gunner's mate, radioman, quartermaster, seaman, signalman, and three enginemen), the new Elco boat featured improved internal structural strength and better crew accommodations.

The effectiveness of PT-launched torpedoes against enemy warships proved disappointing. Surface warship firepower made torpedo runs with unreliable weapons particularly hazardous. By 1944, the Elco evolved into essentially a gun platform, ideally suited for reconnaissance and attacks on enemy small craft and troop and supply barges. Lightweight launching racks and the superior Mark XIII replaced the heavy tubes and unreliable Mark XIV torpedoes. The addition of a rapid-fire 37mm gun forward and a 40mm Bofors gun aft increased firepower. Surface search radars added to stealth and reconnaissance capability. By 1945, 5-inch spin stabilized rockets located forward of the torpedoes further increased firepower. Continual engine upgrades to 1500 hp gave the boats an operational radius of 259 miles at 35 knots.

Higgins Industries of New Orleans produced the other notable American boat of the war, the 78-foot Higgins. The United States exported about two-thirds of the Higgins boats to Britain and the Soviet Union. Slightly shorter and slower than the Elco, the Higgins proved to be more maneuverable and no less effective with equivalent armaments.

The tactical employment of PT boats utilized the advantages of speed, firepower, and stealth. Operating in divisions of three boats in either a "V" or echelon formation, they approached a target at high speed to launch torpedoes usually at night or in low visibility conditions. Against barges and small craft, the division idled close to shore in an ambush position. Upon radar target detection, the division raced to the victim at high speed and raked the heavily armored barges with massive firepower delivered at relatively slow speed. Despite the change in operational missions after 1943, attacks of opportunity against surface warships continued, such as the assault on the Japanese Southern Force to open the action of the Surigao Strait (24 October 1944) in the Battle of LEYTE GULF.

A typical PT squadron consisted of four divisions or 12 boats. Forty-five squadrons (boatrons) participated in World War II. Thirty-three squadrons fought in the Pacific, primarily in the South and Southwest Pacific theaters. On the Atlantic side, six squadrons operated either in the Mediterranean or English Channel. Several squadrons transferred to the Soviet navy. One constituted the Training Squadron at Melville, Rhode Island, operating on Narragansett Bay.

American manufacturers built a total of 768 PT boats of all models, with 511 eventually sent to U.S. squadrons, 166 to the Soviet navy, and 91 to the British Royal Navy. By 1946, only four boats remained in service. Many were stripped of serviceable parts and destroyed in the burning of the boats off Samar, Philippine Islands, at war's end.

See also KENNEDY, JOHN F.

Further reading: Breuer, William B. *Devil Boats: The PT War Against Japan.* Novato, Calif.: Presidio, 1987; Chun, Victor. *American PT Boats in World War II: A Pictorial History.* Atglen, Pa.: Schiffer Military/Aviation History, 1997; Hoagland, Edgar D. *The Sea Hawks: With the PT Boats at War.* Novato, Calif.: Presidio Press, 1999; Keating, Bern. *The Mosquito Fleet.* New York: Putnam, 1963;

Nelson, Curtis L. *Hunters in the Shallows: A History of the PT Boat.* Washington, D.C.: Brassey's, 1998.
— Stanley D. M. Carpenter

Pueblo (23 January 1968) *U.S. Navy electronic intelligence-gathering ship, the capture of which by the Democratic People's Republic of Korea (DPRK, North Korea) precipitated a diplomatic crisis*

The *Pueblo* was a small, 177-foot, 970-ton supply vessel, launched in April 1944 for use by the Army Transportation Corps. In 1967 it was refitted and recommissioned as an auxiliary environmental research vessel (AGER), a cover given to U.S. Navy spy ships. Part of the *Pueblo's* refit gave it the latest electronic and cryptographic intelligence equipment. The ship's armament consisted only of two .50-caliber machine guns.

On 23 January 1968 the *Pueblo,* under Commander Lloyd BUCHER, steamed in international waters 15 miles off the DPRK port of Wonson. There it was intercepted by a DPRK patrol boat, which ordered the *Pueblo* to stop. Bucher's refusal led to an attack on the *Pueblo* by a force that eventually comprised four DPRK patrol boats and two MiG jet aircraft. One U.S. Navy seaman was killed and several others wounded. The *Pueblo* and its 82 surviving crew members were subsequently captured and taken to the DPRK port of Wonson. The ship was the first U.S. warship surrendered to foreign forces since the War of 1812.

During the course of their 11-month captivity, members of the crew were tortured and forced to sign confessions, admitting that they were spies and that they had trespassed into DPRK territorial waters. They were finally released on 22 December 1968 at Panmunjom Bridge between North and South Korea, following a false admission by the U.S. government that the *Pueblo* had indeed entered DPRK territorial waters. The ship was never returned.

The U.S. Navy convened a court of inquiry to investigate the seizure of the *Pueblo* and the conduct of the crew during their captivity. The court's verdict recommended that Bucher and the operations officer in charge of intelligence be court-martialed. Navy Secretary John Chaffee, however, overruled the court and dismissed the charges. He announced that the crew had already suffered sufficient punishment from the episode.

In reality, the decision not to prosecute the men was an attempt to defuse a very embarrassing situation. Not only was the incident a severe blow to American prestige during the COLD WAR, but it was a severe indictment of the U.S. Navy. American intelligence had ample evidence that the DPRK was a well-established ally of the Democratic Republic of Vietnam (DRV, North Vietnam), with which the United States was then at war. Even so, the *Pueblo* had

USS *Pueblo* (AGER-2) off San Diego, California, 19 October 1967   *(Naval Historical Foundation)*

been ordered on its mission with no support and only light armament, inadequate to defend the vessel against an attack.

See also ELECTRONIC WARFARE; INTELLIGENCE.

Further reading: Brandt, Ed. *The Last Voyage of U.S.S. Pueblo.* New York: W. W. Norton, 1969; Lerner, Mitchell B. *The Pueblo Incident: A spy ship and the failure of American Foreign Policy.* Lawrence: University of Kansas Press, 2002; Schumacher, F. Carl, Jr., and George C. Wilson. *Bridge of No Return: The Ordeal of the U.S.S. Pueblo.* New York: Harcourt Brace Jovanovich, 1971.

— Eric W. Osborne

Pulaski, Count Kazimierz (1748–1779) *One of the more colorful but least effective of the foreign volunteer leaders to serve the American revolutionary cause*
Born on 4 March 1748 at Podolia, Poland, to a family of the *szlachta* class (the minor nobility), Kazimierz Pulaski was in 1768 involved in a revolt led by his father, Jozef Pulaski, against Russia. The younger Pulaski became a prominent figure in the military actions, leading a large cavalry organization known as the Knights of the Holy Cross. In 1771, he successfully repulsed a Russian siege of the fortified monastery at Czestochowa, Poland's holiest shrine and site of the venerated Black Madonna.

The revolt ended in April 1772 with the first partition of Poland. Condemned to death by the puppet Polish government, Pulaski fled the country. In 1774, he went to Turkey and tried to incite the Turks to attack Russia. In 1775, he landed in Marseilles, where the French threw him into a debtors prison. When Benjamin Franklin arrived in France, Pulaski immediately volunteered to fight in America.

Pulaski arrived in Boston on 23 July 1777. While the Continental Congress considered his commission, Pulaski served as a volunteer on Continental army commander General George WASHINGTON's staff in the Battle of BRANDYWINE. Shortly after that battle, Congress voted to commission him a brigadier general and commander of the horse. Pulaski thus became the first American cavalry commander.

In December 1777, Washington took the main body of the army into winter quarters at VALLEY FORGE and sent Pulaski and the cavalry to Trenton. In March 1778, Pulaski and Brigadier General Anthony WAYNE engaged in a serious argument over command authority during a foraging expedition, after which Pulaski resigned his command; but with Washington's support, Congress authorized him to raise an independent unit of mixed cavalry and infantry known as the Pulaski Legion.

With 68 horse and 200 foot, Pulaski's legion was barely larger than a company, with 68 cavalry and 200 infantry. On the night of 14 October 1778, near Little Egg Harbor, the British ambushed the legion and inflicted heavy losses on it. In February 1779 Pulaski and his legion were ordered south to support General Major Benjamin LINCOLN. On 19 May, outside of Charleston, South Carolina, Pulaski's force again sustained heavy losses when it attacked a much larger British force under Major General Augustine Prevost.

On 9 October 1779, a combined American and French force under Lincoln and Vice Admiral Count Hector d'Estang attacked British-occupied Savannah, Georgia. Pulaski was mortally wounded while leading a cavalry charge. Evacuated to the American ship *Wasp*, he died at sea two days later. Despite his shortcomings on the battlefield, Pulaski was devoted to the American cause and became a hero of the American Revolution. Hereafter, American cavalry guidons (flags) were red and white, the national colors of Pulaski's native Poland.

See also AMERICAN REVOLUTIONARY WAR: LAND OVERVIEW; CAVALRY.

Further reading: Manning, Clarence A. *Soldier of Liberty: Casimir Pulaski.* New York: Philosophical Library, 1945; Szymanski, Leszek. *Casimir Pulaski: A Hero of the American Revolution.* New York: Hippocrene Books, 1994.

— David T. Zabecki

Puller, Lewis B. ("Chesty") (1898–1971) *U.S. Marine Corps general*
Born on 26 June 1898 at West Point, Virginia, Lewis "Chesty" Burwell Puller entered the Virginia Military Institute in 1917 but, impatient to participate in World War I, left VMI to enlist in the marines in August 1918.

Puller did not see action in World War I. Attending officer candidate school, he was commissioned in the marine reserves in June 1919. Caught in the reduction of the corps following the war, Puller reenlisted as a corporal. From 1919 to 1924, he served in the Haitian gendarmerie as an acting first lieutenant, showing aggressive tactics and leading from the front, two traits that became his hallmarks.

In 1924, Puller was commissioned a second lieutenant. Over the next seven years he served at Philadelphia; Quantico, Virginia; Pensacola, Florida (where he took aviation training but did not earn pilot's wings); Hawaii; and in Nicaragua. He twice commanded the marine detachment on the cruiser *Augusta.* He also served a second time in Nicaragua, and in Beijing (Peking), China, as commander of the marine detachment at the U.S. legation. From 1936 to 1939, Puller was an instructor at the Marine Basic School in Philadelphia, and in 1940–41 he was with the 4th Marine Regiment in Shanghai, China, where he was advanced to major and battalion commander. Puller was next with the 7th Marines at Camp Lejeune, North Carolina, where he helped to pioneer jungle warfare training.

In September 1942, Puller landed with the 7th Marines on GUADALCANAL, where he distinguished himself in the defense of Henderson Field. His half-strength battalion held off an entire Japanese regiment, killing more than 1,400 attackers. Promoted to lieutenant colonel, he next commanded two battalions at Cape Gloucester, New Britain. In February 1944 he took over the 1st Marine Regiment, landing with it on PELELIU in September. In November he returned to the United States on training duty at Camp Lejeune, and shortly thereafter he was promoted to colonel.

In August 1950 he returned to the 1st Marine Regiment at Camp Pendleton, California. Sent to Korea immediately thereafter, Puller led the 1st Marines in the 15 September INCHON LANDING and the recapture of Seoul. He won his 5th Navy Cross, the most awarded in corps history, for his leadership during the withdrawal from the CHANGJIN/CHOSIN RESERVOIR. Promoted to brigadier general in January 1951, Puller for a short time was assistant division commander of the 1st Marine Division under Major General Oliver P. SMITH.

In May 1951, Puller returned to the United States to take command of the 3d Marine Brigade, later redesignated the 3d Marine Division, at Camp Pendleton. Promoted to major general in September 1953, he returned to Camp Lejeune as commander of the 2d Marine Division and later deputy camp commander until his retirement because of disability in November 1955 as a lieutenant general.

Although a competent staff officer, Puller was first and foremost a warrior. During his long career he won 53 decorations, probably the most in Marine Corps history. Chesty Puller was perhaps the most colorful figure in Marine Corps history. He died in Hampton, Virginia, on 11 October 1971.

See also KOREAN WAR, COURSE OF; LATIN AMERICA INTERVENTIONS, EARLY 20TH CENTURY; MARINE CORPS, U.S.

Further reading: Davis, Burke. *Marine! The Life of Lt. Gen. Lewis B. (Chesty) Puller, USMC (ret).* Boston: Little, Brown, 1962; Hoffman, Jon T. *Chesty: The Story of Lieutenant General Lewis B. Puller, USMC.* New York: Random House, 2001; Reynolds, B. L. *The Greatest of the Great: Lt. Gen. L. B. "Chesty" Puller.* New York: Vantage Press, 1983.

— Spencer C. Tucker

Pullman Strike intervention (4–7 July 1894) *One of the major incidents in American labor history*
The Pullman Strike resulted in federal military intervention to break a railroad strike. George Pullman, one of the more notable robber barons of the Gilded Age, prided himself on being a model industrialist. His Pullman Palace Car Company, located on the outskirts of Chicago, was surrounded by worker houses, provided by Pullman, which were of superior quality to those provided by most factory owners for their employees.

Faced with declining revenues as a consequence of the panic of 1893, Pullman opted to reduce wages several times rather than lay off large numbers of employees. The wage reductions were not accompanied by a lowering of rents for the houses, however, and Pullman's workers organized a union. Finding that Pullman was unwilling to negotiate, the workers struck, and Pullman closed the plant to await the collapse of the workers movement. Sympathetic members of the American Railway Union, led by Eugene V. Debs, refused to handle any of the Pullman sleeping cars, and the Pullman closure threatened to escalate into a general railroad strike.

Federal officers in Chicago were told to keep a watchful eye on the developing situation. Matters came to a head on 3 July. A federal court ruled that the railroad action, as a constraint of trade, was a violation of the 1890 Sherman Antitrust Act, and, on the same day, some strikers derailed a train that contained several U.S. mail cars.

Without consulting Illinois governor John Peter Altgeld, President Grover Cleveland dispatched 2,000 federal troops to Chicago to quell the disturbance and terminate the railroad strike. A major riot ensued, resulting in the deaths of nearly two dozen persons, the destruction of several thousand railroad cars, and the arrest of Debs. The use of federal force (legal injunctions and military power) to suppress a strike was upheld by the U.S. Supreme Court in the case of *In re Debs* (1895).

Further reading: Lindsey, Almont. *The Pullman Strike: The Story of a Unique Experiment and of a Great Labor Upheaval.* Chicago: University of Chicago Press, 1942; Papke, David R. *The Pullman Case: The Clash of Labor and Capital in Industrial America.* Lawrence: University Press of Kansas, 1999; Smith, Carl S. *Urban Disorder and the Shape of Belief: The Great Chicago Fire, the Haymarket Bomb, and the Model Town of Pullman.* Chicago: University of Chicago Press, 1995.

— David W. Coffey

punitive expedition into Mexico (14 March 1916–7 February 1917) *Major U.S. military intervention in and occupation of northern Mexico during the administration of President Woodrow Wilson*
After the overthrow of the dictatorship of General Victoriano Huerta in July 1914, President WILSON found it hard to sort out and influence the different revolutionary leaders contending for power in Mexico. Wilson initially favored Francisco "Pancho" Villa, the only major revolutionary

U.S. Commander Brigadier General John J. Pershing is shown here with his aide, 1st Lieutenant Collins.   *(Library of Congress)*

bus, New Mexico. A detachment of U.S. troops—350 men of the 13th Cavalry under Colonel Herbert W. Slocum—was stationed outside of town. The U.S. troops reacted immediately, but the Villistas succeeded in killing 17 Americans and burning and looting much of the town. Villa's forces suffered an estimated 100 casualties.

Although U.S. forces operated under specific instructions not to cross the international boundary, Slocum ordered a detachment of cavalry under Major Frank Tompkins to pursue Villa's troops into Mexico. Tompkins's force of 59 men engaged in four separate actions with the Villistas, killing between 75 and 100 of them on Mexican soil, and returned to the United States after seven hours.

The hot pursuit by Tompkins's cavalry was the forerunner of a much larger military group that would be sent after Villa and his raiders, the punitive expedition. Brigadier General John J. PERSHING assumed command of the force that was assembled at Columbus to pursue Villa and disperse his forces so that they would no longer threaten the border. The first elements of the expedition crossed into Mexico on 15 March, long after hot pursuit was still a possibility. Carranza considered the expedition an invasion of national territory, although initially he was not prepared to resist the incursion with military force.

The punitive expedition was organized as a provisional division with an initial strength of more than 5,000 troops and a peak strength of more than 11,000. The original emphasis was on cavalry, but later infantry, artillery, and even air units joined. The Carranza administration refused to cooperate with the expedition. The most critical example of this was the Mexican government's refusal to let the expedition freely use the Mexican railways that had figured importantly in U.S. logistical planning. This refusal was particularly galling to the Wilson administration, which had earlier permitted Carranza to use U.S. railroads to transfer troops against Villa. The United States would have to supply the expedition overland in an area with few roads, in difficult terrain, and with major weather problems. Expedition planners had to develop a system of motorized supply, despite a shortage of officers, drivers, trucks, and mechanics. By June 1916, the expedition was using more than 300 trucks of 14 different types produced by eight different manufacturers. The U.S. Army used aircraft in combat for the first time in the punitive expedition, dispatching the 1st Aero Squadron (its only air squadron) of eight planes for reconnaissance and communications purposes. By 20 April 1916, the only two planes still operational returned to Columbus, where they were unceremoniously burned by their own pilots after being classified as unfit for service.

One of the biggest fears was a military clash between the expedition and Carranza's forces. As the expedition grew in size and moved farther south, possibilities of an incident increased. By early April, the expedition had

figure who had not denounced Wilson's intervention and occupation of VERACRUZ in April 1914. Forces loyal to First Chief Venustiano Carranza, however, inflicted a series of military defeats on Villa in 1915, eliminating him as a national leader, and the Wilson administration reluctantly recognized Carranza's government in October.

The recognition of Carranza convinced Villa that he had been betrayed by Wilson and that Mexico had been betrayed by Carranza. Despite his defeats, Villa was still a regional military power in northern Mexico with the capability of threatening the U.S.-Mexico border region. In early March 1916 there were reports that Villa's forces were near the border, but U.S. officials discounted them. Before dawn on 9 March, some 500 of Villa's troops crossed the international boundary and attacked the town of Colum-

penetrated more than 300 miles into Mexico and had grown to almost 7,000 troops. The first major encounter came at Parral, Chihuahua, on 12 April. Believing it had the permission of Carranza's officials, a cavalry unit entered the town to purchase supplies. Local citizens opened fire on the U.S. soldiers, who were also attacked by regular troops as they attempted to withdraw. The U.S. unit suffered two dead and several wounded, while Mexican casualties were estimated at 40.

Both Carranza and Wilson prepared for a wider conflict neither wanted. In May, Wilson federalized the National Guards of Texas, New Mexico, and Arizona, sending them to the border to support the punitive expedition. By June, the two countries appeared to be on the brink of full-scale war. Wilson then federalized the National Guards of the other 45 states and sent them to the border. Carranza's forces received orders to resist any movement by units of the expedition unless they were withdrawing to the north.

On 21 June there was another major clash between U.S. troops and Carranza's forces. One of the expedition's reconnaissance patrols violated its orders by trying to enter Carrizal, Chihuahua. The U.S. unit clashed with Carranza's troops and suffered 12 killed (including the patrol's commander), 10 wounded, and 24 taken prisoner. Mexican casualties numbered at least 74. War was avoided when Carranza announced that the U.S. prisoners would be returned, and both sides agreed to submit their grievances to a joint commission.

Although the joint commission produced no tangible results, the punitive expedition began a winding-down process. By September 1916, Pershing, his immediate superior, Major General Frederick FUNSTON, and army chief of staff Hugh SCOTT agreed that there was no longer any military reason for keeping the expedition in Mexico. The expense of military operations was also a consideration. The War Department estimated that the cost of the expedition and the federalized National Guards (more than 100,000 troops) was approximately $15 million per month. The demobilization of National Guard units began in late fall 1916, and a phased withdrawal of the expedition from northern Mexico began on 27 January 1917. The last of the expedition's troops returned to U.S. soil on 5 February 1917.

Many of the troops who marched out of Mexico—including their commander—would soon be in France, fighting in World War I. After almost 11 months, and at a cost of $130 million, the expedition had proved a partial success. It never captured Villa, who would continue to be a problem until 1920, but it had dispersed Villa's forces so that they were no longer a threat to the U.S. border area, and it had provided valuable training both for the regular army and National Guard.

See also LATIN AMERICA INTERVENTIONS, EARLY 20TH CENTURY; ZIMMERMANN TELEGRAM.

Further reading: Clendenen, Clarence C. *The United States and Pancho Villa*. Ithaca, N.Y.: Cornell University Press, 1961; Gilderhus, Mark T. *Diplomacy and Revolution: U.S.-Mexican Relations under Wilson and Carranza*. Tucson: University of Arizona Press, 1977; Hall, Linda B., and Don M. Coerver. *Revolution on the Border: The United States and Mexico, 1910–1920*. Albuquerque: University of New Mexico Press, 1988.

— Don M. Coerver

Pusan Perimeter, Battle of the (5 August–23 September 1950) *First, and pivotal, campaign of the Korean War*

Failure here would have doomed U.S. and Republic of Korea (ROK) forces. The U.S. 24th and 25th Infantry Divisions and 1st Cavalry Division (actually infantry) were dispatched to Korea from Japan beginning on 3 July 1950. Each was at about two-thirds strength, and the men were undertrained, and most of their weapons and equipment were considered unserviceable. The combined U.S.-ROK force fought a delaying action to gain time to establish what became known as the Pusan Perimeter.

Located in the extreme southeast portion of the Korean Peninsula, the perimeter covered the port of Pusan, vital for supply of United Nations Command (UNC) forces from Japan. It was marked by the Naktong River in the west and by high, rugged mountains in the north. U.S. and ROK troops reached this area in the first days of August and dug in. The ROK 1st Infantry Division and the three U.S. divisions were deployed north to south along the Naktong, with frontages ranging from 20 to 40 miles. U.S. Army doctrine stated that an infantry division should man no more than a nine-mile front. The ROK 6th, 8th Capital, and 3d Divisions held the 60-mile long northern front, from west to east.

Along the Naktong from south to north, the North Koreans deployed their 6th Korean People's Army (KPA, North Korean) Division, with the 83d Motorcycle Regiment attached, and the 4th, 3d, and 15th Infantry Divisions. In the north, from west to east, were the KPA 13th, 8th, 12th (the redesignated 7th), and 5th Divisions, and the 766th Independent Infantry Regiment.

Four avenues of attack entered the perimeter, all of which the North Koreans exploited. The southern route ran through Chindong-ni to Masan. The seizure of Masan, 30 miles from Pusan, would outflank the perimeter. To the north was the route from the Naktong to Miryang. If Miryang were lost, the principal highway and rail route would be cut to Taegu, rupturing the perimeter. Another route came down through Taegu, the largest city within the perimeter and a vital crossroads of links south and west, and to the supply and communications links to and among the ROK divisions. Finally, there was the avenue south from Angang-ni through Kyongju to Pusan.

The extended frontages along the Naktong were manned by outposts, depending upon counterattacks to repel KPA penetrations. There, Lieutenant General Walton H. WALKER, commanding U.S. forces (the Eighth Army), conducted the longest, largest, most complex, and most successful mobile defense in U.S. military history (even though the U.S. Army had no such doctrine for infantry divisions). He employed the ROK divisions in a "positional defense."

Although the U.S.-ROK force outnumbered the North Koreans 92,000 to 70,000, the North Koreans had the initiative and were able to concentrate superior numbers at each of their points of attack, while Walker had to spread his troops across the entire front.

Walker carefully analyzed every action in progress or that was imminent, then quickly decided what to do. Although hampered by the lack of adequate reserves, he was always able to commit sufficient resources at the right time to save the day. Walker also faced serious command problems. Since none of his divisional commanders had ever commanded a division in combat, he had to guide each of them, while contending with General of the Army Douglas MACARTHUR's unfriendly chief of staff, Major General Edward ALMOND.

On 9 August, Walker launched a division-sized limited objective attack (Task Force Kean) on his southern flank that was thwarted by stubborn KPA resistance. Between 5 and 8 August, the KPA launched a series of attacks along the other three avenues. Fortunately, Walker received significant reinforcements about this time in the form of the 5th Regimental Combat Team (RCT), two battalions from the 29th infantry, a Marine Brigade, and the 2d Infantry Division. The KPA penetrated deep into the 24th Division sector, and some 27,000 North Koreans attacked the ROK 1st and 6th Divisions and a regiment of the 1st Cavalry Division, striving for Taegu. Reinforcements from elements of the 2d Division, Marine Brigade, and part of the U.S. 27th Infantry Regiment halted the penetration. The ROK 1st Infantry Division and U.S. 27th Infantry Regiment stopped part of the Taegu thrust, while the 1st Cavalry Division, with the 5th Regimental Combat Team attached, almost destroyed the KPA 3d Division. The ROK 8th Division, meantime, slowed, then stopped the KPA 8th Division in the north central mountains. And the KPA 5th Division trapped the ROK 3d along the ocean, forcing its evacuation. The KPA 12th and 5th Divisions then penetrated between the capital and repositioned 3d Divisions but were defeated by ROK and U.S. reinforcements. On 17 and 18 August, elements of the KPA 6th Division struck unsuccessfully into U.S. 25th Infantry Division.

On 27 August the KPA launched its second offensive over the same avenues, but Walker successfully countered each thrust. When the U.S. X Corps landed at INCHON on 15 September, ROK and Eighth Army forces were still locked in battle along the perimeter with the North Koreans. Hampered by insufficient river crossing equipment and a severe shortage of artillery ammunition, the UNC breakout from the perimeter was not completed until 23 September. The Battle of the Pusan Perimeter was an epic stand that enabled UN forces to continue the war.

See also DEAN, WILLIAM F.; KOREAN WAR TASK FORCE SMITH.

Further reading: Appleman, Roy E. *South to the Naktong, North to the Yalu.* Washington, D.C.: Office of the Chief of Military History, Department of the Army, 1961; Ent, Uzal W. *Fighting on the Brink: Defense of the Pusan Perimeter.* Paducah, Ky.: Turner Publishing, 1998.
— Uzal W. Ent

Putnam, Israel (1718–1790) *Militia officer and Continental Army general*
Born on 7 January 1718 at Salem Village, Massachusetts, Israel Putnam received little if any formal education. Around 1740 he moved to Brooklyn, Connecticut, where he became a successful farmer.

On the outbreak of the FRENCH AND INDIAN WAR, Putnam joined the militia as a captain. Distinguishing himself as a scout and in combat, he campaigned at CROWN POINT in 1755 and also took part in the FORT TICONDEROGA CAMPAIGN in 1758. Putnam was captured by Indians and allegedly tortured. Reportedly the Indians were about to kill him when he was saved by a French officer. On his exchange in 1759 he was promoted to lieutenant colonel and took part in the expedition against MONTREAL. He was bringing a 1,000-man relief force to assist in the British siege of Havana, Cuba, when his fleet was wrecked off Cuba. He was one of few survivors.

Putnam again served during PONTIAC'S REBELLION in 1763. With the end of hostilities, he returned to his farm in Connecticut. Active in politics, Putnam was a member of the general assembly, in which he allied with those protesting arbitrary British rule. On the outbreak of the American Revolutionary War, Putnam was lieutenant colonel of the 11th Regiment of Connecticut militia and immediately hastened to Cambridge, Massachusetts, where he was commissioned brigadier general and given command of Connecticut troops.

Putnam helped to organize the Patriot positions on Bunker and Breed's Hills. During the June Battle of BUNKER HILL, he was the ranking officer on the Patriot side and was supposedly responsible for the order "Don't one of you fire until you see the whites of their eyes." The

Israel Putnam   *(Library of Congress)*

battle, although a British victory, was so costly for them that it made Putnam's military reputation. Congress then commissioned him one of the four original major generals in the Continental army under General George WASHINGTON.

Personally fearless in combat, Putnam was less satisfactory as a field commander. He commanded Continental troops at New York City, but his faulty reconnaissance led in part to a British victory in the Battle of LONG ISLAND. He was also partly responsible for the American defeat at Brooklyn Heights. He then commanded the defense of Philadelphia, but Washington was displeased at Putnam's slow response during the Battle of PRINCETON. Transferred to the Hudson Highlands, he failed to prevent the British capture of Forts Montgomery and Clinton on the Hudson in October 1777. Although a court of inquiry exonerated him, Putnam never again held a field command. Suffering a stroke in December 1779, he then retired. "Old Put" nonetheless remained a popular figure, especially in the subsequent embellishment of his exploits. Putnam died at Pomfret, Connecticut, on 29 May 1790.

See also AMERICAN REVOLUTIONARY WAR: LAND OVERVIEW; PRESCOTT, WILLIAM.

Further reading: Niven, John. *Connecticut Hero: Israel Putnam.* Hartford: American Revolution Bicentennial Commission of Connecticut, 1977; Putnam, Hamilton S. *Country on Fire: Israel Putnam and the Colonial Struggle to Survive, 1755–1765.* Concord, N.H.: H. S. Putnam, 1974.

— Spencer C. Tucker

Pyle, Ernest Taylor ("Ernie") (1900–1945) *American war correspondent in World War II*

Born on 3 August 1900 near Dana, Indiana, Ernie Pyle studied journalism at the University of Indiana, but dropped out in 1923 to become a reporter for the *La Porte Herald* in La Porte, Indiana. He held a variety of jobs in journalism over the next 17 years, including managing director of the Washington *Daily News.* At the beginning of World War II, Pyle was a roving reporter for the Scripps-Howard newspaper organization. His columns, always written in a lighthearted, engaging style, won him great popularity among the reading public.

Pyle put his journalistic skills to use during the war when he went to England in November 1940 to report on the German bombing campaign against London. His stories captured the effects of war and entranced readers in the United States.

In 1942 Pyle's writing turned to the average combat soldier, when he went to North Africa and reported on Allied operations there and then in Sicily and Italy. He later reported the Allied drive across France following the June 1944 NORMANDY INVASION.

Pyle's columns, in which he included the names of soldiers and their hometowns, were immensely popular and ultimately ran in 400 daily newspapers. In 1944 he was awarded the Pulitzer Prize for bringing the reality of war to those people who would never experience it firsthand. Pyle also helped to bring about combat pay supplements for GIs and the uniform sleeve-stripe that designated a soldier's six months' overseas service.

In 1945, when fighting in Europe ended, Pyle transferred to the Pacific theater to cover the island-hopping campaigns against Japan. He had produced only a few stories when he was killed during the campaign for OKINAWA. He died on Ie Shima Island, near Okinawa, from Japanese machine gun fire, on 18 April 1945. Pyle's death came as a great blow to soldiers and civilians alike, who had come to respect his talent for revealing the human perspective of war.

See also WAR REPORTING.

Further reading: O'Connor, Barbara. *The Soldier's Voice: The Story of Ernie Pyle.* Minneapolis: Carolrhoda Books, 1996; Tobin, James. *Ernie Pyle's War: America's Eyewitness to World War II.* New York: Free Press, 1997.

— Eric W. Osborne

Quallah Batoo, attack on (Kuala Batu) (6–7
February 1832) *The first military action undertaken by the United States against Asians*

In early 1831, the American merchant ship *Friendship* arrived at Quallah Batoo, Sumatra (Indonesia), one of many ports along the Sumatra coast trading in pepper. The name *Quallah Batoo* means "rocky river," for the river that divided the village.

Captain Charles M. Endicott commanded the 316-ton *Friendship,* with a crew of 17 officers and men. Endicott was trading pepper for Silsbee, Pickman, & Stone, a firm operating out of Salem, Massachusetts.

On 7 February, while Endicott was ashore, a number of armed Sumatrans stormed the ship, killing three of the crew and wounding three others. When Endicott realized what had transpired, he and the remaining members of his crew sought refuge at the next port along the shore. Obtaining assistance from other merchant seamen, he returned to Quallah Batoo on the 9th and retook his ship, by then completely stripped of its goods. Endicott estimated the loss at $12,000 worth of pepper, 12 chests of opium, and other items, all totalling $41,054. Endicott then sailed for the United States, returning to Salem on 16 June. His employers, upset at their loss, petitioned President Andrew JACKSON to recover their investment.

Jackson decided to send a warship to investigate. Captain John Downes of the *Potomac* was ordered to proceed to Sumatra by way of the Cape of Good Hope. His orders called on him to investigate before taking any precipitous action. He also was instructed to hold only the pirates accountable, but Downes found it impossible to determine those responsible and, on the early morning of 6 February 1832, ordered an attack on Quallah Batoo.

Lieutenant Irving Shubrick led an assault force of 282 men ashore, landing about 1.5 miles from the village. The attack lasted about 2.5 hours, and during the fighting two Americans died and 11 were wounded. The number of Sumatran casualties is unknown, but probably was between 60 and 150. Having destroyed three of the four village forts, the U.S. sailors and Marines returned to the *Potomac.* The next day, Downes moved his ship and fired on the remaining fort, on the south side of the river, which quickly surrendered.

Downes's action, which had resulted in the death of Sumatran civilians, guilty and innocent, was soon forgotten by the U.S. government and American people. However, it did halt piratical operations against American commerce in the region.

Further reading: Long, David F. "'Martial Thunder': The First Official American Armed Intervention In Asia," *Pacific Historical Review* 42, no. 2 (1973): 143–62; Neeser, Robert. *Statistical and Chronological History of the United States Navy, 1775–1909.* New York: Macmillan, 1909.

— Ryan N. Peay

Quasi-War with France (1798–1800) *Undeclared naval war that saw the birth of the U.S. Navy*

Following the AMERICAN REVOLUTION and the adoption of the U.S. Constitution, Presidents George WASHINGTON and John Adams attempted to improve commercial and political relations with Great Britain. These efforts bore fruit in the Jay Treaty. Approved by the Senate in 1795, it settled outstanding disagreements with Britain. America's Revolutionary War ally France, however, which began more than 20 years of war with Britain in 1793, deeply resented this action. Determined to coerce the United States into a closer alliance, its ruling Directory in March 1797 ordered its navy to seize U.S. merchant vessels. Several hundred American ships quickly fell into the hands of the French, and American trade dropped precipitously.

Congress met the French challenge by passing a bill in July 1797 granting President Adams the authority to enlist sailors in the infant U.S. Navy, the strength of which at the time rested in only three frigates—the *United States,* the CONSTITUTION, and the CONSTELLATION—although others would soon be ready. Responsibility for command of the navy meanwhile passed from the War Department to the newly created Navy Department, headed by the experienced Maryland merchant and Federalist politician Benjamin STODDERT.

While vigorously supporting a program of naval expansion, Adams also sought a diplomatic solution to the crisis. The Directory refused to receive his envoys, however, unless the U.S. first paid a bribe of $250,000 to each director. The surprised American representatives declined to pay.

Adams related the details of this incident to Congress, referring to the French officials involved as X, Y, and Z. Public outrage in the United States over this "XYZ Affair" pushed the two countries further apart and made a peaceful settlement seem unlikely. Congress enlarged the army, and former president Washington agreed to accept command again. Land forces would not see action in the conflict, however. The Quasi-War would instead be characterized by British and American naval cooperation in guarding merchant vessels in the Caribbean, the scene of most of the conflict's action, through both the use of convoys and attacks on French raiders.

Although the early phases of the war had seen the French visit almost unchecked destruction upon American shipping, with more than 6 percent of the country's overseas trading vessels taken in the first year alone, the tide soon turned. The young U.S. Navy acquitted itself well, capturing nearly 100 French privateers during the two years of the conflict, while losing only one warship, the Retaliation, to enemy action. This ship's unfortunate captain, William BAINBRIDGE, allowed his vessel to be captured because of his misidentification of pursuing frigates as friendly British rather than hostile French ships. The navy's losses due to rough weather and ordinary wear and tear were considerably larger. In one September 1800 storm, two warships, the Insurgent and the Pickering, disappeared in rough seas, along with more than 400 crewmen—the worst disaster suffered by the navy during the war. Yellow fever and other tropical diseases also took their toll of American sailors, particularly when captains gave their restive crews extended shore leave, a practice Adams condemned as immoral and unhealthy, but which nevertheless persisted.

One of the war's few major actions between opposing warships resulted in a spectacular American victory that greatly strengthened the country's fledgling naval tradition. In February 1799, Captain Thomas TRUXTUN, commanding the 36-gun Constellation, pursued and attacked the French vessel l'Insurgente, which mounted an equal number of guns. After several exchanges of broadsides, in which the French ship suffered the greater damage, the captain of l'Insurgente struck his colors. Seventy French sailors had been killed or wounded, with only five American casualties. This resounding victory, made possible partly as a result of poor tactical decisions by the French captain, established Truxton as the navy's premier, although not senior, officer.

The war had a serious impact on the American home front. The generally pro-French and anti-British Republicans, led by Thomas JEFFERSON and James Madison, opposed the war and bitterly criticized the Federalist Adams administration's policies. In order to silence this dissent, and perhaps destroy the opposition party, Congress passed the Alien and Sedition Acts in 1798. The never-invoked Alien Act allowed the president to arrest and expel from the country immigrants suspected of disloyalty, while the Sedition Act provided penalties ranging from heavy fines to imprisonment for writing or uttering statements critical of the government or its officials. The arrest and imprisonment of several prominent Republican editors and party leaders led to bitter resentment of this abridgment of the constitutionally guaranteed right of free speech, and both of these acts expired during the last year of the Adams presidency.

As the war progressed and the British and American navies gained the upper hand in the Caribbean, the French became increasingly willing to negotiate. After Napoleon Bonaparte seized power in November 1799, he quickly decided to pursue a more conciliatory policy toward the United States, intended to isolate the British and deprive them of the military assistance of an increasingly powerful ally. Although Alexander HAMILTON and many other Federalists would have preferred to continue the war in order to justify the enlargement of the army, with the potential intimidation or suppression of the rival Republicans in mind, Adams rejected this. Instead, he again sent envoys to France, and they now met a much friendlier reception. In December 1800 Adams sent the resulting peace treaty to the Senate for ratification, effectively ending the conflict.

Further reading: Allen, Gardner W. *Our Naval War with France.* Boston: Houghton Mifflin, 1909; Palmer, Michael A. *Stoddert's War: Naval Operations During the Quasi-War with France, 1798–1801.* Columbia: University of South Carolina Press, 1987.

— Michael Thomas Smith

Quebec campaign (1759) *Key campaign of the 1754–63 French and Indian War (known as the Seven Years' War in Europe, 1756–1763)*

The FRENCH AND INDIAN WAR reached its climax on the Plains of Abraham, where Major General James Wolfe's victory over Lieutenant General Louis Joseph the Marquis de Montcalm outside Quebec City secured the British conquest of Canada.

The 1758 British victory at LOUISBOURG and their control of Cape Breton Island and Isle Ste. Jean (Prince Edward Island) severely restricted French access to the Saint Lawrence River and its key inland ports of Quebec City and Montreal. In 1759 the British planned to deliver the knockout blow—a two-pronged attack against the French in Canada. The commander of British forces in North America, Major General Jeffrey Amherst, and 11,000 troops, half of them provincials, would capture FORT TICONDEROGA and CROWN POINT and advance down the Lake Champlain corridor to Quebec. There Amherst would join 9,000 men and a strong naval force under Vice Admiral Sir Charles Saunders that were to enter the St. Lawrence and take Quebec. Commanding these land troops was perhaps the ablest British general of the war, James Wolfe.

In June 1759, Wolfe embarked his troops at Louisburg in more than 150 ships and naval craft commanded by Admiral Saunders and began the difficult ascent up the Saint Lawrence. By early July, the British controlled the water approaches to Quebec City. Wolfe's troops occupied Ile d'Orléans, four miles east of the city, and Point Levis on the south bank of the river, within artillery range of the Quebec citadel.

Wolfe's troops conducted forays into the surrounding territory to draw French troops out of the fortress and entrenchments. In the only major action prior to the final battle, British forces lost more than 500 men in an unsuccessful assault on the French lines. The siege of the city continued through August and into September as the British cut off Quebec City from Montreal and mounted raids against nearby French settlements.

Quebec City, however, appeared impregnable. Situated at the eastern end of the Plains of Abraham, Quebec's citadel was located atop sheer cliffs rising directly from the river. An attempt against the nearly vertical walls would invite military disaster.

For two months, all of Wolfe's efforts to gain a foothold met with failure. Saunders, fearing his ships would be trapped in the winter ice, threatened to depart. Then Wolfe's men discovered a narrow footpath winding up the precipitous cliffs just north of the city at Anse de Foulon.

Wolfe's plan called for a night crossing of the river and an attack upstream against Anse de Foulon, with a diversionary attack at Beauport, the site of the earlier British defeat. After midnight on 13 September, an advance element led by Colonel William Howe's light infantry landed unopposed and scrambled up the steep cliffs. Howe's men captured the French guard posts overlooking the landing site, and Wolfe soon followed with the main body of troops. By dawn he had some 4,500 men and some light artillery was on the western heights of the Plains of Abraham.

With the British attackers' rear and flanks exposed, and taking harassing fire from militia and Indian elements, Wolfe quickly formed his regulars in a line facing east on the plain and awaited the French. The surprised Montcalm conducted a personal reconnaissance and decided to attack immediately with as many troops as he could muster to throw the British off the plain and back into the river before they could construct fortifications and solidify their lodgment.

By mid-morning on 13 September Montcalm had assembled some 4,500 men for the assault. At approximately 10:00 A.M., the French attacked. Montcalm's mixed force of poorly trained Canadian militia and French regulars was not well coordinated; moreover, he had only three artillery pieces, because the French governor general, Pierre de Rigaud, marquis de Vaudreuil-Cavagnal, insisted on retaining the remainder for the city's defense.

The disciplined British regulars broke the French with well-aimed and timed volley fire. Wolfe then ordered a bayonet attack against Montcalm's retreating forces. During this assault, Wolfe was mortally wounded. French reinforcements under Count Louis Antoine de Bougainville arrived too late to turn the tide of the battle and stop the rout. The engagement had lasted only 15 minutes, but it had been decisive. Montcalm, also mortally wounded during the battle, was unable to exercise command.

Following the defeat, Vaudreuil decided to abandon the city and join forces with Bougainville. The town major of Quebec, Jean-Baptiste Nicholas Roche de Ramezay, left to negotiate with the British, tried to spin out the talks to allow reinforcements to come up but was obliged on the 18th to surrender Quebec City to Brigadier George Townsend, who had taken command of British forces upon the death of Wolfe.

The Battle of the Plains of Abraham was decisive. The British land victory was sealed by the Battle of Quiberon Bay on 20 November 1759, when ships under Admiral Sir Edward Howe defeated the French Brest Squadron and insured that the French would not be able to resupply America. The French did attempt to retake Quebec City in April 1760 at the Battle of ST. FOY but withdrew when British reinforcements arrived on the Saint Lawrence River. The French retreated to MONTREAL, where they held out until September. On 8 September 1760 Vaudreuil signed articles of capitulation that ceded all Canada to the British.

Further reading: Keegan, John. *Warpaths: Travels of a Military Historian in North America.* Toronto: Key Porter Books, 1995; Lloyd, Christopher. *The Capture of Quebec.* New York: Macmillan, 1959; May, Robin, and Gerry Embleton. *Wolfe's Army.* London: Osprey Books, 1997;

Parkman, Francis. *Montcalm and Wolfe.* New York: Atheneum, 1984.

— J. G. D. Babb

Queen Anne's War (1702–1713) *Anglo-French struggle for North American hegemony occurring during the 1701–14 War of the Spanish Succession*

Although the Treaty of Ryswick had ended KING WILLIAM'S WAR (War of the League of Augsburg) in 1697, it had failed to resolve the conflicting colonial claims of the European powers. The French moved quickly to develop the Louisiana Territory, establishing trading posts at Cahokia (near modern Saint Louis) in 1699 and Fort Louis on the Mobile River in 1702, and signing alliances with the Choctaws and other southern tribes. In addition, the Spanish (from Florida) and English (from South Carolina) raided each other's settlements through the disputed territory that eventually became Georgia. These factors, combined with the death of Charles II of Spain on 1 November 1700 and the succession of Louis XIV's grandson, the duc d'Anjou, to the Spanish throne as Philip V, produced a new round of conflict—the War of the Spanish Succession in Europe and Queen Anne's War in the colonies.

Although England and its allies, which included the Netherlands and Austria, declared war on France and Spain on 15 May 1702, by the time news reached the colonies it was too late in the summer to organize for war in the northern colonies. In South Carolina, however, Governor James Moore organized a force of 500 militiamen and 300 Indian allies for an expedition against Saint Augustine. Although Moore's force sacked the town in December, it failed to take the fort and had to withdraw. In 1703 and 1704, Moore led a series of raids against the Apalachee Indians, capturing some 1,000 as slaves, ending Spanish influence north of Saint John's River and establishing English control over the fur trade in the region. A Franco-Spanish force attempted but failed to take Charleston in 1706, leading the English to launch a retaliatory attack on Fort San Carlos at Pensacola in 1707. Fortunately for the Spanish, French forces from Mobile arrived in time to force the English to abandon their attack.

While the southern theater of Queen Anne's War was important in protecting the frontiers of South Carolina, the conflict in the north would eventually result in the first major territorial changes in North America. At first, however, the fighting was sporadic. Indeed, the governor-general of Canada, Pierre de Rigaud, marquis de Vaudreuil-Cavagnal, reached what amounted to a truce with the governor of New York, Lord Cornbury.

While New York merchants benefited from clandestine trade with the French, New Englanders suffered from raids launched primarily by the Abenaki from Acadia. Between 1703 and 1705, the Abenaki struck at numerous New England frontier settlements, including a raid on Deerfield, Massachusetts, on 28–29 February 1704, during which 38 English colonists were killed and 111 were taken captive. In retaliation for the raids and in hope of shutting off the supplies to the Abenaki, Colonel Benjamin CHURCH led a force of 500 militiamen to destroy the French Acadian settlements of Minas (1 July 1704) and Beaubassin (28 July 1704). In addition, Governor Joseph Dudley of Massachusetts and New Hampshire organized two unsuccessful assaults up the Bay of Fundy in 1704 and 1707 in hope of eliminating French privateers based at Port Royal.

Although Dudley's efforts failed, Samuel Vetch, a Scottish adventurer who had settled in New York, presented a petition to the Board of Trade in 1708, calling for a combined Anglo-Colonial assault on Port Royal, as a prelude to capturing Quebec and driving the French from North America. While the British government was inclined to concentrate on the European theater of the war, the French capture of St. John's in Newfoundland caused it to reconsider Vetch's proposals, lest England lose its fisheries off the Grand Banks.

In February 1709, therefore, Queen Anne commissioned Vetch a colonel and instructed him to raise a colonial force. At the same time, Francis NICHOLSON was given command of approximately 1,500 troops in New York and ordered to invade Canada up the Hudson–Lake Champlain corridor. In the fall of 1710, Nicholson's force was diverted to join Vetch in an assault on Port Royal. On 24 September, Nicholson's British-Colonial force of 2,000 began the siege of Port Royal, which was defended by just 258 troops commanded by Governor Daniel d'Auger de Subercase. On 16 October, Subercase surrendered. In the aftermath of the victory, Port Royal was renamed Port Annapolis in honor of Queen Anne, Vetch was named governor of the new colony of Nova Scotia, and Nicholson returned to London to lobby the government for an invasion of Canada.

The success in capturing Port Royal and acquiring Nova Scotia led the British government to undertake an all-out effort to seize control of Canada in 1711. In May 1711, the British dispatched an expedition of 64 ships, including 11 warships and 6,000 sailors under Admiral Sir Hovenden Walker, and 5,000 troops (including seven regiments who were veterans of the duke of Marlborough's campaigns) under Brigadier General John Hill.

Nicholson had already departed with two warships, supplies for 2,000 colonial troops, and orders to lead an invasion force up the Hudson–Lake Champlain corridor. By the time Nicholson arrived in New York later that summer, Robert Hunter, recently appointed governor of New

York, had already raised some 2,000 men, including approximately 800 Indians (mostly Iroquois).

In the meantime, Walker's flotilla arrived in Boston on 25 June and was soon augmented by approximately 1,000 New Englanders and transports. While Nicholson began his advance up the Hudson toward Montreal, Walker prepared to sail up the Saint Lawrence to Quebec. Unfortunately for the British and fortunately for the French, Walker lacked experienced pilots who could navigate the rocky waters of the lower Saint Lawrence. This, combined with high winds and fog, resulted in the loss of nine ships and 800 lives on the night of 23 August, causing Walker to sail for England. Nicholson, who had advanced to Lake George by the time he learned of Walker's failure, had no choice but to return to Albany.

While Vetch and Nicholson hoped to renew the attack in 1712, events in Europe brought an end to the fighting in the colonies. Although the British had supported Austrian Archduke Charles's claim to the Spanish throne, his brother Joseph I's death in 1711 resulted in Charles's succession to the Austrian throne. For the British and everyone else in Europe, the specter of a renewed Habsburg Empire à la Charles V was worse than two Bourbon kings on the French and Spanish thrones. A truce in 1712 gave way in March 1713 to the Peace of UTRECHT, which among other things recognized English acquisition of Nova Scotia.

Further reading: Craven, Wesley Frank. *The Colonies in Transition, 1660–1713.* New York: Harper & Row, 1968; Eccles, W. J. *France in America.* Rev. ed. Markham, Ontario: Fitzhenry & Whiteside, 1990; Wolf, John B. *The Emergence of the Great Powers, 1685–1715.* New York: Harper & Row, 1951.

— Justin D. Murphy

Queenston Heights, Battle of (13 October 1812)
Battle in Canada between British and U.S. Army troops during the War of 1812

When the war began Washington planned a two-pronged invasion of Upper Canada. Unfortunately for the Americans, these were not simultaneous and the British were able to defeat them piecemeal. The first attack, across the Detroit River, was repulsed, and in August Brigadier General William HULL surrendered DETROIT. The second attack was across the Niagara River in the east. The Americans hoped thereby to sever British supply lines west and gain control of the eastern Great Lakes.

By October 1812 approximately 8,000 regulars and militia had assembled between Buffalo and FORT NIAGARA in New York under Major General Stephen VAN RENSSE-LAER. They lacked adequate provisions, were poorly trained, and there was tension between the regular army officers and militia general Van Rensselaer. Opposing them were nearly 1,000 British regulars and 1,200 Canadian militia and Indians led by commander of British forces in Canada, Major General Sir Isaac Brock, fresh from his triumph over Hull at Detroit.

Early in the morning of 13 October, Van Rensselaer began to send 3,100 troops across the Niagara River at Queenston, six miles south of FORT GEORGE. Approximately 300 soldiers landed, but the token British force nearby counterattacked and inflicted heavy losses, including the commander of the landing party. Finally, Captain John E. WOOL led a detachment of the regulars up the steep bank on a small trail, seized a British redan, and established a foothold on the heights overlooking Queenston. About this time, Brock arrived with light reinforcements and attacked the American position. He was quickly killed, however, and his troops retreated back into the town.

The Americans then consolidated their position, as additional troops crossed the river. Eventually the Americans had about 1,000 men on Queenston Heights. The river's strong current and British artillery fire, however, disabled most of the boats, preventing additional reinforcement. Also, most of the New York militia refused to cross into Canada; the sight of dead and wounded, coupled with the sound of combat, weakened their resolve.

On the Canadian side of the river, meanwhile, British reinforcements, including Indians, arrived under Major General Roger Hale Sheaffe. The presence of the Indians unnerved many of the American troops, who subsequently deserted and tried to recross the Niagara.

In midafternoon, some 930 British regulars, Canadian militia, and Indians attacked the American position, now commanded by Lieutenant Colonel Winfield SCOTT. The American line collapsed as the militia broke and ran, streaming toward the river and trying to get across. Some succeeded, others drowned, and most were captured. The British took 958 prisoners, of whom 450 were regulars. An additional 300 Americans were killed or wounded. British loses totaled just 14 dead, 77 wounded, and 21 missing, including the irreplaceable Brock. The disheartening defeat at Queenston Heights was representative of the early American effort during the War of 1812.

See also WAR OF 1812: LAND OVERVIEW.

Further reading: Berton, Pierre. *The Invasion of Canada: 1812–1813.* Boston: Little, Brown, 1980; Hickey, Donald R. *The War of 1812: A Forgotten Conflict.* Urbana: University of Illinois Press, 1989; Zaslow, Morris, ed. *The Defended Border: Upper Canada and the War of 1812.* Toronto: Macmillan, 1964.

— Michael P. Gabriel

Quesada, Elwood R. **("Pete")** (1904–1993) *U.S. Air*
Force general
Born on 13 April 1904 at Washington, D.C., Elwood R.
Quesada attended the University of Maryland, where he
played quarterback on the football team. He joined the
U.S. Army and from September 1924 to June 1925 under-
went flight training at Brooks Field, Texas, obtaining his
wings and a commission. He then took advanced training at
Kelly Field, Texas.

Quesada briefly left the air service for a professional
baseball contract with the Saint Louis Cardinals. However,
the formation of the U.S. Army Air Corps in 1926 and his
inability to hit a curve ball led him back to army flying, this
time as an engineering officer at Bolling Field, Washington,
D.C. In 1928 he became aide to the chief of the air corps,
Major General James E. Fechet. Also on the staff were
future Air Force leaders Major Carl A. "Tooey" SPAATZ and
Captain Ira C. EAKER. Together with these men and Master Sergeant R. W. Hooe, in 1929 Quesada helped to set a
151-hour world refueling endurance record.

In 1933–34, Quesada was an aide to the assistant secretary of war for air, F. Trubee Davison. Later, in 1934 he
participated in the air corps' ill-fated airmail flights. He
then studied at the Air Corps Tactical School (1935–36)
and the Army Command and General Staff College
(1936–37). From 1938 to 1940, Quesada was technical
adviser to the Argentine air force. During these years, he
conceptualized new tactical close air support theories,
stressing close coordination of ground and air assets.

Quesada was General Henry "Hap" ARNOLD's foreign
liaison chief (1940) and went with him to London in April
1941 to implement LEND-LEASE there. In July 1941 he
took command of the 33d Pursuit Group at Mitchel Field,
New York, which flew P-40 Warhawks. When the United
States entered World War II, Quesada's practical experience with fighters proved invaluable. Promoted to
brigadier general (December 1942), in early 1943 Quesada headed XII Fighter Command in North Africa during
campaigns in Tunisia, Sicily, and Italy. His new tactics were
incorporated into the army air forces' field manual (FM)
100–20, *Command and Employment of Air Power*, first
published in July 1943. Among the key aspects of the new
doctrine were the coequal status of ground and air commanders, centralized command of tactical air assets to
exploit the "inherent flexibility of airpower," and the abso-
lute necessity of air superiority over the battlefield.

In October 1943 Quesada headed IX Fighter Command in Britain, and his pilots soon began to escort Eighth
Air Force bombers on deep raids into France and
Germany. Promoted to major general in April 1944, he led
IX Tactical Air Command to provide support for the invasion of France. In June 1944 his command flew air support
for the NORMANDY INVASION. He also coordinated air
assets during the Battle of the BULGE (December
1944–January 1945). During this time Quesada adapted
and refined such innovations as air-to-ground radio communications, forward air controllers, and collocated air and
ground headquarters.

From March 1946 to September 1947 Quesada com-
manded Third Air Force, the core of the Tactical Air Com-
mand (TAC). He was then the independent air force's first
TAC commander from October 1947 to November 1948.
After a tour as commander of Joint Task Force Three in
Eniwetok (November 1949–October 1951), Lieutenant
General Quesada retired.

Quesada was director of the Federal Aviation Administration (FAA) from 1958 to 1961. Later, he served in executive positions with Olin Industries, Lockheed Aircraft,
Topp Industries, and American Airlines. Quesada died on 9
February 1993 at Jupiter, Florida. Quesada's theories on
how to employ tactical air assets and close air support with
modifications remain in effect today.

Further reading: Copp, DeWitt S. *A Few Great Cap-*
tains: The Men and Events That Shaped the Developments
of U.S. Air Power. Garden City, N.Y.: Doubleday, 1980;
Hughes, Thomas Alexander. *Overlord: General Pete Que-*
sada and the Triumph of Tactical Air Power in World War
II. New York: Free Press, 1995; Kohn, Richard H., and
Joseph P. Harahan, eds. *Air Superiority in World War II*
and Korea: An Interview With General James Ferguson,
General Robert M. Lee, General William Momyer, and
Lieutenant General Elwood R. Quesada. Washington,
D.C.: Office of Air Force History, 1983; Schlight, John.
"Elwood R. Quesada: TAC Air Comes of Age," in John L.
Frisbee, ed. *Makers of the United States Air Force.*
Washington, D.C.: Office of Air Force History, 1987.

— William Head

R

Radford, Arthur W. (1896–1973) *U.S. Navy admiral and chairman of the Joint Chiefs of Staff*

Born on 27 February 1896 in Chicago, Illinois, Arthur William Radford graduated from the U.S. Naval Academy, Annapolis, in 1916. During World War I he served on the battleship *South Carolina,* escorting a transatlantic convoy.

Promoted to lieutenant in November 1920, Radford completed flight training in Pensacola, and for the next two decades alternated between sea duty—invariably as a naval aviator in the Pacific—and shore and staff assignments. Promoted to commander in 1936, he commanded the naval air station (NAS) at Seattle, Washington, from 1937 to 1940, and then established the Trinidad, West Indies, NAS.

After U.S. entry in World War II, Radford, whose superb administrative abilities were widely appreciated, won promotion to captain in January 1942 and was charged with organizing training for the thousands of new pilots the navy's vastly expanded air arm required. Promoted to captain in January 1942 and to rear admiral in July 1943, Radford briefly commanded carrier divisions in the Pacific. After a staff assignment in Washington, he returned in late 1944 to join in the IWO JIMA and OKINAWA invasions.

After the war, Radford's rise continued. In 1947 he commanded the Second Atlantic Task Fleet; in 1948 he served as vice chief of naval operations; and in 1949 he became the Pacific Fleets's commander, responsible for naval operations during the KOREAN WAR, when he would have preferred to follow General of the Army Douglas MACARTHUR's suggestions to bomb Chinese bases in Manchuria. In the fall of 1949 he featured prominently in the so-called Revolt of the Admirals, in which naval aviators fiercely opposed the decision to concentrate funding on nuclear-armed air force bombers rather than an aircraft super carrier. Radford's testimony helped persuade Congress to finance nuclear-powered carriers and submarines.

In 1953 President Dwight D. EISENHOWER appointed the fiercely anticommunist Radford chairman of the Joint Chiefs of Staff. Radford shared the president's own NEW LOOK strategic belief that the threat of "massive retaliation" by strategic nuclear weapons could replace more expensive conventional forces, and his opinion on national security issues carried much weight within the administration. Eisenhower, however, rejected the hawkish Radford's advice to use nuclear weapons in Indochina in 1954 and during the 1955 first Taiwan straits crisis.

Radford opposed Eisenhower's efforts to initiate disarmament negotiations with the Soviet Union and considered the president's later defense budgets inadequate. His outspokenly hard-line views often generated friction with General Matthew B. RIDGWAY, the army chief of staff.

Radford retired in 1957, subsequently advising Republican presidential candidates Richard M. NIXON and Barry Goldwater on military security issues. He died at Bethesda, Maryland, on 17 August 1973.

See also VIETNAM WAR: CAUSES OF U.S. INVOLVEMENT.

Further reading: Barlow, Jeffrey G. *Revolt of the Admirals: The Fight for Naval Aviation, 1945–1950.* Washington, D.C.: Naval Historical Center, Department of the Navy, 1994; Radford, Arthur W. *From Pearl Harbor to Vietnam: The Memoirs of Admiral Arthur W. Radford.* Edited by Stephen Jurika, Jr. Stanford, Calif.: Hoover Institution Press, 1980; Schnabel, James, et al. *The History of the Joint Chiefs of Staff: The Joint Chiefs of Staff and National Policy.* 7 vols. to date. Washington, D.C.: Historical Division, U.S. Joint Chiefs of Staff, 1986–2000; Webb, Willard J. *The Chairmen of the Joint Chiefs of Staff.* Washington, D.C.: Historical Division, U.S. Joint Chiefs of Staff, 1989.

— Priscilla Roberts

Red Cloud (c. 1822–1909) *Oglala Sioux leader*

Like Nez Perce leader Chief JOSEPH, Red Cloud was accorded a stature by whites that he never possessed among the Sioux. Although a gifted leader, ferocious warrior, and man of considerable influence, he never became a true chief. Little about his early life is known with certainty. Likely born in 1822 on the North Platte River in what is now Nebraska, Red Cloud was orphaned as a child. Ambitious and enigmatic, he emerged as a great warrior in the Sioux wars against their Crow and Pawnee enemies.

Following the 1862 Santee Sioux uprising in Minnesota, U.S. military attention shifted to the Teton Sioux to the west. A major expedition into the POWDER RIVER region in 1865 combined with an influx of gold seekers up the Bozeman Trail to Montana stirred Sioux tensions.

In 1866, Red Cloud and other Sioux leaders met with government officials at Fort Laramie. The government offered food and other inducements to get the Indians to yield their Powder River hunting grounds. But part of the deal included forts along the Bozeman Trail, which Red Cloud and most of the Tetons would not accept. The army nonetheless moved up the Bozeman that summer, reactivating Fort Reno and building new Forts Phil Kearny and C. F. Smith.

Over the next two years the Teton Sioux, along with Cheyenne and Arapaho allies, worked to drive the army away. Red Cloud helped plan or participated in numerous raids and larger actions around the new forts, including the December 1866 FETTERMAN MASSACRE and the Wagon Box and Hayfield fights of August 1867. The Indians virtually shut down the Bozeman Trail to emigrant traffic while the soldiers in the forts endured a loose siege. Red Cloud offered to call off the war if the army abandoned its forts. Finally, in the Fort Laramie Treaty of 1868, the government agreed to Red Cloud's demands. Although government officials were relieved, they were mistaken in their understanding of Red Cloud's influence—he did not represent most Sioux bands—and this would come back to haunt them.

Red Cloud kept his word and never again made war on the whites. In 1870 he visited New York and Washington. He advocated peace but leveled numerous complaints against the government, especially its Indian agencies. But in 1873 he took up residence at a new agency in northwest Nebraska that bore his name. For the rest of his life he maintained an ambiguous attitude of compromise. He took no part in the Sioux War of 1876, but in 1877 was moved to the Pine Ridge agency in South Dakota, where he fostered a difficult relationship with agent V. T. McGillycuddy. During the Ghost Dance conflict of 1890 he could do little to impact the events that culminated in the tragedy at WOUNDED KNEE. Blind and in failing health, Red Cloud lived another 19 years at Pine Ridge, where he died on 10 December 1909. He remains among the best-known and most accomplished Native American leaders.

See also AMERICAN INDIAN WARS: OVERVIEW; CRAZY HORSE; SITTING BULL.

Further reading: Larson, Robert W. *Red Cloud: Warrior-Statesman of the Lakota Sioux.* Norman: University of Oklahoma Press, 1997; Utley, Robert M. *The Indian Frontier of the American West, 1846–1890.* Albuquerque: University of New Mexico Press, 1984.

— Angela Kidd

Red River campaign (12 March–18 May 1864)
Major Civil War campaign

Overruling objections from the Union general in chief, Lieutenant General Ulysses S. GRANT, and other senior Union commanders who favored an offensive against Mobile in the West, in the spring of 1864 President Abraham LINCOLN authorized an advance along the Red River into Louisiana and Texas. He believed that eliminating Confederate forces west of the Mississippi would secure Louisiana, show the flag to French and French-backed forces in Mexico, and secure the region's lucrative cotton stores. The campaign's objective was Shreveport, Louisiana, and eventually Texas.

Major General Nathaniel P. BANKS, once opposed to the operation but now sensing personal political and financial rewards, led the expedition, accompanied by Rear Admiral David D. PORTER's gunboat fleet, which would provide transport and artillery support. Banks's 17,000-man force would remain in close proximity to the river to maintain Porter's support. Along the way to Shreveport, other Union commands would reinforce Banks, providing the first of 10,000 troops at Alexandria on March 17 and 15,000 more upon his arrival at Shreveport, scheduled for no later than April 10.

The timetable for the Red River campaign was crucial because Grant had drawn a portion of the force from Major General William Tecumseh SHERMAN and this would be required in Tennessee by mid-April for the march on ATLANTA. Also, Porter's flotilla required high water to navigate the river—and the river would soon begin to recede, making a return trip impossible. Neither Grant nor Porter was optimistic about the chances for success, and Porter was particularly worried about the danger of falling water to his riverine force of 18 ships, including 12 ironclad gunboats.

The operation began as scheduled, but low water levels, numerous confiscation expeditions, and the presence of cotton speculators all hampered Banks's advance. The slow progress compounded pressure on Banks to accelerate his movement before Sherman's troops would be recalled to Tennessee and before the warships became trapped on the river. Reaching Grand Encore on 3 April, Banks made a fateful decision. To save time, he chose to move inland, away from his naval support, and march on Shreveport along an inland route. Unaware of a suitable road parallel

Red River Campaign, March–May 1864. Engraving, *Harper's Weekly*   (Library of Congress)

to the river beyond Grand Encore, and too rushed to send out reconnaissance to scout for a better alternative, Banks turned west away from the lush river valley into a "howling wilderness" of pine thickets and sunken, muddy roads. Porter continued north on the river, plundering ever more cotton as he moved forward.

To oppose the movement toward Shreveport, the Confederacy mustered almost 30,000 men from Louisiana, Arkansas, and Texas under the command of General Edmund Kirby SMITH. Until they arrived, only Major General Richard Taylor's small force of 8,800 Confederates stood against Banks's advance. As per Smith's orders, Taylor provided only token resistance to Federal probes, falling back and avoiding any sustained combat until such time as Smith could reach him with reinforcements.

On 8 April, Taylor's cavalry met Banks's advance column near Sabine Cross Roads, south of Mansfield and 40 miles from Shreveport. Union forces emerged from the woods into a broad open field and deployed behind a rail fence, expecting their foe to retreat. The two forces anxiously faced each other for most of the afternoon. Afraid his enemy might be reinforced during the night, Taylor attacked in the late afternoon and routed the Federals, overrunning their wagon trains and sending them reeling

back three miles toward Pleasant Hill. The assault was costly. Taylor lost 1,000 men, including a division commander and three regimental commanders. Federal casualties were considerably greater—more than 2,200 men. Banks also lost 20 guns and 200 wagons.

Taylor, reinforced overnight by some of Smith's troops, resumed the attack the next morning, but Banks's position at Pleasant Hill held. Each side suffered approximately 1,400 additional casualties during the battle. Exhausted from the contest, both armies withdrew. Smith went north to counter a Federal column advancing on Shreveport from Arkansas, leaving Taylor only a small force to pursue Banks. Meanwhile, Banks realized that he could not reach his objective in time, and retreated south toward Alexandria to rendezvous with Porter.

Porter's gunboats, meanwhile, retraced their route down the Red River, under Confederate fire from the river banks along the way. Porter was forced to abandon a steamer and a gunboat, both badly damaged, and the Confederates captured another steamer. At Alexandria, Porter discovered there was only three feet of water in the river; his gunboats required seven feet. While considering the possibility of scuttling his squadron to prevent its capture, Porter took the suggestion of one of his engineers that they construct a dam to build up sufficient water to enable them to pass. After eight days of hard work the dam was almost completed when it gave way. Although the river fell rapidly, Porter was able to get four of his lighter gunboats out. The engineers then began anew, and on 13 May the remaining ships made it out. A week later they were safely back on the Mississippi.

Banks reached the west bank of the Atchafalaya River in mid-May but found all the bridges over it destroyed. With Banks apparently bottled up, on 18 May the Confederates made a final attempt to crush the Federals at Yellow Bayou. Oppressive heat and the dense vegetation prevented a decisive engagement. The Confederates prepared to resume the offensive the next day, but Federal forces, meanwhile, had constructed pontoon bridges, allowing Banks to cross the river and reach the safety of the east bank.

Upon his return, Banks was relieved of command, and Congress began an extensive investigation into the campaign's conduct and ultimate failure.

See also CIVIL WAR: LAND OVERVIEW; CIVIL WAR: NAVAL OVERVIEW.

Further reading: Brooksher, William Riley. *War Along the Bayous: The 1864 Red River Campaign in Louisiana.* London: Brassey's, 1998; Forsyth, Michael J. *The Red River Campaign and the Loss by the Confederacy of the Civil War.* Jefferson, N.C.: MacFarland, 2002; Johnson, Robert Ludwell. *Red River Campaign: Politics and Cotton in the Civil War.* Baltimore: Johns Hopkins University Press, 1958.

— Derek W. Frisby

Red River War (1874–1875) *Major campaign of the American Indian Wars*

Despite the hopes fostered by the 1867 Medicine Lodge Treaty, the South Plains remained a hotbed of hostile Indian activity and punitive military action. By 1874 the failures of the reservation system and the systematic destruction of the buffalo combined to trigger a major uprising.

On 27 June 1874, several hundred Cheyenne and Comanche warriors attacked a group of 28 buffalo hunters at an old trading post in the Texas Panhandle known as Adobe Walls. Prominent among the attackers was Quanah Parker, son of an influential Comanche chief and his captured white wife. Despite overwhelming odds, the well-protected buffalo hunters devastated the attackers with high-powered rifles.

This action began the Red River War. In July Lone Wolf's Kiowa assailed a Texas Ranger detachment, while Cheyenne warriors struck travel routes in Kansas and Comanche menaced Texas ranches. After years of bristling under President Ulysses S. GRANT's peace policy, army commanding general William Tecumseh SHERMAN unleashed his forces. He directed Lieutenant General Philip SHERIDAN, commanding the Military Division of the Missouri, to bring the uprising to a decisive end. Sheridan, like Sherman an advocate of total war, quickly devised the most ambitious campaign yet mounted by the army against western Indians.

Sheridan's plan called for five independent columns to converge on Indian camps in the Texas Panhandle and punish the Indians to such an extent as to discourage future uprisings. Accordingly, Colonel Nelson MILES marched from Fort Dodge with a large force of cavalry and infantry; Colonel Ranald MACKENZIE, with eight troops of cavalry and five infantry companies, moved northward from Fort Concho; Major William Price led a squadron of cavalry eastward from New Mexico; and Lieutenant Colonels John Davidson and George Buell prepared their commands, including several companies of BUFFALO SOLDIERS (African-American troopers of the 10th Cavalry) to strike westward from Indian Territory. The total force numbered more than 2,000 soldiers and Indian scouts.

In August army units moved onto reservations to separate the peaceful Indians from the hostile. While most Arapaho enrolled as friendly, most Cheyenne refused to submit. Troubles at the Fort Sill agency triggered a confrontation between Davidson's cavalry and a band of Comanche supported by Lone Wolf's Kiowa, most of whom escaped to join hostile factions on the Staked Plains. The army listed almost 5,000 Indians, including 1,200 warriors, as hostile.

A severe drought made water scarce, and late August temperatures reached 110 degrees as Colonel Miles pushed his men southward. On 30 August, near Palo Duro Canyon, the column clashed with Cheyenne warriors, who were soon joined by Kiowa and Comanche. The soldiers prevailed, driving the Indians onto the plains, but supply shortages compelled Miles to disengage.

The drought gave way to torrential rains and dropping temperatures as Miles linked with Price's column on 7 September. Two days later, a band of Kiowa and Comanche assailed a supply train en route to Miles. Following a three-day siege, the Indians abandoned the effort unrewarded, but the incident further complicated Miles's supply crisis.

With Miles temporarily out of action, Colonel Mackenzie and his crack 4th Cavalry took up the fight. After stockpiling supplies, Mackenzie moved in miserable conditions to the rugged canyons of the Caprock escarpment. On 26 September he thwarted a Comanche attempt to stampede his horses. Two days later, Mackenzie struck the most devastating blow of the campaign—a surprise attack in Palo Duro Canyon. Following a harrowing descent, wave after wave of cavalry swept across the canyon floor. The soldiers inflicted few casualties but laid waste to the village, burning lodges, badly needed food stocks, and equipment. Mackenzie's troopers completed the devastation by capturing some 1,500 ponies, a thousand of which the colonel ordered destroyed to prevent their recapture.

Over the next three months, army units scoured the Texas Panhandle, despite freezing temperatures and intense storms. Hungry and demoralized, Indians began to trickle into the reservation by October, but most remained defiant until weather and constant military pressure finally broke their resistance. In late February 1875, 500 Kiowa, including Lone Wolf, surrendered. On 6 March, 800 Cheyenne, among them the elusive Gray Beard, capitulated. But in April some 60 Cheyenne bolted from their reservation in an effort to join the Northern Cheyenne; 27, including women and children, were killed by a cavalry detachment on Sappa Creek in northwestern Kansas. In June, Quanah Parker and 400 Comanche—the last organized band—surrendered to Mackenzie at Fort Sill.

The Red River War was among the most successful campaigns ever conducted by the U.S. Army in the AMERICAN INDIAN WARS. It brought almost complete subjugation to three of America's most powerful and revered tribes. It also provided a model for future campaigns and boldly confirmed the doctrine of total war. Now less concerned with inflicting casualties, the army focused on destroying the Indians' means and will to resist. This, combined with the annihilation of the buffalo, made it impossible for Indians to exist in large numbers outside the reservation.

See also INDIAN WARFARE.

Further reading: Haley, James L. *The Buffalo War: The History of the Red River Indian Uprising of 1874.* Garden City, N.Y.: Doubleday, 1976; Utley, Robert M. *Frontier Regulars: The United States Army and the Indian, 1866–1891.* New York: Macmillan, 1973.

— David Coffey

Reed, Walter (1851–1902) *U.S. Army surgeon and bacteriologist responsible for determining the cause of yellow fever*
Born on 13 September 1851 in Belroi, Virginia, Walter Reed studied medicine at the University of Virginia and at Bellevue Hospital Medical College in New York City. He received a commission as an assistant surgeon in the U.S. Army Medical Corps in June 1875.

Beginning in 1893 Reed served as the curator of the Army Medical Museum in Washington, D.C., while teaching bacteriology at the Army Medical College and Columbia University. He also conducted research to discover the epitogy (cause) and epidemiology (spread) of epidemic diseases. His investigations of typhoid yielded positive results, leading to the prevention of future epidemic breakouts.

In 1900 Reed was appointed to head a commission charged with studying the cause and transmission of yellow fever in Cuba. Assembling a team that included Major James Carroll, Major Jesse W. Lazear, and Major Aristides Agramonte of Havana, Reed investigated possible theories concerning the cause of the disease. The doctors followed up on the work of Dr. Giuseppe Sanarelli, who claimed a casual relationship between yellow fever and *baciullus icteroides,* but the results proved negative. The team then examined the theory of Dr. Carlos Juan Finley, who linked the disease with the *Aedes aegypti* mosquito. Finley had failed to demonstrate the accuracy of his predictions through laboratory tests, but Lazaer successfully contracted the disease after allowing a test mosquito to bite him. Although he died, his journal revealed the key. The mosquito had to bite an infected person during the first three days of the illness and then the disease had to mature in the mosquito for a period of 12 days before it could be transmitted to another host. Reed announced the findings at the 1900 meeting of the American Public Health Association. This discovery allowed Major William Crawford GORGAS, an American sanitation expert, to eradicate yellow fever in Cuba within three months by destroying mosquito breeding areas throughout the island. Shortly after his return to the United States from Cuba, Reed contracted peritonitis after undergoing an appendectomy; he died in Washington, D.C., on 22 November 1902. Walter Reed Army Medical Center was established and named in his honor in 1909.

See also MEDICINE, MILITARY.

Further reading: Bean, William Bennett. *Walter Reed: A Biography.* Charlottesville: University Press of Virginia, 1982; Groh, Lynn. *Walter Reed: Pioneer in Medicine.* Champaign, Ill.: Garrard, 1971.

— Cynthia Clark Northrup

Reeves, Joseph M. ("Bull") (1872–1948) *U.S. Navy admiral and aviation pioneer*
Born on 20 November 1872, in Tampico, Illinois, Joseph Mason Reeves attended local schools. He failed to secure admission to the U.S. Military Academy, WEST POINT, but was accepted by the U.S. Naval Academy, Annapolis, and graduated in 1894.

Reeves served for two years as an engineering officer in a cruiser and then was an assistant engineering officer in the battleship *Oregon,* when it made its famous run from San Francisco to Santiago de Cuba and fought in the Battle of SANTIAGO (3 July 1898). Following the amalgamation of line and engineer officers in 1899, he became a lieutenant, junior grade, in the line. After service as gunnery officer in two battleships and then again in the *San Francisco* (1899–1906), he taught chemistry and physics and was an assistant football coach at the Naval Academy (1906–08). As the gunnery officer of the battleship *New Hampshire,* he won the ship the gunnery efficiency pennant in its first year at sea. In 1913 he obtained his first command, the collier *Jupiter,* an experimental electric-drive ship. In 1915 he commanded the *Oregon;* during World War I he commanded the battleship *Maine* and was also naval attaché in Rome. He then commanded the battleship *Wisconsin* (1921–23) and, because he wore a Vandyke beard, was affectionately nicknamed "Billy Goat" by midshipmen on a summer cruise. In 1923 he attended the Naval War College; he remained on its faculty for a second year. In 1925 he volunteered to take a three-month observer's course at Pensacola Naval Air Station.

In October 1925 Reeves became commander, Aircraft Squadrons, Battle Fleet, Pacific. After observing operations for six weeks on his flagship, the carrier *Langley* (CV-1), he informed his personnel that they did not know how to conduct military operations. He greatly increased the number of takeoffs and landings on the *Langley,* augmented the number of aircraft from eight to 42, and trained pilots for the forthcoming fleet carriers *Lexington* and *Saratoga.* His planes did well in fleet problems VII and VIII (1927, 1928) and performed brilliantly in 1929 but not in 1931, when he ended his connection with aviation.

In succession, Reeves was commandant of the Mare Island Naval Shipyard, the first aviator to command a battleship division, and the second in command of the warships of the fleet as commander, Battle Fleet. He retired in 1936 but was recalled to duty in May 1940 in the Office of the Secretary of the Navy and subsequently served on Justice Owen Roberts's commission in 1942 that held Admiral Husband E. KIMMEL and Lieutenant General Walter SHORT culpable for the Japanese attack on PEARL HARBOR. Roberts was then LEND-LEASE liaison officer for the Navy Department and a member of the Munitions Assignment Board until he retired again in 1946. The man who had prepared U.S. naval aviation for World War II died at Bethesda, Maryland, on 23 March 1948.

See also AIRCRAFT CARRIERS.

Further reading: Coletta, Paolo E. *Admiral Marc A. Mitscher and U.S. Naval Aviation.* Lewiston, N.Y.: Edwin A. Mellen Press, 1996; ———. *Admiral William A. Moffett and U.S. Naval Aviation.* Lewiston, N.Y.: Edwin A. Mellen Press, 1997; Hayes, John D. "Admiral Joseph Mason Reeves, U.S.N. (1872–1946)," *Naval War College Review* 23 (November 1970): 48–57, and vol. 23 (January 1972): 50–64.

— Paolo E. Coletta

Regulators　See WESTERN NORTH CAROLINA UPRISING, 1771.

Resaca de la Palma, Battle of (9 May 1846) *Battle of the Mexican-American War, also known as Resaca de la Guerrero*

The Battle of Resaca de la Palma took place some five miles north of the Rio Grande in present-day Brownsville, Texas. Acting on presidential orders, Brigadier General Zachary TAYLOR crossed the Nueces River and occupied the left bank of the Rio Grande. On 30 April–1 May, Mexican forces crossed the Rio Grande in force and laid siege to Fort Texas.

After the indecisive Battle of PALO ALTO (8 May) Mexican Division General Mariano Arista moved his Division of the North southward to the empty lake bed of Resaca de la Palma. This was good defensive terrain with thickly forested area surrounding a clearing, where the road to Matamoros met the *resaca* (lake). Arista placed skirmishers in front of his line and his infantry to the sides of the ravine and sharpshooters forward in the dense chaparral, hoping thereby to reduce the effectiveness of Taylor's artillery. Arista's artillery was near the road crossing and his cavalry well to the rear.

Taylor decided to continue the advance with his 1,800 men. Once dragoons had located the Mexican army, he deployed advance units on foot under Captain George McCall on either side of the road, while Lieutenant Randolph Ridgely led his artillery battery (known as "the flying artillery" because of its rapid deployment the day before) down the road, closely followed by three infantry regiments.

The thick cactus and briar produced a disjointed fight in which all order was lost. The Americans separated into small groups led by officers or noncommissioned officers. Taylor sent his dragoons under Captain Charles May to locate the Mexican artillery, and they charged the guns and cleared them, but, discovering they were without infantry support, the dragoons charged back again, taking as prisoner Brigade General Rómulo Díaz de la Vega, who refused to leave the guns. McCall silenced the Mexican guns long enough for Ridgely to advance his battery and allow the infantry to come up and control the road crossing. With the Americans in possession of the road to Matamoros and the Mexican left flank crumbling, the right flank soon gave way as well. The Mexicans attempted two unsuccessful cavalry charges, before undertaking a rapid retreat across the river in which they abandoned most of their stores.

U.S. forces relieved Fort Texas that afternoon, and Taylor occupied Matamoros a week later. The battle thus gave the United States control of the disputed land between the Nueces and Rio Grande.

The battle was costly; Mexican losses officially were listed as 154 killed, 205 wounded, and 156 missing. These figures are probably low. Taylor reported that his army buried 200 Mexican soldiers. Estimates of U.S. losses range from 33 to 45 killed and 89 to 98 wounded. The United States declared war on Mexico on 13 May 1846.

See also MEXICAN-AMERICAN WAR.

Further reading: Bauer, K. Jack. *The Mexican War, 1846–1848.* New York: Macmillan, 1974; Eisenhower, John S. D. *So Far From God: The U.S. War Against Mexico, 1846–48.* New York: Anchor Books, 1989; Frazier, Donald S., ed. *The United States and Mexico at War: Nineteenth-Century Expansionism and Conflict.* New York: Macmillan, 1998.

— Sarah Hilgendorff List and Spencer C. Tucker

Reserve Officer Training Corps (ROTC) *Program for training future military officers in civilian schools, colleges, and universities, both public and private*

Reserve Officer Training Corps (ROTC) programs teach military principles and skills needed for each branch of service, develop professionalism, and seek to inculcate attitudes of duty, honor, and love of country. The ROTC has created a large pool of reserve officers with active duty experience who are available in time of national emergency.

The tradition of combining a civilian educational institution's curriculum with military training dates to 1819, when Captain Alden PARTRIDGE, former WEST POINT superintendent, founded the American Literary, Scientific, and Military Academy (now Norwich University) in Vermont. Partridge sought to educate citizen soldiers, well-educated individuals who would pass into the militia and be available in times of need.

Owing to the great expansion of the military during the Civil War, Congress mandated military training at colleges and universities in the Morrill Act (Land-Grant Act) of 1862. It gave grants of public land to state colleges on condition that they would offer military science courses.

In 1916 Congress passed the NATIONAL DEFENSE ACT, which created the ROTC program. The National Defense Act of 1920 expanded the program, which soon operated in hundreds of high schools and colleges. Although pacifists challenged the constitutionality of the program, the Supreme Court ruled that states had the right to make military training compulsory. Compulsory ROTC programs were ended after 1961; however, during the VIETNAM WAR opposition to that conflict led to controversy over the ROTC on many campuses, and a few schools actually dropped their programs. Beginning in World War II, ROTC programs have been the largest single source of officers for the U.S. armed forces, and ROTC officers have attained the highest military ranks.

The army ROTC is the oldest program. It consists of two divisions: junior units in high schools and the senior units in private and state military schools, colleges, and universities. The collegiate program consists of basic ROTC during the freshman and sophomore years, followed by advanced ROTC in the junior and senior years of academics. Transfer students from a two-year community college, where there is no ROTC program, may enter the advanced ROTC program by taking the basic training program the summer between their sophomore and junior years. Students in the advanced program are paid a monthly subsistence allowance.

At the end of the advanced ROTC program the student receives a commission in the Army Reserve. Students with excellent academic and ROTC records may be offered regular army commissions as distinguished military graduates. After being commissioned as second lieutenants in the army, the new officers may serve two years on active duty if they have received a reserve commission or four years for a regular commission.

The U.S. Navy began its ROTC program (the NROTC) in 1926. There are two programs. The regular NROTC seeks to recruit competitively through examinations, grades, and interviews with prospective high school students. Those chosen for the program receive a four-year scholarship that pays most of their college education. They are required to take two summer cruises. Upon graduation they are commissioned as ensigns, and they are required to serve for four years.

The navy also operates a contract NROTC program similar to the advanced army ROTC program. Students pay their own tuition, but receive a monthly subsistence allowance. Graduates are commissioned as ensigns in the naval reserve upon graduation. They serve for three years to fulfill their contract obligation. Some members of the NROTC programs choose to be commissioned as Marine Corps officers.

In 1947, after the air force separated from the army as an independent branch of military service, a separate air force ROTC program (AFROTC) was begun as well. Its junior and senior programs resemble those of the army. Women were first admitted to the program in 1969.

See also HIGHER MILITARY EDUCATION; MILITARY ACADEMIES.

Further reading: Neiberg, Michael S. *Making Citizen Soldiers: ROTC and the Ideology of American Military Service.* Cambridge, Mass.: Harvard University Press, 1999.

— A. J. L. Waskey

Reuben James *U.S. Navy destroyer*

The *Reuben James* was the first U.S. combat ship sunk during World War II, and the only one sunk by the German navy before the U.S. entry into the war. A *Clemson*-class destroyer, the *Reuben James* (DD-245) was named for a hero of the TRIPOLITAN WAR who had saved the life of Lieutenant Stephen DECATUR. Built by the New York Shipbuilding Corporation in Camden, New Jersey, it was launched in October 1919 and placed in service the next year. The *Reuben James* displaced 1,200 tons, was capable of speeds of more than 30 knots, and mounted a main battery of four 4-inch guns. It also carried 21-inch torpedoes.

Decommissioned in 1931, the *Reuben James* returned to duty in March 1932 and served with both the Atlantic and Pacific Fleets. After the beginning of World War II in September 1939, it was assigned to patrol duty off the East Coast. In 1941, "the Rube" was part of Northeastern Escort Force that covered convoys bound for Britain. The U.S. Navy accompanied such convoys as far east as Iceland, at which point they became the responsibility of the British navy.

On 31 October 1941 the *Reuben James*, captained by Lieutenant Commander H. L "Tex" Edwards, was about 600 miles west of Iceland escorting (with four other destroyers) eastbound convoy HX-156, consisting of 44 merchant vessels. Without warning, the *Reuben James* was hit and sunk by a single torpedo fired by German submarine *U-562*. It went down with 115 of its crew, including Edwards and all the officers. Only 45 men survived.

In short order, President Franklin D. ROOSEVELT transferred control of the Coast Guard to the U.S. Navy, and Congress authorized the arming of American merchantmen and abolished restrictions denying European waters to U.S. shipping.

See also ATLANTIC, BATTLE OF THE (WORLD WAR II); DESTROYERS.

Further reading: Morison, Samuel E. *History of United States Naval Operations in World War II*. Vol. 1. *The Battle of the Atlantic (1939–1941)*. Boston: Little, Brown, 1947; Roscoe, Theodore. *United States Destroyer Operations of World War II*. Annapolis, Md.: Naval Institute Press, 1953.

— Spencer C. Tucker

Reynolds, John F. (1820–1863) *U.S. Army general*
Born on 20 September 1820 in Lancaster, Pennsylvania, John Fulton Reynolds graduated from the U.S. Military Academy, WEST POINT, in 1841 and was commissioned in the artillery. During the MEXICAN-AMERICAN WAR he was twice breveted for gallantry—in the Battles of MONTERREY and BUENA VISTA, respectively. Reynolds served in the West in the 1850s and became commandant of cadets and an instructor at West Point in 1860.

With the outbreak of the Civil War Reynolds was promoted to lieutenant colonel and given command of the 14th U.S. Infantry Regiment. In August 1861 he was appointed brigadier general of volunteers and received command of Pennsylvania reserves. As a brigade commander during the Battles of the SEVEN DAYS of the Peninsula Campaign, Reynolds saw extensive combat at Mechanicsville and at Gaines' Mill, where he was captured. Held in Richmond's notorious Libby Prison, Reynolds was part of a general prisoner exchange in August 1862.

Reynolds returned to service in time to command a division in the Second Battle of BULL RUN/MANASSAS. Promoted to major general in November 1862, Reynolds commanded I Corps of the Army of the Potomac in the Battle of FREDERICKSBURG. Major General George G. MEADE's Division of Reynolds's corps was one of the few Union elements that achieved success in the battle, but it went unsupported. Reynolds's corps saw little action at CHANCELLORSVILLE, positioned in reserve when Major General Joseph HOOKER's plans collapsed at the hands of General Robert E. LEE's flanking movement. Reynolds urged Hooker to counterattack against the Confederate left, which might have changed the tide of battle, but his suggestion went unheeded.

As the Army of the Potomac moved northward to counter Lee's invasion, Lincoln considered the respected and well-liked Reynolds for supreme command of the army. Ordered to Washington on 31 May 1863, Reynolds supposedly declined the offer to command when his desire to have a free hand to maneuver was rejected. Instead, the post went to his former subordinate, Meade.

During the march north to GETTYSBURG, Reynolds commanded the Union left wing: his I Corps, along with III and XI Corps. As the Confederates concentrated around Gettysburg on 1 July and battle appeared imminent, Meade ordered Reynolds's I Corps forward to hold the town.

Arriving in Gettysburg ahead of his troops, Reynolds found Brigadier General John BUFORD's cavalry division under heavy Confederate pressure. Reynolds returned to his troops and rushed them forward to reinforce Buford. Assuming command of the 2d Wisconsin Regiment of the Iron Brigade in an effort to steady his right flank, Reynolds was killed by a sniper's bullet. His death was a major blow to the Army of the Potomac.

See also CIVIL WAR: LAND OVERVIEW.

Further reading: Nichols, Edward J. *Towards Gettysburg: A Biography of General John F. Reynolds*. University Park: Pennsylvania State University Press, 1958; Pflanz, Harry W. *Gettysburg: The First Day*. Chapel Hill: University of North Carolina Press, 2001.

— Thomas D. Veve

Rhine crossings (1945) *Action during World War II*
The Rhine River, Germany's natural barrier against invasion from the west, is from 700 to 2,000 feet wide and difficult to ford at low water, with dangerously swift currents. When Allied planners in the fall of 1944 began to draw up an operation to cross the river, they assumed that all bridges would have been destroyed.

OPERATION MARKET GARDEN had attempted to cross the Rhine in Holland in September 1944. The operation failed when British paratroopers were unable to hold a bridge over the Rhine at ARNHEM long enough for ground forces to move up.

On the night of 7 March 1945, however, a task force of the U.S. First Army's 9th Armored Division captured the Ludendorff Bridge at Remagen, despite German attempts to destroy it. This action surprised the Allied high command because the bridge at Remagen had not been part of the planning. General Omar BRADLEY, commander of 12th Army Group, had to improvise exploitation of the bridgehead. In the 24 hours after the bridge was captured, nearly 8,000 men crossed onto the east bank. The bridge collapsed on 17 March; but by that time, engineers had built a number of pontoon bridges in the area.

Lieutenant General George S. PATTON's Third Army crossed the Rhine at Oppenheim on 22 March 1945. Attacking in boats without air or artillery preparation, the forces crossed the river north of Ludwigshafen. The German defenders were taken by surprise and no American soldier was lost.

See also BULGE, BATTLE OF THE; EISENHOWER, DWIGHT D.; HODGES, COURTNEY H.; WORLD WAR II, COURSE OF U.S. INVOLVEMENT: EUROPE.

Further reading: Ambrose, Stephen E. *Citizen Soldiers: The U.S. Army from the Normandy Beaches to the Surrender of Germany, June 7, 1944–May 7, 1945.* New York: Simon & Schuster, 1998; Hechler, Ken. *The Bridge at Remagen.* Missoula, Mont.: Pictorial Histories Publishing, 1998.
— John David Rausch, Jr.

Richmond, Kentucky, Battle of (29–30 August 1862) *Civil War battle, a major Confederate tactical victory*
In the summer of 1862, Confederate major generals Braxton BRAGG and Edmund Kirby SMITH instigated a two-pronged advance into Kentucky to relive pressure on Chattanooga. From Knoxville, Smith advanced on Cumberland Gap. Leaving part of his command to besiege a Federal garrison there, Smith pressed into the bluegrass with his Army of Kentucky.

On 23 August Smith's cavalry, led by Colonel John Scott, defeated a small Union force at Big Hill, outside of Richmond. Learning of this fight, 6,500 green Union troops, led by their equally inexperienced commanders, Brigadier Generals Mahlon Manson and Charles Cruft, moved toward the Confederates. After some sharp skirmishing on the 29th, the Confederates pulled back to consolidate their forces.

At daylight the next day two Confederate brigades and two artillery batteries led by Brigadier General Patrick CLEBURNE advanced on Richmond. Following an artillery duel, the 6,500 Confederates present on the field moved against the Federal lines, located near Mount Zion Church.

The Confederates initially battered both flanks of the Federal army. After a failed Union counterattack, the attackers struck the Federal right and drove it back a mile to White's farm. Although Cleburne had set the stage for a Southern victory, he was shot in the left cheek while speaking to a wounded subordinate. The ball knocked out several of his teeth, and command passed to Colonel Preston Smith.

At White's farm, four miles from Richmond, the Union troops were pushed back from their second position. The remnants of the Federal force made a third stand on the outskirts of town, where part of their line extended into the city cemetery. Union major general William "Bull" Nelson arrived on the field from Lexington, where he vainly attempted to rally the troops. Walking down the Union line, the six foot, four inch, 300-pound Nelson shouted, "If they can't hit me they can't hit anything." He was immediately shot twice in the leg. Three more Confederate volleys then shattered the Union line.

With the Federal army in a shambles, Scott's cavalry rode to the west and cut off the Union retreat. Manson and a majority of his army were captured. The battle was one of the most complete Confederate victories of the entire war. The Union reported 206 killed, 844 wounded, and 4,303 missing and captured (5,353 total). The Confederates suffered 98 killed, 492 wounded, and 10 missing (600 total).

After the fight, Smith's army captured Lexington and Frankfort, and the Confederate force's presence in central Kentucky threatened Louisville and Cincinnati. Despite tactical victories at Richmond and PERRYVILLE, however, the Confederate 1862 Kentucky campaign failed because the armies of Bragg and Smith operated independently from one another and thus were unable to consolidate their gains. With the fall of CORINTH, Mississippi, the Southerners retreated to Tennessee to protect Chattanooga, ending their invasion.

See also CIVIL WAR: LAND OVERVIEW.

Further reading: Lambert, D. Warren. *When the Ripe Pears Fell: The Battle of Richmond, Kentucky.* Richmond, Ky.: Madison County Historical Society, 1995; McDonough,

James Lee. *War in Kentucky: From Shiloh to Perryville.* Knoxville: University of Tennessee Press, 1994.

— Stuart W. Sanders

Rickenbacker, Edward V. ("Eddie") (1899–1973)

U.S. Army officer

Born on 8 October 1890 in Columbus, Ohio, Edward "Eddie" Vernon Rickenbacher (as he was then, using the original spelling of his family name) was forced at age 13 on the death of his father to drop out of school to support his family. By 1908 Rickenbacher was working for an automobile manufacturing company. His fascination with the combustion engine and mechanics led to his entry in several automobile races, including the first 500-mile race at Indianapolis Motor Speedway in 1911.

Rickenbacher became interested in airplanes after a trip to England in 1916, when he saw aircraft of the Royal Flying Corps. Upon the U.S. entry into World War I in April 1917, Rickenbacher joined the army as a sergeant and was shipped to France, where he became driver on the staff of the AMERICAN EXPEDITIONARY FORCE (AEF) commander, General John J. PERSHING. Despite this prestigious assignment, Rickenbacher wanted to see combat. Colonel William MITCHELL arranged a transfer for him to the Army Air Service. Rickenbacher then went through flight training at Tours. In March 1918 he joined the 94th Aero Pursuit Squadron as a captain. With its "hat-in-the-ring" insignia, the 94th was the first U.S. air squadron to see combat.

Rickenbacher's skill in the air was soon revealed. On 29 April he downed his first enemy airplane. By the end of May, he had amassed five kills, which classed him as an ace. He also changed his name to Rickenbacker in an attempt to make it look and sound less German. Rickenbacker's subsequent combat record led to his appointment on 24 September as commander of the 94th Squadron with the rank of major. His greatest victory came the following day when he attacked seven German planes and shot down two of them. By the time of the armistice on 11 November 1918, Rickenbacker had fought in 134 air battles and had 26 confirmed kills, making him the top U.S. ace of the war. He was also one of the war's most decorated fliers, receiving the Medal of Honor, the French croix de guerre, and the American Distinguished Service Cross.

Rickenbacker returned to the automobile industry after the war, but he eventually became the president of

Captain Eddie Rickenbacker with his Spad XIII, the best French fighter aircraft of World War I   *(Library of Congress)*

Eastern Airlines. During World War II he conducted an inspection tour of U.S. Pacific bases for Secretary of War Henry L. STIMSON.

After World War II Rickenbacker returned to Eastern Airlines, becoming chairman of the board in 1954. He retired in 1963. Rickenbacker died in Zurich, Switzerland, on 23 July 1973.

See also WORLD WAR I, U.S. INVOLVEMENT.

Further reading: Adamson, Hans C. *Eddie Rickenbacker.* New York: Macmillan, 1946; Rickenbacker, Edward. *Rickenbacker.* Englewood Cliffs, N.J.: Prentice Hall, 1967.

— Eric W. Osborne

Rickover, Hyman G. (1898–1986) *U.S. Navy admiral,* known as *"the Father of the U.S. Nuclear Navy"*

Born on 27 January 1900 in Makow, Russia (now Poland), Hyman George Rickover was the son of an impoverished Polish tailor who emigrated to the United States with his family from Russia in 1904. He early revealed talent in physics, drawing, and German. Hazed as a Jew while at the U.S. Naval Academy, Annapolis, he lived a solitary life and worked hard, graduating in 1922. He was a student at the navy's postgraduate school in Annapolis from 1928 to 1929 and earned a master's degree in electrical engineering from Columbia University in 1929.

Rickover's sea assignments included assistant engineering officer of a battleship and service in a submarine. He also translated into English Herman Bauer's *Das Unterseeboot.* His only ship command was of a minesweeper on the Asiatic Station in 1937. After that September, when he became an engineering-duty officer only, command afloat was out of the question.

From 1939 to 1945, Rickover was second in command of the Electrical Section of the Bureau of Ships (BuShips). He devised methods of quickly repairing British warships damaged in World War II and reducing damage to their electrical systems. Promoted to captain, he helped to oversee repair on battleships damaged by the Japanese attack on PEARL HARBOR, then brought order to the spare parts establishment of BuShips at Mechanicsburg, Pennsylvania. His last World War II service was in supervising the building of a naval base at Okinawa, only to see a typhoon destroy it.

Beginning in 1946, Rickover was stationed at Oak Ridge Laboratory, Tennessee, studying nuclear technology. In 1948 he headed the Nuclear Power Division of the BuShips. Rickover worked long hours and sought to obtain atomic propulsion for submarines. Demanding "zero defects," he was either hated or loved by his colleagues. In any event, he won the support of the chief of naval opera-

tions, Fleet Admiral Chester W. NIMITZ, as well as that of Secretary of the Navy James V. FORRESTAL and, eventually, the Atomic Energy Commission (AEC), which had concentrated upon atomic bombs rather than propulsion plants. At his request, the AEC established a school to train nuclear engineers at the Massachusetts Institute of Technology. Rickover's poor manners in interviewing candidates for his program became legend.

With the Westinghouse Corporation engaged in solving the engineering problems facing nuclear propulsion, BuShips provided Rickover with the submarine NAUTILUS. Rickover had two mockups of its power plant built, and in June 1952 saw laid the keel of the world's first nuclear-powered ship. Rickover's demand that all large warships be nuclear powered was respected until the days of President Jimmy Carter in the 1970s.

Promoted to rear admiral in 1953, Rickover faced mandatory retirement because of his age, but he used his political connections in Congress to secure an exemption. As deputy commander for nuclear propulsion, Naval Seas System Command, he also helped to develop the POLARIS missile system. Transferred to the retired list in 1964, he remained on active duty until age 81 in 1981. His 64 years on active duty is the longest in U.S. Navy history. Even in retirement he remained outspoken. Rickover died at Arlington, Virginia, on 8 July 1986.

See also NUCLEAR AND ATOMIC WEAPONS; SUBMARINES.

Further reading: Duncan, Francis. *Rickover and the Nuclear Navy: The Discipline of Technology.* Annapolis, Md.: Naval Institute Press, 1998; Hewlett, Richard G., and Francis Duncan. *Nuclear Navy, 1946–1962.* Chicago: University of Chicago Press, 1962; Polman, Norman, and Thomas B. Allen. *Rickover.* New York: Simon & Schuster, 1982; Rockwell, Theodore. *The Rickover Effect: How One Man Made a Difference.* Annapolis, Md.: Naval Institute Press, 1992.

— Paolo E. Coletta

Ridgway, Matthew B. (1895–1993) *U.S. Army general*

Born on 3 March 1895 in Fort Monroe, Virginia, Matthew Bunker Ridgway graduated from the U.S. Military Academy, WEST POINT, in 1917. Commissioned a second lieutenant, he was sent to a border post in Eagle Pass, Texas, where he rose to captain and command of the headquarters company of 3d Infantry Regiment.

Ridgway returned to West Point to teach Spanish and manage the athletics program from 1918 to 1924. Promoted to permanent captain in 1919, in 1925 he graduated from the Infantry School at Fort Benning, Georgia. From

1925 to 1933, Ridgway filled a series of diplomatic assignments in China (with the 15th Infantry in Tianjin [Tsientsin]), Nicaragua (where he helped supervise elections), the Panama Canal Zone (serving with the 33d Infantry), and the Philippines (as military adviser to the governor-general). In 1932 he was promoted to major.

In 1935 Ridgway graduated from the Command and General Staff School at Fort Leavenworth, Kansas, and in 1937 from the Army War College. From 1939 to 1942 he was in the War Plans Division of the War Department's General Staff. Ridgway was promoted to lieutenant colonel in July 1940, to temporary colonel in December 1941, and to temporary brigadier general in January 1942. In March 1942 he became assistant division commander of the 82d Infantry Division, and that June he was named its commander. Two months later he was promoted to temporary major general; in this capacity, he undertook the division's conversion into the 82d Airborne Division. He led the 82d in SICILY; at SALERNO, Italy; and in the NORMANDY INVASION. In August 1944 he took command of the new XVIII Airborne Corps (comprised of the 82d and 101st Airborne Divisions) and directed its operations in Operation MARKET GARDEN in the Netherlands, in the Battle of the BULGE, and in the Rhineland and the Ruhr.

Promoted to lieutenant general in June 1945, Ridgway briefly commanded the Mediterranean theater (November 1945–January 1946). From 1946 to 1948, Ridgway was the U.S. representative to the United Nations (UN) Military Staff Committee, which worked to draft a plan for an international UN military force. He then headed the Caribbean Defense Command (1948–49).

Appointed deputy chief of staff of the army (August 1949), after Lieutenant General Walton H. WALKER was killed in a jeep accident in December 1950, Ridgway was selected to lead the Eighth Army in Korea. He restored its morale, halted the Chinese counteroffensive south of Seoul, and then began a United Nations Command (UNC) offensive, liberating Seoul and recrossing the 38th parallel (March 1951). In April 1951, when President Harry S. TRUMAN fired General of the Army Douglas MACARTHUR, Ridgway took over as commander in chief of U.S. forces in the Far East and as UNC commander.

Appointed supreme commander of Allied Forces in Europe in May 1952, Ridgway was promoted to full general. Appointed army chief of staff in August 1953, he found himself in sharp disagreement with President Dwight D. EISENHOWER's policy of "massive retaliation," which relied on nuclear as opposed to conventional forces. Ridgway retired from the army in June 1955. He then wrote his memoirs and served on the boards of several major corporations. Ridgway criticized the growing U.S. involvement in the VIETNAM WAR and later was one of the group of "Wise Men" who advised President Lyndon JOHN-

SON to deescalate the war. Ridgway died in Fox Chapel, Pennsylvania, on 26 July 1993.

See also AIRBORNE FORCES, DEVELOPMENT AND EMPLOYMENT OF; WORLD WAR II, COURSE OF U.S. INVOLVEMENT: EUROPE.

Further reading: Appleman, Roy E. *Ridgway Duels for Korea*. College Station: Texas A&M University Press, 1990; Blair, Clay. *Ridgway's Paratroopers*. Garden City, N.Y.: Garden Press, 1985; Ridgway, Matthew B. *The Korean War: How We Met the Challenge, How All-Out Asian War Was Averted, Why MacArthur Was Dismissed, Why Today's War Objectives Must be Limited*. Garden City, N.Y.: Doubleday, 1967; ———. *Soldier: The Memoirs of Matthew B. Ridgway, as told to Harold H. Martin*. 1956. Reprint. New York: HarperCollins, 1996.

— Anna Boros

Riflemen, Regiment of *Special U.S. military formation created after the 1807* Chesapeake-Leopard *Affair*
In 1808, determined to enlarge the U.S. Army fourfold, President Thomas JEFFERSON created six new infantry regiments and a cavalry regiment, along with a special formation, the U.S. Regiment of Riflemen. The latter comprised 10 companies, each consisting of 68 privates and requisite numbers of officers, musicians, and sergeants. The unit was equipped with a special weapon, the Harpers Ferry model 1803 rifle, a rather short weapon with a .54 caliber bore that could shoot accurately at ranges of 300 yards. As further indication of their elite status, all ranks were clad in green uniforms with black facings, ideal camouflage coloring for skirmishing and screening work in forested areas.

Republican politics played a direct role in the selection of the regiment's first commanding officers; Alexander Smyth, a politician from Virginia, was appointed colonel, while William Duane, a Philadelphia newspaper editor, became lieutenant colonel. The two men despised each other, and by the advent of the War of 1812, both had been replaced by army veterans Thomas Adams Smith and George Washington Sevier, respectively.

In combat the Regiment of Riflemen proved highly effective and one of the few U.S. Army formations capable of meeting British units in the field. Its first officer of renown was Captain Benjamin FORSYTH, whose company successfully stormed the Canadian villages of Ganaoque and Elizabethtown before being driven out of Ogdensburg, New York, by vengeful British forces. Thereafter, Forsyth distinguished himself in the 1813 captures of YORK/TORONTO and FORT GEORGE. This intrepid light infantry leader ultimately died in a minor skirmish near PLATTSBURG, New York, in June 1814.

Other distinguished officers also came to the fore. On 5 May 1814 a company of riflemen under Captain Daniel Appling ambushed a large British amphibious detachment at Sandy Creek, Lake Ontario, capturing two gunboats, five armed barges, two Royal Navy captains, and 133 sailors and Royal Marines. This victory forced British Commodore Sir James Lucas Yeo to abandon his blockade of the U.S. Navy base at SACKETT'S HARBOR. During initial phases of the siege at FORT ERIE, Ontario, several companies of riflemen under Major Ludowick Morgan arrived for the protection of American supplies at Buffalo, New York. Early on the morning of 4 August 1814, a picked force of 700 British light troops under Colonel John G. P. Tucker attempted to capture Buffalo by crossing Conjockta Creek but were bloodily repulsed by Morgan's sharpshooters. Tucker withdrew with a loss of nearly 50 men. Conjockta Creek was a victory with immense strategic implications for the Americans for Morgan's defense preserved Buffalo and enabled the garrison at Fort Erie to stand.

Ultimately, Congress authorized creation of no fewer than four rifle regiments by the time the war ended in 1815. After the war, all four regiments were consolidated into a single Regiment of Riflemen, stationed at Saint Louis. From there, Colonel Smith directed his riflemen to found Fort Atkinson, Iowa, and Fort Smith, Arkansas, in 1819. However, fiscal retrenchment forced Congress to disband the Regiment of Riflemen in 1821. The U.S. Army thus remained bereft of specialist marksmen until the advent of Berdan's Sharpshooters in 1861.

See also CHESAPEAKE-LEOPARD AFFAIR; WAR OF 1812: LAND OVERVIEW.

Further reading: Fredriksen, John C. *Green Coats and Glory: The United States Regiment of Riflemen, 1808–1821.* Youngstown, N.Y.: Old Fort Niagara Association, 2000.
— John C. Fredriksen

River Raisin battle and massacre (22–23 January 1813) *War of 1812 massacre of American troops, resulting from the Battle of the River Raisin at Frenchtown (now Monroe), Michigan*

During Major General William Henry HARRISON's campaign to recover Detroit, Brigadier General James Winchester led more than 1,000 regulars and Kentucky militia to the Maumee River rapids to establish a base for U.S. forces in the northwest. The expedition arrived at the rapids on 10 January 1813. Soon anxious appeals arrived from residents of Frenchtown, on the River Raisin, 40 miles away, calling for soldiers to protect them from British and Indian marauders.

Winchester convened a council of officers, which urged that he send forces to the town. Winchester conse-quently sent two regiments, a total of some 660 men, to Frenchtown on 17 January. The next day they swept some 200 Canadian militia and 400 Indians from that place at a cost to themselves of 13 killed and 54 wounded. On 20 January, Winchester and his staff and 300 more troops arrived, bringing total U.S. strength there to about 800 Kentucky militia and 175 other soldiers.

While the Kentucky troops encamped behind a puncheon fence, the regulars on the right flank were posted in an open field. British commander Colonel Henry Procter took note of the American salient and organized a counterattack. He assembled almost 600 regulars and militia from Fort Malden, supported by some 600 to 800 Indians commanded by Wyandotte chief Roundhead. Procter also had six artillery pieces.

Although Winchester received reports of a British advance, he discounted these and did not check the American pickets, assuming they already were in place. At dawn on 22 January, the British attacked the sleeping American troops. After the U.S. 17th Infantry Regiment on the right flank came under murderous British artillery and musket fire, it soon withdrew to the river, where the Indians attacked it on the flank. The Kentucky troops behind the fence managed to hold their positions for almost three hours.

Winchester, who came up during the battle from his headquarters, fell prisoner to Roundhead, who forced him to watch atrocities committed by the Indians, inducing the American commander to order the militia to surrender. The British took some 500 prisoners and promised them protection from the Indians. Hundreds of Americans had been slain; of the entire army, only 33 escaped.

The battle cost the British 24 killed and 158 wounded, many of whom required transportation back to Malden. As a result, Procter abandoned almost 80 severely wounded Americans in Frenchtown until transport could be arranged. He perhaps counted on Harrison to march quickly to support Winchester and thereby recover the wounded. However, on 23 January, some 200 Indians attacked the village and, fortified with liquor, burned several buildings that contained wounded Americans. Many other Americans were scalped and their bodies desecrated and scattered along the road. In all, more than 60 Americans were killed.

In Harrison's words, the defeat at Frenchtown was "total and complete." It certainly dashed his plans to continue his campaign until the United States could gain control of Lake Erie; but the barbarity of the British and Indians prompted the rallying cry of "Remember the River Raisin!" Procter's troops heard that cry in October 1813, when the Kentuckians of Harrison's army defeated them at the Battle of the THAMES.

See also TECUMSEH; WAR OF 1812: LAND OVERVIEW.

Further reading: Antal, Sandy. *A Wampum Denied: Procter's War of 1812.* Ottawa, Canada: Carleton University Press, 1997; Quimby, Robert S. *The U.S. Army in the War of 1812: An Operational and Command Study.* East Lansing: Michigan State University Press, 1997; Rosentreter, Roger L. "Condign Punishment Inflicted," *Wild West 2,* no. 1 (June 1989): 35–41.

— Steven J. Rauch

Rodgers, John (1771–1838) *U.S. Navy officer*
Born on 1 August 1771 in Havre de Grace, Maryland, John Rodgers spent 11 years in the merchant marine before joining the navy in 1792 as a lieutenant. He served on the frigate CONSTELLATION during the QUASI-WAR WITH FRANCE, and was present during the victory over the French frigate *Insurgente* on 9 February 1799.

Rodgers rose to captain in 1799; two years later, he commanded the frigate *John Adams* during the TRIPOLITAN WAR. In this capacity he distinguished himself by capturing the Moorish frigate *Meshoda* and several gunboats. In 1805 he was appointed commodore of the Mediterranean Squadron. The following year he returned to the United States, assumed command of the large frigate *President,* and spent several years patrolling coastal waters to prevent the impressment of American sailors by British warships.

On 16 May 1811 the *President* chased an unidentified warship off Cape Henry, Virginia. That night, the two ships exchanged fire. Rodgers silenced his opponent, which turned out to be the British sloop *Little Belt,* a vessel far inferior in armament to his own ship. A court of inquiry acquitted him of any misbehavior in the PRESIDENT–LITTLE BELT ENCOUNTER, and Rodgers enjoyed new-found celebrity as a national hero for having redeemed the honor of the navy for the 1807 CHESAPEAKE-LEOPARD AFFAIR.

When the War of 1812 commenced, Rodgers sailed from New York in concert with several other warships. By then a respected naval officer, he was responsible for a controversial strategy in which the small U.S. Navy was pooled into a single squadron. This had the effect of forcing the British to pool their resources also, giving American merchant vessels at sea more opportunities to escape.

On 23 June 1812 Rodgers fired the first shots of the war while chasing the British frigate *Belvidera.* He was wounded by the explosion of a gun but went on to cruise the Irish Channel, taking 12 prizes. After several more successful outings, Rodgers relinquished command of the *President* to head the Delaware Flotilla. He subsequently played a prominent role in the Battle of BALTIMORE on 13 September 1814.

After the war Rodgers declined President James Madison's invitation to serve as secretary of the navy, preferring instead an appointment as head of the newly constituted Navy Board. He remained in this position for the next 22 years, and in 1827 also commanded the Mediterranean Squadron. Rodgers resigned his commission in 1837 due to poor health. He died at the Philadelphia Navy Yard on 1 August 1838.

See also WAR OF 1812: NAVAL OVERVIEW.

Further reading: Bauer, K. Jack. "John Rodgers: The Stalwart Conservative." In *Command Under Sail: Makers of the American Naval Tradition, 1775–1840,* edited by James C. Bradford. Annapolis, Md.: Naval Institute Press, 1984, 220–47; Paullin, Charles G. *Commodore John Rodgers: Captain, Commodore, and Senior Officer of the American Navy, 1773–1838.* Annapolis, Md.: Naval Institute Press, 1967.

— John C. Fredriksen

Rogers, Robert (1731–1795) *Leader of a force of rangers during the French and Indian War (1754–63)*
Born on 7 November 1731 in Methuen, Massachusetts, Robert Rogers spent his formative years on the fringe of the vast northeastern forests and developed into a skillful woodsman. In 1755 he had to enlist in a provincial New Hampshire regiment to escape a counterfeiting charge. Finding his niche in the military, he quickly gained a commission as captain of an independent ranger company.

Despite British antipathy toward provincial troops, Rogers's skill in unconventional operations during the FRENCH AND INDIAN WAR earned him wide recognition. In 1758 Rogers was promoted to major and given command of nine ranger companies, which became known as Rogers's Rangers. Following the French surrender, Major General Jeffrey AMHERST rewarded Rogers with a regular British commission. Rogers, however, was a poor administrator, and throughout his commissioned service he was constantly in trouble over payroll and supply accounts.

Rogers went to England in 1765 in an attempt to clear up his account problems. He was received as something of a hero in London and returned to America as the commander of Fort Michilimackinac on the eastern end of Lake Huron. Two years later he was charged with embezzlement and treason. Court-martialed in Montreal, he was acquitted for lack of evidence. In 1769 he returned to London, this time to a much colder reception. He spent 22 months in Fleet Street Prison as a debtor.

When Rogers returned to America in mid-1775, he was totally out of touch with the political sentiments of the colonists. In Philadelphia he was arrested because he was a half-pay British officer. The Continental Congress later ordered his release on the condition that he not enter active British military service. In February 1776, Major

General Sir Henry Clinton offered Rogers a British command, but he declined. Later that year, Rogers applied to the Continental Congress for a commission, but the wary Congress wanted no part of him.

In June 1776, Rogers was suspected of being involved in a plot to assassinate Continental Army commander General George WASHINGTON. He maintained his innocence—to no avail. Ordered into confinement, Rogers escaped, now believing he was no longer bound by his oath to the Congress. Rogers accepted a British commission as a lieutenant colonel and raised a Loyalist battalion of rangers. The combat record of the new "Rogers's Rangers" was spotty at best. In 1777, Rogers was forced out of command, and in 1782 he returned to England with the evacuating British army. He spent his remaining years in a drunken fog and died in London on 18 May 1795.

Despite his character flaws and his dismal end, Rogers had a profound impact on both the British and American armies. In the modern British army, rangers are light infantry units, while U.S. Army Rangers are special operations forces. The original Rogers's Rangers performed both roles, and all modern ranger forces still operate by many of the principles first developed and tested in combat by Robert Rogers.

Further reading: Cuneo, John R. *Robert Rogers of the Rangers.* New York: Oxford University Press, 1959; Rogers, Robert. *The Journals of Major Robert Rogers.* Introduction by Howard R. Peckham. New York: Corinth Books, 1961.

— David T. Zabecki

Rolling Thunder, Operation (1965–1968) *Code name for President Lyndon B. Johnson's bombing campaign against the Democratic Republic of Vietnam (DRV, North Vietnam) that lasted from 2 March 1965 to 31 October 1968*

The bombing campaign was the centerpiece of his and Secretary of Defense Robert MCNAMARA's policy of gradually increasing pressure on the DRV in order to force its leaders to quit military efforts against the Republic of Vietnam (RVN, South Vietnam), halt its infiltration of the South, demonstrate U.S. resolve, and raise RVN morale.

Planning began just before the 1964 elections and stemmed from JOHNSON's growing frustration with the VIETNAM WAR. He directed his advisers to formulate a response to DRV infiltration of men and supplies into South Vietnam. Two competing plans emerged.

U.S. military leaders such as General Curtis E. LeMAY, the air force chief of staff, recommended a brief, intense, around-the-clock campaign that would cut off the DRV from its external sources of supply and destroy its ability to produce and transport war matériel south. The second plan, advocated by the State Department, called for interdiction through attacks that would, if necessary, gradually grow in intensity and move north. Advocates of this plan believed that when confronted with U.S. power, Hanoi would negotiate.

Johnson and McNamara, desperate for "a quick victory at an acceptable cost," favored alternating the measured campaign with bombing halts designed to prompt peace talks. Johnson's ultimate objective was to win time for the RVN to secure its national independence, without bringing about Soviet or Chinese intervention. The plan, however, ran counter to the offensive nature of air power, but Johnson hoped it would allow him to support the RVN without losing support for his "Great Society" (antipoverty and civil rights) programs at home. Instead, Rolling Thunder did much to foster the antiwar movement.

Once Rolling Thunder began, targets were selected during Tuesday White House meetings. Johnson, McNamara, Secretary of State Dean Rusk, and selected advisers picked specific targets from a short list prepared by McNamara's staff from targets nominated by military commanders and approved by the Joint Chiefs of Staff (JCS), Admiral Ulysses S. G. Sharp (commander in chief, Pacific), and the State Department. McNamara exercised tactical command and control over precise targets, timing, number and kinds of aircraft, and kinds of ordnance employed.

Rolling Thunder became a source of competition among rival factions in the United States and RVN, with the JCS, CINCPAC, service commanders, presidential advisers, and General William WESTMORELAND (commander of the Military Assistance Command, Vietnam [MACV]) seeking to influence the use of Rolling Thunder assets for their own purposes.

U.S. bombing of North Vietnam was unsuccessful in causing Hanoi to stop its support of the war in South Vietnam. Shown here is a U.S. Air Force B-52 Stratofortress bomber. *(US Air Force)*

The vast majority of Rolling Thunder's 900,000 sorties were flown by navy carrier-based F-4, F-8, A-4, A-6, and A-7 aircraft and air force F-4 and F-105 fighters based in South Vietnam and Thailand.

Over time, the missions became increasingly hazardous, especially with the arrival in North Vietnam of considerable numbers of Soviet surface-to-air missiles (SAMs) and radar-controlled antiaircraft artillery (AAA) batteries. In some units, attrition rates reached 75 percent. Rolling Thunder cost the United States nearly 900 aircraft and more than two-thirds of all airmen lost in the war. Of 654 prisoners of war (POWs) returned by Hanoi after the signing of the Paris peace accords, 457 were Rolling Thunder veterans. While airmen dealt with the dangers of "going downtown," they resented the bureaucratic morass that surrounded these seemingly endless missions, and they were bitter over risking their lives on low-value targets. By 1967 it cost the United States more than nine dollars to inflict for every one dollar's worth of damage.

Rolling Thunder began with 100 sorties by U.S. Air Force and Republic of Vietnam Air Force (VNAF) aircraft striking the Xom Bang ammunition depot 35 miles north of the Demilitarized Zone (DMZ). Rolling Thunder then went through five phases. Phase I lasted from March to late June 1965. During this period, strikes were limited to an area just above the DMZ and south of Vinh. They focused on ammunition depots, barracks, and radar sites. Meanwhile, U.S. diplomats tried, in vain, to persuade Hanoi to negotiate.

Phase II lasted from July 1965 to June 1966. It experienced numerous pauses for bad weather and failed diplomatic efforts. It began with strikes against roads, bridges, and railroads. In September, the target line was moved north to 30 miles south and west of Hanoi. In early 1966, Pentagon sources claimed that Rolling Thunder had destroyed or damaged 9,600 trucks, 1,600 rail cars and 16 locomotives, and 14,400 boats. Later investigations suggest that these numbers were inflated.

To this point, high-value targets such as petroleum, oil, and lubricant (POL) storage facilities, electric power plants, and airfields near Hanoi remained off limits. There was also an off-limits "buffer zone" along the Sino-Vietnamese border. While Johnson justifiably feared that accidental bombings of Chinese personnel and territory might result in a KOREAN WAR–style invasion, this zone remained an open wound, since a growing number of DRV supply routes and POL pipelines ran unimpeded to the South.

Not until July 1966 did CINCPAC and the JCS convince Johnson to attack POL targets near Hanoi, yet some areas around Hanoi and the port city of Haiphong still remained off limits. Phase III lasted into early autumn. Official reports claimed the destruction of 70 percent of the DRV's POL storage capacity, forcing the dispersal of the remainder into small caches in or around cities and villages safe from attacks.

Phase IV began in October 1966 and shifted to industrial and electrical power–generating targets. Targets near Hanoi that were previously off limits for fear of causing collateral civilian damage were now added to the list.

In late 1966, the Rand Corporation sent McNamara its Jason Division report on the effect of the bombing campaign. It concluded that Rolling Thunder had been a failure and that there was little hope of changing this, given the nature and circumstances of the war. McNamara later wrote that this was when he began to oppose the war and that he and Johnson parted ways.

On 25 and 27 December 1966, reports from Hanoi written by Harrison Salisbury appeared in the *New York Times,* accusing the United States of targeting civilians. While this was untrue, the administration stance was undercut when Johnson expressed his "regrets for the bombing of civilians." What he had feared most, a loss of public support, had come to pass.

The climactic fifth phase took place during the first half of 1967. The original 94 targets had grown to 400 and included ammunition depots, storage areas, highways, railroads, bridges, marshaling yards, warehouses, POL storage facilities (the North had no refineries), airfields, barracks, power-generating plants, and the DRV's three major factories. Johnson would not approve strikes against ports, locks, or dams for fear of causing civilian casualties. Rolling Thunder now faced what one expert called the "densest and most sophisticated defenses in the history of aerial warfare."

During the second half of 1967, less frequent attacks (some identify this as Phase VI) continued. The bombing had not produced the desired effect. With domestic support for the war waning, in early 1968 Johnson replaced McNamara with Clark M. Clifford, who soon advised him to end Rolling Thunder and withdraw U.S. forces from Southeast Asia.

On 31 March 1968, following his own lackluster showing in the New Hampshire primary against the antiwar candidate Eugene McCarthy, Johnson appeared on national television. He informed Americans that as a gesture of peace he would limit the bombing below the 19th parallel and, significantly, he would not seek reelection. On 31 October, in a belated effort to boost the election chances of the Democratic presidential nominee, Vice President Hubert H. Humphrey, Johnson ended Rolling Thunder altogether.

Some historians, such as the British diplomat John Colvin, who served in Hanoi, believe that U.S. air power would have succeeded had it been continued. However, most experts credit Rolling Thunder with only limited success. In what became the longest bombing campaign in the history of U.S. air power, Allied aircraft dropped

650,000 tons of bombs and destroyed nearly 10,000 trucks, 2,000 pieces of rolling stock, dozens of locomotives, more than half of the DRV's bridges, two-thirds of its power-generating plants, and virtually all of its POL storage facilities. It killed nearly 52,000 DRV citizens.

Despite this, the air campaign and ground campaigns were never coordinated, allowing the DRV to focus on each threat as it arose. Changes in goals and seven bombing halts also diluted the effect of Rolling Thunder. Critics of Rolling Thunder believe that B-52s should have been employed, although this would have had only a marginal effect as long as the targets and policies remained the same. It was not until mid-1967 that sufficient numbers of B-52D "Big Bellies" were in place and air crews trained to make such raids possible. By then Rolling Thunder was, for all practical purposes, over. As it turned out, bombing never could be effective enough to halt all infiltration of the South, and the degree of damage it inflicted was quite acceptable to Hanoi as the price for continuing the war. While the bombing did lift RVN morale, the 1968 Communist TET OFFENSIVE and its subsequent widespread destruction dashed hopes in the United States of overall success against the Communists in Vietnam.

Further reading: Berman, Larry. *Lyndon Johnson's War: The Road to Stalemate in Vietnam.* New York: W. W. Norton, 1989; Clodfelter, Mark. *The Limits of Air Power: The American Bombing of North Vietnam.* New York: Free Press, 1989; Head, William P., and Lawrence E. Grinter, eds. *Looking Back on the Vietnam War: A 1990s Perspective on the Decisions, Combat, and Legacies.* Westport, Conn.: Greenwood Press, 1993; Momyer, William W. *Air Power in Three Wars: World War II, Korea and Vietnam.* Washington, D.C.: Department of the Air Force, 1978; Thompson, James Clay. *Rolling Thunder: Understanding Policy and Program Failure.* Chapel Hill: University of North Carolina Press, 1979; Tilford, Earl H., Jr. *Crosswinds: The Air Force's Setup in Vietnam.* College Station: Texas A&M University Press, 1993.

— William Head

Roosevelt, Franklin D. (1882–1945) *Assistant secretary of the navy during World War I and president of the United States*

Born on 30 January 1882 at his family's Hyde Park estate in Dutchess County, New York, Franklin Delano Roosevelt studied at Groton School, Harvard College, and Columbia Law School. Emulating his distant cousin President Theodore ROOSEVELT, whose niece Eleanor he married in 1905, Roosevelt entered politics.

A member of the Democratic Party, Roosevelt served two terms as a New York state senator before becoming assistant secretary of the navy in 1913 under President Woodrow WILSON. During World War I Roosevelt, vehemently pro-Allied and interventionist, lobbied strenuously for major increases in defense spending—often differing with his immediate superior, Secretary of the Navy Josephus DANIELS. After war was declared, Roosevelt energetically supervised coastal defenses and interjected himself into discussions of naval tactics and strategy.

In 1920 Roosevelt left his navy post and ran unsuccessfully as the Democratic vice presidential candidate on a pro–League of Nations ticket. Shortly afterward he contracted polio, which left him permanently crippled but failed to discourage his involvement in politics. Elected governor of New York State in 1928, Roosevelt ran successfully for the presidency in 1932, jettisoning his long-standing support for the League of Nations in order to win support from isolationist Democrats.

During his first term, Roosevelt launched a major reform program, the New Deal, to tackle the Great Depression. By the mid-1930s, Roosevelt was growing increasingly concerned over the expansionist fascist dictatorships in Europe and Asia, which he believed ultimately menaced U.S. strategic, economic, and ideological interests. In October 1937, shortly after Japan invaded China, he rather vaguely suggested that peace-loving nations might "quarantine" aggressor nations, but obvious public misgivings dissuaded him from following up this proposal. In September 1938, Roosevelt even congratulated the British prime minister, Neville Chamberlain, on the Munich Agreement, by which Germany obtained the Sudetenland from Czechoslovakia. Despite gradually tightened embargoes, until late 1940 U.S. businessmen also continued to provide considerable quantities of war supplies to Japan, substantially facilitating its ongoing war with China.

When general European war began in September 1939, Roosevelt placed the United States in the antifascist camp. In October 1939, Roosevelt secured revision of the Neutrality Act to permit the Allies to purchase war supplies on a cash-and-carry basis. After France's June 1940 defeat by Germany, despite fears that Britain might not continue the battle alone, Roosevelt ordered the War and Navy Departments to resupply Britain's military, exchanged 50 obsolescent destroyers for long leases of eight British naval bases in the Caribbean, instituted a massive American rearmament program to upgrade the depression-era skeleton U.S. armed forces, and obtained SELECTIVE SERVICE legislation to draft young Americans into the military. He appointed two prominent Republican interventionists, Henry L. STIMSON and Frank KNOX, to head the War and Navy Departments, respectively.

Winning an unprecedented third term in 1940, Roosevelt proceeded even more aggressively. In March 1941 he obtained LEND-LEASE legislation that authorized the government to furnish war supplies on credit to the near-bankrupt British and other nations, such as China. Beginning in early 1941, Britain and the United States privately coordinated their wartime strategies.

Moving ever closer to outright war with Germany, in April 1941 Roosevelt excluded German warships, which were inflicting severe depredations on merchant ships bound for Britain, from the Western Hemisphere and a zone extending halfway across the Atlantic, including Greenland. In July, U.S. Marines occupied Iceland. On several occasions in late 1941, American warships escorting Allied convoys engaged German vessels in direct conflict, and in November Congress permitted the arming of American merchantmen in the war zone, although American public and congressional support for a declaration of war remained problematic. It was during this period that the U.S. destroyer *REUBEN JAMES* was torpedoed and sunk by a German U-boat. Other such sinkings undoubtedly would have brought the United States into the war at some point.

War, however, resulted from the concurrent Pacific crisis. The Tripartite Pact that united Japan, Germany, and Italy, signed in September 1940, obliged each nation to assist the others should one go to war with any opponents in addition to the existing belligerents. The Japanese believed that the preoccupation of France, the Netherlands, and Britain with the European war provided an ideal opportunity to annex their Southeast Asian territories. Although Roosevelt hoped to defer tackling the Pacific situation until the Atlantic war was resolved, in summer 1941 following Japanese military moves into French Indochina, the United States imposed a near-complete embargo on sales of oil and scrap metal to Japan, whose military possessed sufficient fuel for only two years. Despite continuing Japanese-American negotiations, neither side would compromise over their diametrically opposed views on Japan's position in China.

On 7 December 1941, Japanese aircraft and submarines attacked the U.S. Pacific Fleet at PEARL HARBOR, inflicting heavy casualties and outraging Americans. There is no convincing evidence to substantiate repeated allegations then and since that Roosevelt, desperate for full-scale intervention in the war, deliberately exposed the American fleet to Japanese attack and suppressed warning intelligence reports that might have saved it. The following day, Congress declared war on Japan; three days later, Germany and Italy declared war on the United States.

Roosevelt set the parameters of American and Allied strategy, placing the war in Europe ahead of that in the Pacific theater and authorizing the development of the ATOMIC BOMB. He also forged close permanent ties among the U.S. military establishment, science, and industry— links that later hardened into a postwar MILITARY-INDUSTRIAL COMPLEX. His decisions to defer a second front in Europe until 1944 effectively ensured that the Soviet Union would control most of eastern Europe and the Balkans.

Roosevelt himself erroneously assumed that the wartime understanding that he worked to achieve among Britain, the Soviet Union, and the United States would endure beyond victory. He envisaged a peace settlement based upon the delegation to each great power of a regional sphere of influence. During the war Roosevelt endorsed postwar American membership in the United Nations and newly created international economic institutions, effectively setting the United States on the path of continued involvement in international affairs, moves for which he cannily obtained bipartisan political support. Under Roosevelt, the United States became the world's greatest economic and military power, a position it retained throughout the 20th century, and moved decisively away from pre-1940 isolationism. He won reelection to an unprecedented fourth term in 1944; but in poor health in his final year, Roosevelt did not survive to view the results of his labors. He died of a stroke at Warm Springs, Georgia, on 12 April 1945. His successor, Harry S. TRUMAN, continued the war effort to its successful conclusion later that year.

See also COLD WAR; EISENHOWER, DWIGHT D.; MARSHALL, GEORGE C.; WORLD WAR II, CAUSES OF U.S. ENTRY; WORLD WAR II, COURSE OF U.S. INVOLVEMENT.

Further reading: Cole, Wayne S. *Roosevelt and the Isolationists, 1932–45.* Lincoln: University of Nebraska Press, 1983; Dallek, Robert. *Franklin D. Roosevelt and American Foreign Policy, 1932–1945.* New York: Oxford University Press, 1979; Freidel, Frank. *Franklin D. Roosevelt: A Rendezvous with Destiny.* Boston: Little, Brown, 1990; Goodwin, Doris Kearns. *No Ordinary Time: Franklin and Eleanor Roosevelt: The Home Front in World War II.* New York: Simon & Schuster, 1994; Larrabee, Eric. *Commander in Chief: Franklin Delano Roosevelt, His Lieutenants and Their War.* New York: Simon & Schuster, 1987.

— Priscilla Roberts

Roosevelt, Theodore ("Teddy") (1858–1919)

Assistant secretary of the navy, volunteer officer, and president of the United States who pushed an expanded role for the United States on the world stage

Born into a moderately wealthy, established family in New York City on 27 October 1858, Theodore Roosevelt was beset by frail health in childhood. A demanding exercise program overcame this, and two years spent ranching in the Dakota Territory in his late 20s instilled in him a respect for physical hardihood and a passion for what he famously called "the strenuous life," which he always believed inculcated moral and bodily fitness. Roosevelt also wrote several well-received books of popular history, including *The Naval War of 1812* (1882). Atypically for contemporaries of his class, Roosevelt, a Republican, entered politics. Appointed president of New York City's Board of Police Commissioners in 1889, he fought crime energetically.

Roosevelt was one of a small group of Republicans who admired the writings of Captain Alfred Thayer MAHAN and supported a greatly enhanced world role for the United States to include construction of a great steel navy and the acquisition of naval bases and colonies. A social Darwinist and believer in Anglo-Saxon racial superiority, Roosevelt perceived international affairs as characterized by ceaseless fierce competition, in which weaker nations would inevitably falter. Appointed assistant secretary of the navy in 1897, Roosevelt supported American intervention in Cuba, energetically put the navy on a war footing, and urged Admiral George DEWEY, commander of the Asiatic Squadron, to prepare for action. When the SPANISH-AMERICAN WAR broke out in 1898, Roosevelt raised and became colonel of the 1st U.S. Volunteer Cavalry Regiment, the "Rough Riders," serving in Cuba and participating in the well-publicized Battle of SAN JUAN HEIGHTS. When peace came, Roosevelt successfully supported American retention of the Philippine Islands.

Catapulted into national prominence, in quick succession Roosevelt became governor of New York State and vice president of the United States. The assassination of President William McKinley in September 1901 made Roosevelt the youngest U.S. president. Determined to demonstrate his country's international strength, Roosevelt himself proclaimed his policy: "Speak softly but carry a big stick."

Roosevelt facilitated the construction of a canal to link the Atlantic and Pacific Oceans by orchestrating a revolution in Panama, which seceded from Colombia. In 1904 he unilaterally proclaimed the Roosevelt Corollary to the Monroe Doctrine, affirming the U.S. right to intervene in and administer any Latin American state that defaulted on debts to third countries or otherwise mishandled its own affairs. Also in 1904, his policies and personality won him election to a full term in his own right in convincing fashion. In 1906, Roosevelt arbitrated (at Portsmouth, New Hampshire) a settlement of the Russo-Japanese War, thereby winning the Nobel Peace Prize, and later he helped to organize the Algeciras Conference to arbitrate the Franco-German dispute over Morocco. To underline growing American military power, Roosevelt sent the "Great White Fleet" on a 14-month cruise around the world. He also augmented the navy, especially in battleships, although not to the two-ocean navy level he ideally envisaged.

Leaving the presidency in 1909, Roosevelt ran unsuccessfully for office in 1912 on the third-party Progressive ticket, splitting the Republican vote. When World War I began in August 1914, Roosevelt quickly ranged himself on the Allied side. He demanded major increases in American defense spending and the introduction of universal military training, and he forcefully criticized President Woodrow WILSON's diplomatic handling of war-related issues, such as the *LUSITANIA* crisis, as weak, irresolute, and inadequate to defend American national interests.

Roosevelt welcomed American intervention in April 1917 and hoped to raise a volunteer regiment to fight in France, a plan the Wilson administration blocked. When the war ended, Roosevelt opposed the League of Nations that Wilson envisaged, but he apparently favored a long-term Anglo-American entente. Roosevelt died at Sagamore Hill, Long Island, New York, on 6 January 1919.

See also WOOD, LEONARD.

Further reading: Brands, H. W. *T. R.: The Last Romantic.* New York: Basic Books, 1997; Miller, Nathan. *Theodore Roosevelt: A Life.* New York: William Morrow, 1992; Turk, Richard W. *The Ambiguous Relationship: Theodore Roosevelt and Alfred Thayer Mahan.* New York: Greenwood Press, 1987; Walker, Dale L. *The Boys of '98: Theodore Roosevelt and the Rough Riders.* New York: Forge, 1998; Wimmel, Kenneth. *Theodore Roosevelt and the Great White Fleet: American Seapower Comes of Age.* Washington, D.C.: Brassey's, 1998.

— Priscilla Roberts

Roosevelt, Theodore, Jr. (1887–1944) *U.S. Army general*

Born on 13 September 1887 in Oyster Bay, New York, Theodore Roosevelt, Jr., was the son of President Theodore ROOSEVELT. He graduated from Harvard in 1908 and worked with his father and Major General Leonard WOOD in the preparedness campaign prior to the outbreak of World War I. Commissioned a major in the 26th Infantry Regiment, he served with that unit, part of the famed 1st Division, for the duration of the war. He was wounded twice and decorated for heroism. At the end of the war, he transferred to the Army Reserve as a colonel.

Roosevelt was an organizer of the American Legion in the interwar period and was elected to the New York legislature. He was appointed assistant secretary of the navy in 1921, a post that both his father and his distant cousin Franklin D. ROOSEVELT had held. After service with the Washington Arms Limitation Conference in 1922, he ran unsuccessfully for governor of New York State against Alfred E. Smith in 1924.

Roosevelt and his younger brother Kermit both shared their father's love of exploration. Both men mounted expeditions to Asia for the Field Museum of Natural History in

Chicago. In 1929 Roosevelt was appointed governor of Puerto Rico, and in 1932 he served as governor-general of the Philippines. In 1934 he joined the board of American Express as chairman. He was a lifelong supporter of the Boy Scouts. He also wrote himself or coauthored nine books.

When the United States entered World War II, Roosevelt was commissioned colonel of the 26th Infantry Regiment of the 1st Infantry Division. He had the words *Rough Rider* painted on his jeep. Promoted to brigadier general in December 1941 and named assistant commander of the 1st Infantry Division, Roosevelt served in the North African and SICILY campaigns. Adored by the division's soldiers, he was the trusted assistant of division commander Major General Terry de la Mesa ALLEN. As the eldest son of a former U.S. president, Roosevelt's presence in an active combat theater was a matter of some concern. He was relieved of command, along with General Allen, following the successful battle for Troina on Sicily in August 1943, but was reassigned to the 4th Infantry Division as the assistant commander. Despite health concerns, he led the assault wave of that division ashore at Utah Beach during the 6 June 1944 NORMANDY INVASION. He died on 12 July of a heart attack while serving as military governor of Cherbourg. Posthumously awarded the Medal of Honor in September 1944, Roosevelt is buried alongside his brother, Quentin, who was killed in World War I, at the Normandy American Cemetery in Collville-sur-Mer, France.

See also TORCH, OPERATION; WORLD WAR II, COURSE OF U.S. INVOLVEMENT: EUROPE.

Further reading: Jacobs, Bruce. *Heroes of the Army: The Medal of Honor and Its Winners.* Reprint. New York: Jove Books, 1987; Renehan, Edward J., Jr. *The Lion's Pride: Theodore Roosevelt and His Family in Peace and War.* New York: Oxford University Press, 1998.

— John F. Votaw

Root, Elihu (1845–1937) *Secretary of war*
Born on 15 February 1837 in Clinton, New York, Elihu Root graduated from New York University Law School in 1867. He soon became a prominent New York lawyer, whose clients included numerous leading corporations of the period. Like his younger friend Theodore ROOSEVELT, Root a Republican, became active in New York politics.

In 1899 President William McKinley appointed Root secretary of war, with his primary mandate being the establishment of effective governments for the new territories acquired in the SPANISH-AMERICAN WAR, including Cuba, the Philippines, and Puerto Rico. In fulfilling this mission, Root mingled benevolent paternalism with a strong desire to protect his own country's interests. For Cuba, Root endorsed a military government under Brigadier General

Leonard WOOD, which carried out extensive internal improvements before the United States granted the island independence in 1903, as promised by the Teller Amendment of 1898. Personally dubious as to the capacity of Cuba and America's other colonial possessions for self-government, Root insisted that Cuba's new constitution guarantee the United States the right to intervene in the event of future disorders in that island nation.

While remaining an American colony, Puerto Rico obtained extensive export privileges and concessions from the United States, as did the Philippines. Root disciplined individual American offenders for committing atrocities, but he generally endorsed the army's brutal suppression of Filipino guerrillas fighting for independence in the PHILIPPINE-AMERICAN WAR.

With strong presidential backing from Roosevelt, Root moved to professionalize the U.S. Army. He increased its authorized size from 28,000 men to between 60,000 and 100,000, established a centralized general staff to plan and execute military policies, and founded the Army War College to provide specialized military training.

Appointed secretary of state in 1905, Root ably implemented Roosevelt's muscular diplomacy, which sought greatly to expand the U.S. international role. A longtime supporter of the international arbitration movement to resolve peacefully disputes between states, Root represented the United States at the Second Hague Peace Conference of 1907. Staunchly pro-Allied and interventionist during WORLD WAR I and a convinced believer in Anglo-American cooperation, until his death Root doggedly advocated American membership in the International Court of Justice and, with some reservations, in the League of Nations. He died in New York City on 7 February 1937.

Further reading: Herman, Sondra R. *Eleven Against War: Studies in American Internationalist Thought, 1898–1921.* Stanford, Calif.: Hoover Institution Press, 1969; Jessup, Philip C. *Elihu Root.* 2 vols. New York: Dodd, Mead, 1938; Leopold, Richard W. *Elihu Root and the Conservative Tradition.* Boston: Little, Brown, 1954; Roberts, William R. "Reform and Revitalization," in *Against All Enemies: Interpretations of American Military History from Colonial Times to the Present.* Edited by Kenneth J. Hagan and William R. Roberts. Westport, Conn.: Greenwood Press, 1986, 197–218.

— Priscilla Roberts

Rosebud River, Battle of the (17 June 1876) *Major battle of the 1876 Sioux War*
In 1874, Lieutenant Colonel George A. CUSTER led an expedition into the Black Hills on the Great Sioux Reservation. Reports of the region's bounty—especially the presence of

gold—brought an influx of treasure seekers, exacerbating an already volatile situation. Since 1868 the government had labored to bring defiant Sioux, Cheyenne, and Arapaho bands onto reservations, but most refused to oblige. When efforts to buy or lease the Black Hills broke down, the government opted for a military solution.

Lieutenant General Philip SHERIDAN devised a multipronged winter campaign—the sort that had proven so successful on the South Plains. But this time the weather worked against him, and he postponed his action until spring. The targets were numerous villages—most notably, that of Sioux leader SITTING BULL—concentrated along the southern tributaries of the Yellowstone River. All Indians of the region were to report to their respective reservations; those who refused would be labeled hostile. Few came in, while hundreds more left to join the villages south of the Yellowstone.

In the spring of 1876, three heavy columns converged on the Yellowstone country. From Fort Ellis in Montana, Colonel John GIBBON marched eastward with 500 soldiers and Indian scouts. Brigadier General Alfred TERRY pushed westward from Fort Abraham Lincoln in Dakota Territory with more than 900 troops, including the entire 7th Cavalry. And moving up the Bozeman Trail from Fort Fetterman was the largest column—more than 1,000 officers and men in 10 troops of cavalry and five companies of infantry, commanded by the innovative Brigadier General George CROOK. With Crook rode some 160 Crow and Shoshoni auxiliaries.

Crook's mission was to flush what Indians he encountered northward into the clutches of Gibbon or Terry. But the soldiers could only guess at where they might find "hostile" villages; and they had no idea of how many Indians now occupied the Yellowstone country. It was a rare thing to catch a major concentration, and rarer still to engage a large Indian force in anything like a conventional battle. But conditions in 1876 made for such rare occurrences.

Throughout the spring, Indians, drawn by anger or fear and galvanized by Sitting Bull's defiance, gathered in an unprecedented display of unity. Cheyenne and Arapaho joined the many Teton Sioux bands to form one giant village of 10,000 to 15,000 people, including 2,000 to 4,000 warriors. By the middle of June the village was located near the Little Bighorn River in southern Montana.

On 16 June hunting parties reported Crook's column advancing along the Rosebud River. Oglala leader CRAZY HORSE led some 1,200 Cheyenne and Sioux warriors up the Rosebud. On the morning of 17 June they attacked Crook's camp.

Crook's Indian auxiliaries fought tenaciously as the general organized a response, but the broken, hilly terrain hampered his efforts. Cavalry units managed to secure the high ground, which brought some relief, but coordinated action was impossible. Crook tried to move his command

forward, only to be checked. Finally a cavalry squadron commanded by Captain Anson Mills managed to get behind the attackers. After six hours of intense fighting the Indians withdrew to the LITTLE BIGHORN. Crook reported 10 killed and 21 wounded, but his actual losses likely exceeded these figures by a considerable margin. Crazy Horse later admitted to 36 Indians killed and 63 wounded.

Although Crook held the field, the battle on the Rosebud became a major strategic victory for the Indians. In size and sustained intensity, the Indian effort was highly unusual and undoubtedly caught the soldiers by surprise. Crook soon withdrew to his base, his role in the campaign over for the moment. Unaware of Crook's setback, Terry and Gibbon continued. On 25 June, Custer's 7th Cavalry struck the huge village on the Little Bighorn and met with disaster.

See also AMERICAN INDIAN WARS: OVERVIEW; INDIAN SCOUTS; INDIAN WARFARE; SIOUX WAR.

Further reading: Bourke, John G. *On the Border with Crook.* Reprint. Lincoln: University of Nebraska Press, 1971; Crook, George. *General George Crook: His Autobiography.* Edited by Martin F. Schmitt. Reprint. Norman: University of Oklahoma Press, 1960; Utley, Robert M. *Frontier Regulars: The United States Army and the Indian, 1866–1891.* New York: Macmillan, 1973.

— David Coffey

Rosecrans, William S. (1819–1889) *U.S. Army general*

Born on 6 September 1819 in Delaware County, Ohio, William Starke Rosecrans graduated from the U.S. Military Academy, WEST POINT, in 1842. Assigned as a brevet second lieutenant to Engineers and promoted to full-rank second lieutenant in 1843, he performed routine engineering duties and then taught at West Point. Promoted to first lieutenant in 1853, he resigned his commission in 1854. He was engaged in the coal oil and kerosene industry when the Civil War began.

Rosecrans became a volunteer aide on Major General George B. McCLELLAN's staff with the rank of colonel of Volunteers, and in June 1861 was appointed colonel of the 23d Ohio Infantry Regiment. Only days later he was commissioned a brigadier general in the regular army. Rosecrans commanded a brigade under McClellan in western Virginia and was victorious at Rich Mountain. When McClellan took charge of the Army of the Potomac, Rosecrans commanded in western Virginia and directed a successful fall campaign that secured the region for the Union.

Transferred to the Western theater, Rosecrans commanded a wing of Major General John POPE's Army of the Mississippi in the slow advance on Corinth. Heading the army after Pope's transfer to Virginia, Rosecrans, under

Major General Ulysses S. GRANT's overall command, fought the fall 1862 Battles of IUKA and CORINTH. Appointed major general of U.S. Volunteers in September 1862, Rosecrans replaced Major General Don Carlos BUELL as commander of the Department and Army of the Cumberland in October. On 31 December 1862 and 2 January 1863, Rosecrans's forces defeated General Braxton BRAGG's Confederate Army of Tennessee in the bloody Battle of STONES RIVER, for which Rosecrans received the thanks of Congress.

Beginning in June 1863 Rosecrans conducted a brilliant campaign of maneuver (the Tullahoma campaign) that forced the Confederates from central Tennessee and led eventually to the Federal capture of Chattanooga.

Pursuing Bragg's army into northern Georgia, Rosecrans met with disaster. Reinforced by Lieutenant General James LONGSTREET's corps from Virginia, Bragg turned on the Federals along Chickamauga Creek. On the second day of the fierce September Battle of CHICKAMAUGA, Bragg's army exploited Rosecrans's flawed deployment to sweep most of his army from the field and back to Chattanooga. Only a determined stand directed by Major General George THOMAS saved the army from destruction. In October Grant replaced Rosecrans with Thomas.

Assigned to command the Department of the Missouri, Rosecrans was relieved in December 1864 and saw no further duty. Brevetted to major general in the regular army, he was mustered out of the Volunteers in January 1866. Still awaiting orders that never came, he resigned in disgust in March 1867, vacating his brigadier's commission in the regular army. In 1868 he was appointed minister to Mexico, only to be removed the following year when Grant became president. He settled on his ranch in California and in 1880 was elected to the U.S. House of Representatives, rising to chairman of the Military Affairs Committee. In 1889 he was restored to the army rolls and formally retired as a brigadier general. Rosecrans died at his ranch in Redondo, California, on 11 March 1898.

See also CIVIL WAR: LAND OVERVIEW; HALLECK, HENRY.

Further reading: Lamers, William M. *The Edge of Glory: A Biography of General William S. Rosecrans, U.S.A.* Reprint, Baton Rouge: Louisiana State University Press, 1999; Woodworth, Steven E. *Six Armies in Tennessee: The Chickamauga and Chattanooga Campaign.* Lincoln: University of Nebraska Press, 1997.

— David Coffey

Royal American Regiment (1755–1763) *British infantry regiment in the French and Indian War*

In 1755, after the defeat of Major General Edward BRADDOCK by the French and their Indian allies in the Battle of

the MONONGAHELA, London ordered that a new regular regiment of infantry, comprised of four battalions, be raised in the colonies and on the mainland of Europe. Arguably, one of the reasons this unit was formed was to take advantage of the colonists' believed familiarity with fighting Native Americans in the difficult and forested terrain of the North American environment.

The Royal American Regiment, initially designated the 62d of Foot (1755) and later the 60th of Foot (1757), was recruited especially among Germans of Pennsylvania and Maryland, then augmented with non-British mercenary soldiers from continental Europe. The unit was officered predominantly by foreigners, of whom the best known was the 1st Battalion commander, the Swiss-born Major Henry BOUQUET.

Elements of the Royal Americans fought as detached light infantry formations in company to battalion size and took part in virtually all of the major British military campaigns during the remainder of the war. Bouquet's battalion took part in the 1758 FORT DUQUESNE EXPEDITION led by Brigadier General John FORBES. Elements of the Royal American Regiment also participated in the failed 1758 FORT TICONDEROGA CAMPAIGN under Major General James Abercromby. Royal Americans served with Major General James Wolfe in the 1758 expedition against LOUISBOURG and served again under Wolfe in a supporting role in the 1759 QUEBEC CAMPAIGN.

After the FRENCH AND INDIAN WAR, the unit fought in PONTIAC'S REBELLION. It remained in the colonies until moved to the West Indies in 1775. The 60th is in the historic lineage of the King's Royal Rifle Corps, and specifically, the 2d Battalion of the Royal Green Jackets of the British army.

Further reading: Leach, Douglas Edward. *Arms for Empire: A Military History of the British Colonies in North America, 1607–1763.* New York: Macmillan, 1973; May, Robin, and Gerry Embleton. *Wolfe's Army.* London: Osprey Books, 1997; Parkman, Francis. *Montcalm and Wolfe.* New York: Atheneum, 1984; Pargellis, Stanley. *Military Affairs in North America 1748–1765: Selected Documents from the Cumberland Papers in Windsor Castle.* New Haven, Conn.: Archon Books, 1969.

— J. G. D. Babb

Royall, Kenneth C. (1894–1971) *Undersecretary of war, secretary of war, and secretary of the army*

Born on 24 July 1894 in Goldsboro, North Carolina, Kenneth Claiborne Royall earned a bachelor's degree from the University of North Carolina and a law degree from Harvard University. In May 1917 he joined the army and served in France with the AMERICAN EXPEDITIONARY

FORCES (AEF). For the following two decades he practiced law successfully in North Carolina and was active in state Democratic politics.

When the United States entered World War II, Royall emulated many other prominent lawyers and businessmen and joined the wartime bureaucracy, helping to organize the American industrial war effort as a colonel. In 1942 he became chief of the legal section of the Army Service Forces, achieving prominence by doggedly defending eight captured German saboteurs. In 1943 he became deputy fiscal director of the Army Service Forces with the rank of brigadier general. From April to November 1945, he was special assistant to Secretary of War Henry L. STIMSON; when Robert P. PATTERSON succeeded Stimson, Royall became undersecretary in Patterson's place.

Royall specialized in the energetic implementation of technical decisions rather than broad policymaking. In two years he settled almost 480,000 delinquent contracts. He also reduced 30,000 courts-martial sentences and attempted to institute reforms to make the army's legal system more humane.

On Patterson's resignation in July 1947, Royall served briefly as secretary of war. When the National Security Act of 1947 unified all branches of the armed forces, Royall became secretary of the army. He enlarged the army's mission in Europe by securing an additional $500 million to support troops there, but in 1948 his refusal to change the army's segregation policy caused civil rights leaders and the National Association for the Advancement of Colored People to demand his resignation.

Royall left office in April 1949. He then practiced law in New York and openly supported Republican Dwight D. EISENHOWER in the 1952 presidential campaign, despite his own long-standing Democratic political allegiance. In the 1950s and 1960s he supported desegregation in the South, mediating between civil rights groups and local authorities, and he periodically advised the Pentagon on military issues. Royall died at Durham, North Carolina, on 25 May 1971.

See also AFRICAN AMERICANS IN THE MILITARY.

Further reading: Eiler, Keith E. *Mobilizing America: Robert P. Patterson and the War Effort, 1940–1945.* Ithaca, N.Y.: Cornell University Press, 1997; Hooks, Gregory. *Forging the Military-Industrial Complex: World War II's Battle of the Potomac.* Urbana: University of Illinois Press, 1991.

— Priscilla Roberts

Rudder, James E. (1910–1970) *U.S. Army Ranger commander and educator*

Born on 6 May 1910 in Eden, Texas, James Earl Rudder graduated from Texas A&M University in 1932 with a bachelor of science degree and a commission as a second lieutenant of infantry in the U.S. Army Reserve. He was a football coach and teacher until called to active duty in 1941. In 1943, Lieutenant Colonel Rudder was named to command the newly organized 2d Ranger Battalion. After intense training he took the unit to Britain to prepare for the invasion of France.

Named commander of the ranger force for the 6 June 1944 NORMANDY INVASION, Rudder was given the mission of destroying the German heavy guns at Point du Hoc. At 6:30 A.M. on 6 June, as German artillery raked their landing craft, the first rangers landed on the narrow beach below the guns and, utilizing grapnel hooks, ropes, and rope ladders, began to clamber up the steep 100-foot cliffs. Finally, some of the rangers gained a foothold at the top and the remainder swarmed up the cliffs.

After a short, but intense and bloody battle, the Germans were pushed back. By 9:00 A.M. the rangers had seized the heights. Overpowering the German defenders, the rangers discovered that the "guns" in the casemates were telephone poles. Tracks indicated that the 155mm guns that had been there had been removed recently. The rangers had nonetheless carried out a well-executed attack, and they held the position for the next two days.

In accomplishing their mission, Rudder's rangers suffered more than 50 percent casualties. Rudder himself was wounded twice but remained in command. For action that day, he was awarded the Distinguished Service Cross.

Later Rudder led the 109th Infantry Regiment, which was credited with a major role in repulsing the last great German counteroffensive at the Battle of the BULGE. Following victory in Europe, Rudder spent eight months on special War Department missions. Released from active duty with the rank of colonel in April 1946, Rudder remained active in the army reserve, retiring in 1967 as a major general after 35 years of military service.

After the war, Rudder served as land commissioner of Texas and in 1959 became president of Texas A&M University. In 1965 he became president of the Texas A&M university system. He remained in that position until his death in Houston on 23 March 1970.

See also WORLD WAR II, COURSE OF U.S. INVOLVEMENT: EUROPE.

Further reading: Ambrose, Stephen E. *D-Day: June 6, 1944.* New York: Simon & Schuster, 1994; Bradley, Omar N. *A Soldier's Story.* New York: Henry Holt, 1951; Lane, Ronald L. *Rudder's Rangers.* Manassas, Va.: Ranger Associates, 1979; Ryan, Cornelius. *The Longest Day.* New York: Simon & Schuster, 1959.

— James H. Willbanks

Russia, U.S. Intervention following World War I

(1918–1920) *United States contributions to the Allied expeditionary forces operating in Russia during the 1918–20 Russian civil war*

In November 1917, with WORLD WAR I well into its fourth year, a radical Bolshevik regime headed by Vladimir Ilyich Lenin ousted Alexander Kerensky's moderate provisional Russian government. Lenin immediately moved to take Russia out of the war and seek a separate peace with Germany. In March 1918, the Russians signed the Treaty of Brest-Litovsk, which imposed highly disadvantageous terms upon Russia but ended its disastrous participation in the war. Alarmed by Lenin's desertion from the war, his publication of secret Allied treaties regarding the future disposition of Central Powers' territories, and his broad appeals to the international working class to stop fighting the war and instead support worldwide Communist revolution, Britain and France sought both to assist remaining anti-German forces within Russia and to overthrow the Bolsheviks if possible. Japan, eager to expand its Asian sphere of influence, sought to intervene near Vladivostok in Siberia, supposedly to protect Allied supplies and railway communications in the area, although its ultimate objective was widely suspected to be the annexation of substantial Russian territories in the mineral-rich area.

Short of manpower, the Allies attempted to persuade U.S. president Woodrow WILSON to contribute at least some American forces to these ventures. Despite his call for Russia's self-determination, in July 1918 Wilson finally yielded to his associates' pressing entreaties, persuaded in part by their desire to assist the embattled Czech Legion, anti-Hapsburg troops who after Brest-Litovsk sought to journey along the Trans-Siberian Railway line to Vladivostok for evacuation. Wilson attempted to restrict American activities to defending these staunchly anti-German troops, who often became involved in fierce clashes with Communist forces; to protecting large caches of Allied supplies in Vladivostok on the Pacific coast; and to keeping open the Trans-Siberian Railway.

In late August, 4,487 American officers and men, largely conscripts from Michigan and Wisconsin, under Colonel George E. Stewart, sailed for the northern Russian port of Murmansk, arriving there on 4 September. To Stewart's unavailing dismay, almost immediately the British Major General Frederick C. Poole, Allied commander in chief in the area, employed them in extensive anti-Bolshevik offensive operations, including the occupation of Arkhangelsk (Archangel), which brought American and Bolshevik forces into direct conflict. An additional 503 American troops arrived on 30 September 1918, accompanying Major General Sir Edmund Ironside, who replaced Poole. Ironside placed more emphasis upon consolidating a strong defensive position, but American troops still rep-

resented the majority of fighting forces in the region, suffering substantial casualties from Bolshevik counterattacks in late 1918 and January 1919.

In mid-February 1919 the disillusioned Wilson unilaterally announced the withdrawal, when weather conditions allowed, of all American troops in northern Russia. This decision was not fully implemented until July 1919, after further clashes with Bolshevik forces had generated antiwar protests among the U.S. forces.

Concurrently, in August and September 1918 almost 10,000 United States soldiers under the command of Major General William S. GRAVES arrived in Vladivostok. Although ordered to remain neutral in the disorderly fighting then prevalent among various Russian factions, they were instructed to defend Vladivostok and keep open the Trans-Siberian Railway. In practice, the railway carried vital supplies to an anti-Bolshevik regime in Omsk, effectively aligning U.S. forces with that regime.

The United States contingent represented part of a joint Japanese-American intervention force that included smaller contingents from other Allied nations. American troops eventually guarded a 1,000-mile section of track, and in 1919 came close to direct military confrontation with their nominal Japanese partners and Cossack bandits, whose looting of trains the Japanese encouraged. Japanese forces soon outnumbered the Americans tenfold, although in 1922 Allied pressure eventually forced their withdrawal. U.S. soldiers also suffered bloody attacks from partisan forces, whom they assumed to be Bolsheviks, on one occasion losing 25 men killed and a like number of wounded. In spring 1920, as Bolshevik forces advanced eastward, American units were pulled back to Vladivostok and evacuated.

In subsequent years, Soviet historians emphasized the effectively anti-Bolshevik nature of the American intervention in the Russian civil war, which they depicted as the harbinger of subsequent Soviet-American COLD WAR antagonism, and tended to exaggerate the significance of the American contribution to Allied efforts to overthrow the Bolsheviks. Whatever Wilson's intentions, these operations illustrated the manner in which, as many subsequent American military interventions would demonstrate, the initial mission could easily expand and develop in directions very different from those its originators first envisaged.

See also BLISS, TASKER H.; PERSHING, JOHN J.

Further reading: Kennan, George Frost. *Soviet-American Relations, 1917–1920*. 2 vols. Princeton, N.J.: Princeton University Press, 1956–1957; Kettle, Michael. *Russia and the Allies, 1917–1920*. 3 vols. New York: Routledge, 1981–1992; Maddox, Robert J. *The Unknown War with Russia: Wilson's Siberian Intervention*. San Rafael, Calif.:

Presidio Press, 1977; Melton, Carol W. *Between War and Peace: Woodrow Wilson and the American Expeditionary Force in Siberia, 1918–1921.* Macon, Ga.: Mercer University Press, 2001; Rhodes, Benjamin D. *The Anglo-American Winter War with Russia, 1918–1919: A Diplomatic and Military Tragicomedy.* New York: Greenwood, 1988; Unterberger, Betty Miller. *America's Siberian Expedition, 1918–1920: A Study of National Policy.* Durham, N.C.: Duke University Press, 1956.

— Priscilla Roberts

S

Sackett's Harbor, Battle of (29 May 1813) *Battle during the War of 1812*

The Americans had sought to wrest Upper Canada from Britain. Control of Lakes Erie and Ontario was vital to both sides because it would mean control of crucial supply lines.

The U.S. port of Sackett's Harbor, New York, located on the eastern shore of Lake Ontario, was a small, well-protected anchorage and shipbuilding center some 40 miles by water from the principal British base at Kingston, Ontario. On 29 July 1812, a small British squadron attacked Sackett's Harbor but was repulsed. Arriving at Sackett's Harbor in early October, U.S. Navy captain Isaac CHAUNCEY pushed an ambitious naval construction program in an effort to secure command of Lakes Erie and Ontario.

U.S. military strength at Sackett's Harbor had been siphoned off for a planned U.S. assault against FORT GEORGE. In May 1813, only 332 regulars and some 500 militia held the fort, commanded by Brigadier General Jacob Jennings BROWN of the New York militia. Hoping to take advantage of this situation, on 27 May 1813 Lieutenant General Sir George Prevost (the governor-general of Canada) and Commodore Sir James Yeo left Kingston to strike at Sackett's Harbor. They had 1,200 men in six vessels and 40 batteaux. Yeo hoped to destroy the U.S. sloop *General Pike,* then under construction at Sackett's Harbor.

General Brown commanded at Sackett's Harbor but had only 400 regulars and 250 volunteers. He arranged for signal guns to call out the militia and moved volunteers in, but they were poorly armed. Brown positioned his militia in three lines on the beach, with instructions for them to fire only a few rounds before retiring back behind the regulars to form a reserve line. Regulars of the 1st Light Dragoons formed the main defensive line near Fort Tompkins.

At about 1:00 A.M. on 29 May, British troops climbed into the boats for the trip to shore. The landing itself was sufficiently delayed so as to take place in daylight. About 1,000 British regulars landed on Horse Island and then waded across the narrows to the mainland, supported by cannon fire from their ships offshore. The British, using bayonets, easily broke the militia, who fled to the rear. Prevost led the attack in person. Slowly but surely, the British pushed the American regulars back toward the town. However, they failed to evict a small force of regular troops that held the town, and the attack stalled. Brown managed to rally some of the militia and threatened the British flank. Convinced that these were American reinforcements, and much to the dismay of many of his officers, Prevost ordered a withdrawal back to the fleet.

Although the British had outnumbered the defending Americans, they suffered 25 percent casualties: 260 killed, wounded, and missing. The Americans lost only some 100 men. During the battle, however, navy lieutenant Chauncey Wolcott, informed that the battle was lost, set fire to the *General Pike* and stores to keep them from falling into British hands—at a cost of $500,000 in damage.

The Americans subsequently reinforced Sackett's Harbor, and it remained free of attack for the remainder of the war.

See also WAR OF 1812: NAVAL OVERVIEW.

Further reading: Coles, Harry L. *The War of 1812.* Chicago: University of Chicago Press, 1965; Hickey, Donald R. *The War of 1812: A Forgotten Conflict.* Urbana: University of Illinois Press, 1989; Wilder, Patrick A. *The Battle of Sackett's Harbor, 1813.* Baltimore: Nautical and Aviation Publishing Company of America, 1994.

— Sarah Hilgendorff List

St. Clair, Arthur (1736–1818) *U.S. Army general and governor of the Northwest Territory*

Born on 23 March 1736 in Thurso, Scotland, Arthur St. Clair studied for a time at the University of Edinburgh. He joined the British army as an ensign in 1757 and fought in the FRENCH AND INDIAN WAR, participating in the captures of LOUISBOURG and QUEBEC. After the war he married a Boston heiress, resigned his commission, and settled on an estate in western Pennsylvania.

One of the largest property owners in Pennsylvania, St. Clair became a justice of the peace in 1773 and was serving on the Committee of Safety of Westmoreland County when the American Revolutionary War began. Commissioned a colonel of militia in 1775, St. Clair helped to cover the retreat of Brigadier General Benedict ARNOLD from Canada. Promoted to brigadier general in August 1776, St. Clair proved to be a competent staff officer under Continental army commander General George WASHINGTON and fought with distinction in the Battles of TRENTON and PRINCETON in 1776–77. In the spring of 1777 he was promoted to major general and given command of FORT TICONDEROGA. Faced with an invading 10,000-man British army, St. Clair abandoned the fort that July. Ordered to stand trial for this action, St. Clair was exonerated by a court-martial in August 1778. He fought bravely in the Battle of MONMOUTH COURTHOUSE in June 1778. Later he assumed command of the important post of WEST POINT, New York, and then brought reinforcements to Yorktown, Virginia.

Returning to civilian life after the war, St. Clair became active in Pennsylvania politics and was elected to the Continental Congress, in which he served during 1785–87 and was its president in 1787.

In 1787 St. Clair was appointed governor of the new Northwest Territory. After he concluded several treaties with the various tribes of the region at Fort Harmar in January 1789, relations with the Indians worsened because of the influx of white settlers, resulting in war under the leadership of the Miami chief, LITTLE TURTLE, and the Shawnee chief, BLUE JACKET. In October 1790, St. Clair authorized an expedition led by Brigadier General Josiah HARMAR into Indian territory, which the Indians defeated. In March 1791, Secretary of War Henry KNOX authorized St. Clair's promotion to major general, making him the ranking officer in the U.S. Army. St. Clair hoped to raise a force of 3,000 men but had only half that number for a delayed incursion into Indian territory. St. Clair had never served on the frontier and was inexperienced in Indian warfare. He was also in poor health. In any case, he refused to listen to his more knowledgeable subordinates. ST. CLAIR'S EXPEDITION set out in September, three months behind schedule, and was heavily defeated by the Indians on 4 November 1791.

St. Clair then resigned from the army, although a congressional committee cleared him of blame in the defeat. St. Clair continued to serve as governor of the Northwest Territory until 1802, when he retired to his estates. A combination of bad loans and the failure of the U.S. government to reimburse him for his expenses forced him into bankruptcy. He died on 31 August 1818 at his home of Chestnut Ridge, near Ligonier, Pennsylvania.

See also AMERICAN INDIAN WARS; INDIAN WARFARE.

Further reading: Kohn, Richard H. *Eagle and Sword: The Federalists and the Creation of the Military Establishment in America, 1783–1812.* New York: Free Press, 1975; Mackesy, Piers. *The War for America, 1775–1783.* Cambridge, Mass.: Harvard University Press, 1964; Middlekanff, Robert. *The Glorious Cause: The American Revolution, 1763–1789.* New York: Oxford University Press, 1982.

— J. W. Thacker

St. Clair's expedition (September–November 1791)
Expedition by U.S. forces against Native American tribes in the Old Northwest

Although the end of the American Revolutionary War gave the United States control of the Great Lakes Region, the British were slow to relinquish this vast area. President George WASHINGTON was faced with the challenges of evicting the British, making peace with the many American Indian tribes, and supporting growing encroachments by settlers on Indian lands in the area.

Initial U.S. military operations went poorly. In 1790, LITTLE TURTLE's Miami Indians defeated Brigadier General Josiah HARMAR's expedition into the area and American settlers left their homes and sought protection from the U.S. forts that dotted the frontier. Washington suspected that the British were supplying the Wabash tribes. In any case, the Miami warriors, invigorated by their victory, attacked more U.S. settlements.

Although Washington ordered a renewed peace initiative, he appointed Arthur ST. CLAIR (the governor of the Northwest Territories) major general of the army and ordered him to advance against Little Turtle and his warriors. St. Clair planned to march across the Ohio region, building forts along the way, but he failed to drill his men adequately; moreover, he had insufficient equipment for the task at hand—only 15 hatchets, 18 axes, 12 hammers, and 24 handsaws.

After numerous delays, St. Clair set out north from Fort Washington (present-day Cincinnati) on 17 September 1791. He commanded 1,453 men, of whom only 320 were disciplined regulars. Desertions were common and discipline poor, and St. Clair barely communicated with his staff.

As planned, St. Clair built two small forts. By late October, he had departed the second of these, Fort Jefferson, and moved toward the Wabash River. As St. Clair stumbled through the wilderness, Little Turtle prepared to receive him. When Native American scouts located St. Clair's force, Little Turtle moved south with about 1,000 warriors to counter it.

On 3 November 1791, St. Clair made camp near a tributary of the Wabash River. The next day, Little Turtle attacked St. Clair's camp, devastating the U.S. force. Militia units crumbled and the defenders were forced into a bloody three-hour retreat until they reached safety.

This remains one of the worst defeats ever for the U.S. military. Fully 55 percent of the American force fell during the initial onslaught and retreat. The fiasco claimed 630 soldiers dead or missing. Officer casualties alone came to 69 killed, wounded, or missing. St. Clair also abandoned materiel valued at more than $33,000. Although a congressional committee cleared St. Clair of any wrongdoing, he resigned from the army.

Although the battle was a major victory for the Native Americans, they could not maintain the advantage. Cold weather compelled much of the Indian force to scatter, and a bad crop year pressured Little Turtle to send his men home. The territory remained in a state of limited war for nearly four years before Washington appointed Major General Anthony WAYNE to organize, train for, and launch a third, successful expedition against Little Turtle and his people.

See also AMERICAN INDIAN WARS; BLUE JACKET; FALLEN TIMBERS, BATTLE OF; INDIAN WARFARE; LEGION OF THE UNITED STATES; MILITIA, ORGANIZATION AND ROLE OF.

Further reading: Edel, Wilbur. *Kekionga! The Worst Defeat in the History of the U.S. Army.* Westport, Conn.: Praeger, 1997; Perry, James M. *Arrogant Armies: Great Military Disasters and the Generals Behind Them.* New York: John Wiley & Sons, 1996; Rafert, Stewart. *The Miami Indians of Indiana: A Persistent People, 1654–1994.* Bloomington: Indiana University Press, 1999; Sword, Wiley. *President Washington's Indian War: The Struggle for the Old Northwest, 1790–1795.* Norman: University of Oklahoma Press, 1993.

— Patrick R. Jennings

Sainte-Foy, Battle of (28 April 1760) *Last French victory in the French and Indian War*
Realizing that Montreal did not offer a good defensive position, the commander of French forces in Canada, General François-Gaston, chevalier de Lévis, determined to retake Quebec in 1760 in the hope of dragging out the war until peace could be established in Europe. Toward this end, he dispatched a messenger to France in late 1759, requesting reinforcements and matériel before the English could resupply Brigadier General James Murray's forces at Quebec.

Leaving behind a small force under Captain Pierre Pouchot, recently repatriated after losing FORT NIAGARA the previous year, Lévis departed Montreal on 20 April with approximately 7,000 men and 12 old cannon aboard bateaux and barges escorted by two frigates, the *Atalante* and the *Pomone.* Arriving at Pointe-aux-Trembles on 24 April, Lévis unloaded his men and supplies and moved overland toward Quebec. On the morning of 27 April, Lévis reached the village of Sainte-Foy, six miles from Quebec, only to find the road blocked by 3,800 men under Murray, who had been warned of the French approach only that morning. Fearing that his men could not withstand a siege, particularly if French reinforcements arrived by sea, Murray had brought his men out into the open—not so much to force a battle as to keep from being confined behind Quebec's walls.

Rather than attack Murray's position, Lévis waited for nightfall in hope of moving his forces through the woods and outflanking him. Realizing Lévis's intentions, Murray withdrew to the Plains of Abraham, where on the morning of 28 April he established his men and 20 cannon on the same ridge that Lieutenant General Louis Joseph, marquis de Montcalm, had held during the previous year's battle. When Murray realized that Lévis was still bringing about half of his forces up, he moved to the low ground in order to strike Lévis's flank. Unfortunately for Murray, his cannon became stuck in mud and could not be moved. After an hour's fighting, superior numbers forced Murray to withdraw behind the walls of Quebec.

Lévis, having lost only 12 percent of his force (193 dead and 640 wounded), besieged Murray, who had lost 28 percent of his effective force (259 dead and 829 wounded). For the French, this taste of victory proved short-lived. Although Lévis completed his siege lines and began to bombard Quebec on 11 May, the arrival of British ship of the line *Vanguard* (70) on 12 May forced him to evacuate on 13 May. Within four months the British captured MONTREAL, bringing an effective end to the FRENCH AND INDIAN WAR.

See also QUEBEC CAMPAIGN.

Further reading: Anderson, Fred. *Crucible of War: The Seven Years' War and the Fate of Empire in British North America, 1754–1766.* New York: Knopf, 2000; Eccles, W. J. *France in America.* Rev. ed. Markham, Ontario: Fitzhenry & Whiteside, 1990.

— Justin D. Murphy

Saint-Mihiel offensive (12–16 September 1918) *First independent offensive by the American Expeditionary Forces (AEF) during World War I, and the largest U.S. military operation since the Civil War*
The opportunity for a major U.S. operation arose from the successful Allied counteroffensive in July that reduced the

AISNE-MARNE salient. From that point forward, the initiative lay with the Allies under the overall command and direction of Marshal Ferdinand Foch of France. General John J. PERSHING's dream of an independent American field army became reality in July–August 1918, and he secured approval from Foch to reduce the Saint-Mihiel salient.

Colonel Hugh A. Drum, First Army chief of staff, directed planning. The salient, northwest of Toul near the right extremity of the Allied battle line, was oriented to the southwest with the village of Saint-Mihiel at its apex. It was 25 miles across its base and 16 miles deep into Allied territory, cutting the rail line from Verdun to Toul and from Paris to Nancy. This fortified triangular position had remained almost unchanged since 1914. Much to Pershing's dismay, Foch insisted on limiting the scope of the American attack in order to permit the MEUSE-ARGONNE OFFENSIVE two weeks later.

The U.S. I and IV Corps launched the main attack against the south face of the salient on 12 September. Major General Hunter LIGGETT commanded I Corps, consisting of four divisions on the right of the First Army line. Major General Joseph DICKMAN's IV Corps, consisting of three divisions, operated on the left. Major General George H. Cameron's V Corps of two divisions and one brigade held the left (northern) end of the line; to its right was the French II Colonial Corps of three divisions. In all, 500,000 Americans and more than 110,000 French soldiers participated in the operation. Thousands of airplanes and tanks added to the combat power of First Army, and 2,900 guns laid down a four-hour barrage prior to the attack. A deception plan, the so-called Belfort Ruse, drew attention away from the Saint-Mihiel area.

Opposing this massive Allied force were nearly 14 German divisions. They were in the process of withdrawing to shorten their lines at the very time the Allies attacked.

After the preparatory barrage the infantry jumped off at 5:00 A.M. Progress of the main attack against the south face of the salient was excellent, although at other points it was slower. The infantry units with engineer assistance had managed to get through the wire entanglements quite effectively simply by moving over the entanglements where they were unable to cut them quickly. Prior to this innovation, attackers had relied on artillery preparation to cut the wire.

After the solid progress of the first day, Pershing directed that the units driving north and those driving east link up near Vigneulles to pinch off the nose of the salient. Thiaucourt fell to the combined efforts of the 2d and 89th Infantry Divisions at 11:00 A.M. on 12 September. Mont Sec in the IV Corps zone, on the left flank of the 1st Division, had threatened the advance because it dominated the entire area, but the fast pace of the attack put the Americans beyond the hill. By noon on the 13th, about 15,000 Germans and 400 guns had been captured. Allied casualties at that point were about 5,000. By the 15th, the salient was occupied by Allied troops, and the campaign was concluded on the 16th. In all, the First Army incurred about 7,000 casualties while capturing 16,000 Germans and 443 guns.

By all measures the reduction of the salient was a successful operation. The AEF had proved its worth in battle. Foch rejected Pershing's plan to continue the offensive toward Metz, and 10 days later these same forces were relocated and launched the Meuse-Argonne Offensive.

See also AMERICAN EXPEDITIONARY FORCES; WORLD WAR I, COURSE OF U.S. INVOLVEMENT.

Further reading: Coffman, Edward M. *The War to End All Wars: The American Military Experience in World War I.* New York: Oxford University Press, 1968; Liggett, Hunter. *A.E.F.: Ten Years Ago in France.* New York: Dodd, Mead, 1928; ———. *Commanding an American Army: Recollections of the World War.* Boston: Houghton Mifflin, 1925; Marshall, George C. *Memoirs of My Services in the World War 1917–1918.* Boston: Houghton Mifflin, 1976; Trask, David F. *The AEF And Coalition Warmaking, 1917–1918.* Lawrence: University Press of Kansas, 1993; *United States Army in the World War 1917–1919.* Vol. 8. Washington, D.C.: Historical Division, Department of the Army, 1948.

— John F. Votaw

Salerno invasion (9–17 September 1943) *World War II Allied invasion of the Italian mainland*
The successful Allied conquest of SICILY had brought about the overthrow of Benito Mussolini's fascist government on 25 July 1943. Marshal Pietro Badoglio, Mussolini's successor, immediately initiated secret negotiations with the Allies. Meanwhile, British prime minister Winston Churchill urged an Allied attack on the Italian mainland, and the Americans agreed, in part because it might facilitate Italy's withdrawal from the war before the Germans could react. The Salerno attack, designated Operation Avalanche, was timed to coincide with the announcement of Italy's surrender. Salerno was chosen as the point of attack because of its proximity to the port of Naples, which the Allies needed as an entry point for supplies, and because it was within the limits of fighter cover from aircraft based in Sicily.

Unfortunately for the Allies, difficulties arose even before the landings began. General Bernard Montgomery's British Eighth Army crossed to the mainland on 3 September, but it did not provoke a significant German response; the German commander in Italy, Field Marshal Albert Kesselring, relied on the difficult terrain, demolition of transportation facilities, and a small screening force to delay the British. Even worse for the Allies, the Germans had expected Italy's surrender, which was announced on 8 September, and had forces in position to occupy the country and disarm Italian troops. Thus, although the Allies would face limited resistance on landing, Kesselring could quickly mobilize powerful reinforcements to resist an invasion, and he had already guessed Naples as the likely target.

The landings were carried out on 9 September by the British X Corps, commanded by Lieutenant General Richard McCreery, and the U.S. VI Corps, under Major General Ernest Dawley, both part of Lieutenant General Mark CLARK's Fifth Army. The British corps of two divisions landed on the northern side of the Gulf of Salerno, while the VI Corps, which consisted of only Major General Fred Walker's 36th Division, landed farther south. The British and Americans were separated by the Sele River, which made it difficult for the two corps to support one another. Further complicating the Allied situation was the terrain: The beaches at Salerno were surrounded by a ring of high ground that made a naturally strong defensive position.

Although the British landings met determined opposition, the Americans encountered less resistance and came ashore with minimal losses despite Clark's orders that there would be no supporting naval bombardment. The following day both British and American forces, the latter reinforced by elements of the 45th Infantry Division, pushed inland. But German reinforcements counterattacked later in the day and drove back the Allies, who were separated by a seven-mile gap. On 11 September, the Allies again advanced and again were driven back. German air attacks on the invasion fleet supported the Germans' land effort.

By 12 September, the Germans had assembled sufficient armored forces to launch a major assault against the British in the northern section of the beachhead. The attacks were extended to the American sector on 13 September with the intention of driving a wedge between the British and Americans, so that each force could be destroyed separately. American troops were driven from the town of Persano, and in one place German tanks pushed to within a mile of the beaches before their assault was halted by naval gunfire. Clark therefore stopped the unloading of ships in the southern sector and made plans to reembark the American troops and transfer them to the British sector if necessary. On learning of this, both British General Harold Alexander, Allied commander in chief in the Mediterranean, and General Dwight D. EISENHOWER ruled out any withdrawal.

The Allies now rushed reinforcements to Salerno. Part of the Eighty-second Airborne Division was dropped directly onto the beaches that evening, with the remainder dropping on 14 September. Allied naval gunfire and more

effective air support prevented German attacks from making any appreciable gains that day.

Both sides spent 15 September regrouping, but by this time the Allies had seven divisions ashore with some 200 tanks in support, a force nearly twice as large as the Germans could muster. Alexander visited the beachhead that day to encourage the troops, and at his urging Clark relieved Dawley from command of VI Corps. Although Dawley had performed adequately, neither Alexander nor Clark had confidence in him, and they thought that a change in command was necessary after the near-disastrous battle.

Realizing that he lacked the strength to destroy the Allied invasion force, on 16 September Kesselring ordered his forces to withdraw to a defensive line to the north. Late that day American troops in the southern sector made contact with the advance guard of Montgomery's army. The Germans withdrew on the 17th, covered by limited attacks. American casualties totaled 1,649, while British losses amounted to 5,259. German casualties were 3,472. The difficult fight for Italy had only begun.

See also WORLD WAR II, U.S. INVOLVEMENT: EUROPE.

Further reading: Hickey, Des, and Gus Smith. *Operation Avalanche: The Salerno Landings, 1943.* New York: McGraw-Hill, 1984; Lamb, Richard. *War in Italy, 1943–1945: A Brutal Story.* New York: St. Martin's Press, 1993; Morris, Eric. *Salerno: A Military Fiasco.* New York: Stein & Day, 1983.

— Jim Piecuch

Salt Creek Prairie Raid (Warren wagon train raid)
(18 May 1871) *Pivotal event of the American Indian Wars*

Prompted by vociferous complaints about Indian raids on the Texas frontier, in the spring of 1871, Lieutenant General William Tecumseh SHERMAN, commanding general of the army, conducted a tour of Texas posts from Fort Clark near the Mexican border to Fort Sill in Indian Territory. Sherman long believed Texan claims to be grossly exaggerated, and nothing he witnessed during the tour had caused him to change his opinion. Traveling with Inspector General Randolph Marcy and a small escort of 10th Cavalry troopers, Sherman indeed enjoyed an uneventful journey. On 18 May, en route from Fort Griffin (near present Albany, Texas) to Fort Richardson at Jacksboro, the general's entourage crossed Salt Creek Prairie in Young County and arrived that evening at Fort Richardson.

Unknown to Sherman, as he rode across Salt Creek Prairie in a military ambulance he did so under the watchful eyes of a large Kiowa raiding party that numbered some 100 warriors. As with their Comanche allies, many Kiowa raided ranches and settlements in northwestern Texas, only to return to the protection of the Fort Sill Agency—the very behavior about which Texans had complained to the government. But under President Ulysses S. GRANT's peace policy, neither the state of Texas nor the U.S. Army could do much about it. The Kiowa, led by the notorious Satanta, could not have known that Sherman passed before them; on the advice of a medicine man, who promised a more lucrative target, they opted not to attack.

Only hours after Sherman's party passed, the Kiowa struck a large wagon train hauling freight to Fort Griffin. Although five of the teamsters somehow escaped, seven others were tortured, killed, and mutilated. The raiders burned the wagons and made off with more than 40 mules, which they took with them back to the Fort Sill Agency.

That night a wounded teamster arrived at Fort Richardson with the news. After a patrol reported the ghastly scene on Salt Creek Prairie, Sherman ordered post commander Colonel Ranald S. MACKENZIE of the 4th Cavalry to pursue the raiders while he moved on to Fort Sill.

On 27 May, after Satanta boasted of the raid to the Indian agent at Fort Sill, Sherman and post commander Colonel Benjamin GRIERSON of the 10th Cavalry confronted Kiowa leaders at Grierson's headquarters. Satanta proudly confirmed his participation in the raid, and Sherman ordered him arrested along with Satank and Big Tree. The Kiowa leveled weapons, at which point Sherman signaled and dozens of black troopers from the 10th Cavalry appeared. The confrontation ended without bloodshed and the three Indian leaders were taken into custody for transfer to Jacksboro, where they would stand trial in civil court.

Shortly thereafter Sherman left Fort Sill, and on 4 June Mackenzie and his command arrived after a grueling and fruitless pursuit to escort the prisoners to Jacksboro. En route old Satank, a revered member of an elite Kiowa warrior society, shed his restraints, attacked a guard, and was gunned down. A Jacksboro jury convicted Satanta and young Big Tree of murder and sentenced them to death. Texas governor E. J. Davis reduced the sentence to life at the state penitentiary at Huntsville. In 1873 both were released over much opposition and returned to raiding. Satanta surrendered during the 1874–75 RED RIVER WAR and was returned to prison, where he committed suicide in 1878.

The Salt Creek Prairie Raid did not bring an immediate change in Indian policy, but it did lead to a new aggressiveness among military units in Texas. Persistent campaigning coupled with the systematic slaughter of the buffalo triggered major Indian uprisings in 1873 and 1874 that finally toppled the peace policy. The hugely successful Red River War, commenced only three years after the raid, brought final subjugation to the Indians of the southern plains.

See also AMERICAN INDIAN WARS; INDIAN WARFARE.

Further reading: Capps, Benjamin. *The Warren Wagontrain Raid: The First Complete Account of an Historic Indian Attack and Its Aftermath.* New York: Dial Press, 1974; Haley, James L. *The Buffalo War: The History of the Red River Indian Uprising of 1874.* Garden City, N.Y.: Doubleday, 1976.

— David Coffey

Saltville, Virginia, massacre at (2 October 1864)

One of the most brutal acts of the Civil War, which occurred during the Union attempt to capture the town of Saltville in southwestern Virginia

Saltville produced salt, which was vital in the preservation of food and tanning. It was also on the Virginia and Tennessee Railroad, which moved men and equipment between the eastern and western military theaters.

On 27 September 1864, U.S. Army brigadier general Steven G. Burbridge launched a raid from Kentucky to destroy the salt works. Burbridge commanded some 5,000 men, including Colonel James Brisbin's 5th U.S. Colored Cavalry Regiment (USCC) and two companies of the 6th USCC Regiment.

Confederate colonel Henry L. Giltner's cavalry brigade delayed the Union advance as long as possible to give Confederate reinforcements time to come up. The attackers arrived at Saltville on 1 October, but Burbridge delayed the assault to allow his men a chance to rest. Had he struck immediately, his forces would easily have overpowered the few Confederates then defending Saltville.

While General Burbridge delayed, the Confederates hastily reinforced Saltville. By the time battle was joined in midmorning on 2 October, the Confederates had some 2,800 men under Brigadier General John S. Williams. Although Burbridge still had a numerical advantage, the odds were not as great as he had previously enjoyed.

Most of the Union attacks were made on foot. After numerous attempts to secure Cedar Ridge, the main hill before Saltville, the 5th Cavalry, 12th Ohio Cavalry, and 11th Michigan Cavalry finally broke through the defenders' lines. Out of ammunition, however, they were forced to withdraw. Short of supplies and having suffered heavy casualties, Burbridge decided to withdraw without having accomplished his mission. In his hasty retreat, Burbridge left many Union dead and wounded on the battlefield. The next morning, Confederate soldiers, including men of Brigadier General Felix H. Robertson's brigade and a company of bushwhackers under Captain Champ Ferguson, gave no quarter to the Union troops, especially not to

African Americans of the 5th and 6th Cavalry. They slaughtered them and left most of the white soldiers for dead. The number murdered probably was in excess of 100. The battle thus became known as the Saltville Massacre. Total losses on the Union side in the battle and its aftermath came to 329 men, while the Confederates lost only 190.

Two months later, the Federals took and destroyed much of Saltville. Ferguson was eventually captured, charged with murder, tried, and convicted; he was hanged on 20 October 1865. Robertson escaped justice.

See also CIVIL WAR, LAND OVERVIEW.

Further reading: Marvel, William. "The Battle of Saltville: Massacre or Myth?" *Blue and Gray Magazine* (August 1991): 10–19, 46–60; Mays, Thomas D. *The Saltville Massacre.* Abilene, Tex.: McWhiney Foundation Press, 1995.

— Joseph R. Rubin

Sampson, William T. (1840–1903) *U.S. Navy admiral*
Born on 9 February 1840 in Palmyra, New York, William Thomas Sampson graduated from the U.S. Naval Academy, Annapolis, in 1861. During the Civil War he served with the Gulf and South Atlantic Blockading Squadrons. Following the war, Sampson served on the European Station in his first command, the gunboat *Alert,* and later commanded *Swatara,* another gunboat, on the Asiatic Station. He next commanded the cruiser *San Francisco.* His final ship command was the *Iowa,* the navy's newest battleship.

Sampson also served three tours as an instructor at the Naval Academy (1862–64, 1867–71, and 1874–78). With a strong background in science, especially astronomy, he was chief of the Bureau of Ordnance (1893–97). He was on the board that inspected coastal defenses, a member of the International Prime Meridian and Time Conference, and a delegate to the 1887 International Maritime Conference.

Sampson was superintendent of the Naval Academy from 1886 to 1890. Promoted to captain in 1889, he helped establish the Naval War College. As a founder and later president of the Naval Institute (1898–1902), he sought to enhance professionalism. After the MAINE blew up in Havana harbor on 15 February 1898, Sampson presided over the board of inquiry.

With war with Spain looming, in February 1898 Sampson took command of the North Atlantic Squadron. He vaulted to this position over more senior officers, and his appointment won him few friends. Following the declaration of the SPANISH-AMERICAN WAR, his squadron blockaded SANTIAGO, bottling up a Spanish squadron there under Rear Admiral Pascual Cervera.

On 3 July 1898, as Sampson was departing in his flagship, the *New York,* for a meeting with his army counterpart, Major General William SHAFTER, Cervera's ships began to sortie. Ships of the squadron then under Commodore Winfield Scott SCHLEY destroyed the Spanish squadron. Despite Sampson's immediate return, he played no substantive role in the battle. Controversy over who had won the battle—Sampson or Schley—reflected little credit on either man and polarized the navy.

Sampson was promoted to rear admiral in March 1899 and retired in February 1902. No doubt the controversy with Schley abetted his deteriorating health. Sampson died on 6 May 1902, in Washington, D.C.

Further reading: Bradford, James C. *Admirals of the New Steel Navy: Makers of the American Naval Tradition, 1880–1930.* Annapolis, Md.: Naval Institute Press, 1990; Goode, William A. M. *With Sampson through the War.* New York: Doubleday & McClure, 1899; West, Richard S. *Admirals of American Empire.* Indianapolis: Bobbs-Merrill, 1948.

— Michael S. Casey

Sand Creek Massacre (29 November 1864)
Unwarranted attack by Colorado militia on the Southern Cheyenne village on Sand Creek in eastern Colorado
The Minnesota Sioux uprising of 1862 spread fear among white settlements in the West. With the federal government understandably preoccupied with the Civil War, westerners believed themselves vulnerable. In Colorado, Governor John Evans forecast a major war. Minor raids on stock herds and white property brought a heavy-handed response from Colorado troops that ignited the war Evans had predicted. During the summer of 1864, as Cheyenne and Arapaho warriors struck across Kansas and Colorado, Chief Black Kettle sought peace.

Sixty-year-old Black Kettle had long believed that the continued freedom of his people rested not in war but in accommodation. Although he did not represent most Cheyenne, he approached military authorities at Fort Lyon with an offer of peace and backed his words by surrendering four white captives. Major Edward Wynkoop, who was sympathetic to Black Kettle, agreed to escort a delegation to Denver. Governor Evans found the peace overtures problematic. He had promised an active campaign against the Indians and raised the 3d Colorado Cavalry for that purpose. The appearance of prominent peace chiefs complicated the matter.

Colonel John M. Chivington, an ambitious former minister known as "the Fighting Parson," commanded the District of Colorado with much autonomy. He had distinguished himself during the Confederate invasion of New Mexico and now planned to make a bigger name for himself by striking a major blow against the Indians. His political aspirations would not be served by making peace. He informed the delegation that if they wanted peace, they could surrender to Major Wynkoop at Fort Lyon. The chiefs thought they had an understanding.

In October, Little Raven's Arapaho arrived at Fort Lyon on the Arkansas in southwestern Colorado. Wynkoop issued them rations. But when Black Kettle arrived in early November, he found that the trusted major had been summoned to Kansas to explain his actions. Before leaving, Wynkoop and his successor, Major Scott Anthony, informed Black Kettle that they lacked the provisions to feed so many Indians and that Wynkoop needed to obtain authorization to accept them as prisoners. In the meantime, the Arapaho should return to their hunting grounds and Black Kettle's people should remain in their village on Sand Creek, some 40 miles northeast of the fort.

Prodded by the public and the press to strike a definitive blow against the Indians, Chivington chose an easy target. Conveniently, he considered Black Kettle and his people hostile. He quietly assembled a force comprising the 3d Colorado Cavalry, a 100-day-enlistment unit that contained many men of dubious character, part of the veteran 1st Colorado, and four mountain howitzers. Chivington marched to Fort Lyon and on the night of 28 November led his command of 700 men toward Sand Creek.

At dawn, Chivington positioned his troopers for the attack. In Black Kettle's village, 500 people, some 300 of them women and children, slept as the soldiers charged. In disbelief, Black Kettle raised the U.S. flag and a white flag above his lodge. It did no good. Chivington wanted no prisoners, and his men cut down every Indian they came across. Pockets of resistance formed only to be wiped out. For hours bloodthirsty men of the 3d Colorado combed the village and surrounding area killing, scalping, and mutilating men, women, and children. Amazingly, Black Kettle and more than 200 of his people managed to escape.

Chivington and his men, bearing bloody trophies of their conquest, returned to Denver as heroes. By the time the army and Congress acted on reports of the slaughter, the colonel and the 3d Colorado had mustered out of service. Despite the massacre at Sand Creek, Black Kettle still advocated peace. He and his band eventually settled on a reservation in Indian Territory, where, almost four years after Sand Creek, in a similar attack by Lieutenant Colonel George A. CUSTER's 7th Cavalry, Black Kettle, his wife, and more than 100 of his people were killed in the Battle of the WASHITA RIVER.

See also AMERICAN INDIAN WARS; SIOUX WARS; WOUNDED KNEE INCIDENT.

Further reading: Hoig, Stan. *The Sand Creek Massacre.* Norman: University of Oklahoma Press, 1963; Utley,

Robert M. *Frontiersmen in Blue: The United States Army and the Indian, 1848–1865.* New York: Macmillan, 1967.
— David Coffey

Sandy Creek expedition of 1756 (18 February–15 March 1756) *Unsuccessful expedition of Virginia militia and Cherokee Indians against the Shawnee Indians in the Ohio country during the 1754–63 French and Indian War*

Following the defeat of British Major General Edward BRADDOCK's expedition against FORT DUQUESNE in 1755, the Shawnee Indians terrorized the colonial frontier of the Ohio River valley. In an effort to stop the raids and prevent further attacks, Virginia formed an alliance with the Cherokee Indians. Virginia governor Robert Dinwiddie also planned an expedition to the mouth of the Great Sandy River to construct a military post, from which to fight the Indians and contest the French for control of the Ohio River valley. The expedition, however, was hastily mounted and poorly planned.

On 18 February 1756, 340 Virginia militiamen and 130 Cherokee Indians set out from Fort Frederick, near Salem, Virginia. The force was commanded by Major Andrew Lewis, who commissioned two Cherokee warriors, Round O and Yellow Bird, as captains.

The expedition headed to the New River and then on to the Blue River before reaching the Big Sandy River at Dry Fork on 28 February 1756. Lewis planned to move down the Big Sandy River to the forks of the Ohio River and there attack the Shawnee. To facilitate rapid movement, Lewis carried only limited supplies and planned to live off the land as much as possible. Because of heavy rains and resultant flooding of the river, the expedition was forced to continue on foot. This slowed it considerably, and the loss of several canoes carrying valuable supplies and a lack of game in the Ohio River valley led to a mutiny among Lewis's men.

On 13 March, Lewis called his men together. Addressing his troops, he drew a line and called on all those willing to share his fate to cross it and continue. All officers crossed the line, but only 30 men did so. This, and a council of war with his officers two days later, convinced Lewis to turn back without ever having confronted the Shawnee. The expedition had failed, the consequence of poor planning and organization, a lack of resources, and bad luck. The failure of the expedition resulted in additional Indian attacks along the frontier that exposed militia ineffectiveness.

See also FRENCH AND INDIAN WAR.

Further reading: Johnston, David E. *A History of Middle New River Settlements and Contiguous Territory.* Huntington, W.Va.: Standard Printing and Publishing,

1906; Rice, Otis K. *West Virginia: A History.* Lexington: University Press of Kentucky, 1985; Rice, Otis K. *The Allegheny Frontier.* Lexington: University Press of Kentucky, 1970; Thwaites, Reuben G. *Chronicles of Border Warfare.* Cincinnati: Stewart and Kidd, 1920.

— Jason S. Boncher

San Gabriel, Battle of (8 January 1847) *Final decisive battle of the Mexican-American War in California*

The battle was fought between a mixed force of U.S. Marines, navy seamen, and dragoons against native Californians supported by the Mexican government. Two previous campaigns had initially captured, then lost, Los Angeles. The commander of the U.S. Pacific Squadron, Commodore Robert F. Stockton, began the third and final campaign for Los Angeles from San Diego on 29 December 1846. The American column consisted of marines and navy seamen from the Pacific squadron, California volunteers, and six pieces of artillery. Stockton was joined by Brigadier General Stephen KEARNY and 100 horsemen of the 1st U.S. Dragoons.

The Americans were opposed by a Mexican force of some 450 mounted votunteers and California lancers, supported by four pieces of artillery, all under Captain José Flores. Flores set up an ambush position at a ford of the San Gabriel River. An American reconnaisance of the ford revealed the ambush, and Stockton moved to an upstream crossing. When Flores discovered that the Americans had changed their line of march, he quickly led his small army to the upstream crossing, placing his men on a series of rises on the western bank of the river. Flores positioned two artillery pieces in the center to cover the actual crossing spot, and one on each flank.

In approaching the ford on 8 January, Stockton formed his entire command into a large square. Cattle, spare oxen, and supply wagons were placed in the middle of the square. As soon as the Americans crossed the San Gabriel River, the battle was joined. Both of the flanks of the American square broke ranks, formed squares of their own, and continued forward.

Flores ordered his left and right wings to attack, but these efforts were repulsed. Stockton then formed a battle line and ordered his entire force to make a bayonet charge. This drove the remainder of Flores's troops from the heights. Flores then counterattacked, but effective American artillery forced the Californians back toward Los Angeles.

The following day, 9 January, the American force moved in the direction of Los Angeles across a wide plain called La Mesa. Flores and 300 men established another defensive line before the road to Los Angeles crossed the Rio Los Angeles. Stockton deployed his troops to the left of the road in square formation and followed a route parallel to the road. The American artillery, manned by navy pikemen, drove the California artillery from the field, at which time Flores ordered his mounted lancers to charge the right flank of the American formation, consisting of marines and seamen. The Americans hurled the lancers back in confusion. Stockton's men occupied Los Angeles on 10 January.

In the campaign there were only light casualties on both sides. Low-quality Mexican gunpowder and poor artillery practice contributed to the American victory, which insured that California would remain in American hands.

See also MEXICAN-AMERICAN WAR.

Further reading: Bauer, K. Jack. *Surfboats and Horse Marines: U.S. Naval Operations in the Mexican War, 1846–48.* Annapolis, Md.: Naval Institute Press, 1978; Santelli, Gabrielle M. Neufeld. *Marines in the Mexican War.* Washington, D.C.: History and Museums Division, Headquarters, U.S. Marine Corps, 1991.

— Michael J. Manning

San Jacinto, Battle of (21 April 1836) *Final and deciding battle of the Texas War of Independence*

March 1836 had proved a disastrous month for Texans fighting for independence from Mexico. The fall of the ALAMO on 6 March had been followed by the massacre of more than 300 Texan prisoners at Goliad on 27 March. What remained of the Texan army under General Sam HOUSTON was in retreat to the northeast, accompanied by large numbers of terrified civilians.

General Antonio López de Santa Anna was so convinced that the Texans were beaten that he thought the campaign was at an end. His officers, however, persuaded him to pursue Houston's fleeing forces and put a definitive end to the Texas Revolution. The retreating Houston attempted to recruit and train a force despite bad weather, disease, and poor discipline. Houston was under growing pressure from both his own troops and the provisional government to make a stand and fight.

In the meantime, Santa Anna had decided to pursue the members of the fleeing provisional government, who reportedly was heading for Harrisburg. This decision distracted Santa Anna from his main goal of destroying Houston's army, and further divided the Mexican forces. It also brought Santa Anna to the decisive battle of the campaign, for Houston had decided to fight and was also on the road to Harrisburg. The Texan forces had captured Mexican couriers and were aware of the size and the location of Santa Anna's force.

On the morning of 21 April 1836, both armies were encamped less than a mile apart where Buffalo Bayou met the San Jacinto River. Houston's forces numbered 918, while

Santa Anna had approximately 1,400 men. The possibility of further Mexican reinforcements induced Houston to attack. Santa Anna assumed that the Texans would be on the defensive and was planning his own attack for the next day.

Houston held a rare war council that recommended a defensive stance. Houston, however, decided to attack on the afternoon of 21 April. The Mexican forces were resting and had neglected to post sentries. The Texans moved across a relatively open area, but still took the Mexican forces completely off guard. With cries of "Remember the Alamo" and "Remember Goliad," the Texans pounced on the surprised Mexicans. The battle lasted only about 15 minutes, but the killing continued for another hour. When the fighting was done, the Mexicans had suffered 630 killed and 730 taken prisoner. Santa Anna had fled from the battlefield. On the Texan side, 9 were killed and some 30 wounded, including Houston, shot in the ankle. The day after the battle, Santa Anna was captured and brought before Houston. While many Texans demanded Santa Anna's immediate execution, Houston recognized that Santa Anna was worth much more alive to Texas independence than he was dead.

The victory at San Jacinto led directly to the signing of the Treaties of Velasco on 14 May 1836. A public treaty called for the withdrawal of all Mexican forces beyond the Rio Grande and the return of Santa Anna to Mexico as soon as possible. A second secret treaty called for Santa Anna's immediate release in exchange for his efforts to have the Mexican government recognize Texas independence and the Rio Grande as the Texas boundary. The outcome of the Texas Revolution and War of Independence had come down to this one battle. The independence of Texas, however, was still not assured. The Mexican government disavowed Santa Anna's recognition of independence and vowed to reconquer Texas, a position that would lead to a decade of border conflict and boundary disputes, contributing to the outbreak of the MEXICAN-AMERICAN WAR in 1846.

See also MEXICAN-AMERICAN WAR, CAUSES OF; TEXAS WAR FOR INDEPENDENCE.

Further reading: Hardin, Stephen L. *Texan Iliad: A Military History of the Texas Revolution.* Austin: University of Texas Press, 1994; Peña, José Enrique de la. *With Santa Anna in Texas: A Personal Narrative of the Revolution.* College Station: Texas A&M University Press, 1975; Pohl, James W. *The Battle of San Jacinto.* Austin: Texas State Historical Association, 1989.

— Don M. Coerver

San Juan Heights, Battle of (1 July 1898) *American victory in Cuba during the SPANISH-AMERICAN WAR*
After Spanish rear admiral Pascual Cervera y Topete slipped his squadron of seven ships into Santiago Harbor

on 19 May 1898, U.S. secretary of the navy John D. Long pressured President William McKinley and the cabinet to attack Santiago instead of Havana. Toward this end, the cabinet voted on 26 May to dispatch Major General William R. SHAFTER's V Corps to Cuba with the objective of taking Santiago.

Comprised of some 17,000 regulars (two divisions of infantry, one division of dismounted cavalry, and one artillery battalion) and volunteers (including Lieutenant Colonel Theodore ROOSEVELT's Rough Riders), V Corps departed Tampa, Florida, on 14 June. Although the navy had sought an attack on the fortresses guarding the entrance to Santiago harbor, Shafter decided to land at Siboney and Daiquiri, then march overland and seize the heights overlooking Santiago.

Shafter's Spanish counterpart, Major General Arsenio Linares y Pombo, had approximately 28,000 soldiers (half Spanish regulars and half militia), but they were widely scattered across eastern Cuba. Linares intended to drag out the fighting in hope of securing a negotiated settlement to end the war. On 22 June, V Corps began landing operations. In the first major engagement, on 24 June, dismounted cavalry under Major General Joseph WHEELER, a former Confederate cavalry commander, pushed back a numerically superior Spanish force at Las Guasimas. Shafter then moved his troops, who had been reinforced by approximately 4,000 Cubans from General Calixto Garcia's rebel army, to within five miles of Santiago.

Although Shafter had received reports that Santiago was on the verge of starvation, several factors induced him to attack rather than delay. He feared that his troops would succumb to tropical diseases and become ineffective. He also had been informed that Colonel Federico Escario was leading a relief column (falsely numbered at 8,000 men) overland to Santiago. Wheeler's success at Las Guasimas convinced Shafter that he easily could defeat the Spaniards holding San Juan Heights and the nearby village of EL CANEY, which were lightly defended according to Cuban insurrectionists and balloon reconnaissance.

Shafter therefore decided to launch a two-pronged attack on 1 July, with Brigadier General Henry W. LAWTON's 2d Infantry (supported by the 2d Massachusetts Volunteers and an artillery battery) moving against El Caney and Brigadier General Jacob F. Kent's 1st Infantry and Wheeler's dismounted cavalry (supported by the Rough Riders and the 71st New York Volunteers) moving against San Juan Heights—a mile-long ridge approximately 125 feet above the landscape, overlooking Santiago. At its highest point, San Juan Hill, the Spanish had constructed a blockhouse to defend the approach. A similar blockhouse lay to the east on Kettle Hill. Both blockhouses had been reinforced just the day before. Not expecting much resistance, Wheeler and Kent sent some 8,000 troops forward in one column down a narrow road that stretched some four miles from Shafter's headquarters through dense jungle to the crest of San Juan Hill.

Although Lieutenant Colonel Edward J. McClernand tried to direct operations from El Poso, a hill about 1.5 miles east of San Juan Heights, once the Spanish opened fire at 10:00 A.M. ground commanders had to improvise plans. Initially, American forces congested on the small road provided easy targets for Spanish snipers firing from treetops and Spanish defenders firing from the ridge above. Although the congestion was relieved after an observation balloon spotted trails that branched off the road and led through the jungle to the flanks of the heights, American units still faced heavy fire when they emerged from the jungle and tried to climb the relatively open slopes of the ridge. The 71st New York, poorly equipped with old single-shot Springfields, disintegrated after a few minutes. The 6th Infantry Regiment lost almost 25 percent of its 463 men within just a few minutes of emerging from the jungle. While Captain George S. Grimes had been fairly ineffective in directing artillery fire from El Poso, the tide began to turn around 1:15 P.M., when Lieutenant John H. Parker brought three Gatling guns to within 800 yards of San Juan Hill and opened fire. It was at about this time that Roosevelt's Rough Riders swept up Kettle Hill, then regrouped for the famous charge up San Juan Hill. Although accounts vary, Parker's Gatling guns were probably the key factor in forcing the Spaniards from their positions. The Americans lost approximately 140 dead and 940 wounded at San Juan Heights, compared to total Spanish casualties of 650 at San Juan Heights and El Caney.

With the Americans controlling the heights overlooking Santiago, Cervera attempted to escape on 3 July, leading to the destruction of his fleet in the Battle of SANTIAGO DE CUBA. Santiago capitulated on 17 July, effectively bringing the Cuban portion of the Spanish-American War to an end.

Further reading: Cosmas, Graham. "San Juan Hill and El Caney, 1–2 July 1898," in *America's First Battles, 1776–1965.* Edited by Charles E. Heller and William A. Stofft. Lawrence: University Press of Kansas, 1986; O'Toole, G. J. A. *The Spanish War: An American Epoch, 1898.* New York: W. W. Norton, 1984.

— Justin D. Murphy

Santiago de Cuba, Battle of (3 July 1898) *Key naval battle of the 1898 Spanish-American War*

Commodore (soon Rear Admiral) William T. SAMPSON commanded the U.S. Atlantic Squadron. Although junior to Commodore Winfield Scott SCHLEY, the latter agreed when Secretary of the Navy John D. Long asked him to be

Sampson's second in command and lead a flying squadron in Norfolk that could operate either northward or southward in support.

Sampson believed that Admiral Pascual Cervera's squadron of four fast cruisers and three destroyers in the Cape Verdes Islands would coal at San Juan, Puerto Rico, and then operate off the U.S. east coast or in Caribbean waters. Instead, Cervera outfoxed him by reaching Santiago de Cuba on 19 May via Martinique and Curaçao. Sampson, retiring from bombarding San Juan, Puerto Rico, where he thought Cervera would be, ordered Schley to reconnoiter Cienfuegos, where Cervera might be. Learning that Cervera was in Santiago, he ordered Schley there. When Schley reported that bad weather made it impossible for him to coal his ships and would return to Key West to do so, Sampson ordered him to turn around, but Schley did not reach Santiago until 28 May. Sampson joined him there on 1 June and established a semicircular blockade about the entrance to Santiago Channel and at night had his battleships in turn shine their searchlights on it.

A month of humdrum blockade work was replaced by great excitement on 3 July when, after Spanish defeats on land at SAN JUAN HEIGHTS and EL CANEY, Cervera tried to escape. Sampson was on his way in his flagship, the heavy cruiser *New York,* to a meeting with U.S. Army commander ashore Major General William R. SHAFTER when the Spanish began to exit the harbor, and he quickly turned back. Believing that Cervera, in the lead ship, would ram his own ship, the heavy cruiser *Brooklyn,* Schley turned it to starboard, rather than parallel Cervera's course to starboard, his port. After opening distance to some 1,500 yards, however, his and other ships, especially the battleship *Oregon,* destroyed all four Spanish cruisers in a four-hour battle, while other American ships destroyed Cervera's destroyers.

Both Schley (in tactical command during Sampson's absence off Santiago on 3 July) and Sampson claimed victory, even though the latter was engaged but briefly. Both the naval corps and popular opinion split for decades between the two men, with Schleyites holding that it had been wrong to subordinate him to a junior and that he had been in command during Sampson's absence in the battle. However, a court of inquiry held in 1901 at Schley's request upheld Sampson. Destruction of the Spanish cruiser-destroyer squadron in this battle, following the annihilation of one in MANILA BAY on 1 May, effectively ended the SPANISH-AMERICAN WAR.

Further reading: Chadwick, French Ensor. *The Relations of the United States and Spain: The Spanish-American War.* 2 vols. New York: Charles Scribner's Sons, 1911; Coletta, Paolo E. *French Ensor Chadwick: Scholarly Warrior.* Washington: University Press of America, 1980;

Trask, David F. *The War with Spain in 1898.* New York: Macmillan, 1981.

— Paolo E. Coletta

Saratoga, campaign and Battles of (18 January– 17 October 1777) *Pivotal campaign and battle of the American Revolutionary War*

The Saratoga campaign began in the winter of 1776–77, when the British minister of colonies, Lord George Germain, approved a three-pronged summer offensive designed by Major General John Burgoyne to end the war. Centered on upstate New York, the offensive aimed to split the colonies along the Hudson River and isolate rebel strongholds in New England. Forces under Burgoyne were

Burgoyne surrenders at Saratoga, 17 October 1777. *(Library of Congress)*

to move south from Canada along the Lake Champlain–Hudson River corridor and then turn west; Lieutenant Colonel Barry St. Leger was to move eastward into New York from Lake Ontario; and Major General Sir William Howe was to move northward from New York City and join Burgoyne and St. Leger at Albany.

Burgoyne's army of approximately 8,000 moved south in June, defeating the Americans at HUBBARDTON and capturing FORT TICONDEROGA on 6 July. From then on, however, the campaign fell apart. Major General Philip SCHUYLER, the American regional commander, delayed the British advance by all means possible. Rebels destroyed bridges, flooded low-lying trails, and blocked fords with boulders. Burgoyne's men took 22 days to advance the 24 miles to Fort Edward, which Schuyler burned and evacuated before retreating.

Meanwhile, St. Leger's British, Hessian, Tory, and Indian force of only 1,900 men had been halted by Continental army and militia forces at FORT STANWIX (Fort Schuyler), at present-day Rome, New York. Howe, who had also received Germain's approval for his own plan of operation, moved south against Philadelphia. He did leave a corps behind in New York under Major General Henry Clinton, and it advanced up the Hudson above Hyde Park. Howe had informed Burgoyne he would not be driving north, but Burgoyne had proceeded nonetheless. Burgoyne's army was on its own.

Short of food, Burgoyne detached a foraging expedition that was also to raise Loyalist supporters in BENNINGTON, Vermont. A mixed force of Continentals and militia commanded by Brigadier General John STARK crushed the expedition on 16 August, then defeated a relief column, killing more than 200 British soldiers and taking 700 prisoners and their equipment.

Undeterred, Burgoyne maintained his advance, crossing to the west bank of the Hudson on 13 September and continuing south. Crossing the river cut his supply lines to Canada, however, and his army shrank as casualties, malnutrition, and disease took their toll. When he crossed the Hudson, Burgoyne was already down to 6,000 effectives, and he faced an American army of more than 10,000, moving to block his advance.

The Americans, commanded by Major General Horatio GATES following the dismissal on 19 August of Schuyler (who was blamed for the loss of Ticonderoga and the constant retreat), prepared defensive positions near Bemis Heights, New York, under the warchful eyes of Major General Benedict ARNOLD and the Polish engineer Colonel Tadeusz KOŚCIUSZKO. When Burgoyne attacked with three columns on 19 September, Colonel Daniel MORGAN's riflemen and a spirited charge led by Arnold blunted the British assault in the Battle of Freeman's Farm, at a cost of 566 British and 313 American casualties. Burgoyne brought up

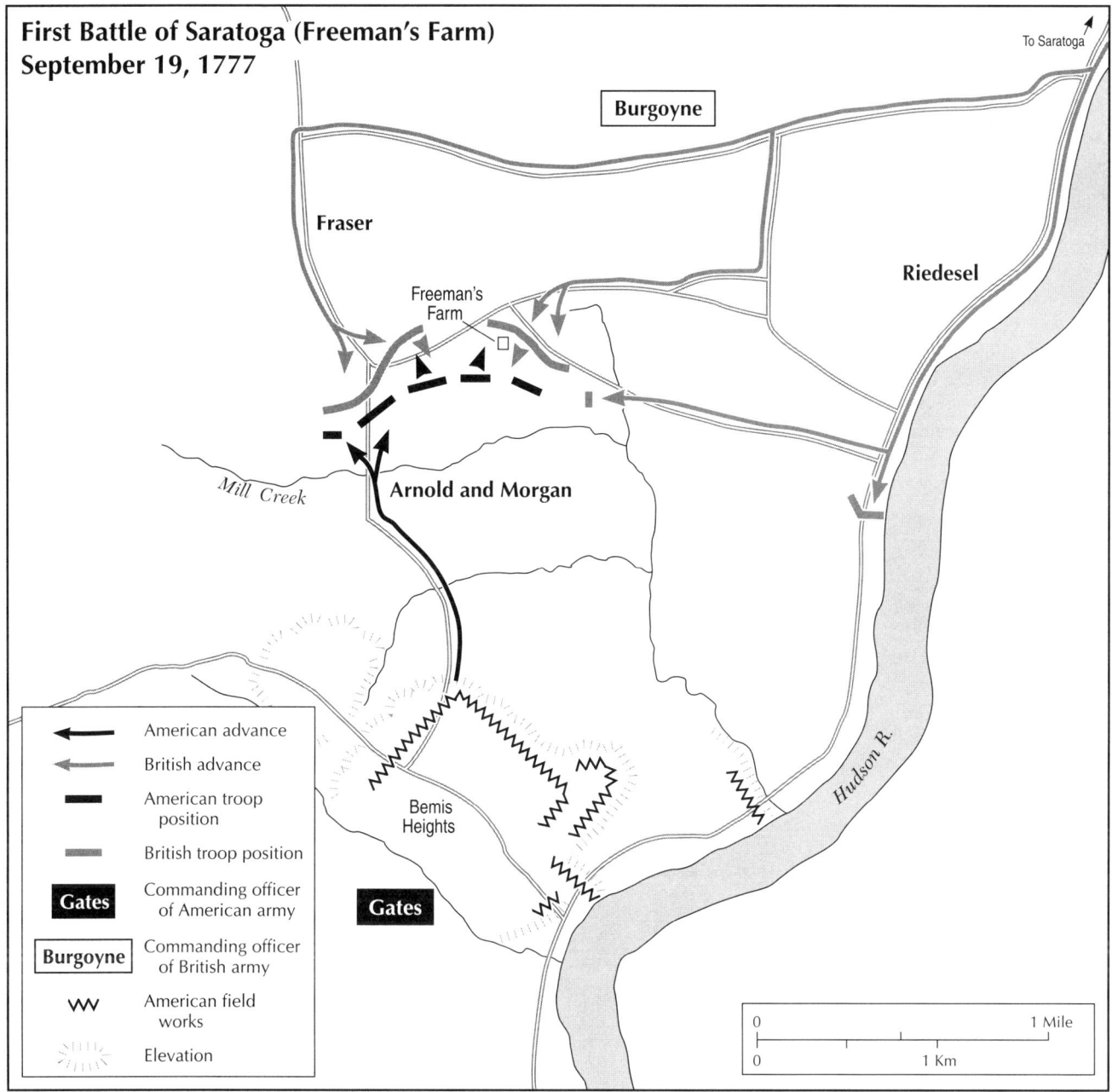

First Battle of Saratoga (Freeman's Farm)
September 19, 1777

To Saratoga

Burgoyne

Fraser

Riedesel

Freeman's
Farm

Arnold and Morgan

Mill Creek

Hudson R.

Bemis
Heights

	American advance
	British advance
	American troop position
	British troop position
Gates	Commanding officer of American army
Burgoyne	Commanding officer of British army
᭢	American field works
	Elevation

Gates

0   1 Mile

0   1 Km

more men and artillery and tried again on 7 October. In the Second Battle of Freeman's Farm (also known as the Battle of Bemis Heights), Arnold led another counterattack, despite having been relieved of command and confined to his tent by Gates. Arnold suffered a leg wound while driving the British from the field at a cost of 631 British and 130 American casualties.

Outnumbered and short of supplies, Burgoyne realized the impossibility of further advance. The proximity of the Americans and the great distance back to Canada precluded retreat, as did the looming onset of winter. Although

Clinton finally had moved north and seized Hudson River Forts Clinton and Montgomery on 6 October, Burgoyne had no knowledge of his advance and little hope of relief. He fell back to Saratoga, New York, and surrendered his army of 5,895 on 17 October 1777.

Saratoga ranks among the worst defeats in the history of the British army, and it marked a decisive turning point in the American Revolutionary War. This American victory convinced France to sign a treaty of alliance with the rebels and to intervene openly on the American side, tipping the scales of war in favor of the United States.

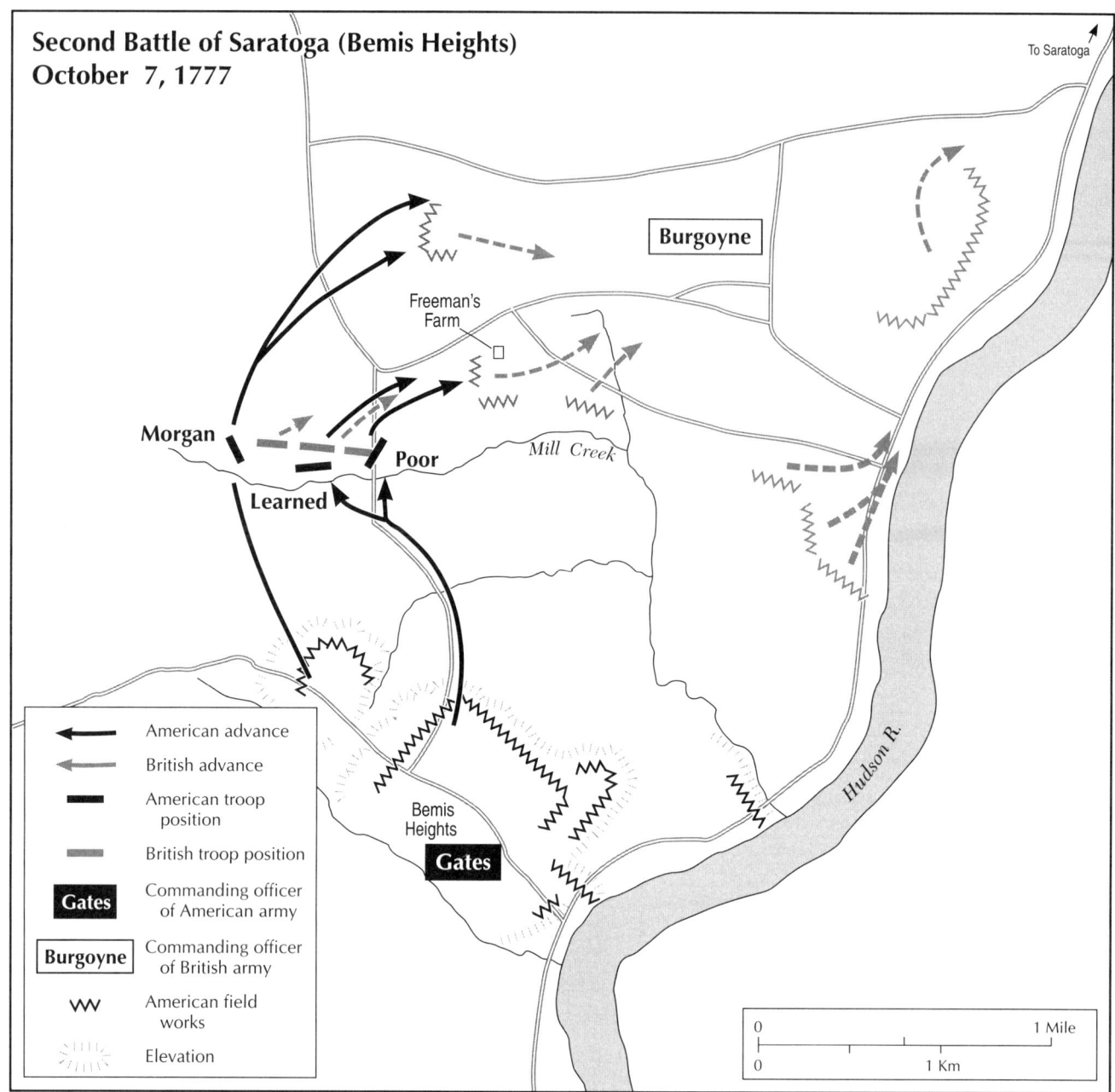

Second Battle of Saratoga (Bemis Heights)
October 7, 1777

To Saratoga

Burgoyne

Freeman's
Farm

Morgan

Poor

Mill Creek

Learned

Hudson R.

Bemis
Heights

Gates

American advance

British advance

American troop
position

British troop
position

Gates Commanding officer
of American army

Burgoyne Commanding officer
of British army

American field
works

Elevation

0   1 Mile

0   1 Km

See also AMERICAN REVOLUTIONARY WAR: LAND OVERVIEW; FRANCE AND THE AMERICAN REVOLUTION.

Further reading: Ketchum, Richard M. *Saratoga: Turning Point of America's Revolutionary War.* New York: Owl Books, 1999; Mintz, Max M. *The Generals of Saratoga: John Burgoyne and Horatio Gates.* New Haven, Conn.: Yale University Press, 1992; Sobel, Robert. *For Want of a Nail: If Burgoyne Had Won at Saratoga.* New York: Stackpole Books, 1997.

— Lance Janda

Savannah, British capture and subsequent Franco-American siege of (1778–1779) *Actions by which the British took and held Savannah during the American Revolutionary War*

The 1778 Franco-American alliance changed the complexity and breadth of the American Revolutionary War. It gave the Americans and their allies naval strength to counter the British navy, providing the means to move troops quickly up and down the American coast. Following the British defeat in the Battle of SARATOGA in late 1777, London adopted a Southern strategy. The American South was closer to British West Indian bases and the British hoped to take advantage of Loyalists there to assume military roles once an area had been conquered. London hoped to subdue the colonies of the South one at a time, beginning with Georgia.

The first blow fell against Savannah, when Lieutenant Colonel Archibald Campbell and 3,500 troops from New York were ordered to cooperate with British commander in Florida, Colonel Augustine Prevost, to capture that port city. Campbell arrived near Savannah in late December 1778 and saw an immediate opportunity to seize it on the 29th. The Patriots had only a small force of Continentals and Georgia militia, under Brigadier General Robert Howe.

Alerted to British intentions, Howe moved his force to a point southeast of Savannah to block the British advance. Although outnumbered four to one, the Americans occupied a defensible position. As the main part of his force moved against the American front, Campbell sent his light infantry up a little-known path around the American right flank and attacked from the rear. The Patriot force soon disintegrated and retreated in disorder. The British then quickly occupied Savannah and eventually drove most American forces out of Georgia.

In September 1779, Admiral Charles-Henri Comte d'Estaing's French fleet of 33 warships and transports carrying 4,000 French soldiers arrived off the Georgia coast. His orders were to assist the Americans if the opportunity arose. D'Estaing decided to strike at Savannah and notified Continental army Major General Benjamin LINCOLN in Charleston of his plans. Lincoln then marched south with a mixed force of 1,300 Continentals and South Carolina militia, supported by cavalry under Brigadier General Kazimierz PULASKI.

After a difficult landing on 11–12 September, the French moved slowly toward Savannah. Early on the 16th, before Lincoln arrived, d'Estaing demanded Savannah's surrender "to the arms of the King of France." French disregard for American authority created difficulties with the Americans throughout the campaign. General Prevost, commanding the Savannah garrison, requested and was granted 24 hours to consider the ultimatum, during which he was reinforced by 800 men, giving him 3,200 regulars and Loyalist militia. The British and Loyalists manned extensive earthworks surrounding the city, centered on Spring Hill, the probable line of advance by an attacking force.

As soon as they discovered Prevost had been reinforced, d'Estaing and Lincoln decided to besiege Savannah. The allied troops then began the construction of siege works. While this was in progress, d'Estaing was forced to yield to a demand by his captains for departure because of shipboard sickness and the approach of hurricane season.

Given this situation, early on 9 October, the Americans and French assaulted the British defenses. They feinted attacks against both British flanks, but, as Prevost had predicted, they made their main effort at Spring Hill. The well-entrenched British defenders cut up both main allied columns and threw them back with heavy losses.

The French then returned to their ships and the American troops retraced their steps to Charleston. Georgia continued under British control the remainder of the war.

See also AMERICAN REVOLUTIONARY WAR: LAND OVERVIEW.

Further reading: Coleman, Kenneth. *The American Revolution in Georgia, 1763–1789.* Athens: University of Georgia Press, 1958; Lawrence, Alexander A. *Storm Over Savannah: The Story of Count d'Estaing and the Siege of the Town in 1779.* Savannah, Ga.: Tara Press, 1979; Searcy, Martha C. *The Georgia-Florida Contest in the American Revolution, 1776–1778.* University: University of Alabama Press, 1985.

— Michael J. Manning

Savo Island, Battle of (9 August 1942) *World War II Pacific theater naval battle, perhaps the worst defeat ever suffered by the U.S. Navy in a stand-up fight*
On 7 August 1942, U.S. landings began on Tulagi and GUADALCANAL, whereupon Japanese vice admiral Mikawa Gunichi, on Rabaul, promptly assembled a force to attack the U.S. invasion site at Guadalcanal.

Mikawa set out on the evening of 7 August with five heavy cruisers, two light cruisers, and a destroyer. He planned to enter in the early hours of the 9th what would become known as Ironbottom Sound, attack Allied warships protecting the invasion force, and then destroy the transports. The operation was risky, because the Japanese ships would have to steam down the "Slot" of the central Solomons during daylight.

The Japanese crews were well trained in night fighting, and they had the superb Long Lance torpedo. Allied crews were inexperienced at night fighting and were exhausted from having been at general quarters for nearly two days. The Allies also suffered from inadequate aerial reconnaissance and mishandled information.

Rear Admiral Victor Crutchley, a Royal Navy officer serving in the Australian navy, commanded Allied screening forces. Two light cruisers and two destroyers between Tulagi and Guadalcanal protected the eastern approach. Six heavy cruisers and four destroyers guarded the two western approaches on either side of Savo Island. Two other destroyers with new radars served as pickets father west. Crutchley commanded the southern group, consisting of the cruisers HMAS *Australia* (flag) and *Canberra,* the USS *Chicago,* and two destroyers. Captain Frederick Riefkohl commanded the northern approach force of three cruisers—the USS *Vincennes* (flag), *Astoria,* and *Quincy*—and two destroyers. Crutchley neither conferred with his cruiser captains before the battle nor issued a battle plan.

At about 6:10 P.M. on 8 August, Admiral Frank J. FLETCHER began to withdraw his covering force of three carriers, depriving the landing force of air cover. Two days of operations had sharply reduced his fighter strength and the carriers were short of fuel, but the real reason was that Fletcher had already lost two carriers and he did not intend to lose another. Fletcher did not consult with his subordinate Rear Admiral Richmond K. TURNER, beforehand. This prompted Turner, convinced there would be no Japanese attack that night, to call a sudden meeting with Major General A. A. VANDEGRIFT and Crutchley aboard his flagship. Crutchley then pulled the *Australia* out of formation. He and the *Australia* did not return in time for the battle.

Mikawa's task force, steaming at high speed in radio silence, escaped detection by the destroyer pickets, both of which were spotted by Japanese lookouts. Beginning at 11:45 P.M., Mikawa's cruiser-launched floatplanes made several flights over the transports and Allied warships, passing back valuable information on Allied dispositions. These flights elicited no response from observers, who assumed the planes were friendly.

Mikawa ordered his one destroyer at the rear of his column to protect his rear from the two American picket destroyers, while the rest of the task force then moved to attack the southern force before turning north to engage the northern force behind Savo Island. Mikawa opened the attack at 1:33 A.M. on the 9th, firing torpedoes. The floatplanes then dropped flares to silhouette the American ships, and the Japanese cruisers opened gunfire. The *Canberra* was hit by two torpedoes and literally taken apart by gunfire. The *Chicago* took one shell hit and a torpedo forward but made for Mikawa's lone destroyer, taking it out of the battle. Mikawa's cruisers then steamed for the second western defense group and engaged it. The cruisers *Astoria, Quincy,* and *Vincennes* were all sunk by gunfire and torpedoes.

Mikawa now committed his only mistake. At 2:40 A.M., fearful of a daylight air attack on his ships from Fletcher's carriers (which were then steaming away from the battle), he ordered his ships to return to Rabaul. In the half-hour Battle of Savo Island he had sunk four Allied heavy cruisers and one destroyer and heavily damaged three other ships. Some 1,270 officers and men were killed and another 709 wounded. Mikawa's ships sustained only light damage and lost only 35 men killed and 57 wounded. On the return trip to Rabaul, however, an American submarine sank one of the heavy cruisers.

All Allied transports and supply ships were unloaded quickly and withdrawn, leaving the marines ashore with scant ammunition for their heavy guns and only a month's supply of food. In not striking at the amphibious force, Mikawa had missed a chance to alter the strategic balance.

See also WORLD WAR II, U.S. INVOLVEMENT: PACIFIC THEATER.

Further reading: Loxton, Bruce, with Chris Coulthard-Clark. *The Shame of Savo: Anatomy of a Naval Disaster.* Annapolis, Md.: Naval Institute Press, 1994; Morison, Samuel Eliot. *History of United States Naval Operations in World War II.* Vol. 5, *The Struggle for Guadalcanal.* Boston: Little, Brown, 1989.

— Spencer C. Tucker

Schlesinger, James R. (1929–) *Economist, strategic analyst, secretary of defense, and first secretary of the Department of Energy*
Born on 15 February 1929 in New York City, James Rodney Schlesinger earned a B.A. and a Ph.D. from Harvard University before teaching economics at the University of Virginia (1955–63).

Next came service at the Rand Corporation as senior staff member (1963–67) and director of strategic studies (1967–69). Schlesinger entered government service in 1969 as assistant director of the Bureau of the Budget. In 1971 he became chairman of the Atomic Energy Commission, and in 1973 he was appointed director of the Central Intelligence Agency. Later that year, President Richard M. NIXON named Schlesinger his secretary of defense. Schlesinger was perhaps the best prepared man ever to hold the position. He served at Defense from 1973 to 1975, a turbulent period marked by the final stages of the VIETNAM WAR, the end of conscription and the shift to reliance on a volunteer military force, and the struggle to maintain an adequate defense establishment in the face of severe downward pressures on the defense budget.

In testimony before Congress, Schlesinger forthrightly portrayed the impact of declining budgets, inflation, and spiraling personnel costs on force structure, modernization, and readiness. The United States, he maintained, could not escape great responsibilities at a time when "military power remains relevant." In his first defense report, he quoted from Proverbs: "Where there is no vision, the people perish." Schlesinger offered a vision of continued American involvement in world affairs based on strength, prudence, and reliability.

Schlesinger's contribution to strategic thinking about nuclear deterrence was essential, exposing as "a dangerous illusion" the idea that, at a time when the United States no longer dominated in nuclear terms, deterrence could reasonably be based on inflicting unacceptable retaliatory damage. "Deterrence is not a substitute for defense," he stressed; nor was the concept of détente.

In 1976 Schlesinger was named assistant to the president to develop a national energy policy. When the Department of Energy was established the following year, he became its first secretary, continuing in that position until 1979. In later years he served as senior adviser to Lehman Brothers, as counselor to the Center for Strategic and International Studies, and as chairman of the Board of the Mitre Corporation.

See also COLD WAR; CONTAINMENT, DOCTRINE AND COURSE OF.

Further reading: Schlesinger, James. *The Political Economy of National Security.* New York: Praeger, 1960; ———. *America at Century's End.* New York: Columbia University Press, 1989.

— Lewis Sorley

Schley, Winfield Scott (1839–1911) *U.S. Navy admiral*

Born on 9 October 1839 in Richfields, Maryland, Winfield Scott Schley was named after the American general Winfield Scott, a friend of his father. He attended St. John's College in Frederick, Maryland, in 1855 and entered the U.S. Naval Academy, Annapolis, in 1856, graduating in 1860.

Schley's first sea duty was aboard the screw frigate *Niagara,* which visited Japan and South Africa. Although from a border slave state, he sided with the Union during the Civil War and served in the North Atlantic Blockading Squadron, the Western Gulf Blockading Squadron, and in riverine duty along the Mississippi. He then toured ports of Central and South America (1864–68). As a lieutenant commander he taught language at the Naval Academy from 1866 to 1969, after which he cruised in the Far East and saw action in gunboat diplomacy in Korea, where he also fought ashore.

From 1872 to 1875, Schley headed the department of foreign languages at Annapolis; he was promoted to commander in 1874. He next served in the South Atlantic Squadron and was a lighthouse inspector. In 1884, after two army expeditions had failed to do so, he rescued Lieutenant Adolphus W. Greely's Arctic expedition.

From 1884 to 1889, Schley was chief of the Bureau of Equipment and Recruiting, and then served on the Lighthouse Board. He later obtained command of the heavy cruiser *Brooklyn.* When the 1898 SPANISH-AMERICAN WAR began, Secretary of the Navy John D. Long appointed Commodore William T. SAMPSON to command the North Atlantic Squadron and Schley to head a flying squadron at

Norfolk that could either defend the northeastern coast of the United States or support Sampson in West Indies waters.

Although senior to Sampson, Schley let him know that he would support him unreservedly. When ordered to seek Spanish rear admiral Pascual Cervera, who commanded four fast cruisers and three torpedo boat destroyers, Schley dallied before Cienfuegos. Worried about his coal supply, he actually started to return for coal at Key West before Sampson, returning from bombarding San Juan, Puerto Rico, where he thought Cervera might be, turned him around. Schley's subsequent blockade of Santiago Channel, within which Cervera's squadron lay, was poor indeed. Worse, when Cervera did sortie, on 3 July 1898, Schley feared that he would be rammed and turned to starboard rather than paralleling the Spanish ships' course to port. He opened distance some 1,500 yards, but he also destroyed all of Cervera's forces. He then claimed that in Sampson's absence from the battle he had been in command of the squadron.

After the war, Schley served as a member of the American commission that planned the transportation home of Spanish troops in Cuba. He ended his naval career in command of the South Atlantic Squadron, 1899–1901. In 1901, upon reading severe criticism of his actions in the Battle of SANTIAGO in a history of the navy by Edgar S. Maclay, he demanded a court of inquiry. Explanations for his actions failed to clear his name, and the Sampson-Schley controversy continued to split the service and the nation. He died in New York City on 1 October 1911.

See also CIVIL WAR, NAVAL OVERVIEW.

Further reading: Chadwick, French Ensor. *The Relations of the United States and Spain: The Spanish-American War.* 2 vols. New York: Charles Scribner's Sons, 1911; Schley, Winfield Scott. *Forty-five Years Under the Flag.* New York: Appleton, 1904; West, Richard S. *Admirals of American Empire: The Combined Story of George Dewey, Alfred Thayer Mahan, Winfield Scott Schley, and William Thomas Sampson.* Indianapolis: Bobbs-Merrill, 1948.

— Paolo E. Coletta

Schofield, John M. (1831–1906) *U.S. Army general*

Born on 29 September 1831 in Gerry, New York, John McAllister Schofield graduated from the United States Military Academy, WEST POINT, in 1853. Commissioned a second lieutenant and assigned to artillery, he served on garrison duty in Florida and taught at West Point. Promoted to first lieutenant, he took a leave of absence to teach physics at Washington University in Saint Louis.

Schofield was promoted to captain, 1st Artillery, in 1861, and entered the Civil War as a major in the 1st Missouri

Infantry, a regiment he later reorganized as the 1st Missouri Light Artillery. Serving on the staff of Brigadier General Nathaniel Lyon, he participated in the capture of Camp Jackson and fought in the Battle of WILSON'S CREEK (for which he later received the Medal of Honor). Appointed brigadier general, U.S. Volunteers in November 1861, he commanded the District of Saint Louis and the Missouri militia.

After a succession of district commands, in November 1862 Schofield was appointed major general of Volunteers and commanded the Army of the Frontier until March 1863, when his appointment to major general lapsed for lack of Senate confirmation. He briefly headed a division in the Army of the Cumberland and in May 1863 was reappointed and confirmed as major general to rank from November 1862. Schofield commanded the Department of Missouri until February 1864, when he assumed command of the Department and Army of the Ohio.

Schofield led his army, XXIII Corps, throughout Major General William Tecumseh SHERMAN's ATLANTA CAMPAIGN. After that city's surrender, Schofield was dispatched to oppose General John B. HOOD's invasion of Tennessee. In November 1864 he escaped disaster at Spring Hill, only to engage Hood's advancing army in a desperate battle at FRANKLIN. Although not victorious, his force severely mauled the Confederates.

Schofield then led XXIII Corps under Major General George H. THOMAS in the rout of Hood's army at NASHVILLE. Promoted directly from captain to brigadier general in the regular army, Schofield moved with his corps to North Carolina to participate in Sherman's final offensive. At the close of the war he was in command of the Department of North Carolina.

Breveted major general in the regular army, Schofield was sent to France to negotiate an end to the French intervention in Mexico. Continuing in the army, he also served as secretary of state from 1868 to 1869, during which time he recommended the acquisition of Pearl Harbor, in the Hawaiian Islands, as a naval base. In 1869, with the inauguration of President Ulysses S. GRANT and the promotions of Sherman to full general and Philip SHERIDAN to lieutenant general, Schofield returned to active duty as a major general. A tireless advocate of military reforms, he served as superintendent of West Point from 1876 to 1881 and presided over the exoneration of Fitz John Porter, who had been wrongly court-martialed after the Second Battle of BULL RUN/MANASSAS. In 1888 he succeeded Sheridan as commanding general of the army.

Promoted to lieutenant general in 1895, Schofield was retired later that year by operation of the law on his 64th birthday. Schofield died at Saint Augustine, Florida, on 4 March 1906.

See also CIVIL WAR, LAND OVERVIEW.

Further reading: McDonough, James L. *Schofield: Union General in the Civil War and Reconstruction.* Tallahassie: Florida State University Press, 1972; Schofield, John McAllister. *Forty-Six Years in the Army.* Reprint. Norman: University of Oklahoma Press, 1998.

— David Coffey

Schriever, Bernard A. (1910–   ) *U.S. Air Force general*
Born on 14 September 1910 in Bremen, Germany, Bernard Schriever moved to the United States in January 1917. Gaining a commission as a second lieutenant in the army on graduation from Texas A&M University in 1931, Schriever after a brief stint in the field artillery switched to the U.S. Army Air Corps. Qualifying as a bomber pilot in 1933, he also flew test aircraft. In 1942 he earned a graduate degree in aeronautical engineering from Stanford University.

Serving with bomber commands in the Pacific during World War II, Schriever flew 63 combat missions. In 1946 he began a rapid rise in the field of advanced weaponry. At air force headquarters, Schriever served as chief of scientific liaison in matériel. He graduated from the National War College in 1950. Promoted to brigadier general in 1953, the following year Schriever joined the Air Research and Development Command with responsibility for accelerating the new Atlas intercontinental ballistic missile (ICBM) program. By 1961 he had brought not one but four major ballistic missile systems to fruition: Atlas; Thor, an intermediate-range missile; Titan, the second generation ICBM; and Minuteman, the solid-fuel silo-launched ICBM. For these weapons, Schriever also managed the development of the launch and tracking facilities as well as the ground support equipment. In this remarkable effort, he oversaw 6,400 research and development contracts, involving 1,500 major companies. In terms of scientific difficulty, budget, and number of personnel, this effort rivaled—and in some respects surpassed—the MANHATTAN PROJECT.

Not only did these missiles give the United States a credible land-based nuclear deterrent force, but they also provided an essential basis for the country's satellite reconnaissance program and, indeed, for its entire space effort. For example, Schriever oversaw the modification of both Atlas and Titan boosters for the Mercury man-in-space initiative and many later programs sponsored by the National Aeronautics and Space Administration (NASA). Promoted to lieutenant general in 1959 and then to general in 1961, Schriever in 1965 became director of the Manned Orbiting Laboratory project to test military defense in space.

Schriever retired from the air force in August 1966. Although this modest officer never received the public recognition that his work warranted, within the air force he was known as "the father of the air force space program." In 1998 he was present for the renaming of Falcon Air Force Base at Colorado Springs in his honor.

See also BALLISTIC MISSILES; MISSILE GAP.

Further reading: Futrell, Robert Frank. *Ideas, Concept, Doctrine: Basic Thinking in the United States Air Force, 1961–1984.* Maxwell AFB, Ala.: Air University Press, 1989; Gorn, Michael H. *Harnessing the Genie: Science and Technology Forecasting for the Air Force, 1944–1986.* Washington, D.C.: Office of Air Force History, 1988; Neufeld, Jacob. "Bernard A. Schriever: Challenging the Unknown," in *Makers of the United States Air Force.* Edited by John L. Frisbee. Washington, D.C.: Office of Air Force History, 1987.

— Malcolm Muir, Jr.

Schuyler, Philip J. (1733–1804) *Continental army general*

Born on 11 November 1733 into a very wealthy and influential Dutch family at Albany, New York, Philip John Schuyler joined the British army during the FRENCH AND INDIAN WAR, obtaining the rank of major. Schuyler was heavily involved as a supply agent during the war, a role that prompted him to travel to England in 1761 to negotiate settlement of colonial claims against the British army.

Schuyler chose the Patriot cause early in the AMERICAN REVOLUTION and represented New York as a delegate to the Continental Congress in 1775. Following the outbreak of the American Revolutionary War, Congress commissioned Schuyler a major general, subordinate only to Continental army commander General George WASHINGTON, in part because of his prior military experience but also because of the need to retain the allegiance of New Yorkers.

Schuyler took command of the Northern Department and oversaw the initial stages of the American invasion of CANADA in 1775. His overly cautious preparations and poor relationship with the many New England soldiers under his command delayed the start of the invasion until October. Plagued by chronic gout, Schuyler fell ill just as the invasion got underway and field command fell to his chief subordinate, Brigadier General Richard MONTGOMERY. Despite his infirmity, Schuyler worked to support the invasion from his headquarters at Albany by obtaining supplies and reinforcements for Montgomery's army in Canada. Nonetheless, when the invasion faltered after a disastrous assault against Quebec on New Year's Eve 1775, Schuyler took the brunt of criticism and found himself embroiled in a struggle for command throughout 1776 with Major General Horatio GATES.

Schuyler retained his tenuous hold over the Northern Department until July 1777, when he was officially cen-

sured and demoted by the Congress following the British army's almost effortless capture of FORT TICONDEROGA. He was replaced by Gates—but not before Schuyler organized widespread resistance to the advancing British under Major General John Burgoyne that proved instrumental in the American victory at SARATOGA.

Schuyler demanded a court-martial to clear his name in the Ticonderoga debacle; he was exonerated on all counts in 1778. He resigned his army commission the following year and resumed his political appointment to the Continental Congress.

After the revolution, Schuyler served multiple terms in the New York Senate and became a United States senator in 1789. Poor health forced his retirement from politics in 1798 and he died on 18 November 1804 at his estate in Albany.

See also AMERICAN REVOLUTIONARY WAR: LAND OVERVIEW.

Further reading: Bush, Martin H. *Revolutionary Enigma: A Re-Appraisal of General Philip Schuyler of New York.* Port Washington, N.Y.: I. J. Friedman, 1969; Gerlach, Don R. *Proud Patriot: Philip Schuyler and the War for Independence, 1775–1783.* Syracuse, N.Y.: Syracuse University Press, 1987.

— Daniel P. Barr

Schwarzkopf, Herbert Norman (1934–) *U.S. Army general*

Born on 22 August 1934 in Trenton, New Jersey, Norman Schwarzkopf was the son of an army brigadier general. A year in Iran in the late 1940s gave him a lasting interest in Islamic culture. He graduated from the U.S. Military Academy, WEST POINT, in 1956. Commissioned in the infantry, in 1964 he earned a master's degree in guided-missile engineering at the University of Southern California.

Schwarzkopf interspersed teaching assignments at West Point with two highly decorated combat tours in the VIETNAM WAR (1965–66 and 1969–70) as a captain and lieutenant colonel, and during 1972–73 he studied international defense and national security issues at the Army War College. Assignments in Alaska, Washington State, Hawaii, Germany, and Washington, D.C., brought promotion to brigadier general in 1978 and major general in 1982. Schwarzkopf distinguished himself in the 1983 U.S. intervention in GRENADA, earning his third and fourth stars in 1985 and 1988.

After a year as deputy army chief of staff, in 1988 Schwarzkopf became commander in chief of the United States Central Command, covering the Middle East and Southwest Asia. Although Schwarzkopf supported President George H. W. BUSH's efforts to improve U.S.-Iraqi

General H. Norman Schwarzkopf, here receiving Kuwait's highest decoration. *(US Air Force)*

ties, by early 1990 he publicly expressed misgivings over the potential Iraqi threat to neighboring Kuwait and Saudi Arabia and held military exercises predicated on an Iraqi invasion of Kuwait—an invasion that indeed occurred in August 1990. Schwarzkopf immediately briefed Bush and the National Security Council on the strengths and weaknesses of the Iraqi armed forces, and he moved his headquarters to the Saudi capital, Riyadh. Schwarzkopf, who enjoyed good relations with his Saudi counterpart, General Khalid Bin Sultan, played a key role in building the 27-nation Arab-Western coalition that implemented the United Nations mandate to restore Kuwaiti sovereignty and effectively served as its leader. The tensions of this role may have contributed to his sometimes explosive temper, one source of his nickname "Stormin' Norman."

Schwarzkopf consistently sought a force of at least 400,000 troops before attacking Iraq; doubted the ability of air power alone to compel Iraq's leader, Saddam Hussein,

to withdraw; and demanded effective latitude in conducting the campaign. Beginning on 17 January 1991, massive air attacks weakened Iraqi defenses, and on 24 February Schwarzkopf launched a western flank attack against Iraqi forces in Kuwait that overwhelmed them within 100 hours. Reportedly over the strong objections of Schwarzkopf, who would have preferred to topple Saddam's regime, on 28 February President Bush declared the campaign over, on the grounds that it had fulfilled the United Nations mandate to liberate Kuwait. Reportedly Bush was unwilling to incur substantial American casualties in a lengthy campaign and sought to preserve Iraq as a buffer against Iran.

Returning to the United States a national hero, Schwarzkopf retired from the army later in 1991. He published a best-selling autobiography in 1992.

See also DESERT SHIELD, OPERATION; DESERT STORM, OPERATION; GULF WAR, CAUSES OF; POWELL, COLIN L.

Further reading: Atkinson, Rick. *Crusade: The Untold Story of the Persian Gulf War.* New York: Houghton Mifflin, 1993; Cohen, Roger, and Claudio Gatti. *In the Eye of the Storm: The Life of General H. Norman Schwarzkopf.* New York: Farrar, Straus & Giroux, 1992; Schwarzkopf, H. Norman. *It Doesn't Take a Hero.* New York: Bantam Books, 1992; Woodward, Bob. *The Commanders.* New York: Simon & Schuster, 1991.

— Priscilla Roberts

Schweinfurt and Regensburg raids (1943) *U.S. Army Air Forces (AAF) strategic bombing raids on Germany during World War II, part of the bomber offensive initiated by the Combined Chiefs of Staff (CCS) on 10 June 1943*

In spite of growing doubts about the effectiveness of largely unescorted daylight bombing raids on Germany, AAF leaders were determined to prove that bombers could win the war. They thus scheduled simultaneous assaults on the ball bearing plants at Schweinfurt and on the Messerschmitt aircraft complex at Regensburg. Success at Schweinfurt would force the Germans to disperse their ball bearing industry, while success at Regensburg would mean a marked reduction in German aircraft production.

Lieutenant General Ira EAKER's Eighth Air Force performed the raids. On 17 August, his bombers made their deepest penetration into the Reich. The 3d Bombardment Division attacked Regensburg and the 1st Bombardment Division struck Schweinfurt. The 1st was to hit Schweinfurt 10 minutes after the 3d struck Regensburg. Both targets were far beyond normal B-17 range. Regensburg was more than 500 miles from the English coast, while Schweinfurt was nearly 400 miles away. The Luftwaffe thus would have ample time to deploy and hit the B-17s coming and going.

AAF planners decided that the Regensburg force would fly on to North Africa. Fighter support could extend only about 40 percent of the way to Regensburg and not much further for the 1st Division against Schweinfurt, which would return the same way it came. Eighteen squadrons of P-47s and 16 squadrons of RAF Spitfires would fly as escorts, but these lacked the drop tanks that allowed long-range capability.

Early morning fog on the 17th forced a change in the plan. The 3d departed at about 6:30 A.M., while the 1st launched five hours later. Of the 3d's 146 B-17s, 122 reached the target and dropped 250 tons of bombs. Four hours later, 184 of the 1st's original 230 bombers dropped 380 tons of bombs on Schweinfurt. Of the total of 376 B-17s, 60 (36 over Regensburg and 24 over Schweinfurt) were lost to enemy fire. More than 25 percent of the 306 bombers that returned were damaged beyond repair. Eighth Air Force lost 601 airmen killed, wounded, or captured. U.S. aircrews claimed 208 German fighters downed; the Germans admitted to 25.

Nearly half of the machine tools in the Regensburg assembly plant were destroyed. Although the plant was back in production in fewer than four weeks, German estimates put overall fighter production losses at 800 to 1,000. Not known at the time, the attack destroyed new jigs for the fuselage of the Me-262 jet fighter, which German managers later speculated delayed the production of these jets by a critical four months. At Schweinfurt, ball bearing production suffered a temporary 50 percent drop-off. After the war, German leaders expressed surprise that the Allies had not immediately sent follow-up raids, but such an effort would have been too costly in terms of bombers lost. In spite of later criticism of the tactics employed, the limited success of the raids had less to do with flaws in the concept of STRATEGIC BOMBING and more to do with the inability of 500- and 1,000-pound bombs to destroy the machine tools.

A far too belated attempt to renew the assault on Schweinfurt on 14 October (so-called Black Thursday) cost the Americans 60 of 291 aircraft and more than 600 aircrew, again with limited success. This second raid left 133 planes so badly damaged that it took four months to bring Eighth Air Force back to anything approaching full strength. The Germans lost perhaps 35 fighters. The attacks proved to Allied leaders that deep raids were impossible without long-range fighter escort.

Nonetheless, the raids forced Germany's already depleted industrial resources to concentrate on antiaircraft artillery and defensive fighter production. They siphoned fighters away from close air support, leading to a dramatic rise in German ground force casualties beginning in the autumn of 1943.

See also LeMAY, CURTIS.

Further reading: Coffey, Thomas. *Decision over Schweinfurt: The U.S. 8th Air Force Battle for Daylight Bombing.* New York: David McKay, 1977; Copp, DeWitt. *Forged in Fire: Strategy and Decisions in the Air War over Europe, 1940–1945.* Garden City, N.Y.: Doubleday, 1982; Craven, Wesley Frank, and James Lea Cate. *The United States Army Air Forces in World War II.* Vol. 2, *Europe: Torch to Pointblank, February 1942 to December 1943.* Reprint. Washington, D.C.: Office of Air Force History, 1983; Middlebrook, Martin. *The Schweinfurt-Regensburg Mission.* New York: Scribner's, 1983.

— William Head

Scott, Hugh L. (1853–1934) *U.S. Army general and chief of staff*

Born on 23 September 1853 at Danville, Kentucky, Hugh Lenox Scott graduated from the U.S. Military Academy, WEST POINT, in 1876. He spent most of his time until 1898 on the United States frontier, becoming a recognized expert on Native American customs and language. Frustrated that during the SPANISH-AMERICAN WAR he was confined to a training assignment, after the conflict he served as Brigadier General Leonard WOOD's adjutant during the military occupation of Cuba and Wood's subsequent tour as military governor of the Philippines. From 1903 to 1906, Scott was governor of the Philippine Sulu Archipelago, gaining substantial combat, negotiation, and administrative experience. Following four years as superintendent of West Point, Scott returned to the Southwest as a unit commander, negotiating various Native American land and other disputes.

In 1914 President Woodrow WILSON, an old friend of Scott's brother, a distinguished Princeton paleontologist, appointed Scott brigadier general and army chief of staff, in which capacity Scott forcefully advocated increased preparedness, defended the new general staff system, and directed the early months of his country's military involvement in World War I. Initially a supporter of a national volunteer force, when such a system proved unfeasible Scott became a convinced convert to conscription, laying the foundations of the wartime SELECTIVE SERVICE system. In 1914 and 1915, early in the Mexican Revolution, Scott functioned as a conduit between Wilson and the Mexican rebel leader Pancho Villa, and he represented the United States in several Southwest border meetings with Mexican authorities to resolve Mexican-American conflicts, including those caused by the 1916–17 American PUNITIVE EXPEDITION INTO MEXICO, which seemed likely to precipitate war just as a German-American crisis peaked.

Scott apparently regarded the Mexican enterprise as an excellent opportunity to train troops for the forthcoming European war, which the United States finally entered in

April 1917. Scott recommended Brigadier General John J. PERSHING to lead the AMERICAN EXPEDITIONARY FORCES (AEF) dispatched to Europe. In his remaining days as chief of staff, Scott quashed politically motivated military appointments and encouraged American annexation of the Virgin Islands. He supported Pershing's opposition to amalgamation of American recruits into Allied units, preferring to keep an all-American force. Retiring in the summer of 1917, he joined the mission headed by former Secretary of War Elihu ROOT that unavailingly attempted to keep Russia in the war. He subsequently visited Britain and France as a military observer and oversaw the training of the 78th Division at Camp Dix, New Jersey. After an active and productive retirement, Scott died in Washington, D.C., on 30 April 1934.

See also BAKER, NEWTON D.; BLISS, TASKER H.; MARCH, PEYTON C.; MILITARY TRAINING CAMPS ASSOCIATION; NATIONAL DEFENSE ACT OF 1916; PLATTSBURG MOVEMENT.

Further reading: Bell, William. *Commanding Generals and Chiefs of Staff 1775–1995: Portraits and Biographical Sketches of the United States Army's Senior Officer.* Washington, D.C.: U.S. Army Center of Military History, 1999; Coffman, Edward. *The War to End All Wars: The American Military Experience in World War I.* New York: Oxford University Press, 1968; Scott, Hugh L. *Some Memories of a Soldier.* New York: Appleton-Century, 1928.
— Priscilla Roberts

Scott, Winfield (1786–1866) *U.S. Army general*
Born on 13 June 1786 in Laurel Branch, Virginia, Winfield Scott entered the army by direct commission in 1807. Sent to New Orleans, he soon quarreled with his nefarious superior, Major General James WILKINSON, and was suspended without pay for a year. Scott first saw action in the WAR OF 1812 at QUEENSTON HEIGHTS, where, unsupported by militia, he was taken prisoner. Soon exchanged and promoted to colonel, he henceforth harbored a distrust of the part-time soldier. He drilled his troops rigorously, training that paid dividends in 1813 when he captured FORT GEORGE (where he was wounded). Promoted to brigadier general in March 1814, Scott led his forces in the Battle of CHIPPEWA. His were the first U.S. troops in the war to stand up to British regulars in an even fight. In the Battle of LUNDY'S LANE, Scott was wounded twice. His outstanding record won the Thanks of Congress, a gold medal, and promotion to brevet major general. Scott's concern for the welfare of his men was unusual for the age.

Following the war Scott wrote a drill manual, *Infantry Tactics,* which remained a standard for decades. He rendered excellent peacetime service by smoothing relations with South Carolina over nullification in 1832 and with Britain after crises along the Canadian frontier in 1837 and 1839. On three occasions he carried out government directives relating to Indians: negotiating in 1832 the Treaty of Fort Armstrong with the Sauk and Fox tribes, campaigning in 1836–37 against the Seminole, and overseeing the Cherokee removal in 1838. On 5 July 1841, Scott was promoted to major general and placed in command of the army, a post he would hold for more than 20 years.

During the 1846–48 MEXICAN-AMERICAN WAR, Scott planned and executed the great 1847 campaign that forced the Mexicans to terms. Commanding the first large American amphibious landing, Scott captured VERACRUZ and moved inland. Outnumbered, advancing into easily defendable terrain, and vulnerable to the guerrilla attacks of a potentially hostile populace, Scott managed, largely by maneuver, to win five major battles and, by strict control of his troops, to placate the Mexican people. This performance, unique in the annals of American military history, brought Scott further awards from Congress (including the brevet rank of lieutenant general) and incurred the enmity of President James K. Polk. Scott's leadership in the war offers enduring lessons as to what a small, well-disciplined professional force can accomplish.

Fearing Scott as a presidential contender, Polk ordered a court of inquiry into Scott's relations with his key subordinates, especially Major General Gideon Pillow, a Polk protégé. Although Scott won exoneration, he forfeited his best chance at the White House. In 1852, as the last Whig presidential candidate, Scott carried just four states. His quarrels with the new secretary of war, Jefferson DAVIS, became legend. In 1859, the aged Scott made the arduous journey to Washington Territory to settle with Great Britain the status of the San Juan Islands.

As civil war approached, Scott made clear to President-elect Abraham LINCOLN his loyalty to the United States. Too old and infirm for campaigning, Scott tried futilely to persuade Colonel Robert E. LEE to accept field command of the U.S. Army. One of the few to anticipate a long war, Scott predicted a three-year struggle with victory for the Union if it employed its superior resources. His strategy, derisively labeled the ANACONDA PLAN, ultimately proved successful.

Treated badly by "the Young Napoleon," Major General George B. MCCLELLAN, Scott left the army on 1 November 1861, after 54 years in its uniform. Scott must rank as one of the greatest American generals. His professionalism elevated standards in the army. Scott retired to WEST POINT, where he wrote his memoirs, died on 29 May 1866, and is buried.

See also CIVIL WAR, LAND OVERVIEW; SEMINOLE WAR, SECOND; WAR OF 1812: LAND OVERVIEW.

Further reading: Eisenhower, John S. D. *Agent of Destiny: The Life and Times of General Winfield Scott.* Norman:

University of Oklahoma Press, 1997; Johnson, Timothy D. *Winfield Scott: The Quest for Military Glory.* Manhattan: University Press of Kansas, 1999; Scott, Winfield. *Memoirs.* 2 vols. New York: Sheldon, 1864.

— Malcolm Muir, Jr.

Second Amendment to the U.S. Constitution *The right to keep and bear arms*

In order to quiet fears that the new central government would encroach upon the rights of the states or the people, the first Congress adopted a Bill of Rights with 12 proposed amendments fashioned primarily by James Madison from 210 proposals introduced in Congress. Of the 12 submitted to the states for ratification, 10 were ratified in 1791 and are commonly referred to as the Bill of Rights. Few of the amendments have generated more controversy than the Second Amendment, which declares: "A well-regulated Militia being necessary to the security of a free State, the right of the people to keep and bear Arms shall not be infringed."

Interpretations of the Second Amendment vary depending upon the standards used to interpret the Constitution. Liberal organizations such as the American Civil Liberties Union commonly make a strict textual argument that emphasizes the first clause, interpreting it as a preamble that conditions the right expressed in the second clause. Thus, the right of the people to keep and bear arms is viewed as guaranteeing only a state's right to maintain an adequate police and military, not as a constitutionally protected right of an individual to possess firearms. On the opposite extreme, conservative organizations such as the National Rifle Association generally emphasize the second clause as an individual right since the Framers understood the "militia" of the first clause to be the armed citizenry, as evidenced by the MILITIA ACT OF 1792, which recognized all able-bodied males between 18 and 45 as the militia. A third standard of interpretation relies upon viewing the Constitution as a living document that provides a framework of government that should be interpreted in the present context. Thus, those who seek to prohibit private ownership of guns emphasize that, because the Framers could never have conceived of modern assault weapons, the Second Amendment does not prevent efforts to ban such weapons and that the violence in modern society demands that restrictions be imposed. Yet this utilitarian frame of reference has its dangers, for gun advocates can just as easily argue that such violence should guarantee the right of law-abiding citizens to bear arms for self-defense.

Equally important in the debate over how the Second Amendment should be interpreted is the question of application: Does it apply only to the federal government, or does it also apply to the states through the Fourteenth Amendment? If the Second Amendment was intended simply to prevent the federal government from prohibiting state militias, then states would be free to regulate, restrict, and even prohibit gun ownership. Thus far, federal courts have not used the Fourteenth Amendment to apply the Second Amendment to the states as they have other provisions of the Bill of Rights. In *Presser v. Illinois* (1886), for example, the U.S. Supreme Court upheld an Illinois law that forbade anyone other than a member of the militia or regular military from drilling or parading with weapons without a license. Gun control advocates also point to *United States v. Miller* (1939), in which the Supreme Court unanimously upheld the National Firearms Act of 1934 and its ban against sawed-off shotguns. Yet this case was based on the premise that because the Second Amendment had been intended to guarantee the militia, it protected only weapons of war, and thus did not apply to sawed-off shotguns. Because the Court also defined the militia as all well-bodied males, *United States v. Miller* could be used by gun advocates to protect the right to own assault weapons.

Since a constitutional change to the Second Amendment is doubtful in the foreseeable future, it will continue to generate controversy, as it is viewed either as "the palladium of American liberty," to paraphrase Justice Joseph Story, or as "a source of embarrassment," to paraphrase several modern scholars.

Further reading: Bogus, Carl T., ed. *The Second Amendment in Law and History: Historians and Constitutional Scholars on the Right to Bear Arms.* New York: New Press, 2001; Levinson, Sanford. "The Embarrassing Second Amendment." *Yale Law Journal* 99 (December 1989): 637–59.

— Justin D. Murphy

Selective Service *U.S. conscription system, used in the 20th century (from World War I through the Vietnam War) to raise manpower*

Since the early 1900s, the question of how to mobilize manpower for war service has been a controversial issue in United States politics. The Civil War experience—the United States drafted young men of military age but permitted the reluctant draftee to pay a substitute a bounty to replace them—was widely criticized as undemocratic and favoring the wealthy. All-volunteer armies were inadequate to meet the demands of a major war, and many supporters of universal military training argued that it could provide a shared national democratic experience, uniting all American young men in common patriotic service.

The first Selective Service Act, passed in 1917, specifically outlawed the old substitute-bounty practice and established a network of thousands of local draft boards empowered to grant deferments to conscientious objectors, the physically unfit, and those with dependents or engaged in vital jobs, on a largely discretionary basis. Although America's involvement in World War I was somewhat unpopular among the general population and military conscription often was resented, the close connection of draft boards with their local communities substantially mitigated public dissatisfaction with the system, facilitating the induction of some 60 to 70 percent of the 5 million men and women who served in the World War I U.S. armed forces, more than 2 million of whom served in Europe.

Conscription quickly was abandoned after World War I, but the experience set the prototype for subsequent Selective Service legislation. In September 1940, as American intervention in the European war (which began in September 1939) seemed increasingly likely, President Franklin D. ROOSEVELT obtained a Selective Service Act from Congress, establishing a draft to raise an army of no more than 900,000 men. Terms of service would be restricted to 12 months, and draftees would be deployed only in the Western Hemisphere. By a one-vote margin, in August 1941 Congress removed these restrictions.

The Washington-based Office of Selective Service supervised the entire draft system, determining national manpower needs and general principles for induction, which a network of local draft boards, numbering 6,400 at the war's peak, then implemented, enlisting more than 13 million men relatively efficiently and fairly. World War II's huge scale and the military demand for manpower meant that relatively few deferments were granted, while discontented workers in vital industrial jobs were liable to be threatened with induction, ordered to either "work or fight."

The original draft law expired in 1947, but within a year growing COLD WAR tensions and political reluctance to authorize universal military training, which the army supported, led Congress to pass the Selective Service Act of 1948, reestablishing the Office of Selective Service under its former director, Major General Lewis B. HERSHEY, and as before leaving implementation to local draft boards. During the KOREAN WAR conscription was reimposed, inducting 550,000 men. Until the 1960s, the harshest criticism of the system was that stringent physical and mental testing of recruits excluded unqualified men from the educational and economic opportunities military service offered.

During the VIETNAM WAR, however, registration and induction under the draft, reimposed in 1965 as the number of American troops in Vietnam skyrocketed, with call-ups rising within a year from 10,000 to 30,000 a month, quickly became a focus of opposition to the war. Student protestors habitually burned draft cards, and reluctant potential draftees often feigned illness, obtained deferments, or manipulated the rules, while the truly intransigent occasionally fled to Canada or other countries rather than serve. Still, only 8,750 of a probable 570,000 draft offenders were ever prosecuted. Hershey's attempts to target student protestors for drafting, revealed in 1967, outraged many opponents of the war and contributed to his dismissal in 1970 by President Richard NIXON. Dr. Curtis Tarr, Hershey's successor, sharply cut back deferments and instituted a random lottery, and draft calls fell to insignificant levels by 1971.

As the war continued, it became apparent that the wealthier and better educated were far better placed to evade the draft than were the poor. For example, only 11 percent of all draft-age men were black, but African-American men comprised 31 percent of all U.S. combat troops in Vietnam. Among recruits overall, the working class and poorly educated made up a disproportionate number of the American fighting force. This was a source of concern both to professional military officers and to those critics who regarded this skewed distribution as unjust and undemocratic.

In 1973, the draft was abolished and the Selective Service system dismantled, although some officers believed that, given the competition numerous other attractive employment opportunities presented, only conscription would succeed in providing the army with well-qualified manpower. After major American diplomatic setbacks in Iran and Afghanistan, beginning in 1980 young men were again required to register with the federal government so that a system would be in place if a draft was reinstituted. As the 21st century began, however, the U.S. armed forces remained voluntary.

See also MILITARY TRAINING CAMPS ASSOCIATION; PLATTSBURG MOVEMENT.

Further reading: Baskir, Lawrence M., and William A. Strauss. *Chance and Circumstance: The Draft, the War, and the Vietnam Generation.* New York: Knopf, 1978; Chambers, John Whiteclay, II. *To Raise an Army: The Draft Comes to Modern America.* New York: Free Press, 1987; Clifford, J. Garry, and Samuel R. Spencer. *The First Peacetime Draft.* Lawrence: University Press of Kansas, 1986; Flynn, George Q. *The Draft, 1940–1973.* Lawrence: University Press of Kansas, 1993; Gerhardt, James M. *The Draft and Public Policy: Issues in Military Manpower Procurement, 1945–1970.* Columbus: Ohio State University Press, 1971; Tarr, Curtis W. *By the Numbers: The Reform of the Selective Service System, 1970–1972.* Washington, D.C.: National Defense University Press, 1981.

— Priscilla Roberts

Selma and Columbus, Battles of (Wilson's Raid)

(March–April 1865) *Two of the largest clashes of Union brigadier general James Wilson's cavalry raid through the Deep South in the waning days of the Civil War. The raiders also captured the fleeing Confederate president, Jefferson Davis, in what was the largest Union cavalry raid of the war.*

Following Confederate defeats in the Battles of FRANKLIN and NASHVILLE in December 1864, the western theater was quiet. This led Union Major General George THOMAS to order WILSON to conduct a cavalry raid into Alabama. He was ordered to destroy the "military school" at the University of Alabama; to capture and destroy the Confederate arsenal and foundry at Selma; and to destroy iron furnaces supplying Confederate arms manufacturing. Wilson also was ordered to take the capital city of Montgomery if possible.

On 22 March 1865, Wilson's force of 13,500 cavalrymen left their winter camps in northwest Alabama, moving southward on three separate routes to mislead the Confederates while remaining close enough to provide each other mutual support if necessary. Meanwhile, a second cavalry raid, initiated from southeast Alabama, successfully diverted attention from Wilson. Wilson's three columns rejoined near Elyton (present-day Birmingham). Confederate lieutenant general Nathan Bedford FORREST commanded the cavalry opposing Wilson but found it difficult to gather his scattered forces because of rain-swollen waterways.

The first clash occurred on 31 March, when Wilson's force drove Forrest's troopers back at Montevallo. Union detachments then destroyed the school at Tuscaloosa and the ironworks at Tannehill and Brierfield, and burned a strategic bridge across the Cahaba River at Centreville. This latter action further complicated Forrest's attempt to gather his various columns. Forrest again failed to stop Wilson at Ebenezer Church along the main road to Selma. His small force of militia—mostly old men and boys—was driven back into the Selma defenses.

Selma's defensive works consisted of earthen redoubts, abatis, redans, and trenches, all in a large semicircle around the city and anchored on the Alabama River. Forrest had only 5,000 troops to garrison defenses designed for 20,000.

On 2 April, Wilson sent one division in a dismounted attack that overran Forrest's right flank, while a second division moved through a swamp and broke through the Confederate left. Wilson and another force then charged down the main Selma road and penetrated the Confederate center. Most Selma defenders quickly capitulated, although Forrest and others escaped across the river. The Union troopers then destroyed the Confederate arsenal and foundry. Wilson's command moved east and easily captured Montgomery but, misled by a poor map, missed a chance to destroy the last Confederate arms factory at Tallassee, Alabama.

The final attempt to stop the Union advance came at Columbus, Georgia, on 16 April. The defenders established a mile-long entrenchment on the Alabama side of the Chattahoochee River garrisoned with small detachments of the Confederate army and militia. This defense was easily overrun, and Wilson took the Confederate Naval Iron Works and destroyed it. Wilson's Raid continued until he reached Macon, Georgia, on 20 April. There he learned of the war's end. His troopers captured Jefferson DAVIS on 10 May. Wilson's losses were minor.

See also CAVALRY; CIVIL WAR, LAND OVERVIEW.

Further reading: Jones, James Pickett. *Yankee Blitzkrieg: Wilson's Raid Through Alabama and Georgia.* Lexington: University Press of Kentucky, 1987; Keenan, Jerry. *Wilson's Cavalry Corps: Union Campaigns in the Western Theater, October 1864 Through Spring 1865.* New York: McFarland, 1998.

— Michael J. Manning

Seminole War, First (1817–1818) *One of the American Indian Wars; it ended Spanish control of East Florida*

Early in the 18th century, a number of Creek Indians in present-day Florida withdrew from the Creek Confederacy. Known as Seminole by whites, they intermarried with runaway slaves and remnants of other Indian bands—Apalachicola, Yamaee, Uchee, Tallahassee, Oconee, and Mikasuki. By 1816 there was a long history of hostility between the Seminole and the United States, in part because of Indian raids on American settlements and in part because the Seminole provided sanctuary to runaway slaves. Added to these provocations was the American desire to oust Spain from Florida.

Fighting began in the spring of 1816 after Brigadier General Edmund P. GAINES constructed Fort Scott on the Flint River in southwestern Georgia and dispatched forces to attack runaway slaves who had established Negro Fort on the site of an old British outpost at Prospect Bluff on the Apalachicola River. When American gunboats opened fire on 27 July, the first round of heated shot struck the fort's power magazine, causing an enormous explosion that killed 270 of the defenders. Although the attack was successful, it led to a series of raids and counterraids that produced the First Seminole War.

After several whites were killed in Seminole raids in 1817, Gaines demanded that Neamathla, chief of Fowltown (just north of the Florida border), surrender those responsible. When Neamathla refused, Gaines dispatched forces under Major David Twiggs, who attacked Fowltown on 12 November, driving the Indians deep into the swamps and in effect beginning the Seminole War.

In retaliation for the burning of Fowltown, the Seminole ambushed a boatload of troops and their dependents traveling on the Apalachicola River on 30 November, killing 36 soldiers, four children, and six of seven women. As a result of this incident, President James Monroe ordered Major General Andrew JACKSON, commander of the Southern Division, to move into Florida and punish the Seminole. Although Jackson was not officially authorized to attack Spanish fortifications, he wrote Monroe on 6 January 1818, asserting that he could occupy Florida within 60 days. When neither Monroe nor Secretary of War John C. CALHOUN responded, Jackson interpreted their silence as an unofficial endorsement of his subsequent actions.

With an army of 4,000 men, half of them friendly Creek, Jackson invaded Florida. After arriving at the site of Negro Fort on 15 March 1818, Jackson rebuilt the fort, naming it Fort Gadsden. Resupplied by boat, Jackson then marched northeast to Fort St. Marks (San Marcos), where on 6 April he demanded that the Spanish commander surrender. Although the commander initially refused, he surrendered the next morning after Jackson mounted a brief attack.

Two days after taking Fort St. Marks, Jackson marched toward Chief Billy Bowlegs's town, some 100 miles to the east on the Suwannee River. Along the way he fought several minor engagements against Seminole and blacks. On 12 April, Jackson's men took Peter McQueen's Red Stick village. On 16 April, the Americans attacked Nero, a settlement of several hundred fugitive slaves led by a mulatto of the same name. Although the outnumbered blacks and Seminole were forced to withdraw, the conflict alerted Seminole in nearby Bowlegs's Town. By the time Jackson's men arrived there at dusk, most of the Indians had fled. Jackson burned the village and reprovisioned his forces with Indian food.

After resting his men for several days, Jackson moved west to Pensacola, which he took on 24 May after only token Spanish resistance. With Spanish authority in Florida in effect extinguished, Jackson installed a provisional U.S. government.

While the invasion obviously had offended Spain, the British were perhaps even more outraged: Jackson had executed two British subjects—former Royal Marine Robert Armbrister and Scots trader Alexander Arbuthnot—for providing arms to the Indians. Although Jackson's arbitrary handling of the situation created an international incident that led Calhoun and the majority of the cabinet to recommend that Monroe censure Jackson, Secretary of State John Quincy Adams defused British anger by blaming Spanish officials for failing to maintain order in Florida.

With the Indians and Spanish defeated, Jackson departed Florida on 30 May. In the aftermath of the First Seminole War, Adams successfully used Jackson's actions as leverage to compel Spain to cede Florida to the United States for $5 million in the Adams-Onís Treaty. Jackson's role in acquiring Florida greatly increased his popularity and paved his way to the White House.

See also AMERICAN INDIAN WARS; CREEK WAR; SEMINOLE WAR, SECOND; SEMINOLE WAR, THIRD.

Further reading: Heidler, David S., and Jeanne T. Heidler. *Old Hickory's War: Andrew Jackson and the Quest for Empire.* Mechanicsburg, Penn.: Stackpole Books, 1996; Owsley, Frank L., and Gene A. Smith. *Filibusters and Expansionists: Jeffersonian Manifest Destiny, 1800–1821.* Tuscaloosa: University of Alabama Press, 1997; Remini, Robert V. *Andrew Jackson and His Indian Wars.* New York: Viking Penguin, 2001.

— A. J. L. Waskey

Seminole War, Second (1836–1842) *Longest and most expensive of all the American Indian Wars*
After the acquisition of Florida from Spain in 1819 there was a growing demand in the United States for the Seminole Indians there to be removed and relocated to the West. The Seminole were neither a single tribe nor a united nation, but a loose association of Native American bands collectively called "Seminoles" by the whites. The Seminole were pressured into signing several treaties that called for their removal. Many Seminole, however, resisted removal.

In June 1835 Seminole resistance turned violent in a skirmish with militia at Hickory Sink. By September many Seminole began to gather around OSCEOLA, the leader of those opposing removal. By December 1835, hundreds of moderate Seminole who accepted removal fled to several U.S. Army forts for protection. These Seminole were soon moved to the West.

The war intensified when a detachment of troops under Major Frances L. Dade was wiped out on 28 December 1835. In what is often referred to as Dade's Massacre, Dade and all but two of his 108-man force were killed. This event began the Second Seminole War. By September 1836 the Seminole controlled most of Florida. However, Oceola became ill with malaria, and Seminole leadership fragmented back into disparate bands.

Brigadier General Duncan Lamont Clinch commanded U.S. forces at the beginning of the war. He was only the first of many, as a parade of commanders and even the territorial governor attempted to defeat the Seminole.

In January 1836 President Andrew JACKSON gave Brigadier General Winfield SCOTT command in Florida.

Scott had little success in employing conventional tactics against the Seminole, and his efforts to force a decisive battle met with failure. In February 1836, Brigadier General Edmund P. GAINES, commander of the Western Department, landed at Tampa. A large Seminole force attacked his 1,100 troops on the Withlacoochee River, besieging it for eight days until Gaines's army was relieved by reinforcements under General Clinch.

Brigadier General Thomas Jesup replaced Scott but, before Jesup arrived, Territorial Governor Richard Keith Call, who was also a militia brigadier general, began a summer campaign against the Seminole. In November 1836 he tried to lure the Seminole into battle at Withlacoochee but they refused and retreated into the swamps. Call accomplished little.

Jesup was probably the most successful of all the generals during the war. On two occasions he seized large groups of Indians, but under flag of truce. He used this technique to capture Osceola on 27 October 1837. Vehemently criticized for this violation of the rules of war, Jesup justified the action as preferable to the Seminole being killed.

On 25 December 1837, in the largest engagement of the war, Colonel Zachary TAYLOR and 1,000 troops engaged and defeated 400 Seminole in a pitched battle at Lake Okeechobee. The battle was inconclusive, however; the Indians and their African-American allies merely withdrew into the swamps. Moreover, Taylor's force suffered 150 casualties, against only 24 for the Indians.

In March 1838 Jesup reversed a previous policy and promised African Americans siding with the Seminole that they would be given freedom if they would join the army and fight against their former allies. Four hundred accepted the offer. Jesup served 18 months before he resigned over criticism of the method he employed to capture Osceola, taking him prisoner under a flag of truce. During that time more than 2,000 Seminole were captured and 300 killed.

Jesup was replaced by Taylor in May 1838. Taylor wanted to divide the disaffected area into 20-square-mile districts, each with a stockade and garrison. Each district commandant would comb his district on alternate days. This strategy might have worked in time, but it would have required substantial resources. When the War Department optimistically ordered Taylor to suspend hostilities and the Indians renewed their raids, Taylor asked to be relieved of his command.

Major General Alexander MACOMB replaced Taylor in April 1839. He burned a number of Seminole villages, but the Seminole continued to attack the troops. Soon, Brigadier General Walker Keith Armistead replaced Macomb. He introduced bloodhounds to track the Seminole, but was largely unsuccessful. Meanwhile, expenses and troop losses from disease continued to mount.

In August 1841 Colonel William J. WORTH took command. For months he relentlessly hunted the Seminole. He used combined navy, army, and marine operations to comb the waterways of the Everglades. He also waged war against Seminole crops, destroying their means of subsistence. The last major action with the Seminole was fought on 19 April 1842 near Fort King. In July 1842, negotiations led to an agreement that allowed the approximately 600 remaining Seminole to stay in far south Florida. The war had cost the United States 1,500 casualties and $20 million.

See also AMERICAN INDIAN WARS; SEMINOLE WAR, FIRST; SEMINOLE WAR, THIRD.

Further reading: Mahon, John K. *History of the Second Seminole War, 1835–1842.* Gainesville: University Presses of Florida, 1967; Peters, Virginia Bergman. *The Florida Wars.* Hamden, Conn.: Archon Books, 1979; Walton, George. *Fearless and Free: The Seminole Indian War, 1835–1842.* Indianapolis: Bobbs-Merrill, 1977.

— A. J. L. Waskey

Seminole War, Third (1855–1858) *The final war to remove the Seminole Indians from Florida to Indian Territory in the West*

In the years following the end of the Second SEMINOLE WAR, the Seminole remained quiet in their swampy south Florida isolation until white encroachment upon their lands renewed the conflict.

The Third Seminole War began on 20 December 1855, when an 11-man reconnaissance patrol led by Lieutenant George Hartsuff was attacked by the Billy Bowlegs Seminole band in the Big Cyprus Swamp. Several members of Hartsuff's patrol were killed. Hartsuff was wounded but managed to return to Fort Myers. The Seminole then raided farms and plantations. Clashes continued through 1856, but neither the 700 regulars available nor militia units were effective against the elusive Seminole in their swamp hiding places.

In the autumn of 1856 Colonel William S. Harney, a veteran of the Second Seminole War, took command of regular army forces in Florida. Employing the same strategy of attrition that had worked in the previous conflict, he ordered constant patrols, even utilizing shallow-draft whaleboats to pursue the Seminole deep into the Everglades.

The Seminole, who numbered only a few hundred people, were badly outnumbered. Exhausted, ragged, and with little ammunition remaining, the Billy Bowlegs band and others accepted removal by terms of an agreement signed in Washington, D.C., on 27 March 1858. However, this entitled the Sam Jones band of fewer than 150 Seminole to remain in the Everglades.

See also AMERICAN INDIAN WARS; SEMINOLE WAR, FIRST; SEMINOLE WAR, SECOND.

Further reading: Covington, James W. *The Billy Bowlegs War, 1855–1858.* Chuluota, Fla.: Mickler House, 1982; Peters, Virginia Bergman. *The Florida Wars.* Hamden, Conn.: Archon Books, 1979.

— A. J. L. Waskey

Semmes, Raphael (1809–1877) *Confederate navy officer*

Born on 27 September 1809 in Charles County, Maryland, Semmes was orphaned at an early age and raised by relatives in Georgetown, District of Colombia. Semmes entered the navy as a midshipman in 1826. There were too many officers for active duty slots, and during his extended leaves of absence Semmes took up the practice of law. In 1837 he was promoted to lieutenant. He served with distinction in the MEXICAN-AMERICAN WAR. Although he lost his ship, the brig *Somers*, during a storm in December 1846, Semmes was cleared in a subsequent court of inquiry; indeed, the court praised him for his seamanship. Semmes subsequently participated in the capture of VERACRUZ and the expedition against Tuxpan, and he accompanied troops ashore in the campaign against Mexico City.

In 1852 Semmes published a book about his experiences, *Service Afloat and Ashore during the Mexican War.* In 1855 he was promoted to commander. After the secession of his adopted state of Alabama, Semmes resigned his commission in the U.S. Navy and joined the Confederate navy in February 1861. He and the Confederate secretary of the navy, Stephen R. MALLORY, met and agreed on the need for the Confederacy to adopt a GUERRE DE COURSE to drive up insurance rates for Northern shippers and dissipate Union naval assets. Given command of the first Confederate commerce raider, the *Sumter*, between June 1861 and January 1862 Semmes took 18 Union merchant ships, most of which he burned.

Advanced to captain in August 1862, Semmes took command of a sloop built in Britain, which he named the *Alabama.* Over a period of nearly two years until July 1864, the *Alabama* took 66 prizes and sank the Union warship

Captain Raphael Semmes on the CSS *Alabama,* 1863.   *(Naval Historical Foundation)*

Hatteras. Estimates of the damage he inflicted range upwards of $6 million. Semmes captured more enemy merchant ships than any other cruiser captain in maritime history. Finally, with his ship in need of overhaul, Semmes put in to Cherbourg, France. Cornered there by the U.S. Navy steam sloop *Kearsarge,* on 19 June 1864 Semmes ordered the *Alabama* out to sea to engage the *Kearsarge.* In the ensuing fight, the *Alabama* was sunk. Semmes was rescued by a British yacht and taken to England, from where he returned to the Confederate States. Promoted to rear admiral in February 1865, he took command of the James River Squadron for three months. When the Confederates abandoned Richmond, on 2 April Semmes scuttled his vessels. He then briefly commanded a naval brigade on land as a brigadier general, surrendering in North Carolina.

Arrested by U.S. authorities after the war and held to await trial, Semmes was released when the Supreme Court refused jurisdiction. Semmes subsequently was briefly a probate judge, professor at Louisiana State Seminary (now Louisiana State University), and a newspaper editor. He then resumed the practice of law. In 1869 he published *Memoirs of Service Afloat* about his Civil War experiences. Semmes died at Point Clear, Alabama, on 30 August 1877.

See also CIVIL WAR, NAVAL OVERVIEW.

Further reading: Roberts, W. Adolphe. *Semmes of the Alabama.* Indianapolis: Bobbs-Merrill, 1938; Semmes, Raphael. *Memoirs of Service Afloat, During the War Between the States.* Baltimore: Kelly, Piet & Co., 1869; Spencer, Warren F. *Raphael Semmes: The Philosophical Mariner.* Tuscaloosa: University of Alabama Press, 1997; Taylor, John M. *Confederate Raider: Raphael Semmes of the Alabama.* Washington, D.C.: Brassey's, 1994; Tucker, Spencer C. *Raphael Semmes and the Alabama.* Abilene, Tex.: McWhiney Foundation Press, 1996.

— Stephen L. Skakandy

Seven Days, Battles of the (Seven Days' Battles)

(26 June–2 July 1862) *Series of attacks by General Robert E. Lee's Confederate forces against Major General George B. McClellan's Union army during the Peninsula campaign in the Civil War*

As MCCLELLAN approached Richmond, he prepared for a long struggle for the capital. After the inconclusive Battle of SEVEN PINES (23 May–1 June 1862) and the wounding of General Joseph E. JOHNSTON, LEE took command of the Southern forces defending the capital.

Lee was determined to take the offensive. In mid-June the Southern cavalry, commanded by Brigadier General James E. B. "Jeb" STUART, rode around the Union army and reported that Major General Fitz-John Porter's V Corps was isolated on the north side of the Chickahominy River. In addition, Stuart's raid encouraged McClellan to shift his supply base to the James River.

Lee left a small force south of the Chickahominy, gambling that the cautious McClellan would not attack. The bulk of his army assembled north of the river to crush Porter. A key part of the plan was for Major General Thomas J. "Stonewall" JACKSON's forces from the Shenandoah Valley to march 120 miles and be in position to hit Porter's right flank by 26 June.

Unfortunately for the Southerners, Jackson's tired troops were late. The first of the Seven Days battles, Mechanicsville (or Beaver Dam Creek), did not begin until midafternoon on 26 June when Major General Ambrose P. HILL's Confederate Division attacked Porter's lines without orders. Porter repulsed all of the Southern attacks with relative ease, but realizing that Jackson was poised on the Union right flank, McClellan ordered V Corps to pull back to a new position at Gaines's Mill.

Lee ordered attacks on the Union position at Gaines's Mill on 27 June, but again the Confederates were unable to coordinate their assaults and Jackson was late. For almost five hours the Union forces repulsed the piecemeal Southern attacks. Finally, in the evening, Lee had all of his forces in position. Brigadier General John Bell HOOD's Texas Brigade penetrated Porter's position with a spirited charge. Although defeated, Porter skillfully withdrew his forces across the Chickahominy during the night of 27 June.

McClellan decided to abandon his position in front of Richmond and pull the army back to the James River. He ordered two of his corps to move immediately, while his other three corps were to cover the retreat. The next day, Lee realized that McClellan was in retreat, and the Confederate commander made new plans to strike the withdrawing Union forces. He ordered Jackson to join Major General John Magruder's troops already south of the Chickahominy; then their combined forces would pin the Union units near Savage's Station.

On 29 June, Jackson—clearly tired and not up to his usual standards—was again late. A nervous Magruder attacked the Union rear guard at Savage's Station, but the Union forces easily repulsed the outnumbered Confederates. This successful defense allowed the bulk of the Union army to move through White Oak Swamp. However, part of the Union army was still strung out on the road from the swamp to Malvern Hill. Lee was determined to attack.

Jackson hit the Union rearguard on the southern edge of White Oak Swamp on 30 June. Two Union divisions repulsed his attack and then pulled back at nightfall. Several miles to the southwest, at the small village of Glendale, a Confederate division under Major General Benjamin Huger struck the Union column midway between Malvern

Hill and White Oak Swamp. Huger was thrown back; but, again, the Southerners had difficulty coordinating their assaults. Later in the day, two more Confederate divisions struck the Federals, but Jackson and Huger did not join in the attacks. Major General Edwin V. Sumner's II Corps parried these assaults and the Federals continued their march to the James.

On 1 June, Lee found a major part of the Union forces positioned on Malvern Hill. He believed that the Union forces, which had been in constant retreat for several days, might be demoralized. However, the Federals held a superb position on Malvern Hill. Porter's corps manned much of the first line, with Sumner's corps in support, and Federal artillery was skillfully positioned to resist any assault. The Confederates attacked on the afternoon of 1 July and suffered a costly rebuff. Nonetheless, McClellan decided to complete his withdrawal, and by 2 July the entire Army of the Potomac was positioned at Harrison's Landing on the James.

The results of the Seven Days' battles offer an interesting contrast. The Federals had skillfully shifted their base while inflicting 20,614 casualties on the Confederates (Union losses were 15,849). However, Lee had maintained the initiative despite being outnumbered, and he had imposed his will on McClellan, removing the threat to Richmond. It was, in fact, a clear Confederate victory.

See also CIVIL WAR, LAND OVERVIEW.

Further reading: Cullen, Joseph P. *The Peninsula Campaign 1862: McClellan and Lee Struggle for Richmond.* Harrisburg, Pa.: Stackpole Books, 1973; Dowdey, Clifford. *The Seven Days: The Emergence of Robert E. Lee.* Lincoln: University of Nebraska Press, 1993; Sears, Stephen W. *To the Gates of Richmond: The Peninsula Campaign.* New York: Ticknor & Fields, 1992.

— Curtis S. King

Seven Pines, Battle of (Fair Oaks) (31 May–1 June 1862) *Civil War battle during the Peninsula campaign, pitting Confederate forces under General Joseph E. Johnston against Major General George B. McClellan's Union Army of the Potomac*

MCCLELLAN began the campaign with a slow advance up the Virginia Peninsula that finally reached the outskirts of Richmond in May. The Union commander made his dispositions to facilitate a link with Major General Irvin MCDOWELL's I Corps to arrive from the north. McClellan decided to place three of his five corps north of the Chickahominy River, while two corps remained south of the river on the direct route to Richmond.

JOHNSTON recognized the vulnerability of the Union position and planned for an attack. Learning that McDowell was not moving to reinforce McClellan, he decided to strike the Federals on the south side of the river. In fact, Confederate Major General Thomas J. "Stonewall" JACKSON's campaign in the Shenandoah Valley had successfully diverted McDowell's troops from the peninsula.

After a reconnaissance on 30 May, Johnston ordered an attack for the next day. He divided his army into two wings. The northern wing under Major General Gustavus W. Smith was to watch Union forces north of the Chickahominy and lend one division to the attack. Major General James LONGSTREET's southern wing was to advance on three separate routes that converged on the lead Union division near the crossroads of Seven Pines. The plan was well conceived, but perhaps too complicated for the raw Southern troops and staffs.

Mistakes in Confederate orders and Longstreet's confusion over routes delayed the attack. Finally, the Southern assault began in the afternoon with an attack by Major General Daniel H. HILL's Division. Hill's troops drove back the lead Union division under Brigadier General Silas Casey. However, because the other Confederate columns had still not developed their attacks, Union IV Corps commander Major General Erasmus D. Keyes was able to bring forward reinforcements to stabilize the line at Seven Pines.

Later in the afternoon, the other Confederate columns began to arrive. Several Confederate brigades waged a back and forth struggle with Major General Philip KEARNY's division south of Seven Pines. To the north, near a village called Fair Oaks, a major battle developed with an assault by Major General W. H. C. Whiting's Confederate division. Johnston, who had been occupied with untying the confused Southern columns, personally took control of the battle at Fair Oaks, but he was severely wounded toward dusk. McClellan took little part in the battle, except to direct Major General Edwin V. Sumner to send reinforcements across the swollen river to help Keyes.

After Johnston's wounding, Major General Gustavus Smith took command of the Confederate forces. He planned to renew the attack the next day, with the main effort at Seven Pines. D. H. Hill's division again led the attack on 1 June, but the Federals repulsed his efforts. By the end of the day, the Confederates were back in their original positions and the battle had ended in a stalemate.

The Confederate attack at Seven Pines had almost succeeded, but the Federals recovered and remained close to Richmond. Perhaps more importantly, Johnston's wounding and Smith's subsequent removal brought General Robert E. LEE to command the Confederate forces defending Richmond.

See also CIVIL WAR, LAND OVERVIEW; JACKSON'S SHENANDOAH VALLEY CAMPAIGN; SEVEN DAYS, BATTLES OF THE.

Further reading: Catton, Bruce. *Mr. Lincoln's Army.* Garden City, N.Y.: Doubleday, 1951; Cullen, Joseph P. *The Peninsula Campaign, 1862: McClellan and Lee Struggle for Richmond.* Harrisburg, Pa.: Stackpole Books, 1973; Newton, Steven Harvey. *Joseph E. Johnston and the Defense of Richmond.* Lawrence: University of Kansas Press, 1989; Sears, Stephen W. *To the Gates of Richmond. The Peninsula Campaign.* New York: Ticknor & Fields, 1992.

— Curtis S. King

Shafter, William R. (1835–1906) *U.S. Army general*
Born on 16 October 1835 in Kalamazoo County, Michigan, William Rufus Shafter taught school prior to the Civil War. Commissioned a first lieutenant in the 7th Michigan Infantry, he served in the Peninsula campaign and was wounded in the May 1862 Battle of SEVEN PINES (in 1893 he received the Medal of Honor for his actions there). Returning to duty as a major in the 19th Michigan in September 1862, Shafter moved to the western theater. He was captured at Thompson's Station, Tennessee, in March 1863. Exchanged in May, Shafter was promoted to lieutenant colonel in June.

In April 1864 Shafter was appointed colonel of the 17th United States Colored Infantry. He remained with this unit for the duration of the war, leading it in action in the Battle of NASHVILLE in December 1864. In March 1865 he received a brevet to brigadier general of U.S. Volunteers, and after the war mustered out of that organization.

As with many of the civilian officers who performed well during the war, Shafter received several strong recommendations for a permanent appointment in the regular army. Offered a regular commission, he entered the army as lieutenant colonel of the 41st Infantry, one of the newly authorized African-American regiments. In the 1869 army reorganization, the 41st was merged into the new 24th Infantry. Over the next 10 years, he served with great distinction on the Texas frontier, supporting the campaigns of Colonel Ranald MACKENZIE and leading extensive scouting expeditions in the trans-Pecos country. Shafter's arduous service in West Texas brought him the sobriquet "Pecos Bill."

In 1879 Shafter was promoted to colonel of the 1st Infantry, a position he held for nearly 18 years. During that time, he commanded his regiment in the Dakotas, Texas, and Arizona. He also served as superintendent of the Recruiting Service in New York and was post commandant at Angel Island, California, from 1891 to 1897. Promoted to brigadier general in May 1897, Shafter took command of the Department of California.

With the outbreak of the 1898 SPANISH-AMERICAN WAR, Shafter was appointed major general of Volunteers and given command of V Corps for the invasion of Cuba.

Weighing more than 300 pounds and suffering from gout, Shafter directed the campaign against Santiago de Cuba, which included the attacks on SAN JUAN HEIGHTS and EL CANEY. Although his campaign was successful, Shafter bore the brunt of criticism for the numerous problems that confounded the U.S. effort in Cuba, most of which were beyond his control.

Following the war, Shafter returned to his regular duties in California. He retired from the army in 1901 and settled near Bakersfield, California, where he died on 12 November 1906.

See also AMERICAN INDIAN WARS; CIVIL WAR, LAND OVERVIEW; MERRITT, WESLEY; MILES, NELSON A.; RED RIVER WAR.

Further reading: Carlson, Paul H. *"Pecos Bill": A Military Biography of William R. Shafter.* College Station: Texas A&M University Press, 1989; Cosmas, Graham H. *An Army for Empire: The United States Army in the Spanish-American War.* College Station: Texas A&M University Press, 1994.

— Angela Kidd

Shaw, Robert Gould (1837–1863) *U.S. Volunteer officer during the Civil War*
Born on 10 October 1837 in Boston, Massachusetts, Robert Gould Shaw was the only son of wealthy reformers and early supporters of militant abolitionism. Raised for a life of privilege and principle, Shaw spent his youth in Massachusetts, New York, and Europe. Although he did not fully share his parents' antislavery zeal, Shaw developed into an ardent patriot. In 1856 he enrolled in Harvard College, but withdrew in 1859 to join an uncle's business in New York City.

Anticipating the breakup of the Union, Shaw enlisted in the 7th New York State Militia. When the Civil War began in April 1861, Shaw and his regiment rushed to Washington, D.C., for 30 days of emergency service. On 10 May, Shaw received a second lieutenant's commission in a three-year regiment, the 2d Massachusetts Volunteer Infantry. During the next 20 months, he suffered two slight wounds and rose to captain while serving in the Shenandoah Valley and at ANTIETAM.

On 26 January 1863, the Union War Department authorized Governor John A. Andrew of Massachusetts to raise a model black regiment, the 54th Massachusetts Volunteer Infantry. Andrew offered the colonelcy of the regiment to Shaw. After some hesitation, Shaw committed himself to proving that African Americans could fight as well as whites did.

Following three months of training, the 54th Massachusetts sailed from Boston on 28 May 1863 for the

Department of the South. Unsatisfied with garrison duty, Shaw succeeded in getting the 54th incorporated into the army that Brigadier General Quincy Adams Gillmore assembled to besiege CHARLESTON, South Carolina.

The late afternoon of 18 July 1863 found the 54th Massachusetts on Morris Island with the bulk of Gillmore's forces. Gillmore intended to storm FORT WAGNER, which blocked his advance to the mouth of Charleston Harbor. Asked if the 54th Massachusetts would spearhead the assault, Shaw eagerly accepted.

Shaw led his regiment through concentrated cannon and rifle fire and became the first man to mount Fort Wagner's south curtain. Confederate riflemen shot him down as he urged his men forward. The 54th Massachusetts matched Shaw's courage, suffering 272 casualties out of 622 personnel engaged.

Instead of returning Shaw's remains to his friends, Confederate troops dumped him into a common trench with 25 dead black soldiers. The circumstances of Shaw's death and burial transformed him into a Union martyr.

See also AFRICAN AMERICANS IN THE MILITARY; CIVIL WAR, LAND OVERVIEW.

Further reading: Duncan, Russell, ed. *Blue-Eyed Child of Fortune: The Civil War Letters of Colonel Robert Gould Shaw.* Athens: University of Georgia Press, 1992; Duncan, Russell. *Where Death and Glory Meet: Colonel Robert Gould Shaw and the 54th Massachusetts Infantry.* Athens: University of Georgia Press, 1999; Emilio, Luis F. *A Brave Black Regiment: The History of the 54th Massachusetts, 1863–1865.* New York: Da Capo Press, 1995; Wise, Stephen R. *Gate of Hell: Campaign for Charleston Harbor, 1863.* Columbia: University of South Carolina Press, 1994.

— Gregory J. W. Urwin and William Dwight Peveler

Shays, Daniel (ca. 1747–29 September 1825) *Former Continental army officer who led SHAYS'S REBELLION*
Born in 1747 at Hopkinton, Massachusetts, Daniel Shays grew up in relative poverty. After working as a farm laborer, he moved to Pelham in Hampshire County, where he acquired a small farm. In the aftermath of the Battles of LEXINGTON AND CONCORD, Shays joined the Continental army and fought in several engagements during the American Revolutionary War over the next five years. After the Battle of BUNKER HILL, Shays was cited for bravery by his commander and promoted to sergeant. Commissioned a captain of the 5th Massachusetts Regiment in January 1777, Shays fought under Major Generals Benedict ARNOLD and Horatio GATES at SARATOGA and under Brigadier General Anthony WAYNE at STONY POINT.

After leaving the Continental army in 1780, Shays returned to Pelham, where he soon became involved in protests against the Massachusetts legislature's increase of poll and personal property taxes. As with many other small farmers in western Massachusetts, Shays had difficulty meeting the requirement that taxes be paid in specie (hard currency). On at least one occasion he was almost imprisoned for debt. When the Massachusetts legislature adjourned in July 1786 without addressing the grievances of western farmers, Shays joined in popular protests. Although the radical demagogues Samuel Ely and Luke Day were responsible for inciting the rebellion that bears his name, Shays's military experience in the American Revolutionary War made him a natural leader of the insurgents who sought to end foreclosures on farmlands.

On 26 September 1786, Shays led a force of approximately 500 men to Springfield, forcing the Massachusetts Supreme Court to adjourn. When Governor James Bowdoin responded by mobilizing some 4,400 militiamen to put down the rebellion, Shays attempted to seize the federal arsenal at Springfield on 25 January 1787, but was driven off by artillery. Defeated at Petersham on 4 February, Shays fled to Vermont. Eventually pardoned on 13 June 1788, Shays moved to New York State, where he lived in relative obscurity until his death in Sparta on 29 September 1825.

See also AMERICAN REVOLUTIONARY WAR: LAND OVERVIEW.

Further reading: Morris, Richard B. *The Forging of the Union, 1781–1789.* New York: Harper & Row, 1987; Palmer, Davew R. *1794: America, Its Army, and the Birth of the Nation.* Novato, Calif.: Presidio Press, 1994.

— Justin D. Murphy

Shays's Rebellion (August 1786–4 February 1787)
Tax protest in Massachusetts
After the American Revolutionary War, Massachusetts, like many other states, suffered from a postwar depression that hit western farmers especially hard. Making matters worse, in the early 1780s the Massachusetts government not only increased poll and personal property taxes but also required that taxes be paid in specie (hard currency), rather than the paper money issued by the state. Farmers would have had difficulty paying the tax anyway, but the specie requirement made it next to impossible. Since the Massachusetts Constitution of 1780 retained property qualifications for voting and appointive judges, small farmers in western Massachusetts, who had long resented the political dominance of eastern merchants, felt as if an unresponsive government was destroying them. By 1786, debt prosecutions in Hampshire County were 262 percent higher than they had been before independence, while in Worcester County there were 4,000 debt suits, and debtors accounted for 80 percent of county inmates.

When the Massachusetts legislature adjourned in July 1786 without redressing their grievances, farmers in western Massachusetts rebelled. Although the rebellion was soon named after Daniel SHAYS, it owed its outbreak more to Samuel Ely, an itinerant preacher who had been leading protests since 1782, and Luke Day, a brevet during the Revolutionary War who by 1786 commanded his own militia.

On 15 August 1786, a Worcester town meeting condemned the state's tax policies; one week later (22–25 August), a Hampshire County convention attended by delegates from 50 towns demanded that foreclosures cease. A mob of farmers prevented court proceedings in Northampton on 31 August and in Worcester on 5 September. In response, Governor James Bowdoin dispatched 600 militia under Major General William Shepherd to Springfield to protect the state supreme court.

It was at this stage that Shays, who had been a captain in the Continental army, was chosen by insurgents to command a "militia." On 26 September, Shays led 500 rebels to Springfield, confronting the state militia and forcing the supreme court to adjourn. Because the Confederation government maintained an arsenal in Springfield, Congress authorized Major General Henry KNOX to intervene. Before Knox could act, however, Bowdoin dispatched 4,400 militiamen (raised in eastern counties) under Major General Benjamin LINCOLN and Brigadier General Rufus PUTNAM to crush the rebellion.

Although Putnam, who had commanded Shays during the war, tried to mediate, Shays departed Worcester on 26 December with 1,200 men, expecting to join forces with Day for an attack on Springfield. Day did not arrive as expected, but Shays went ahead with his attack on Springfield on 25 January 1787. Shepherd's artillery drove the Shaysites off, leaving four dead. After arriving in Springfield on 27 January, Lincoln hurriedly organized his forces and attacked Shays at Petersham on 4 February, capturing 150 rebels, dispersing the rest, and effectively ending the rebellion.

In the aftermath of the fighting, Massachusetts voters elected John Hancock as governor and a majority of moderates to the legislature. The new legislature not only offered pardons to everyone except Shays, Day, and two other leaders, but also met the rebels' demands for lower court costs, reduced taxes, and exemptions on household goods and trade tools. Convicted and sentenced to death in absentia, Shays was pardoned eventually on 13 June 1788. Most important, Shays's Rebellion convinced leaders like George WASHINGTON and James Madison of the need for a stronger central government, thus adding greater urgency to the Constitutional Convention.

See also CONSTITUTION OF 1789.

Further reading: Morris, Richard B. *The Forging of the Union, 1781–1789. The New American Nation Series.* New York: Harper & Row, 1987; Palmer, Davew R. *1794: America, Its Army, and the Birth of the Nation.* Novato, Calif.: Presidio Press, 1994.

— Justin D. Murphy

Shelby, Joseph O. (1830–1897) *Confederate cavalryman*

Born on 12 December 1830 at Lexington, Kentucky, Joseph Orville Shelby studied at Transylvania University from 1845 to 1848 and then spent an additional year of study in Pennsylvania. Returning to Lexington, he engaged in the manufacture of rope. In 1852 Shelby migrated to Berlin, Missouri, then to Waverly, where he became a leading hemp planter and rope manufacturer. In 1854 Shelby began active participation in the Border Wars in order to protect his slavery-related assets.

On the outbreak of the Civil War, Shelby rejected a commission in the U.S. Army and raised a company of volunteers for the Missouri State Guard. During the war, Shelby swiftly rose from captain of a company of volunteers to a colonelcy and command of a brigade (June 1862). He led Confederate units in Arkansas, Missouri, Texas, Louisiana, and Mississippi.

In 1863, Shelby directed a brigade of cavalry on a raid of Union-controlled Missouri, thereby gaining recognition as one of the finest cavalry commanders of the Civil War. With typical panache and courage, the dashing raider and his troops covered an astonishing 1,500 miles in 36 days, all the while eluding 50,000 Union soldiers. The longest cavalry raid of the war, it resulted in 600 Federal casualties and only 150 for his own force. He destroyed 10 Union forts, inflicted $800,000 worth of property damage, and captured 600 rifles, 300 wagons, and 6,000 horses and mules. More important, Shelby prevented Union reinforcements from aiding major offensives in Tennessee. The raid won Shelby belated promotion to brigadier general and command of a division of cavalry (December 1863). Although he held a regular commission, Shelby frequently operated in more of a partisan role.

Throughout the war, Shelby brilliantly carried out all the functions of the mounted service, including reconnaissance, fighting as dismounted cavalry, screening retreats, supplying and recruiting for the army, and guarding the flanks. His use of guerrilla tactics and his execution of black United States soldiers, however, diminished his reputation. Following the war, in June 1865 Shelby led several hundred men into Mexico, where he offered his services to Emperor Maximilian, who declined but gave Shelby land, which Shelby occupied until Maximilian's fall. He returned to Missouri in 1867 and became a Republican. Shelby served as a U.S. marshal until his death in Adrian, Missouri, on 13 February 1897.

See also CAVALRY; CIVIL WAR, LAND OVERVIEW.

Further reading: Fellman, Michael. *Inside War: The Guerrilla Conflict in Missouri During the American Civil War.* New York: Oxford University Press, 1989; Oates, Stephen B. *Confederate Cavalry West of the River.* Austin: University of Texas Press, 1961; O'Flaherty, Daniel. *General Jo Shelby: Undefeated Rebel.* Chapel Hill: University of North Carolina Press, 1954.

— Dallas Cothrum

Shenandoah, CSS *Confederate navy commerce raider*
Purchased in England in September 1864 by Confederate navy agent James D. Bulloch, the *Shenandoah* was the world's first composite auxiliary screw steamship. Launched in August 1863 as the *Sea King*, it displaced 1,160 tons and measured 230 feet by 32 feet. Capable of a speed of nine knots under steam, it had one screw.

On 8 October, a British merchant captain took the *Sea King* out on what appeared to be a merchant voyage, but then proceeded to Funchal, Madeira, to rendezvous with a supply ship that had sailed the same day with Lieutenant Commander James I. Waddell and the remainder of its crew and armament. Armed with four eight-inch and two 12-pounder smoothbore cannon, and two 32-pounder rifled guns, it had a crew of 73 men. On 19 October 1864, Waddell officially commissioned the ship the *Shenandoah* and began to cruise in search of Union vessels.

The *Shenandoah* took six Union prizes in the Atlantic. It arrived in Melbourne, Australia, on 25 January 1865 and there underwent repairs, sailing again on 18 February. It then cruised the whaling grounds in the Pacific Ocean and off Alaska. Its long stay at Melbourne allowed U.S. whaling vessels in the South Pacific to disperse, but Waddell then took the *Shenandoah* north and decimated the Union whaling fleet.

Waddell refused to believe reports of the end of the war. Only after he had left northern waters did he accept as proof a report from an English captain on 2 August 1865. Waddell then sailed the *Shenandoah* 17,000 miles to Liverpool without stopping at any port. Arriving on 6 November 1865, he turned over his ship to British authorities. The *Shenandoah* was the only Confederate warship to sail around the world. In all, it captured 38 Union vessels, 32 of which Waddell burned. Damage to Union shipping amounted to some $1.36 million.

In 1866 the *Shenandoah* was sold to the sultan of Zanzibar. Renamed *El Majidi*, it was damaged in a hurricane off Zanzibar in April 1872; that September, it sank in the Indian Ocean while on the Zanzibar-Bombay route.

See also CIVIL WAR, NAVAL OVERVIEW.

Further reading: Hearn, Chester G. *Gray Raiders of the Sea: How Eight Confederate Warships Destroyed the Union's High Sea Commerce.* Camden, Me.: International Marine Publishing, 1992; Horn, Stanley F. *Gallant Rebel: The Fabulous Cruise of the C.S.S. Shenandoah.* New Brunswick, N.J.: Rutgers University Press, 1947; Morgan, Murray. *Dixie Raider: The Saga of the C.S.S. Shenandoah.* New York: Dutton, 1948; Waddell, James T. *C.S.S. Shenandoah: The Memoirs of Lieutenant Commanding James I. Waddell.* Edited by James D. Horan. New York: Crown, 1960.

— Spencer C. Tucker

Shenandoah Valley campaigns, 1864 *Major Civil War campaign*
With its fertile farms and numerous mills and as a key communications route via the Valley Turnpike, the Shenandoah Valley was much contested during the war. This north-south route was formed by the Blue Ridge Mountains to the east and Alleghenies to the west. From the beginning of the Civil War until the last half of 1864, the Confederacy controlled this strategically critical area.

In the spring of 1864 Union major general Franz Sigel commanded the Department of West Virginia, stationed at the northern end of the Shenandoah Valley. Although his primary mission was defensive, in April Sigel received orders from Lieutenant General Ulysses S. GRANT to move south, up the Shenandoah Valley (the river runs north) and divert attention from a thrust by Brigadier General George CROOK with three brigades of some 6,000 men from the Kanawha Valley, which had as its goal destruction of the Virginia and Tennessee Railroad bridge over the New River. Another cavalry force of 2,000 men, under Brigadier General William Averell, would strike the salt works at SALTVILLE. Both objectives were located in southwestern Virginia. Grant's overall objective was to reduce General Robert E. LEE's ability to wage war by destroying his communications and food resources.

Sigel's force of about 6,500 infantry and cavalry started out on 30 April 1864. His objective was Staunton, where he could threaten the Virginia Central Railroad. Major General John C. BRECKINRIDGE, who commanded about 5,000 Confederates in the valley, opposed him. A battalion of about 250 cadets from the Virginia Military Institute (VMI) augmented Breckinridge's forces. The antagonists clashed at New Market on 15 May. Breckinridge had hoped to hold the cadets in reserve, but they had to be used, and they helped turn the tide of battle. Sigel managed the battle badly and was out maneuvered and defeated. The Confederate victory bought some time for the valley and allowed the wheat crop to be harvested. It also protected the western terminus of the Virginia Central Railroad. Losing that supply line might have forced Lee to dispatch part of the Army of Northern Virginia to the valley when Grant's pressure on him at SPOTSYLVANIA COURTHOUSE was the heaviest.

But in June, with his army backed into Petersburg, Lee dispatched Lieutenant General Jubal EARLY with most of II Corps to thwart Federal efforts in the valley and, it was hoped, relieve some of the pressure on Lee's front. In the meantime, Major General David Hunter replaced Sigel. After defeating Confederate forces in the Battle of Piedmont, Hunter moved to Lexington, where his men burned VMI. But Hunter's advance was checked on 18 June by Early's newly arrived command at Lynchburg.

Hunter now withdrew, and Early had the initiative. His force moved into Maryland, threatening Harpers Ferry and exacting cash ransoms from Hagerstown and Frederick. The Confederates defeated a rag-tag Federal force commanded by Major General Lew Wallace at Monocacy, Maryland, but Wallace had bought time for Union authorities to ready Washington's defenses. Early pushed on to the outskirts of the capital before turning away. He returned to the valley in mid-July.

In order to deal with Early and complete the destruction of the valley, Grant turned to his aggressive cavalry commander Major General Philip SHERIDAN, and bolstered the Valley forces with major additions from the Army of the Potomac. Sheridan commanding the newly formed Army of the Shenandoah, ordered a general advance that caused Early to withdraw south from Bunker Hill, West Virginia, to Fishers Hill, Virginia. A week later, Sheridan sent cavalry to seize or destroy livestock and grain in the area. This initiated the scorched-earth policy that characterized Sheridan's Shenandoah Valley campaign.

On 17 September Grant approved Sheridan's new plan to attack. Learning of this decision, Early quickly ordered his troops to consolidate at Winchester. On 19 September, Union cavalry initiated the Battle of the Opequon, also known as the Third Battle of Winchester. After a delayed start by Sheridan, a late afternoon cavalry charge down the Martinsburg Road sent Confederate troops streaming south through Winchester to establish a new line at Fishers Hill, 20 miles away. The cost to Sheridan was about 5,000 casualties, to Early's 4,000.

On 22 September Sheridan attacked Early's poorly defended left flank, causing another rout, in which Early lost more than 1,300 men, mostly prisoners, and 11 guns. Union losses were only about 400 men. By 25 September, Early was in Port Republic.

On 6 October, Sheridan started back north, continuing to carry out Grant's directive to destroy the valley's crops. The Federals devastated the valley, destroying 400 square miles of prime farmland. They burned 2,000 barns and 70 grain mills, ran off 4,000 cattle, and butchered 3,000 sheep.

Sheridan stopped at Cedar Creek and Early returned to Fisher's Hill. On 19 October Early struck before dawn and caught the Union army off guard. Within two hours, the Confederates had sent the Federals scurrying north toward Winchester. Sheridan, receiving reports of firing from the direction of Cedar Creek, left Winchester at 9:00 A.M. and arrived on the scene at 10:30 A.M. during a lull in the fighting. He quickly assessed the situation, stopped the retreat, and re-formed the Union lines. Around 4:00 P.M. he attacked Early. Union cavalry turned the Confederate left, and by 5:30 P.M. the battle was over. Union losses were about 5,700 men, while the Confederates lost almost 3,000. From 19 September to 19 October Sheridan had won three major battles, earned the rank of permanent major general, and gained national fame.

In November Sheridan sent cavalry into Fauquier and Loudoun Counties on a raid of destruction. In four days his men caused more than $1 million worth of damage.

Although Sheridan's Shenandoah Valley campaign was essentially over, Early's army would not be truly eliminated until its defeat at Waynesboro on 2 March 1865.

See also CIVIL WAR, LAND OVERVIEW; SALTVILLE MASSACRE.

Further reading: Heatwole, John L. *The Burning: Sheridan in the Shenandoah Valley.* Charlottesville, Va.: Rockbridge Publishing, 1998; Mahon, Michael G. *The Shenan- doah Valley, 1861–1865: The Destruction of the Granary of the Confederacy.* Mechanicsburg, Pa.: Stackpole Books, 1999; Morris, Roy, Jr. *Sheridan: The Life and Wars of General Phil Sheridan.* New York: Crown, 1992; Osborne, Charles C. *Jubal: The Life and Times of General Jubal A. Early.* Chapel Hill, N.C.: Algonquin Books, 1992.

— Richard C. Halseth

Shepherd, Lamuel C., Jr. (1896–1990) *U.S. Marine Corps general and commandant*

Born on 10 February 1896 in Norfolk, Virginia, Lamuel Cornick Shepherd graduated from Virginia Military Institute in 1917. Securing a commission as a second lieutenant in the marines, he was ordered to France during World War I in June 1917 with the 5th Marine Regiment, which was attached to the 2d Army Division. Shepherd fought in the Battle of Belleau Wood and in the AISNE-MARNE, SAINT-MIHIEL, and MEUSE-ARGONNE offensives. He was wounded three times.

In 1919 Shepherd won promotion to captain. A year later he became aide to the Marine Corps commandant, General John Archer LEJEUNE. During the 1920s he held a variety of assignments, including service aboard battleships *Nevada* and *Idaho* (1922–25), commanding the Sea School in Norfolk (1925–27), and serving with the 4th Marines in Tsientsin and Shanghai, China (1927–29).

After graduating from the field officer course at Quantico, Virginia, in 1930 he was assigned to Haiti. Shepherd was promoted to major in 1932 and to lieutenant colonel in 1935. Returning from Haiti in 1934, he served on the Marine Corps Institute staff for two years. After graduating from the Naval War College at Newport, Rhode Island, in 1937, Shepherd was selected to command the 2d Battalion of the 5th Marines at Quantico. In 1940 he was promoted to colonel.

After the United States's entry into World War II, in 1942 Shepherd formed the 9th Marine Regiment as part of a new 3d Marine Division. A year later he became a brigadier general and assistant commander of the 1st Marine Division, which he led in the Battle of Cape Gloucester. In July–August 1944, he commanded the 1st Provisional Marine Brigade in the reconquest of GUAM. The following year, as a major general, Shepherd commanded the 6th Marine Division in the OKINAWA campaign. In 1946 he became assistant commandant of the Marine Corps. From 1948 to 1950 he was the commandant of Marine Corps Schools at Quantico, Virginia.

In 1950, after being promoted to lieutenant general, Shepherd took command of the Fleet Marine Force in the Pacific. During the KOREAN WAR he served on General of the Army Douglas MACARTHUR's staff and participated in the planning of the INCHON LANDING, but he did not secure command of X Corps as he had hoped.

In January 1952 Shepherd won promotion to general and became commandant of the Marine Corps. The first marine commandant to be a member of the Joint Chiefs of Staff, Shepherd enjoyed a cordial working relationship with the other members. He was largely successful in minimizing the impact of President Dwight D. EISENHOWER's reductions in defense spending and a shift to reliance on nuclear weaponry.

Shepherd retired from the marines in January 1956, but a few months later he returned to chair the Inter-American Defense Board. He retired again in September 1956. Shepherd died in La Jolla, California, on 6 August 1990.

See also WORLD WAR I, U.S. INVOLVEMENT; WORLD WAR II, COURSE OF U.S. INVOLVEMENT: PACIFIC THEATER.

Further reading: Heinl, Robert Dobs, Jr. *Soldiers of the Sea: The United States Marine Corps, 1775–1962*. Baltimore: The Nautical & Aviation Publishing, 1991; Millett, Allan R. *Semper Fidelis: The History of the United States Marine Corps*. New York: Macmillan, 1990.

— Anna Boros

Sheridan, Philip H. (1831–1888) *U.S. Army general*

Born on 6 March 1831, reportedly to Irish immigrant parents in Albany, New York, Philip Henry Sheridan was raised in Ohio. He entered the U.S. Military Academy, WEST POINT, with the class of 1852, but a disciplinary suspension delayed his graduation until 1853. Posted to the infantry, he served on the frontier as a second lieutenant until the eve of the Civil War. He was promoted to first lieutenant in March 1861 and to captain in May of that year.

In the early stages of the war Sheridan served as chief quartermaster and commissary for the Army of Southwest Missouri. He joined Major General Henry W. HALLECK's staff during the slow advance on CORINTH. Sheridan entered the Volunteer establishment in May 1862 as colonel of the 2d Michigan Cavalry, but in July he was appointed brigadier general, U.S. Volunteers. After commanding an infantry division in the Battles of PERRYVILLE and STONES RIVER, he was promoted to major general of Volunteers, to rank from December 1862. In September 1863 his division was shattered in the Battle of CHICKAMAUGA, but his men rebounded that November at CHATTANOOGA, spearheading the unauthorized assault that drove the Confederates from Missionary Ridge.

When Lieutenant General Ulysses S. GRANT became overall commander of Federal forces, he selected the fiery Sheridan to command the Army of the Potomac's cavalry corps. Throughout the spring and summer of 1864, Sheridan's troopers battled the once-superior Confederate cavalry, with mixed results. Sheridan claimed victory at Yellow

Major General Philip H. Sheridan *(Library of Congress)*

Tavern, where Confederate cavalry commander Major General J. E. B. STUART was mortally wounded. When Confederate forces under Lieutenant General Jubal EARLY threatened Washington, D.C., Grant created the Middle Military Division and placed Sheridan in command. Sheridan's Army of the Shenandoah defeated Early's forces at Winchester and Fisher Hill but was surprised at Cedar Creek. Sheridan, who was away when the latter battle began, galloped from Winchester and helped to rally his army to victory. He then proceeded to lay waste to the Shenandoah valley, depriving the Confederates of much needed supplies.

Promoted to brigadier general in the regular army in September 1864 and to major general that November, he rejoined Grant's army with the bulk of his command on the PETERSBURG front. Sheridan played a major role in the final defeat of General Robert E. LEE's Army of Northern Virginia. His troopers crushed the Confederates at FIVE FORKS and Sayler's Creek before trapping Lee's army near APPOMATTOX Court House.

Following Lee's surrender, Sheridan was dispatched to Texas with a large force to discourage French intentions in Mexico. He remained in Texas as commander of the Fifth Military District during Reconstruction, until his heavy-handed management brought his removal. In March 1869, when Grant became president and General William T. SHERMAN filled the post of commanding general, Sheridan assumed command of the Military Division of the Missouri with the rank of lieutenant general. He thus became chief prosecutor of the federal effort against the Indians of the West. In 1870 he went to Germany as an official observer of the Franco-Prussian War.

Sheridan succeeded Sherman as commanding general in 1884, and in June 1888 he became only the third full general (four-star rank) in the history of the U.S. Army. He died at Nonquitt, Massachusetts, on 5 August 1888.

See also AMERICAN INDIAN WARS; CIVIL WAR, LAND OVERVIEW; CROOK, GEORGE; CUSTER, GEORGE A.; MACKENZIE, RANALD S.; MERRITT, WESLEY; SHENANDOAH VALLEY CAMPAIGN.

Further reading: Morris, Roy. *Sheridan: The Life and Wars of General Phil Sheridan.* New York: Crown, 1992; Hutton, Paul Andrew. *Phil Sheridan and His Army.* Lincoln: University of Nebraska Press, 1985; O'Connor, Richard. *Sheridan the Inevitable.* Indianapolis: Bobbs-Merrill, 1953.

— Roger W. Caraway

Sherman, Forrest P. (1896–1951) *U.S. Navy admiral*
Born on 30 October 1896 in Merrimack, New Hampshire, Forrest Percival Sherman attended the Massachusetts Institute of Technology before graduating from the U.S.

Naval Academy, Annapolis, in 1917. During World War I he served on destroyers in European waters.

After the war, Sherman became involved in naval aviation. In 1922, he completed flight training at Pensacola and then served in a squadron on the aircraft carrier *Saratoga.* He returned to Pensacola as a flight instructor in 1924 for two years. Sherman graduated from the Naval War College in 1927, then served on carriers and taught at Annapolis. Sherman became known as a naval thinker through articles published in the Naval Institute *Proceedings.* He held a variety of assignments before serving in the War Plans Division of the Office of the Chief of Naval Operations (CNO) from 1940 to 1942.

In 1942 Captain Sherman commanded the carrier *Wasp* and fought in battles off GUADALCANAL. Following the loss of his ship to a Japanese torpedo attack in September 1942, Sherman became chief of staff to the commander of Pacific Fleet Air Force. Promoted to rear admiral in April 1943, he was then deputy chief of staff and head of the War Plans Division for Pacific Fleet commander Admiral Chester NIMITZ.

After the end of the war, Sherman took command of Carrier Division 1 in October 1945, but two months later he was promoted to vice admiral and made deputy CNO, in which role he defined the navy's position in interservice rivalries following the war and also was an architect of the 1947 National Security Act. A strong advocate of a U.S. naval presence in the Mediterranean Sea, during 1948–49 Sherman commanded the naval forces there that soon were designated Sixth Fleet.

Promoted to admiral, in November 1949 Sherman was appointed CNO, marking the triumph of aviation in the navy. Sherman worked to strengthen the fleet and to advance research into nuclear power and oversaw navy activities at the beginning of the KOREAN WAR. He died in Naples, Italy, while on a diplomatic mission, on 22 July 1951.

See also COLD WAR.

Further reading: Barlow, Jeffrey G. *Revolt of the Admirals: The Fight for Naval Aviation, 1945–1950.* Washington, D.C.: Naval Institute Press, 1994; Palmer, Michael A. *Origins of the Maritime Strategy: American Naval Strategy in the First Postwar Decade.* Washington, D.C.: Naval Historical Center, 1988; Reynolds, Clark G. "Forrest Percival Sherman, 2 November 1949–22 July 1951," in *The Chiefs of Naval Operations.* Edited by Robert W. Love, Jr. Annapolis, Md.: Naval Institute Press, 1980: 208–32.

— Spencer C. Tucker

Sherman, William Tecumseh (1820–1891) *U.S. Army general*
Born on 8 February 1820 in Lancaster, Ohio, William Sherman graduated from the United States Military

Academy, WEST POINT, in 1840. Commissioned a second lieutenant of artillery, he served in Florida. In 1841 he earned promotion to 1st lieutenant. Serving in California during the MEXICAN-AMERICAN WAR, Sherman won a brevet to captain; the substantive rank followed in 1850.

In 1853 Sherman resigned his commission to become a banker in California. In 1957 his parent bank failed. He briefly practiced law in Kansas, and from 1859 to 1861 he was superintendent of the Louisiana Military Seminary (later Louisiana State University). Sherman had great affection for the South, but with Louisiana's secession, he resigned his position and moved to Saint Louis.

In May 1861 Sherman reentered the U.S. Army as colonel of the new 13th Infantry and commanded a brigade in the First Battle of BULL RUN/MANASSAS. He entered the Volunteers as a brigadier general in August 1861 and was sent to the West. However, his eccentric behavior prompted questions about his sanity. Temporarily relieved, he returned to duty in February 1862.

Commanding a division under Major General Ulysses S. GRANT, Sherman and his men were surprised at SHILOH but rallied to share in the victory. Slightly wounded in the battle, he was promoted to major general of Volunteers. Sherman developed a close friendship with Grant during this period, and by summer he had emerged as Grant's chief subordinate.

In July 1862 Sherman became military governor of Memphis. During the preliminary actions against VICKSBURG, he was defeated at Chickasaw Bluffs and served under Major General John McClernand in the capture of Arkansas Post. Sherman led XV Corps, Army of the Tennessee, in the capture of Vicksburg, after which he was promoted to brigadier general in the regular Army. In October 1863 he assumed command of the Army of the Tennessee, but its performance at CHATTANOOGA did not compare favorably with that of the Army of the Cumberland. Still, most of Grant's praise went to Sherman.

In February 1864 Sherman conducted the MERIDIAN CAMPAIGN in Mississippi; but, when Grant became Union general in chief, Sherman assumed direction of the Military Division of the Mississippi—essentially, overall command of the western theater. In May 1864 Sherman launched a campaign against General Joseph E. JOHNSTON's Confederate Army of Tennessee. Pushing to ATLANTA, Sherman fought a series of battles with Johnston's replacement, General John B. HOOD, finally capturing the city in September. For this he received the Thanks of Congress and promotion to major general in the regular army.

Sending part of his force to deal with Hood in Tennessee, Sherman commenced his MARCH TO THE SEA. A firm believer in total war, Sherman cut a swath of desolation through Georgia and presented Savannah to President Abraham LINCOLN as a Christmas gift. Turning

northward in 1865, Sherman carried his campaign of destruction to the Carolinas. On 26 April he accepted Johnston's surrender in North Carolina.

In 1866 Sherman received promotion to lieutenant general; in 1869, when Grant entered the presidency, Sherman became commanding general with full (four-star) rank, only the second man after Grant to serve at that grade in the U.S. Army. During his years in command, the army successfully prosecuted the AMERICAN INDIAN WARS in the West; these wars had largely ended by the time of his retirement in 1884. Rejecting several requests to run for the presidency, Sherman settled in New York City, where he died on 14 February 1891.

See also CIVIL WAR, LAND OVERVIEW; SALTCREEK PRAIRIE RAID.

Further reading: Kenneth, Lee. *Sherman: A Soldier's Life.* New York: HarperCollins, 2001; Marszalek, John F. *Sherman: A Soldier's Passion for Order.* New York: Free Press, 1993; Sherman, William T. *Memoirs of General William T. Sherman.* 2 vols. Reprint. Bloomington: Indiana University Press, 1957.

— Mark N. Calandra

Shiloh/Pittsburg Landing, Battle of (6–7 April 1862) *Bloody Civil War battle in which Confederate forces tried but failed to reverse the course of early Union successes in the West*

After Major General Ulysses S. GRANT captured FORT HENRY and FORT DONELSON in February 1862, his department commander, Major General Henry W. HALLECK, ordered him to encamp at Pittsburg Landing on the Tennessee River and await his own arrival as well as that of the armies of Major General Don Carlos BUELL and Major General John POPE. Then Halleck himself would personally lead the combined force against CORINTH, Mississippi, about 30 miles from Pittsburg Landing.

Meanwhile, Confederate commander General Albert Sidney JOHNSTON used Halleck's delay to regroup after recent defeats and concentrate at Corinth all his available forces along with heavy reinforcements from all over the western Confederacy. Johnston sought to crush Grant's army before it could be joined by the other Union forces. On 2 April 1862, with scouts reporting Buell's army only a few days' march from Grant, Johnston advanced.

The detailed plan of attack, drawn up by Johnston's second in command, General Pierre G. T. BEAUREGARD, called for Confederate troops to make a 25-mile approach march on 3 April, then attack at dawn on the 4th. Heavy rain, inexperienced troops, and Beauregard's too complicated plan combined to slow the march and force postponement of the attack until the morning of 6 April.

The "Hornets' Nest," Battle of Shiloh, 6 April 1862. Painting by Lewis Prang.   *(Library of Congress)*

Remarkably, Grant did not expect the attack, despite scouting reports of Confederates in the area, and his troops were largely unprepared when the Confederates struck. In those divisions immediately in the path of the onslaught, some Federals fled in confusion at the sudden attack, but most resisted stoutly.

Contrary to Johnston's directions, Beauregard had arranged the three corps of the Confederate army one behind the other in long thin lines spanning the battlefield. This arrangement, coupled with the wooded terrain, led to the breakdown of command at higher levels. The attack was pressed forward by assorted regiments in piecemeal assaults, urged on by generals the troops did not know.

The Union divisions, however, were deployed for convenience of camping rather than for strength of defense, and had difficulty supporting each other or forming a continuous front. The Confederate attackers repeatedly forced them back. On the Union left-center, defenders took position in a peach orchard, a nearby "sunken" road, and adjoining thickets that the Confederates were soon calling "the Hornets' Nest" for the swarms of bullets that poured out of them.

With his army stalled before this position in midafternoon, Johnston personally directed a charge against the peach orchard, sustaining a leg wound from which he bled to death. Still, the Hornets' Nest held out against furious Confederate assaults until 4:30 P.M., when it collapsed and several thousand Union soldiers were captured.

Grant, meanwhile, had been organizing a final line of resistance directly in front of the landing. A fifth of his men were casualties and as many more cowered in abject terror on the riverbank, intent on nothing but escape. One of his six divisions had, through its commander's misunderstanding of Grant's orders, failed to move the six miles from Crump's Landing to help the rest of the army as it fought for its life. Despite this, Grant's final line was his strongest and most compact. All the army's reserve and siege artillery was on line, and additional fire support came from two gunboats in the river. The errant division was at last approaching, and the lead division of Buell's army had arrived on the far bank of the river and a handful of its

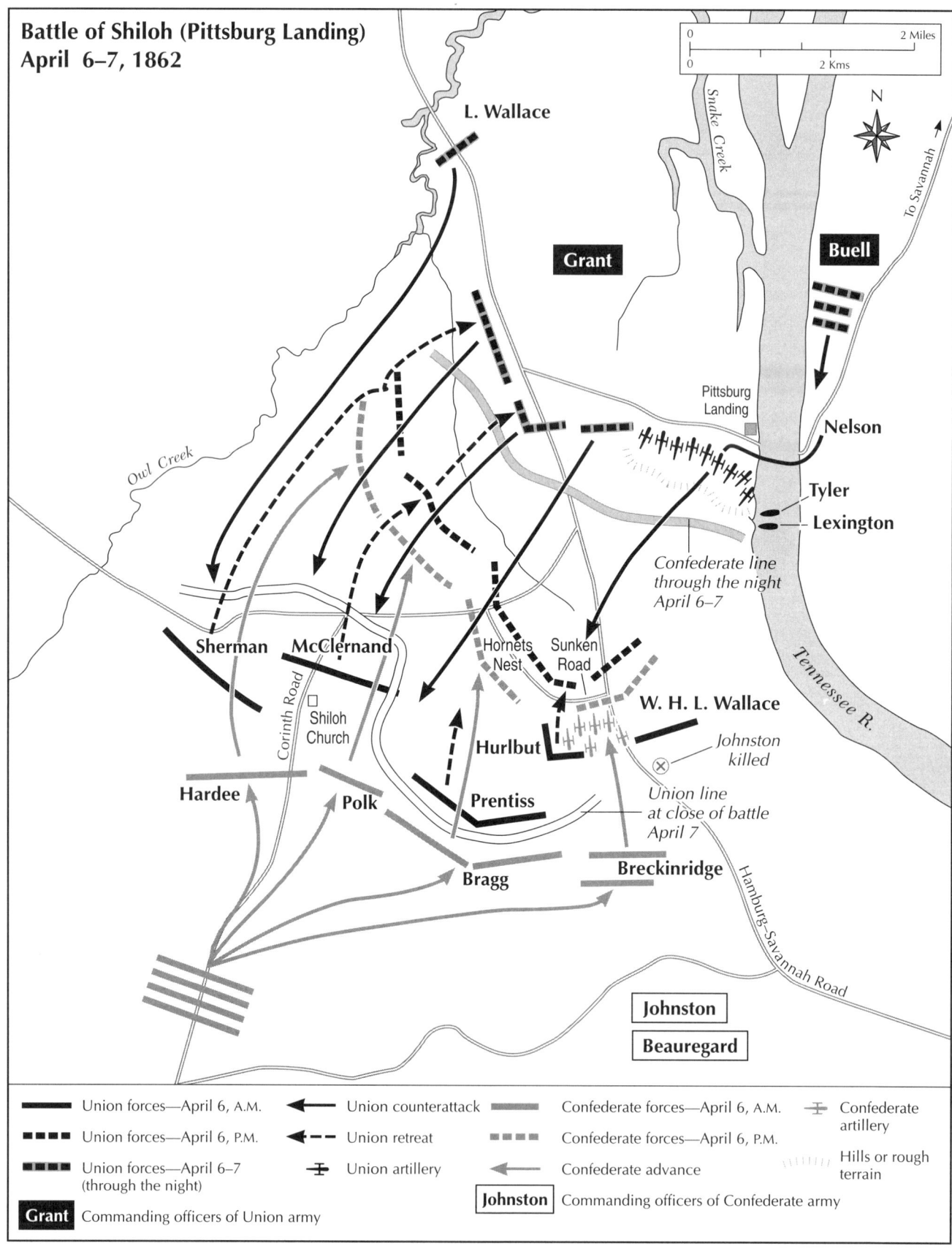

Battle of Shiloh (Pittsburg Landing)
April 6–7, 1862

troops, having been ferried across, were even now coming into line.

In the event, the final line was never tested. Beauregard, who assumed command upon Johnston's death and directed the battle from a command post in the rear, ordered the attack suspended with about a half hour of daylight left.

The following morning Grant, now reinforced by all of Buell's army, launched a counterattack and, in heavy fighting that lasted until midafternoon, drove the Confederates back out of the Union encampments they had captured. Beauregard ordered his devastated army back to Corinth; Grant's force was too battered to mount a vigorous pursuit.

The country was shocked by the unprecedented casualties of the battle that some called Pittsburg Landing and others Shiloh, after a small country church on the battlefield. Union losses were 1,754 killed, 8,408 wounded, and 2,885 captured; Confederates casualties were 1,723 killed, 8,012 wounded, and 959 missing. Grant was temporarily semidiscredited. Still, the Confederacy had struck an all-out blow and yet failed to arrest the flow of Union successes in the West.

See also CIVIL WAR, LAND OVERVIEW.

Further reading: Daniel, Larry J. *Shiloh: The Battle that Changed the Civil War.* New York: Simon & Schuster, 1997; McDonough, James L. *Shiloh: In Hell Before Night.* Knoxville: University of Tennessee Press, 1977; Simpson, Brooks D. *Ulysses S. Grant: Triumph over Adversity, 1822–1865.* Boston: Houghton Mifflin, 2000; Sword, Wiley. *Shiloh: Bloody April.* Dayton, Ohio: Morningside, 1995.

— Steven E. Woodworth

ships of the line *Largest warships of the age of sail*
These three-masted square-rigged vessels, boasting massive firepower, were capable of standing in the main battle line. They also were known as line-of-battle ships. Such vessels were ship rigged, but larger than FRIGATES. By the time of the American Revolutionary War, most had 74 or more guns.

The United States built one ship of the line during the war. The *America* (74), never entered American service, however. Launched in November 1782, it was presented to France in September 1782 and completed in June 1783. Congress authorized six ships of the line in 1799, but only one—the *Franklin*—was even begun. All were canceled in 1800. It was not until the WAR OF 1812 that the United States again built a ship of the line. Congress authorized four 74-gun vessels, but none were in service by war's end. The *Independence* was launched in June 1814 and commissioned in July 1815; the *Washington* was launched in October 1814 and commissioned in August 1815; the

Franklin was launched in August 1815 and commissioned thereafter; and the *Columbus* was launched in March 1819 and commissioned that September.

In April 1816, Congress authorized a total of nine ships of the line "to rate not less than 74 guns each." This *Delaware*-class program was later cut back; only four were built and only two were commissioned as 74s: the *Delaware*, launched in October 1820 and commissioned in February 1828, and the *North Carolina*, launched in 1820 and commissioned in 1825. The *New Hampshire* (the renamed *Alabama*) was commissioned in 1864 as a storeship. The *New York* and the *Vermont* (the renamed *Virginia*) both were launched but never commissioned.

The *Ohio* (74), launched in 1820 and commissioned in 1838, was considered one of the finest 74s in the world. The *Pennsylvania* (120), launched in 1837 and commissioned in 1841, was the largest sailing warship ever in the U.S. NAVY—and, for a time, the largest in the world. It saw little service and was burned in April 1861 at the Norfolk Navy Yard to prevent capture during the Civil War.

By the mid-1850s, these titans of the seas were obsolete. They gave way to new classes of small steam-powered, iron-hulled ships.

Further reading: Gardiner, Robert. *The Line of Battle: The Sailing Warship, 1650–1840.* Annapolis, Md.: Naval Institute Press, 1992; Lavery, Brian. *The Ship of the Line.* Vol. 1: *The Development of the Battle Fleet, 1650–1850.* Annapolis, Md.: Naval Institute Press, 1983; Silverstone, Paul H. *The Sailing Navy, 1775–1854.* Annapolis, Md.: Naval Institute Press, 2001.

— Sarah Hilgendorff List and Spencer C. Tucker

Shirley, William (1694–1771) *British colonial governor of Massachusetts and military planner*
Born on 2 December 1694 in Sussex County, England, William Shirley was the eldest son of an English gentleman and textile merchant. Educated at Pembroke College, Cambridge, and the Inner Temple, he was admitted to the bar in 1720. Around 1719, he married the daughter of a prominent London merchant, but financial problems forced him to take a government position in America and he won appointment to the Vice-Admiralty Court in Boston. Shirley soon made many powerful friends in the Massachusetts merchant community; and in 1741 their influence proved decisive in getting him appointed governor of the colony.

Shirley's tenure as governor came in the midst of KING GEORGE'S WAR, and Shirley made the most of it, winning army contracts and commissions for the colony. He proved instrumental in planning the 1745 military expedition to capture Fort Louisbourg. He commissioned William

PEPPERELL to command colonial forces and worked tirelessly to arrange the logistical and strategic support the British navy offered the campaign. The expedition was a great success, and the capture of Louisbourg was celebrated throughout the colonies and in England. Shirley was deeply involved in the preparations for future campaigns when word of peace reached Boston.

In 1749, Shirley went to France to negotiate a treaty that would have divided North America between the two colonial powers. The plan failed and Shirley returned to Massachusetts, where once again war loomed along the frontier. Shirley urged Massachusetts to attend the Albany Conference in 1754. This meeting, which failed, sought to unite the English colonies for defensive purposes.

Once the FRENCH AND INDIAN WAR began, Shirley made plans for a campaign to blunt French incursions into northern New York and western Pennsylvania by leading an expedition against FORT NIAGARA. He worked closely on this with British major general Edward BRADDOCK. Following the latter's death in 1755, Shirley was unable to win support for his plan from the other colonies. By 1756, his military policies were so discredited that he was recalled to England.

In 1759, Shirley received the honorary military rank of lieutenant general and governorship of the Bahamas. He remained in the post for eight years, resigning in 1767 in favor of his son. Shirley returned to Massachusetts in 1768 and lived on his estate in Roxbury, where he died on 24 March 1771.

Further reading: Schutz, John A. *William Shirley: King's Governor of Massachusetts.* Chapel Hill: University of North Carolina Press, 1961; Shirley, William. *Correspondence of William Shirley, Governor of Massachusetts and Military Commander in America, 1731–1760.* Edited by Charles Lincoln. New York: Macmillian, 1912; Wood, George A. *William Shirley, Governor of Massachusetts, 1741–1756.* New York: Columbia University Press, 1920.

— Kyle F. Zelner

Short, Walter C. (1880–1949) *U.S. Army general*
Born on 30 March 1880 at Fillmore, Illinois, Walter Campbell Short graduated from the University of Illinois in 1901 and was commissioned a second lieutenant in the 25th Infantry in February 1902. His first assignments took him to the Presidio of San Francisco, to posts in the Southwestern United States, and to the Philippines in 1907. After tours in Alaska and Fort Sill, Oklahoma, he participated in the PUNITIVE EXPEDITION INTO MEXICO.

In June 1917, after U.S. entry into World War I, Short was assigned to the 1st Division and accompanied it to France. He served as a training officer in the 1st Division and as a staff officer in the AMERICAN EXPEDITIONARY FORCES (AEF) headquarters. During the occupation of the Rhineland after the war, he was chief of staff, Third Army. Short rose to temporary colonel, but was returned to his permanent grade of captain in 1920.

During the 1920s, Short served as an instructor at the Command and General Staff School (C&GSS), on the War Department General Staff, and with the 65th Infantry in Puerto Rico. He finished the decade as an instructor at Leavenworth. From 1930 to 1934 he was assigned to the Bureau of Indian Affairs; then, upon promotion to colonel, he commanded the 6th Infantry at Jefferson Barracks, Missouri, for two years. Short was next the assistant commandant of the Infantry School at Fort Benning, Georgia, during which time he was promoted to brigadier general in 1937.

In March 1937, Short received command of the 2d Infantry Brigade at Fort Ontario, New York. In January 1938 he took command of the 1st Division at Fort Hamilton, New York. During First Army maneuvers near Canton, New York, in August 1940, Short commanded the provisional II Corps. He was promoted to major general to command the I Corps shortly thereafter. In January 1941, he transferred to command the Hawaiian Department at Fort Shafter, and he was promoted to lieutenant general the following month.

Short had command of all army ground and air forces in Hawaii when the Japanese struck PEARL HARBOR on 7 December 1941. He and Admiral Husband E. KIMMEL, commander of naval forces at Pearl Harbor, were held responsible for the success of the Japanese attack. Short was relieved of command on 17 December 1941. Investigations into the attack in 1942 and again in 1944 upheld Short's responsibility. Since that time, Short's relief has been the subject of controversy among historians.

Short retired from the army in 1942 and worked for the Ford Motor Company for four years. He died 3 September 1949 in Dallas, Texas.

See also WORLD WAR II, COURSE OF U.S. INVOLVEMENT: PACIFIC THEATER.

Further reading: Beach, Edward L. *Scapegoat: A Defense of Kimmel and Short at Pearl Harbor.* Annapolis, Md.: Naval Institute Press, 1995; Prange, Gordon W. *At Dawn We Slept: The Untold Story of Pearl Harbor.* New York: McGraw-Hill, 1981.

— Steven E. Clay

Sicily invasion (Operation Husky) (July–August 1943)
Major Allied amphibious operation of World War II
In the early morning hours of 10 July 1943, armed forces of the United States and Britain conducted what was at

A U.S. armored column rolls through the streets of Palermo, Sicily, on 22 July 1943. *(National Archives)*

that time the largest amphibious invasion in history. The operation was part of the Allied effort to drive Italy from the war. Located off the southwestern tip of the Italian Peninsula, Sicily was a stepping stone to the mainland and a decisive location from which to control sea lanes to and from the Suez Canal. The island was defended by General Alfredo Guzzoni's Italian Sixth Army, which consisted of seven static coastal divisions and four maneuver divisions, and by Lieutenant General Hans Hube's XIV Panzer Corps, consisting of the 15th Panzer Grenadier Division and the Hermann Göring Division. On 10 July the 1st Parachute Division and the 29th Panzer Grenadier Division reinforced German forces, resulting in a combined Axis force of more than 300,000 men.

The invasion of Sicily was British-inspired. Opposed by General George C. MARSHALL and other U.S. generals, the plan nonetheless won the approval of President Franklin ROOSEVELT. It was code-named Husky. General Dwight D. EISENHOWER had overall command of Allied Mediterranean forces. British general Sir Harold Alexander, commanding Fifteenth Army Group, had charge of the attacking ground forces. Admiral Sir Andrew B. Cunningham commanded Allied naval forces, and Air Chief Marshal Sir Arthur Tedder had charge of Allied air forces. Thus, all senior operational commanders were British. Disharmony characterized the planning and conduct of the campaign.

Fifteenth Army Group consisted of Lieutenant General George S. PATTON's U.S. Seventh Army and General Bernard L. Montgomery's British Eighth Army. Prior to the invasion, Allied air forces methodically bombed key Axis installations.

The Sicily invasion was unprecedented. More forces would be landed than at Normandy on 6 June 1944. More than 2,500 ships and craft were deployed, and this was the first landing in which newly designed landing ships and craft were utilized, including the DUKW amphibious truck. On 10 July 1943 the British Eastern Naval Task Force landed four Allied divisions on the southeast coast of Sicily between Syracuse and the southernmost tip of the island. The American Western Naval Task Force landed four divisions on the southwest coast of the island in the vicinity of Gela. An airborne drop, the objective of which was to neutralize Axis beach defenses, preceded the amphibious landing. An unfortunate incident occurred during the landing: U.S. Navy gunners, who had shortly before come under German air attack, mistakenly attacked and shot down a number of second-wave U.S. transport aircraft. Despite this, the landings were successful. By nightfall the assault divisions had secured their assigned beachheads.

At Gela, the Hermann Göring Division counterattacked the U.S. 1st Infantry Division. Naval gunfire played a key role in driving off the Germans. Vice Admiral H. Kent Hewitt, commander of U.S. naval forces, noted that this was the first cruiser-versus-tank battle in history, and the cruiser won.

Montgomery's Eighth Army was to conduct the main attack north to Messina, while Patton's Seventh Army conducted a supporting attack and protected Montgomery's left flank. Patton disapproved of Alexander's operational plan and developed his own. The two armies competed, and Alexander tended to favor Montgomery. The rugged, mountainous terrain and stubborn German resistance slowed the Allied advance; however, on 22 July Patton's forces reached Palermo and a few days later bisected the island.

On 25 July King Victor Emmanuel III dismissed Benito Mussolini as premier of Italy and initiated actions to withdraw Italy from the war. Thus Husky's primary strategic objective was achieved. Nevertheless, German and Italian forces continued to fight tenaciously, defending from three successive perimeters as they skillfully withdrew toward Messina. On 11 August, German field marshal Albert Kesselring ordered the evacuation of Axis forces. Allied air and naval forces proved ineffective in stopping the withdrawal. The Italians evacuated 62,000 soldiers, 227 vehicles, and 41 artillery pieces; the Germans removed 38,846 men, 10,356 vehicles, and 14,949 tons of supplies. The campaign cost the Americans 7,319 casualties and the British 9,353. Axis losses were much higher: 164,000, including 32,000 Germans. The Allies' failure to complete the destruction of Axis forces in Sicily, however, made the ongoing Allied task in Italy much more difficult.

On 16 August Patton's forces reached Messina ahead of the British. Early the next morning the Germans completed their evacuation. On 3 September the Italians signed a secret armistice. Finally, during the Sicilian campaign, Patton lost the chance to command U.S. forces in the invasion of Europe and almost ended his career by slapping two soldiers suffering from battle fatigue (posttraumatic stress disorder). These incidents were reported in the press and led to Lieutenant General Omar N. BRADLEY's promotion ahead of Patton.

See also AIRBORNE FORCES, DEVELOPMENT AND EMPLOYMENT OF; GAVIN, JAMES M.; WORLD WAR II, COURSE OF U.S. INVOLVEMENT: EUROPE.

Further reading: D'Este, Carlo. *Bitter Victory: The Battle for Sicily, 1943.* London: Collins, 1988; Morison, Samuel Eliot. *History of United States Naval Operations in World War II.* Vol. 9: *Sicily-Salerno-Anzio, January 1943–June 1944.* Boston: Little, Brown, 1954; Smyth, Howard McGraw, and Albert N. Garland. *Sicily and the Surrender of Italy.* Washington, D.C.: U.S. Government Printing Office, 1965.

— Adrian R. Lewis

Signal Corps, U.S. Army *Army branch responsible for providing command and control communications and computer support (C4) between the deployed army and its fixed posts, sister services, coalition partners, and the Department of Defense*

The Signal Corps uses all available media to provide secure voice, data, and video services for customers worldwide. In 1986 the Signal Corps became a regiment and is now comprised of uniformed and civilian C4 personnel assigned throughout the Department of Defense. Additionally, today's Signal Corps leverages existing commercial infrastructure, technology, and expertise from America's leading information technology (IT) firms to augment portions of the strategic and tactical networks.

The father of the U.S. Army Signal Corps was Albert Myer. A former employee of the New York State Telegraph Company who had joined the army as an assistant surgeon, Myer developed a form of optical telegraphy using a binary code derived from his medical dissertation, "A New Sign Language for Deaf Mutes." Myer recommended his system—which became known as "wigwag"—as the means to overcome the major obstacles to efficient battlefield command and control (C2): weather, distance, time, and terrain. Myer's persistence culminated in the Appropriations Bill of 1860, which authorized a single major to take "charge of all signal duty, and all books, papers, and apparatus connected therewith." With Myer's own appointment to that position, the U.S. Army Signal Corps became history's first separate signal branch within an armed force.

The extensive use of wigwag during the Civil War provided glimpses of the promise of an effective C2 system.

Union hot air balloon during the Battle of Seven Pines/Fair Oaks, 31 May–1 June 1862 *(National Archives)*

During the battle of ATLANTA, when the Confederate army threatened to cut off the Union's northern line of communications by attacking the supply base at Allatoona, Georgia, signalers conveyed on three occasions Major General William T. SHERMAN's order to "hold out" until reinforcements arrived. Signal stations also frequently doubled as observations posts, conveying valuable intelligence regarding troop movements. On the second day of the Battle of GETTYSBURG, Lieutenant General James LONGSTREET, aware that he was under observation by the signal station on Little Round Top, ordered the famous countermarch that gave Major General George MEADE time to reinforce his exposed flank.

Despite the corps' successes, Myer's place in history was assured by the ambitious nature of his wartime failures. Although wigwag never overcame the fog of battle, its human architecture of signal "sets," or stations, would

mature into today's electronic network of switchboards, radio relays, satellite transponders, and data routers. Myer's *Manual of Signals* (1864), published a year following his removal as chief of signal, formed the basis of signal doctrine for decades to follow. Myer's aversion to the system of "detailing" officers for signal duty and his fight to establish a permanent corps assigned to commands throughout the army were vindicated by the explosion of communications technologies that required dedicated expertise. His contract with Henry Rogers for a failed field telegraph initiated the rich tradition of civilian-military cooperation in the field of research and development, one that has seen the Army Signal Corps midwife the airplane, wireless telephony, radar, communications satellites, and today's sophisticated data networks.

After Secretary of War John SCHOFIELD testified in 1869 that a permanent peacetime Signal Corps was unnecessary, Myer convinced Congress that the Signal Corps could fulfill the mission of its 1870 joint resolution calling for the War Department to establish a national weather service to reduce weather-related loss of life, crop, and property. At its height, the Signal Corps' National Weather Service controlled 5,000 miles of telegraph, connected more than 100 domestic weather stations, and assimilated observations from myriad domestic and international sources. Myer contracted with commercial firms, railroads, and retail outlets to distribute nationwide thrice-daily weather reports, daily crop bulletins, and domestic and international weather maps.

After President Benjamin Harrison transferred the Weather Service to the newly created Department of Agriculture, Chief of Signal Adolphus GREELY refocused the Signal Corps' attention on providing military communications. Barely prepared for the SPANISH-AMERICAN WAR, the corps eventually employed a nationalized telegraph system, improved field telegraph trains, and the new media of telephony to establish seamless connectivity between the War Department and field telephone stations on the front lines in Cuba. The war also exposed the danger of wire-based signal systems. Cut underwater cables left both armies dependent on pretechnological signal systems. Dewey's decision to sever Spain's cable between Manila and Hong Kong had the unintended consequence of delaying the arrival of news of the cease-fire protocol that would have made the Battle of Manila unnecessary.

The war highlighted one of the Signal Corps' new duties, a natural extension of its observer role in the Civil War: aeronautical reconnaissance. During the Battle of SAN JUAN HEIGHTS, a Signal Corps balloon floated lethargically above the jungle terrain—and the American forces—to convey INTELLIGENCE regarding entrenched Spanish forces. It also served to direct withering fire upon soldiers of the 10th Cavalry who were gathering below for the assault, inviting the bitter scorn of its regimental quartermaster, First Lieutenant John J. PERSHING. More successful was the Signal Corps' use of combat camera to document the war, a responsibility it carries out to this day.

Expanding the search for a more survivable form of reconnaissance, the Signal Corps awarded a contract to Wilbur and Orville WRIGHT for the purchase of their heavier-than-air flying machine. The Army Signal Corps' 1st Aero Squadron and its eight planes deployed in support of Pershing's 1916–17 PUNITIVE EXPEDITION INTO MEXICO. The failure of a single plane to survive the expedition in working condition or to spot Pancho Villa moved Pershing to conclude that the airplane was useful neither as a scout nor as an alternate means of communications. As the commander of the AMERICAN EXPEDITIONARY FORCE (AEF), under European skies dominated by the employment of thousands of combat airplanes, Pershing established a separate Air Corps and gave it a combat mission. In May 1918 the army followed suit, severing the Signal Corps from its aviation role.

Although the Signal Corps had made tantalizing progress in the field of wireless telegraphy by 1917, its capability to support voice traffic did not mature in time for employment during WORLD WAR I. Wired telephony provided poor C2 on a front line that was heavily bombed and regularly raked by machine gun fire.

Unable to communicate by voice or signal, commanders on the move could not call for reinforcements, exploit tactical opportunities, or adjust artillery fire. The commander of the famous "Lost Battalion," savaged by friendly artillery while trapped behind enemy lines in October 1918, was down to his final communications option: the use of Cher Ami, a member of the newly authorized Signal Corps' Pigeon Service. Despite loss of limb and organ, Cher Ami successfully delivered the message, earning for his heroics a medal and a pension. As for the Signal Corps' human members, their dangerous mission of repairing damaged cable resulted in casualties exceeded only by the infantry.

In the interwar period, the Signal Corps exploited the U.S. Navy's invention of a radio detection and ranging capability to build the military's first radar system. One of the Signal Corps' first-deployed radar systems detected Japanese aircraft approaching PEARL HARBOR in the early hours of 7 December 1941. Unfortunately, the Air Corps lieutenant on duty discounted the signal soldiers' radar readings as evidence of operator inexperience or merely the approach of friendly aircraft.

The use of vacuum tubes to generate continuous waves enabled the transmission of voice over radio, sparking a revolution in radio technology that would produce the first

serious rival to wire-based battlefield C2 systems. Radio relay, or microwave, solved the problem of division command posts outrunning their wired connectivity to higher headquarters. Microwave also enabled isolated units to communicate over the heads of their enemy. During the Battle of the BULGE in December 1944, the 101st Airborne Division maintained radio relay contact with General Omar BRADLEY's 12th Army Group's communications network, despite being entirely surrounded at Bastogne. At the small-unit level, the infantry used backpacked FM walkie-talkies and handheld AM handie-talkies. Although neither could communicate with the other, nor with the vehicular mounted FM tank version, radio contributed immeasurably to the generally decisive nature of mobile battle during WORLD WAR II.

The KOREAN WAR provided the Signal Corps with some of the most formidable challenges in its history. Steep terrain, extreme climates, and an obsolete Signal Corps inventory forced small-unit commanders to rely heavily on messenger for battlefield C2. For its long-distance communications, the Signal Corps' VHF radio system provided reliable communications between major headquarters. Its reliance on line of sight required signal units to occupy high, exposed, key terrain. During the fighting for the CHANGJIN/CHOSIN RESERVOIR, a detachment from the 4th Signal Battalion participated in some of the most difficult fighting of the war, maintaining communications in the face of the Chinese onslaught. The name of the small knoll they fought so hard to defend, Communications Hill, honored their courage.

The COLD WAR, fueled by competition between superpowers, accelerated an extraordinary era of technological exploitation, and the Signal Corps was in the middle of it. Signal Corps' collaboration with industry produced the transistor. The invention of an electric version, the microchip, signaled the birth of the digital age, and the Signal Corps' Fieldata Program was the first of its kind to envision a worldwide computer-based communications network. Its Project Diana proved that humans could send electronic signals to space; 12 years later, Project Score successfully launched the Signal Corps'—and the world's—first communications satellite.

The VIETNAM WAR marked America's first significant commercialization of the battlefield. The political nature of the war required a network that supported operations from a multitude of fixed bases, a requirement that soon overwhelmed the Signal Corps' tactical capabilities. The army contracted Page Commercial Engineers to build and operate the Integrated Wideband Communications System (IWCS) that connected bases throughout Southeast Asia. Infantry, artillery, and armor units employed the new family of interoperable FM radios to achieve remarkable combined arms effects. During the Battle of the IA DRANG, the

13th Signal Battalion employed aircraft-mounted radio relays to provide leaders of the 1st Cavalry Division with continuous C2 during its bloody fight with experienced North Vietnamese regulars.

Operation DESERT STORM in 1991 marked a return to mobile warfare, as the U.S.-led coalition against the Iraqi army amassed the largest concentration of armored vehicles since World War II. The Signal Corps provided commanders with exceptional operational flexibility. Special Forces units used manpacked tactical satellites to achieve C2 well behind enemy lines. Leaders successfully navigated the theater's deserts thanks to a network of orbiting satellites called the Global Positioning System (GPS). The army's first fully tactical digital network (MSE) instantaneously distributed surveillance data, resulting in vastly improved target engagement. The Gulf War foreshadowed the army network at the end of the 20th century, where frontline soldiers enjoy Internet-like services, and commanders use videoteleconferencing (VTC) to project their presence to leaders and staffs separated by oceans, deserts, and mountains.

Albert Myer's unfulfilled promise to provide the commander with the eyes to see a battlefield increasingly beyond his scope of control is closer to fulfillment. Space-based technology, computer networking, and "smart" applications will one day extend a seamless network from president to the soldier in the foxhole, conveying tailored intelligence to each desired echelon of command. That such a battlefield is even feasible is due in great measure to the Army Signal Corps' tradition of pioneering bold, battlefield C2 innovations.

Further reading: Davis, H., and F. Fasset. *What You Should Know About the Signal Corps.* New York: W. W. Norton, 1943; Marshall, Max. *The Story of the U.S. Army Signal Corps.* New York: Franklin Watts, 1965; Army Times. *A History of the United States Signal Corps.* New York: G. P. Putnam's Sons, 1961; Raines, Rebecca Robbins. *Getting the Message Through: A Branch History of the U.S. Army Signal Corps.* Washington, D.C.: Center of Military History United States Army, 1996.

— George H. Cushman and Jeffrey G. Smith, Jr.

Simpson, William H. (1888–1980) *U.S. Army general*
Born on 19 May 1888 in Weatherford, Texas, William Hood Simpson graduated from the U.S. Military Academy, WEST POINT, and was commissioned a second lieutenant of infantry in June 1906. Assigned to the 6th Infantry, he moved with the regiment on successive assignments to the Philippines; to the Presidio of San Francisco; to El Paso, Texas; and took part in the PUNITIVE EXPEDITION INTO MEXICO in 1916–17. During World War I he served in suc-

cession as aide to Brigadier General George Bell, Jr.; assistant G3 of the 33rd Division; and chief of staff, 33d Division. Rising to temporary lieutenant colonel, he reverted to his permanent rank of captain in June 1920, but then was immediately promoted to major.

Simpson was assigned to the Office of the Chief of Infantry in 1921, after which he attended the Infantry School at Fort Benning, Georgia. He attended the Command and General Staff School at Fort Leavenworth, Kansas, from which he graduated with distinction in 1925.

From July 1925 to August 1927 Simpson commanded Fort Washington, Maryland, and the 3d Battalion, 12th Infantry. He attended the Army War College in 1927 and 1928, then was assigned to the Intelligence Division of the War Department General Staff. From 1932 to 1936 Simpson was professor of military science and tactics at Pomona College, Claremont, California. From there, he served a year as instructor at the Army War College and two years as the director of the War Department G2 (Intelligence) Division, during which time he was promoted to colonel in 1938.

In August 1940 Simpson took command of the 9th Infantry Regiment at Fort Sam Houston, Texas. Two months later he was promoted to brigadier general and made assistant division commander of the 2d Division. In April 1941 he was transferred to command the Infantry Replacement Training Center at Camp Wolters, Texas, where he was promoted to major general in September.

Over the next two and a half years, Simpson commanded, in succession, the 30th Division, 35th Division, XII Corps, and Fourth Army, gaining promotion to lieutenant general. In May 1944 he assumed command of the U.S. Ninth Army in England. He then led that force in fighting in France as part of General Omar N. BRADLEY's 12th Army Group in reducing the fortress of Brest in August, then in fighting in Holland and Belgium. In November, units of the Ninth broke through the Siegfried line; after some of the toughest fighting on the Western front, they advanced to the Roer River by February 1945. Simpson's troops crossed the Rhine River in late March and, in conjunction with Lieutenant General Courtney HODGES's First Army, had encircled the massive industrial area of the Ruhr River Valley by 1 April. The Ninth Army continued the advance across central Germany and crossed the Elbe River in late April.

Simpson's primary postwar assignment was command of Second Army at Memphis, Tennessee, and Baltimore, Maryland. He retired in November 1946 and was promoted to general on the retired list in July 1954. He died at San Antonio, Texas, on 15 August 1980.

See also BULGE, BATTLE OF THE; EISENHOWER, DWIGHT DAVID; PATTON, GEORGE S.; WORLD WAR II, U.S. INVOLVEMENT: EUROPE.

Further reading: *Conquer: The Story of the Ninth Army, 1944–45.* Washington, D.C.: Infantry Journal Press, 1947; Stone, Thomas R. "He Had the Guts to Say 'No': A Military Biography of General William H. Simpson." Unpublished doctoral dissertation. Ann Arbor, Mich.: University Microfilms, 1974.

— Steven E. Clay

Sims, William S. (1858–1936) *U.S. Navy admiral*
Born on 15 October 1858 in Port Hope, Ontario, Canada, William Sowden Sims graduated from the United States Naval Academy, Annapolis, 1880. He spent almost a decade in ship assignments before embarking on yearlong French-language studies in Paris and four years of teaching on a training ship.

An assignment to the China Station, serving in two of the modern steel ships of the "modern American navy," marked the beginning of Sims's interest in enhancing his service's equipment, technology, and doctrine. Intelligence reports that Sims sent the Office of Naval Intelligence during the 1894–95 Sino-Japanese War carefully analyzed the performance of the various vessels involved and suggested ways in which this information might be used to enhance the effectiveness of the U.S. fleet. Sims's reports won praise from his superiors and Assistant Secretary of the Navy Theodore ROOSEVELT, as did information he provided on European naval innovations while naval attaché in Paris and Saint Petersburg.

During three years on the China Station from 1900 to 1902, Sims further crystallized and developed his ideas on naval gunnery reform and a general staff system. Recalled to Washington in 1902 by Roosevelt, for seven years Sims—the father of the "gun club"—incorporated his new gunnery tactics in naval training and agitated for organizational improvements, including the introduction of an Office of Naval Operations, efforts that achieved only modest success. Tours commanding the battleship *Minnesota*, the Atlantic fleet's torpedo flotilla, and the battleship *Nevada,* and an assignment as instructor at the Naval War College, enabled him to implement new tactical doctrines. Promoted to rear admiral in 1916, the next year he became the president of the Naval War College.

Sims was in Britain in April 1917 when the United States entered World War I. He was immediately given charge of U.S. ships operating from European bases. Promoted to vice admiral and appointed commander of U.S. naval forces in Europe in May, he deluged Washington with recommendations on convoying, antisubmarine warfare, intelligence gathering, and strategic planning, urging that American warships be assigned primarily to escort duties, convoying supplies and men across the Atlantic.

His insistence on a CONVOY SYSTEM, supported by British prime minister David Lloyd George, brought drastic reductions in Allied shipping losses but generally reassigned overall control of American naval operations in Europe to British admirals. Sims won promotion to full admiral in December 1918.

Sims's attitude and his excellent relations with his British counterparts led Washington officials, including Secretary of the Navy Josephus DANIELS and Chief of Naval Operations Admiral William S. BENSON, to characterize him as an Anglophile. For his part, Sims judged his superiors' failure to implement some of his suggestions—and what he viewed as their earlier reluctance to prepare the navy for a major conflict—responsible for its somewhat disappointing initial wartime performance. He aired these charges to Congress during a 1920 investigation that he largely precipitated, provoking bitter feuding within the navy.

Reverting to the rank of rear admiral at war's end, from 1919 until 1922, when he retired, Sims again headed the Naval War College. In his final years he spoke and wrote extensively on naval matters, forcefully urging the development of naval aviation. He even declared battleships to be obsolete. Promoted to admiral on the retired list in 1930, Sims died in Boston on 25 September 1936.

See also ATLANTIC, BATTLE OF THE (WORLD WAR I); ROOSEVELT, FRANKLIN D.; WORLD WAR I, COURSE OF U.S. INVOLVEMENT.

Further reading: Hagan, Kenneth J. "William S. Sims: Naval Insurgent and Coalition Warrior," *The Human Tradition in the Gilded Age and Progressive Era.* Edited by Ballard C. Campbell. Wilmington, Del.: Scholarly Resources, 2000: 187–203; Sims, William Sowden. *The Victory at Sea.* Garden City, N.Y.: Doubleday, Page, 1920; Simpson, Michael, ed. *Anglo-American Naval Relations, 1917–1919.* Brookfield, Vt.: Gower, 1991; Trask, David F. "William Sowden Sims: The Victory at Sea," *Admirals of the New Steel Navy: Makers of the American Naval Tradition, 1880–1930.* Edited by James C. Bradford. Annapolis, Md.: Naval Institute Press, 1990: 282–99.

— Priscilla Roberts

Sioux Wars (1862–1891) *American Indian Wars on the northern Great Plains*
Between 1862 and 1891, the Teton Sioux fought a series of wars against the U.S. government. These wars were initially directed against local settlers, but they grew into a highly organized war of independence against the government's attempts to confine the Sioux to rapidly shrinking reservations. The Sioux Wars comprised three phases: the early period between 1862 and 1865, the middle period between 1873 and 1881, and the closing period of 1890–91. U.S.

Army leaders continued to refine their tactics as they pursued the Sioux relentlessly. Eventually, the army defeated the Sioux, killing or resettling all their leaders and confining the people to barren reservations.

The Sioux Wars opened on 17 August 1862 when a band of four Wahpeton warriors killed five Minnesota settlers. The following day the local Sioux war chief, LITTLE CROW, led an attack through the Redwood Agency. With 800 warriors he struck Fort Ridgely, Minnesota, on 20 August. In the first week of attacks throughout the Redwood Agency, New Ulm, and Fort Ridgely areas, Little Crow's band killed nearly 800 settlers.

To defeat Little Crow, Major General John POPE, commander of the Department of Missouri, launched a two-pronged offensive with Colonel Henry H. Sibley and Brigadier General Alfred Sully, in which the Sioux sustained heavy casualties. On 23 September 1862, the Sioux ambushed Sibley's column at Wood Lake, Minnesota, but Sibley's troops drove them off. Little Crow's band scattered into Dakota and Canada, while its leader was shot by a farmer shortly thereafter.

Sioux operations increased after the notorious SAND CREEK MASSACRE in November 1864. The Sioux spent January and February 1865 in vengeful raids, burning nearly every ranch and stagecoach station on the South Platte.

Relations with the Sioux stabilized after the 1868 Treaty of Fort Laramie. This ceded to the Sioux the Black Hills of Dakota as a reservation in perpetuity. Despite these promises, military expeditions cut through the heart of this reservation—notably the columns of Colonel David S. Stanley in 1873 and of Lieutenant Colonel George A. CUSTER in 1874. These expeditions distressed the Sioux and led to frequent skirmishes with the army. Gold prospectors, lured by enthusiastic newspaper stories about gold reported by Custer's expedition, also invaded the Black Hills reservation. Sioux bands not only attacked these prospectors, but also raided outside the reservation into settled areas of Dakota and Nebraska.

To drive the Sioux back to the reservation, the army sent three converging columns. One, under Brigadier General Alfred TERRY, marched west from Fort Abraham Lincoln, North Dakota. The second, under Brigadier General George CROOK, marched north from Fort Fetterman, Wyoming. The third, under Colonel John GIBBON, marched east from Fort Ellis, Montana. Sioux warriors turned back Crook's entire column in the Battle of the ROSEBUD RIVER on 17 June. Custer, who continued on in defiance of orders, divided his 7th Cavalry Regiment at the LITTLE BIGHORN, where the Sioux camp had drawn an unusually large spring migration of Cheyenne. These warriors, led by CRAZY HORSE, overwhelmed Custer's command, killing Custer and all 204 troops who accompanied him into battle.

The unsuccessful campaign of 1876 was eclipsed by the success of the campaign of 1877. Colonel Nelson A. MILES succeeded by employing mixed forces of light artillery, cavalry, mounted infantry, and INDIAN SCOUTS. His aggressive use of infantry instead of cavalry, employment of Indian scouts, and relentless year-round campaigning all wore down his adversaries. The last actively campaigning Sioux chief, SITTING BULL, surrendered on 19 July 1881.

WOUNDED KNEE was the last major violent confrontation between Indians and the army. The Ghost Dance movement that spawned it reflected the agitation of Sioux warriors who sought to reconcile their subjugation with their glorious past and martial culture. As in nearly all the previous military engagements, the 29 December 1890 Battle of Wounded Knee arose from mutual suspicion and misunderstanding. The Sioux, led by Big Foot and escorted by Colonel James W. Forsyth and the 7th Cavalry, were camped at Wounded Knee Creek. Before continuing the march to the Pine Ridge Agency, the white troops attempted to disarm the Indians of their Winchester repeating rifles. The Indians attempted to hide their arms; in the confusion, a shot rang out. The troops fired into the camp with their own rifles and four Hotchkiss cannon firing exploding shells. The Sioux suffered more than 200 deaths, while army losses numbered 25 killed and 39 wounded. Miles relieved Forsyth of his command following the massacre, although subsequent military judicial appeals overturned the relief.

The Sioux were a relentless adversary. They were finally conquered by technologically superior, better-organized, and better-disciplined regular army units that were capable of sustained pursuit and campaigning. Deprived of safe havens, the Sioux were driven by exhaustion and continuous casualties onto the reservations prepared by their conquerors.

See also AMERICAN INDIAN WARS; FETTERMAN DISASTER; INDIAN WARFARE; POWDER RIVER EXPEDITION; RED CLOUD.

Further reading: Clodfelter, Michael. *The Dakota War: The United States Army Versus the Sioux, 1862–1865.* Jefferson, N.C.: McFarland, 1998; Utley, Robert M. *Frontiersmen in Blue: The United States Army and the Indian, 1848–1865.* New York: Macmillan, 1967; ———. *Frontier Regulars: The United States Army and the Indian, 1866–1891.* Lincoln: University of Nebraska Press, 1984; ———. *The Indian Frontier of the American West, 1846–1890.* Albuquerque: University of New Mexico Press, 1984; Wooster, Robert. *The Military and United States Indian Policy 1865–1903.* New Haven, Conn.: Yale University Press, 1988.

— Kevin Gould

Sitting Bull (Tatanka Iyotake) (ca. 1831–1890)
Hunkpapa Sioux leader

The actual date and place of Sitting Bull's birth are not known; most estimates fix his birth around 1831, along the Grand River, a tributary of the Missouri River in the present state of South Dakota. His name, Tatanka Iyotake, means literally "buffalo bull sitting on its haunches." At a young age he showed potential of being a great warrior, and by age 10 he had killed his first buffalo. His first combat experience came against the neighboring Crows. During the 1850s he became leader of the elite Strong Heart warrior society and also emerged as a spiritual leader.

Sitting Bull's first serious encounter with whites came in 1863 during the campaign of retaliation that followed LITTLE CROW's Minnesota uprising, in which his band played no part. In 1864 Sitting Bull fought unsuccessfully in defense of the Sioux village at Killdeer Mountain. In 1865 and 1866 his warriors battled army units in the POWDER RIVER country, and in attacks on Forts Rice and Buford in the Dakota Territory. In 1868, after RED CLOUD accepted a treaty and moved onto a reservation, Sitting Bull was selected to lead an unprecedented military alliance of the various bands of Teton (Lakota) Sioux, who continued to oppose white encroachment on the northern plains.

In 1874, gold was discovered in the Black Hills of Dakota Territory, an area that had been set aside as a reservation in the Fort Laramie Treaty of 1868 and that was considered sacred by the Sioux. Prospectors illegally rushed into the Black Hills, provoking a confrontation. When government attempts to buy the land from the Sioux failed, authorities ordered all Teton bands onto reservations by 31 January 1876; after that date, defiant bands would be considered hostile. Many Sioux refused the order, while increasing numbers of agency Indians left reservations to join them. As promised, in March soldiers took the field to bring in the "hostiles." By June, three columns converged on southeastern Montana Territory, where the Sioux, now bolstered by Cheyenne and Arapaho allies, gathered in large villages along the Rosebud and Little Bighorn Rivers. On 17 June, Oglala chief CRAZY HORSE's warriors turned back Brigadier General George CROOK's large column on the ROSEBUD RIVER and then joined Sitting Bull's village on the Little Bighorn.

Sitting Bull presided over a massive village of more than 1,000 lodges and commanded a force of perhaps 2,000 warriors. Days before, he had had a vision that foretold a spectacular victory. On 25 June, Lieutenant Colonel George A. CUSTER made the vision a reality when his 7th Cavalry imprudently attacked without reconnoitering, in what became known as the Battle of the LITTLE BIGHORN. But the Indian victory on the Little Bighorn brought massive army retaliation. The great Indian coalition broke up into small bands, most of which fell prey to the army during the following winter.

Sitting Bull led his band to Canada, where he remained for five years. Compelled by hunger, in July 1881 he and his people returned to the United States. Sitting Bull surrendered at Fort Buford and spent many months in the stockade before taking up residence at the Standing Rock Agency. He toured briefly with Buffalo Bill's Wild West show, but remained a symbol of resistance for his people. In December 1890, fear aroused by the Ghost Dance religious movement prompted agent James McLaughlin to order Sitting Bull's arrest. On 15 December, when 43 tribal policemen attempted to take him into custody, a fierce fight erupted between the police and Sitting Bull's followers in which Sitting Bull was killed. This was a contributing factor in the catastrophe at WOUNDED KNEE two weeks later.

See also AMERICAN INDIAN WARS; SIOUX WARS.

Further reading: Utley, Robert M. *The Lance and the Shield: The Life and Times of Sitting Bull.* New York: Holt, 1993; Vestal, Stanley. *Sitting Bull: Champion of the Sioux.* Norman: University of Oklahoma Press, 1957.

— Jim M. Kerbow

Slocum, Henry W. (1827–1894) *U.S. Army general*

Born on 24 September 1827 in Delphi Falls, near Syracuse, New York, Henry Warner Slocum worked his way through several schools by teaching in a neighboring county. He earned an appointment to the U.S. Military Academy, WEST POINT, and graduated in 1852.

After serving four years in the artillery, Slocum resigned his commission upon the death of his daughter. He returned to Syracuse and took up the practice of law, having studied for the bar while on garrison duty at Charleston, South Carolina. He also pursued various business interests and served a term in the New York state legislature.

In early 1861, with civil war approaching, Slocum was appointed colonel of the 27th New York Regiment from Elmira. He led this unit in the First Battle of BULL RUN/MANASSAS and was badly wounded in the thigh. Upon his recovery, he was appointed brigadier general of Volunteers and took command of a brigade in the Army of the Potomac in September 1861. During the Peninsula Campaign he commanded a division through the SEVEN DAYS battles. He was promoted to major general of Volunteers in July 1862.

After participating on the periphery of the Second Battle of BULL RUN/MANASSAS, Slocum and his division fought in the Battle of Crampton's Gap on their way to ANTIETAM. After the death of Major General Joseph Mansfield,

Slocum received command of XII Corps. During the Battle of CHANCELLORSVILLE, he helped to stop the rout of XI Corps, and he commanded the Union right flank during the Battle of GETTYSBURG.

Slocum's XII Corps was transferee to the western theater, but a long-standing conflict with Major General Joseph HOOKER led to Slocum's reassignment when the XI and XII Corps were consolidated to form XX Corps. He commanded at Vicksburg until Hooker resigned during the ATLANTA CAMPAIGN. Recalled to command XX Corps, Slocum led it through the end of the campaign and accepted the city's surrender on 2 September 1864. He commanded the left wing (the Army of Georgia) during Major General William Tecumseh SHERMAN's MARCH TO THE SEA and through the Carolinas. He resigned his Volunteer commission in September 1865.

After the war, Slocum became a Democrat and moved his family to Brooklyn, New York. He served three terms in Congress, became a successful businessman, and remained active in veterans' affairs. Slocum died in Brooklyn on 14 April 1894.

See also CIVIL WAR, LAND OVERVIEW.

Further reading: Gettysburg Monument Committee. *In Memoriam: Henry Warner Slocum.* Albany, N.Y.: J. B. Lyon, 1904; Howard, Oliver O., Thomas E. Hilton, ed. "To the Memory of Henry Slocum: A Eulogy by Oliver O. Howard," in *Civil War Times Illustrated* (21 March 1982): 39–41; Slocum, Charles E. *The Life and Services of Major General Henry Warner Slocum.* Toledo, Ohio: Slocum Publishing, 1913.

— Brian C. Melton

small arms: pistols

Although handguns were used in the American Revolutionary War and War of 1812, it was with the invention of the revolver, roughly coinciding with the MEXICAN-AMERICAN WAR, that the handgun began to supplant the saber as the primary weapon for the cavalry. After the Civil War the pistol was the preferred weapon, but carbines were used on skirmish line or for dismounted fighting. While the handgun has little importance in combat, it remains a symbol of authority for officers and a primary weapon for individuals assigned to units such as military police.

American military pistols span the period from flintlock to self-loading semiautomatic. During the American Revolutionary War, the Continental army used flintlock pistols of various caliber and manufacturer. In many instances, gunsmiths turned out pairs of pistols made to order for an individual. Congress attempted to equip the fledgling cavalry with two pistols per man, to be carried in holsters mounted on the saddle. Many mounted soldiers procured their own weapons and certainly supplemented any regulation issue with additional pistols. During this period, the preferred weapon of the mounted army was the saber; handguns were either a self-defense weapon or used to dispatch wounded horses—hence the name "horse pistol" given to the large caliber issue pistols of the period.

With the founding of the new republic in 1789, the government built two ARSENALS for the production of small arms. The Springfield arsenal in Massachusetts and the HARPERS FERRY arsenal in Virginia (now in West Virginia) produced both muskets and pistols for the army and navy. Many smaller forges produced weapons to supplement arsenal production.

One of the most important innovations in manufacturing technology was factory mass production. In 1799 Eli WHITNEY designed and manufactured muskets with interchangeable parts, and Simeon North began to experiment with similar technology for the manufacture of pistols. While Whitney is generally credited with the idea of interchangeable parts, North may have independently arrived at the same idea at the same time.

In the 1830s and 1840s, the U.S. military began the conversion from flintlock- to percussion-firing systems. The percussion system was more reliable than the flintlock and took fractionally less time to load after each round was fired. Most flintlock pistols in service from 1819 onward were either scrapped or converted to percussion by plugging the vents by the pan and mounting the nipple over it, thereby channeling the igniting charge from the percussion cap directly into the chamber.

Additionally, in 1855 the Harpers Ferry and Springfield arsenals began to manufacture detachable shoulder stocks for their pistols. Such weapons were known as *pistol carbines.* Some had longer barrels than was usual in order to enhance accuracy. Other manufacturers, such as Johnson, Ames, and Deringer, produced pistols under government contract.

The most important advance in handgun technology was the invention of the revolving pistol, or revolver. In 1836, Samuel COLT, while serving as a merchant seaman, carved a model of a pistol that had a cylinder holding six rounds of ammunition; the gun fired as a hammer struck the percussion nipple at the end of each of the firing ports on the cylinder. From this model, Colt went on to manufacture the Colt revolver, known as the Patterson after its place of manufacture (Patterson, New Jersey). It was a .36 caliber weapon, lacking a trigger guard; in fact the trigger dropped down from the frame when the revolver was cocked.

The U.S. Ordnance Bureau was slow to show any interest, but Colt's pistol gained wide acceptance from settlers on the frontier. One of the first organizations to adopt the revolver was the Texas Rangers. This weapon proved to be decisive in frontier history, as the person employing it no longer had to go through the cumbersome reloading process necessary with single-shot weapons. Other law enforcement agencies began to look with interest at the revolver. In 1850, the New York Police Department purchased Colt's "Pocket," or "Sheriff's," model. These weapons had a shorter barrel than the Patterson.

The Mexican-American War won over the military establishment. One of the complaints Colt received was that the Patterson was too flimsy. In 1845 army captain Samuel Walker met with Colt at his New Haven plant and the two designed a larger, heavier pistol to correct previous flaws. The result was the two-pound Colt Walker, which fired a .44-caliber bullet. Shortly thereafter, Colt followed with the Dragoon, purchased by the U.S. military in 1855.

At the beginning of the Civil War, the U.S. Army accepted delivery of Colt's 1860 Army model, while the navy preferred a smaller version, the .36-caliber Navy model. Both weapons were standard issue for each side during the war, the "Navy" being especially popular in the South and manufactured in the Confederacy by a number of factories. Samuel Colt died in 1860, but his role as the primary provider of pistols to the U.S. military was secure. The only competition came from the new firm of Smith and Wesson, which provided a line of pistols that were much sought after by both Union and Confederate soldiers. In fact Confederate General Robert E. LEE had a Colt Army model, but he carried a .28-caliber Smith and Wesson on his person, preferring it to the heavier Colt. Some other models appeared during the war in small numbers.

In 1872 Colt, Smith and Wesson, and other small arms designers improved on the invention of the metallic cartridge, and Colt sold the government perhaps its most famous pistol. In 1873, the army adopted the single-action Army model with a six-inch barrel. The civilian version, with a four-inch barrel, became known as the Peacemaker. This weapon was in production from 1873 until 1941. This model became known as "the gun that won the West." The army also procured several thousand Smith and Wesson "Schofield" model top-break pistols. The Schofield was named for Major General George W. Schofield, who designed the ejector system that threw out six empty shell casings simultaneously when the pistol was opened. There were actually more Smith and Wessons on the frontier, and these were much less expensive than the Colt, but the latter remained the preferred sidearm of soldier and settler alike. Interestingly enough, Smith and Wesson enjoyed great success in foreign sales with its Schofield model. The pistol was even licensed for manufacture in Russia, that model being produced in the United States as the Smith and Wesson

.44 "Russian." A number of Remington revolvers also saw extensive use.

In 1898–1900 Colt introduced the "New Service" revolver in .38 caliber. This was adopted by both the army and navy and used in the SPANISH-AMERICAN WAR and the PHILIPPINE-AMERICAN WAR. However, the .38 caliber bullet was ineffective against Moro tribesmen in the latter conflict; in response, the United States conducted trials to find a new service pistol.

The U.S. military expressed interest in the self-loading, semiautomatic pistol, specifically in designs of Georg Luger and John BROWNING. The Luger 9mm Parabellum (meaning "for war") was similar to the .38, but its bullet had a higher velocity. Based on ballistic trials conducted in 1903, the U.S. Army decided that a heavier-caliber pistol was needed. Between 1905 and 1911, numerous companies tested their handguns, but in 1911 the army adopted the Browning design, and classified the new pistol the M1911. Heavy at two pounds, the pistol fired a massive .45 caliber bullet. Few handguns exist, even today, with its stopping power. Many experts regards the M1911 and the M1911A1 as the best combat handguns ever devised.

The M1911A1 incorporates improvements based on the U.S. experience in World War I. It was introduced into service in 1921. More than 2.5 million of these weapons were produced, and they were distributed worldwide during World War II.

The great demand for pistols during World War II by the U.S. military and its Allies also ensured that the revolver would remain a service pistol. Colt as well as Smith and Wesson manufactured revolvers in both .45 and .38 calibers. With the .38 being used by police and units in the United States, the priority of issue of the M1911A1 was to units deployed overseas. Aircrews especially found the short barrel or "snubnose" .38-caliber pistols convenient when in flight clothing. In fact, the U.S. Air Force continued to issue it as its primary side arm until the 1980s. The OFFICE OF STRATEGIC SERVICES (OSS) issued the Colt 1903 or 1908 in .32 caliber or .38 caliber. German and other foreign self-loading pistols were often issued to OSS agents because the 9mm Parabellum was fairly standard throughout Europe.

In the 1980s, the U.S. military sought a replacement for the aging M1911A1, one compatible with other NATO countries employing the 9mm cartridge. After numerous tests, the American military adopted the Beretta Model 92. A robust and large pistol, it has a 15-round capacity magazine and chambers the almost-universal 9mm cartridge. It is type-classified as the M9 pistol. The production contract calls for the manufacture of more than 315,000 of these weapons. The M9 is the current service pistol for all branches of the U.S. military.

See also SMALL ARMS: RIFLES.

Further reading: Bishop, Chris, and Ian Drury. *Combat Guns: An Illustrated Encyclopedia of Twentieth Century Weapons.* Secaucus, N.J.: Chartwell Books, 1987; Kalman, James, and C. Meade Patterson. *U.S. Single Shot Martial Pistols.* New York: Scribner, 1949.

— Julius A. Menzoff

small arms: rifles

Technically the term *rifle* refers to a firearm with a rifled (grooved) barrel. During the Colonial period and the American Revolutionary War, the vast majority of American troops were equipped with muzzle-loading flintlock smoothbore muskets. The musket's chief advantage was its relatively rapid rate of fire; its major drawback was its lack of accuracy.

Rangers on the frontier were armed with a new weapon, the Pennsylvania or Kentucky rifle. It resembled a musket in size and firing device but differed from it in having rifling in the barrel. These grooves gave a spin to the ball. Its accurate range was much greater than a musket— up to 400 yards, as opposed to 50–100 yards. It was, however, a weapon of restricted use. It took three times as long to load—the ball had to be rammed down the barrel, and repeated discharges made this increasingly more difficult—and it could not mount a bayonet. Hence it was impractical for conventional battles. It was, however, well suited to guerrilla tactics.

During the American Revolutionary War, the mainstay of the Continental army was the .69-caliber Charleville musket, named for the principal French arsenal that produced it. An excellent weapon, it remained the standard American infantry weapon into the War of 1812.

The first rifle issued by the U.S. Army was the Harpers Ferry Model 1803, a short weapon of Jaeger derivation that saw effective service with the Regiment of RIFLEMEN during the War of 1812. Nearly four decades passed before a new weapon, the Model 1841, was introduced. A muzzle-loading .54 caliber percussion rifle, it was four feet long and weighed almost 10 pounds. This rifle suffered from many of the same problems that plagued early rifles—difficulty in loading and a tendency toward fouling.

In 1849 a French army officer, Claude-Étienne Minié, revolutionized rifle technology with a new type of bullet. The Minié bullet, rather than being a round ball, was an elongated cylindro-conoidal lead projectile that had a hollow base. When the rifle was fired, the force of the explosion forced the edges of the soft lead bullet into the rifling of the barrel and created a tight seal. The minié bullet, therefore, eliminated the two principal problems of the rifle. It was easy to load because it could be smaller than the barrel diameter and still engage the rifling, and, because it engaged the rifling with such a tight seal, it prevented excessive fouling of the barrel. It thus combined the chief advantages of both musket and rifle.

The first mass-produced American rifle created for the Minié bullet was the Model 1861. The Springfield Model 1861 rifle (along with the almost identical Model 1863) was carried by most Union and many Confederate soldiers during the Civil War. The Model 1861, a muzzle-loading .58-caliber percussion rifle, was four and a half feet long and weighed almost nine pounds.

During the Civil War, both sides utilized a wide variety of rifles. One of the most often issued rifles among Confederate forces was the British Enfield Model 1853. A muzzle-loading .557 caliber percussion rifle, it was four and a half feet long and weighed almost nine pounds. While the Enfield and Model 1861 were relatively conventional weapons for the time, many other Civil War rifles were much more innovative. The Sharps New Model Rifle and Carbine were just such innovations. The Sharps, a single-shot breech-loading .56 caliber percussion rifle, was four feet long and fired a paper (or linen) cartridge. While the carbine was very popular with cavalrymen, the full-sized rifle was issued to the 1st and 2d U.S. Sharpshooters Regiments.

The Civil War also saw the first two repeating rifles used by the U.S. Army: the Spencer and the Henry. The Spencer, produced in both full-sized and carbine models, was a .56 caliber rifle that held seven rimfire cartridges in a tubular magazine inside the butt of the weapon. The rifle was armed by pulling the trigger guard down; this action both ejected the spent cartridge and inserted a new one. The hammer then had to be cocked manually, but with practice a soldier could fire as many as 12 rounds a minute. The Henry, a .44-caliber rifle, was four feet long, weighed 10 pounds, and held 16 rimfire rounds in a tubular magazine under the barrel. The rifle was armed by pulling down the lever trigger guard, which simultaneously ejected the spent cartridge, inserted a new one, and cocked the hammer. Even the most inexperienced soldier could fire its entire 16 rounds in less than a minute.

Following the Civil War, the U.S. Army Ordnance Department, which had resisted any use of the Spencer and Henry repeating rifles, decided that since these weapons "wasted ammunition," neither would be designated as the official army rifle. Instead, the Ordnance Department rechambered the Model 1861 and 1863 rifles to accommodate a .45–.70-caliber centerfire cartridge. Later models of this single-shot rifle, known as the Springfield (for the Springfield arsenal, Massachusetts), were produced from scratch specifically for the .45–.70 cartridge. The Model 1873 Springfield remained the standard rifle of the U.S. Army until 1892.

In 1892, the Ordnance Department, under pressure from both the U.S. Congress and the combat arms of the

U.S. Army, adopted a new rifle to replace the aged Springfield. The new rifle, the first repeating rifle to be designated as the official rifle of the U.S. Army, was the Danish-designed Krag-Jorgensen. It saw extensive service during the SPANISH-AMERICAN WAR and the PHILIPPINE-AMERICAN WAR, although Volunteer units were still armed with the antiquated Springfield. The Krag-Jorgensen was a bolt-action .30 caliber rifle that was three and a half feet long, weighed eight pounds, and held five centerfire rounds in an internal box magazine. Its cartridges used smokeless powder. Although the Krag-Jorgensen was a great improvement over the single-shot Springfield, it did not compare well with the British Lee-Enfield or the German Mauser. Within only a few years, therefore, the Ordnance Department introduced a new rifle of its own design, but based on the Mauser: the Springfield Model 1903. It was a bolt-action .30 caliber rifle. Almost four feet long, it weighed almost nine pounds and held five rounds in an internal box magazine. Later the U.S. Army was forced to pay Mauser for the patent infringements.

During the late 1920s and early 1930s, a completely new rifle was designed to replace the Springfield 1903. Invented by John Garand, an employee at the Springfield arsenal, in 1932 the M1, commonly known as the Garand, became the first semiautomatic rifle adopted by the U.S. Army. The Garand, a .30-caliber rifle, was three and a half feet long, weighed almost 10 pounds, and held eight rounds. The Garand was a significant improvement over earlier designs and provided American soldiers with a firepower advantage during World War II. While the Garand was the primary rifle used by American forces during the war, another rifle was also widely issued. The M1 Carbine was a lightweight and easy-to-use rifle designed for rear-echelon soldiers and as a personal defense weapon for officers instead of a handgun. A .30-caliber rifle, the M1 Carbine was three feet long, weighed five and a half pounds, and held 15 or 30 rounds in an external magazine. While the Carbine was popular for its light weight and ease of use, the .30-caliber pistol-style cartridge was considered underpowered.

In the late 1950s, the army decided to replace the already outdated Garand with a rifle capable of both semi- and full-automatic fire. Its replacement was the M14, for all practical purposes, an updated version of the Garand capable of full-automatic fire. The M14, a 7.62mm rifle, was almost four feet long, weighed eight and a half pounds, and held 20 rounds in an external magazine. While the M14 was a reliable and accurate rifle, its large 7.62mm cartridge made the weapon almost impossible to control on full-automatic fire. Therefore, only a few years after adopting the M14, the U.S. Army replaced it with a new rifle, the M16. A significant change in rifle design, the M16 utilized light metal alloys and black plastic to create what was, at the time, a futuristically styled rifle. A 5.56mm rifle, the M16 was three feet long, weighed eight pounds, and held 20 or 30 rounds in an external magazine. During the VIETNAM WAR the M16 saw extensive combat service during which it proved its worth against the Soviet-designed AK47. Although early versions of the rifle did suffer from lack of reliability and lack of accuracy, these problems were largely solved by the M16A1. In the 1970s the M16 was redesigned to accommodate a new cartridge, and the result was the M16A2, which served into the Gulf War and beyond.

See also SMALL ARMS: PISTOLS.

Further reading: Canfield, Bruce N. *U.S. Infantry Weapons of World War I.* Lincoln, R.I.: Andrew Mowbray Publishers, 2000; Canfield, Bruce N. *U.S. Infantry Weapons of World War II.* Lincoln, R.I.: Andrew Mowbray Publishers, 1994; Coggins, Jack. *Arms and Equipment of the Civil War.* New York: Barnes & Noble Books, 1990; Hallahan, William H. *Misfire: The History of How America's Small Arms Have Failed Our Military.* New York: Scribner, 1994.

— Alexander M. Bielakowski

Smalls, Robert (1839–1915) *African-American Civil War naval hero and congressman*
Born on 5 April 1839 into slavery of a white father at Beaufort, South Carolina, Robert Smalls was permitted by his owner to learn the skill of ship rigging. He was subsequently employed as a seaman aboard the *Planter,* a steamship operating in the waters around Charleston, South Carolina.

In 1861 the Confederate government chartered and armed the *Planter,* and Smalls soon became its pilot. By May 1862 he devised a daring plan to commandeer the *Planter* and pilot it through Charleston harbor to refuge with the blockading U.S. Navy fleet.

At approximately 3:00 A.M. on 13 May 1862, while the *Planter's* white officers were ashore, Smalls and eight black crew members took it through Charleston harbor, stopping only to bring aboard Small's wife and two children and five other slave refugees. By sunrise the *Planter* was passing under the guns of FORT SUMTER and Fort Johnson. Smalls stood in the pilot house wearing the captain's familiar straw hat and sounded the authorized whistle signals. The *Planter* then steamed out to sea toward the Union blockaders and freedom.

Shortly thereafter, Smalls surrendered the *Planter* to the USS *Onward.* As well as the ship itself, Smalls also delivered cannon intended for Forts Sumter and Ripley. More significant, Smalls also provided intelligence information

Robert Smalls   *(Library of Congress)*

that proved invaluable to the Union in its subsequent conquest of eastern South Carolina.

His exploit made Smalls an instant hero throughout the Union. For delivering the *Planter* he was awarded $1,500 prize money. Smalls then was appointed a pilot in the U.S. Navy and piloted the monitor *Keokuk* during Rear Admiral Samuel DU PONT's 7 April 1863 attack on Charleston. His bravery while piloting the *Planter* during another coastal attack earned him promotion to captain in December 1863, making him the highest-ranking African-American officer in the Union navy. During the war, Smalls piloted several warships and commanded the *Planter* in 17 engagements.

During Reconstruction in South Carolina, Smalls capitalized on his Civil War fame by entering politics. Commissioned in 1870 as a lieutenant colonel in the state militia, he rose to major general until forced out of the militia at the end of Reconstruction in 1877. His Sea Island black neighbors elected Smalls to Congress for five terms (1875–79 and 1881–87). Robert Smalls died in Beaufort, South Carolina, on 23 February 1915.

See also AFRICAN AMERICANS IN THE MILITARY; CIVIL WAR, NAVAL OVERVIEW.

Further reading: Meriwether, Louise. *The Freedom Ship of Robert Smalls.* Englewood Cliffs, N.J.: Prentice-Hall, 1971; Miller, Edward A., Jr. *Gullah Statesman: Robert Smalls from Slavery to Congress, 1839–1915.* Columbia: University of South Carolina Press, 1995; Uya, Okron Edet. *From Slavery to Public Service: Robert Smalls, 1839–1915.* New York: Oxford University Press, 1971.

— Theodore D. Harris

Smith, Edmund Kirby (1824–1893) *Confederate army general*

Born on 16 May 1824 at Saint Augustine, Florida, Edmund Kirby Smith graduated from the U.S. Military Academy, WEST POINT, in 1845. A second lieutenant of infantry, he served in the MEXICAN-AMERICAN WAR, earning two brevets for gallantry. From 1849 to 1852 he taught mathematics at West Point. Promoted to first lieutenant and then captain, in 1855 he was assigned to the elite new 2d Cavalry. Promoted to major in 1860, he was on duty in Texas when the secession crisis erupted.

Resigning his commission in April 1861, Smith entered Confederate service as a lieutenant colonel of cavalry. He was General Joseph E. JOHNSTON's chief of staff in the Shenandoah Valley and received a promotion to brigadier general in June 1861. Smith was severely wounded while commanding an infantry brigade in the First Battle of BULL RUN/MANASSAS. Clearly a rising star in the Confederacy, Smith was promoted to major general in October and assigned to command a division in northern Virginia. In March 1862 he assumed command of the Department of East Tennessee.

In July, Smith moved into Kentucky in conjunction with General Braxton BRAGG's invasion of that state. Despite Smith's impressive victory in the Battle of RICHMOND, the campaign stalled and both columns were forced to withdraw. Promoted to lieutenant general in October 1862, Smith was transferred to the Trans-Mississippi Department, assuming command in March 1863. The fall of VICKSBURG in July left Smith's department ("Kirby Smithdom") isolated from the rest of the Confederacy, and as a result he exercised almost total authority for the balance of the war, appointing a number of general officers who were never confirmed by the Senate. In February 1864 he became the seventh full general of the Confederacy.

That spring, during the RED RIVER CAMPAIGN, Smith directed the repulse of Major General Frederick Steele's advance in Arkansas while his chief subordinate, Major General Richard Taylor, turned back Union Major General Nathaniel P. BANKS in Louisiana. With the collapse of the Confederacy, on 2 June 1865 Smith confirmed surrender, at Galveston, Texas, of the last organized Southern force.

Fearing imprisonment, Smith fled to Mexico. Returning to the United States, he became president of an insurance company and later the Atlantic and Pacific Telegraph Company. Failing in business, in 1870 he became president of the University of Nashville, and in 1875 he joined the faculty of the University of the South at Sewanee, Tennessee. The last survivor of the Confederacy's full generals, he died at Sewanee on 28 March 1893.

See also CIVIL WAR, LAND OVERVIEW.

Further reading: Kerby, Robert Lee. *Kirby Smith's Confederacy: The Trans-Mississippi South, 1863–1865.* New York: Columbia University Press, 1972; Parks, Joseph H. *General Edmund Kirby Smith, CSA.* Baton Rouge: Louisiana State University Press, 1992.

— Roger W. Caraway

Smith, Holland M. ("Howlin' Mad") (1882–1967)
U.S. Marine Corps general

Born on 20 April 1882 at Seale, Alabama, Holland McTyeire Smith graduated from the Alabama Polytechnic Institute (now Auburn University) in 1901 and completed a law degree at the University of Alabama two years later. Commissioned a second lieutenant in the U.S. Marine Corps in 1905, Smith served in the Philippines, Panama, and the Dominican Republic.

After the United States entered World War I, Smith was assigned command of a machine gun company in June 1917. On arrival in France, however, he was the first marine officer chosen to attend the Army General Staff College at Langres. Smith then served as a staff officer with I Corps, First Army.

Graduating from the Naval War College in 1921, Smith was the first Marine officer assigned to the Joint Army-Navy Planning Committee. Receiving various appointments and promotions, Smith in 1939 was named assistant to Marine Corps commandant Major General Thomas HOLCOMB. Smith focused on innovations in equipment and amphibious landing methods, and he is often considered the father of modern amphibious warfare because of his contributions to its technology and tactics.

Training the 1st Marine Brigade at GUANTANAMO, Cuba, Smith won promotion to major general in February 1941. His brigade was augmented to become the 1st Marine Division, which was then incorporated into the Amphibious Force, Atlantic Fleet. Given command of the V Amphibious Corps, Smith deployed to the Pacific theater in June 1943. His troops took TARAWA and MAKIN that fall. In 1944 they secured Kwajalein, Eniwetok, Saipan, Tinian, and Guam. In a controversial decision, Smith removed U.S. Army major general Ralph Smith from command at Saipan, claiming he was not sufficiently aggressive;

this action soured interservice relations. Holland Smith was known by his men as "Howlin' Mad Smith" for his aggressive leadership.

In August 1944, Smith was promoted to lieutenant general and named commander of the new Fleet Marine Force. He accompanied his troops when they seized IWO JIMA in February 1945. That July, he left the Pacific theater to direct the Marine Training and Replacement Command at San Diego, California. Smith was only the third Marine officer to receive four stars. He retired in August 1946. Smith then wrote his memoirs, *Coral and Brass* (1948). He died at San Diego on 12 January 1967.

See also MARSHALL ISLANDS, BATTLE FOR THE; MARIANAS, BATTLE FOR THE; WORLD WAR II, COURSE OF U.S. INVOLVEMENT: PACIFIC THEATER.

Further reading: Cooper, Norman V. *A Fighting General: The Biography of Holland McTyeire "Howlin' Mad" Smith.* Quantico, Va.: Marine Corps Association, 1987; Gailey, Harry A. *Howlin' Mad v. the Army: Conflict in Command, Saipan, 1944.* Novato, Calif.: Presidio Press, 1986; Isley, Jeter A., and Philip A. Crowl. *The U.S. Marines and Amphibious War.* Princeton, N.J.: Princeton University Press, 1951; Hough, Frank O., Verle E. Ludwig, and Henry I. Shaw, Jr. *History of U.S. Marine Corps Operations in World War II.* 5 vols. Washington, D.C.: Historical Branch, G-3 Division Headquarters, U.S. Marine Corps, 1956–1971.

— Elizabeth D. Schafer

Smith, John (1580–1631) *Leader of the English settlement at Jamestown, Virginia*

Born in 1580 in Lincolnshire, England, John Smith attended school and served a brief apprenticeship. He then journeyed to the Netherlands in 1596, where he fought in the Dutch army against the Spaniards. After a short period of service, he returned to England. To improve his martial skills, he studied military books and learned horsemanship.

In 1600, Smith left England to join Archduke Ferdinand's Austrian forces fighting the Turks. Smith rose to the rank of captain and distinguished himself when he killed three Turkish champions in tournament combat. Wounded in Transylvania and left for dead, Smith was taken as a slave to Turkey. He killed his master and escaped, returning to England in 1603.

Seeking new adventures, Smith sailed in 1606 with the English expedition to the Chesapeake and was appointed a councilor of the Virginia colony. He assumed responsibility for Indian relations. Smith recognized the colony's weakness and the threat posed by the Indians, so he adopted a confrontational policy to keep them in awe of the English.

His goals were to protect the colony and procure supplies from the Indians while avoiding a full-scale war. In December 1607 he was captured by Powhatan Indians after a skirmish, sentenced to death, and then reportedly saved by Pocahontas, the daughter of Powhatan, chief of a dozen Indian tribes of the region, in what was probably a ritual intended to impress Smith and win more equitable treatment from him.

Smith continued his tough policies, however, using intimidation to secure food and, when he met resistance, seizing corn, burning houses, and killing Indians or taking hostages to enforce compliance with the colonists' demands. Smith was elected president of the colony in September 1608. He placed Jamestown on a military footing, organizing the settlers into companies and drilling them weekly.

In January 1609 a trading expedition nearly erupted into a battle when Smith's men believed that OPECHAN-CANOUGH's Pamunkey warriors were about to attack them. Smith averted a crisis by seizing Opechancanough and threatening him with a pistol. Although Indian relations improved thereafter, further problems arose when settlers at outlying posts abused nearby Indians. Concerned that such actions might provoke war, Smith ordered a more conciliatory policy but was ignored. In September he was injured in an explosion, forcing him to return to England. He wrote extensively of his experiences and promoted colonization efforts until his death in London on 21 June 1631.

See also ANGLO-POWHATAN WAR; POWHATAN.

Further reading: Lemay, J. A. Leo. *The American Dream of Captain John Smith,* Charlottesville: University Press of Virginia, 1991; Vaughan, Alden T. *American Genesis: Captain John Smith and the Founding of Virginia.* Boston: Little, Brown, 1975.

— Jim Piecuch

Smith, Oliver P. (1893–1977) *U.S. Marine Corps general*

Born on 26 October 1893 in Menard, Texas, O. P. (Oliver Prince) Smith graduated from the University of California, Berkeley, in 1916. A Christian Scientist, Smith remained a deeply religious person who neither drank nor swore. He went to work for the Standard Oil Company; but when the United States entered World War I, he applied for a Marine Corps reserve commission, which was granted in May 1917. Stationed in Guam, he received a regular commission.

In 1919 Smith was assigned to Mare Island Marine Barracks, San Francisco. He commanded the Marine detachment on the battleship *Texas* (1921–24). From 1924 to 1928 he was in the Personnel Section of Marine Headquarters in Washington. Following three years in Haiti, in 1932 Smith graduated from the Army Infantry School, Fort Benning, Georgia. He was then an instructor in the Marine Corps Schools at Quantico, Virginia. He served on the staff of the naval attaché at the U.S. embassy in Paris from 1934 to 1936, returning to Quantico as an instructor from 1936 to 1939. After a year with the Fleet Marine Force, Pacific, in 1940 he took command of a battalion of the 6th Marine Regiment, and was with it in Iceland from 1941 to 1942. After two years with headquarters staff, in January 1944 he commanded the 5th Marine Regiment of the 1st Marine Division, leading it through the New Britain campaign.

Promoted to brigadier general in April, Smith became assistant commander of the 1st Division. He saw action on PELELIU in September-October, and in November became deputy chief of staff of the Tenth Army. He next fought on OKINAWA in April–June 1945, then became commandant of Marine Corps Schools at Quantico.

In April 1948, Smith became assistant commandant and chief of staff of the Marine Corps. Promoted to major general, in June 1950 he took command of the 1st Marine Division at Camp Pendleton, California. On 15 September 1950 Smith led the division as part of X Corps in the INCHON LANDING.

Smith then relocated with his division by sea to Wonsan on the west coast of Korea, and at the end of October began an advance to the Yalu River. Smith had serious misgivings about General of the Army Douglas MacARTHUR's troop dispositions for the push to the Yalu in the dead of winter and with a wide gap between his division and Eighth Army on his left. Smith slowed his advance and hurried the establishment of a base at Hagaru-ri, probably saving his division from annihilation in the next weeks.

When the Chinese People's Volunteer Army (CPVA) resumed its offensive at the end of November, Smith's division was trapped with its main elements 78 miles north of the port of Hungnam at the CHANGJIN/CHOSIN RESERVOIR. Ultimately, the Chinese fed 12 divisions into the battle, but the marines carried out an epic 13-day retreat, bringing out their wounded and their equipment in one of the most masterful operations in military history.

Following the HUNGNAM EVACUATION at the end of December, Smith's division joined Eighth Army as part of IX Corps. During February and March 1951, Smith commanded IX Corps—one of the rare instances in which a marine general has commanded army troops at that level. In April 1951, Smith returned to the United States to command Camp Pendleton, California. Promoted to lieutenant general in 1953, he had charge of the Fleet Marine Force, Atlantic, from July 1953 to September 1955, when he retired as a full general. Smith died at Los Altos, California, on 25 December 1977.

See also KOREAN WAR, COURSE OF; WORLD WAR II, U.S. INVOLVEMENT: PACIFIC THEATER.

Further reading: Blair, Clay. *The Forgotten War: America in Korea, 1950–1953.* New York: Times Books, 1987; Heinl, Robert D. *Victory at High Tide: The Inchon-Seoul Campaign.* Philadelphia: J.B. Lippincott, 1968; Montross, Lynn, et al. *U.S. Marine Operations in Korea, 1950–1953.* 5 vols. Washington, D.C.: U.S. Marine Corps Historical Branch, 1954–1972.

— Spencer C. Tucker

Smith, Walter Bedell (1895–1961) *U.S. Army general, director of the Central Intelligence Agency, and undersecretary of state*

Born on 5 October 1895 in Indianapolis, Indiana, Walter Bedell Smith was educated at Manual Training High School, Indianapolis. He briefly attended Butler University. He early determined on a military career, and in 1910 enlisted as a private in the Indiana National Guard. He secured a commission in the guard and served during World War I in the 39th Infantry. Badly wounded in the AISNE-MARNE COUNTEROFFENSIVE in August 1918, he was invalided home.

During the interwar years Smith, who rose to major by the end of the 1930s, acquired the organizational, administrative, and planning skills essential to managing modern warfare. He served with the Bureau of Military Intelligence, the Bureau of the Budget, and the Federal Liquidation Board, and had several assignments either studying or instructing at the Infantry School at Fort Benning, Georgia, the Command and General Staff School at Fort Leavenworth, Kansas, and the Army War College. General George C. MARSHALL, appointed chief of staff of the army in 1939, noted Smith's abilities and that October summoned him to Washington to assist in swiftly building up the military from its existing weakness to full wartime strength and capability. In September 1942, Smith was assigned as chief of staff to Lieutenant General Dwight D. EISENHOWER, commander of the European theater. He held this post until the end of 1945, winning a stellar reputation.

Smith returned to Washington in January 1946 as chief of the Operations and Planning Division of the Joint Chiefs of Staff, but two months later President Harry S. TRUMAN appointed him ambassador to the Soviet Union, where he remained until 1949. Smith's experiences in this post, as the COLD WAR steadily and rapidly intensified, convinced him that the United States must take a firm line to contain Soviet expansion, but also that the Soviets did not wish war and would back down when confronted by American strength.

In late June 1950 Truman named Smith, then commanding First Army, director of the CENTRAL INTELLIGENCE AGENCY (CIA). Smith was advanced to full general in July 1951. Truman hoped that Smith would improve leadership and organization within the agency, then attracting heavy criticism for its failure to predict the KOREAN WAR. Smith's reputation as an outstanding bureaucrat and a staunch anticommunist helped to deflect further criticism from the CIA, which he centralized and coordinated, persuading General of the Army Douglas MACARTHUR not only to allow the agency to operate in Korea but also to utilize its intelligence.

Under Smith the CIA nonetheless incorrectly predicted that China would not intervene in the Korean War, and it also failed to anticipate assorted coups in Latin America. Smith tightened the flow of INTELLIGENCE, restricting it to a few high-ranking officers, and instituted a training program to develop a group of career intelligence officers.

As undersecretary of state in the Eisenhower administration, Smith provided a degree of continuity. After his retirement in 1954, an embittered Smith, who never received either a fifth star or the promotion to chief of staff of the army that he believed he deserved, turned to business, amassing a substantial estate. In 1958, Secretary of State John Foster Dulles appointed Smith, a staunch and vocal supporter of nuclear expansion, his special adviser on disarmament. Smith died in Washington, D.C., on 9 August 1961.

See also CONTAINMENT.

Further reading: Crosswell, D. K. R. *The Chief of Staff: The Military Career of General Walter Bedell Smith.* New York: Greenwood Press, 1991; Mayers, David. *The Ambassadors and America's Soviet Policy.* New York: Oxford University Press, 1995; Montague, Ludwell Lee. *General Walter Bedell Smith as Director of Central Intelligence, October 1950–February 1953.* University Park: Pennsylvania State University Press, 1992; Smith, Walter Bedell. *My Three Years in Moscow.* Philadelphia: J. B. Lippincott, 1949.

— Priscilla Roberts

Solomon Islands campaign (1942–1944) *Major campaign in the Pacific theater during World War II*

Symbolized by the epic naval and land battles of GUADALCANAL, the Solomon Islands campaign lasted from August 1942 to March 1944. During that time U.S. forces, with significant assistance from Australia and New Zealand, seized the islands comprising the larger Solomons chain. The bloody combat in the Solomons forced each branch of the military to reexamine its strategies and tactics and make adjustments for future operations. Thus, the seizure of the Solomons played a significant role in the eventual defeat of Japan.

Situated east of New Guinea and northeast of Australia, the Solomons comprise hundreds of islands, most of them heavily jungled. Japan planned to use Solomon bases for future assaults on Australia. Possession of the islands would also allow it to disrupt supply lines between the United States and Australia. If the United States could take and hold the islands, it would impede significantly Japan's ability to carry out operations in the South Pacific.

The Solomon Islands campaign was part of a two-pronged strategy to capture the Japanese stronghold at Rabaul on the island of New Britain. This operation, code-named Cartwheel, called for U.S. Army and Allied troops to capture New Guinea and parts of New Britain, while marines, assisted by the navy, would seize strategic locations in the Solomons. The campaign to drive the Japanese out of the Solomons was known as Operation WATCH-TOWER. It began with the U.S. attack on Guadalcanal in August 1942 and did not end until Bougainville was officially secured in March 1944.

The recapture of Guadalcanal proved the most difficult and costly of all the battles in the Solomons. Initiated only nine months after PEARL HARBOR, the attack was carried out with the slimmest margin for error. Vice Admiral Robert GHORMLEY initially commanded the operation, Rear Admiral Richmond Kelly TURNER had charge of the amphibious landing, and Major General Alexander VAN-DEGRIFT commanded the 1st Marine Division ashore. Although the marines landed with little difficulty, they soon found themselves involved in a deadly battle of attrition.

In many ways, the battle for Guadalcanal was key to the entire operation in the Solomons. Whoever prevailed would more than likely have command of the air and the surrounding seas for future operations. From 7 August 1942 to 7 February 1943, U.S. and Japanese forces slugged it out. The marines managed to take the airfield, renamed Henderson Field. There were 10 major battles for it. Almost daily Japan attempted to send naval forces down the Slot, the middle passage through the Solomons, to reinforce its defenders and to shell the marines ashore. Seven major naval battles occurred between U.S. and Japanese squadrons, including the Battle of SAVO ISLAND (8–9 August 1942), the costliest defeat ever for the U.S. Navy. While the battle was often in doubt, the last Japanese forces were withdrawn from the island in early February 1943.

The remainder of the Solomons campaign involved LEAPFROGGING—bypassing Japanese strong points, such as Rabaul. From the end of June 1943 to March 1944, U.S. forces launched a series of amphibious assaults to seize three strategic locations: New Georgia, Vella Lavella, and Bougainville. The Allies seized New Georgia in July and

early August, Vella LaVella during the second half of August, and Bougainville in a campaign that lasted from November 1943 to March 1944. The capture of Bougainville marked the end of the Solomon Islands part of Operation Cartwheel. Along with the successful capture of most of New Britain and several other islands, American and Allied forces had successfully isolated Rabaul and rendered it useless as a Japanese base.

See also KENNEY, GEORGE C.; MacARTHUR, DOUGLAS; NIMITZ, CHESTER W.

Further reading: Hoyt, Edwin P. *The Glory of the Solomons.* New York: Stein & Day, 1983; Koburger, Charles W., Jr. *Pacific Turning Point: The Solomon Campaign, 1942–1943.* Westport, Conn.: Praeger, 1995; Miller, John, Jr. *CARTWHEEL: The Reduction of Rabaul.* Washington, D.C.: United States Government Printing Office, 1959; Shaw, Henry I., Jr., and Douglas T. Kane. *History of the U.S. Marine Corps, Operations in World War II.* Vol. 2, *Isolation of Rabaul.* Washington, D.C.: United States Government Printing Office, 1963.

— David L. Snead

Spaatz, Carl A. ("Tooey") (1891–1974) *Army Air Forces general and first chief of staff of the U.S. Air Force*

Born on 28 June 1891 in Boyerstown, Pennsylvania, Carl ANDREW Spaatz graduated from the U.S. Military Academy, WEST POINT, in 1914. In October 1915 Spaatz entered the army's San Diego flying school, earning his wings six months later and serving in Brigadier General John J. PERSHING's 1916 PUNITIVE EXPEDITION INTO MEXICO. In July 1917 Spaatz went to France as a major, assigned to the Issoudun training center for fighter pilots, rapidly rising to command. During the 1918 SAINT-MIHIEL and MEUSE-ARGONNE offensives, he flew missions with a British pursuit squadron, downing several German aircraft and winning the Distinguished Service Medal.

In 1918 Spaatz met the like-minded Colonel Henry H. ARNOLD, then assistant director of military aeronautics, with whom he immediately formed a lasting bond. The two headed a small but dedicated interwar band of military aviators who pioneered the development of army airpower. In 1925 both risked their careers as defense witnesses for Brigadier General William MITCHELL, whose intemperate crusade for an independent air force brought his court-martial. Spaatz subsequently undertook air power publicity stunts, in 1929 taking part in an endurance refueling flight that remained aloft continuously for 150 hours.

By the 1930s Spaatz firmly believed that strategic bombing of industrial facilities would be crucial in any future war. In 1939 Arnold, now chief of staff of the Army

Air Corps, summoned him to Washington as executive assistant, and in 1940 Spaatz, now a brigadier general, visited London, establishing links with British airmen that facilitated subsequent coalition warfare. As Arnold's deputy commander, in 1941 Spaatz pushed to develop the B-29 bomber and STRATEGIC BOMBING doctrine. In 1942 he took command of the new Europe-based Eighth Air Force, which for three years launched massive air offensives against German targets. Under General Dwight D. EISENHOWER, he served as air commander in the November 1942 invasion of North Africa. Promoted to lieutenant general in March 1943, Spaatz assumed command of the Allied Northwest Africa Air Forces.

In January 1944, Spaatz returned to Britain as head of the Strategic Air Force in Europe, consisting of the Eighth Air Force in Britain and the Twelfth Air Force in Italy. In recognition of his success in crushing German aerial resistance, he was promoted to full general in March 1945. After Germany's surrender that May, Spaatz moved to Asia to command the final bombing campaigns against Japan, including the August 1945 detonation of ATOMIC WEAPONS over Hiroshima and Nagasaki.

Spaatz ended the war convinced that airpower and strategic bombing had been predominant in attaining Allied victory, and that still heavier bombing might have precluded the need for the D day invasion. In October 1945 he headed a board that recommended that atomic weapons should form the backbone of postwar American defense planning. In 1946, Spaatz succeeded Arnold as commanding general of the U.S. Army Air Forces. During the postwar interservice unification battles preceding the 1947 National Security Act, Spaatz successfully continued his predecessor's drive for a separate and independent air force. He mounted a tremendous publicity campaign for this and became its first chief of staff. In April 1948 Spaatz retired, but until 1961 he wrote military affairs columns for *Newsweek* magazine. This enabled him to continue promoting his favored air power doctrines. Spaatz died in Washington, D.C., on 4 July 1974. With Mitchell and Arnold, he was an organizational and intellectual founder of the U.S. Air Force.

See also AIR FORCE, U.S.; QUESADA, ELWOOD.

Further reading: Copp, DeWitt S. *A Few Great Captains: The Men and Events That Shaped the Development of U.S. Air Power.* Garden City, N.Y.: Doubleday, 1980; Davis, Richard G. *Carl A. Spaatz and the Air War in Europe.* Washington, D.C.: Smithsonian Institution Press, 1993; James, D. Clayton. *A Time for Giants: The Politics of the American High Command in World War II.* New York: Franklin Watts, 1987; Mets, David R. *Master of Airpower: General Carl A. Spaatz.* Novato, Calif.: Presidio Press, 1988.
— Priscilla Roberts

Spain in the American Revolution

Spain provided secret assistance to the Patriots from 1775 to 1778 during the American Revolutionary War. From 1778 to 1783, Spain fought on the side of France against Great Britain, although it never officially recognized the United States during the war. Ultimately, the Spanish alliance proved to be a significant diplomatic accomplishment for the new nation.

Spain's decision to support the American Revolution signaled the isolation of Great Britain and substantially benefited France and the American Patriots. France considered Spanish aid so valuable that it was willing to assist Spain in regaining Gibraltar. Similarly, in order to gain Spain's aid, the Americans agreed not to challenge Spanish control of the Mississippi River and to limit territorial expansion.

Spain entered the war to diminish the size of the British Empire and protect its own colonial holdings. Foremost among Spanish objectives included the return of Gibraltar from Britain and an end to trading privileges gained by the British in the New World during the colonial wars. Spain also hoped to regain East Florida, which had been lost to Britain in the 1763 Treaty of PARIS, and deny the British claims to West Florida and the lower Mississippi, thereby controlling navigation on that river. Finally, Spain hoped to drive British logwood cutting establishments from Central America and regain Jamaica.

Spain's strategic aspirations exceeded its grasp; nevertheless, it played a significant role in the war. Initially, Spain's entry lifted American morale, galvanizing Patriot resolve. Spanish forces successfully captured portions of Florida, forcing British troops from the Gulf Coast. Likewise, Spanish expeditions from Saint Louis and Arkansas claimed lands above and below the Ohio River.

Spain's most significant role in the war, however, came with its navy. The addition of its 25 ships of the line forced the British to station sizable forces in the North Sea and Gibraltar, as well as to convoy ships to North America. This dissipation of British navy strength proved fatal to its land cause at YORKTOWN in 1781.

During the course of the war, John Jay attempted to gain formal recognition of the United States by Spain. He made little headway; Spain adamantly refused to recognize the United States until the British did so. Jay received only small sums of money and promises of future consideration, while Spain used the relationship as a lever in negotiations with Great Britain. Spain's actions demonstrated its belief that its own North American colonies would be safer with U.S. independence.

Spain's military and diplomatic efforts during the war accomplished little. Britain retained Gibraltar, although Spain did regain Minorca and Florida and managed to restrict British woodcutting to the Honduran coast. Such limited accomplishments, however, could have been reached through diplomacy rather than war. Spain's position in North America also laid the groundwork for later conflict with the United States. Faced with growing unrest in its own colonies, Spain was unable to prevent U.S. western expansion or to protect Florida adequately. This led Spain to cede Florida to the United States in 1819 for $5 million in U.S. citizens' claims against that country.

See also FRANCE IN THE AMERICAN REVOLUTION; PARIS, TREATY OF (1782).

Further reading: Bemis, Samuel Flagg. *The Diplomacy of the American Revolution.* Bloomington: Indiana University Press, 1935; Cummins, Light Townsend. *Spanish Observers and the American Revolution, 1775–1783.* Baton Rouge: Louisiana State University Press, 1991.

— Dallas Cothrum

Spanish-American War, causes of (1898)

On 21 April 1898 President William McKinley signed congressional resolutions declaring war on Spain over its treatment of Cuba. His action was the culmination of several years of strained Spanish-American relations, beginning in the early 1890s, when Cuban insurrectionists started a lengthy rebellion against Spanish colonial rule, an uprising that Spanish troops endeavored to suppress. Ever since proclaiming the Monroe Doctrine in 1823, the United States had asserted special rights in the Western Hemisphere and viewed unfavorably efforts by European imperial powers forcibly to retain their colonies against insurgent challenges. In the late 19th century the American government and general public were increasingly assertive internationally, fueled by a nationalistic sense that their country, already one of the world's largest states and strongest industrial economies, had the potential to be a great power.

Initially American officials, including McKinley's predecessor, Grover Cleveland, and the latter's secretary of state, Richard W. Olney, attempted to mediate in the Cuban conflict, hoping to persuade the Spanish to moderate their repressive scorched earth and concentration camp tactics, which caused more than 200,000 civilian deaths, and grant Cuba independence. McKinley continued these efforts, which both Spanish officials and Cuban insurgents distrusted; but, increasingly, American public opinion—always pro-Cuban—favored war with Spain. Within the administration, an aggressive internationalist faction romanticized war and sought to wield the new American "steel fleet" to win Cuban independence, an event they believed would enhance American prestige and also facilitate the construction of a transisthmian canal, enhancing United States national security and commercial interests.

Businessmen and other American residents in Cuba, who desired the restoration of peace and stability and restitution for their wartime property and other losses, came to support American intervention. In Congress the Democrats, led by William Jennings Bryan, strongly supported intervention in Cuba, leading Republicans to pressure McKinley to take decisive action before the next election.

In January 1898 McKinley dispatched the battleship USS *MAINE* to Havana harbor, ostensibly to protect U.S. lives and interests. A few weeks later the *Maine* blew up from an unexplained explosion (now thought to have been caused by spontaneous combustion in a coal bunker) that, at the time, was ascribed to Spanish sabotage. As further mediation attempts proved unavailing, public opinion was continuously inflamed by the fiercely pro-interventionist "yellow journalism" of newspapers owned by William Randolph Hearst and Joseph Pulitzer, and swung toward intervention. On 11 April 1898, McKinley asked Congress to declare war against Spain.

See also PARIS, TREATY OF (1898); SPANISH-AMERICAN WAR, COURSE OF.

Further reading: Musicant, Ivan. *Empire by Default: The Spanish-American War and the Dawn of the American Century.* New York: Henry Holt, 1998; Offner, John L. *An Unwanted War: The Diplomacy of the United States and Spain Over Cuba, 1895–1898.* Chapel Hill: University of North Carolina Press, 1992; Smith, Angel, and Emma Dávila Cox, eds. *The Crisis of 1898: Colonial Redistribution and Nationalist Mobilization.* New York: St. Martin's Press, 1999; Smith, Joseph. *The Spanish-American War: Conflict in the Caribbean and the Pacific, 1895–1902.* New York: Longman, 1994; Trask, David F. *The War with Spain in 1898.* New York: Macmillan, 1981; Traxel, David. *1898: The Birth of the American Century.* New York: Knopf, 1998.

— Priscilla Roberts

Spanish-American War, course of (1898) *Conduct of the conflict over Cuba that propelled the United States to the status of a world power*

On 25 April 1898 the United States declared war on Spain with the sole stated purpose of bringing about the independence of Cuba. While the new U.S. "steel navy" was capable of quick action, the U.S. Army was not well prepared to wage a major offensive land campaign. The regular army totaled fewer than 30,000 troops and had not engaged in large land campaigns since the Civil War. In fact, the top army leaders in the war of 1898—Major Generals William SHAFTER, Nelson MILES, and Wesley MERRITT—were all Civil War veterans who were still much influenced by that experience. Secretary of War Russell Alger feuded continuously with Miles, the commanding general of the army.

Spanish-American War, 1898—Pacific and Caribbean Campaigns

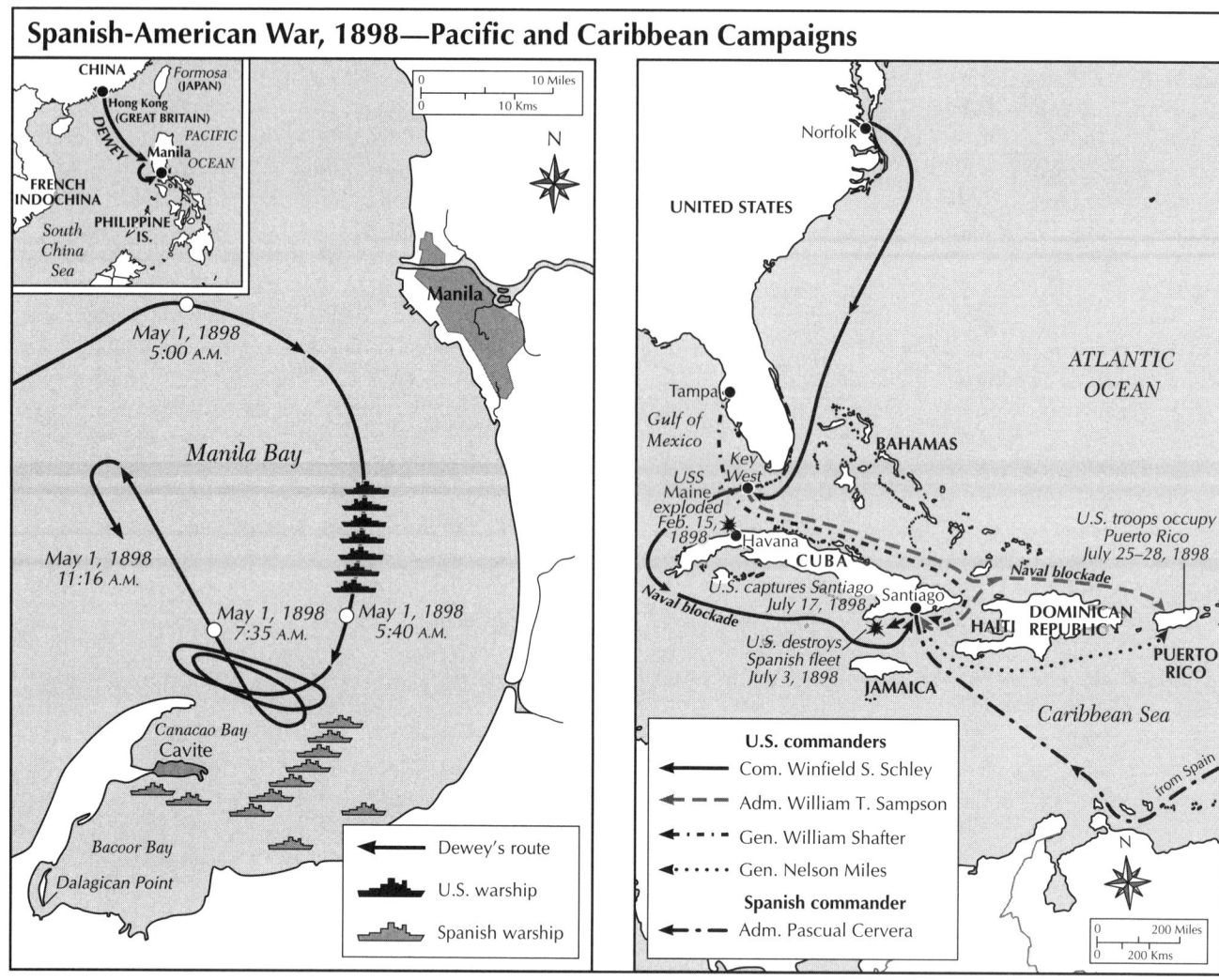

The army had no formal board or organization to engage in strategic planning.

The main problem confronting the army was how to expand the force. Army officials recommended an expansion of the regular army to more than 100,000 men with an additional 50,000 in volunteers. Political pressures, however, forced a much greater emphasis on volunteers. President William McKinley shocked the army brass by calling for a total of 200,000 volunteers.

Recruiting such a large force proved surprisingly easy; equipping, training, and supplying it, however, overwhelmed the War Department bureaucracy. The situation was particularly chaotic in Tampa, Florida, where logistical problems hampered efforts to launch an invasion of Cuba.

With the army facing major organizational problems, it was not surprising that the U.S. Navy dominated operations in the early months of the war. What was surprising to many Americans was where the navy's first major action

took place: the Philippines, another—but distant—Spanish colony. Commodore George DEWEY had assumed command of the navy's Asiatic Squadron in January 1898. In early February, Assistant Secretary of the Navy Theodore ROOSEVELT instructed him to move the fleet from Japan to Hong Kong, placing it in a better position to move against Spanish naval forces in the Philippines in the event of war. On 25 April Washington notified Dewey that war had been declared and that he was to move against the Spanish fleet in the Philippines as soon as possible. On 1 May Dewey's force of nine ships attacked the Spanish fleet in MANILA BAY near Cavite, inflicting an overwhelming defeat on the Spanish. Spanish losses included seven ships and 370 killed. Dewey did not lose any ships, and the only American fatality was a sailor who died from heat exhaustion.

The original Cuban invasion plan called for a force of some 70,000 troops, led by General Miles, to strike at Havana on the northern coast. Because such a large force was not available, the main landing was shifted to the port of Santiago in southeastern Cuba, where the Spanish naval squadron, under the command of Rear Admiral Pascual Cervera y Topete, was located. The Santiago campaign also necessitated extensive cooperation between the army and the navy, but the two service branches found it difficult to agree on operations and coordinate activities. The commander of U.S. naval forces in the region, Rear Admiral William SAMPSON, saw the Santiago campaign as basically a navy operation aimed at destroying the Spanish fleet and opening the harbor. Sampson wanted the army to move along the coast and attack the fortress at the entrance of Santiago Bay, opening the way for the navy to destroy the Spanish fleet. Army commander Major General William Shafter wanted to follow an inland route that would capture the high ground to the north and east of Santiago,

dooming the Spanish forces there. Shafter's view prevailed, and army-navy cooperation never went beyond the landing of troops.

On 22 June, Shafter's force of some 17,000 men began to land at the towns of Daiquirí and Siboney, east of Santiago. As U.S. forces moved inland, they first encountered Spanish troops at the town of Las Guásimas on 24 June. A U.S. force of almost 1,000 dismounted cavalry, under Major General Joseph WHEELER, confronted a Spanish contingent of some 1,500 holding the town. The battle lasted for about two hours, when Spanish forces—already under orders to withdraw—retreated toward Santiago. Two major battles on 1 July 1898 opened the way to the siege of Santiago. One took place at the town of EL CANEY, which controlled the water supply for Santiago. Shafter dispatched Brigadier

Lieutenant Colonel Theodore Roosevelt (center, with suspenders) and the Rough Riders   *(Library of Congress)*

U.S. Navy armored (1st Class) cruisers USS *New York* (left, in distance) and USS *Brooklyn* (center) were significant ships of the Spanish-American War.   *(Library of Congress)*

General Henry LAWTON with some 6,600 men, most of them regulars. There were only 520 Spanish defenders of El Caney, but they were well entrenched and better armed than the Americans. The U.S. plan had called for El Caney to be taken in two hours, with Lawton's force then joining in the attacks on SAN JUAN HEIGHTS. However, it took U.S. forces almost 11 hours to drive out the Spaniards, preventing Lawton's troops from assisting in the later attack. Some 8,000 U.S. troops sent to attack San Juan Heights encountered approximately 500 well-entrenched and well-armed Spaniards defending the heights. The Americans were not well informed about the terrain and found it difficult to move through the jungle leading to the heights. After fierce fighting the Spaniards retreated from both positions. Total U.S. casualties for the three engagements were 205 killed and 1,180 wounded. Spanish losses were 215 killed and 376 wounded.

The loss of the heights forced the Spaniards to take action. Admiral Cervera received orders to make a dash for the open sea. Although he considered it hopeless,

Cervera followed orders, directing his six ships to run the U.S. blockade on the morning of 3 July. In the Battle of SANTIAGO DE CUBA, none of the ships escaped. Two were sunk; three were badly damaged and beached; and one surrendered after being hit. More than 300 Spaniards were killed and 1,700—Cervera among them—taken prisoner. Only one U.S. sailor was killed.

The one-sided battle at Santiago Bay did not bring an immediate end to the Santiago campaign nor to the fighting in Cuba. The arrival of Commanding General of the Army Nelson Miles with reinforcements led to an ultimatum to the Spaniards in Santiago to surrender or face a full-scale attack. On 16 July, the Santiago garrison laid down its arms with the understanding that Spanish soldiers would be returned directly to Spain at U.S. expense.

Miles had come to Cuba primarily to lead the campaign against Spanish troops in Puerto Rico. The original invasion plans called for Miles to use part of the forces involved in the Santiago campaign, but they were so weakened by disease that Miles departed Cuba on 21 July with a much smaller force of 3,300, with additional troops from the United States to follow. Miles also made a major change in his plan of attack, switching the landing from Puerto Rico's northeast coast—near the capital, San Juan—to the southwest coast, near Ponce. The first U.S. troops landed on 25 July, meeting little resistance. Additional troops soon began to arrive, bringing the total U.S. force to 17,000. Spanish forces, meanwhile, were rapidly declining. Puerto Rican volunteers, who made up about half of the Spanish forces, deserted en masse after the U.S. landing, leaving only about 8,000 regular Spanish troops to contest the Americans. After occupying Ponce, Miles launched a four-column offensive on 9 August, with the ultimate goal of taking San Juan. The attack met little resistance as Spanish forces fell back toward the capital. Miles's triumphal march toward San Juan was interrupted when the United States and Spain agreed to a general armistice on 12 August. His troops had conquered most of Puerto Rico, with total American casualties of four killed and some 40 wounded.

There was still unfinished business in the Philippines. Dewey's early triumph at Manila Bay had eliminated the Spanish navy there, but he did not have sufficient forces to occupy the capital, Manila. A further complication was the presence of some 12,000 Filipino rebels, led by Emilio AGUINALDO, who were besieging the Spanish forces in Manila. The first U.S. ground forces—approximately 2,500 men—arrived in the Philippines on 30 June. More U.S. troops arrived in July, bringing the total to some 12,000, which was approximately the number of Spanish forces at Manila. The Spanish commander was willing to surrender—but only to the Americans, and only after a face-saving "battle." The U.S. commander, Major General Wesley Merritt, agreed to the conditions and told Aguinaldo to keep his men out of the fighting. On the morning of 13 August, Merritt launched his "attack," unaware that a general armistice had just been signed between Spain and the United States. There was some unexpected heavy fighting when Filipino rebels joined in the attack, but combat lasted only a few hours. As agreed earlier, the Spanish force surrendered to the Americans, not to the Filipinos.

The 12 August armistice applied to all fronts. Although the conduct of the war provoked a postwar investigation of the War Department, the war itself had been brief—fewer than four months of fighting—and had a low number of combat-connected deaths—fewer than 400. (Tropical disease and the heat, however, claimed another 2,000 U.S. soldiers and sailors.) The conduct of the war did much to shape the 10 December 1898 Peace Treaty of PARIS. The war began a period of U.S. intervention in the Caribbean and Central America that would continue until the mid-1930s.

See also GUANTÁNAMO NAVY BASE; MacARTHUR, ARTHUR; MANILA, SIEGE OF; PHILIPPINE-AMERICAN WAR; SCHLEY, WINFIELD SCOTT; SPANISH-AMERICAN WAR, CAUSES OF; WOOD, LEONARD.

Further reading: Cosmas, Graham A. *An Army for Empire: The United States Army in the Spanish-American War.* Columbia: University of Missouri Press, 1971; Musciant, Ivan. *Empire by Default: The Spanish-American War and the Dawn of the American Century.* New York: Henry Holt, 1998; Trask, David F. *The War with Spain in 1898.* Lincoln: University of Nebraska Press, 1996.

— Don M. Coerver

Spotsylvania Courthouse, Battle of (7–20 May 1864) *Battle, during the Overland Campaign of the Civil War, between Union forces under Lieutenant General Ulysses S. Grant and Confederate forces led by General Robert E. Lee*

After the battle of the WILDERNESS (5–6 May 1864), Grant ordered Major General George G. MEADE's Army of the Potomac to take the crucial crossroads at Spotsylvania. Meade selected Major General Gouverneur K. WARREN's V Corps to lead the movement. On the night of 7–8 May, Warren's troops were delayed by Confederate cavalry that blocked the roads at Todd's Tavern. As a consequence, Confederate major general Richard H. Anderson's I Corps arrived in Spotsylvania just minutes before the Union forces on 8 May. Warren's troops, later joined by Major General John Sedgwick's VI Corps, launched poorly coordinated attacks throughout the day, and the Confederates held their positions.

Fighting was light on 9 May as the remaining forces on both sides arrived near Spotsylvania. During the sporadic firing, a Confederate sharpshooter killed Sedgwick, who was replaced by Brigadier General Horatio G. Wright.

GRANT and Meade issued orders for an attack on 10 May. Believing that Union moves on LEE's flanks had spread the Southern line too thin, they directed a concerted attack on Lee's center. However, Union coordination broke down. Warren's corps attacked too early, and Anderson easily threw back its assault. The only Union success was by Colonel Emory UPTON's brigade. It penetrated Lieutenant General Richard S. EWELL's II Corps lines. However, the Southerners brought up reinforcements and forced Upton to retreat.

Grant and Meade used 11 May to plan for a major assault on a salient in the Confederate lines known as the "mule shoe." Major General Winfield S. HANCOCK's II Corps moved on the night of 11 May and spearheaded the Union assault the next morning. The Federals pierced the Confederate line at the tip of the salient, but a counterattack by Major General John B. GORDON's division drove Hancock's men back. Later in the morning, Wright's VI Corps

The Battle of Spotsylvania Court House, 7–20 May 1864. Painting by Lewis Prang.   *(Library of Congress)*

joined in the attack in an area that became known as the "bloody angle." The struggle raged all day in one of the most vicious fights of the war. Finally that night, Lee pulled his troops back to a new trench line at the base of the salient.

After the battle of 12 May, both sides rested. Grant devised a new plan that moved the Union V and VI Corps to the Union left in an attempt to turn Lee's flank. However, bad weather on 13 and 14 May slowed the Union move, and Lee shifted forces that blocked it. Both sides then paused while Grant worked out another plan.

Convinced that Lee's most recent shift of forces must have weakened the Southerners' left flank, Grant directed V and VI Corps to shift back to the Union right and launch an attack. This assault took place on 18 May, but the Confederates were well posted in strong entrenchments, and they repulsed the Federals. Before the Federals could make another move, Lee struck the Union right flank with Ewell's corps on 19 May. The Northerners rebuffed this final attack at Spotsylvania.

The two-week engagement at Spotsylvania Court House was a tactical draw, with heavy casualties on both sides. The Federals had made penetrations of the Confederate positions, but could not achieve a decisive victory. In the end, Lee continued to hold fortified lines while Grant retained the initiative.

See also CIVIL WAR: LAND OVERVIEW; OVERLAND CAMPAIGN.

Further reading: Matter, William D. *If It Takes All Summer: The Battle of Spotsylvania.* Chapel Hill: University of North Carolina Press, 1988; Rhea, Gordon C. *The Battles for Spotsylvania Court House and the Road to Yellow Tavern: May 7–12, 1864.* Baton Rouge: Louisiana State University Press, 1997; Rhea, Gordon C. *To the North Anna River. Grant and Lee, May 13–25, 1864.* Baton Rouge: Louisiana State University Press, 2000.

— Curtis S. King

Sprague, Clifton A. F. ("Ziggy") (1896–1955) *U.S. Navy admiral*
Born on 8 January 1896 in Dorchester, Massachusetts, Clifton Albert Furlow Sprague entered the U.S. Naval Academy, Annapolis, in 1914 and was graduated a year early

(in 1917) because of World War I. He spent his war service in a gunboat. He was a student at Pensacola Naval Aviation Station (NAS) (1920–22) and then was a pilot and section leader of scouting group VS-1. From 1923 to 1926 he was the flight officer and executive officer at NAS Anacostia, District of Columbia. Sprague did development work on the arresting gear for the new fleet carriers *Lexington* and *Saratoga* (1926–28) and served as the *Lexington's* flight deck officer and assistant air officer before becoming executive officer of VN-8-D5 at the Naval Academy (1929–31). Sprague was squadron commander of fighter group VF-8 at Panama and Hawaii (1931–34), and in February 1934 became the first naval aviator to complete the 2,650-mile round-trip flight from Hawaii to Midway Island. He served as the air operations officer at NAS Norfolk and air officer of the carrier *Yorktown* before attending the Naval War College in 1939. He then commanded the *Patoka,* a tanker fitted with a mooring mast for dirigibles. From 1940 to 1943 he commanded the seaplane tender *Tangier* and, as a captain, was air officer of the Eastern Sea Frontier, commander NAS Seattle, and captain of the carrier *Wasp.* Under his command, the *Wasp* engaged in the raids on Marcus and WAKE Islands during the MARIANAS ISLANDS campaign, and in the Battle of the PHILIPPINE SEA.

Promoted to rear admiral in July 1944, Sprague assumed command of Carrier Division 25, six escort carriers and their escorts, with which he supported the invasion of Morotai and on 25 October 1944 fought in the Battle off Samar in the larger Battle of LEYTE GULF.

On that date, Japanese admiral Takeo Kurita transited San Bernardino Strait and entered Leyte Gulf with four battleships, eight cruisers, and 11 destroyers. Sprague launched aircraft as 14-, 16-, and 18-inch shells straddled his carriers. He made smoke, headed into a nearby rain squall, radioed for help in plain language, and made many course changes before turning south. With Kurita's ships about to box him in, he took the extraordinary measure of ordering his escorts to undertake suicide attacks. Three of the U.S. attackers were sunk and the rest damaged, but torpedoes put a Japanese heavy cruiser out of action, caused the battle line to scatter and lose ground, and confused the tactical situation for Kurita even though he closed in and sank the CVE *Gambier Bay.* Then an attack by planes from a nearby CVE group crippled two heavy cruisers, and torpedo attacks by planes caused Japanese ships to scatter. Kurita thereupon withdrew. Sprague had calmly but quickly made vital decisions that saved most of his force and defended the Allies' invasion forces in Leyte Gulf.

In February and March 1945, Sprague fought in the IWO JIMA campaign and at OKINAWA. The war over, he commanded navy air in Operation Crossroads at Bikini Atoll and was chief of basic air training at Corpus Christi NAS. He commanded first a carrier group in the Mediterranean,

then the naval air bases of the 11th and 12th naval districts from San Diego. As the commander of the Alaska Sea Frontier, he flew over the North Pole. Sprague retired in November 1951. He died in San Diego, California, on 13 April 1955.

See also AIRCRAFT CARRIERS; WORLD WAR II, COURSE OF: PACIFIC THEATER.

Further reading: Cutler, Thomas J. *The Battle of Leyte Gulf, 23–26 October 1944.* New York: HarperCollins, 1994; Morison, Samuel E. *History of United States Naval Operations in World War II.* Vol. 12, *Leyte, June 1944–August 1944.* Boston: Little, Brown, 1958; Wheeler, Gerald E. *Kinkaid of the Seventh Fleet: A Biography of Admiral Thomas C. Kinkaid, U.S. Navy.* Washington, D.C.: Naval Historical Center, 1995; Wukowitz, John F. *Devotion to Duty: A Biography of Admiral Clifton A. F. Sprague.* Annapolis, Md.: Naval Institute Press, 1995.

— Paolo E. Coletta

Spruance, Raymond Ames (1886–1969) *U.S. Navy admiral and commander of Fifth Fleet in World War II*
Born on 3 July 1886 in Baltimore, Maryland, Raymond Ames Spruance graduated from the U.S. Naval Academy, Annapolis, in 1906. He participated in the circumnavigation of the globe with the Great White Fleet and was commissioned an ensign in 1908. He served with both the Atlantic and Asiatic Fleets before being promoted to lieutenant junior grade and taking command of the destroyer *Bainbridge* (1913–14). During World War I he rose to the rank of commander and was executive officer of a troop transport.

From 1919 to 1921, Spruance commanded destroyers. He then headed the Electrical Division at the Bureau of Engineering (1921–24) before serving on board the *Pittsburgh* (1924–25). Spruance commanded another destroyer (1925–26) and then attended the Naval War College (1926–27). He served at the Office of Naval Intelligence (1927–29) and in 1931 returned to the Naval War College to head correspondence courses until 1933. He earned promotion to captain in 1932. Spruance served aboard the *Raleigh* (1933–35), before returning for a third tour at the Naval War College, where he headed three departments and taught naval command as well as strategies for fighting a Pacific war. In 1938 he took command of battleship *Mississippi.* He was promoted to rear admiral in 1939.

In July 1941 Spruance took command of Cruiser Squadron Five at Pearl Harbor. As surface screen commander for Admiral William F. HALSEY's carrier forces, he took part in the raids on the Gilbert, Marshall, WAKE, and Marcus Islands in February and March 1942. He also

Admiral Raymond A. Spruance, April 1944   *(Naval Historical Foundation)*

served in this capacity for Halsey's fleet as it launched Lieutenant Colonel James DOOLITTLE's TOKYO RAID that April.

In May 1942 Spruance relieved Halsey as commander of Task Force 16 on board the carrier *Enterprise.* He was junior to Admiral Frank J. FLETCHER at the Battle of MIDWAY, but emerged as the victorious commander during the course of the fight. His brilliant ship disposition and use of available aircraft, despite the fact that he was not an aviator, proved decisive in the sinking of four Japanese carriers.

Two weeks later Spruance became chief of staff and deputy to Pacific Fleet Commander Admiral Chester W. NIMITZ. In May 1943 he was promoted to vice admiral and in August received command of the Central Pacific offensive that he had helped to plan. Spruance oversaw the invasion of the Gilbert Islands in November 1943 and of the MARSHALL ISLANDS in January–February 1944. He led the raid on the Japanese base at Truk later in February. In March 1944 Spruance became a full admiral, and in April he was redesignated commander of Fifth Fleet and led the raid on Palaus. During the summer of 1944, Spruance directed the invasion of the MARIANA ISLANDS; in June he won the Battle of the PHILIPPINE SEA, including the so-called Great Marianas Turkey Shoot, which destroyed most of the Japanese carrier-based aircraft.

Spruance planned and commanded the invasions of IWO JIMA and OKINAWA in February and March–May 1945, respectively. He helped prepare plans for the proposed invasion of the Japanese home islands and served briefly in the occupation.

Spruance is considered by many to be the most brilliant fleet commander of World War II. A superb combination of fighter and intellectual, he maintained a dispassionate respect for the Japanese throughout the war. He encouraged initiative and avoided details. He also was known for his integrity and during the war spoke out against the internment of Japanese Americans. He avidly avoided publicity. A master of naval warfare, he nonetheless suffered from periodic bouts of seasickness.

In November 1945 Spruance became commander in chief, Pacific Fleet, serving in this capacity until his appointment in February 1946 as president of the Naval War College. He retired in July 1948 but later served as ambassador to the Philippines (1952–53). Spruance died at Pebble Beach, California, on 13 December 1969.

See also WORLD WAR II, COURSE OF U.S. INVOLVEMENT: PACIFIC THEATER.

Further reading: Buell, Thomas B. *The Quiet Warrior: A Biography of Admiral Raymond A. Spruance.* Annapolis, Md.: Naval Institute Press, 1992; Forrestal, Emmet P. *Admiral Raymond A. Spruance, USN: A Study in Command.* Washington, D.C.: U.S. Government Printing Office, 1966.

— Laura Matysek Wood

Squalus, USS   *U.S. Navy submarine*

On 23 May 1939 the new 1,450-ton submarine USS *Squalus* (SS-192), skippered by Lieutenant Oliver Naquin, sortied from the Portsmouth Navy Yard (New Hampshire) to conduct final test dives, only to land on the bottom at a depth of 243 feet with its rear compartments flooded. When expected reports were not received in Portsmouth, Admiral Cyrus Cole alerted the submarine rescue ship *Fulton* at New London, Connecticut, and the submarine desk in the Office of the Chief of Naval Operations, and asked for Charles "Swede" Momsen, the navy's foremost submarine salvage man. He also sent the submarine *Sculpin* and a tug to locate the *Squalus.* Naquin had sent up smoke rockets and a marker buoy containing a telephone line, but its cable broke. The tug finally located the *Squalus,* and Momsen, aboard the *Fulton,* lowered a McCann Rescue Chamber over its forward escape hatch and rescued 33 of the 57 men, 23 men trapped aft died, including Naquin. In September, the navy raised the *Squalus* and refitted it. Renamed the *Sailfish,* it served in World War II in the

Pacific theater and was decommissioned in October 1945 and sold in June 1948.

See also SUBMARINES.

Further reading: Barrows, Nathaniel. *Blow all Ballast! The Story of the Squalus.* New York: Dodd, Mead, 1940; Gray, Edwyn. *Few Survived: A Comprehensive Survey of Submarine Accidents and Disasters.* London: Leo Cooper, 1996; Maas, Peter. *The Terrible Hours: The Man Behind the Greatest Submarine Rescue in History.* New York: HarperCollins, 1999.

— Paolo E. Coletta

Standish, Miles (ca. 1584–1656) *Military leader of the Plymouth Colony*

Born around 1584 in Lancashire, England, Miles (or Myles) Standish was trained as a professional soldier. He served as a mercenary in the Netherlands during the Dutch War of Independence. In 1620, Pilgrim separatists exiled in Holland hired him as their military adviser and a leader of their American colonization effort. While not himself a separatist, Standish's military expertise and devotion to the colony made him a crucial figure in the early history of the Plymouth colony. He led the first landing party when the *Mayflower* reached Plymouth in 1620, and he was elected captain general of the Pilgrim militia in 1621.

Standish gave shape to the colonists' Indian policy and became the colony's chief negotiator with the local Indians. His expertise in dealing with the Indians kept the peace for many years. He established the Pilgrim militia system based on the English model and organized it into four units, each with specialized duties. He also oversaw the building of defensive fortifications at Plymouth. Over the years, Standish led expeditions against Indian, French, and English threats to the Pilgrim community.

Standish traveled to England in 1625 as an agent for the colony, securing new loans and purchasing supplies. Having returned to America, in June 1628 he led the Pilgrim expedition against the heretic Thomas Morton at his settlement of Merry Mount; he then arrested Morton and sent him back to England in chains. Standish, along with John Alden, established the outlying town of Duxbury in 1631 and settled there in 1637. In 1633 Standish was made an assistant in the colonial government. In 1644 he became treasurer and assistant governor of the colony, posts in which he served until 1649. Standish remained instrumental in the military and political life of Plymouth until his death in Duxbury on 3 October 1656.

See also PEQUOT WAR.

Further reading: Bradford, William. *Of Plymouth Plantation.* Edited by Harvey Wish. New York: Capricorn Books, 1962; Leach, Douglas Edward. "The Military System of Plymouth Colony," *New England Quarterly* 26 (1951): 342–64; Peterson, Harold L. "The Military Equipment of Plymouth and Bay Colonies, 1620–1690," *New England Quarterly* 20 (1947): 197–208; Salisbury, Neal. *Manitou and Providence: Indians, Europeans, and the Making of New England, 1500–1643.* New York: Oxford University Press, 1982.

— Kyle F. Zelner

Stanton, Edwin M. (1814–1869) *U.S. secretary of war during the Civil War*

Born on 19 December 1814 in Steubenville, Ohio, Edwin McMasters Stanton as a child developed an asthmatic condition that continued to plague him the remainder of his life. When he was 13, his father died, forcing Stanton to leave school and work in a bookstore to supplement the family's income. In 1831 he entered Kenyon College, but he was forced to leave after two years when his funds ran out. He read for the law at the offices of his guardian and was admitted to the bar in 1836. From 1849 to 1856, Stanton was counsel for the state of Pennsylvania, in which position he acquired a national reputation. His work as a special counsel for the U.S. government in 1858, litigating fraudulent land claims in California, led to his appointment as attorney general under President James Buchanan in December 1860. He did all he could to stiffen Buchanan's resolve to preserve the Union. Stanton left office when President Abraham LINCOLN became president, but he remained in Washington. He returned to the cabinet as secretary of war in February 1862.

A friend of U.S. Army commander Major General George B. MCCLELLAN, Stanton quickly became disillusioned with him and recommended to Lincoln that McClellan be removed from supreme command. McClellan falsely blamed Stanton for the failure of his Peninsula campaign, and the two men became bitter enemies. Stanton played a key role in the appointment of successive commanders of the army, and he oversaw the operations of Union forces in the field and helped Lincoln formulate strategy. A staunch patriot with an unyielding desire to preserve the Union, Stanton was also an advocate of the concept of total war.

Stanton was a gifted administrator. His blunt manner and zeal in rooting out waste and fraud in procurement practices won the enmity of many. He rigidly enforced the new draft laws and on occasion restricted the freedom of a press that too often reportedly military information of great use to the Confederacy.

Although Stanton and Lincoln complemented one another, Stanton often disagreed with the president, and he was not hesitant to express that displeasure to others when he believed Lincoln was not prosecuting the war with sufficient vigor. The sometimes stormy relationship between the two men later led to stories that Stanton was associated with Lincoln's assassination, although there is no basis for this in fact.

Stanton kept his cabinet position under President Andrew Johnson until May 1868, when a struggle between Congress and Johnson over his tenure forced him from office. Worn out by his exertions, he turned down opportunities to run for public office in order to recover his strength. Nominated for the Supreme Court by President Ulysses S. GRANT, Stanton died in Washington, D.C., on 24 December 1869, four days after the Senate confirmed his nomination.

See also CIVIL WAR, CAUSES OF; CIVIL WAR, LAND OVERVIEW.

Further reading: Allison, Amy. *Edwin Stanton: Union War Secretary.* Philadelphia: Chelsea House, 2001; Pratt, Fletcher. *Stanton: Lincoln's Secretary of War.* Westport, Conn.: Greenwood Press, 1970; Thomas, Benjamin P., and Harold M. Hyman. *Stanton: The Life and Times of Lincoln's Secretary of War.* New York: Knopf, 1962.

— Spencer C. Tucker

Stapp, John P. (1910–1999) *U.S. Air Force officer and pioneer in aviation medicine*
Born on 11 July 1910 in Bahia, Brazil, to missionary parents, John Paul Stapp graduated from Baylor University in 1931 and earned a Ph.D. in biophysics from the University of Texas and an M.D. from the University of Minnesota. Serving in the U.S. Army Medical Corps during World War II, Stapp became a flight surgeon at Wright Field.

In 1947 Stapp began to investigate the effects of violent deceleration on the human body. Acting as his own guinea pig, he rode a rocket-propelled sled at Muroc, California, and proved that humans could survive much greater g forces than hitherto believed possible. As aircraft speeds increased, Stapp's test runs kept pace, probing human tolerance to impact forces and windblast.

In 1954 Stapp simulated an ejection from a supersonic aircraft at high altitude by riding a sled to 632 mph and, while decelerating to zero in 1.4 seconds, experiencing forces in excess of 40g. His body weighed momentarily 6,800 pounds. During his 29 sled rides, Stapp paid a heavy personal price, losing fillings from his teeth, cracking ribs, breaking wrists, and suffering retinal hemorrhages. With his insights into collisions gained at such expense, Stapp in 1957 founded and headed the Aeromedical Field Laboratory, Holloman Air Force Base, where he helped to design better aircraft restraint systems, ejection seats, and escape capsules.

Realizing that the principal killer of air force personnel during peacetime was auto accidents, Stapp also worked on improved seat belts and was the first to conduct car collision tests using anthropomorphic dummies. His efforts in this field led the air force in 1967 to loan Stapp to the Department of Transportation as chief scientist in the highway and traffic safety program. Upon his retirement from the air force as a colonel three years later, Stapp continued as a consultant with the Department of Transportation, and in 1972 he joined the faculty of the University of California's Institute of Safety and Systems Management. Later he advised the surgeon general of the United States as well as the National Aeronautics and Space Administration. Stapp's work was recognized with honorary degrees and numerous decorations. He died in Alamogordo, New Mexico, on 13 November 1999.

See also MEDICINE, MILITARY.

Further reading: Armstrong, Harry G., ed. *Aerospace Medicine.* Baltimore, Md.: Williams, 1961; Robinson, Douglas H. *The Dangerous Sky: A History of Aviation Medicine.* Seattle: University of Washington Press, 1974; U.S. Air Force Missile Development Center. *History of Research in Space Biology and Biodynamics at the Air Force Missile Development Center, Holloman Air Force Base, New Mexico, 1946–1958.* Holloman AFB, N.M.: Air Research and Development Command, 1958.

— Malcolm Muir, Jr.

Stark, Harold R. (1880–1972) *U.S. Navy admiral and chief of naval operations*
Born on 12 November 1880 in Wilkes-Barre, Pennsylvania, Harold Raynsford Stark graduated from the U.S. Naval Academy, Annapolis, in 1903. Commissioned an ensign in the U.S. Navy in 1905, he participated in the Great White Fleet's 1907–09 around-the-world cruise and subsequently captained torpedo boats, destroyers, and an armored cruiser. During World War I he commanded a flotilla in the Mediterranean, undertaking antisubmarine and escort duties, and served on the staff of Admiral William S. SIMS, commander of U.S. naval forces in Europe, coordinating collaborative Anglo-American naval operations.

Between the two world wars, Stark alternated sea duty, courses, and service as aide to the secretary of the navy. Promoted to rear admiral, from 1934 to 1937 Stark headed the Bureau of Ordnance; in August 1939, President Franklin D. ROOSEVELT named Stark, who was then commanding Cruisers Battle Force, as chief of naval operations (CNO). The next month, World War II began in Europe.

Stark, who shared Roosevelt's profoundly interventionist outlook, immediately instituted major naval rearmament, winning congressional appropriations for a shipbuilding program intended to make the U.S. Navy the world's largest, and a rapid expansion of naval facilities and personnel. His memorandum Plan D or Dog, prepared for Roosevelt in November 1940, delineated what became the fundamental American wartime strategy, that Germany, the greatest threat, must be defeated first. Convinced that Britain's survival was essential to United States national security, in early 1941 Stark proposed and held staff talks with a high-level British delegation, whose ABC-1 (America-Britain-Canada) Rainbow 5 strategic agreement, much of which he drafted, became the basis of wartime Anglo-American cooperation. Stark constantly urged Roosevelt to do more to assist Britain, and by autumn 1941 American naval forces were effectively at war with Germany in the Atlantic.

Although Stark attempted to improve Pacific fortifications and naval strength, viewing this theater as secondary, he opposed measures, such as an oil embargo, that might provoke forceful Japanese reactions. As with other American military and civilian officials, he failed to interpret correctly or transmit to U.S. Commander in Chief in the Pacific Admiral Husband E. KIMMEL deciphered cable traffic indicating that Japan might attack PEARL HARBOR, a misjudgment for which one investigation later faulted him.

Shortly after the Pearl Harbor attack Stark lost his control over U.S. naval forces, and in March 1942 Roosevelt dispatched him to Europe as commander of U.S. naval forces there. In this position he performed valuable liaison functions between London and Washington; established and later dismantled American naval bases in Britain, France, and Germany; directed logistical support for U.S. naval forces; and served as Washington's unofficial envoy to Free French leader General Charles de Gaulle. Stark retired from active duty in 1946. He died in Washington, D.C., on 20 August 1972.

See also KING, ERNEST J.; LEAHY, WILLIAM D.; STIMSON, HENRY LEWIS.

Further reading: Cline, Ray S. *Washington Command Post: The Operations Division.* Washington, D.C.: Office of the Chief of Military History, Department of the Army, 1951; Cowman, Ian. *Dominion or Decline: Anglo-American Naval Relations in the Pacific, 1937–1941.* Washington, D.C.: Berg, 1996; Reynolds, Clark G. *Famous American Admirals.* New York: Van Nostrand Reinhold, 1978; Simpson, B. Mitchell, III. *Admiral Harold R. Stark: Architect of Victory, 1939–1945.* Columbia: University of South Carolina Press, 1989.

— Priscilla Roberts

Stark, John (1728–1822) *Continental army general*
Born on 28 August 1728 in Londonderry, New Hampshire, John Stark grew up in Manchester. Although a farmer like his father, Stark had an adventurous side and spent his early adult years in hunting and exploration trips in the northwest country, often dealing with or fighting with the Abnaki

Indians. During this time, friction between the French and British continued to increase, and in 1756 Stark joined Robert ROGERS's famed rangers as a first lieutenant.

Stark was involved in several actions during the FRENCH AND INDIAN WAR, including the siege of FORT WILLIAM HENRY. He managed to escape the infamous Indian attack on the surrendered British column, and came home with a wealth of military knowledge.

At war's end, Stark returned to civilian life, but word of the 19 April 1775, Battles of LEXINGTON AND CONCORD led him to make his way to Medford, Massachusetts, leaving orders for the local militia to meet him there. When the New England militias were organized as the Army of Observation, Stark became colonel of the 1st New Hampshire Regiment.

Stark's first engagement was the 27 May 1775 raid on Noddles Island. He and his men played a crucial role in the 17 June 1775 Battle of BUNKER HILL. Stark later joined Continental army commander General George WASHINGTON at the Delaware River, and he and his regiment fought in the 26 December 1776 Battle of TRENTON.

In early 1777, when the Continental army was reorganized, Stark was passed over for promotion. He resigned his commission in protest, but agreed to return to the defense of New Hampshire if the northern frontier was threatened. The British advance down the Hudson did threaten the frontier, so Stark organized short-term militia forces and, with Seth Warner's Vermont troops, stopped the British advance in the August Battle of BENNINGTON. Ordered to join Major General Horatio GATES at SARATOGA, Stark nonetheless departed when the militia's term of enlistment expired.

A grateful Congress promoted Stark to brigadier general, and he returned to duty to serve in the New York/New Jersey area. At war's end, Stark won promotion to major general for his dedicated service. Stark lived long enough to be recognized as the last surviving Continental army general. He died in Manchester on 8 May 1822.

See also AMERICAN REVOLUTIONARY WAR: LAND OVERVIEW; MILITIA, ORGANIZATION AND ROLE OF (1603–1815).

Further reading: Foster, Herbert D. *Stark's Independent Command at Bennington.* Manchester, N.H.: Standard Book Co., 1918; Stark, Caleb. *Memoirs and Official Correspondence of General John Stark.* Boston: Harvard University Press, 1972.

— Patrick R. Jennings

state navies (American Revolution) *Navies of the individual colonies during the American Revolutionary War*
Eleven of the 13 colonies developed some naval force; each remained under the control of that individual state. While

the Continental navy built warships as large as FRIGATES to do battle with British warships and merchantmen on the seas, the small state forces were intended to defend the individual state coasts and to protect seaports and coastal trade.

With several colonies considering the establishment of navies, the Continental Congress passed a resolution on 10 July 1775 supporting the idea. The largest state navies were those of Massachusetts, Connecticut, Pennsylvania, Maryland, Virginia, and South Carolina. For the most part, the state navies consisted of row galleys and smaller armed craft. Many of these were modified merchant ships. During the War of Independence the states commissioned some 100 vessels altogether. Combined with the Continental navy, these vessels accounted for 200 British ships sunk or captured; another 600 British ships were taken by privateers.

The first state navy, that of Massachusetts, began when the people of Maine captured two small armed British vessels—the renamed sloop *Machias Liberty* and schooner *Diligent.* In January 1776, Massachusetts ordered 10 new sloops; however, this order soon was modified to five new ships and five converted merchant ships. The Massachusetts navy eventually numbered 32 vessels, although many of these were lost in the PENOBSCOT BAY EXPEDITION, in which 37 American vessels were deliberately destroyed to prevent their capture.

The Connecticut, Pennsylvania, Maryland, and North and South Carolina navies were all smaller. The Connecticut navy consisted of only 10 vessels, while the Pennsylvania navy numbered 20 armed boats, two floating batteries, 10 fire rafts, and 13 40-foot row galleys. The Maryland navy had numerous one-gun galleys and armed boats and barges, which operated on the shallow waters of the Chesapeake Bay. Eighteen of the small vessels saw service, along with the 22-gun *Defense,* two schooners, and one sloop. The North Carolina navy mainly comprised three brigantines. It played only a minimal role in the war because of scant British interest in the North Carolina coast. The Virginia navy numbered 10 ships, eight brigs, a sloop, nine galleys, and six armed boats. Virginia also had the largest naval shore establishment.

In July 1775, South Carolina captured a British supply ship carrying eight tons of gunpowder. A month later it captured another with six additional tons of gunpowder. In 1779, South Carolina added the 44-gun frigate *Bricole.* This French-designed and -funded ship had been built for the Continental navy and was intended for John Paul JONES. Learning of its intended destination, the British pressured the Dutch builders. The ship ultimately sailed to France and was then delivered to South Carolina.

Although poorly funded and lacking supplies and qualified leadership, and short of sailors, the various state navies performed a useful service. They and many privateers impacted the British war effort.

See also AMERICAN REVOLUTIONARY WAR: NAVAL OVERVIEW; PRIVATEERS IN THE AMERICAN REVOLUTIONARY WAR.

Further reading: Jackson, W. John. *The Pennsylvania Navy, 1775–1781. The Defense of the Delaware.* New Brunswick, N.J.: Rutgers University Press, 1974; Miller, Nathan. *Sea of Glory: The Continental Navy Fights for Independence, 1775–1783.* New York: David McKay, 1974.

— William Martin Boulware

Sternberg, George M. (1838–1915) *U.S. Army surgeon general and renowned bacteriologist*
Born on 8 June 1838 in Otsego County, New York, George Miller Sternberg received his schooling at the Hartwick Seminary. He taught at various schools, including Hartwick, and took up the study of medicine.

In 1860 Sternberg graduated with an M.D. degree from the College of Physicians and Surgeons in New York. In May 1861, shortly after the beginning of the Civil War, he became an assistant surgeon in the U.S. Army, assigned to the Army of the Potomac. During the war he held many different positions: assistant to the medical director for the Department of the Gulf in New Orleans; executive officer of the U.S. General Hospital at Portsmouth Grove, Rhode Island; and director of the U.S. General Hospital in Cleveland, Ohio, and, simultaneously, assistant medical director at Columbus, Ohio (until 1866).

Sternberg's interest in science led to his greatest work, on yellow fever. He began this in 1870 at Governor's Island in New York Harbor. From 1872 to 1875 he was an army surgeon at Fort Barrancas, Florida, where he encountered yellow fever epidemics. During 1875 he almost died of yellow fever; although it took six months for him to recover, he developed a permanent immunity.

Briefly stationed at Walla Walla, Washington Territory, as a lieutenant colonel, Sternberg worked in bacteriology and the study of surgical disinfectants. The army next assigned him to the National Board of Health, and this led to his membership on the Havana Yellow Fever Commission in 1879. In 1886 he became the director of the Hoagland Laboratory at Long Island Medical College, Brooklyn, New York. Sternberg also traveled to Brazil, Mexico, and Havana to research yellow fever. When at the Hoagland Laboratory, he published *A Manual of Bacteriology* (1892), which became the standard reference for bacteriology. Later he published *Immunity, Protective Inoculations in Infectious Diseases and Serum Theory* (1895), and *Infection and Immunity with Special Reference to Prevention of Infectious Diseases* (1903).

President Grover Cleveland appointed Sternberg army surgeon general in May 1893. In that position he worked to provide temporary hospitals, medical personnel, and supplies, and he tried to improve sanitation. He worked with the Dodge Commission to reorganize the Army Medical Department, forming the Medical Reserve Corps, the Corps of Dental Surgery, and the ARMY NURSE CORPS. In 1898 he formed the Typhoid Fever Board with the help of Major Walter REED, Edwin Shakespeare, and Victor C. Vaughn. The board found that human contact with flies was the cause of the transmission of the deadly typhoid fever. Two years later, in 1900, Sternberg presided over the Yellow Fever Board.

Sternberg retired in 1902. He died in Washington, D.C., on 3 November 1915.

See also MEDICINE, MILITARY.

Further reading: Gibson, John M. *Soldier in White: The Life of General George Miller Sternberg.* Durham, N.C.: Duke University Press, 1958.

— Brandon R. Matthews

Steuben, Friedrich von (1730–1794) *Continental army general*

Born on 17 September 1730 in Magdeburg, Prussia, Friedrich Wilhelm Augustin von Steuben became a soldier at 16. During the 1756–63 Seven Years War he rose to the rank of captain in the Prussian army and was for a time attached to the general staff of King Frederick II (the Great). After the war, Steuben retired from the army and became court chamberlain for the prince of Hohenzollern-Hechingen.

Recruited to fight in the American Revolutionary War by the American minister to France, Benjamin Franklin, Steuben was given a letter of introduction to Continental army commander General George WASHINGTON as a "lieutenant general in the King of Prussia's service" and ardent supporter of the American cause.

Arriving in America in December 1777, Steuben impressed the Continental Congress with his fictitiously high rank, his pleasant personality, and with Washington's favorable comments; Congress appointed him to train the Continental forces stationed at the winter encampment of VALLEY FORGE, Pennsylvania. Thereafter, American forces were better prepared to confront their professional British army adversaries in the field.

With the rank of major general and the position of inspector general, Steuben wrote *Regulations for the Order and Discipline of the Troops of the United States.* Also known as the "Blue Book," it became the standard drill manual for the entire army and served as the country's official military guide until 1812. He also remodeled the army's organization, improving its discipline and creating an efficient staff. In 1780 he sat on the court-martial of British army officer Major John André, who was charged with ESPIONAGE. Steuben later secured a field command and served as a division commander in Virginia, participating in the decisive 1781 siege of YORKTOWN.

After the war, Steuben became an American citizen and settled in New York City, where he lived so extravagantly that, despite large grants of money from Congress and the grant of 16,000 acres of land by New York state, he fell into debt. Finally, in 1790 he was voted a life pension of $2,500 per year, which was enough to maintain him on his farm near Remsen, New York, until he died on 28 November 1794.

See also REVOLUTIONARY WAR: LAND OVERVIEW.

Further reading: Palmer, John M. *General von Steuben.* Port Washington, N.Y.: Kennikat Press, 1966; Tolzmann, Don H., ed. *The Army of the American Revolution and Its Organizer: Rudolf Cronau's Biography of Baron von Steuben.* Bowie, Md.: Heritage Books, 1998.

— Alexander M. Bielakowski

Stewart, Alexander P. (1821–1908) *Confederate army general*

Born on 2 October 1821 in Rogersville, Tennessee, Alexander Peter Stewart graduated from the U.S. Military Academy, WEST POINT, in 1842. Commissioned a second lieutenant and posted to artillery, he served on garrison duty and taught at West Point. He resigned his commission in 1845 to teach mathematics and philosophy at Cumberland University and the University of Nashville. Although he opposed secession, when Tennessee left the Union, Stewart offered his services to the Confederacy, becoming a major of artillery.

After seeing action in Kentucky and Missouri early in the Civil War, Stewart was appointed brigadier general in November 1861. He led a brigade at SHILOH, PERRYVILLE, STONES RIVER/MURFREESBORO, and in the Tullahoma campaign. Promoted to major general in June 1863, he commanded a division at CHICKAMAUGA, where he was slightly wounded, and at CHATTANOOGA. During the ATLANTA CAMPAIGN he assumed command of the Army of Mississippi (redesignated Stewart's Corps, Army of Tennessee) upon the death of Lieutenant General Leonidas POLK in June 1864.

Promoted to lieutenant general, Stewart led his corps with great distinction throughout the balance of the campaign, most notably at Peachtree Creek on 20 July. He was wounded in the action at Ezra Church on 28 July, but quickly returned to duty and rendered strong service during General John B. HOOD's disastrous Tennessee campaign, after which he and what remained of the Army of Tennessee joined General Joseph E. JOHNSTON's command in North Carolina. He surrendered with Johnston in April 1865.

After the war, Stewart returned to teaching and engaged in the insurance business. In 1874 he was named chancellor of the University of Mississippi, a position he held until 1886. He later became commissioner of the Chickamauga-Chattanooga National Military Park. He died in Biloxi, Mississippi, on 30 August 1908.

See also CIVIL WAR, LAND OVERVIEW.

Further reading: Connelly, Thomas L. *Autumn of Glory: The Army of Tennessee, 1862–1865.* Baton Rouge: Louisiana State University Press, 1971; Elliott, Sam Davis. *Soldier of Tennessee: General Alexander P. Stewart and the Civil War in the West.* Baton Rouge: Louisiana State University Press, 1999.

— David Coffey

Stewart, Charles (1778–1869) *U.S. Navy admiral*
Born on 29 July 1778 at Philadelphia, Pennsylvania, Charles Stewart emulated his merchant captain father, beginning his life at sea as a cabin boy on a merchant ship in 1791. Soon he commanded his own ship.

In March 1798 during the QUASI-WAR WITH FRANCE, Stewart received a commission in the U.S. Navy as a lieutenant. First assigned to the West Indies in the frigate *United States* under Commodore John BARRY, Stewart then served on the *Enterprise.* In July 1800, as senior lieutenant in the navy, he took command of the schooner *Experiment,* capturing near Guadeloupe the French privateers *Deux Amis* in September and *Diane* in October 1800.

Following the outbreak of the TRIPOLITAN WAR, in 1802 Stewart was first lieutenant on the *CONSTELLATION* in the blockade of Tripoli. He then commanded the new brig *Siren* (1803–05) and supported Lieutenant Stephen DECATUR's 16 February 1804 raid to destroy the captured U.S. frigate *PHILADELPHIA* in Tripoli Harbor. Promoted to master commandant in 1804, Stewart took command of the *Essex* at Tunis in September 1805. He was promoted to captain in April 1806, after his return to the United States.

From 1806 to 1807 Stewart oversaw the building of gunboats at the New York Navy Yard. After that he took a leave of absence to work as a merchant captain (1808–12).

When the WAR OF 1812 began, Stewart returned to U.S. Navy service in command of the brig *ARGUS,* the sloop *Hornet,* and then, in December 1812, the frigate *CONSTELLATION.* When the British blockade off Norfolk prevented his departure, Stewart took command of the frigate *CONSTITUTION* at Boston in the spring of 1813.

Stewart finally got to sea in December 1813 and raided British commerce until April 1814, taking a number of merchant ships as prizes before returning to Boston. Again blockaded by the British, the *Constitution* was unable to get to sea again until December 1814. During the period, until April 1815, *Constitution* took several more prizes. On 20 February 1815, in a brilliant fight, Stewart captured two British warships, the frigate *Cyane* and the corvette *Levant*—although the latter ship was recaptured by the British on the return to Boston.

After the war, from 1816 to 1820 Stewart commanded the Atlantic Squadron, with his flag in the *Franklin.* In 1820 he took the *Franklin* to the Pacific for four years. He was president of the Examining Board in 1829 and a member of the Board of Naval Commissioners from 1830 to 1833. He commanded the Philadelphia Navy Yard from 1838 to 1841, the Home Squadron from 1841 to 1843, and returned to command the Philadelphia Navy Yard from 1846 to 1849 and again from 1853 to 1860. Stewart was promoted to senior flag officer (the first to hold this title) in April 1859 and retired in December 1861. Promoted to rear admiral on the retired list in July 1862, Stewart died in Bordentown, New Jersey, on 6 November 1869.

See also JEFFERSONIAN GUNBOAT PROGRAM.

Further reading: Martin, Tyrone G. *A Most Fortunate Ship: A Narrative History of Old Ironsides.* Annapolis, Md.: Naval Institute Press, 1997; Reynolds, Clark G. *Famous American Admirals.* New York: Van Nostrand Reinhold, 1978.

— Sarah Hilgendorff List

Stilwell, Joseph W. ("Vinegar Joe") (1883–1946)
U.S. Army general
Born on 19 March 1883 in Palatka, Florida, Joseph Warren Stilwell graduated from the U.S. Military Academy, WEST POINT, in 1904. Until 1917, he alternated tours in the Philippines with spells of language instructing at West Point. During World War I, Stilwell was chief intelligence officer of IV Corps in France. In 1920 he volunteered to become a language officer for China, studying Chinese in California and Beijing. In the 1920s and 1930s he served 10 years in China—on general duties from 1920 to 1923; as an infantry battalion commander from 1926 to 1929, in which capacity he served under and impressed Lieutenant Colonel George C. MARSHALL; and as military attaché from 1935 to 1939. Stilwell also took various courses; taught at the Infantry School, Fort Benning; trained and organized reserves; and held commands in Texas and California. He was promoted to brigadier general in April 1939, to major general in September 1940, and to lieutenant general in January 1942.

Marshall named Stilwell concurrently commander of all American forces in the CHINA-BURMA-INDIA theater and chief of staff to Generalissimo Jiang Jieshi (Chiang Kaishek), the leader of America's ally, Nationalist China, who himself made Stilwell commander of the Fifth and Sixth Chinese armies. On arrival at the Nationalist headquarters of Chongqing, Stilwell attempted to revitalize the demoralized CBI theater, demonstrating considerable tactical, organizational, and leadership ability as he gradually reclaimed northern Burma.

In 1943, Stilwell also became deputy to British admiral Lord Louis Mountbatten, Allied head of the Southeast Asian Command. In 1944, a renewed Japanese offensive and American demands that Stilwell, promoted temporary full general (August 1944), assume genuine control of all Chinese forces provoked a crisis with Jiang, with whom the undiplomatic Stilwell's relations were already strained. Whereas Stilwell sought to create a strong ground force capable of defeating Japan and to mount an aggressive land campaign, Jiang preferred to take the advice of the American flier Major General Claire L. CHENNAULT to rely on air missions against Japanese bases, and to reserve his troops for his own purposes—predominantly, to quash a growing internal Chinese Communist challenge.

On Jiang's insistence, Stilwell was replaced and CBI itself now became two commands. Although Stilwell was difficult and abrasive, his assorted and sometimes conflicting duties carried variegated responsibilities almost certainly beyond any single man's strength to shoulder. After a short training assignment in the United States, in June 1945 he took command of the Eighth Army in OKINAWA, expecting to take part in the final invasion of Japan, which Tokyo's surrender made unnecessary. Scheduled to retire in late 1946, Stilwell took over the Sixth Army Western Defense Command in San Francisco, where he died on 12 October 1946. His volatile temper and acerbic personality led to Stilwell's unflattering nickname, "Vinegar Joe."

See also MERRILL'S MARAUDERS; WORLD WAR II, COURSE OF U.S. INVOLVEMENT: PACIFIC THEATER.

Further reading: Prefer, Nathan N. *Vinegar Joe's War: Stilwell's Campaigns for Burma.* Novato, Calif.: Presidio Press, 2000; Romanus, C. F., and R. Sunderland. *United States Army in World War II: China-Burma-India Theater.* 3 vols. Washington, D.C.: Office of the Chief of Military History, Department of the Army, 1953–1959; Sunderland, Riley, and Charles F. Romanus. *Stilwell's Personal File: China, Burma, India, 1942–1944.* 5 vols. Wilmington, Del.: Scholarly Resources, 1976; Tuchman, Barbara. *Stilwell and the American Experience in China, 1911–45.* New York: Macmillan, 1970; White, Theodore H., ed. *The Stilwell Papers.* New York: W. Sloane Associates, 1948.

— Priscilla Roberts

Stimson, Henry L. (1867–1950) *Secretary of war and state*

Born on 21 September 1867 in New York City, Henry Lewis Stimson was educated at Phillips Academy, Yale University, and Harvard Law School. In 1891 Stimson entered the law firm of Root and Clarke. Its leading partner, Elihu ROOT, a future secretary of war and secretary of state, became one of two role models. The other was future president Theodore ROOSEVELT.

As with Roosevelt, Stimson found public service more satisfying than the pursuit of a career, and he soon became active in New York Republican politics, becoming in 1906 the energetic district attorney for New York City's Southern District. Appointed secretary of war in 1911, Stimson followed in Root's footsteps in attempting to modernize the army, improving troop training and the efficiency of the general staff, although congressional opposition blocked his contemplated consolidation and rationalization of army posts around the country.

When World War I began in Europe in 1914, the staunchly interventionist and pro-Allied Stimson campaigned ardently for "preparedness," massive increases in U.S. military budgets in anticipation of war with Germany. He was active in the PLATTSBURG MOVEMENT, which called for universal military training. After American intervention, Stimson volunteered, serving in France as a lieutenant colonel of artillery. He returned from France convinced that the United States must assume a far greater international role.

As governor general of the Philippines in 1928, Stimson ruled in the spirit of benevolent paternalism. Appointed secretary of state in 1929, he played a prominent role in negotiating the 1930 London Naval Treaty, and he attempted to strengthen the League of Nations. He protested firmly against Japan's establishment in 1931 of the puppet state of Manchukuo, instituting the policy of American nonrecognition that endured throughout the 1930s.

In the later 1930s, Stimson was among the strongest advocates of firm American opposition to the demands of the fascist states. When World War II began in September 1939, Stimson, a convinced believer in an Anglo-American alliance, outspokenly demanded massive American assistance to the Allies.

In 1940, President Franklin D. ROOSEVELT recruited Stimson as secretary of war, a position Stimson held throughout the conflict. He attracted an able group of younger lawyers and businessmen such as Robert A. LOVETT, Robert P. PATTERSON, and John J. McCloy, who not only oversaw the massive recruitment and industrial mobilization programs the war effort demanded, but also accepted and wished to carry forward the forceful internationalist tradition their revered chief embodied. In the final days of the war, Stimson approved the use of the ATOMIC BOMB against Japan; he also initially suggested that the Allies should share the secrets of nuclear power with the Soviet Union.

After retiring in 1945, Stimson endorsed a greatly enhanced American international role. He died on 20 October 1950 in Huntington, New York.

Further reading: Hodgson, Godfrey. *The Colonel: The Life and Wars of Henry Stimson, 1867–1950.* New York: Knopf, 1990; Isaacson, Walter, and Evan Thomas. *The Wise Men: Six Friends and the World They Made.* New York: Simon & Schuster, 1986; Morison, Elting E. *Turmoil and Tradition: A Study of the Life and Times of Henry L. Stimson.* Boston: Houghton Mifflin, 1960; Schmitz, David F. *Henry L. Stimson: The First Wise Man.* Wilmington, Del.: Scholarly Resources, 2001; Stimson, Henry L., and McGeorge Bundy. *On Active Service in Peace and War.* New York: Harper & Brothers, 1948.

— Priscilla Roberts

Stimson, Julia C. (1881–1948) *Director of the Army Nurse Corps and nursing educator*
Born on 26 May 1881 in Worcester, Massachusetts, Julia Catherine Stimson was one of seven children expected to continue a family tradition of professional and public service. Stimson's early years were influenced by her father, a Congregational minister, and by family moves to Saint Louis in 1886 and to New York City in 1893.

Stimson earned a B.A. from Vassar College in 1901 but struggled with a career choice following graduation. She settled on nursing and enrolled in the New York Hospital Training School for Nurses in 1904. She completed her training in 1908 and worked in supervisory positions in Harlem and Saint Louis. She also lent her expertise to the AMERICAN RED CROSS (ARC).

When the United States entered World War I in April 1917, Stimson enlisted in the ARMY NURSE CORPS. Assigned to a hospital in Rouen, France, Stimson proved an able administrator. In April 1918 she received temporary appointment as chief of all ARC nurses in France. Designated director of the American Expeditionary Forces Nursing Service, Stimson remained in Europe at the war's end to facilitate demobilization of American nurses.

Stimson returned to the United States in 1919 and served until the mid-1930s in a dual capacity as an administrator of the Army School of Nursing and as superintendent of the Army Nurse Corps. Promoted to major in 1920, she was the first army nurse to hold that rank; however, as it was not commissioned rank, it was without benefit. Stimson retired in 1937. She briefly returned to active duty in 1942 as an army nurse recruiter.

Following her six months of service during World War II, Stimson retired to Briarcliff, New York. Six weeks prior to her death she was promoted to the rank of colonel on the retired list. Stimson died in Pougheepsie, New York, on 29 September 1948.

See also WOMEN IN THE MILITARY.

Further reading: Dock, Lavinia, et al. *History of American Red Cross Nursing.* New York: Macmillan, 1922.

— Tracy M. Shilcutt

Stockdale, James B. (1923–) *U.S. Navy admiral*
Born on 23 December 1923 in Abingdon, Illinois, James Bond Stockdale graduated from the U.S. Naval Academy, Annapolis, in 1943. He spent three years in destroyers and then became a naval aviator. He was a carrier fighter pilot, test pilot, and test pilot instructor. In 1962 he received a master's degree from Stanford University.

During the VIETNAM WAR, as commanding officer of Squadron 51 on the aircraft carrier *Ticonderoga*, Commander Stockdale participated in the August 1964 TONKIN GULF INCIDENTS. During his second Vietnam tour, while in command of Air Group 16 on the carrier *Oriskany*, Stockdale was shot down on 9 September 1965. He was confined at the "Hanoi Hilton" prison as the senior navy prisoner of war until his release in 1973. During his captivity, he spent two years in leg irons and four years in solitary confinement. He was tortured 15 times.

Repatriated in 1973, Stockdale was promoted to rear admiral in 1974 and awarded the Medal of Honor in 1976. After an antisubmarine warfare command, Stockdale served in the Pentagon. Promoted to vice admiral, he was president of the Naval War College from 1977 to 1979 and then retired from the navy.

Stockdale was president of the Citadel during 1979–80, then senior research fellow at the Hoover Institution on War, Revolution, and Peace, 1980–96. In 1992 he ran unsuccessfully for vice president on the Reform Party ticket headed by H. Ross Perot. Stockdale's many books include *A Vietnam Experience: Ten Years of Reflection* and *In Love and War.*

Further reading: Stockdale, James B. *A Vietnam Experience: Ten Years of Reflection.* Stanford, Calif.: Hoover Institution Press, 1991; Stockdale, James B., and Sybil Stockdale. *In Love and War.* New York: Harper & Row, 1984.

— Scott Blanchette

Stoddert, Benjamin (1751–1813) *First U.S. secretary of the navy*
Born in 1751 in Charles County, Maryland, Benjamin Stoddert was a veteran of the American Revolutionary War and

served as secretary of the Board of War. He was at the time a member of a prosperous mercantile firm and a loyal Federalist.

After England and France went to war in 1793, American shipping came under threat from both nations, while Algerine pirates resumed predatory activities. These problems became enmeshed in partisan politics. Federalists demanded protection for American ships, while Republicans were opposed. The Federalists won in the Navy Act of 1794, which called for the building of six frigates. There being no separate navy department, during 1789–95 naval affairs were handled by Secretary of War Henry KNOX. Knox used naval agents to build ships and to provide their materials and personnel. The system did not work well. Moreover, when France seized American ships, the United States waged an undeclared QUASI-WAR WITH FRANCE (1798–1800). Federalists thereupon overcame strenuous Republican objections and, in a law dated 30 April 1798, created the Navy Department.

President John Adams chose Stoddert as its first secretary. He entered office just as the Quasi-War began. By the end of the year he had increased the number of ships from five to 20 and had established cruising grounds for the warships in the West Indies to defend American ships. To defend the nation he called for the building of 12 74-gun ships of the line, 12 frigates, and many smaller vessels. He would buy warehouses, a naval hospital, and six sites for drydocks in which ships could be repaired. He revised both the *Navy Regulations* and the naval penal code, drafted a bill for the governance of the Marine Corps, and demanded protection of needed timber reserves.

In June 1800 Stoddert moved his office from Philadelphia to the new national capital in Washington. By September, with the Quasi-War about to end, the navy had 35 major vessels that had taken 84 French ships and recaptured many French prizes. With Thomas JEFFERSON about to enter the presidency, Stoddert recommended that the peacetime navy retain 13 frigates and that work on the six 74s continue. Congress decreed that only six frigates would operate, and stopped work on the 74s. Stoddert also suggested that a board of three to five senior officers be created to advise the secretary on nautical matters; however, Congress failed to do so until 1815. All in all, Stoddert had provided the ships, navy yards, and personnel with which an infant but permanent navy could protect national interests.

Stoddert left office in March 1801. He died in Georgetown, Maryland, on 12 December 1813, in the midst of another war.

See also NAVY, U.S.

Further reading: Carrigg, John J. "Benjamin Stoddert, 18 June 1798–31 March 1801," in Paolo E. Coletta, Robert J. Albion, and K. Jack Bauer, eds. *Secretaries of the*
American Navy. 2 vols. Annapolis, Md.: Naval Institute Press, 1981; Paullin, Charles O. *Paullin's History of Naval Administration, 1775–1911.* Annapolis, Md.: U. S. Naval Institute, 1968; Smelser, Marshall. *Congress Founds the Navy, 1787–1798.* Notre Dame, Ind.: University of Notre Dame Press, 1959.

— Paolo E. Coletta

Stones River/Murfreesboro, Battle of (31 December 1862–2 January 1863) *Sanguinary Civil War battle fought between Major General William S. Rosecrans's Union Army of the Cumberland and General Braxton BRAGG's Confederate Army of Tennessee*

Although he was under pressure from the Union political leaders to invade eastern Tennessee, ROSECRANS hesitated to move until he had accumulated sufficient supplies. His army of 44,000 men entered Nashville in early November, but Rosecrans waited until Christmas to move against Bragg's army of 38,000 men, which was encamped near Murfreesboro on Stones River. The Federals approached the Confederate forces on 29 December, and the next day both commanders made their plans for battle. Coincidentally, they came up with virtually identical plans: to hold with their right flank and attack with their left. Much would depend on who struck first.

Bragg delivered the first blow, and his attack caught the Union right flank unprepared. Lieutenant General William J. HARDEE's Confederate corps drove back a Federal corps under Major General Alexander McDowell McCook. A spirited defense by Brigadier General Philip H. SHERIDAN's division bought some time, but by midmorning the entire Union flank was in retreat.

Rosecrans worked hard to rally his army and used reinforcements to rebuild his line. An effective defense of Round Forest helped to steady the center of the Union line. Rosecrans's best corps commander, Major General George H. THOMAS, was able to build a new Federal defensive position at right angles to the original Union lines.

After the beginning of the battle, Bragg did little to influence the struggle. When he belatedly ordered Lieutenant General Leonidas POLK to have his corps join the attack, Polk committed his troops piecemeal. The Federals were able to repulse each of Polk's attacks. By the end of the day, the Confederates had battered their opponents, but Rosecrans's army was holding in its new lines.

Bragg believed that he had won a decisive victory, and throughout New Year's Day he expected the Federals to withdraw. On 2 January, Bragg was perplexed to find Rosecrans's army still in position. That afternoon, Bragg ordered Major General John C. BRECKINRIDGE's division to attack the Union left flank on the east side of Stones River. The

Confederates charged gallantly across an open field, but were repulsed with heavy casualties. During the night, Bragg decided to withdraw. After the Confederate departure, the Federals occupied Murfreesboro.

The battle had been a costly tactical draw. Rosecrans suffered almost 13,000 casualties, while Bragg's approached 12,000. Rosecrans had barely averted disaster, but he held possession of the battlefield. It would be six more months before the Federals resumed their offensive.

See also CHICKAMAUGA, BATTLE OF; CIVIL WAR, LAND OVERVIEW; PERRYVILLE, BATTLE OF.

Further reading: Connelly, Thomas L. *Autumn of Glory: The Army of Tennessee, 1862–1865.* Baton Rouge: Louisiana State University Press, 1971; McDonough, James Lee. *Stones River—Bloody River in Tennessee.* Knoxville: University of Tennessee Press, 1980.

— Curtis S. King

Stoney Creek, Battle of (6 June 1813) *War of 1812 battle*

The failure of U.S. forces to mount an effective pursuit of the British following the 27 May 1813 capture of FORT GEORGE enabled the garrison under Major General John Vincent to escape intact. Four days later, U.S. Major General Henry DEARBORN assigned two brigades, under Brigadier Generals John Chandler and William H. Winder, to the task. They commenced a leisurely advance along the southern shore of Lake Ontario and did not reach Stoney Creek, seven miles from Vincent's position, until 5 June 1813.

The Americans encamped 1,300 men below the creek, with another 1,300 located three miles distant to guard boats and supplies on the lake. However, security was lax. At length, their entire position was personally reconnoitered by British lieutenant colonel John Harvey. He reported back to Vincent and impressed upon him the possibility for a surprise nighttime attack. Vincent, faced with possible abandonment of the Niagara peninsula, agreed to the stratagem. Rounding up 700 veteran soldiers from the 8th and 49th Regiments, the British stealthily advanced upon the unsuspecting Americans.

At around 3:00 A.M. on 6 June, Vincent's men successfully eliminated most American sentries and commenced a bayonet charge into the center of the camp. The surprised defenders, driven up a steep hill in their midst, could then clearly see their attackers backlit by numerous campfires. A heavy fusillade followed that inflicted many casualties, until Major Charles Plenderheath's company, the 49th, carried a battery commanded by Captain Nathan Towson. In the redundant melee that followed, both Chandler and Winder blundered into British lines and were captured. Vincent himself endured a close call when he was unhorsed in the dark and became separated from his command for several hours. Although hard pressed, the Americans continued to rally in larger and larger numbers, being materially assisted by a valiant stand by Colonel Joseph Lee Smith's 25th Infantry. Just prior to the battle, Smith redeployed his men on higher ground and repulsed several attempts by Harvey to reach him. With daylight approaching and Vincent nowhere to be found, Harvey called off the attack at dawn and retreated. As they departed, a section of the 16th U.S. Infantry charged and recaptured one of Towson's cannon; the British retained the remaining three.

U.S. losses in the Battle of Stoney Creek tallied 17 killed, 30 wounded, and 99 missing. Despite the advantage of surprise, British losses were also considerable, amounting to 23 killed, 136 wounded, and 55 captured. The British scored considerable success, however, in the capture of Winder and Chandler. Colonel James Burn of the dragoons, who succeeded Winder and Chandler as U.S. commander, decided against pursuing Vincent (who rejoined his forces a day later) and fell back to Forty Mile Creek. Stoney Creek thus represented the farthest penetration of Niagara ever achieved by American forces. Burn's survivors fell back to Fort George on the Niagara River, where they camped for the remainder of the year. The defeat also stimulated calls for Dearborn's removal.

See also WAR OF 1812: LAND OVERVIEW.

Further reading: Stanley, George F. G. *Battle in the Dark: Stoney Creek, 6 June 1813.* Toronto, Canada: Balmuir Book Publishing, 1991.

— John C. Fredriksen

Stony Point, Battle of (15–16 July 1779) *Battle between the British and Americans during the American Revolutionary War*

On 1 June 1779, 6,000 British troops under Major General Henry Clinton scattered two small American detachments and seized Stony Point, on the west bank of the Hudson River, and Verplanck's Point, directly opposite it. Surrounded by water on three sides, Stony Point was connected to the mainland by a swampy ravine crossed by a causeway. The British added to this natural strength by constructing a fort, fronted by two lines of abatis, and garrisoned the whole with more than 600 men. Seeing this as a threat to WEST POINT, only 10 miles to the north, Continental army commander General George WASHINGTON ordered Brigadier General Anthony WAYNE and his 1,350-man light infantry brigade to recapture Stony Point.

Wayne conducted an extensive reconnaissance and then decided to assault Stony Point with the bayonet alone and at night. After carefully deploying his troops, he attacked at around 11:00 P.M. on 15 July. The British sentries spotted the Americans and opened fire as they crossed the ravine, but the Americans continued their advance. Only one American battalion had loaded muskets, and it stopped outside the first line of abatis, returning the British fire. The firing drew many British soldiers out of the fort and diverted their attention from the main American assault.

The principal attack came in the form of simultaneous blows against both the northern and southern ends of the abatis. Each was led by some 150 men with axes, who cut openings in the lines of tangled trees and sharpened branches. Behind them was a small unit that immediately passed through the breach and engaged the British, clearing the way for the main body.

Once inside the works, the American charge was irresistible. In 30 minutes of fierce hand-to-hand combat, the Americans carried the fort. In all, the Americans killed 63 British troops, wounded 70, and captured 543 others. They also took 15 cannons, which they immediately turned on Verplanck's Point, though to no effect. American losses at Stony Point came to 15 dead and 80 wounded. The latter included Wayne, grazed in the head by a musket ball.

Following the capture of Stony Point, Washington decided that it could not be held and ordered that the fortifications there be destroyed and evacuated. The British later reoccupied and strengthened the site. Still, the assault, which showed the value of Major General Friedrich STEUBEN's training, inflicted heavy casualties, yielded a large quantity of military provisions, and proved to be a great boost to American morale. For Wayne, it was also revenge for his earlier humiliation at PAOLI.

See also AMERICAN REVOLUTIONARY WAR: LAND OVERVIEW; SHAYS, DANIEL.

Further reading: Nelson, Paul David. *Anthony Wayne: Soldier of the Early Republic.* Bloomington: Indiana University Press, 1985; Sklarsky, I. W. *The Revolution's Boldest Venture: The Story of General "Mad Anthony" Wayne's Assault on Stony Point.* Port Washington, N.Y.: Kennikat Press, 1965; Ward, Christopher. *The War of the Revolution.* 2 vols. New York: Macmillan, 1952.

— Michael P. Gabriel

Strategic Air Command (SAC) *U.S. Air Force branch charged with long-range, strategic bombing*
U.S. Army Air Forces Commanding General Carl "Tooey" SPAATZ created the Strategic Air Command (SAC) on 21 March 1946. SAC's primary mission during the COLD WAR was the delivery of atomic bombs in the event of war with the Soviet Union.

Spaatz's successor in 1948, air force chief of staff General Hoyt VANDENBERG, was not convinced that SAC could do the job and entrusted Lieutenant General Curtis E. LeMAY to rebuild it. LeMay found SAC unable to perform its primary mission of bombing the Soviet Union. In May 1948, when 180 SAC bombers were ordered to conduct a mock raid on New York City, only 101 bombers managed to get off the ground.

SAC suffered from insufficient funding, improper equipment, and a lack of trained personnel. It comprised two air forces: the Eighth and the Fifteenth, both commanded by men who had served under LeMay in the Pacific theater during World War II. Despite budget problems and general public apathy, by 1949 LeMay had built SAC into a force of 1,000 aircraft and 65,000 personnel in three heavy bomb wings, 11 medium bomb wings, two fighter escort wings, three reconnaissance wings, and six air refueling squadrons located at 22 bases within the continental United States and abroad.

SAC's principal bomber was the Boeing B-29 Superfortress. The Consolidated B-36 Peacemakers, a true intercontinental bomber capable of penetrating deep within the Soviet Union, entered service in 1949.

During the KOREAN WAR, SAC proved its worth when its B-29 bombers destroyed a large portion of North Korea's industrial capacity and Communist lines of communication south. SAC greatly benefitted from the sharp increase in defense spending that accompanied the war. The B-36 was soon replaced by the Boeing B-47

U.S. Air Force B-52 aircraft coming in for a landing after a mission over South Vietnam *(National Archives)*

Stratojet, which was produced in greater numbers than any other postwar bomber. The B-47 led directly to the B-52 Stratofortress, which in various modifications remains in service as the principal SAC bomber. Advances also occurred in onboard equipment technology, and significant sums were expended on navigation and bombing equipment and electronic countermeasures. There were also changes in tactics. As opposed to the massed bomber formations of World War II and the Korean War, B-52s flew singularly or in cells of three aircraft.

The B-52's size and versatility allowed it to fly a variety of missions, from delivering nuclear weapons to serving as a low-level penetrator, carrying precision cruise missiles with conventional warheads. During the VIETNAM WAR, SAC bombers were even employed in direct support of ground troops in Arc Light strikes within South Vietnam. SAC B-52s carried the war to North Vietnam in Operations LINEBACKER I and LINEBACKER II.

B-52s continued in service after the end of the cold war. They participated in Operation DESERT STORM during the Gulf War and also took part in strikes against al-Qaeda and Taliban targets in Afghanistan in 2001–02.

The SAC bomber fleet has sharply shrunk in size, from approximately 2,000 aircraft in 1961 to only 200 at the beginning of the 21st century. These, however, include B-1 and B-2 aircraft, the most capable—and expensive—bombers ever designed.

See also AIRCRAFT, FIXED WING; AIR FORCE, U.S; BALLISTIC MISSILES; NUCLEAR AND ATOMIC WEAPONS.

Further reading: Anderton, David A. *Strategic Air Command: Two Thirds of the Triad.* New York: Scribner, 1976; Coffey, Thomas M. *Iron Eagle: The Turbulent Life of General Curtis Lemay.* New York: Crown, 1986; Boyne, Walter J. *Beyond the Wild Blue: A History of the United States Air Force, 1947–1997.* New York: St. Martin's Press, 1997.
— Jason M. Halin

strategic bombing, World War II (1942–1945)

Massive bombing raids against Germany and Japan, used extensively by the United States and Great Britain
In World War II, for the first time, the United States and the European powers employed air warfare and strategic bombing on a massive scale, in the process developing doctrines of air warfare that would guide subsequent American policies. As early as the 1920s, army airpower advocates such as Brigadier General William "Billy" MITCHELL and his followers urged the development of American aviation capabilities, which they believed would be crucial in any future war. The German blitzkrieg of western Europe and bombing raids on Britain in 1940 further confirmed them in this outlook.

As early as the spring of 1941, British and American military leaders opened secret discussions, drawing up the joint global Basic War Plan Rainbow No. 5. This envisioned a strategic air offensive against Germany preparatory to a European invasion, close air support for both the invasion and subsequent offensives, and the use of air power for strategic defensive operations in the Pacific.

After the Japanese attack on PEARL HARBOR, these plans were modified. Primarily to raise American morale, in April 1942 Chief of Naval Operations Admiral Ernest J. KING and Commander of Army Air Forces Lieutenant General Henry "Hap" ARNOLD approved and launched an aircraft carrier–based raid by 16 B-25 bombers, led by Lieutenant Colonel James "Jimmy" DOOLITTLE, on five Japanese cities, including TOKYO. The latter raid inflicted little material damage but had considerable psychological impact and caused the Japanese to shift military resources for defense of their capital. Two months later, U.S. Army Air Forces in Europe used Egyptian air bases to mount an attack on the German-controlled PLOESTI oil fields in Romania.

Over the longer term, in Europe the Eighth Air Force established 52 support installations and 75 airfields in the United Kingdom, from which, in collaboration with the British Royal Air Force, it sought to exert air supremacy prior to a European invasion. Initially, U.S. officers, who believed that with the NORDEN bombsight and B-17 Flying Fortress bomber they could conduct daylight precision bombing raids, broke with the British preference for nighttime area bombing, a tactic adopted primarily because it kept aircraft losses relatively low. General Carl A. SPAATZ, commander of the Eighth and Fifteenth U.S. Army Air Forces, and Colonel Curtis E. LeMAY, who headed the 305th Bomb Ardment Group, initially sent B-17s on daylight precision bombing raids, a tactic they abandoned temporarily after suffering heavy losses, particularly in the October 1943 massive raids on ball bearing plants in SCHWEINFURT, Germany. Daylight raids were resumed in March 1944, after the arrival of the long-range P-47 Thunderbolt and P-51 Mustang fighter escort plane. Massive raids on Germany, often utilizing more than 1,000 aircraft, became common, culminating in the February 1945 destruction of Dresden. One of the most destructive air raids in history, it killed up to 135,000 people and destroyed much of the "Florence of the Elbe."

Despite diverting considerable resources to support the June 1944 NORMANDY INVASION, bombing raids razed large areas of most German cities, and devastating attacks on oil refineries and communications caused the German transportation system to collapse. Beginning in late 1942, British and American bombers based in the Mediterranean wreaked great damage on Italian cities, reducing the country's industrial output by 60 percent before Italy switched

Boeing B-17 Flying Fortresses of the 303rd Bomb Group dropping bombs over Nazi-occupied Europe in 1944

sides in September 1943. After October 1943, Romanian oil fields and oil refineries elsewhere also suffered repeated attacks from the Fifteenth U.S. Army Air Force.

Overall, the strategic air offensive cost American and British forces around 50,000 aircrew apiece, while killing between 750,000 and 1,000,000 Germans. The terror bombing of German cities did not bring the war to a speedier conclusion, however; in totalitarian Germany, the Nazi grip on power was such that it was not possible for civilians to topple the Hitler regime. Indeed, such bombing only served to make civilians more determined. In September 1944, Allied planners made their priority the destruction of the petroleum industry and, above all, gasoline. But it was only in 1944 and 1945 that Allied air power was concentrated effectively against industrial targets and lines of communication. The Strategic Bombing Survey, conducted by the United States Eighth Air Force after the war, showed that bombing—while important in the war—was not the decisive element envisioned. Strategic bombing was important in the European theater in many ways—in disrupting the German transportation system, in isolating the Normandy invasion site, and in destroying Germany's capacity to produce key industrial components. But German inventiveness and dispersal of industry meant that Germany actually increased production of armaments at the end of the war, achieving its highest levels in early 1945, just as the war was ending. But the Germans lacked both fuel for their new planes and trained pilots to fly their new jet aircraft.

The full-scale strategic air offensive against Japan, almost exclusively a United States operation, only began on 15 June 1944, when Twentieth Air Force, based in China and India under LeMay, began limited attacks on

U.S. strategic bombing in World War II reached its apogee at the end of the war in the bombing of Japan. The photograph shows a B-28 Superfortress of the 500th Bomb Group of Twentieth Air Force on Saipan.   *(San Diego Aerospace Museum)*

the Japanese home islands. The campaign intensified dramatically in November, when American forces seized the MARIANA ISLANDS, from whose range B-29 Super Fortresses of XXI Bomber Command, directed by Arnold in Washington, could comfortably mount raids on Japanese cities. Initially, the campaign concentrated almost exclusively on precision bombing of Japanese industrial targets. This was hindered by relatively high aircraft loss rates, difficult wind conditions, and the high altitudes at which the bombers flew.

Dissatisfied with the results, in January 1945 Arnold replaced Brigadier General Haywood S. Hansell with LeMay, who abandoned high-altitude precision daytime bombing in favor of low-level area night bombing with incendiaries. During the night of 9–10 March 1945, 325 B-29s of XXI Bomber Command conducted the single most destructive air raid in history, killing more than 83,000 people and destroying some 267,000 buildings in Tokyo, along with 18 percent of the city's industrial capacity. In the weeks that followed, Japan's most important industrial

cities were similarly struck. In early June 1945, the United States targeted 60 second-rank Japanese cities, subjecting them to both incendiary bombing and precision attacks on industrial facilities. Then, on 6 and 9 August, B-29 bombers dropped the ATOMIC BOMB over Hiroshima and Nagasaki, respectively.

After World War II, many questioned the morality of British and American political and military leaders in mounting the highly destructive and indiscriminate fire raids on both Germany and Japan that inflicted heavy civilian casualties. Some lawyers considered such bombing equivalent to war crimes. Postwar analyses of the effectiveness of such bombing raids suggested that, although highly destructive, their impact on morale and infrastructure was still insufficiently detrimental to coerce a nation to surrender, and that unless nuclear weapons were employed, only a successful ground invasion would bring an enemy's capitulation.

Despite such caveats, from 1945 onward heavy reliance upon airpower would characterize accepted American strategic doctrine. Persistent United States reluctance to risk high casualties among American troops led American leaders to use strategic bombing extensively in the subsequent KOREAN WAR and VIETNAM WAR, and to depend yet more significantly upon airpower in campaigns against Iraq in 1991 during Operation DESERT STORM and against Serbia in 1999.

See also BRERETON, LEWIS H.; DE SEVERSKY, ALEXANDER; EAKER, IRA C.; MANHATTAN PROJECT; TWINING, NATHAN F.

Further reading: Copp, Dewitt S. *Forged in Fire: Strategy and Decisions in the Air War Over Europe, 1940–45.* Garden City, N.Y.: Doubleday, 1982; Futrell, Robert F. *Ideas, Concepts, Doctrine: A History of Basic Thinking in the United States Air Force, 1907–1964.* 2 vols. Maxwell Air Force Base, Ala.: Aerospace Studies Institute, Air University, 1971; Kennett, Lee. *A History of Strategic Bombing.* New York: Scribner's, 1982; MacIssac, David. *Strategic Bombing in World War Two: The Story of the United States Strategic Bombing Survey.* New York: Garland Publishing, 1976; Schaffer, Ronald. *Wings of Judgment: American Bombing in World War II.* New York: Oxford University Press, 1985.

— Priscilla Roberts

strategic defense *Defense of the United States from intercontinental attack*

Serious planning and experimentation relating to strategic defense began during WORLD WAR II with the formation of the Air Defense Command (ADC) in February 1940. Although only a small planning headquarters, during its brief 17-month existence it laid the groundwork for postwar air defense through research, planning, and coordination with its more experienced counterpart in Britain. With the exception of some minor attacks by Japanese balloons, however, intercontinental air attack remained only a theoretical problem.

The theory became much more frightening, however, with the first Soviet atomic test of 29 August 1949, at least three years earlier than expected. Although Soviet NUCLEAR WEAPONS could be delivered to the continental United States only via one-way missions carried out with copies of a crashed wartime U.S. B-29 (Tu-4 "Bulls"), by 1949 the Soviet Air Force already possessed hundreds of these aircraft, and U.S. intelligence believed them fully capable of carrying out such attacks. In the early postwar years, the U.S. military did place some emphasis on "continental defense" (as it was then known), but in 1949 this was still woefully inadequate.

The best "all-weather" fighter available, the F-82 Twin Mustang, in fact performed miserably in poor weather and darkness and was barely able to reach the cruising altitude of a Tu-4. Radar coverage was provided only by sporadic groupings of World War II–era radars, collectively (and aptly) known as "Lashup."

In February 1950, the air force concluded that attacking Soviet aircraft could likely hide themselves amid routine domestic commercial air traffic, and that the first warning of an attack would probably be the explosion of the weapon over its target. Two months later, the CENTRAL INTELLIGENCE AGENCY (CIA) estimated that the delivery of as few as 200 bombs "might well knock the U.S. out of the war," and further estimated that the Soviet stockpile would reach that level within four years. Soviet CHEMICAL AND BIOLOGICAL WARFARE capabilities, possibly delivered along with nuclear weapons via clandestine means, only heightened fears of what was often referred to as a potential "nuclear PEARL HARBOR."

Progress came slowly. Following a series of reorganizations associated with the budget cuts of the late 1940s, ADC finally reemerged as the major command with primary responsibility for strategic defense in 1951. Despite air force fears that attempting to create a "perfect defense" would divert funds from the STRATEGIC AIR COMMAND (SAC), the importance of continental defense as a matter of national policy increased dramatically in 1953 within the context of President Dwight D. EISENHOWER's NEW LOOK STRATEGY.

The 1954 creation of the joint Continental Air Defense Command (CONAD) institutionalized interservice cooperation, followed three years later by formalized international cooperation in the form of the new joint U.S.-Canadian North American Air Defense Command (NORAD). In late 1956, President Eisenhower predelegated the authority to use nuclear weapons in air defense of the United States to the commander of CONAD. By the late 1950s, ADC's budget rivaled that of SAC, with ADC's quarter of a million personnel overseeing a vast strategic defense system that included more than 2,000 modern fighter-interceptors and several different series of radar installations sprawling from Alaska to Greenland.

Following the Soviet intercontinental BALLISTIC MISSILE (ICBM) tests of August 1957, charges of a "bomber gap" were replaced by even greater fears of a "MISSILE GAP," fears made public in dramatic fashion by the Soviet launch of the *Sputnik* satellite on 4 October 1957.

Much of the continental defense system was immediately threatened with irrelevance just as many of its most complex and expensive systems were finally coming online. Throughout the 1960s and into the 1970s, many components of the air defense system were allowed to wither away, most of their tasks eventually relegated by reserve and National Guard forces, as attention shifted to launch warning and attempts to create an antiballistic missile (ABM) defense.

The first generation of U.S. ABM weapons emerged from existing surface-to-air missile research, but little progress was made as the technical challenges associated with "hitting a bullet with a bullet" proved immense, even for interceptor missiles that were themselves armed with nuclear warheads. By the late 1960s, even as the number of Soviet ICBM launchers approached 1,000, a viable ABM system remained out of reach. Critics argued that the defense of cities was an unrealistic goal, and that trying to do so would only fuel the arms race and challenge the prevailing doctrine of Mutual Assured Destruction (MAD).

In 1969, President Richard NIXON's administration modified the existing Sentinel program, the ambitious attempt at population defense still in development, into a much more limited program for the defense of ICBM fields, renamed Safeguard. The 1972 ABM treaty restricted research to the laboratory and limited the United States and the Soviet Union to two ABM sites each (reduced to one in 1974). In 1975 Congress canceled the sole U.S. site in North Dakota only months after it became operational.

ABM research continued in both superpowers, however, fueled anew by President Ronald Reagan's dramatic March 1983 announcement of his Strategic Defense Initiative (SDI). The advent of PRECISION-GUIDED MUNITIONS made possible research into various nonnuclear means of intercepting incoming ballistic missiles, including technologies as exotic as lasers and "brilliant pebbles" (and earning SDI the derisive nickname of "Star Wars"). Although no such system has yet been deployed, its specter played an important role in the arms race during the final years of the COLD WAR. In the 1990s, funding for strategic defense was reduced but not eliminated by President Bill Clinton's administration, and as of 2002, despite several well-publicized failures, a program to create a limited system of national missile defense (NMD) was still underway.

See also AIRCRAFT, FIXED WING; COAST DEFENSE.

Further reading: Baucom, Donald R. *The Origins of SDI, 1944–1983.* Lawrence: University Press of Kansas, 1992; Bruce-Briggs, B. *The Shield of Faith: A Chronicle of Strategic Defense from Zeppelins to Star Wars.* New York: Simon & Schuster, 1988; Schaffel, Kenneth. *The Emerging Shield: The Air Force and the Evolution of Continental Air Defense, 1945–1960.* Washington, D.C.: Office of Air Force History, United States Air Force, 1991.

— David Rezelman

Stratton, Dorothy C. (1899–) *World War II director of the Coast Guard Women's Reserve*
Born on 24 March 1899 in Brookfield, Missouri, Dorothy Constance Stratton graduated from Ottawa College in Kansas and earned a master's degree in psychology at the University of Chicago and a doctorate from Columbia University. As dean of women and professor of psychology at Purdue University, she took a leave of absence on U.S. entry into World War II and was commissioned a lieutenant in the WAVES in 1942.

On 23 November 1942, the U.S. COAST GUARD WOMEN'S RESERVE was created, and Stratton became its first director. Upon her transfer to the Coast Guard, she was promoted to lieutenant commander; she later rose to captain. She was the originator of the nickname SPARs— from the Coast Guard's motto of *Semper Paratus,* Always Ready. During World War II, more than 11,000 women served in the SPARs under Stratton's leadership. Stratton returned to civilian life in January 1946, and was presented with the Legion of Merit for her wartime service upon her retirement.

After the war, Stratton was director of personnel for the International Monetary Fund from 1947 to 1950 and national executive director of the Girl Scouts from 1950 to 1960. In 1962, she was appointed to a presidential commission on employment of the handicapped.

In March 1999, Dorothy Stratton celebrated her 100th birthday, with many congratulations from her Coast Guard family.

See also WOMEN IN THE MILITARY.

Further reading: Thomson, Robin J. *The Coast Guard & the Women's Reserve in World War II.* Washington, D.C.: U.S. Coast Guard, 1992; Tilley, John A. *A History of Women in the Coast Guard.* Washington, D.C.: U.S. Coast Guard, 1996.

— Marie-Beth Hall

Streeter, Ruth Cheney (1895–1990) *World War II director of the Marine Corps Women's Reserve*
Born on 2 October 1895 in Brookline, Massachusetts, Ruth Cheney attended Bryn Mawr College, but left school to marry Thomas W. Streeter in 1917; they had four children. Always interested in aviation, she earned a commercial pilot's license in 1942 and was active in the CIVIL AIR PATROL and on various national defense committees. On 13 February 1943, the MARINE CORPS WOMEN'S RESERVE was established; Streeter became its director, with the rank of major. During World War II, 23,145 officer and enlisted women reservists served in the corps under Streeter's leadership, freeing the equivalent of an entire marine division to fight in the field. Streeter was promoted to lieutenant colonel in November 1943 and to colonel in 1945. She served until December 1945, after which she returned to her home in Morristown, New Jersey. In February 1946 she was presented with the Legion of Merit for her wartime service.

After the war, Streeter was active in the American Legion, as well as in several state organizations, and served as a delegate to the New Jersey Constitutional Conventions. She died at Morristown, New Jersey, on 30 September 1990.

See also WOMEN IN THE MILITARY.

Further reading: Soderberg, Peter A. *Women Marines: The World War II Era*. Westport, Conn.: Praeger, 1992; Stremlow, Mary V. *A History of the Women Marines, 1946–1977*. Washington, D.C.: Headquarters Marine Corps, 1986.

— Marie-Beth Hall

Stuart, James Ewell Brown ("Jeb") (1833–1864)
Confederate army general

Born on 6 February 1833 in Patrick County, Virginia, J. E. B. "Jeb" Stuart attended Emory and Henry College, 1848–50, before entering the U.S. Military Academy, WEST POINT, from which he graduated in 1854. Commissioned brevet second lieutenant and assigned to the mounted rifles, Stuart received his regular commission in October 1854 and joined his command in Texas that December. In 1855 Stuart was transferred to the newly formed 1st Cavalry Regiment. He spent most of the next six years on the western frontier.

In December 1855 Stuart received promotion to first lieutenant. In 1859, while on leave in Washington, he assisted Colonel Robert E. LEE in capturing John Brown at HARPERS FERRY. Promoted to captain in April 1861, Stuart resigned his commission a month later when Virginia seceded from the Union. He had accepted a lieutenant colonelcy in Virginia's state organization, but in July he became colonel of the 1st Virginia Cavalry in Confederate service.

Major General J. E. B. Stuart, CSA   *(Library of Congress)*

Stuart attracted high praise for his performance in the First Battle of BULL RUN/MANASSAS and was promoted to brigadier general. He commanded General Joseph E. JOHNSTON's cavalry during the Peninsula campaign, and during the fighting around Richmond in June 1862 he mounted a spectacular raid around the Federal Army of the Potomac, gathering valuable intelligence and humiliating his opponents.

Promoted to major general in July 1862, Stuart commanded a two-brigade cavalry division in General Robert E. Lee's Army of Northern Virginia. Stuart's cavalry mounted another productive raid prior to the Second Battle of BULL RUN/MANASSAS and rendered valuable assistance to Lee's army during the Maryland campaign and at FREDERICKSBURG.

In May 1863, Stuart temporarily commanded Lieutenant General Thomas J. "Stonewall" JACKSON's Corps when Jackson was wounded at CHANCELLORSVILLE. In June, Stuart performed well in the giant cavalry clash at BRANDY STATION, although critics accused him of being caught by surprise. At this point, Stuart was one of the most popular generals in the Confederacy, and already recognized as a gifted cavalry commander; but the Federals were gaining ground, and the South's dwindling resources rendered his job increasingly difficult.

During Lee's July invasion of Pennsylvania, Stuart was assigned to screen Lee's right flank, but Union dispositions led him farther east. As a result, Lee operated blind, only narrowly averting diaster. Stuart did not appear until the second day of the Battle of GETTYSBURG. Federal cavalry repulsed Stuart's sweep to cut Union lines of communication on the final day of that pivotal battle. That September, when Lee created a cavalry corps, Stuart was not promoted to lieutenant general, the appropriate rank for a Confederate corps commander.

Stung by criticism over Gettysburg and his failure to win promotion, Stuart entered 1864 determined to restore his reputation. He performed well in the opening stages of Lieutenant General Ulysses S. GRANT's OVERLAND CAMPAIGN, and when Major General Philip SHERIDAN's superior Federal cavalry mounted a major effort against Richmond, Stuart met the advance only miles from the capital. In fierce fighting at Yellow Tavern on 11 May, the flamboyant cavalryman was mortally wounded. He died in Richmond the following day.

See also CAVALRY; CIVIL WAR, LAND OVERVIEW.

Further reading: Freeman, Douglas Southall. *Lee's Lieutenants: A Study in Command*. 3 vols. New York: Scribner, 1942–1944; Thomas, Emory M. *Bold Dragoon: The Life of J. E. B. Stuart*. New York: Harper & Row, 1986.

— Shane Nall

Stuyvesant, Peter (1592–1672) *Director-general of New Netherlands*

Born sometime in 1592 in West Friesland, Peter Stuyvesant entered the service of the Dutch West India Company, serving first in Brazil (1635–43) before being appointed governor of Curaçao, one of the Leeward Islands in the Caribbean, in 1643. While leading a siege against Saint Martin in 1644, Stuyvesant lost his right leg; he was forced to return to the Netherlands to recover. On 28 July 1646, he was commissioned director-general of New Netherlands, and upon arriving in New Amsterdam on 11 May 1647 immediately set out to improve the colony's defenses.

Although Stuyvesant's imperious manner and rigid conformity to the Dutch Reformed Church won him few admirers in New Netherland, his success is destroying Sweden's colony along the Delaware River insured the support of officials at home. After failing to maintain Fort Beversrede, constructed in April 1648 near modern Philadelphia, Stuyvesant founded Fort Casimir (modern Newcastle, Delaware) on 5 November 1651 to control the approach to Fort Christina, New Sweden's main outpost on the Delaware River. Although Swedish director Johann Rising seized control of Fort Casimir in May 1654, Stuyvesant recaptured it on 18 August 1655, then proceeded to capture Fort Christiana, completing the conquest of New Sweden.

While the undermanned Swedes proved to be an easy foe, the English in 1664 posed a far greater challenge. In March of that year, English towns on Long Island forced Stuyvesant to grant them autonomy. On 22 March, King Charles II granted his brother, the duke of York (the future King James II), a charter to territory, including New Netherland, in the New World. Although Stuyvesant vowed to fight when four frigates carrying troops under the command of Colonel Richard Nicolls appeared in New Amsterdam Harbor on 29 August, Dutch settlers led by Johannes and Samuel Megapolensis surrendered. Stuyvesant refused to sign the articles of surrender, and in 1665 he traveled to the Netherlands to defend his actions. In 1667 he returned to his estate along the East River, where he died in February 1672.

See also ANGLO-DUTCH WARS.

Further reading: Craven, Wesley Frank. *The Colonies in Transition, 1660–1713.* New American Nation Series. New York: Harper & Row, 1968; Pomfret, John E., with Floyd M. Shumway. *Founding the American Colonies, 1583–1660.* New York: Harper & Row, 1970.

— Justin D. Murphy

submarines *Naval craft capable of subsurface operations*

The United States early led in submarine development, and the U.S. Navy has been the most effective practitioner of submarine warfare in history. Until the beginning of the 20th century, submarines were limited by the state of technology and had only a marginal impact. The first U.S. submarine was David BUSHNELL's *TURTLE*. Built in 1776, during the American Revolutionary War, the *Turtle* became the world's first submarine to conduct a combat mission when its operator endeavored, without success, to attach a mine to the hull of a British warship at New York. Robert FULTON also contributed an early design, the *Nautilus.*

During the Civil War, a Southerner, H. L. Hunley, was involved in the construction of several submarines, including one named after him. The 40-foot-long *H. L. HUNLEY* had a crew of nine, eight of whom turned hand cranks along a single screw shaft that served to propel the craft. Shipped to Charleston for use against the Union blockading fleet there, the *Hunley* sank on two occasions, killing a number of crew members, including its inventor. A third crew volunteered and, on 17 February 1864, utilizing a spar torpedo, the *Hunley* sank the Union screw sloop *Housatonic.* Although the *Hunley* sank shortly thereafter, it was the first submarine to claim an enemy vessel.

The U.S. Navy also experimented with submarines, but none saw action during the war. The navy continued experiments after the Civil War, but it was not until the end of the 19th century that inventors developed a truly effective submarine.

John HOLLAND, an Irish expatriate, built a number of submarines, and in 1897 launched the *HOLLAND.* Purchased by the navy in 1900, the *Holland* marked the effective beginning of the U.S. submarine service. The *Holland* incorporated both a gasoline internal combustion engine for surface cruising and an electric engine for submerged operation. It incorporated a set of horizontal planes to assist in submerging, and mounted a single bow torpedo tube for three Whitehead torpedoes. American Simon Lake also made important contributions to the evolution of submarines, and his *Seal* featured a rotating periscope and diving planes.

The first U.S. diesel-powered submarines, the E-boats, appeared in 1912. Each E- and F-class boat was armed with six Bliss Leavitt Mk VI torpedoes (1,500 lbs., 200-lb. charge, 35-knot speed). Submarines EB-18 through EB-20 displaced 340 to 435 tons and had a range of 2,475 nautical miles (nm) at 11 knots, and 3,465 nm with fuel in the ballast tanks. The E-boats were the first U.S. submarines with permanent radios on board. They were also the first submarines to cross the Atlantic, but they saw only limited action in World War I.

The first all-electric-driven submarine, the *Porpoise,* joined the fleet in 1933, but it was not until World War II that the submarine became a decisive element of U.S. naval strategy. Following the U.S. declaration of war after the December 1941 Japanese Attack on PEARL HARBOR,

U.S. submarine on war patrol in the Pacific, 1945   *(National Archives)*

submarines and aircraft carriers were the only naval forces capable of carrying the war to the Japanese. U.S. submarine capabilities were enhanced with the launching of the *Gato/Balao*-class boats in 1942; these were specifically designed for long-range operations. This class constituted the standard U.S. submarine type during the war, although the navy had in its inventory a wide variety of hull designs from the 1918 O-class, displacing 521 tons (surfaced) to the *Gato/Balao* class (1,526 tons surfaced, 2,410 tons submerged). The *Gato/Balao*-class, with a complement of six officers and 54 enlisted personnel, were capable of 21 knots on the surface and eight knots submerged. Each boat carried 24 torpedoes, with bow- and stern-launch capability.

U.S. submarines had a deep-dive capability, a well-kept secret during the war. *Balao*-class submarines could dive to 400 feet, while the normal distance was only 300 feet. This enabled them to survive many depth charge attacks. Unfortunately, they also were armed with ineffective torpedoes that dove too deep and had a magnetic pistol that often did not work, a problem that was later remedied.

Allied strategic plans called for concentration on the European theater of operations against Germany; but with few German ships at sea, most U.S. submarines were deployed in the Pacific theater, where the commander in chief of the U.S. Pacific Fleet, Admiral Chester NIMITZ, greatly accelerated U.S. submarine operations. On 7 December 1941, the U.S. Navy had 112 submarines; by war's end, the United States had built an additional 203. During the war, U.S. submarines sank 60 percent of

Japanese merchant shipping and perhaps 200 Japanese naval vessels. Fifty-two subs were lost during the war, 48 of them to Japanese attack, and more than 3,500 submariners perished.

Research into nuclear power during the late 1940s and early 1950s brought significant changes in submarine design. Prior to these advances, the diesel-battery-powered submarine was tied to the atmosphere for all except relatively short runs. As a result, most of the time it operated on the surface, cruised at reduced speed while submerged, and was always constricted by the necessity of reaching air again within a reasonable time to recharge its batteries.

The NAUTILUS was the world's first nuclear-powered submarine. Commissioned in 1955, it vastly increased the range and duration of subsurface operations. On 10 May 1960, the nuclear-powered *Triton* surfaced off the northeast coast of the United States after completing the first submerged circumnavigation of the globe.

The arrival of the nuclear-powered and nuclear-armed ballistic missile submarine (SSBN) marked a revolutionary change in naval warfare. The *George Washington*, launched in 1959, carried the Polaris sea-launched ballistic missile (SLBM). When it achieved operational status in November 1960, global strategy was unequivocally altered. Virtually undetectable and thus able to survive in a nuclear first strike, a submerged U.S. nuclear ballistic missile submarine insured that an enemy nation launching first would not be able to avoid a devastating response. U.S. nuclear missile submarines thus became the third leg of the nation's triad of deterrence, joining ground-based nuclear-tipped ICBMs and long-range nuclear-armed B-52 bombers in promising the assured destruction of any nation contemplating a nuclear strike against the United States.

U.S. Navy SSBNs progressed through a series of classes, including the first of five *Ethan Allen*–class subs in 1961; 19 *Lafayette*-class subs, beginning in 1963; and 12 *Benjamin Franklin*–class subs, the first of which became operational in 1965. All were armed with the Polaris SLBM system. At the beginning of the 21st century, the 18,700 ton *Ohio*-class, first launched in 1981, was the premier "boomer" U.S. Navy submarine. Armed with 24 highly accurate 7,000-mile-range D-5 Trident II SLBMs, the *Ohio*-class continues to provide the United States with an effective sea-based deterrent. Each of the navy's ballistic missile submarines has more firepower than all the armies and navies of World War I and World War II combined.

To protect their own SSBN submarines and to hunt down enemy missile-carrying submarines, the U.S. Navy developed a special class of attack submarines, designated SSN and known as "hunter-killers." First at sea in 1976, these *Los Angeles*–class attack subs became the front-line counter to the threat posed by Soviet submarines. Hunter-killers were also designed to destroy surface targets both in the ocean and on land. With the capacity to launch cruise missiles (SLCMs) through standard torpedo tubes, SSNs are able to project naval power inland in excess of 1,400 miles. The first naval vessel to open fire during Operation DESERT STORM in 1991 was the *Louisville* (SSN-724), which attacked inland targets.

When the Soviet Union disintegrated in late 1991, the navy had plans to build several advanced and expensive submarines. With the changed strategic environment, the numbers were subsequently scaled back. In 1997, the USS *Seawolf* was launched. The largest, fastest attack sub ever built, it carries 50 torpedoes plus Tomahawk cruise missiles. The navy plans to build a smaller, less-expensive submarine, the *Virginia*-class. These subs, the lead unit of which is projected for 2004, feature a conical covering over the propellers to serve as a muffler, making this class the quietest submarines ever built.

Recent arms control treaties and the changed strategic environment mandated a reduction in the SSBN fleet from 18 *Ohio*-class submarines to 14. These subs have an estimated 20 years of hull life, and the navy plans to utilize two of the four in intelligence-gathering and special-operations missions. The remaining two will have their 24 vertical tubes retooled to allow each to launch a cluster of cruise missiles. The 154-missile arsenal will allow each of the submarines to match the cruise-missile capacity of an entire carrier battle group.

See also AMERICAN REVOLUTIONARY WAR: NAVAL OVERVIEW; BALLISTIC MISSILES; CIVIL WAR, NAVAL OVERVIEW; RICKOVER, HYMAN G.; SUBMARINE WARFARE AGAINST JAPAN, WORLD WAR II; WORLD WAR II, U.S. INVOLVEMENT: PACIFIC THEATER.

Further reading: Bagnasco, Erminio. *Submarines of World War II.* New York: Sterling Publishing, 2000; Friedman, Norman. *U.S. Submarines Through 1945: An Illustrated Design History.* Annapolis, Md.: Naval Institute Press, 1995; ———. *U.S. Submarines Since 1945: An Illustrated Design History.* Annapolis, Md.: Naval Institute Press, 1994; Keunne, Robert E. *The Attack Submarine: A Study in Strategy.* New Haven: Yale University Press, 1965; Weir, Gary E. *Building American Submarines, 1914–1940.* Washington, D.C.: Naval Historical Center, Department of the Navy: U.S. Government Printing Office, 1991.

— James B. McNabb

submarine warfare against Japan, World War II

(1942–1945) U.S. Navy submarine forces in the Pacific inflicted decisive damage against Japan in World War II

Indeed, U.S. SUBMARINES in World War II were the most successful practitioners of submarine warfare in history.

Their efforts disrupted Japan's military-industrial complex, preventing the delivery of raw materials, especially oil, to the Japanese home islands; this, in turn, hindered manufacture of required military hardware. Submarine interdiction of Japanese supply lines also severely limited the ability of dispersed Japanese forces to prosecute the war. In addition, U.S. submarine support for conventional military forces allowed the Allies to project power throughout the Pacific.

The destruction of the U.S. Pacific Fleet at PEARL HARBOR on 7 December 1941 left few options for U.S. naval planners. All U.S. battleships had either been sunk or were disabled. Unable to rely on the battleship as the centerpiece of its strategic plan, the navy used aircraft carriers and submarines to carry the war to Japan.

The U.S. Navy entered the war with 112 submarines. In the course of the conflict, the United States built an additional 203 submarines, while Japan built only 112. The United States lost 52 submarines, Japan 130. U.S. submarines also had a deep-dive capability, one of the best-kept secrets of the war. The usual diving depth was 300 feet, but U.S. submarines could dive to 400 feet. Most Japanese depth charges exploded above them. Unfortunately, U.S. submarines for the first two years of the war were forced to operate with highly ineffective torpedoes. The magnetic pistols often did not work, and torpedoes sometimes circled around their target (one even sank the submarine, *Tang*, which had fired it). It was not until late 1943 and early 1944 that these problems were solved.

Japan began the war with 6 million tons of merchant shipping. During the war, it built another 2 million tons. Of this total, 4.8 million tons, or 60 percent, were sunk by submarines. Between the summer of 1943 and the summer of 1944, Japanese oil imports fell from 1.75 million barrels per month to 360,000 barrels per month. The Japanese navy required 1.6 million barrels monthly to operate. These oil shortages also impacted training time for Japanese pilots. By 1944, the Allies had eliminated more than 90 percent of all raw-material shipping to the Japanese home islands, largely as a result of U.S. undersea warfare.

U.S. submarines also sank 30 percent—200 ships in all—of all Japanese navy ships lost during the war. This included eight aircraft carriers, one battleship, and 11 cruisers. U.S. submarine operations against Japan were not without cost. The Japanese sank 48 of the 52 U.S. submarines lost in the war, and more than 3,500 submariners perished. American submariners had more than a one in five chance of being killed in action, a mortality rate higher than that of any other branch within the military.

See also WORLD WAR II, COURSE OF U.S. INVOLVEMENT: PACIFIC THEATER.

Further reading: Blair, Clay. *Silent Victory: U.S. Submarine War Against Japan.* 2 vols. New York: Lippincott, 1975; Galantin, I. J. *Take Her Deep!: A Submarine Against Japan in World War II.* New York: Unwin Hyman, 1988; Milton, Keith W. *Subs Against the Rising Sun.* Las Cruces, N.M.: Yucca Tree Press, 2000; Padfield, Peter. *War Beneath the Sea: Submarine Conflict During World War II.* New York: Wiley, 1995.

— Scott Blanchette

Sullivan, John (1740–1795) *Continental army general*
Born on 14 February 1740 at Somersworth, New Hampshire, John Sullivan studied law and was admitted to the bar. He first practiced in Berwick, Maine, but in 1763 moved to Durham, New Hampshire, becoming the first lawyer there. Between 1764 and 1772 he won a number of cases. A delegate to the First Continental Congress in September 1774, that December he organized two successful raids on a British fort in Portsmouth Harbor. Sullivan represented New Hampshire in the Second Continental Congress in May 1775.

Sullivan welcomed the American Revolutionary War and in July 1775 joined the Continental army at Cambridge as a brigadier general. With his striking appearance and erect posture, Sullivan had the bearing of a leader of men. Unfortunately, this bearing was not matched with military ability. His lack of success on the battlefield earned him the title of "the Luckless Irishman."

After the end of the siege of Boston, Continental army commander General George WASHINGTON ordered Sullivan to lead six regiments north as reinforcements for the invasion of CANADA. Arriving at Saint John's, Sullivan led an unsuccessful assault on British positions at TROIS RIVIÈRES and then returned to CROWN POINT. Learning that Congress had appointed Major General Horatio GATES to relieve him, the contentious Sullivan threatened to resign. In August, Congress promoted him to major general.

Washington then ordered Sullivan to Long Island, to replace Major General Nathaniel GREENE, who was ill. Sullivan took part in the Battle of LONG ISLAND in August 1776, but he and 400 men were trapped by the British and taken prisoner. Taken aboard Vice Admiral Lord Richard Howe's flagship, he agreed to accept a parole to present Howe's peace proposals to Congress.

Exchanged for a British general, by September Sullivan was back with Washington and participated in the retreat from New York City and in the Battles of TRENTON and PRINCETON. In the summer of 1777 he led a raid from New Jersey against the British on Staten Island, but the operation was largely unsuccessful. He then fought in the Battle of BRANDYWINE CREEK (11 September 1777) and at GERMANTOWN (4 October). Initially with Washington at VALLEY FORGE, he insisted on an independent command, and Washington finally gave him one in Rhode Island. He was ineffective in the siege of NEWPORT in August 1778, although he did carry out a skillful withdrawal.

Sullivan remained in Rhode Island until Washington gave him command of an expedition against the Iroquois in the Finger Lakes region of New York. His troops burned Indian villages and destroyed food stocks. Although the campaign was called a success, it failed to prevent the Indians from mounting raids along the frontier. When Congress appointed an investigating committee, Sullivan resigned in November 1779, citing poor health.

Sullivan returned to Durham. Elected to the Continental Congress in September 1780, he promoted efforts to produce a stronger central government. He returned to New Hampshire in August 1781. He later served as state attorney general and was for three terms president of the state in the late 1780s. He played an active role in putting down SHAYS'S REBELLION in 1786 and he supported ratification of the federal Constitution. In 1789, President Washington appointed him a federal district judge, a post Sullivan held until the spring of 1792. Sullivan's last years were spent in senility, the result of excessive drinking and a nervous disorder. He died on 23 January 1795.

See also AMERICAN REVOLUTIONARY WAR: LAND OVERVIEW.

Further reading: Billias, George Athan. *George Washington's Generals.* New York: William Morrow, 1964; Whittemore, Charles P. A. *A General of the Revolution: John Sullivan of New Hampshire.* New York: Columbia University Press, 1961.

— Nathan W. Charles

Sullivan's Island, Battle of (28 June 1776) *British naval attack on Charleston, South Carolina, early in the American Revolutionary War*

In 1775, London planned to send five regiments from Cork, Ireland, to cooperate with Loyalists in North Carolina. The expedition was delayed, and it was not until May 1776 that the force arrived off Cape Fear, where it was joined by some 2,000 men under Major General Henry Clinton, who assumed command of the ground troops. Commodore Sir Peter Parker, with his flag in the *Bristol,* commanded the naval force.

The North Carolina Loyalists had taken up arms, only to be crushed in the 27 February 1776 Battle of MOORE'S CREEK BRIDGE. Orders called for Clinton and Parker to participate in the assault on New York; but, with some time available before that attack, they decided to take CHARLESTON, the South's largest and wealthiest city. They left Cape Fear for Charleston on 31 May.

Fort Sullivan, located north of the harbor's mouth on an island of the same name, guarded the entrance to Charleston. Constructed of palmetto logs enclosing dirt walls 16 feet thick, only its southern and western walls were completed. Colonel William Moultrie commanded the fort, which mounted 31 guns and had a garrison of 420 men.

The British arrived off Charleston Bar on 4 June. An immediate attack might have taken the city, but Parker delayed to reconnoiter. Most of his ships crossed the bar on 7 June, but the *Bristol* had to be lightened by removing some of its guns and did not cross until the 10th. By the 15th, Clinton had landed all his troops on Long Island, separated from Sullivan's Island by a narrow channel. Clinton believed the channel could be forded, but it turned out to be seven feet deep at low water. Before Clinton could attempt a boat assault, the Americans emplaced field pieces and riflemen, preventing any assault there.

Parker apparently did not see the need to work with the army and was convinced he could force his way into the harbor with ships alone. In any case, he delayed, allowing the Americans to reinforce and strengthen their defenses. On 27 June the *Experiment* (50 guns) arrived. Lightened, it too crossed the bar and then took its guns on board again.

On 28 June eight warships, mounting a total of 260 guns, and the bomb vessel *Thunderer* opened a heavy fire on Fort Sullivan. They scored repeated hits but did little damage as the spongy ramparts absorbed the cannon balls. After nearly an hour, three of the vessels tried to maneuver around the end of the island to enfilade the fort but ran aground. Two were eventually refloated, but the other, the new 20-gun frigate *Actaeon,* remained fast. The *Thunderer*'s mortar also became dismounted.

Moultrie returned a slow, accurate fire, concentrating on the two largest British vessels. The American gunners riddled the *Experiment* and the *Bristol.* They then raked the *Bristol* when its cable was cut and its stern swung toward the island. Finally, at 9:00 P.M., Parker withdrew. The British suffered 64 killed and 161 wounded, mostly aboard the *Bristol* and *Experiment.* Parker and two ship captains were among the wounded. The next morning, the *Actaeon*'s crew abandoned and burned the ship.

American losses in the battle were only 17 dead and 20 wounded. The British would not return to the southern colonies for another two and a half years.

Further reading: Buchanan, John. *The Road to Guilford Courthouse: The American Revolution in the Carolinas.* New York: Wiley, 1997; Clowes, William Laird. *The Royal Navy. A History from the Earliest Times to 1900.* Vol. 3. London: Sampson Low, Marston & Co., 1898; Lumpkin, Henry. *From Savannah to Yorktown: The American Revolution in the South.* Columbia: University of South Carolina Press, 1981; Syrett, David. *The Royal Navy in American Waters, 1775–1783.* Aldershot, England: Scolar Press, 1989.

— Michael P. Gabriel and Spencer C. Tucker

Sultan, Daniel I. (1885–1947) *U.S. Army general*
Born on 9 December 1885 in Oxford, Mississippi, Daniel Isom Sultan attended the University of Mississippi from 1901 to 1903 before entering the U.S. Military Academy, WEST POINT, where he graduated in 1907. Commissioned in the engineers, Sultan graduated from the Engineer School in 1910. He returned to West Point as a member of the staff and instructor (1912–16) and was promoted to captain in 1914.

Sultan did not see combat in World War I. Assigned to the Philippines, he supervised construction of fortifications on CORREGIDOR, 1916–18. These fortifications, which were surrendered by U.S. forces to the Japanese in 1942, were never breached.

Sultan then joined the War Department General Staff for a year before a succession of other engineer assignments, including the Nicaragua Canal Survey (1929–31). He graduated from the Command and General Staff School in 1923 and the Army War College in 1926. Promoted to colonel in 1935, he then commanded 2d, Engineers. Promoted to brigadier general in 1938, he was, despite his lack of command experience, a contender for the position of army chief of staff, which went to General George C. MARSHALL. Sultan commanded the 22d Infantry Brigade in Hawaii from January 1939 to April 1941. Promoted to major general in April 1941, he subsequently commanded the 38th Infantry Division (May 1941–April 1942) and VIII Corps (April 1942–November 1943).

Promoted to lieutenant general in September 1943 and regarded as an excellent engineer and highly competent staff officer with careful attention to planning and detail, Sultan became chief of staff to Lieutenant General Joseph STILWELL, commander of U.S. forces in the CHINA-BURMA-INDIA theater. He served in that post from November 1943 to November 1944. When Stilwell was recalled, his command was split and Sultan became the U.S. commander of the India-Burma theater (November 1944–July 1945). With two Chinese armies and the British 36th Division, Sultan carried out operations in north Burma. His forces opened the Burma Road in June 1945.

Returning to the United States, Sultan was inspector general of the army from July 1945 until his death at Washington, D.C., on 14 January 1947. Sultan was the first member of the army to receive four Distinguished Service Medals.

See also WORLD WAR II, COURSE OF U.S. INVOLVEMENT: PACIFIC THEATER.

Further reading: Anders, Leslie. *Ledo-Road: General Joseph W. Stilwell's Highway to China.* Norman: University of Oklahoma Press, 1965; Tuchman, Barbara W. *Stilwell and the American Experience in China, 1911–45.* New York: Macmillan, 1971.

— Spencer C. Tucker

Summerall, Charles P. (1867–1955) *U.S. Army general*
Born on 4 March 1867 in Lake City, Florida, Charles Pelot Summerall graduated from secondary school and worked briefly as a teacher until he was appointed to the U.S. Military Academy, WEST POINT, in 1888. Commissioned in the infantry in 1892, he soon transferred to the artillery. As a young artillery officer in China during the relief expedition in July 1900 following the BOXER UPRISING, Summerall showed both his leadership and his personal courage while a member of Reilly's Battery (Light Battery F, 5th Artillery). Following assignments in Washington and Alaska, Captain Summerall was a senior instructor of artillery tactics at West Point from 1905 to 1911. He then commanded the 2d Battalion, 3rd Field Artillery, in Texas and Pennsylvania.

Major Summerall then served in several assignments on the War Department General Staff and was promoted to colonel. In April 1917, the United States entered World War I. Four months later, Summerall was promoted to brigadier general, and the next month Summerall took command of the 67th Field Artillery Brigade of the 42d (Rainbow) Division at Camp Mills, New York. He deployed with his brigade to France in October, then was assigned to command the 1st Field Artillery Brigade of the 1st Division in December. Summerall was welcomed by his old colleague Major General Robert L. BULLARD, commanding general of the 1st, with whom he had served in the Philippines. When Bullard was promoted to corps command after the CANTIGNY operation, in June Summerall was promoted to temporary major general and assumed command of the 1st Division, three days before the Soissons attack commenced on 18 July 1918. Following the SAINT MIHIEL OFFENSIVE, he was assigned to command the U.S. V Corps, which he led until the ARMISTICE. Along the way he picked up the nickname of "Sitting Bull," which the war correspondents ensured stuck for the rest of his life.

During the war General Summerall was decorated for valor with the Distinguished Service Cross and won four Silver Stars. At the end of the war he commanded the U.S. IX Corps in France and the U.S. IV Corps in Germany. Upon his return to the United States he again commanded the 1st Division in Kentucky and New Jersey from 1919 to 1921.

From November 1926 until November 1930, General Summerall was chief of staff of the army, after which he retired. From 1931 to 1953 he was president of the Citadel, in Charleston, South Carolina. Summerall died in Washington, D.C., on 14 May 1955.

See also AISNE-MARNE COUNTEROFFENSIVE; WORLD WAR I, COURSE OF U.S. INVOLVEMENT.

Further reading: Bullard, Robert L. *Personalities and Reminiscences of the War.* Garden City, N.Y.: Doubleday,

Page & Co., 1925; Pratt, Fletcher. "Charles P. Summerall: Sitting Bull II," in *Eleven Generals: Studies in American Command*. New York: William Sloane Associates, 1949.

— John F. Votaw

Summers, Harry G., Jr. (1932–1999) *U.S. Army officer and influential American military thinker*
Born on 6 May 1932 at Covington, Kentucky, Harry Summers enlisted in the U.S. Army in 1947 by falsifying his age. During the earliest days of the KOREAN WAR he served as an infantry squad leader with the 24th Infantry Division. After earning a college degree while still in the army, he received a direct commission as a 2nd lieutenant of infantry in 1957.

From February 1966 to June 1967, Summers fought in the VIETNAM WAR—initially as an assistant operations officer for II Field Forces; then as operations officer (S-3) of the 1st Infantry Division's 1st Battalion, 2d Infantry; then again as assistant operations officer at II Field Forces. He was wounded twice and received the Silver Star and the Bronze Star with V Device. Returning from Vietnam, Summers attended the U.S. Army Command and General Staff College.

Summers returned to Vietnam in July 1974 as chief of the Negotiations Division of the Four Party Joint Military Team. Operating from Saigon, he frequently traveled to Hanoi to negotiate with members of the People's Army of Vietnam (PAVN or North Vietnamese Army, NVA) General Staff. When PAVN forces overran Saigon on 30 April 1975, Summers was on the last helicopter to leave the American embassy.

In 1979, the same year he was promoted to full colonel, Summers joined the faculty of the U.S. Army War College Strategic Studies Institute. Assigned the task of distilling the lessons of the Vietnam War, he wrote *On Strategy: A Critical Analysis of the Vietnam War,* a brilliant and scholarly book that remains one of the most influential analyses of America's failure. After retiring from the army in 1985, Summers became a widely noted military commentator and writer and the founding editor of *Vietnam* magazine.

On Strategy in particular had a profound impact on American military thinking. In the debate over America's performance in Vietnam, Summers was a strong advocate of the argument that U.S. forces never lost on the battlefield. His critics insist that American combat tactics failed dismally. Tactical performance, however, was only a small piece of Summers's broader, more significant argument.

On Strategy focused primarily on the strategic level of war. Summers showed that America had no clearly defined strategic objective in Vietnam. He also argued that the lack of internal political support for the war violated Karl Clausewitz's concept of the "Remarkable Trinity," which requires a unity of purpose among the government, the military, and the people, before any nation's war effort can hope to succeed.

Summers's arguments were tremendously influential, both inside and outside of the military. They underlie many of the key statements of American security policy in the 1980s and early 1990s, most significantly the 1984 Weinburger Doctrine. Many of the ideas in the U.S. Army's 1993 capstone manual of war doctrine, *FM 100-5 Operations,* were paraphrased directly from *On Strategy.* Summers also influenced all of America's senior service colleges (war colleges) to return the study of Clausewitz's writings to their curriculums. Summers died at Walter Reed Army Hospital on 14 November 1999.

Further reading: Bassford, Christopher. *Clausewitz in English: The Reception of Clausewitz in Britain and America, 1815–1945.* New York: Oxford University Press, 1994; Summers, Harry G. *On Strategy: A Critical Analysis of the Vietnam War.* Novato, Calif.: Presidio Press, 1982; Zabecki, David T. "A Tribute to Colonel Harry G. Summers, Jr.," *Vietnam* (April 2000): 62–68.

— David T. Zabecki

Sumter, Thomas ("Gamecock") (1734–1832) *South Carolina partisan leader and general during the American Revolutionary War*
Born on 14 August 1734 in Louisa County, Virginia, Thomas Sumter had a limited education before working as a miller. From 1756 to 1761 he served in the Virginia militia against the French and in the CHEROKEE WAR.

After the war Sumter was imprisoned for debt, but he escaped to South Carolina. He settled at Eutaw Springs in 1764 and became a storekeeper. He served as a militia captain in the 1776 campaign against backcountry Loyalists. That February, he was appointed lieutenant colonel, commanding a state infantry regiment, which he led in the defense of Charleston in June and in the autumn campaign against the Cherokees.

Sumter campaigned along the Georgia–East Florida border in 1777 and 1778. Although his regiment was incorporated into the Continental army and he was promoted to colonel, illness and military failures led him to resign in September 1778. He remained inactive until the British capture of CHARLESTON in May 1780. As the British advanced into South Carolina, Sumter returned to military service, leaving his home hours before Lieutenant Colonel Banastre Tarleton's cavalry burned it.

In June, Sumter took command of a combined partisan force, with the rank of brigadier general in the state militia. His troops were the only organized Patriot unit in the state at the time. Sumter's first operations were unsuccessful, and on 18 August Tarleton surprised Sumter's camp at Fishing Creek, inflicting more than 400 casualties. Sumter, however, continued to fight, earning the name "Gamecock" for his relentless determination. On 9 November, he was again surprised, at Fish Dam Ford, but his troops rallied and fought off the attack. On the 20th, he repulsed Tarleton's attack at Blackstock's farm.

In January 1781 Sumter assumed command of all state militia. He quarreled with Major General Nathaniel GREENE and other officers over issues of command and recruiting practices. Sumter offered enlistment bounties in the form of slaves seized from Loyalists and shares in plundered Loyalist property. This practice, known as "Sumter's Law," attracted needed recruits, but many Americans denounced it as robbery.

After a feeble effort to delay Colonel Lord Francis Rawdon's relief march to Ninety Six, Sumter attacked a British force at Quinby Plantation on 17 July and was repulsed. He then resorted to plundering to pay his troops.

This angered Greene and Governor John Rutledge, sparking new quarrels that led Rutledge to remove Sumter from command. Sumter took no further part in the war, but it was his persistence that had kept the revolutionary cause alive in South Carolina.

After the war, Sumter served in the state legislature, the U.S. House of Representatives, and the U.S. Senate. He died at his plantation, South Mark, near Stateburg, South Carolina, on 1 June 1832. Fort Sumter, South Carolina, where the first shots of the Civil War were fired, was named for him.

See also AMERICAN REVOLUTIONARY WAR: LAND OVERVIEW; GREENE'S OPERATIONS; MARION, FRANCIS; PICKENS, ANDREW.

Further reading: Bass, Robert D. *Gamecock: The Life and Campaigns of General Thomas Sumter.* New York: Holt, Rinehart & Winston, 1961.

— Jim Piecuch

T

Tailhook Association convention (7 September 1991) *Event at which an incident occurred that adversely affected the navy*

Charges of scandalous, drunken behavior by naval aviators at this event in a Las Vegas hotel led to official investigations and prosecutions. In its wake Congress admonished the naval leadership, the secretary of the navy resigned, several senior officers were reprimanded, and hundreds of officers had their reputations tarnished and careers stalled. The public reaction that followed the event hastened abolition of barriers that had prevented women naval aviators from serving in squadrons with combat missions.

A group of carrier-based naval aviators formed the Tailhook Association in 1956. The organization took its name from the hook on aircraft that engaged arresting gear on an aircraft carrier deck. The annual Tailhook conventions offered a weekend of professional networking among the aviators and industry representatives, plus a degree of revelry both celebrated and infamous.

In years preceding the 1991 convention, the association had urged restraint. Notwithstanding, private parties during the convention featured licentious behavior and large quantities of liquor. On 7 September a group of male aviators lined up along a third-floor hallway to jeer at, molest, and even assault passing women. One of those assaulted Lieutenant (junior grade) Paula Coughlin, a navy helicopter pilot, who later testified that as an admiral's aide and naval aviator she believed herself safe from harm and was stunned and frightened when she was accosted.

The next morning and twice more in the next few days, Coughlin reported the events to her superior, Rear Admiral John W. Snyder, Jr., but he took no action. She then went to higher-ranking officers. When portions of the story became public in October, the navy began a formal investigation. In November it transferred Coughlin's boss to a lesser post. Subsequent investigations reported that 26 women, about half of them naval officers, had been similarly assaulted, but only two suspects were identified. No charges were brought because so many witnesses refused to cooperate, or misled or lied to investigators. One investigation charged both the Tailhook Association and the naval aviation community with "lack of moral courage and failed leadership."

Secretary of the Navy Lawrence Garrett subsequently withdrew all navy support from the association. Publication of the details and charges of a cover-up aroused public opinion outside the navy and provoked controversy within it. Garrett resigned in June 1992. More investigation was followed by military judicial proceedings. In the end, although dozens of navy and Marine Corps officers were prosecuted, not one was convicted, and 50 received only administrative punishment.

In the spring of 1994, Chief of Naval Operations and Chairman of the Joint Chiefs of Staff Admiral Frank Kelso retired two months early. Coughlin resigned from the navy.

See also WOMEN IN THE MILITARY.

Further reading: Ebbert, Jean, and Marie-Beth Hall. *Crossed Currents: Navy Women in a Century of Change.* 3rd ed. Washington, D.C.: Brassey's, 1999; Zimmerman, Jean. *Tailspin: Women at War in the Wake of Tailhook.* New York: Doubleday, 1995.

— Jean Ebbert and Marie-Beth Hall

tanks *Tracked, armored fighting vehicles armed with a high-velocity, flat-trajectory main gun*

The tank's main armament is designed for direct-fire engagement; artillery, on the other hand, primarily employs indirect fire. Tanks first appeared during World War I. Developed by the British beginning in 1915, they were prematurely deployed in September 1916 in an attempt to break the deadlock in the Battle of the Somme. Only Britain, France, and Germany produced tanks that saw combat in World War I, and Germany produced very few.

French-built FT-17 (Renault) Tank of C Company, 327th Tank Battalion, 3d Brigade, 1st Infantry Division, American Expeditionary Forces, in action in the St. Mihiel Sector, 12 September 1918.   *(U.S. Army Military History Institute)*

When the United States entered the war, getting American manpower to Europe was much more important than equipment. U.S. forces used a great deal of British and French equipment, and no American-made tank saw combat in the war. The U.S. Tank Corps, created in December 1917, for the most part employed the Renault light tank, which was well suited to American theories of mobile warfare. Weighing seven tons, it had a crew of two men, maximum half-inch armor, and a 37mm gun or 8mm machine gun in a fully rotating top turret. U.S. tank units, which made their first appearance in the September 1918 SAINT MIHIEL OFFENSIVE, utilized the Renault and also Schneider CA.1 heavy tanks. The latter had a 75mm gun in a turret on the right side and two 8mm machine guns.

Another U.S. tank unit, the 301st Heavy Tank Battalion, served with the British army and was equipped with British Mark V and Mark V Star tanks. The 30-ton Mark V mounted two 6-pounder guns and four machine guns in the "male" version, and six machine guns in the "female" version.

The 36-ton Mark V Star was somewhat longer and added another machine gun (giving the "male" five and the "female" seven). In 1918, the Americans began production of a Renault clone, the 1917 six-ton, but none were delivered in time to see action.

In the drawdown of U.S. forces following the war, the Tank Corps was abolished in 1919. The National Defense Act of 1920 assigned the tanks to the infantry, consistent with the army belief that they should support attacking infantry. The few resources available for tank development were expended on "light" tanks of no more than five tons and "medium" types of no more than 15 tons. The budgets of the 1920s allowed production of only two experimental models per year, which nonetheless led to the development of the T1E4 light tank with its sprocket drive and rear engine, both adopted in subsequent light tank models.

In 1927 the army set up the small experimental Mechanized Force built of light tanks. In 1931, however, Chief of

Staff General Douglas MACARTHUR decreed that tanks would have an exploitation role apart from infantry support, and the cavalry took over the Mechanized Force. In order to get around the 1920 defense act, however, the tanks were described as "combat cars."

Experimentation led to the T2 light tank, with a leaf-spring suspension, and to a similar vehicle for cavalry use known as the T5 Combat Car, which entered service as the M1 Combat Car in 1937 and became the Light Tank M1A1 in 1940. Weighing 9.7 tons with a crew of four, the M1A1 had maximum 16mm armor and was armed with one .30-caliber and one .50-caliber machine gun in the turret and a .30-caliber machine gun in the hull. An improved model, the M2 Combat Car, incorporated a trailing idler for better traction and improved ride.

In 1940 the Armored Force, led by Brigadier General Adna Romanaza CHAFFEE, Jr., came into being. It abolished the distinction between infantry and cavalry tank units. The M1 and M2 Combat Cars now became the M1A1 and M1A2 light tanks. Declared obsolete in 1940, they did not see combat in World War II but were utilized extensively as training vehicles and as the basis for subsequent light-tank design.

The M3 Stuart light tank incorporated lessons learned in the early fighting in Europe in World War II. It entered service in March 1941. The M3 went through three different models but eventually incorporated a gyro-stabilizer for the main gun, an all-welded turret and hull (the first being all-riveted), and a diesel engine. The M3 weighed 16 tons, had a crew of four, maximum 51mm armor, and was armed with a 37mm gun in the turret and 3 x .30 machine guns. It saw extensive service in North Africa with the British and Americans. Too light and underpowered, it was declared obsolete in July 1943.

The M3 was followed by the M5 General Stuart, which was the same basic design but with twin Cadillac automobile engines. Originally to be the Light Tank M4, it was designated the M5 to avoid confusion with the M4 medium Sherman tank, then entering production. Recognizable by its stepped-up rear deck, the General Stuart had a crew of four, weight of 16.5 tons, maximum 67mm armor, and armament of one 37mm gun and two .30-caliber machine guns.

The M24 Chaffee appeared late in the war, answering the need for a light tank with heavier armament. Entering production in March 1944, this highly successful design was manufactured in a variety of models. The 20-ton M24 had a crew of five, maximum 38mm armor, and mounted a 75mm gun, and three machine guns: two .30-caliber (one coaxial) and one .50-caliber.

The M2 medium tank with a 37mm gun, which was to enter production in 1941, was rendered obsolete by the Battle of France and heavier-gunned German tanks. The M2 was used only for training purposes in the United States and was superseded by the M3 Medium Lee and Grant series. These latter weighed 30 tons combat-loaded, had a crew of six, maximum 51mm armor, and mounted a 75mm gun in the right sponson with secondary armament of one 37mm gun and three .30-caliber machine guns.

The M3's successor, the M4 Sherman medium tank, was produced in a wide variety of models. It was certainly the most widely used Allied tank of the war. In all, some 49,000 M4s were built. The M4 continued in service after the war and was widely used by the Israeli army.

The M4 utilized the lower hull of the M3 with a redesigned upper hull, mounting a central turret with a 75mm gun. It weighed 33 tons, had a crew of five, maximum 51mm armor, and mounted a 75mm main gun and one .50-caliber and two .30-caliber machine guns. The Sherman first saw service in North Africa in 1942. It had two great advantages over the German tanks: its powered turret that enabled crews to react and fire more quickly, and greater mechanical reliability and reparability. Rugged, maneuverable, and easy to maintain, the M4 was consistently upgraded in main gun and armor during the course of the war.

The Sherman's great disadvantages were its engine and main gun. Its gasoline (vice diesel) engine earned it the GI nickname of "Ronson Lighter—lights first time, every time." The Sherman was also consistently outgunned by the larger German tanks against which it had to fight. Its 75mm gun was relatively ineffective, but a replacement 76mm gun with much higher muzzle velocity was far more effective. The British were the first to use the 76mm gun on their Shermans, which they called the Sherman Firefly; the Americans soon followed suit.

Indeed, one of the major problems for the U.S. Army in the war was the lack of a heavy tank. German tanks had thicker frontal armor and a much higher velocity gun: the German Tiger mounted an 88mm. The 88mm German Panzerschreck antitank weapon could easily knock out the Shermans, whereas the U.S. 2.36-inch BAZOOKA, from which it was copied, was only effective against German side armor. Also, the Sherman tread mark was only 14 inches; German tanks had a track twice as wide and thus were not as easily bogged down.

In the course of 1944–45, the 3d Armored Division alone lost 648 Sherman tanks completely destroyed in combat and another 700 knocked out, repaired, and put back into operation—a loss rate of 580 percent. In fact, the U.S. lost 6,000 tanks in Europe in World War II. The Germans never had more than half that total.

The answer to the German tanks, the M26 Pershing heavy tank, was not available until after the December 1944–January 1945 Battle of the BULGE. The failure to have the M26 available in large numbers earlier was in part because influential Lieutenant General George S. PATTON insisted on concentrating on high production of M4 Shermans since the army needed a fast, medium tank and because he believed that "tanks do not fight other tanks." Patton counted on tank destroyers to protect the U.S. tanks, but the M10 Wolverine tank destroyer of 1942 had only a 76mm gun. The M36 Jackson, introduced in 1944, had a 90mm gun, which could indeed take on the German Panthers and Tigers on an equal footing. Both the M10 and M36 used the Sherman chassis.

The Battle of the Bulge, which again revealed the weakness of the M4 against heavy German tanks, led to the prompt shipment to Europe of the first M26 Pershing heavy tanks, the prototypes of which had been produced only in November 1944. Weighing 46 tons, the M26 had a crew of five, maximum 102 mm (4 inch) armor, and a 90mm gun, along with one .50-caliber and two .30-caliber machine guns. The muzzle velocity of its main gun did not match the 88mm German tank guns, but it was almost a match for the fearsome Tiger in firepower and surpassed it in terms of reliability and mobility.

During the KOREAN WAR, the Korean People's Army (KPA, North Korean) and Chinese People's Volunteer Army (CPVA, Chinese Communist) employed the Russian-built T34 tank, mounting an 85mm gun; it had been one of the best tanks in World War II. The United States principally employed the M24 light tank, the M4A3 medium Sherman (76 mm gun) in a number of variants, the M26 Pershing, and the M46 Patton.

The M46 Patton was an improved model of the M26, developed in 1947. Weighing 48.5 tons, it had a crew of five, and maximum 102mm (4 inch) armor. It mounted a 90mm gun, along with one .50-caliber gun atop the turret for the tank commander and two .30-caliber machine guns (one coaxially). In 1952 an improved version, the M47, appeared.

Most of the time during the Korean War, United Nations Command tanks were employed as mobile pillboxes, providing fire support to infantry units. Korea's geography precluded large-scale tank battles. The same was largely true during the VIETNAM WAR. Some lighter U.S. tanks, such as the M551 Sheridan, which appeared in 1966, were ill suited for this combat environment. Intended as an air-transportable vehicle with superior hitting power, the M551 sported aluminum armor and a 152mm gun that could also fire an antitank missile, along with two machine guns. Intended as a quantum leap in technology, it also suffered from many problems.

The M48 Patton served well. Introduced in 1953, the M48 was an entirely new design and the first U.S. medium tank to do away with the hull-mounted machine gun. Weighing 46.4 tons, it had a crew of four men, and maximum 120mm armor. It mounted a 90mm gun and two machine guns: one .50-caliber external and one .30-caliber coaxial. The M48 went through a variety of models up to the M48A5 with a 105mm gun.

In Vietnam, the M48 was commonly used to create paths through dense vegetation and to assault Communist bunkers and grind them down beneath its tracks. Tanks were employed to help clear out Communist strong points, patrol secure areas, and engage in sweeps and ambushes. Armor was never a strong point for the People's Army of Vietnam (PAVN, North Vietnamese) forces. The optic systems of their Soviet-built T54 and T55 tanks were inferior to that of the M48. The PAVN did employ significant numbers of tanks late in the war, however.

The U.S. Army M60 medium tank, the prototype of which appeared in 1958, was derived from the M48. The M60A3 weighed 51.8 tons, had a crew of four, maximum 120mm armor, and mounted a 105mm gun and one 50 caliber and one 7.62mm coaxial machine guns. It employed a new fire-control computer and laser rangefinder.

The epitome of armor development for the United States, as well as that of the world, is the M1A1 Abrams MBT (Main Battle Tank). The 1991 Gulf War (Operation DESERT STORM) provided a perfect venue for it in what were some of the largest tank battles in history. Derived from the M1, which first went into production in 1980, the M1A1 appeared in 1985. The M1 mounted a 105mm main gun while the 57-ton M1A2 is armed with a 120mm smoothbore gun. The M1 and M1A2 also have one .50-caliber and two 7.62mm machine guns (one coaxial). It has a crew of four men and laminate steel armor, which proved highly effective in the Gulf War. The tank's superior optics enabled it to engage Iraqi tanks at twice their own effective range and to fight effectively in obscured conditions. Of 1,956 M1A1s in theater during Operation Desert Storm, none were destroyed by Iraqi fire and only eight were damaged or disabled; all of those were repairable. Production of the M1A2 began in 1992. It sports improved armor.

See also AMERICAN EXPEDITIONARY FORCE; CHRISTIE, JOHN W.; WORLD WAR I, COURSE OF U.S. INVOLVEMENT; WORLD WAR II, U.S. INVOLVEMENT: EUROPE.

Further reading: Chamberlain, Peter, and Chris Ellis. *British and American Tanks of World War II.* New York: Arco Publishing Co., 1969; Cooper, Belton Y. *Death Traps: The Survival of an American Armored Division in World War II.* Novato, Calif.: Presidio Press, 2000; Dunstan, Simon. *Vietnam Tracks: Armor in Battle, 1945–1975.* Novato, Calif.: Presidio Press, 1982; Macksey, Kenneth, and John H. Batchelor. *Tank: A History of the Armoured Fighting Vehicle.* New York: Scribner, 1976.

— Spencer C. Tucker

Tarawa and Makin, Battles for (November 1943)

Significant battles in the Pacific theater during World War II

Makin and Tarawa were two of the 16 atolls in the Gilbert chain to be captured in Operation Galvanic. This was the first step in Admiral Chester NIMITZ's Central Pacific campaign, which was to work its way toward the Japanese home islands. At the time, the Gilberts were Japan's most easterly outpost, and Betio, Tarawa's largest atoll, contained an airfield from which Japanese planes could threaten U.S. shipping lanes to Australia.

Vice Admiral Raymond A. SPRUANCE, commander of Fifth Fleet, had overall operational command of the operation. Rear Admiral Richmond K. TURNER's Fifth Amphibious Force lifted Marine Major General Holland M. "Howlin' Mad" SMITH's V Amphibious Corps. In addition to fleet air and naval gunfire assets, Seventh Air Force provided support. The army's 27th Division, a National Guard outfit, with the 6th Marines in reserve, was to secure Makin while the 2d Marine Division took Tarawa. The two islands were some 100 miles apart.

The assault of the Gilberts began on 20 November. Makin proved to be lightly defended and was easily secured in four days. Tarawa was much more difficult. Rear Admiral Keiji Shibasaki and 4,700 defenders had spent 15 months building bunkers and defensive positions. Betio island, only two miles long and several hundred yards across, had 400 concrete pillboxes and bunkers, covered with logs and sand, that were impervious to all but a direct hit. Mines and barbed wire inhibited movement, while defensive firepower included up to 8-inch guns. Coral reefs ringing the island provided a natural defensive barrier.

The invasion of Tarawa was the first assault against a defended coast since the struggle for Gallipoli in World War I. Marine colonel David Shoup both planned and led the assault, which took place on its more lightly defended north side. Preparatory naval gunfire and air strikes proved largely ineffectual, and three hours of naval gunfire preceding the assault itself was halted prematurely for fear that the shells would hit the marine amphibious tractors (amtracs, or LVTs). Although the amtracs could make it over the shallow reefs, the following landing craft hung up on them, forcing the marines they were carrying to wade ashore in waist-deep water, where they were easy prey for Japanese defensive fire.

Of the 5,000 marines who landed on the first day, 1,500 were killed or wounded. For a day and half, the issue was in doubt, and 2d Marine commander Major General Julian Smith called for the 6th Marines to be landed. On the Japanese side, Admiral Shibasaki's early death prevented effective Japanese counterattacks until late in the battle.

Tarawa was taken on 24 November, but the battle for the atoll was one of the bloodiest battles in Marine Corps history. It claimed 985 marines killed and 2,193 wounded. The Japanese lost 4,690 men killed. The marines took only 17 prisoners, along with 129 Korean laborers.

While the assault proved the validity of marine amphibious operational doctrine, it had also provided many hard lessons. These led to improvements in reconnaissance, radio communications, naval gunfire and close air support, additional amphibious tractors, and improved assault weapons. The latter included more infantry firepower, flamethrowers, and demolition charges. Most of these were available for the MARSHALL ISLANDS campaign six weeks later.

See also WORLD WAR II, COURSE OF U.S. INVOLVEMENT: PACIFIC THEATER.

Further reading: Alexander, Joseph H. *Utmost Savagery: The Three Days of Tarawa.* Annapolis, Md.: Naval Institute Press, 1995; Graham, Michael B. *Mantle of Heroism: Tarawa and the Struggle for the Gilberts, November 1943.* Novato, Calif.: Presidio Press, 1993; Wilson, Earl J., et al. *Betio Beachhead: The U.S. Marines' Own Story of the Battle for Tarawa.* New York: G. P. Putnam's Sons, 1945.

— Stephen L. Skakandy

Task Force Smith *Initial U.S. ground response to the North Korean invasion of South Korea*

On the evening of 30 June 1950, Major General William F. DEAN ordered Lieutenant Colonel Charles B. Smith to prepare his 1st Battalion of the 21st Infantry, 24th Infantry Division, to move to Korea.

The next day the battalion, less its A and D companies, flew from Itazuke Air Base in Japan, to Pusan, South Korea, in C-54 transports. The men were then transported by train to Teajon, arriving there on 2 July. As finally constituted on 4 July, Task Force Smith comprised the infantry as well as the 52d Field Artillery with five 105mm howitzers. The entire force numbered 540 officers and men. Poorly trained, it had little antitank ammunition.

Smith selected defensive positions north of the city of Osan, where the men were expected to stop two Korean People's Army (KPA, North Korean) infantry regiments supported by dozens of tanks. Task Force Smith met defeat in the subsequent 5 July Battle of OSAN.

See also KOREAN WAR, COURSE OF.

Further reading: Appleman, Roy E. *United States Army in the Korean War: South to the Naktong, North to the Yalu, June–November 1950.* Washington, D.C.: Government Printing Office, 1961; Sandler, Stanley. *The Korean War: No Victors, No Vanquished.* Lexington: University Press of Kentucky, 1999.

— Troy D. Morgan

Taylor, David W. (1864–1940) *U.S. Navy admiral*
Born on 4 March 1864 in Louisa County, Virginia, David Watson Taylor entered Randolph-Macon College in 1877. He graduated at the head of his class from the U.S. Naval Academy, Annapolis, in 1885. Following brief sea service, Taylor pursued a three-year postgraduate course in naval architecture and maritime engineering at the Royal Naval College, Greenwich, England. His scholastic records at the Naval Academy and at Greenwich have never been equaled.

In 1886 Taylor was appointed assistant naval constructor and after his graduation in 1888 from the Royal Naval College was appointed assistant inspector at the Cramp's Shipyard, Philadelphia. A year later he reported to the Bureau of Construction and Repair in Washington, where he worked on designs for the battleships *Oregon, Massachusetts,* and *Indiana.* Promoted to naval constructor in 1892, he was recalled to the Bureau of Construction and Repair to act as the principal assistant to the chief constructor.

Taylor immediately began the task of improving U.S. naval design facilities and built the Washington model ship basin. The basin, the first of its kind in the United States, allowed study of such problems as hull and propeller designs, gyroscopic control of ship rolling, and the effect of suction on vessels passing close to each other. As a result of these studies, Taylor set standards for calculating displacement, stability, and other elements for the navy that remain in use to the present.

Taylor was the first to suggest a change in the design of battleship turrets, an improvement adopted by both American and British navies. He testified in 1911 as an expert witness in a lawsuit resulting from a collision of the liner *Olympic* and the British cruiser *Hawke.* His testimony on the theory of suction was the principal piece of evidence in deciding the case in favor of the Royal Navy.

Promoted to rear admiral, in 1914 Taylor became chief of the Bureau of Construction and Repair, holding that post until 1922. Promoted to rear admiral in 1916, during World War I he was responsible for the design and construction of more than 1,000 ships. Prior to 1921 he was also in charge of the design of naval aircraft and helped to produce the NC flying boat for strategic bombing operations.

Taylor retired from the navy in January 1923. He continued as a consultant in naval architecture after his retirement. Taylor wrote two books, *Resistance of Ships and Screw Propulsions* (1893) and *Speed and Power of Ships* (1910). In his honor, the American Society of Naval and Marine Engineers established the Taylor Medal, awarded annually for notable achievements in naval engineering. Taylor died in Washington, D.C., on 28 July 1940.

Further reading: Carlisle, Rodney P. *Where the Fleet Begins: A History of the David Taylor Research Center, 1898–1998.* Washington, D.C.: Government Printing Office, 1998; Reynolds, Clark G. *Famous American Admirals.* New York: Van Nostrand Reinhold, 1978.

— Stephen P. Ward

Taylor, Maxwell D. (1901–1987) *U.S. Army general and chairman of the Joint Chiefs of Staff*
Born on 26 August 1901 in Keytesville, Missouri, Maxwell Davenport Taylor graduated fourth in his class in 1922 from the U.S. Military Academy, WEST POINT. An able linguist, he later taught languages at West Point, completed foreign assignments in Paris and Tokyo during the 1920s and 1930s, and undertook intelligence duties in China in 1937, when the Sino-Japanese War began. He graduated from the Army War College in 1940.

Promoted to colonel, Taylor became chief of staff to Major General Matthew RIDGWAY's 82d Infantry Division, soon the army's first airborne division. As a brigadier general, Taylor accompanied the Eighty-second to North Africa in March 1943 and helped to plan the July assault on SICILY, in which he participated. He then undertook a secret mission to Rome to discuss an airborne assault there. His negative assessment led to cancellation of the plan. Ordered to Britain in March 1944, he took command of the 101st Airborne Division and jumped with it in the NORMANDY INVASION and Operation MARKET GARDEN. He commanded the 101st for the remainder of the war.

When the war ended, Taylor became commandant of West Point, instituting reforms designed to modernize military training. He later served in Germany and as assistant chief of staff in Washington. In February 1953, Taylor took command of the Eighth Army in Korea, at a time when an armistice was imminent. Promoted to full general, in August 1953 he took command of U.S. forces in the Far East. In February 1955 he became army chief of staff. Although Taylor served out his four-year term and did not, as is often alleged, resign in protest, he differed sharply with President Dwight D. EISENHOWER'S NEW LOOK STRATEGY, which relied on massive nuclear retaliation. Taylor favored building up conventional forces to enable the United States to fight limited wars, the strategy of FLEXIBLE RESPONSE. In his book *The Uncertain Trumpet* (1959), Taylor publicly aired his views, winning the attention and approval of Eisenhower's successor, John F. KENNEDY.

Although Taylor retired from the army in 1959, Kennedy brought him out of retirement, initially as military adviser to investigate the 1961 BAY OF PIGS fiasco. Taylor quickly assumed other responsibilities. In late 1961 Taylor and Deputy National Security Advisor Walt W. Rostow headed a mission of experts to South Vietnam. Their report recommended the introduction of 6,000 to 8,000 American troops in the guise of a flood relief force, a suggestion that

President Kennedy rejected; however, Taylor and Rostow were successful in advocating a major expansion in the numbers of U.S. military advisers in Vietnam and of military and economic aid, together with an increase in American responsibilities for Vietnam. As chairman of the Joint Chiefs of Staff from 1962 to 1964, Taylor opposed the commitment of further American troops to Vietnam but supported the escalation of the war through United States air strikes within Vietnam and bombing raids on North Vietnam. During a one-year term as United States ambassador to South Vietnam, which began in August 1964, he continued to oppose the commitment of American ground forces—advice that President Lyndon B. JOHNSON ignored. On his return to the United States Taylor served three years as a special consultant to Johnson, in which capacity he frequently and publicly defended U.S. policies in Vietnam. In March 1968 Taylor was one of only three senior advisers or "Wise Men" to dissent from the view that the United States should seek a negotiated settlement to end the war. In 1972 he advised Secretary of State Henry A. KISSINGER that the United States should resolve the issue of North Vietnamese troops remaining in the South and several other contentious matters before reaching a peace agreement—advice that Kissinger largely ignored. For the rest of his life Taylor continued to defend U.S. policies in Vietnam and to blame his country's defeat largely upon criticism by the media and public opinion, which in his view had sapped American resolve to win. Taylor died in Washington, D.C., on 19 April 1987.

See also AIRBORNE FORCES, DEVELOPMENT AND DEPLOYMENT OF; ARMY, U.S.; GAVIN, JAMES; MCAULIFFE, ANTHONY C.; MCNAMARA, ROBERT S.; VIETNAM WAR, COURSE OF; WESTMORELAND, WILLIAM C.

Further reading: Buzzanco, Robert. *Masters of War: Military Dissent & Politics in the Vietnam Era.* New York: Cambridge University Press, 1996; Kinnard, Douglas. *The Certain Trumpet: Maxwell Taylor and the American Experience in Vietnam.* Washington, D.C.: Brassey's, 1991; Taylor, John M. *General Maxwell Taylor: The Sword and the Pen.* New York: Doubleday, 1989; Taylor, Maxwell D. *Swords and Plowshares.* New York: W. W. Norton, 1972.

— Priscilla Roberts

Taylor, Zachary (1784–1850) *U.S. Army general and president of the United States*
Born on 24 November 1784 near Barboursville, Virginia, Zachary Taylor moved in 1785 with his family to the Kentucky frontier near Louisville. Taylor received only a limited education. In the spring of 1808, Congress responded to the *CHESAPEAKE-LEOPARD* AFFAIR by nearly tripling the size of the army. In May 1808, Taylor secured a commission as a first lieutenant in the 7th Infantry Regiment.

First stationed at New Orleans, Taylor then commanded Fort Pickering near present-day Memphis. Promoted to captain in November 1810, he commanded Fort Knox, at Vincennes, Indiana Territory. Shortly before the beginning of the War of 1812 he took command of Fort Harrison (present-day Terre Haute), Indiana, on the Wabash River. When 400 Indians attacked the fort in September 1812, Taylor and 50 defenders held them off, for which Taylor was promoted to brevet major. Promoted to major, in the summer of 1814 he led an expedition against the Indians in the upper Mississippi area and up the Des Moines River, but was intercepted by a British-Indian force at Rock River, in Illinois, in September and forced to withdraw. He saw no further action.

Reverting to the rank of captain with the return of peace, Taylor resigned his commission, but he returned to military service in 1816, when President James Madison ordered him restored to major. Assigned to Green Bay on Lake Michigan, he helped to direct the construction of Fort Howard. In April 1819, Taylor won promotion to lieutenant colonel and was posted to Florida with the 4th Infantry. From 1819 until 1832 he served in various installations, chiefly in Louisiana. In April 1832, Taylor was promoted to colonel and joined the 1st Infantry, fighting Chief BLACK HAWK's Sauk and Fox warriors.

In November 1837 Taylor joined the Second SEMINOLE WAR. On 25 December 1837 he won the Battle of LAKE OKEECHOBEE, for which he was promoted to brevet brigadier general. In May 1838 he received command of the Department of Florida, and for the next two years he chased the remaining Seminole forces in a campaign that earned him the nickname "Old Rough and Ready."

During much of 1840 Taylor was on leave. Securing command of the Second Department, Western Division, he was stationed at Fort Smith, Arkansas. By this time Taylor had developed a reputation for complete indifference to military etiquette and dress, although his concern for his men won their respect and affection.

Following the annexation of Texas, President James K. Polk ordered forces under Taylor to occupy territory to the Rio Grande, precipitating the MEXICAN-AMERICAN WAR. On 8 May 1846 Taylor won the Battle of PALO ALTO, and the next day he defeated the Mexican Army of the North at RESCA DE LA PALMA. On 11 May 1846 Congress declared war on Mexico. Taylor invaded Mexico as ordered and captured Matamoros. Breveted major general and named commander of the Army of the Rio Grande in July, Taylor then advanced on MONTERREY in September. His attempt to take the heavily fortified city bogged down, and he agreed to an armistice whereby Mexican forces were allowed to withdraw, and Taylor's forces entered the city. With the majority of Taylor's northern force then siphoned off by Major General Winfield SCOTT for his landing at VERACRUZ, General Antonio López de Santa Anna marched north to try to catch Taylor. Although he faced a much larger force, Taylor won the February 1847 Battle of BUENA VISTA.

With Taylor now a national hero, Whig party leaders persuaded him to run for the presidency. Taylor won the election of 1848 with Millard Filmore as his running mate. Taylor was president for only 16 months, and his tenure was dominated by the issue of slavery. A Southerner by birth and a slave owner, Taylor nonetheless opposed the expansion of slavery into the territories taken from Mexico. He died of food poisoning at the White House in Washington, D.C., on 9 July 1850.

See also WAR OF 1812: LAND OVERVIEW.

Further reading: Bauer, K. Jack. *Zachary Taylor: Soldier, Planter, Statesman of the Old Southwest.* Baton Rouge: Louisiana State University Press, 1985; Hamilton, Holman. *Zachary Taylor: Soldier of the Republic.* 2 vols. Hamden, Conn.: Archon Books, 1966.

— A. J. L. Waskey

Tecumseh (1768–1813) *Shawnee Indian Leader and general in the British army*

Born in March 1768 near Old Piqua, Ohio, to a Shawnee father and Creek mother, Tecumseh fought in several raids and skirmishes against white settlers in Ohio during and after the American Revolutionary War. He served as a scout and warrior during the Northwestern Indian Wars (1790–94) and was present during the Battle of FALLEN TIMBERS. Tecumseh refused to sign the 1795 Treaty of Greenville imposed by Major General Anthony WAYNE upon the Indians that opened the Ohio region to further white settlement.

Tecumseh joined with his half brother TENSKWATAWA, known as "the Prophet," to work for a confederacy of Native American tribes that would oppose further white settlement in the northwest. The Prophet also preached a return to Native American religion and values and a renunciation of white habits and associations. Tecumseh believed in common ownership of land by all the Indians, and hence land could not be ceded without consent of all the tribes. He traveled to tribes as far away as Iowa and Florida to spread his message of Indian nationalism.

William Henry HARRISON, the governor of Indiana Territory, opposed Tecumseh. Harrison persisted in entreating with separate tribes. In August 1810 the two men met at Vincennes (in present-day Indiana) and almost came to blows over that issue. The Prophet also upset Tecumseh's plans. While Tecumseh was away seeking to gain the support of the southeastern tribes, the Prophet

attacked Harrison's army at TIPPECANOE. Harrison defeated the Native American forces, but this drove Tecumseh into closer ties with the British in Canada.

In the War of 1812, Tecumseh sided with the British in hope of gaining an independent Indian state. Tecumseh commanded both Indian and British forces in many engagements during the 1812 DETROIT campaign. For his success in battle and his support of the British effort, he was awarded an appointment as a brigadier general in the British army. Tecumseh played a significant role during the British invasions of Ohio in summer 1813, leading Indian forces in the sieges of FORT MEIGS and FORT STEPHENSON.

With American success on LAKE ERIE, Harrison prepared to invade Canada. Tecumseh urged British brigadier general Henry Procter to stand firm against the invasion. Procter's decision to retreat into Upper Canada signaled the end of a political and military relationship between the Indians and British to oppose U.S. expansion. As Harrison advanced, Tecumseh and his warriors found themselves committed to a final battle near the THAMES River on 5 October 1813. Tecumseh was killed, supposedly by Colonel Richard M. Johnson; however, no trace of his body was found. His death signaled the end of organized Indian resistance in the northwest, opening American expansion westward to the Mississippi River. Tecumseh's intelligence, military skill, and determination to unite his people against American expansion have enhanced his legacy as one of the greatest Native American leaders.

See also AMERICAN INDIAN WARS; CREEK WAR; INDIAN WARFARE; WAR OF 1812: LAND OVERVIEW.

Further reading: Antal, Sandy. *A Wampum Denied: Procter's War of 1812.* Ottawa, Canada: Carleton University Press, 1997; Edmunds, R. David. *Tecumseh and the Quest for Indian Leadership.* Boston: Little, Brown, 1984; Sugden, John. *Tecumseh: A Life.* New York: Henry Holt, 1997.

— Steven J. Rauch

Tenskwatawa (1775–1836) *Shawnee prophet and brother of Tecumseh*

Born in early 1775 at Old Piqua in western Ohio, one of a set of triplets, the future prophet, originally named Lalawethika, had a troubled childhood and adolescence. His father, Puckeshinwa, a Shawnee war chief, had been killed in the Battle of POINT PLEASANT in October 1774. In 1779 his Creek mother, Methoatske, abandoned him to be raised by an older sister. Accidently blinded in his right eye by one of his own arrows when he was a teenager, Lalawethika became a drunk as a young adult.

After receiving a vision in April 1805, however, Lalawethika transformed himself into a holy man, Tenskwatawa ("the Open Door"). Known as The Prophet, he preached a revivalist message that promised protection from disease and white settlers if the Shawnees and other tribes renounced alcohol, returned to their traditional lifestyles, and practiced proscribed rituals and ceremonies. At first received with some skepticism, Tenskwatawa won many converts after he "predicted" a solar eclipse on 16 June 1806 (he had learned from traveling astronomers when the eclipse would occur).

In 1808 Tenskwatawa established Prophetstown at the mouth of the Tippecanoe River. With TECUMSEH using the religious movement (and British support) to unite tribes against further land cessions, Indiana territorial governor William Henry HARRISON decided to strike at Prophetstown while Tecumseh was visiting the Creeks in 1811. Although Harrison greatly exaggerated the extent of his victory in the Battle of TIPPECANOE (7 November 1811), the battle nevertheless destroyed Tenskwatawa's credibility.

When the WAR OF 1812 began, Tenskwatawa fled to Canada, where he remained in exile under British protection until 1825, when he returned to Ohio. In his later years he cooperated with federal officials in removing the Shawnees to Kansas. He died near modern-day Kansas City in November 1836.

See also AMERICAN INDIAN WARS.

Further reading: Edmunds, R. David. *The Shawnee Prophet.* Lincoln: University of Nebraska Press, 1983; ————. *Tecumseh and the Quest for Indian Leadership.* Boston: Little, Brown, 1984.

— Justin D. Murphy

Terre-aux-Boeufs affair (1808–1809) *Event that erupted over a malarial U.S. Army encampment in Louisiana*

In 1808, with tensions rising with Britain because of the *CHESAPEAKE-LEOPARD AFFAIR*, the federal government massed troops in New Orleans to protect the city. By April 1809, Brigadier General James WILKINSON had 2,000 soldiers under his command, many of whom were recent enlistees. Ill-disciplined and lacking knowledge of basic camp hygiene, the troops were highly susceptible to the humid climate and the city's numerous diversions; these conditions left nearly a third of them incapacitated. Therefore, Secretary of War William EUSTIS ordered the army to a healthier location near Natchez, 300 miles upriver. Wilkinson, however, instead chose to relocate his troops to Terre-aux-Boeufs, 12 miles south of New Orleans, in order to maintain his personal dealings in the city.

The soldiers began to arrive at Terre-aux-Boeufs on 9 June. Thick jungle-like vegetation covered most of the swampy 30-acre site that was three feet lower than the adjacent Mississippi River. Wilkinson's men spent much of the next several months clearing the land and building levies. The exhausted soldiers suffered greatly from intense heat and from torrential rains that overflowed the sewage-filled drainage ditches. Swarms of flies and mosquitoes descended on the camp, spreading diseases and overwhelming the undersized medical staff. The army's tents leaked profusely, and many of them did not have wooden floors, causing the men to lie on the wet ground. Furthermore, the soldiers lacked adequate food and clothing, partly because of a stringent spending policy that Eustis imposed and partly because Wilkinson conspired with the contractor. Vermin infested the army's flour and meat, and the men could not replace their worn, muddy uniforms. On 22 June, Eustis, learning of the miserable conditions, ordered Wilkinson to relocate immediately to Natchez, but the general delayed.

Wilkinson finally got under way on 10 September. Rather than dividing his command into several small detachments for the difficult trip upriver, Wilkinson jammed his entire force aboard a number of boats. As it moved north, the army left behind scores of sick troops, many of whom later died. In late October, after a six-week ordeal, the bedraggled survivors reached Natchez. Better provisions and cooler temperatures alleviated the suffering, but many soldiers remained ill, their morale shaken. Between February 1809 and January 1810, 186 soldiers deserted and more than 900 died, out of 2,036 rank and file. Approximately 40 officers also died or resigned. A congressional investigation of the Terre-aux-Boeufs affair found irregularities, but did not censure Wilkinson for his role in the debacle.

Although an extreme case, the Terre-aux-Boeufs affair demonstrated not only problems that disease and logistics posed for the military, but also the incompetence of much of the U.S. Army leadership in the period.

See also MEDICINE, MILITARY.

Further reading: Coffman, Edward M. *The Old Army: A Portrait of the American Army in Peacetime, 1784–1898.* New York: Oxford University Press, 1986; Jacobs, James Ripley. *The Beginning of The U.S. Army, 1783–1812.* Princeton, N.J.: Princeton University Press, 1947; Jacobs, James Ripley. *Tarnished Warrior: Major-General James Wilkinson.* New York: Macmillan, 1938.

— Michael P. Gabriel

terrorism *In its official U.S. definition, the premeditated, politically motivated violence perpetrated against noncombatant targets by subnational groups, usually intended to influence events*

The United States has a long history of dealing with both domestic and international terrorism. When George

WASHINGTON became president, 21 Americans were being held hostage by the Barbary pirates. Washington negotiated a treaty that paid a ransom for them. Currently, U.S. law prohibits the government paying ransoms to terrorists.

Prior to the 11 September 2001 attacks on the World Trade Center and the Pentagon, U.S. government policy had preferred military force as a last resort against terrorism, opting instead for a traditional legalistic/law enforcement approach. While employing military force against terrorists demonstrates resolve and determination to defeat terrorism and can also be an effective deterrent for future terrorist attacks, the use of military force is not without difficulties and dangers. One of the most difficult obstacles is gathering the necessary INTELLIGENCE to wage an effective campaign. By their very nature terrorist organizations are secretive. Another problem is that the employment of force often puts American lives in jeopardy, although risks to military personnel can be reduced by striking targets with stand-off weapons such as the Tomahawk cruise missile or naval bombardment. While designed to reduce American casualties, such weapons can cause collateral damage, creating a propaganda tool for terrorists and increasing their local support.

Beginning with the TRIPOLITAN WAR, the United States has waged war against terrorism. More recently, in Operation Eagle Claw in April 1980, U.S. military personnel attempted to rescue 55 U.S. embassy personnel held hostage in Iran. The operation was a disaster, with the attempt aborted before it could take place. A report concerning the operation cited faulty intelligence, lack of planning and practice, and a dearth of inter- and intraservice coordination.

The 1980s nonetheless saw widespread use of U.S. military force to combat international terrorism. On 18 April 1983, the U.S. embassy in Beirut, Lebanon, was attacked by a van filled with explosives. The detonation flattened most of the building, killing 63, including 17 Americans. The loss of life and humiliation were far greater on 23 October when a truck raced past a lone U.S. Marine guard and crashed into the center of the building serving as the marine barracks at the Beirut airport. The suicide bomber killed 241 marines in what was then the worst single surprise attack on U.S. forces since PEARL HARBOR. This action led to the withdrawal of the marines from Lebanon. Subsequent offshore bombardment of terrorist camps by the guns of the battleship *New Jersey* produced hundreds of collateral casualties and helped recruit new converts to the war against America.

Emboldened by the seemingly impotent American response, Libya's leader Muammar Gadhafi stepped up his sponsorship of anti-American terrorism. Attacks occurred against Americans in Paris, Beirut, Rwanda, and Sudan. The 5 April 1986 bombing of a West Berlin discothèque killed three (two Americans) and wounded 229 others (79 Americans). Intelligence sources confirmed Libyan sponsorship.

Nine days after the disco bombing, U.S. forces conducted Operation Eldorado Canyon, an air strike against targets in Libya. Eighteen air force F-111s based in Great Britain and more than 70 carrier-based navy and Marine Corps aircraft participated in the attack. The mission had mixed results. Collateral damage was high. Reports vary, but perhaps 37 people were killed and 93 were wounded. The raid did not kill Gadhafi, but it did kill his young adopted daughter and seriously injured two of his sons. After the raid, however, the level of Libyan rhetoric and sponsorship of terrorism decreased.

In the 1990s, a new terrorist threat emerged. Islamic extremist Osama bin Laden was connected to the March 1993 bombing of the World Trade Center in New York, two attacks in Saudi Arabia, the 1995 bombing in Riyadh that killed seven Americans, the 1996 bombing in Dhahran that left 19 Americans dead, and the simultaneous bombings of U.S. embassies in Nairobi, Kenya; and Dar es Salaam, Tanzania, in which 224 died (12 Americans) and nearly 5,000 were wounded.

In response, less than three weeks after the embassy bombing, the U.S. military carried out Operation Infinite Reach. U.S. warships fired 70 Tomahawk cruise missiles against targets in Afghanistan and Sudan. In Afghanistan, the damage was significant, with more than 100 terrorists estimated killed, bin Laden not among them. The attack on a Sudanese pharmaceutical factory, suspected of being a chemical weapons plant, was more controversial. Many critics argued that evidence was at best tenuous that bin Laden was tied to the factory or that it had been producing chemical weapons.

On 12 October 2000, the U.S. guided missile destroyer *Cole* was entering the port of Aden, Yemen, when explosives were detonated against its hull by suicide bombers in a small boat. The explosion blew a hole in the side of the ship. Although the vessel was saved, the blast killed 17 sailors and wounded 31 others.

On 11 September 2001, Arab terrorists hijacked four U.S. commercial airliners. They flew two of the planes directly into the World Trade Center in New York City, collapsing both towers; a third slammed into the Pentagon in Washington, D.C.; a fourth airplane, believed heading toward another target in Washington, crashed outside Pittsburgh, apparently when passengers attacked the hijackers. Total casualties were in excess of 3,000 lives, making it the worst terrorist attack in history and second only to the Battle of ANTIETAM/SHARPSBURG as the bloodiest day in U.S. history. President George W. Bush then commenced Operation Infinite Justice forcibly to extricate Osama bin Laden from his refuge in Afghanistan, destroy the al-Qaeda terrorist network there, and topple the Taliban regime that sheltered the terrorists.

The effectiveness of military force in combatting international terrorism has been mixed. With the increasing possibilities of biological, chemical, and even nuclear terrorism, pressure for quick military solutions will be even greater. The stakes will be higher, and the chances for catastrophic mistakes will be compounded.

Further reading: Laqueur, Walter. *The Age of Terrorism.* 2nd ed. Boston: Little, Brown, 1987; Heymann, Philip B. *Terrorism and America.* Cambridge: Massachusetts Institute of Technology Press, 1998.

— Craig T. Cobane

Terry, Alfred H. (1827–1890) *U.S. Army general*
Born on 10 November 1827 in Hartford, Connecticut, Alfred Howe Terry attended law school at Yale University, but left in 1850 without graduating. Admitted to the bar, he was appointed clerk of the New Haven County Superior Court. In 1861, with the outbreak of the Civil War, Terry raised the 2d Connecticut Militia (a 90-day regiment) and was appointed its colonel. He led his troops in the First Battle of BULL RUN/MANASSAS. Raising a second regiment, the 7th Connecticut Infantry, he saw action at Port Royal and FORT PULASKI.

Appointed brigadier general in the Volunteers in April 1862, Terry spent most of the next year in operations against CHARLESTON. Transferred with X Corps to Virginia, he led a division and on several occasions the corps in the Army of the James during operations against Richmond and PETERSBURG. In January 1865, after Major General Benjamin BUTLER's failure, Terry took charge of the effort against FORT FISHER and captured the fort in two days. Wilmington, North Carolina, the Confederacy's last open port, fell to Terry's forces days later. For these achievements, he received the Thanks of Congress and provisional promotion to major general of Volunteers. In a rare case, he also was commissioned a brigadier in the regular army, having never served in the regular establishment.

During the war's final weeks, Terry commanded his corps in conjunction with Major General William Tecumseh SHERMAN's campaign in North Carolina. His promotion to major general of Volunteers was confirmed in April 1865.

Remaining in the army after the war, in 1866 Terry assumed command of the Department of Dakota, but he was called upon frequently to serve on various commissions and boards. In 1869 Terry was transferred to the Department of the South for Reconstruction duty. Returning to the Department of Dakota in 1872, he provided military support for the exploration of the Yellowstone region and for the Canadian border survey.

In 1876 Terry commanded a campaign against the Sioux, in which Lieutenant Colonel George A. CUSTER disregarded his orders and met with disaster in the Battle of the LITTLE BIGHORN. Terry endured the resulting criticism in silence, never casting blame on Custer or his men. Throughout 1876 and 1877 troops within Terry's department subdued the Sioux and Cheyenne and brought an end to the Nez Perce bid for freedom. Over the next few years, Terry worked to bring a final peace to the northern plains.

In 1886 Terry assumed command of the Military Division of the Missouri with the rank of major general. Two years later, he was retired at his own request because of serious illness. Terry died in New Haven, Connecticut, on 16 December 1890.

See also CIVIL WAR, LAND OVERVIEW; MILES, NELSON A.; NEZ PERCE WAR; SIOUX WARS.

Further reading: Gragg, Rod. *Confederate Goliath: The Battle of Fort Fisher.* New York: HarperCollins, 1991; Utley, Robert M. *Frontier Regulars: The United States Army and the Indian, 1866–1891.* Lincoln: University of Nebraska Press, 1973.

— Jim M. Kerbow

Tet Offensive (January–February 1968) *Vietnam War campaign; one of the few decisive battles in military history in which the side that won on the battlefield lost the war*
The Tet Offensive was a tactical and operational disaster for the People's Army of Vietnam (PAVN; North Vietnamese Army, NVA) forces, but ultimately it became a strategic victory.

The basic concept for the Tet Offensive originated with the Democratic Republic of Vietnam (DRV, North Vietnam) defense minister, General Vo Nguyen Giap. Militarily, the war had not been going well for the Communists since the Americans intervened on a large scale. Apparently abandoning the idea of a protracted war, Giap looked for a quicker solution that would neutralize the overwhelming American advantages in battlefield firepower and mobility. Giap based his plan on the notion of the "General Offensive," a key element of Chinese Communist doctrine. He combined the General Offensive with the "General Uprising," a distinctly Vietnamese element of revolutionary dogma, in which the South Vietnamese people were expected to rally to the Communist cause and overthrow the government of the Republic of Vietnam (RVN, South Vietnam).

Giap's plan depended on three key assumptions: First, the Army of the Republic of Vietnam (ARVN) would not fight and would collapse under the initial shock of the General Offensive; second, the people of South Vietnam—with a little prodding from Communist cadres—would follow

A marine from the 3rd Platoon, Company 2nd H, 2nd Battalion, 5th Marines, carries a Vietnamese woman from Hue Hospital to safety during the battle for Hue. *(National Archives)*

through with the General Uprising; and third, American will would break from the shock of the one-two punch.

Giap planned to launch the General Offensive at the start of Tet 1968, the beginning of the Lunar New Year, the most important Vietnamese holiday. The overall plans were a close secret, with the exact timing and objectives of the attacks withheld from local commanders until the last possible moment. Meanwhile, Giap staged a masterful deception campaign designed to draw American forces away from the primary objectives, the major population centers. Starting in the fall of 1967, South Vietnamese Communist Vietcong (VC) and PAVN forces launched a series of bloody but seemingly pointless attacks along the Cambodian border. Battles at LOC NINH and DAK TO also were intended to give Communist forces more experience in conducting large-scale conventional attacks.

In January 1968, several PAVN divisions also began to converge on the isolated U.S. Marine Corps outpost at KHE SANH, far to the north, near the Demilitarized Zone (DMZ). The assault on Khe Sanh was a classic feint. Giap depended on the Americans misreading history to see another Dien Bien Phu in the making, but he also wanted to take the outpost. The deception worked. From 21 January 1968 until the eruption of the country-wide attacks at Tet, the attention of U.S. Military Assistance Command, Vietnam (MACV) headquarters and the National Command Authority in Washington remained riveted on Khe Sanh. The battle so obsessed President Lyndon B. JOHN-SON that he had a scale terrain model of the base installed in the White House situation room.

Meanwhile, Communist commanders used the Christmas 1967 cease-fire to move forces into position and reconnoiter objectives. In November 1967, the U.S. 101st Airborne Division captured a Communist document outlining the General Offensive/General Uprising, but American intelligence officers dismissed it as propaganda. They simply did not believe the Communists had the capability to launch an operation on such a scale.

Lieutenant General Frederick C. WEYAND, commander of U.S. II Field Forces, was not deceived by Giap's peripheral campaign. He noticed the pattern of increased Communist radio traffic around Saigon, which did not fit with the too few contacts his units were making in the border areas. On 10 January 1968, Weyand persuaded General William WESTMORELAND, the commander of U.S. forces in Vietnam, to let him pull more American maneuver battalions back toward Saigon. When the attack came, therefore, 27 American battalions, instead of 14, were in the Saigon area. Weyand most likely made the key allied decision of the entire battle.

The attacks were supposed to start country-wide on 31 January. Coordination, however, suffered from Giap's tight security measures. Shortly after midnight on the morning of 30 January, the Communists attacked Dá Nang, Pleiku, Nha Trang, and nine other cities in the center of South Vietnam. Vietcong Region 5 had started the offensive 24 hours too early. The Americans and South Vietnamese immediately canceled the Tet holiday cease-fire, ARVN troops were called back to their units, and American forces took up alert positions in key areas. Tactically, at least, Giap lost the element of surprise.

The following day at 1:30 A.M., Communist sappers attacked the presidential palace in Saigon, followed by attacks on the U.S. embassy, MACV headquarters, the huge American logistics base at Long Binh, and ARVN III Corps headquarters in Bien Hoa. The ancient capital of HUE was attacked at 3:40 A.M., and by dawn the full Tet Offensive was under way. Before the end of 31 January, five of six South Vietnamese autonomous cities, 36 of 44 provincial capitals, and 64 of 245 district capitals were under attack.

With the exception of Khe Sanh, Hue, and the area around Saigon, Long Binh, and Bien Hoa, the fighting was over in a few days. The allied forces retook Hue on 25 February after bitter fighting and cleared the Cholon area of Saigon on 7 March. By 20 March, PAVN units around Khe Sanh began to disperse in the face of overwhelming American firepower. By the end of March 1968, the Communists had failed to achieve a single one of their military objectives, losing more than 58,000 VC and PAVN troops dead in the process. The Americans suffered 3,895 dead, the ARVN lost 4,954, and other allied forces lost 214. More than 14,300 South Vietnamese civilians also died, including some 6,000 the Communists massacred in Hue.

Even though Giap had lost tactical surprise, he still achieved great surprise on the operational and strategic levels. He was unable to exploit it, however. He violated the principle of mass by attacking everywhere, and he therefore had superior strength nowhere. All across South Vietnam, Communist forces attacked piecemeal and were repulsed piecemeal. Giap also was wrong on two of his three key assumptions. The people of the South did not rise up in support of the Communist cause. The General Uprising never took place—even in Hue, where Communist forces held the city for the longest time. Also, the ARVN did not collapse. It required significant stiffening in certain areas, but generally it fought—and fought well.

The Vietcong were the biggest losers of the battle. While much of the PAVN was committed to the diversionary attack at Khe Sanh, the VC main force guerrilla units carried the major attacks in the South, and they suffered the heaviest casualties. The guerrilla infrastructure developed over so many years was shattered. After Tet, the VC were a far less significant force in the war. When Saigon fell in 1975, it was to four regular PAVN corps.

Giap, however, had been right on his third major assumption. His primary enemy did not have the will to do what was necessary to win. The United States handed the Communists a crushing tactical defeat and simultaneously handed them a strategic victory. Thus, the Tet Offensive is one of the most paradoxical of history's decisive campaigns.

As in the Battle of the BULGE in World War II, the American military had made the mistake of grossly underestimating its enemy but still won overwhelmingly. Detecting the opportunity, American military leaders immediately began to formulate plans to finish off the Communist forces in the South. Westmoreland and JCS chairman General Earl WHEELER wanted to request 206,000 additional troops to finish the job. However, a disgruntled staffer in the Johnson White House leaked the plan to the press, and the story broke in the *New York Times* on 10 March 1968.

With the fresh images of the besieged U.S. embassy in Saigon still in their minds, the press and the public immediately concluded that the extra troops were needed to recover from a massive defeat. Under the pressure of widespread accusations that the government had lied to the American people, President Johnson announced just three weeks later that he would not run for reelection. The Tet Offensive was the psychological turning point of the VIETNAM WAR.

Further reading: Braestrup, Peter. *The Big Story.* Boulder, Colo.: Westview Press, 1977; Oberdorfer, Don. *Tet!* New York: Doubleday, 1971; Palmer, Bruce, Jr. *The 25-Year War: America's Military Role in Vietnam.* Lexington: University Press of Kentucky, 1984; Palmer, Dave. *Summons of the Trumpet.* Novato, Calif.: Presidio Press, 1978;

Summers, Harry G. *On Strategy: The Vietnam War in Context.* Novato, Calif.: Presidio Press, 1982; Zabecki, David T. "Battle for Saigon," *Vietnam* (summer 1989): 19–25.

— David T. Zabecki

Texas War for Independence (1835–1836)

Revolution turned independence movement in Texas during 1835–36

The Mexican government had welcomed American immigrants into Texas in the 1820s in hope of winning their loyalty and using them to block official U.S. expansion. The American immigrants soon greatly outnumbered the Mexican settlers and resisted official efforts to "Mexicanize" them. The immigrants were generally successful in securing concessions from the state government on such issues as slavery, taxation, and the requirement to convert to Catholicism.

The drive to centralize power, which began in 1834 under General Antonio López de Santa Anna, was viewed as a major threat by the American immigrants and an issue the state government could not control. Matters came to a head in 1835 when Santa Anna sent additional troops to Texas and threatened to subordinate state power. The first military conflict between the Texans and Mexican forces took place at Gonzales in October 1835.

Colonel Domingo de Ugartechea, the Mexican commander at San Antonio, dispatched 100 dragoons under Lieutenant Francisco de Castañeda to recover a cannon given to the settlers at Gonzales in 1831 for defense against Indian attacks. The settlers defied an order to return the cannon, hoisting a flag with the words *come and take it.* After a brief skirmish and considerable talking, the Mexican force returned to San Antonio without the cannon.

Soon after the skirmish at Gonzales, the immigrants held a convention in which they voted to remain part of Mexico but to establish a provisional state government loyal to the federalist principles of the 1824 Constitution. The convention also called for the creation of a regular army, organization of militias, and even purchase of ships for a navy.

The next military move by the Texans was to lay siege to San Antonio, recently reinforced by troops under the command of Division General Martín Perfecto de Cos, Santa Anna's brother-in-law. A volunteer army of approximately 600 men maintained the siege from October until 5 December 1835, when the Texans launched an assault on the town. On 9 December, Cos surrendered. The Texans had suffered approximately 30 casualties, while Mexican losses were about 150. The Mexican troops were allowed to keep their weapons but had to leave behind all surplus military supplies and promise to withdraw south of the Rio Grande. After their victory, most of the Texas volunteers went home, an indication of problems to come in maintaining a force in the field.

Sam HOUSTON, the new commander in chief of Texas's mostly nonexistent army, endeavored to organize one. This was delayed when the provisional government instructed him to negotiate a peace treaty with the Cherokee Indians in the crucial month of February 1836. In the meantime, Santa Anna—having ruthlessly crushed a similar federalist revolt in the Mexican state of Zacatecas—crossed into Texas with an army of 6,000 in January 1836, intending to do in Texas what he had done in Zacatecas.

Santa Anna targeted San Antonio, with its greatly reduced force of fewer than 200 volunteers and regulars, including Davy Crockett and James Bowie. He surprised the Texans, commanded by William Barrett Travis, when he arrived in the San Antonio area on 23 February 1836, three weeks earlier than the Texans expected. The Texans hastily withdrew to the old mission-fortress of the ALAMO, and the Mexicans initiated a siege. Santa Anna grew impatient and wanted to make an example of the Texans, so on 6 March he ordered an assault by some 1,800 troops. The Mexican forces soon overran the Alamo; most defenders died in the fighting, while a small number were captured and executed almost immediately thereafter. Mexican forces suffered some 600 casualties and experienced a delay of almost two weeks to take a position of limited military significance. As the Alamo was under siege, a convention at Washington-on-the-Brazos proclaimed the independence of Texas on 2 March.

The next major military development was not a battle but a mass execution. Colonel James Fannin had assembled a large force at the town of Goliad. When the Alamo fell, Houston ordered Fannin to destroy the fortifications at Goliad and move his force to the town of Victoria. Fannin, however, received contradictory orders from the provisional government, instructing him to remain in Goliad. On 19 March 1836 Fannin decided to follow Houston's orders to move to Victoria. The following day his force was surrounded by Mexican troops and Fannin surrendered, believing his men would be treated as prisoners of war. Santa Anna, however, ordered all of the prisoners executed in accordance with a decree issued in December 1835, which directed that all foreigners captured in rebellion against the Mexican government would be considered as pirates and subject to immediate execution. On 27 March Mexican troops executed some 400 Texans, including the wounded; only about 25 managed to escape.

Santa Anna believed that the fall of the Alamo and the mass execution at Goliad signaled the end of the Texas revolution and considered withdrawing his troops. His top officers, however, convinced him to pursue and destroy what was left of the fleeing Texas forces under Houston, who was attempting to recruit and train an army while retreating before Santa Anna's advancing forces. Pressured by his own officers and the provisional government to make a stand, Houston ended the retreat and turned to take on Santa Anna, who was pursuing the fleeing Texas government. The two armies—both moving toward Harrisburg—met where the San Jacinto River joined Buffalo Bayou.

Although they were encamped less than a mile apart and each knew of the presence of the other, in the Battle of SAN JACINTO, Houston's force of 918 men successfully surprised Santa Anna's some 1,400 Mexicans on the afternoon of 21 April. The Texans were victorious in a matter of minutes but pursued and killed the fleeing Mexicans for another hour. The Mexicans suffered 630 killed and 730 captured; Texan casualties were nine killed and 30 wounded, including Houston. The following day Texas soldiers captured Santa Anna, who was later forced to sign two treaties calling for the recognition of Texas independence and the withdrawal of Mexican forces beyond the Rio Grande.

The war for Texas independence came down to one battle—San Jacinto. Although Texans were good fighters and often displayed great courage, they achieved military success almost in spite of themselves. Most of the Texan forces involved at the Alamo, Goliad, and San Jacinto were volunteers only recently arrived in Texas. Mexican forces outnumbered Texan forces in every major engagement. Efforts to raise a regular Texas army were unsuccessful. Texas troops preferred the shorter enlistments, looser discipline, and election of officers associated with volunteer forces. Likewise, a conscription system for the militia—authorized in March 1836—was never implemented. At San Jacinto, Texas achieved but did not secure independence. It would take another war with Mexico, this time by the United States, to accomplish that.

See also MEXICAN-AMERICAN WAR, CAUSES OF.

Further reading: Hardin, Stephen L. *Texan Iliad: A Military History of the Texas Revolution.* Austin: University of Texas Press, 1994; Lack, Paul D. *The Texas Revolutionary Experience. A Political and Social History.* College Station: Texas A&M University Press, 1992; Peña, José Enrique de la. *With Santa Anna in Texas: A Personal Narrative of the Revolution.* College Station: Texas A&M University Press, 1975.

— Don M. Coerver

Thames, Battle of the (5 October 1813) *Important battle of the War of 1812 in the Northwest*

Also known as Moraviantown, it marked the end of British and Indian influence on the Great Lakes frontier. Following victories at DETROIT and RIVER RAISIN, the British and

their Indian allies, commanded by Major General Henry Procter and the Shawnee war chief TECUMSEH, frustrated efforts by Major General William Henry HARRISON to regain U.S. control of the region. The key to American success was control of Lake Erie, which was achieved by Master Commandant Oliver H. PERRY on 10 September 1813. The Battle of LAKE ERIE enabled Harrison to begin his offensive to recapture Detroit and invade Canada.

With loss of the waterways and deteriorating logistics, Procter hoped to avoid engaging Harrison's army by withdrawing along the Thames River through Upper Canada. Tecumseh opposed Procter's decision, seeing it as another abandonment by the British, who had promised the Indians their own lands. Eventually the allies reached a compromise: to retreat, but to make a stand somewhere along the route. The march began on 24 September with about 880 troops, almost 1,000 Indians, their families, and much baggage.

On 27 September, Harrison's army landed in Canada. He had almost 5,000 men: 2,000 regulars and 3,000 Kentucky militia. Harrison's mobility was greatly enhanced by mounted Kentucky riflemen, led by Colonel Richard M. Johnson. On 5 October, Johnson's men overtook Procter's army along the Thames River, a few miles from Moraviantown.

Procter deployed his regulars in a clearing in a beech forest. The men were in two thin lines about 250 yards apart. Their left flank rested on the river. A 6-pounder gun anchored the center on the road. Tecumseh's Indians held the right flank, making effective use of cover near a marsh.

Harrison decided to attack the regulars with Johnson's mounted riflemen. They charged with the cry "Remember the Raisin!" recalling the earlier massacre. The Kentuckians quickly drove through the British lines, then attacked from the rear. The British line crumbled, and even Procter was caught up in the chaos and pursued by mounted American infantry. The Indians held their ground and Tecumseh led an attack, in which he was killed. Tecumseh's body was never recovered, but Johnson is generally credited with having killed him.

The whole engagement lasted less than an hour. The British suffered 12 killed and the Indians 33, but Procter's force lost 600 men taken prisoner. The Americans had only seven killed and 22 wounded. Procter was later courtmartialed and found guilty of poor judgment. He was publicly reprimanded, and left the service in 1816.

Although a relatively minor action in terms of men involved and the numbers of casualties, the Thames provided a rare victory for the United States and helped to renew public support to sustain the war. It also resolved a 60-year-long struggle for control of the Northwest and opened new territory for American expansion to the

Mississippi River, crushing Tecumseh's dream of an Indian state.

See also WAR OF 1812: LAND OVERVIEW.

Further reading: Antal, Sandor. *A Wampum Denied: Procter's War of 1812.* Ottawa, Canada: Carlton University Press, 1997; Freehoff, William. "Tecumseh's Last Stand," *Military History* 13, no. 4 (October 1996): 30–36; Sudgen, John. *Tecumseh's Last Stand.* Norman: University of Oklahoma Press, 1985.

— Steven J. Rauch

Thayer, Sylvanus (1785–1872) *Military educator*
Born on 9 June 1785 in Braintree, Massachusetts, Sylvanus Thayer attended Dartmouth College for three years before receiving an appointment to the U.S. Military Academy, WEST POINT. Upon graduation in 1808 (he was only the 33rd graduate in history), Thayer was commissioned a 2nd lieutenant in the Corps of Engineers. In the four years that followed his graduation, Thayer divided his time between supervising the construction of coastal fortifications and serving as an instructor at West Point.

The War of 1812 provided Thayer with both quick promotion and battlefield experience. During the Battle of CHÂTEAUGUAY (October 1813), Thayer, by then a captain and aide-de-camp to Major General Wade Hampton, had his first and only combat experience in his long military career. The battle, part of the unsuccessful U.S. attempt to invade Canada, left a lasting impression on Thayer. The incompetence or outright cowardice of many of the officers involved convinced him that it was essential to train officers properly before they commanded troops in combat.

In 1815, Brevet Major Thayer was sent to France to study European engineering, fortification, and instructional techniques. Upon his return to America in 1817, he succeeded Alden PARTRIDGE as superintendent of West Point. He initiated a series of reforms in the curriculum of instruction that would remain relatively unchanged for more than a century. Between 1817 and 1833, the course of study at West Point was formalized, the fourth-class system was established, and a professional sense of both instruction and military discipline was created. With the addition of both better-educated instructors and more diverse subjects of study, Thayer converted West Point from an academically undisciplined environment into the first—and for most of the century, only—engineering school in the United States.

The election of President Andrew JACKSON in 1828 found both the military academy and its superintendency under attack. "Jacksonian Democracy" held professional soldiers in disdain, and West Point was the most obvious symbol of the "elitist" professional military. The strict discipline with which Thayer oversaw the military academy did little to help matters. Many graduates and ex-cadets disliked what they perceived as Thayer's harsh administration. Although Jackson did not personally make any negative comments regarding either West Point or Thayer, it seemed clear that he disapproved of the "military aristocracy" created by the academy.

In 1833, after five years of defending both himself and the military academy against the Jacksonian Democrats in Congress, Thayer resigned as superintendent, believing this would divert much of the Democrats' anger away from the academy. Thayer then became responsible for the design and construction of the coastal fortifications at Boston Harbor. Promoted to lieutenant colonel in 1838, Thayer, who regularly worked 12-hour days, found his new position insufficiently challenging when compared with his duties at West Point. After serving briefly as acting chief of the Army Corps of Engineers, Thayer asked to be put on sick leave in 1858. Promoted to colonel in March 1863 and brevetted brigadier general in the regular army in May 1863, Thayer retired that June. Later he endowed the Thayer School of Engineering at Dartmouth College. A lifelong bachelor, Thayer died in Braintree, Massachusetts, on 7 September 1872. He is buried at West Point.

See also MAHAN, DENIS HART; MILITARY ACADEMIES.

Further reading: Dupuy, R. Ernest. *Sylvanus Thayer: Father of Technology in the United States.* West Point, N.Y.: Association of Graduates of the United States Military Academy, 1958; Kershner, James W. *Sylvanus Thayer: A Biography.* New York: Arno Press, 1982.

— Alexander M. Bielakowski

Thomas, George H. (1816–1870) *U.S. Army general*
Born on 31 July 1816 in Southampton County, Virginia, George Henry Thomas graduated from the U.S. Military Academy, WEST POINT, in 1840. As a second lieutenant assigned to artillery, he served on the frontier and in coastal defenses. Thomas fought in the Second SEMINOLE WAR in Florida and earned two brevets for gallantry during the MEXICAN-AMERICAN WAR. Rising steadily through the ranks, he returned to West Point, where he taught artillery and cavalry tactics, and in 1855 he became junior major in the newly formed 2d Cavalry Regiment, an elite unit that included such future Civil War generals as Albert S. JOHNSTON, Robert E. LEE, John B. HOOD, William J. HARDEE, Earl Van Dorn, and George Stoneman. For the next six years Thomas served on the Texas frontier. In April 1861, as the secession crisis erupted into war, Thomas was promoted to lieutenant colonel. A week later he became colonel when the 2d was redesignated the 5th Cavalry.

Although a Virginian, Thomas remained loyal to the Union and was disowned by his family. Appointed a brigadier general of U.S. Volunteers in August 1861, he served briefly in the Shenandoah Valley but soon transferred to the western theater. He won the battle at Mill Springs, Kentucky, and fought at SHILOH, CORINTH, and PERRYVILLE. Promoted to major general of Volunteers in April 1862, he commanded a division in the Battle of STONES RIVER. In September 1863 he commanded XIV Corps, Army of the Cumberland, during the Battle of CHICKAMAUGA. Gathering the remnants of Major General William S. ROSECRANS's shattered force, he held his ground long enough to prevent the army's total destruction, for which he earned the sobriquet "the Rock of Chickamauga."

Promoted to brigadier general in the regular army in October 1863, Thomas received command of the Department and Army of the Cumberland. During the struggle for CHATTANOOGA his command, acting without orders, drove the Confederates from Missionary Ridge. Thomas's Army of the Cumberland comprised more than half of Major General William T. SHERMAN's force during the 1864 ATLANTA CAMPAIGN, winning the Battle of Peachtree Creek and playing a significant role in the actions that compelled the Confederate evacuation of Atlanta.

Detached with part of his army to oppose General John B. Hood's drive into Tennessee, Thomas carefully prepared his forces (too slowly for Lieutenant General Ulysses S. GRANT, who planned to relieve him) and in December 1864 routed Hood at NASHVILLE in one of the most complete victories of the war. Promoted to major general in the regular army shortly thereafter, Thomas received the Thanks of Congress for the Nashville victory.

After the war, Thomas remained on duty in Tennessee before assuming command of the Military Division of the Pacific. Thomas died at his headquarters at San Francisco on 28 March 1870.

See also CIVIL WAR, LAND OVERVIEW; HOOKER, JOSEPH; MCPHERSON, JAMES B.; SCHOFIELD, JOHN M.

Further reading: Cleaves, Freeman. *Rock of Chickamauga: The Life of General George H. Thomas.* Reprint. Norman: University of Oklahoma Press, 1986; McKinney, Francis. *Education in Violence: The Life of George H. Thomas and the History of the Army of the Cumberland.* Detroit: Wayne State University Press, 1961.

— David Coffey

Thompson, John T. (1860–1940) *U.S. Army officer, engineer, and arms inventor*

Born on 30 December 1860 at Newport, Kentucky, John Taliaferro Thompson entered Indiana University in 1877 but left after a year to attend the U.S. Military Academy, WEST POINT. Graduating in 1882, he was commissioned in the artillery. Following his completion of the torpedo course at the Engineering School of Application at Willet's Point, New York, beginning in 1884 he served at numerous armories and garrisons. In 1890 he graduated from the U.S. Artillery School.

Promoted to first lieutenant in 1889, Thompson transferred to the Ordnance Department in December 1890. From 1896 to 1898 he was senior assistant instructor of ordnance and gunnery at West Point. Promoted to captain in 1898, during the SPANISH-AMERICAN WAR he was the chief ordnance officer of IV Corps and was promoted to lieutenant colonel of Volunteers. He then commanded the Tampa Ordnance Depot and was the secretary of the Board of Campsites and other military locations in Cuba. From 1899 to 1907 he was stationed at arsenals at Rock Island, Illinois, and Springfield, Massachusetts. Promoted to major in June 1906, from 1907 to 1914 he was chief assistant to the chief of Army Ordnance. Promoted to lieutenant colonel in January 1909 and to colonel in October 1913, he was then a lecturer at the Army War College.

In November 1914, Thompson retired from the army and went to work as a consultant for the Remington Arms–Union Metallic Cartridge Company. With this firm he built a new plant in Eddystone, Pennsylvania, to produce rifles for the Allied effort in World War I. In April 1917, soon after the United States had entered the war, Thompson returned to active duty, and in August 1918 he was promoted to temporary brigadier general. Placed in charge of small arms and ammunition design and production, he became aware of the fact that the .303-caliber Enfield rifle could be produced privately in surplus for the Allies, while the 1903 Springfield rifle, produced at Springfield and Rock Island, could not meet production needs. By the November 1918 Armistice, American plants had produced 2.5 million M1917 American Enfield rifles, which Thompson had redesigned to employ the U.S. Army standard .30-caliber round.

After World War I, Thompson worked for the Auto-Ordnance Corporation as a consultant in 1919. In 1920 he patented the Thompson submachine gun, a fully automatic shoulder weapon, firing a .45-caliber round. This reliable weapon, first used by U.S. Marines in Nicaragua in 1925, was adopted by the army for the mechanized cavalry in 1928. The navy also adopted it. Popularly known as the "tommy gun," it was also sold abroad, and it became the weapon of choice of both the Federal Bureau of Investigation and gangsters of the 1920s.

Thompson left Auto-Ordnance in 1930, and Thompson Automatic Arms Company, headed by his son, took over production of the weapons after 1939. Thompson died on 21 June 1940, in Great Neck, Long Island, New York.

See also SUBMACHINE GUNS.

Further reading: Hobart, Frank W. A. *Pictorial History of the Sub-Machine Gun.* New York: Scribner's, 1973.

— Benjamin J. Midura

Tippecanoe, Battle of (7 November 1811) *Important battle between U.S. military forces and Native-American tribes in the Old Northwest, fought on the banks of the Wabash River near the Native-American village of Prophetstown*

TENSKWATAWA and TECUMSEH, two half brothers and sons of a Shawnee chief, took the lead in forming a confederation of tribes to resist expansion of white settlement. Tenskwatawa, known as "the Prophet," had established Prophetstown in 1807, and encouraged Native Americans of different tribes to settle there. Located on the west bank of the Wabash river, approximately three miles from the mouth of Tippecanoe Creek (near present-day Lafayette, Indiana), it was an attempt to minimize tribal differences and present a united front to white expansion and threats to the Native-American way of life.

The governor of the Indiana Territory, William Henry HARRISON, viewed the existence of Prophetstown and the efforts of Tecumseh and the Prophet as a threat, as did other American officials. With War Department approval, Harrison ordered Tecumseh and his supporters to disband and disperse. When they did not, he decided on force. In the fall of 1811, Harrison organized Indiana militia, Kentucky volunteers, and regular soldiers of the U.S. 4th Infantry Regiment. With some 1,000 men, Harrison left the territorial capital of Vincennes and moved north, up the east side of the Wabash River. Crossing to the west bank of the river just below the mouth of the Vermilion River, Harrison then proceeded toward Prophetstown. On 6 November he set up camp at Burnett Creek, a scant two miles west of Prophetstown.

Although instructed by Tecumseh, who was away, to avoid a confrontation, Tenskwatawa was determined to fight. He crafted a plan that called for a predawn attack to increase surprise. Early on 7 November 1811, some 600 to 700 Native-American warriors, drawn from a number of tribes but predominately Kickapoos, Winnebagos, and Potawatomies, surrounded Harrison's camp. While most of the Indians attacked the camp perimeter, a small group of warriors sought to penetrate the camp and locate and kill Harrison. They hoped that this would panic his troops and bring about their retreat.

As the Indian infiltrators moved into the camp, sentry fire alerted the defenders. The attempt to kill Harrison failed when his aide, Colonel Abraham Owen, was mistaken for him and shot. Although there was initial panic and confusion, Harrison and his officers eventually were able to form a line of battle and beat back the assault.

With daylight, Harrison ordered his men forward, and they quickly dispersed the Indian attackers, ending the battle.

After spending the next day securing his position, Harrison sent out a detachment to reconnoiter Prophetstown. Finding the Indian encampment deserted, they destroyed it. Despite Harrison's claims for the Battle of Tippecanoe, the whites had actually suffered more casualties than their opponents—68, to perhaps 50 for the Indians. The battle did weaken the prestige of Tecumseh, and it completely destroyed that of the Prophet. It also provided some evidence of British military support to the Indians, and thus helped to fuel demand for military action against the British in Canada, leading to the War of 1812. Finally, it drove the Indians to fury and caused them to side openly with the British—a major factor in British military successes early in the War of 1812.

See also WAR OF 1812: CAUSES.

Further reading: Cleaves, Freeman. *Old Tippecanoe: William Henry Harrison and His Times.* Port Washington, N.Y.: Kennikat Press, 1939; Sudgen, John. *Tecumseh: A Life.* New York: Henry Holt, 1997.

— Bruce Tap

Tokyo, raid on (18 April 1942) *The first United States bombing mission against the Japanese home islands in World War II*

In early 1942, President Franklin D. ROOSEVELT sought a means to boost the morale of U.S. servicemen and citizens in general and pressed for a strike against Japan. The idea for an air attack on Tokyo was the work of Captain Francis S. Low, an operations officer on the staff of Chief of Naval

B-25 Mitchell bomber flying off the USS *Hornet* on its way to bomb Tokyo, 18 April 1942   *(National Archives)*

Operations Admiral Ernest J. KING. Low suggested to King that army bombers launched from an aircraft carrier could bomb Japan. Army Air Forces commanding general Lieutenant General Henry "Hap" ARNOLD embraced the plan and picked Lieutenant Colonel James DOOLITTLE as army coordinator and, ultimately, leader of the mission.

The plan was complicated because U.S. forces would risk detection by Japanese picket boats at 500 miles from the Japanese home islands. Despite Low's hope, army bombers could take off from a carrier but would not be able to return to it. The plan developed therefore called for army twin-engine B-25 bombers, modified for greater fuel capacity and economy, to launch from a carrier and bomb the cities of Kobe, Osaka, Nagoya, Tokyo, and Yokohama. The planes would then fly to China, where they would land at specially prepared airfields.

The aircraft carrier selected for the operation was the *Hornet,* commanded by Captain Marc MITSCHER. The *Hornet,* carrying 16 B-25s, sortied from San Francisco on 2 April 1942, as part of Task Force 16 under the command of Vice Admiral William HALSEY. The force comprised carriers *Hornet* and *Enterprise,* four cruisers, eight destroyers, and two oilers. Two U.S. submarines operating in Japanese waters provided Halsey with intelligence on Japanese naval movements and weather information.

On the morning of 18 April Japanese picket ships discovered the task force at a range of 600 miles and Halsey promptly ordered the launch of Doolittle's bombers and then led his task force out of the area. The first plane was away by 8:20 A.M. At 12:30 P.M., the first bombs fell on Tokyo. Although one plane received damage from antiaircraft fire, none were lost over Japan. One plane landed at Vladivostok; the crew was promptly interned by the Soviets. The airfields in China stipulated in the plan were not finished, forcing the remaining air crews to bail out or attempt crash landings. Three crewmen were killed. Eight were captured by the Japanese and were later brought to trial; three were executed for their role in the operation.

The slight damage that Doolittle's bombers inflicted on Japan belied the great value of the mission. The Tokyo raid boosted American morale, and it greatly embarrassed the Japanese. It forced Japan to shift air assets to the defense of the home islands; and, more importantly, it increased support in Tokyo for extending Japan's defensive perimeter and for Admiral Isoroku Yammamoto's plan to lure the U.S. fleet out and destroy it—a fateful decision leading to the decisive Japanese defeat in the Battle of MIDWAY.

See also WORLD WAR II, COURSE OF U.S. INVOLVEMENT: PACIFIC THEATER.

Further reading: Glines, Carroll V. *The Doolittle Raid: America's Daring First Strike Against Japan.* New York: Orion Books, 1988; Morison, Samuel Eliot. *History of* *United States Naval Operations in World War II.* Vol. 3, *The Rising Sun in the Pacific.* Boston: Little, Brown, 1961.
— Eric W. Osborne

Tokyo, raid on (9–10 March 1945) *U.S. bombing raid during World War II and the single most destructive bombing raid to date*
As a major political, administrative, and military-industrial center of the Japanese Empire, Tokyo had been under more or less constant U.S. bombing attack since November 1944. The U.S. conquest of the MARIANA ISLANDS allowed the United States to intensify the air campaign against Japan.

In March 1945 Lieutenant General Curtis LeMAY, the new commander of the Mariana-based 21st Bomber Command, introduced new bombing tactics that followed techniques of the air war against Germany and took advantage of the vulnerability of the largely wooden structures of the Japanese cities. LeMay planned to remove much of the B-29's armament to increase bomb loads, and to conduct low-level (6,000–8,000 feet) night raids that would take advantage of the limited Japanese nightfighter capability. The planes would drop incendiary bombs filled with jellified petroleum.

On the night on 9–10 March 1945, 279 B-29 Superfortress bombers, flying from Mariana bases, struck Tokyo in a spectacular three-hour night raid. The planes dropped more than 1,665 tons of incendiaries, which caused a massive firestorm in central Tokyo. Temperatures grew so high in the heart of the firestorm that water in Tokyo's canals boiled. The fire consumed about 16 square miles—40 percent of the city's area—and 267,000 buildings. Some 83,800 people died, and more than 160,000 were wounded. Japanese authorities later declared that 130,000 people died in the bombing attack. The Americans lost only 14 aircraft. The raid was replicated over other Japanese cities in the months to follow.

The 9–10 March 1945 Tokyo raid significantly reduced industrial capacity and communication ability in the city and adversely affected civilian morale. At the same time, this deliberate bombing of civilians, with such an enormous attendant death toll, made easier the subsequent decision to deploy the ATOMIC BOMB. The bomb's use against Hiroshima and Nagasaki produced fewer casualties in each case than the Tokyo attack.

See also STRATEGIC BOMBING, WORLD WAR II; TOKYO, RAID ON (1942); WORLD WAR II, COURSE OF U.S. INVOLVEMENT: PACIFIC THEATER.

Further reading: Caidin, Martin. *A Torch to the Enemy.* New York: Ballantine Books, 1960; Edoin, Hoito. *The Night Tokyo Burned.* New York: St. Martin's Press, 1987;

Hoyt, Edwin P. *Inferno: The Firebombing of Japan, March 9–August 15, 1945.* Lanham, Md.: Madison Books, 2000.

— Peter Rainow

Tompkins, Sally L. (1833–1916) *Confederate hospital administrator*

Born on 9 November 1833 in Mathews County, Virginia, Sally Louisa Tompkins grew up on her father's Tidewater Virginia plantation. She developed a reputation at a young age for her abilities to care for the sick. When her father died, she moved with her mother to Richmond. They were living there when the CIVIL WAR began.

Following the First Battle of MANASSAS/BULL RUN in July 1861, the Confederate government appealed to the citizens of Richmond to open their homes to the wounded. Tompkins secured a private residence and devoted her energies to adapting the house to serve as a health-care center. In August 1861 she opened the Robertson Hospital. The facility had a 25-bed capacity and supported a small staff that included Tompkins, a chief surgeon, four women slaves, two disabled veterans, and a contingent of local female volunteers.

There were several private and government-run hospitals located in Richmond, but Tompkins's facility soon developed the reputation of a model institution. The army often sent her the most desperate cases because of her hospital's high rate of healing.

Tompkins advocated sanitation and prayer as vital components of the recovery process. Her commitment to cleanliness and godliness bolstered morale and promoted healing. She served as spiritual adviser and constantly read patients passages from the Bible.

In September 1861, Confederate authorities closed private hospitals as a means of centralizing the control of medical services, but Tompkins's reputation caused President Jefferson DAVIS to commission her as a captain of cavalry. This allowed the hospital to remain open, and Tompkins received authorization to draw medical supplies from the Confederate government.

Nicknamed "Captain Sally," Tompkins ran the Robertson Hospital until it closed on 13 July 1865. During the time the hospital was open, only 73 of more than 1,300 patients admitted died. After the war, Tompkins performed charity work; but as her health failed in her later years, she moved to Richmond's Home for Confederate Women. Tompkins died in Richmond on 25 July 1916 and was accorded a military funeral.

See also BARTON, CLARISSA H.; BICKERDYKE, MARY ANN; DIX, DOROTHEA LYNE; MEDICINE, MILITARY.

Further reading: Coleman, Elizabeth Dabney. "The Captain Was a Lady," *Virginia Cavalcade* (summer 1956): 35–41.

— Tracy M. Shilcutt

Tonkin Gulf incidents (August 1964) *Clashes between U.S. and North Vietnamese naval units in the Gulf of Tonkin*

One of the VIETNAM WAR's most controversial episodes, the Tonkin Gulf incidents demonstrated the complex and multifaceted interplay of military and political factors in the formation of U.S. policy.

On 31 July 1964, the U.S. destroyer *Maddox*, captained by Commander Herbert L. Ogier, began a signals intelligence-gathering Desoto patrol in the Gulf of Tonkin. Commander of the Seventh Fleet Destroyer Division 192 Captain John J. Herrick headed the operation. The *Maddox* was to monitor Democratic Republic of Vietnam (DRV, North Vietnam) naval activity and locate and identify radar stations and collect radio signals along the North Vietnamese coastline. The operation was controlled by the Pacific Fleet at Pearl Harbor.

At the same time, Military Assistance Command, Vietnam (MACV) in Saigon was running Oplan 34A operations that utilized fast patrol boats and South Vietnamese commandoes to conduct hit-and-run raids against the DRV coast and offshore islands. On the evening of 1 August, the *Maddox* approached within gun range of Hon Me Island, which had been shelled by Oplan 34A boats on the night of 30–31 July.

On the afternoon of 2 August, three high-speed North Vietnamese PT boats came out from the island and attacked the *Maddox*, launching torpedoes and firing machine guns at the ship. The destroyer escaped the torpedo attack by evasive movement and returned fire with its 5-inch and 3-inch guns. Four F-8 aircraft scrambled from the aircraft carrier *Ticonderoga* also attacked the withdrawing patrol boats with air-to-surface rockets and cannon fire. One PT boat was sunk and two were damaged. One U.S. plane received minor damage.

While U.S. military leaders, including the Joint Chiefs of Staff and U.S. ambassador in Saigon General Maxwell D. TAYLOR, wanted military retaliation, President Lyndon B. JOHNSON limited the U.S. response to a diplomatic protest to Hanoi and naval reinforcement. On 3 August, the destroyer *C. Turner Joy*, under Commander Robert C. Barnhart, Jr., joined the *Maddox*. Both destroyers were ordered to remain farther from the North Vietnamese coast.

On the moonless night of 4 August, both destroyers detected objects, which they identified as surface high-speed vessels, and opened fire, believing that they were under attack. They called for air support from the *Ticonderoga* and *Constellation*. Sixteen aircraft were scrambled to assist, but they could find no DRV vessels in the vicinity. Radar and sonar operators on the destroyers insisted they had contacts, but poor visibility, ineffective operators, stress, and high-speed maneuvering were probably responsible for the report. Even Herrick later expressed doubts that the attack had occurred, and DRV officials, including Defense Minister Vo Nguyen Giap, steadfastly denied there was a second attack. Nevertheless, President Johnson decided to teach Hanoi a lesson.

On the afternoon of 5 August, Operation Pierce-Arrow saw 64 sorties of naval aircraft strike DRV targets, including four coastal bases, two support oil storage facilities, and patrol boats along a 100-mile stretch of coast. Perhaps half of some 40 vessels in the DRV navy were sunk or damaged, along with 10 percent of the country's oil storage facilities and seven antiaircraft installations. U.S. losses were one aircraft shot down, one plane lost at sea, and two aircraft damaged. One U.S. pilot was killed and one captured.

Politically, the Tonkin Gulf incidents had far-reaching effects. On 7 August Congress almost unanimously passed the TONKIN GULF RESOLUTION, which authorized President Johnson to employ whatever force he deemed necessary to protect U.S. interests in Southeast Asia—in effect, a blanket authorization for him to make war.

The Tonkin Gulf incidents sparked much future controversy. Washington's reaction appears to have been an honest mistake, rather than a deliberate deception, as so many critics of the Johnson administration later came to believe.

See also COLD WAR; INTELLIGENCE; VIETNAM WAR, CAUSES OF.

Further reading: McNamara, Robert S., with Brian Van-DeMark. *In Retrospect: The Tragedy and Lessons of Vietnam.* New York: Vintage Books, 1996; Moïse, Edwin E. *Tonkin Gulf and the Escalation of the Vietnam War.* Chapel Hill: University of North Carolina Press, 1996; Windchy, Eugene G. *Tonkin Gulf.* Garden City, N.Y.: Doubleday, 1971.

— Peter Rainow

Tonkin Gulf Resolution (7 August 1964)

Congressional resolution authorizing President Lyndon B. JOHNSON to take whatever measures he considered appropriate to deal with the growing crisis in Vietnam

As the military situation in Vietnam deteriorated in early 1964, Johnson and his advisers decided that only heavy U.S. support would enable the government of South Vietnam to survive. Johnson, running for reelection against Senator Barry Goldwater, feared that a major escalation might jeopardize his campaign, so he relied extensively on covert operations, including DeSoto signals intelligence-gathering missions undertaken by American destroyers, to monitor Democratic Republic of Vietnam (DRV, North Vietnam) radar and radio transmissions, and Operations Plan 34A raids by South Vietnamese forces along the North Vietnamese coast.

After the TONKIN GULF INCIDENTS of 2 August, in which North Vietnamese torpedo boats attacked the destroyer *Maddox* on a DeSoto patrol in international waters, and 4 August, in which the *Maddox* and destroyer *Turner Joy* reported hostile attacks that probably did not occur, Johnson moved quickly to preempt further criticism that his Vietnam policy was irresolute and ineffective. Without waiting for an investigation of the 4 August attack—many within the military questioned whether the attack actually had occurred—Johnson announced that American ships had encountered an unprovoked, "deliberate attack" and ordered retaliatory bombing raids on an oil storage depot and North Vietnamese patrol boat bases. More important, he submitted to Congress a draft resolution that would authorize him to "take all necessary measures" to "repel any armed attack" on U.S. forces and "prevent further aggression" and to give any aid necessary, "including the use of armed force," to help any country that requested assistance under the Southeast Asian Treaty Organization.

The Tonkin Gulf Resolution, following debate that clearly dealt with its implications, was passed unanimously by the House and with only two dissenting votes in the Senate. It provided the legal basis for the conflict's future expansion, including massive bombing raids on North Vietnam (which began in February 1965) and (in April 1965) a major deployment of American ground troops and the drastic expansion of such forces' operational activities within Vietnam.

Only on 30 December 1970, after the CAMBODIAN INCURSION authorized by President Richard M. NIXON that spring, did an increasingly restive Congress repeal the Tonkin Gulf Resolution. Congressional reluctance ever again to give a president a similar blank check was a major factor in the passage of the 1973 War Powers Act, drastically limiting the chief executive's future ability to deploy United States troops in combat situations.

See also VIETNAM WAR, CAUSES OF; VIETNAM WAR, COURSE OF.

Further reading: Austin, Anthony. *The President's War: The Story of the Tonkin Gulf Resolution and How the Nation Was Trapped in Vietnam.* Philadelphia: Lippincott, 1971; Galloway, John. *The Gulf of Tonkin Resolution.* Rutherford, N.J.: Fairleigh Dickinson University Press, 1970; Moïse, Edwin E. *Tonkin Gulf and the Escalation of the Vietnam War.* Chapel Hill: University of North Carolina Press, 1996; Siff, Ezra Y. *Why the Senate Slept: The Gulf of Tonkin Resolution and the Beginning of America's Vietnam War.* Westport, Conn.: Praeger, 1999.

— Priscilla Roberts

Torch, Operation (8 November 1942) *World War II Allied invasion of North Africa, the largest amphibious operation to that point in the war*

The U.S. Chiefs of Staff favored an early 1943 direct cross-Channel attack against the European continent; the British, most notably Prime Minister Winston Churchill, preferred a peripheral attack, which would have the added advantage of protecting their colonial possessions in the Middle East. The Americans feared that such an operation in 1942 would delay invasion of the Continent. However, British experience and the shortage of Allied resources, especially landing craft, eventually led to the decision to invade North Africa.

Operation Torch, the invasion of North Africa, resulted from many factors: Soviet insistence on a second front, which President Franklin D. ROOSEVELT had promised Soviet leader Joseph Stalin would occur before the end of 1942; the desire to bring French colonial possessions into the war against the Axis powers; Allied desire to clear the Mediterranean for its shipping; the desire to secure bases from which to mount operations against southern Europe; and its usefulness as a means to relieve pressure on the British Eighth Army in Egypt.

When the agreement to undertake Torch was made, debate still flourished over precisely where to land. The British favored landings directly at Tunis and Bizerta—the keys to Tunisia—or at least at nearby Bône in Algeria. The Americans favored a more cautious approach, recommending at least one landing at Casablanca, on the Atlantic coast. The final plan called for three initial landing sites—two within the Mediterranean, at Oran and Algiers, Algeria, and the third at Casablanca, Morocco. The Casablanca invasion force, numbering 38,000 men and commanded by Major General George S. PATTON, Jr., would travel all the way from Norfolk, Virginia—making it the longest expeditionary effort to that point in U.S. history. The other two invasion forces would sail from Britain. Major General Lloyd Fredendall commanded Center Task Force of nearly 41,000 men (37,100 Americans and 3,600 British), bound for Oran. Eastern Task Force, destined for Algiers, was largely a British affair with 45,000 British troops and 10,000 American; however, in order to give the illusion that the invasion of French Northwest Africa was an American affair, an American, Major General Charles Ryder, commanded it. Once Algiers was secured, a British lieutenant general, Kenneth A. N. Anderson, would take over. U.S. Lieutenant General Dwight D. EISENHOWER had overall command of the Allied expeditionary forces.

The first operational objective of Torch was the occupation of Tunisia—particularly the port city of Tunis—to prevent Axis reinforcement and resupply of their forces in Libya. This would allow the Allies to crush Axis forces in North Africa between the Torch forces and the British Eighth Army. The second objective was the buildup of a force in French Morocco in order to strike into Spanish Morocco if necessary to protect the Strait of Gibraltar should Spain renounce its neutrality and join the Axis, or should Axis forces invade Spain in order to take Gibraltar.

On 8 November 1942, U.S. and British assault forces conducted near-simultaneous amphibious landings to seize the ports and airfields at Casablanca, Oran, and Algiers. The invasion caught the Axis by surprise. French forces, loyal to the Vichy government, did fight the invaders until a cease-fire could be arranged. While there were casualties, the operation provided useful training for the green U.S. troops. After buildup and consolidation, Anderson's First Army drove east from Oran and Algiers to occupy Tunisia and cut German lines of communication, while Patton's Casablanca force and units from Oran linked up to establish the striking force in French Morocco to protect Gibraltar.

German leader Adolf Hitler responded to the landings by ordering the immediate occupation of Vichy France. He also rushed troops to Tunisia. On 10 November, two German regiments arrived in Tunisia; they were followed by other German and also Italian reinforcements, including tank units.

Although the Allies occupied Bône on 12 November and Allied troops were 25 miles southwest of Tunis by the 25th, the rapid German response led to a stalemate by Christmas. German field marshal Erwin Rommel smashed the Americans in the February 1943 Battle of KASSERINE PASS, yet Axis forces could only delay the inevitable. In May the campaign for North Africa ended with the surrender of 250,000 Axis troops.

See also WORLD WAR II, COURSE OF U.S. INVOLVEMENT: EUROPE.

Further reading: Howe, George F. *The United States Army in World War II. Northwest Africa: Seizing the Initiative in the West.* Washington, D.C.: U.S. Government Printing Office, 1957; Meyer, Leo J. "The Decision to Invade North Africa (Torch)," in *Command Decisions.* Edited by Kent Roberts Greenfield. Washington, D.C.: U.S. Government Printing Office, 1987; Rolf, David. *The Bloody Road to Tunis.* Mechanicsburg, Pa.: Stackpole Books, 2001; Watson, Bruce A. *Exit Rommel: The Tunisian Campaign, 1942–1943.* Westport, Conn.: Praeger, 1999.

— Arthur T. Frame

torpedoes *A weapon for destroying ships by blowing them up*

The term *torpedo* was first used to describe sea MINES during the Civil War. These were usually stationary and detonated by either contact or electrical charge. One variant was the spar torpedo—a mine attached to the end of a spar.

It could be carried by a small boat that would approach the target vessel. The crew would then lower the mine and detonate it.

In the 1860s Robert Whitehead, a British engineer working for the Austrian government, developed the modern self-propelled torpedo. It operated on compressed air and had equipment to control its depth and balance. Whitehead's Mark I torpedo was 14 feet long and had a range of 600 yards at a speed of 17.5 knots. It had an 18-pound warhead. In 1895, a directional control came into use; this made it possible to hit a target not in line with the torpedo tubes. The Mark II torpedo was 14 feet six inches in length but could travel 1,000 yards at 30 knots, or 1,500 yards at 24 knots.

The self-propelled torpedo was initially deployed on torpedo boats. In 1878, two Russian craft of this type used torpedoes to sink a Turkish boat—the first such sinking on record. Self-propelled torpedoes were even more ideally suited to the new submarine, which during World War I sank more ships than mines or gunfire.

Torpedoes were also carried by aircraft, beginning in 1911. On 12 August 1915 a British Short 184 aircraft, specifically designed to launch torpedoes, became the first aircraft to sink a boat with a torpedo (the victim again was a Turkish craft).

The effectiveness of air-deployed torpedoes was demonstrated during World War II by the British navy at Taranto, Italy, in November 1940, and by the Japanese navy at PEARL HARBOR on 7 December 1941. During that war there were great advances in torpedo technology, such as homing devices that sensed propeller noise.

The most effective torpedo at the start of the war was the Japanese Long Lance. Deployed at Pearl Harbor, it was used throughout the war. It appeared in different types, although submarine version Mk-95 had a 900-pound warhead and was propelled by a wakeless oxygen-fueled turbine engine. It could travel for five miles at 49 knots. This was twice the speed and twice the range of the comparable U.S. torpedo. The U.S. torpedo also left a wake and was notoriously unreliable. The magnetic pistol to explode the charge under the target ship often did not work, and the torpedoes also circled; one U.S. submarine, the *Tang*, was sunk by one of its own "fish." By late 1943, contact pistols were installed, and by 1944, a new magnetic pistol was developed.

Today's torpedoes are highly accurate and can travel at up to 45 knots speed. They have a maximum distance of 25,000 yards and carry an 800-pound high-explosive warhead.

See also CIVIL WAR, NAVAL OVERVIEW; SUBMARINE WARFARE AGAINST JAPAN, WORLD WAR II; SUBMARINES.

Further reading: Gannon, Robert. *Hellions of the Deep. The Development of American Torpedoes in World War II.* University Park: Pennsylvania State University Press, 1996;

Harris, Brayton. *The Navy Times Book of Submarines.* New York: Berkley Books, 1997; Tucker, Spencer C. *Handbook of 19th Century Naval History.* Annapolis, Md.: Naval Institute Press, 2000.

— Samuel D. Carney

***Trent* affair** (8 November 1861) *Anglo-American diplomatic crisis during the Civil War*

On 8 November 1861, Captain Charles WILKES of the USS *San Jacinto* halted and boarded the British steamship *Trent* in the Caribbean, forcibly removing two prominent Southerners, James Mason and John Slidell, who were en route to Europe to assume their posts as Confederate ministers to Great Britain and France, respectively. They were subsequently imprisoned in Boston. Public opinion in the North initially strongly favored this action, as both a blow to the Confederacy and to Britain, the United States's opponent during both the American Revolutionary War and the War of 1812. The House of Representatives voted its

Engraving of the *Trent* Affair, 8 November 1861   *(Library of Congress)*

thanks and a medal to Wilkes, who instantly became a national hero. His action, not sanctioned by international law respecting the rights of neutral shipping, precipitated the greatest diplomatic crisis of the Civil War.

When the Union cabinet first met and discussed the removal of the Confederate commissioners, Postmaster General Montgomery Blair warned his colleagues and President Abraham LINCOLN that Mason and Slidell should be released and sent on their way to Europe. The outraged British response to the *Trent* affair soon confirmed the wisdom of Blair's assessment and brought the two countries to the brink of war. Prime Minister Henry John Temple, Viscount Palmerston, informed his cabinet colleagues that he would be damned if he would stand for such an insult, and he immediately dispatched reinforcements to Canada, strengthened Britain's Atlantic fleet, and halted shipments of saltpeter to the Union. He also directed Foreign Minister John Earl Russell to send a note to U.S. secretary of state William H. Seward, demanding an apology and the release of the prisoners. Richard Bickerton Pemell, Lord Lyons, the British minister in Washington, was instructed to return home if a favorable response to this communication was not received in seven days. In a crucial move, however, the fatally ill Prince Albert, in a rare exercise of the royal prerogative to revise diplomatic correspondence, toned down the message by suggesting that Russell demand an explanation rather than an apology. The British were by no means sure that the Union would back down, however, and continued to prepare for armed conflict.

President Lincoln carefully weighed his options in the wake of the unexpectedly strong British reaction. Along with most Northerners, he was reluctant to surrender the Southern diplomats; but war with Britain, the world's strongest naval power, would certainly have resulted in the breaking of the blockade of the Southern ports, and ultimately in Confederate independence. Accepting the necessity of compromise, the cabinet and congressional leaders agreed with Lincoln's decision to release Mason and Slidell. In the official diplomatic response to Russell's note, Seward explained that Wilkes had acted illegally and without orders, and that the administration therefore would not sanction his actions. Seward did not, however, formally apologize. Anglo-American relations thereafter improved considerably, as it became increasingly clear to each side that neither wanted war.

Further reading: Ferris, Norman B. *The Trent Affair: A Diplomatic Crisis.* Knoxville: University of Tennessee Press, 1977; Jones, Howard. *Union in Peril: The Crisis over British Intervention in the Civil War.* Chapel Hill: University of North Carolina Press, 1992.

— Michael Thomas Smith

Trenton, Battle of (26 December 1776) *Pivotal battle of the American Revolutionary War*

British commander Major General William Howe had decided in late November 1776 to go into winter quarters after his army forced Continental army commander General George WASHINGTON's force to abandon New York and retreat across New Jersey. Confidence in the Patriot cause was waning, many enlistments would expire at year's end, and a number of the men were sick. In these circumstances, Washington desperately needed a victory. Toward this end Washington ordered Major General Charles LEE to bring his 2,700-man force from upstate New York to join him and called upon Quartermaster General Thomas Mifflin to raise militia in Pennsylvania.

On 11 December, Washington crossed the Delaware into Pennsylvania to gather his forces. Although Lee was captured by a British patrol at Basking Ridge on 13 December, Major General John SULLIVAN, who succeeded to the command, successfully brought the troops across the river. Meanwhile, Brigadier General James Ewing arrived with 2,000 Pennsylvania militiamen to bring Washington's total force up to approximately 6,000 men by 20 December.

Receiving reports that Howe had transferred most of his regulars back to New York, leaving Hessians in garrisons at Princeton, Bordentown, and Trenton, Washington decided to attack the more isolated Trenton, where Colonel Johann Gottlieb Rall commanded 1,500 Hessians. Washington planned to cross the Delaware on the night of 25 December, hoping not only to surprise the Hessians but also to find them off guard following their Christmas revelry. While Washington crossed the Delaware to the north of Trenton with 2,400 regulars, Ewing was supposed to cross to the south with 1,000 of his Pennsylvanians to prevent a Hessian retreat toward Bordentown. At the same time, Colonel John Cadwalader was to cross at Bristol with 2,000 men (mostly militia) in a feint toward Bordentown to prevent the 2,000 Hessians garrisoned there from reinforcing Rall.

Before marching his troops toward the Delaware on late Christmas afternoon, Washington had Thomas Paine's *The Crisis* read to his men, lifting their spirits before the dangerous crossing. Although Ewing never made it across and Cadwalader was delayed by the difficulty of landing his artillery, Washington's main force of 2,400 men and 18 cannon successfully made the crossing of the icy Delaware under the supervision of Colonel John Glover, whose 14th Regiment was comprised primarily of fishermen from Marblehead, Massachusetts.

After marching to within four miles of Trenton, Washington split his forces into two columns. Major General Nathaniel GREENE, accompanied by Washington, led about half of the force down the Pennington Road, striking Trenton from the northeast, while Sullivan led the remainder

General George Washington at the Battle of Trenton, 26 December 1776. Engraving.   *(National Archives)*

down the River Road, hitting Trenton from the north. Washington's two columns startled the Hessians, who never expected an attack in such awful weather.

After Rall was mortally wounded trying to rally his hung-over troops, resistance collapsed. Fewer than 500 Hessians escaped; 918 were captured, and approximately 100 were killed or wounded. Washington suffered just five casualties, including Lieutenant (and future president) James Monroe, who was wounded.

Because Ewing had failed to cross and Cadwalader had been delayed, Washington canceled plans to march immediately to Princeton and Brunswick, choosing instead to take the captured Hessians back across the Delaware to Pennsylvania.

Although Washington would recross the Delaware a week later to take PRINCETON, the vital element of surprise had been lost. Yet, while the battle of Trenton hardly compensated for the loss of New York, it and the subsequent victory at Princeton largely restored both Patriot morale and Washington's reputation as a military commander.

See also AMERICAN REVOLUTIONARY WAR: LAND OVERVIEW.

Further reading: Alden, John Richard. *The American Revolution, 1775–1783.* New American Nation Series. New York: Harper & Row, 1954; Fast, Howard. *The Crossing.* New York: Simon & Schuster, 1999; Flexner, James Thomas. *Washington: The Indispensable Man.* Boston: Little, Brown, 1969.

— Justin D. Murphy

Tripolitan War (1801–1805) *Conflict between the United States and the Barbary states, principally Tunis, over neutral shipping rights*

Independence from Great Britain meant that American merchant ships were no longer under the protection of British warships or British-paid tributes. Therefore, after independence, the United States had suffered obstruction of trade in the Mediterranean from the Barbary regencies of Tripoli, Tunis, Algiers, and Morocco. U.S. vessels were seized and its citizens held for ransom.

Secretary of State Thomas JEFFERSON was reluctant to pay ransom and tribute for fear of setting a precedent the meager U.S. budget could not support. He argued that the

Battle off Tripoli involving Commodore Edward Preble's U.S. squadron, 3 August 1804   *(Naval Historical Foundation)*

cost of a navy to protect shipping would be less expensive than tribute, while Vice President John Adams favored tribute. After France and Britain went to war in 1793, France attempted to invoke the mutual defense treaty made with the United States during the American Revolutionary War, but the United States resisted. With Britain also exerting pressure on the United States, war with one or the other power seemed likely.

Under the threat of war with a European state, and in view of the situation with the Barbary regencies, in 1794 Congress appropriated funds to construct a small navy of six frigates. These would eventually make up the nucleus of the Mediterranean Squadron.

War came first with neither Britain nor the Barbary states, but with France. During the QUASI-WAR (1798–1800), there were a number of naval engagements in which the infant U.S. Navy gained combat experience at the expense of the less capable French. At the same time,

the United States negotiated agreements with the Barbary states that freed American captives, exempted U.S. merchant shipping from attack, and provided for an annual tribute in naval stores. The treaties also established American consuls in Tangier, Algiers, Tunis, and Tripoli. The United States failed to meet the promised payments, however. Problems ensued from all of the Barbary states, but the bashaw (or pasha) of Tripoli presented the most persistent difficulties.

Because of perceived diplomatic slights and a desire to increase his prestige, in October 1800 the bashaw of Tripoli demanded a new treaty from the United States, increasing the amount of tribute. When this was not forthcoming, in February 1801 he repudiated the treaty of 1797 and declared war on the United States. Jefferson, now president, had anticipated hostilities and in June dispatched a squadron of four ships to the Mediterranean. Commanded by Commodore Richard DALE, the squadron arrived in the

Mediterranean in July and found that Tripoli had declared war. Dale engaged in offensive operations, but he lacked sufficient force and the requisite instructions to bring an end to the conflict. He returned to the United States in his flagship in March 1802, leaving only three warships in the area.

After Congress authorized the use of force against Tripoli in February 1802, a second squadron of six ships, commanded by Commodore Richard V. MORRIS, arrived off Gibraltar in May, bringing the total number of U.S. ships to nine. About the same time, Morocco declared war on the United States, making impossible demands but taking no hostile action. Morris remained near Gibraltar until August, when Morocco agreed to resume peaceful relations. Leaving Gibraltar, Morris still did not sail to Tripoli, but instead conducted a cruise around the Mediterranean with his wife and children aboard his flagship.

Not until February 1803 did Morris near Tripoli, and then it was to go ashore at Tunis, which was threatening war. He persuaded the Tunisian leader, the bey, to maintain the peace, but initially refused to pay the American Consul William EATON's debt and was himself arrested. Scraping together enough funds to pay Eaton's debts and his own ransom, he left Tunis and sailed again to Gibraltar. Finally, on 27 May 1803, he led a poorly conceived attack on Tripoli's harbor. Morris then concluded that a blockade of Tripoli was unfeasible and withdrew to Malta. He was called home to the United States in the summer of 1803.

As Morris left the Mediterranean, the first elements of a third squadron arrived in September 1803 under Commodore Edward PREBLE. Preble conducted the war more aggressively than had his predecessors. Not only did he blockade Tripoli, but Preble also made a show of force before Tangier that persuaded Morocco, again threatening war, to keep the peace. Approaching Tripoli in November, Preble learned that the 38-gun frigate PHILADELPHIA had run aground and that Captain William BAINBRIDGE and his crew had been taken captive by the bashaw. When the Tripolitans managed to refloat the frigate, in February 1804 Lieutenant Stephen DECATUR and a crew of volunteers entered the harbor and burned the *Philadelphia* without losing a man.

Before Preble could make any more raids in Tripoli Harbor, the bey of Tunis again began to make hostile noises. After quieting this saber rattling, Preble returned to Tripoli in June. Between June and September, Preble's forces made numerous forays into the harbor, sinking Tripolitan vessels, bombarding the city, and blasting the harbor forts. These actions were interspersed with fruitless negotiations. Preble was unable to subdue the Tripolitans, despite his aggressive actions, so President Jefferson sent a reinforcing squadron that brought a total of 23 vessels into the Mediterranean during the summer of 1804.

Preble sailed for home in September, replaced by Captain Samuel BARRON as commodore of the force. Unfortunately, Barron soon became ill and lethargic. However, accompanying Barron was the former consul to Tunis, William Eaton, with a plan that might end the war.

Eaton was authorized to undertake an overland expedition against Tripoli, which if successful would install Hamet Caramanali, the brother of the bashaw of Tripoli, as the new bashaw. Eaton gathered a force in Egypt that consisted of 40 Greek infantrymen, 28 artillerymen of Levantian origin, about 300 Arabs, and his own staff, which included a U.S. Navy midshipman, a marine lieutenant, and seven marines. In March 1805 Eaton and Hamet set off for Tripoli, 1,000 miles across the desert.

After Eaton captured DERNA, the largest city next to Tripoli, and with a U.S. naval force before Tripoli now under Captain John RODGERS, the bashaw on 4 June 1805 formally agreed to a peace treaty favorable to the United States. While challenges from the Barbary regencies continued to rise periodically until 1815, this treaty effectively ended the Tripolitan War.

See also JEFFERSONIAN GUNBOAT PROGRAM; HULL, ISAAC; MARINE CORPS.

Further reading: Kitzen, Michael L. S. *Tripoli and the United States at War.* Jefferson, N.C.: McFarland, 1993; Tucker, Glenn. *Dawn Like Thunder: The Barbary Wars and the Birth of the U.S. Navy.* Indianapolis: Bobbs-Merrill, 1963; Whipple, A. B. C. *To the Shores of Tripoli: The Birth of the U.S. Navy and Marines.* New York: Morrow, 1991.

— Arthur T. Frame

Trois Rivières, Battle of (8 June 1776) *Revolutionary War battle*

The Battle of Trois Rivières was the Continental army's last effort to take Canada following the failed invasion of 1775. On 6 July 1776, Continental army brigadier general John SULLIVAN detached 2,000 troops to attack the British army at the small Canadian settlement of Trois Rivières on the Saint Lawrence River, between Montreal and Quebec. Sullivan hoped that a victory over the advancing British army under Sir Guy Carleton might reverse American fortunes in Canada and halt the American retreat.

The American force consisted of the 4th and 6th Pennsylvania Regiments under Brigadier General William Thompson, along with the 2d New Jersey regiment commanded by Colonel William Maxwell. Thompson's force descended the Saint Lawrence in small boats and landed nine miles south of Trois Rivières, where it formed into four columns under Colonels Maxwell, William Irvine, Anthony WAYNE, and Arthur ST. CLAIR. A reserve force of 250 men was left to guard the boats and secure an avenue of retreat. At dusk on 7 June, the Americans advanced within a few miles of Trois Rivières, where they were fired upon by the British ship *Martin,* lying at anchor in the river. The ship's cannon sent the Americans sprawling into the woods, where they soon became mired in a large swamp.

While the Americans blundered about in the marshy woods during the night, the British at Trois Rivières turned out for battle. Sullivan's intelligence indicated that only a small British contingent occupied the town, but the advance units of the main British army under Major General John Burgoyne (more than 1,000 troops) had arrived that morning. These collided with Wayne's 4th Pennsylvania Regiment as it emerged from the swamp at dawn on 8 June. Wayne's column, soon reinforced by Thompson and the main body of American troops, pushed the British back to Trois Rivières, where, however, they ran into the recently arrived 20th and 62d Regiments of the British army. Assisted by two companies of grenadiers and several light field cannon, Burgoyne broke the American attack at Trois Rivières and repulsed Wayne and his Pennsylvanians from the small village.

As the battle turned, Burgoyne sent Brigadier General Simon Fraser and nearly 1,000 British soldiers by ship upriver to cut off the American retreat. Fraser's force assaulted the retreating Americans' southern flank around noon, driving the Americans back into the wooded swamps, where Thompson called for a general retreat. The beleaguered Americans reached their embarkation point on 9 June only to find that the reserve force had retreated with all the boats at the first hint of combat. As the British closed in, some 200 Continental soldiers, including Thompson, surrendered. Wayne took command of the remainder of the army and organized a daring escape through the woods to the American base at Sorel.

Trois Rivières was a disaster for American military interests in Canada. The Americans suffered 50 killed and 236 captured, while even greater numbers deserted. Only 1,100 of the 2,000 men who began the mission returned. Citing insurmountable odds, incompetent subordinates, and smallpox-ravaged troops, Sullivan ordered the wholesale American withdrawal from Canada on 13 June 1776.

See also AMERICAN REVOLUTIONARY WAR: LAND OVERVIEW; CANADA, INVASION OF, 1775–1776.

Further reading: Hatch, Robert McConnell. *Thrust for Canada: The American Attempt on Quebec in 1775–1776.* Boston: Houghton Mifflin, 1979. Stanley, George F. G. *Canada Invaded, 1775–1776.* Toronto: Hakkert, 1973; Stille, Charles Janeway. *Major General Anthony Wayne and the Pennsylvania Line in the American Revolution.* Reprint. Port Washington, N.Y.: Kennikat Press, 1968.

— Daniel P. Barr

Truman, Harry S. (1884–1972) *President of the United States, 1945–53*

Born on 8 May 1884 in Lamar, Missouri, Harry S. Truman spent most of his formative years on the family farm in Grandview, Missouri. Truman had a first-class intellect, a keen memory, and was well read; however, poor eyesight kept him out of the U.S. Naval Academy, Annapolis, and the U.S. Military Academy, West Point. Instead, Truman read law at night in the Kansas City School of Law, but never did formally attend college. During World War I he served in France with Battery D of the 129th Field Artillery, ultimately rising to captain.

After the war Truman entered politics and was elected—with the backing of "Boss" Tom Pendergast, the local Democratic power broker—to a judgeship on the Jackson County court in Missouri. He sat on the court from 1926 to 1934, when he was elected to the U.S. Senate. He was reelected in 1940. A relatively obscure senator until the United States entered World War II, Truman earned national exposure and notoriety as the chairman of the Senate committee charged with rooting out procurement waste during the war effort.

In 1944, President Franklin D. ROOSEVELT, dissatisfied with Vice President Henry A. Wallace, tapped Truman as his new vice presidential running mate. Roosevelt was reelected, to an unprecedented fourth term, and Truman was sworn in as vice president in January 1945. In office less than three months, on 12 April Truman became president upon Roosevelt's sudden death from a cerebral hemorrhage. Although inexperienced in foreign policy and largely ignorant of substantive policy matters—Roosevelt had not even told him about the development of the ATOMIC BOMB—Truman characteristically moved forward with confidence to pilot the United States through the last months of World War II. In the first few months of his presidency, Truman oversaw the defeat of Germany, attended the last wartime conference at Potsdam, and made the decision to unleash the atomic bomb against the Japanese, a decision he claimed he never regretted or agonized over.

Truman was generally less diplomatic and more intransigent toward the Soviets than was his predecessor. In only a matter of months, and certainly by mid-1946, he became America's first COLD WAR leader, repeatedly demonstrating his firm anti-Soviet stance that would soon include some of the most far-ranging and bold American foreign and military policies in the nation's history. In the 1947 Truman Doctrine, the president committed the United States to a policy of CONTAINMENT of communism. That same year, his administration pledged to help the ailing Western European economy and to protect it from Communist influences by initiating a five-year, $13.5 billion aid program known as the Marshall Plan, after his secretary of state,

George C. MARSHALL. In 1948, the same year he was reelected president, Truman stood firm during the first BERLIN crisis of the cold war, forcing the Soviets to back down. In 1949, his administration engineered the NORTH ATLANTIC TREATY ORGANIZATION (NATO), the first formal politico-military alliance in which the nation had engaged itself since the Franco-American alliance of the American Revolutionary War.

In July 1948, Truman ordered the racial integration of the U.S. armed forces. Although highly controversial both inside and outside of the military establishment, it, along with the congressional act to allow women broader access to military careers, helped to ease manpower concerns and advanced civil rights.

By late 1949, however, the Communist victory in China, combined with the shocking news of the Soviet atom-bomb test, significantly accelerated cold war hostilities. At home, the politics of anticommunism became vicious with the advent of McCarthyism—the witch-hunt tactics of Senator Joseph McCarthy. In response, Truman approved the development and deployment of the hydrogen (or thermonuclear) bomb in January 1950; this bomb was successfully detonated in 1952. In April 1950, Truman's national security advisers, the State Department, and the Pentagon drafted the top-secret defense report known as NSC-68, which called for massive increases in the nation's defensive and offensive capabilities. Truman, always something of a fiscal conservative, initially demurred on its implementation. The outbreak of the KOREAN WAR in June 1950 helped change his mind, and by September, he reluctantly approved NSC-68, which would stand as the nation's cold war blueprint for the next 25 years.

The only U.S. president to preside during two major wars, Truman always cited the decision to intervene in the Korean War (1950–53) as the toughest one he had to make as president. But, convinced that Moscow had engineered the North Korean assault against South Korea, and determined to contain the spread of communism, the president acted decisively, authorizing U.S. troop deployments within a week of the attack. The Korean War was frustrating for the U.S. public, and its mounting casualty toll was politically damaging to the Truman administration and the Democratic Party. Truman's decision to relieve General of the Army Douglas MACARTHUR of his command in April 1951, combined with the strategic stalemate reached by the summer of 1951, turned public opinion against the war and Truman's handling of it. As a result, Truman declined to seek another term in office. He was succeeded by Republican Dwight D. EISENHOWER in January 1953.

Upon leaving office, Truman retired to his family home in Independence, Missouri. He spent his retirement building and organizing his presidential library, writing his memoirs, and giving occasional speeches and addresses. He died in Kansas City, Missouri, on 26 December 1972.

See also FORRESTAL, JAMES; KOREAN WAR, CAUSES OF.

Further reading: McCoy, Donald R. *The Presidency of Harry S. Truman.* Lawrence: University Press of Kansas, 1984; McCullough, David. *Truman.* New York: Simon & Schuster, 1992; Pemberton, William E. *Harry S. Truman: Fair Dealer and Cold Warrior.* Boston: Twayne Publishing, 1989; Truman, Harry S. *Memoirs.* 2 vols. Garden City, N.Y.: Doubleday, 1955–56.

— Paul G. Pierpaoli, Jr.

Truscott, Lucian King (1895–1965) *U.S. Army general*
Born on 9 January 1895 in Chatfield, Texas, Lucian King Truscott enlisted in the army when the United States entered World War I. Selected for officer training, he was commissioned in the cavalry in 1917 but remained in the United States during the war.

From 1919 to 1921, Truscott served at Schofield Barracks, Hawaii. He was promoted to captain in 1920, major in 1926, and lieutenant colonel in 1935. He was an instructor at both the Cavalry School and the Command and General Staff School.

Promoted to colonel in December 1941 and to brigadier general in May 1942, Truscott joined Admiral Lord Louis Mountbatten's Allied combined staff and developed the Ranger units for special operations. Truscott led the Rangers in the raid on Dieppe, France, in the summer of 1942. Promoted to major general in November 1942, he led his Rangers to liberate Port Lyautey in French Morocco from Vichy French forces as a part of Operation TORCH.

During the fighting for Tunisia, Truscott was General Dwight D. EISENHOWER's field deputy in charge of training. Known for his rigorous training and flamboyant attire, he prided himself on having the fastest-moving troops, stepping up their cadence early in a march. Truscott took command of the 3d Infantry Division in March 1943, and participated with it in the July-August invasion of SICILY. He established his reputation as a fine combat commander who led from the front. He led the division ashore at SALERNO, Italy, and then participated in the landing at ANZIO. When Lieutenant General Mark CLARK relieved VI Corps commander Major General John P. Lucas of his command, Truscott succeeded Lucas. In this role, Truscott orchestrated a major counterattack that made possible the Allied capture of Rome in June 1944.

VI Corps was then withdrawn from Italy and on 15 August 1944 participated in Operation DRAGOON, the invasion of southern France. In September, Truscott was promoted to lieutenant general and returned to Italy to replace Clark as commander of Fifth Army. In October 1945,

Truscott replaced General George S. PATTON as commander of Third Army and military governor of Bavaria. He returned to the United States in May 1946 and retired from the army in 1947.

During his retirement, Truscott wrote his memoirs and served in a number of advisory roles. President Dwight D. Eisenhower promoted him to general on the retired list in July 1954. Truscott died in Washington, D.C., on 13 September 1965.

Further reading: Morris, Eric. *Circles of Hell: The War in Italy, 1943–1945.* New York: Crown, 1993; Truscott, Lucian King. *The Twilight of the U.S. Cavalry: Life in the Old Army, 1917–1942.* Lawrence: University Press of Kansas, 1989; ———. *Command Decisions: A Personal Story.* Novato, Calif.: Presidio, 1990; Wilt, Alan F. *The French Riviera Campaign of August 1944.* Carbondale: Southern Illinois University Press, 1981.

— John David Rausch, Jr.

Truxtun, Thomas (1755–1822) *U.S. Navy captain*
Born on 17 February 1755 in Hempstead, Long Island, Thomas Truxtun went to sea as an apprentice at 12. Three years later, he was pressed into Royal Navy service on the frigate *Prudent.* Later released, he returned to the merchant service. The naval experience, however, fostered in him a preference for military efficiency and harsh discipline.

In 1775, Truxtun captained his first ship, the merchantman *Charming Polly.* During the American Revolutionary War, Truxtun built his reputation as a daring seaman, transporting invaluable munitions to Philadelphia. Following the British seizure of his vessel, he became a lieutenant on the privateer *Congress.* Participating in several captures, he worked his way to command in succession the privateers *Independence, Mars, Commerce,* and *St. James.* Truxtun fought many engagements against more heavily armed opponents, winning acclaim as a daring and successful seaman.

After the war, Truxtun entered the China trade and published a treatise on navigation. When Congress established the U.S. Navy in 1794, Truxtun became one of the first six captains, although last in seniority. Truxtun never reconciled this "insult," which hampered his professional relationships for the remainder of his career.

From 1795 to 1797, Truxtun oversaw construction of and then commanded the frigate *Constellation.* On 9 February 1799, during the 1798–1800 QUASI-WAR WITH FRANCE, his outgunned ship hammered the French frigate *Insurgente* into submission, a victory that gained him lasting fame. On 1–2 February 1800, again outgunned, he won a bloody duel with *La Vengeance,* but the loss of his own mainmast prevented the capture of the crippled French warship. The victory, nonetheless, cemented Truxtun's fame, and Congress struck a medal in his honor.

On the commencement of the TRIPOLITAN WAR, Truxtun was in line to command the U.S. squadron headed for the Mediterranean. In a dispute with the Jefferson administration over seniority, Truxtun's complaints were "accepted" as his resignation, despite his repeated protests.

Recruited by Aaron BURR, Truxtun did not participate in Burr's treason, even testifying against Burr in the former vice president's 1807 trial. In 1810 he ran unsuccessfully for a seat in Congress. He was sheriff of Philadelphia from 1816 to 1819, and he also published several books on naval tactics. Truxtun died in Philadelphia on 5 May 1822.

See also PRIVATEERS IN THE AMERICAN REVOLUTION.

Further reading: Ferguson, Eugene S. *Truxtun of the Constellation: The Life of Commodore Thomas Truxtun, U.S. Navy, 1755–1822.* Baltimore, Md.: Johns Hopkins University Press, 1956; Guttridge, Leonard F., and Jay D. Smith. *The Commodores. The U.S. Navy in the Age of Sail.* New York: Harper & Row, 1969. 1984; Sprout, Harold, and Margaret Sprout. *The Rise of American Naval Power, 1776–1918.* Princeton: Princeton University Press, 1939.

— Michael S. Casey

Tryon, William (1729–1788) *Royal governor of North Carolina and New York, and general in the British army during the American Revolutionary War*
Born on 8 June 1729 in Surrey, England, William Tryon was privately educated. He secured a lieutenant's commission in the Foot Guards in 1751; by 1758, he had risen to lieutenant colonel.

In 1757, Tryon married a relative of English statesman Lord Hillsborough, who was secretary of state for colonies (1768–72). During the Seven Years' War he participated in operations in France. Worried that peace would limit his military opportunities, in June 1764 he secured an appointment as lieutenant governor of North Carolina through Hillsborough's influence. He became governor when his predecessor died the following year. He built a spectacular capital building and governor's residence, Tryon Palace, at New Bern.

In 1768, settlers in western North Carolina formed the Regulator Association to protest high taxes and corrupt local officials. When armed Regulators assembled in the spring of 1771 to resist the government, Tryon, though sympathetic to many of their grievances, marched 1,300 militia to their camp near Alamance Creek. On 16 May he attacked and defeated the Regulators in the Battle of ALAMANCE, effectively ending the movement.

In July 1771, Tryon assumed the governorship of New York. He went to England in 1774 and returned to New York in June 1775 to find royal authority in tatters. He worked to restore British control, including an attempt to recruit loyalists from among the Continental troops in New York. Tryon hoped to use these men to kidnap Continental army commander General George WASHINGTON, but American leaders discovered the plot.

After the British captured New York, Tryon recruited several Loyalist battalions and served as an adviser to Major General Sir William Howe; however, he became frustrated with the latter's conciliatory approach. Tryon advocated harsh policies to suppress the rebellion. London's refusal to restore civil authority in New York led Tryon to become active in military service himself. In 1777 he was named major general of provincial troops, and he led several attacks on American supply depots, including the destructive DANBURY RAID in Connecticut. His troops helped to repulse Washington's probing attacks at King's Bridge in August.

Lieutenant General Governor Sir Henry Clinton's refusal to approve his plans for further raids angered Tryon, and he rejected Clinton's invitation to command British forces in Georgia. When the British ministry ordered a renewal of coastal raiding, Tryon led a series of raids in Connecticut in 1779. Employing the destructive measures he favored, his troops inflicted heavy damage at New Haven, Fairfield, and Norwalk. He returned to England in September 1780 and saw no further service. He was promoted to lieutenant general in 1782 and was a staunch advocate of the Loyalists until his death in London on 27 January 1788.

See also AMERICAN REVOLUTIONARY WAR: LAND OVERVIEW; WESTERN NORTH CAROLINA UPRISING.

Further reading: Nelson, Paul David. *William Tryon and the Course of Empire: A Life in British Imperial Service.* Chapel Hill: University of North Carolina Press, 1990.

— Jim Piecuch

Turner, Richmond K. (1885–1961) *U.S. Navy admiral*
Born on 27 May 1885 in Portland, Oregon, Richmond Kelly Turner graduated near the top of his class at the U.S. Naval Academy, Annapolis, in 1908 and became a gunnery specialist. He later underwent aviation training, and received his wings at age 42, and won promotion to captain in 1935. After attending the Naval War College he remained there as head of the Strategy Section. In 1938 Turner returned to the sea as skipper of the heavy cruiser *Astoria.*

In 1940 Turner became director of War Plans Division in Washington. Disregarding recommendations from other staff officers, he refused to send clear warnings of possible Japanese aggression to Pacific Fleet commander Admiral Husband KIMMEL, even when it became apparent that war in the Pacific was imminent. As with most observers, Turner believed the Japanese would begin hostilities in the western Pacific, not at PEARL HARBOR. When the Japanese struck there, Turner still refused to admit personal culpability, and he became a witness against Kimmel in later investigations.

After the U.S. declared war on Japan, Turner became assistant to Chief of Staff Fleet Admiral Ernest KING, with responsibility for planning amphibious operations in the Pacific. Rear Admiral Turner left Washington in July 1942 to command Amphibious Forces, South Pacific. He directed amphibious support for the GUADALCANAL campaign (7 August 1942–9 February 1943) and was severely criticized for the defeat of his second in command, Rear Admiral Victor Crutchley, in the first battle of SAVO ISLAND on the night of 8–9 August 1942. An investigation concluded that no one officer could be held responsible for all the mistakes involved in that operation. Turner directed the Russell Island assault in late August 1942, and he later planned the New Georgia and Rendova assaults. On 24 July 1943

Rear Admiral Richmond K. Turner, February 1944   *(Naval Historical Foundation)*

he was designated commander, Fifth Amphibious Forces, Pacific. Turner formed a new administrative command ashore so that he could be at sea for the conquest of the Gilbert Islands in late 1943.

Promoted to vice admiral in February 1944, Turner directed all subsequent major amphibious operations in the central Pacific, including those at Saipan and the MARIANAS ISLANDS, IWO JIMA, and OKINAWA. In June 1945 he was promoted to full admiral and began to plan the invasion of Japan.

With the end of the war, Turner served on the General Board until December 1945, when he was appointed U.S. Navy representative on the United Nations Military Staff Committee. After serving in New York and London, he retired on 30 June 1947. Turner died in Monterey, California, on 12 February 1961.

See also WORLD WAR II, COURSE OF U.S. INVOLVEMENT: PACIFIC THEATER.

Further reading: Dyer, George Carroll. *The Amphibians Came to Conquer: The Story of Admiral Richmond Kelly Turner.* 2 vols. Washington, D.C.: U.S. Government Printing Office, 1971; Morison, Samuel E. *History of United States Naval Operations in World War II.* Vols. 5, 6, 7, 8, 12, 13, and 14. Boston: Little, Brown, 1949–1960.

— Lisa L. Beckenbaugh

Turtle (1776) *The world's first true submarine, developed by American David Bushnell during the American Revolutionary War*

Bushnell had already developed an underwater mine; then, in 1776, at Saybrook on the Connecticut River, he built a means to deliver it—what he called a "sub-marine."

BUSHNELL's craft consisted of two great tortoise-like shells made of oak staves and clamped together by iron hoops. It resembled an egg in appearance and rode upright in the water with its smaller end facing down. An entry hatch at the top of the craft had eight small windows to provide light for the operator below, and a 900-pound keel provided stability. Measuring seven and a half feet by six feet, the tar-coated craft had two brass pipes, with check valves, to provide both fresh air and a means of exhaust. A valve admitted water to submerge, and a pump expelled it to ascend. The craft was driven forward and up and down by means of two sets of screw-like paddles operated manually by inside cranks—one on top of the craft and the other in front of the operator. A rudder moved by a tiller steered the craft. The operator could use a release chain to detach 200 pounds of the lead keel, which could also be let down as an anchor. The craft even had a depth gauge and a compass. It was called the *Turtle* because of its appearance.

The *Turtle's* destructive power came from a cask that contained 150 pounds of gunpowder. A bolt attached the mine to the submarine. Withdrawing the bolt released the mine and activated the timer, a clockwork device that exploded the mine after about an hour by means of a flint lock. The submarine was to dive beneath its target and the operator would screw an auger, which was attached to the mine, into the target vessel's hull. Once this was accomplished, the auger was released and the mine floated free against the target's hull. The *Turtle's* chief drawback was that the operator had only 30 minutes of air once the craft submerged. This meant that an attack had to be mounted at night or in a period of poor visibility in order for the *Turtle* to get as close as possible before it submerged.

Bushnell successfully tested the *Turtle* in the Connecticut River. In 1776, when Vice Admiral Lord Richard Howe's fleet arrived at New York, the *Turtle* was sent there. Bushnell was too frail, and his brother Ezra, who was to make the attempt, fell ill. Bushnell then quickly trained a volunteer, Sergeant Ezra Lee, in the *Turtle* on Long Island Sound.

Lee made his attempt shortly after midnight on 7 September. He finally reached the target vessel, Admiral Howe's 64-gun *Eagle*, but he was unable to get the auger to enter its hull. In his escape he released the mine, which exploded an hour afterward. Several other attempts were made to sink British ships in the Hudson, without success. The *Turtle* was later destroyed, probably to prevent it from falling into British hands.

See also SUBMARINES.

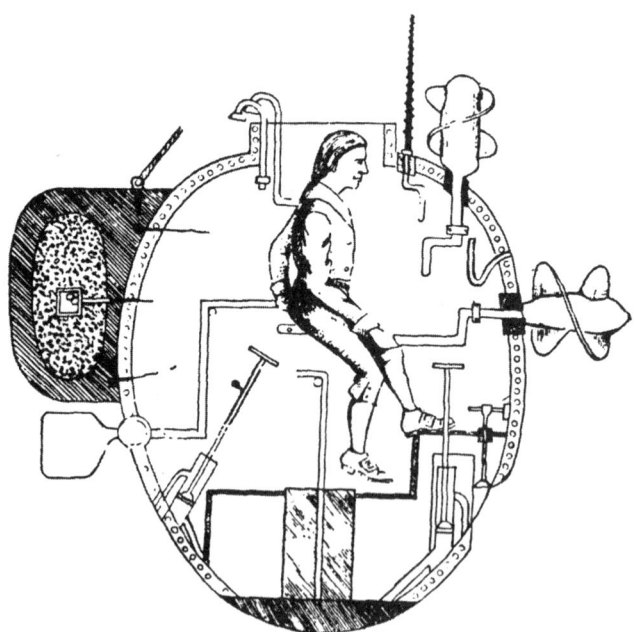

David Bushnell's *Turtle* submarine   *(Library of Congress)*

Further reading: Roland, Alex. *Underwater Warfare in the Age of Sail.* Bloomington: Indiana University Press, 1977; Miller, Nathan. *Sea of Glory: The Continental Navy Fights for Independence, 1775–1783.* New York: David McKay, 1974.

— Spencer C. Tucker

Tuscarora War (1711–1713) *War between the Tuscarora Indians of eastern North Carolina and the expanding North Carolina colony*

The first English settlers in North Carolina arrived from Virginia in what is now the upper northeastern corner of the state. It was not until the beginning of the 18th century that white settlers began to move south of the Albemarle Sound. A decisive moment occurred in 1710 with the arrival of a group of Swiss and Germans, led by Baron Christoph von Graffenried, who settled on the Neuse River and created the town of New Bern. This arrival of some 400 people in an area previously untouched by whites, and most of whom claimed farms of 250 acres apiece, intensified growing Indian resentment.

The Tuscarora (an Iroquoian-speaking people) and other coastal Algonquian tribes had long complained of encroachment on their lands, the taking of Indians as slaves, and the shady trading practices of the whites. Their complaints, while legitimate, were generally ignored. The sudden arrival of this new group, despite Graffenried's sincere effort to establish friendly relations with the local Indians, was spark to the tinder.

On 22 September 1711, 500 Tuscarora, Coree, Pamlico, Machapunga, and Bear River Indians attacked the outlying farms on the Pamlico, Neuse, and Trent Rivers. New Bern itself was left alone, but the isolated farms were hit hard, with some 130–140 whites killed and 20–30 prisoners taken on that first day. The colonists' efforts at retaliation were weak, hampered by internal divisions and by the impulse of most settlers to shut themselves up in "garrison" houses. The Indians gained confidence, and after learning that the colonists had captured and apparently roasted to death a Bay River chieftain, they escalated their attacks.

North Carolina appealed for help, but only South Carolina provided material assistance, dispatching a force of 33 whites and about 500 Indians (mostly Yamassee) under the command of Colonel John Barnwell. During January and February 1712, Barnwell destroyed nearly 400 Indian houses, burned thousands of bushels of corn, and forced the Tuscarora to flee their newly constructed forts. After a pause, Barnwell returned to the offensive in April, this time reinforced by North Carolina troops and other local Indians. Barnwell marched to the Tuscarora main defensive position, Hancock's Fort, and after a lengthy siege successfully negotiated its surrender and the return of the white prisoners. Barnwell then returned to South Carolina, believing the war over. "King Hancock," the leader of the Tuscarora pro-war faction, had fled but was captured by Tom Blount, leader of the northern Tuscarora, who had remained allied to the English. Blount handed Hancock over to the whites, who promptly executed him.

Barnwell's expedition, however, did not end the war. Raids began anew after the Tuscarora discovered that some of their captured people had been sold into slavery in violation of the truce terms. Their fresh attacks led to yet another expedition of 33 whites and 1,000 "friendly Indians" from South Carolina under Colonel James Moore. This army, again working with North Carolina militia and local allied Indians, caught and wiped out a large group of Tuscarora on Contentnea Creek in March 1713. They killed or captured probably 950 men, women, and children; the captives were then sold as slaves. A treaty drawn up in April 1713 ensconced Tom Blount as the new nominal leader of all the Tuscarora. Many Tuscarora fled to New York, however, and joined the Five (now Six) Nations of the Iroquois, while sporadic violence continued in North Carolina until early 1715.

See also AMERICAN INDIAN WARS; INDIAN WARFARE.

Further reading: Lefler, Hugh T. *Colonial North Carolina: A History.* New York: Scribner's, 1973.

— Wayne E. Lee

Twining, Nathan F. (1897–1982) *U.S. Air Force general, chief of staff of the Air Force, and chairman of the Joint Chiefs of Staff*

Born on 11 October 1897 in Monroe, Wisconsin, Nathan Farragut Twining was called up for National Guard duty on the border during the PUNITIVE EXPEDITION INTO MEXICO in 1916. During World War I he briefly attended WEST POINT; he received a commission, and remained in the army.

In the early 1920s, Twining developed an interest in aviation. After receiving flight training, he formally transferred to the Air Service in 1926. In the 1930s he served on aviation bases in Hawaii, Texas, and Louisiana, and took various courses. From August 1940 through early 1942, Twining held assorted staff positions in Washington, D.C. Promoted to brigadier general, he transferred to the South Pacific in July 1942 to become chief of staff of Army Ground and Air Forces. Promoted to major general, in 1943 he commanded the new Thirteenth Air Force in the SOLOMON ISLANDS CAMPAIGN. In 1944 and 1945 he headed the Fifteenth Air Force, based in southern Italy, which mounted numerous raids against German and Balkan targets, especially oil refineries, and provided air support for ground campaigns in Italy and southern

France. Promoted to temporary lieutenant general, at the end of the war Twining commanded Twentieth Air Force in the final bombing of Japan, including the two ATOMIC BOMB missions.

After heading the Army Matériel Command (1945–47) and the Alaska Command, Twining was promoted to full general and became air force vice chief of staff in 1950. In 1953 he succeeded General Hoyt S. VANDENBERG as chief of staff. Under Twining, the STRATEGIC AIR COMMAND expanded and acquired B-52 and XB-70 bombers to become the keystone of the "massive retaliation" nuclear strategies favored by President Dwight D. EISENHOWER. Twining also forcefully advocated the development of assorted intercontinental BALLISTIC MISSILE programs, including Jupiter and Atlas, and Polaris submarine-launched weapons, as part of a full and coordinated American nuclear defense strategy. Twining opposed the decreases in conventional defense forces envisaged by Eisenhower's 1953 NEW LOOK strategy. In 1957 his repeated assertions of a "bomber gap" between the United States and the Soviet Union persuaded Congress to increase air force appropriations by $1 billion. As with Joint Chiefs of Staff chairman Admiral Arthur W. RADFORD, whom he succeeded in 1957, Twining unsuccessfully advocated a nuclear strike against Indochinese Communist Vietminh forces during the 1954 siege of Dien Bien Phu, and he also supported an uncompromising American commitment to defend Taiwan. By the late 1950s, some critics questioned his reliance on nuclear weapons, preferring a more flexible response capacity.

Twining retired in 1960. He vehemently supported American involvement in Vietnam, advised Republican presidential candidate Barry Goldwater in the 1964 election campaign, and, in the book *Neither Liberty nor Safety* (1966), fiercely criticized President Lyndon B. JOHNSON's administration's reluctance to modernize American nuclear weaponry. Arguing that they compromised American national security, in the 1970s he opposed the Strategic Arms Limitation and Antiballistic Missile Treaties. Twining died at Lackland Air Force Base, San Antonio, Texas, on 29 March 1982.

See also LeMAY, CURTIS E.; NUCLEAR AND ATOMIC WEAPONS; SPAATZ, CARL; VIETNAM WAR, CAUSES OF; WORLD WAR II, COURSE OF U.S. INVOLVEMENT: PACIFIC THEATER.

Further reading: Moody, Walton S. *Building a Strategic Air Force*. Washington, D.C.: Air Force Museums and History Program, 1996; Mrozek, Donald J. "Nathan F. Twining: New Dimensions, A New Look," in *Makers of the United States Air Force*. Edited by John L. Frisbee. Washington, D.C.: Office of Air Force History, United States Air Force, 1987: 257–80; Schnabel, James, et al. *The History of the Joint Chiefs of Staff: The Joint Chiefs of Staff and National Policy*. 7 vols. to date. Washington, D.C.: Historical Division, U.S. Joint Chiefs of Staff, 1986–2000; Webb, Willard J. *The Chairmen of the Joint Chiefs of Staff*. Washington, D.C.: Historical Division, U.S. Joint Chiefs of Staff, 1989.

— Priscilla Roberts

U

U-2 incident (1 May 1960) *International crisis provoked when the Soviet Union captured the pilot of a United States U-2 spy plane downed on an espionage mission over Soviet territory*

On 1 May 1960 a Soviet missile battery downed an American U-2 surveillance plane deep over Soviet territory. The pilot, Francis Gary POWERS, was captured alive and publically confessed that he had undertaken an espionage mission planned by the CENTRAL INTELLIGENCE AGENCY (CIA).

Between 1956 and 1960, the United States used the U-2 to undertake from 20 to 30 high-altitude photographic reconnaissance flights along an arc from Pakistan to Norway, violating Soviet airspace but providing vital information on the number, strength, and location of Soviet nuclear missiles and other weapons. Numerous other less controversial missions were flown along the Soviet borders. Pilots, who could rejoin the American military without loss of seniority after their tour, were officially employed by Lockheed and attached to a weather observation squadron based in Turkey. The missions also utilized bases in Pakistan.

The United States government, assuming Powers to be dead, initially denied any espionage, claiming that a meteorological observation flight had accidentally violated Soviet airspace. Allowing Washington to be trapped in a lie, not until 7 May did Soviet authorities reveal that Powers was alive and had informed his captors of his CIA affiliation and provided numerous details of his espionage mission and the program of which it was part. Turkey, Pakistan, and Norway all protested publicly to the United States over the use of their facilities in the American surveillance program. Ignoring Soviet hints that he should disavow all knowledge of the operation, President Dwight D. EISENHOWER then took full responsibility, arguing that failure to do so would suggest that as chief executive he was incompetent to control his own government. He declined either to promise to cease all such flights or publicly to apologize for them.

The capture of Powers effectively derailed Eisenhower's hope that, before he left office in early 1961, the United States and Soviet Union might conclude a nuclear test ban treaty and settle their ongoing dispute over West Berlin, which the Soviet leader Nikita Khrushchev claimed should be entirely under East German control. In early 1960, the two superpowers and Britain progressed steadily toward acceptable treaty terms, expecting to finalize the agreement at a May 1960 Paris summit meeting between Eisenhower and Khrushchev. An atmosphere of acute hostility pervaded the summit; no progress was made toward the contemplated treaty, and Eisenhower left Paris after only two days.

Powers stood trial in Moscow, receiving a 10-year prison sentence, but in 1962 the Soviet Union exchanged him for one of their prominent intelligence operatives, Colonel Rudolf Abel, then held by the United States. Although the U-2 incident embarrassed the United States internationally and generated some tensions with its allies, the U-2 program overall provided much valuable information on Soviet nuclear installations and capabilities and proved that there was no "MISSILE GAP" with the Soviet Union.

No further U-2 flights were made over Soviet territory, and by the early 1960s satellites began to provide similar data without risk. However, U-2 aircraft were still used for reconnaissance missions over other hostile states, such as China and Cuba, where the danger of interception was considered small. Given the difficulties of verification on the ground, reliable information from satellites and spy planes came to be considered an important safeguard, ensuring mutual compliance and confidence in the implementation of the arms limitation agreements concluded under the détente policies of the 1970s.

See also INTELLIGENCE; NUCLEAR AND ATOMIC WEAPONS.

Further reading: Beschloss, Michael R. *Mayday: Eisenhower, Khrushchev and the U-2 Affair.* New York: Harper

& Row, 1986; Pedlow, Gregory W., and Donald E. Welzenbach. *The CIA and the U-2 Program, 1954–1974.* Washington, D.C.: Central Intelligence Agency, Center for the Study of Intelligence, 1998; Peebles, Curtis. *Shadow Flights: America's Secret Air War Against the Soviet Union.* Novato, Calif.: Presidio Press, 2000; Prados, John. *Presidents' Secret Wars: CIA and Pentagon Covert Operations from World War II through Iranscam.* New York: Morrow, 1986.

— Priscilla Roberts

Ultra secret and codebreaking *Vital Allied intelligence operation during World War II*

Accounts about Ultra are frequently incomplete, often slanted by claims that Ultra—an early British cover name for intercepted Enigma communications—was developed by British cryptanalysts early in World War II. On balance, however, the foremost actors in the larger Enigma story were first the Poles, then the British and French, and finally the United States.

Restored as an independent nation in 1919, Poland found itself situated between two traditional adversaries, Germany and Russia. It was thus logical that the Polish Biuro Szyfrów (cipher service) showed earlier interest in solving the Reichswehr's new Enigma cipher system than did the British or French cryptology services. Study started in Warsaw in 1928, soon after new Enigmas were introduced in the German army, but no significant progress was made at the outset. In 1929 the Biuro Szyfrów organized a special course on cryptology for advanced mathematicians at Adam Mickiewicz University in Poznan. The most gifted mathematicians were Marian Rejewski, Henryk Zygalski, and Jerzy Rózycki, who were given appointments in the Biuro Szyfrów and moved to Warsaw in September 1932. Soon Rejewski was given the secret task of reconstructing the German military Enigma. However, a French contribution proved crucial to Rejewski's eventual success.

In late 1931, French intelligence officials bought some invaluable Enigma secret documents from a German civil servant (code-named Asche) working in the cipher service of the War Ministry. Higher French military authorities judged these documents unusable but granted permission for the transfer of copies to the cipher services of allied countries. The British refused to cooperate, but the Poles enthusiastically accepted the Asche materials. They promised to keep the French informed about their progress in attacking the Enigma system—a promise they failed to keep until the summer of 1939.

After much hard work Rejewski and his two colleagues were able to reconstitute the Enigma machine's internal wiring, and by the time Hitler came to power the Poles were reading most German army messages transmitted via Enigmas. This flow of secret information continued until the end of 1938, when the Germans introduced sophisticated modifications to their Enigmas that the Poles were unable to penetrate.

Simultaneous with the blackout of Enigma traffic with which the Poles were confronted, French patience became exhausted. The French had supplied the Poles with expensive Asche documents for seven years and received nothing in exchange. In early January 1939 French intelligence officials hosted a meeting with their Polish and British counterparts. The British, who by 1936 had changed their minds about the German threat and thus requested and started to receive Asche material from the French, admitted that they had been unable to reconstitute the German machine. The French had nothing to offer, and the Poles revealed nothing of their work. The cryptologic experts promised to meet again if new conditions or developments warranted. The time was soon ripe for another meeting after the German takeover of Czechoslovakia in March, followed by British diplomacy that committed the West to the defense of Poland. In late July, Polish intelligence specialists hosted a meeting with the French and British near Warsaw. Secrets were openly shared and the French and British were each given a Polish-made Enigma machine.

Within weeks Germany invaded Poland, and the long-anticipated general European war was unleashed. The British and French were anxious for the team of Polish cryptographers to escape, and when some of them were traced to the Kalimanesti Camp in Romania, the Western Allies helped to organize their escape. Dozens, including the three Poznan mathematicians, reached safety in the West, most in Paris—only to be forced to escape again following the May 1940 German invasion of France. Their new home was the Government Code and Cypher School (GC&CS) at Bletchley Park, 50 miles northwest of London.

The British cryptographic infrastructure was superb; indeed, the British were quick to perfect and elaborate on earlier Polish work. GC&CS produced the first Enigma decrypts of intelligence of operational value in late May 1940. Nonetheless, the Polish cryptographers were marginalized in Britain, and the contingent was not incorporated at Bletchley Park. GC&CS grew very rapidly, from a few dozen people in 1939 to a staff of more than 7,000 by 1944.

As the war became more perilous for Britain, and United States assistance appeared more forthcoming, British cryptographers sought a broad exchange of secret technical information with their American counterparts. Washington then sent a team of intelligence specialists to Britain in February 1941. Many American cryptographic secrets were shared openly with the British, and GC&CS was given an American analog of the Japanese Purple cipher machine as well. Since September 1940, Purple had been producing intelligence, known by the cover name Magic, primarily by deciphering Japanese diplomatic traffic. In exchange, the American team received general technical briefings about the German military Enigma system.

The British and Americans gradually became more cooperative in cryptographic intelligence matters, particularly after U.S. entry in December 1941. Several Anglo-American intelligence agreements were concluded at different bureaucratic levels, but problems resulted in their modification or disregard. Central to all of the changes were two overriding conditions. First, the strain of war prevented the British from developing and delivering on time to the United States some promised high-speed, costly, and sophisticated cryptographic equipment essential for combatting the U-boats in the Battle of the ATLANTIC. Second, the United States, with its enormous resources and engineering talent in the field of cryptographic equipment, pushed ahead to design and build new intelligence matériel for domination in the Atlantic and defeat of Hitler's U-boats.

The British role should not be minimized. They supplied the Americans with key elements, such as wheel wirings, and their wartime experience in the entire Enigma field was without equal. They also had captured German cryptographic equipment and documents. Yet, some of what the British gave the Americans was based on the original Polish gifts. The efforts and sacrifices of many obviously helped to end the war. Since the public revelation of the Ultra secret in 1974, independent scholars have estimated that the Western Allies' ability to act on information obtained by reading German military Enigma traffic shortened the war in Europe by two to four years. Had far-reaching cooperation among the Poles, British, and French been fully exploited before the summer of 1939, Hitler's lust for war and conquest might have been severely tempered.

See also INTELLIGENCE; WORLD WAR II, U.S. INVOLVEMENT: EUROPE; WORLD WAR II, U.S. INVOLVEMENT: PACIFIC THEATER.

Further reading: Benson, Robert Louis. *A History of U.S. Communications Intelligence During World War II: Policy and Administration.* Fort George G. Meade, Md.: National Security Agency, 1997; Boyd, Carl. *Hitler's Japanese Confidant: General Oshima Hiroshi and MAGIC Intelligence, 1941–1945.* Lawrence: University Press of Kansas, 1993; Hinsley, F. H., et al. *British Intelligence in the Second World War: Its Influence on Strategy and Operations.* Vols. 1–3. New York: Cambridge University Press, 1979–88; Hinsley, F. H., and Alan Stripp, eds. *Codebreakers: The Inside Story of Bletchley Park.* New York: Oxford University Press, 1993; Kohnen, David. *Commanders Winn and Knowles: Winning the U-Boat War with Intelligence, 1939–1943.* Krakow, Poland: The Enigma Press, 1999: Kozaczuk, Wladyslaw. *Enigma.* Edited and translated by Christopher Kasparek. Frederick, Md.: University Publications of America, 1984; Rowlett, Frank B. *The Story of MAGIC: Memoirs of an American Cryptologic Pioneer.* Laguna Hills, Calif.: Aegean Park Press, 1998; Skillen, Hugh. *Enigma and Its Achilles Heel.* Pinner, Middlesex, England: by the author, 1992.

— Carl Boyd

unarmored fighting vehicles

Unarmored fighting vehicles are a form of military fighting vehicle used in scouting, raiding, perimeter defense, terrain seizure, ambushes, and, in some instances, indirect artillery support. They are also used in noncombat roles such as personnel and cargo transport, ammunition resupply, and general hauling. Generally these vehicles tend to be lighter, faster, more maneuverable and transportable, and cheaper than their armored counterparts. However, their soft unarmored skins make them highly vulnerable to small arms fire, shell fragmentation, and vehicular mine blasts. In some cases, while some armor protection is afforded to critical components of these vehicles, the crews are often left totally exposed or sit in unarmored compartments.

Five basic forms of unarmored fighting vehicles have existed in U.S. motor pools and inventories since the early 20th century: tracked, half-tracked, wheeled, amphibious, and marginal terrain. Tracked vehicles are represented by gun carriages, artillery movers, and personnel and cargo carriers. An unarmored gun carriage mates an artillery piece to the top of a vehicle, while an unarmored artillery mover tows an artillery piece. An example of an early gun carriage would be the 75mm self-propelled Holt 5-ton artillery tractor of the 1920s, which had an exposed driver and gun crew. Numerous artillery movers with exposed driver cabs were utilized from WORLD WAR I into the 1930s. In both cases, newer generations of these vehicles provided armor protection for their personnel.

Unarmored cargo and personnel carriers developed after the World War I but never existed in great numbers. The better-known ones were the Model T Ford and Dodge tracked cars and trucks, the Studebaker T15 Cargo Carrier, and various tracked Jeeps. While not normally utilized, machine guns could be fitted to these vehicles. By 1950, true armored personnel carriers began to develop and made extinct these earlier unarmored oddities.

Unarmored half-tracks were principally produced during the years between World War I and WORLD WAR II. They were superseded by armored half-track production that took place relatively late, toward the end of the 1930s. Half-tracks were developed by the army; their concept dated back to 1916. These vehicles were used for troop transport and hauling. While they were typically unarmed, one variant known as the T1E2 (or M1) carried two Browning .30-caliber (M1919 series) machine guns and was organized into the 1st Machine Gun Company, 1st Cavalry Regiment, Mechanized, found during the mid-1930s.

Wheeled vehicles have been the mainstay of U.S. unarmored fighting forces. Early cars such as the Model T Ford and various motorcycles gave way to the much celebrated U.S. Army one-quarter-ton truck, the Jeep. The Jeep was so important to the World War II effort that its contribution was singled out by General George C. MARSHALL. This four-wheel-drive vehicle was produced in the hundreds of thousands and had a maximum speed of 60 miles per hour. It was used for scouting, patrolling, officer transport, and myriad other duties. For combat purposes, it could be fitted with a pedestal-mounted .50-caliber machine gun or a 106mm recoilless rifle, or could tow a 37 mm antitank gun. More than 650,000 jeeps were produced during World War II. The original M38A1 vehicle saw service throughout the war and the KOREAN WAR. It was subsequently upgraded to the larger M151 model with a longer wheelbase and more unitized body. This vehicle saw service during the VIETNAM WAR.

The Jeep was replaced by the M998-series High Mobility Multipurpose Wheeled Vehicles (HMMWV), nicknamed the Hummer, with production of more than 70,000 of these vehicles beginning in 1985. An odd assortment of M274 (quarter-ton Mules), M561 (one-and-a-quarter-ton Gama Goats), and M880 (one-and-a-quarter-ton pickup trucks) were also replaced by the HMMWV. Fifteen HMMWV configurations were designated, ranging from cargo and troop carriers to weapons carriers, ambulances, and shelter carriers. Armament for this vehicle can include either a 7.62 mm or .50-caliber machine gun, MK19 40mm automatic grenade launcher, or TOW antitank missile launcher. While the basic HMMWV is unarmored, variants exist with minimal bullet and fragmentation protection and up-armored kits.

Although it was not strictly a fighting vehicle, mention must be made here of the World War II two-and-a-half-ton truck ("deuce-and-a-half"), a troop and cargo carrier that served into the Vietnam War. Developed by the Yellow Truck Company in 1940, and a generation ahead of other military trucks, it was both rugged and reliable and had three axles and a six-wheel drive. Its controls were similar to that of the jeep, so that it was easy for a driver to shift from one vehicle to another. The deuce-and-a-half was the mainstay of the "Red Ball Express" across Europe, and General of the Army Dwight D. EISENHOWER pointed to it as a key factor in the Allied victory.

Amphibious vehicles can be of either the tracked or air-cushion variety. Unarmored wheeled amphibians existed only in prototype form. These vehicles allowed personnel and cargo to be transported from ships through the surf and onto a beach. In the case of tracked amphibious vehicles, they have the capability to penetrate deeper inland and serve as normal troop carriers.

Tracked amphibians and landing vehicles emerged during the 1920s and 1930s and were basically a Marine Corps endeavor. Many of these early designs were unarmored. Some of these unarmored or under-armored variants were probably used in amphibious operations against Japanese-held islands early in World War II. Unarmored versions of the LVT-3 and LVT-4 were known to be employed by the army in that war. Typically, they had two machine gun mounts.

Air-cushion vehicles have great cargo-hauling capability—in the tens of tons—and can achieve speeds between 15 and 40 knots. Normally, they have been used to transport armored fighting vehicles and bulk containers to the shore since the Vietnam era. The army's Lighter Amphibious Air Cushion Vehicle (LACV-30) and the navy's Landing Craft Air Cushion (LCAC) are representative of this type of vehicle. A handful of SK-5 air-cushion assault and transport vehicles were also produced and used in Vietnam operations. Armament consisted of .50-caliber or 7.62mm machine guns and/or an M5 automatic grenade launcher. These vehicles were unarmored except for key mechanical component protection.

Within the marginal terrain category, more exotic vehicular types exist. Many of these vehicles were designed to be used in the difficult terrain found in Southeast Asia and in harsh arctic climates. All were unarmed and intended for transport use. Archimedes-screw vehicles were developed for use in riverine and snow-covered terrain and include the Sno-Jeep, Marsh Screw Amphibian, and Riverine Utility Craft. Propeller-driven sleds, used in the arctic, are represented by the Sno-Peep and Kee Bird. Individual lift (jet propulsion) and walking-machine vehicles were also developed but were not practically employed in the field.

See also TANKS.

Further reading: Crimson, Fred W. *U.S. Military Tracked Vehicles.* Osceola, Wis.: Motorbooks International Publishers, 1992; Green, Michael. *Hummer: The Combat and Developmental History of the AM General High Mobility Multipurpose Wheeled Vehicle.* Osceola, Wis.: Motorbooks International Publishers, 1992; Fowler, Will. *Jeep Goes to War.* Leicester, U.K.: Magna Books, 1993.

— Robert J. Bunker

Underhill, John (1597–1672) *Colonial militia officer and military adviser*

Born in England around 1597, John Underhill was raised in the Netherlands, where his father was a mercenary soldier.

Trained as a professional soldier, he moved to Massachusetts Bay in 1630 to act as a military adviser to the Puritans. Made a captain of militia, he received a land grant. Underhill was troubled at the colonists' lack of concern over defense matters.

In 1637, during the PEQUOT WAR, Underhill commanded of 20-man force, reinforcing Fort Saybrook. Once Connecticut declared war against the Pequot Indians, his unit joined Connecticut forces commanded by John Mason. Assisted by a large contingent of as many as 500 friendly Narragansett and Mohegan Indians, Mason and Underhill's combined force of at most 80 men attacked the Pequot fort at Mystic, Connecticut, on 26 May 1637. The colonists and their Indian allies surrounded the fort, and Underhill and Mason entered the fort to fire it. The colonists and Indians outside shot any Pequot who tried to escape. Within an hour, the village was destroyed and somewhere between 300 and 700 Pequot—men, women, and children—were dead. The colonists lost two killed and 26 wounded; their Narragansett allies sustained 40 wounded. The attack broke Pequot resistance, and the war soon ended.

Underhill then returned to Massachusetts Bay, where he spent the next years in turmoil among his Puritan neighbors. He joined the Antinomians and was excommunicated and banished in 1638, only to be forgiven after an emotional recantation. In 1642 he moved to the New Netherlands to act as the governor's military adviser. In 1644 he led a massacre of 420 Indians on Long Island. Underhill was active during the ANGLO-DUTCH WARS. In 1652, on the outbreak of fighting, he captured Fort Good Hope for the English. He then settled down in New York. He again fought on the English side in 1664–65, helping the English exert control over their newly won territory around New Amsterdam and serving in various government posts. He retired to Long Island in 1667 and died there on 21 September 1672.

Further reading: Cave, Alfred A. *The Pequot War.* Amherst: University of Massachusetts Press, 1996; Malone, Patrick. *The Sulking Way of War: Technology and Tactics Among the New England Indians.* Lanham, Md.: Madison Books, 1991; Orr, Charles, editor. *History of the Pequot War: The Contemporary Accounts of Mason, Underhill, Vincent, and Gardiner.* Cleveland: Helman-Taylor Co., 1897; Winthrop, John. *The Journal of John Winthrop, 1630–1649.* Edited by Richard S. Dunn, James Savage, and Laetitia Yeandle. Cambridge, Mass.: Harvard University Press, 1996.
— Kyle F. Zelner

United Colonies of New England   See NEW ENGLAND CONFEDERATION.

United States v. *Macedonian*   (25 October 1812)
Important frigate engagement of the War of 1812

In October 1812, Captain Stephen DECATUR and the large frigate *United States* (affectionately known as "Old Wagon"), carrying 44 guns, departed Boston in concert with the sloop *Argus.* Decatur's mission was to attack British shipping in and around the Canary Islands. On the morning of 25 October, he spotted a sail, which turned out to be the British frigate *Macedonian,* carrying 38 guns, under Captain John S. Carden.

Since the startling 19 August 1812 victory of U.S. frigate *Constitution* over British frigate *Guerriere,* which the Royal Navy dismissed as something of a fluke, the British had been eager to reassert their traditional superiority in single-ship engagements, despite common knowledge that the American vessels were much stouter and more heavily armed than British warships of the same class. Carden, a veteran commander and a fine sailor, cleared for action and approached to give battle.

By 9:00 A.M., both vessels had maneuvered into position and commenced a long-range duel with little effect. When Decatur perceived that his opponent was reluctant to close, he closed range and unleashed broadsides with his 24-pounder guns. Carden, whose ship mounted lighter 18-pounder ordnance, replied ineffectually at this range. The *Macedonian,* a crack ship, was slowly pounded by superior firepower. Within 30 minutes, Carden realized the hopelessness of his position and maneuvered his ship to close with the Americans. Decatur, alert to such a move, adroitly kept his distance and continued firing at his quarry. By 10:30 A.M., with the *Macedonian* a near-wreck and most of its starboard cannon out of commission, Carden struck his flag.

Decatur's victory was significant in being the second consecutive victory over the heretofore seemingly unbeatable Royal Navy. Damage to the *United States* was minor, but the British frigate was extensively injured in the hull, mainmast, and rigging. Worse, Carden lost 36 dead and 68 wounded out of a crew of 301. American losses amounted to 7 dead and 5 wounded. Decatur was determined to repair the *Macedonian* at sea and convey it home as a prize. The damaged ship was gingerly nursed toward New London, where it arrived on 4 December 1812, amidst public celebrations. The victory cemented Decatur's reputation as the nation's foremost naval hero, and he received a gold medal from Congress and $30,000 in prize money. The *Macedonian* was subsequently taken into active service—as a reminder of U.S. naval prowess—until decommissioned in 1828.

See also WAR OF 1812: NAVAL OVERVIEW.

Further reading: De Kay, James T. *Chronicles of the Frigate Macedonian, 1809–1922.* New York: W. W. Norton,

1995; Gardiner, Robert. *The Naval War of 1812.* Annapolis, Md.: Naval Institute Press, 1998.

— John C. Fredriksen

Upton, Emory (1839–1881) *U.S. Army officer, tactician, and military reformer*

Born on 27 August 1839 near Batavia, New York, Emory Upton was an ardent abolitionist who attended Oberlin College before graduating from the U.S. Military Academy, WEST POINT, in May 1861. Upton served with distinction in the Union forces throughout the Civil War, from 1862 onward commanding artillery, infantry, and cavalry in a variety of engagements, including the Battles of First BULL RUN/MANASSAS, Salem Church, GETTYSBURG, Rappahannock Station, SPOTTSYLVANIA COURTHOUSE, Opequon, and SELMA. At Selma, Alabama, he defeated forces under Confederate lieutenant general Nathan Bedford FORREST. Upton's undoubted courage and his military skills, particularly his 1864 organization of regiments in columns as opposed to a line frontal assault, won him commendations and promotion to brevet major general.

After the war Upton reverted to his permanent rank of captain, but in July 1866 he was appointed lieutenant colonel of the 25th Infantry Regiment. Upton quickly became one of the army's leading intellectuals and reformers, a protégé of William Conant Church, editor of the *Army and Navy Journal.* He spent 1866–67 instructing at West Point and working on his new manual, *Infantry Tactics* (1867), the first of three linked books whose successors, published in 1874 and 1875, respectively, covered cavalry and artillery tactics. For several decades these remained highly influential military training guides. Upton emphasized reliance upon open formations, forming soldiers into squads of four men; the three-battalion regiment; and employment of the rifled breechloader.

From 1870 to 1875, Upton was commandant of cadets at West Point. Commanding General of the Army William T. SHERMAN sent Upton on a yearlong world tour to inspect European and Asian armies. He returned an admirer of the German model of a strong standing army that would provide the nucleus and officer cadre around which, when war began, conscription and training—as opposed to the National Guard citizen-soldier model—rapidly could create a large and effective force. He also applauded the general staff system and its frequent rotation of officers between staff and line assignments. Upton expressed these views in *The Armies of Asia and Europe* (1878) and an influential manuscript work, *The Military Policy of the United States* (1904). Congress, reluctant to finance a substantial permanent army or affront the state organizations, largely ignored his recommendations.

Within the army, Upton's writings remained basic texts, and he became revered as the father of modern army organization and tactics, although some historians later criticized him for encouraging the United States military to disregard democratic values. In 1880, Colonel Upton took command of the 4th Artillery Regiment at the Presidio, San Francisco, where on 15 March 1881, plagued by agonizing headaches perhaps caused by depression, he committed suicide.

See also EDUCATION: HIGHER MILITARY SCHOOLS.

Further reading: Ambrose, Stephen E. *Upton and the Army.* Baton Rouge: Louisiana State University Press, 1964; Michie, Peter S. *The Life and Letters of Emory Upton, Colonel of the Fourth Regiment of Artillery, and Brevet Major-General, U.S. Army.* New York: Appleton, 1885; Reardon, Carol. *Soldiers and Scholars: The U.S. Army and the Uses of Military History, 1865–1920.* Lawrence: University Press of Kansas, 1990; Upton, Emory. *The Military Policy of the United States.* Washington, D.C.: Government Printing Office, 1904; Weigley, Russell F. *Towards an American Army: Military Thought from Washington to Marshall.* New York: Columbia University Press, 1962.

— Priscilla Roberts

Urban, Matt L. (1919–1995) *Medal of Honor winner in World War II*

Born 25 August 1919 in Buffalo, New York, Matt Louis Urban graduated from Cornell University in June 1941. Urban began active-duty army service as a volunteer in July 1941, reporting to the 60th Infantry Regiment, 9th Infantry Division, at Fort Bragg, North Carolina. During World War II, Urban advanced from platoon leader to battalion commander and from second lieutenant to lieutenant colonel. He participated in the invasion of North Africa (Operation TORCH) and fought in SICILY before participating in the NORMANDY INVASION.

During the period of 14 June to 3 September 1944, Captain Urban was involved in a series of actions in France. The citation for his Medal of Honor describes how, on 14 June, near Renouf, Urban, while leading a company of the 9th Infantry Division, encountered two German tanks. Picking up a BAZOOKA, he worked his way through heavy fire to the tanks and destroyed both. During the next 24 hours, Urban was wounded twice and evacuated to a hospital in England. A few weeks later, learning that his company was suffering heavy casualties, he left the hospital and returned to France. Urban found his unit under fierce German attack, taking cover behind an American tank, the gunner of which had been killed. Although wounded in the leg, Urban ran through enemy fire and mounted the tank. He ordered the tank forward and fired its machine gun on the Germans. His actions motivated the rest of the battalion, which then attacked and destroyed the German position.

Known as "the Ghost" because he left the battlefield badly wounded and returned soon afterward to lead his troops, Urban was wounded seven times in all during tours in Africa and Europe. He left the army in 1946 as a lieutenant colonel with 29 medals: seven Purple Hearts, two Bronze Stars, a Silver Star, and 18 other decorations. Urban, in fact, had as many medals as Audie MURPHY, another veteran of World War II.

The recommendation for the Medal of Honor was misplaced by the army when it was submitted in 1945. Urban inquired about it in 1978, and in July 1980 President Jimmy Carter presented the medal to him in Washington, D.C. After World War II, Urban was recreation director for the city of Holland, Michigan. He retired in 1989 and died on 4 March 1995, from complications related to his wartime wounds.

See also COBRA, OPERATION.

Further reading: Boven, Robert W. *Most Decorated Soldier in World War II: Matt Urban.* Victoria, British Columbia, Canada: Trafford, 2000; Urban, Matt, with Charles Conrad. *The Matt Urban Story.* Holland, Mich.: Matt Urban Story, Inc., 1989.

— John David Rausch, Jr.

Utah War (Mormon Expedition) (1857–1858)
Military expedition ordered by President James Buchanan and Secretary of War John B. Floyd to punish alleged resistance to federal authority by the Mormons led by Brigham Young, the first territorial governor of Utah

It is also known as the Mormon War, Mormon Expedition, or Utah Expedition. The Compromise of 1850 admitted California to the Union as a free state and established the territories of New Mexico and Utah without specification with respect to slavery. That year, President Millard Fillmore appointed Brigham Young, the religious and secular leader of the Mormons, as territorial governor and superintendent of Indian affairs.

In 1854, the Kansas-Nebraska Act granted the two territories popular sovereignty on the question of slavery. In an attempt to resist a popular vote on the extension of slavery into the territories, the newly created Republican Party associated the support for slavery with support for the Mormon practice of polygamy in the Utah Territory. The Democrats then felt obliged to denounce polygamy—and therefore the Mormons—in order to distance their support of slavery from the Mormon marriage practice.

Democrat James Buchanan won the presidential election of 1856. To show Southern extremists that Washington would not tolerate rebellion, he seized upon allegations by non-Mormon federal officials in Utah that Mormons, especially Governor Young, were defying federal authority. The allegations were in fact based upon personal animosities engendered by the federal appointees' often public antagonism toward Mormons and the Mormons' greater trust in and allegiance to their religious leaders, particularly Brigham Young.

In 1857, Buchanan decided to reinvoke federal control by appointing a new governor in Utah and, to insure no resistance to his installation, secretly ordered a military force sent there to guarantee it. General orders were issued on 28 May 1857 to assemble about 2,500 troops, including two artillery batteries, at Fort Leavenworth, Kansas, to be dispatched to Utah under the eventual command of Colonel Albert Sidney JOHNSTON. The troops began their westward march on 18 July 1857, proceeding over the Oregon Trail toward South Pass in present-day Wyoming. The first contingents of infantry and artillery, along with 100 wagons of provisions and supplies, arrived near the Green River in late September.

The Mormons, members of the Church of Jesus Christ of Latter-day Saints, had emigrated to the valley of the Great Salt Lake in 1847, after previously being driven out of New York, Ohio, Missouri, and Illinois by violent local mobs. (Those mobs often were supported by organized militias that in theory should have protected the Mormons.) In 1844, Mormon church founder and leader Joseph Smith had been murdered while being held in a county jail supposedly under the protection of Illinois militia. Under these circumstances, it is not surprising that the Mormons, when hearing reports of U.S. Army troops advancing on their settlements, feared for their safety.

The Mormons evacuated their homes in northern settlements, preparing to burn those homes and their businesses if the troops proved hostile. The Mormons also burned their own outposts of Fort Bridger and Fort Supply. On 5 October, they captured and burned two trains with a total of 52 freight wagons of army provisions east of Green River.

The army troops spent the severe winter of 1857–58 in the vicinity of Fort Bridger. There they experienced great difficulties in securing sufficient supplies, and follow-on contingents lost hundreds of horses to the weather, while beef cattle and oxen belonging to provision trains were lost to Mormon raids. There was little actual bloodshed, however.

On 19 November 1857, the newly appointed governor, Alfred Cummings, along with other new federal appointees, arrived in Johnston's camp. Aided by the mediation of Colonel Thomas Kane, a nonmember friend of the

Mormons, and against the advice of now Brevet Brigadier General Johnston, Cummings entered Salt Lake City in February 1858 without military escort. Upon Mormon acceptance of Cummings as governor, Johnston's forces peacefully entered Salt Lake City in June. They remained there until their recall after the beginning of the Civil War.

See also CIVIL WAR, CAUSES OF; DRAGOONS.

Further reading: Arrington, Leonard J. *Brigham Young: American Moses.* New York: Knopf, 1985; Furniss, Norman F. *The Mormon Conflict, 1850–1859.* New Haven, Conn.: Yale University Press, 1960; Long, E. B. *The Saints and the Union: Utah Territory During the Civil War.* Urbana: University of Illinois Press, 1981.

— Arthur T. Frame

Utrecht, Peace of (11 April 1713) *Peace settlement that concluded the 1701–14 War of the Spanish Succession, known in the colonies as Queen Anne's War*

In 1713, representatives of the warring powers met at Utrecht in the Netherlands to negotiate a settlement to conclude the War of the Spanish Succession. The European portion of the Peace of Utrecht brought several important changes: Philip V retained Spain and the Spanish overseas colonies in exchange for renouncing all rights to the French throne; Austria gained the Spanish Netherlands, Milan, Sardinia, and Naples; Savoy received Sicily (exchanged for Sardinia in 1721); England acquired Gibral-tar and Minorca; Prussia secured Upper Guelderland and recognition of its king's royal status; Bavaria was restored to Elector Maximilian, who also gained Mindelhelm; France had to dismantle privateer bases at Dunkerque; and the United Netherlands was allowed to build fortifications in the Austrian Netherlands.

The colonial portion of the settlement was equally important. France ceded Newfoundland, the West Indies island of Saint Kitts, and Acadia to its "ancient boundaries" (which the French interpreted as the peninsula of modern Nova Scotia); France recognized the rights of the Hudson's Bay Company and English suzerainty over the Iroquois; it also retained Cape Breton Island and fishing rights off Newfoundland, including the right to maintain unfortified fishing stations on the coast. Portugal received recognition of its control over Brazil and the Amazon Basin, which effectively restricted French Guiana; and Spain granted England the right of *asiento*—that is, the right to bring slaves to its colonies. Failure to resolve the precise borders of Acadia was the chief shortcoming of the treaty and would lead to future wars between Britain and France.

See also KING GEORGE'S WAR; QUEEN ANNE'S WAR.

Further reading: Craven, Wesley Frank. *The Colonies in Transition, 1660–1713.* New York: Harper & Row, 1968; Eccles, W. J. *France in America.* Revised ed. Markham, Ontario, Canada: Fitzhenry & Whiteside, 1990; Wolf, John B. *The Emergence of the Great Powers, 1685–1715.* New York: Harper & Row, 1951.

— Justin D. Murphy

V

Valcour Island, Battle of (11–13 October 1776) *The culminating event in the British expulsion of American military forces from the 1775–76 invasion of Canada during the American Revolutionary War*

By July 1776, the British liberation of CANADA was complete and British governor Sir Guy Carleton was prepared to invade northern New York by way of Lake Champlain. The British advance was slowed, however, by the presence of a small American fleet on the lake. The result was a three-month arms race at either end of the lake as both the British and the Americans hastily built ships and gunboats in an effort to control the lake.

By early October, both fleets were ready for action. They clashed near Valcour Island on 11 October in the first of two engagements. The American squadron, under Brigadier General Benedict ARNOLD, was smaller and possessed fewer guns than the British fleet. Arnold knew the British could outgun him on the open lake, so he anchored his ships in a defensive arc near a narrow inlet on the western side of the island. The British fleet was forced to tack into a contrary wind in order to engage Arnold's defensive line, and the larger vessels struggled for most of the day to get into the action. In the interim, Arnold's smaller but more maneuverable vessels pounded the British during the early stages of the battle. By midafternoon, however, the larger British vessels, including the three-masted frigate *Inflexible*, came within range of Arnold's anchorage and unleashed a devastating cannonade. Two of Arnold's ships went down, and his own flagship, the galley *Congress*, and two other vessels were damaged severely.

Darkness brought a cessation of hostilities and allowed Arnold to engineer a daring escape by his 13 remaining vessels, slipping past the British fleet during the night. The majority of the next 36 hours were spent in flight from the British fleet, which on 13 October finally caught Arnold halfway down the lake, near Split Rock. The ensuing battle was entirely one-sided, as the British punished Arnold's limping squadron on the open lake. Nearly half of the American fleet broke off from the battle in the early going and set course up the lake toward FORT TICONDEROGA. Arnold remained behind with a handful of vessels and fought a determined delaying action, allowing the remainder to escape. The British forced several of Arnold's remaining warships to strike their colors, but Arnold grounded his own vessel along the eastern shore and escaped with his crew overland to the fort.

A military defeat for the Americans, the battle was in reality a strategic victory. The naval contest for Lake Champlain delayed the British until the season was too far advanced to sustain a long-term invasion. Unwilling to commit to a winter siege of Fort Ticonderoga, Carleton withdrew his army to Montreal, leaving his subordinate, Major General John Burgoyne, to renew the invasion in 1777. The result was the American victory at SARATOGA.

See also AMERICAN REVOLUTIONARY WAR: LAND OVERVIEW.

Further reading: Fowler, Richard M. *Rebels under Sail: The American Navy During the Revolution.* New York: Scribner's, 1976; Martin, James Kirby. *Benedict Arnold: Revolutionary Hero.* New York: New York University Press, 1997.

— Daniel P. Barr

Valley Forge (December 1777–June 1778) *Winter encampment for the Continental army during 1777–78*

At the end of British major general William Howe's 1777 Pennsylvania campaign, on 19 December CONTINENTAL ARMY commander General GEORGE WASHINGTON withdrew his army of some 9,000 men to Valley Forge. Its location, some 20 miles from Philadelphia and the British camp, gave Washington the means to maneuver and also allowed him to protect his main supply routes. Although there was some skirmishing between the two armies during the winter, the main task confronting the Continental army was the struggle simply to survive.

At first there were only tents as shelter; Washington set the example by remaining in his own tent until the men were housed in crude huts, some 800 of which were constructed. Weeks passed with no meat, and fuel was in short supply. In part this was because of the inefficiency of the commissariat services, but it was also because the individual states failed to get provisions to the camp, and many individual merchants preferred to sell their goods to the British in Philadelphia instead.

Valley Forge was important to the Continental army in another sense. In early 1778, Frederick Wilhelm August Hendrik Ferdinand, the self-styled Baron von STEUBEN, arrived. He volunteered to serve as drillmaster to the Continental army. Soon known simply as "the Baron," von Steuben had served during the Seven Years' War as a captain on the personal staff of Frederick the Great, which did not keep him from representing himself to the Americans as a lieutenant general. Steuben was exceptionably able, and Washington soon appointed him inspector general of the Continental army. Steuben immediately began to organize, discipline, and train the army. This was immensely important, because after Valley Forge, the Continentals fought on equal terms with British army regulars in the open field.

The Americans departed Valley Forge on 19 June 1778, in pursuit of British forces, now under Lieutenant General Henry Clinton, who had evacuated Philadelphia. The experience of Valley Forge was critical for the Continental army. It emerged from the encampment well trained and disciplined, ready to perform well in battle. Although the suffering at Valley Forge was deeply engrained in the American psyche, the winter encampment of 1779–80 at Morristown, New Jersey, was actually worse.

See also AMERICAN REVOLUTIONARY WAR: LAND OVERVIEW.

Further reading: Reed, John F. *Valley Forge: Crucible of Victory.* Monmouth Beach, N.J.: Philip Freneau Press, 1969; Stoudt, John T. *Ordeal at Valley Forge: A Day-By-Day Chronicle from December 17, 1777 to June 18, 1778.* Philadelphia: University of Pennsylvania Press, 1963.
— Spencer C. Tucker

Vandegrift, Alexander A. (1887–1973) *U.S. Marine Corps general and commandant*

Born on 13 March 1887 in Charlottesville, Virginia, Alexander Archer VANDEGRIFT attended the University of Virginia from 1906 to 1908. He joined the Marine Corps in 1908 and was commissioned a 2d lieutenant in 1909. In 1910 he was assigned to marine barracks at Portsmouth Navy Yard, New Hampshire. During the next four years he served in Panama and Nicaragua, and at VERACRUZ, Mexico. In 1915, Vandegrift was sent to Haiti, where he was part of the Haitian Constabulary (1916–18 and 1919–23). He did not see action in World War I.

Following his second tour with the Haitian Constabulary, Vandegrift served in various staff jobs at Quantico (1923–26). He was with the marine expeditionary force in China (1927–28) and held various postings in Washington and Quantico (1928–35). Vandegrift returned to China in 1935 to command the marine guard at the Peking (Beijing) embassy.

In 1937 Vandegrift returned to Washington as secretary and later assistant commandant for Marine Corps commandant Lieutenant General Thomas HOLCOMB. Promoted to brigadier general in 1940, he became assistant commander of the 1st Marine Division in November 1941. After the United States entered World War II, he was promoted to major general in March 1942 and took command of the division.

Vandegrift commanded the 1st Marine Division in the Battle of GUADALCANAL, landing with his division there in August 1942. For the next four months, Vandegrift and his men fought off Japanese attempts to recapture Henderson Field. The battle was marked by a lack of adequate logistical and naval support, and there were command disputes between Vandegrift and Rear Admiral Richmond K. TURNER. Relieved in December, Vandegrift and his division went to Australia to rest and refit. His inspirational leadership on Guadalcanal earned him both the Navy Cross and the Medal of Honor. Vandegrift then assumed command of I Corps for the November 1943 invasion of Bouganville. In January 1944, Vandegrift took over from General Holcomb as commandant. In April 1945, Vandegrift was promoted to full general—the first active-duty marine officer to attain that rank.

After the war, Vandegrift oversaw the demobilization of the corps and fought to preserve its existence during efforts to unify the armed forces. Vandegrift retired from active duty in December 1947. He died in Bethesda, Maryland, on 5 May 1973.

See also LATIN AMERICA INTERVENTIONS, EARLY 20TH CENTURY; MARINE CORPS, U.S.; SOLOMON ISLANDS CAMPAIGN; WORLD WAR II, COURSE OF U.S. INVOLVEMENT: PACIFIC THEATER.

Further reading: Asprey, Robert B., and Alexander Archer Vandegrift. *Once a Marine: The Memoirs of General A. A. Vandegrift.* New York: W. W. Norton, 1964; Foster, John. *Guadalcanal General: The Story of A. A. Vandegrift, USMC.* New York: William Morrow, 1966.
— Trevor K. Plante

Vandenberg, Hoyt S. (1899–1954) *U.S. Army Air Force and U.S. air force general and chief of staff*

Born on 24 January 1899 in Milwaukee, Wisconsin, the nephew of future U.S. senator Arthur H. Vandenberg, whose political influence probably smoothed his career, Hoyt Sanford Vandenberg graduated from the U.S. Military Academy, WEST POINT, in 1923 and immediately joined the Army Air Service. Selected in October 1927 as a flight instructor, until 1939 he rotated between teaching and taking advanced flying and staff courses.

In 1939, Vandenberg joined the Plans Division under Chief of the Army Air Corps and Brigadier General Henry H. ARNOLD. His excellent staff work in directing the rapid air force expansion at the beginning of World War II won him promotion to colonel in 1942. In summer 1942, Vandenberg moved to Britain to help Major General Carl A. SPAATZ and Brigadier General James H. DOOLITTLE plan and provide air support for the forthcoming North African invasion. Promoted to brigadier general that December, Vandenberg accompanied Doolittle to Northwest Africa as his chief of staff, flying 26 combat missions, and attended the 1943 Quebec, Tehran, and Cairo conferences. After helping General Dwight D. EISENHOWER to plan the NORMANDY INVASION, in August 1944 Vandenberg took command of Ninth Air Force, with more than 4,000 aircraft, winning high praise from his colleagues for his skill in providing tactical support to Allied ground forces throughout the West European theater. He won promotion to major general in March 1945.

Following staff appointments in Washington, in 1946 Vandenberg became director of the Central Intelligence Group, the forerunner of the CENTRAL INTELLIGENCE AGENCY (CIA), substantially expanding and centralizing its activities and laying the groundwork for further such developments.

Made full general in October 1947, he became the newly independent air force's vice chief of staff; six months later, Vandenberg succeeded Spaatz as chief of staff. Almost immediately the air force faced the BERLIN BLOCKADE crisis, sustaining a massive airlift to keep West Berlin supplied. Vandenberg sought a 70-group air force, but President Harry S. TRUMAN's stringent budgetary policies initially restricted him to 55 or fewer. Vandenberg concentrated resources on developing strategic air offensive capabilities, ably presenting air force views in the heated 1949 controversy over the navy's strategic deterrent role, and strongly supporting development of the hydrogen bomb. When the KOREAN WAR began in June 1950, the U.S. Air Force quickly achieved air superiority, providing effective support to United Nations ground forces. War also brought the expansion Vandenberg had long advocated, doubling the air force to 106 wings, although he furiously protested the decision to defer for several years after his June 1953 retirement a promised further increase to his ideal 143 wings. He died in Washington, D.C., on 2 April 1954. His ceaseless efforts to build up the air force effectively ensured the United States a strategic striking strength far surpassing that of any other nation.

See also COLD WAR; CONTAINMENT; NUCLEAR AND ATOMIC WEAPONS; STRATEGIC AIR COMMAND; STRATEGIC BOMBING; TORCH, OPERATION.

Further reading: Meilinger, Phillip S. *Hoyt S. Vandenberg: The Life of a General.* Bloomington: Indiana University Press, 1989; Parrish, Noel F. "Hoyt S. Vandenberg: Building the New Air Force," in *Makers of the United States Air Force.* Edited by John L. Frisbee. Washington, D.C.: Office of Air Force History, United States Air Force, 1987: 205–228.

— Priscilla Roberts

Van Fleet, James A. (1892–1992) *U.S. Army general*
Born on 19 March 1892 in Coytesville, New Jersey, James Alward Van Fleet graduated from the U.S. Military Academy, WEST POINT, in 1915. He saw service in the 1916–17 MEXICAN PUNITIVE EXPEDITION and in World War I, fighting with the AMERICAN EXPEDITIONARY FORCE in the MEUSE-ARGONNE OFFENSIVE. Between the wars he served in the infantry and as an instructor.

In 1941 Van Fleet, now a colonel, took command of the 8th Infantry Regiment of the 4th Infantry Division, directing its assault on Utah Beach in the WORLD WAR II 1944 NORMANDY INVASION. Promoted first to brigadier and then to major general, during the drive against Germany, Van Fleet led various divisions in heavy fighting at Metz, in the ARDENNES, at Remagen, and in the Ruhr and Austria.

After the war, Van Fleet served in the United States and Germany. In February 1948, promoted to lieutenant general, he led the Athens-based Joint U.S. Military and Planning Group, advising the Greek government in fighting Communist insurgents. Appointed to the Greek National Council, for two years Van Fleet directed the training and employment of Greek military forces in that civil war.

In April 1951, Van Fleet took command of Eighth Army in Korea when General Matthew B. RIDGWAY replaced General of the Army Douglas MACARTHUR as commander of the United Nations forces. For much of 1951 his troops saw fierce fighting, driving north in mid-1951 and again after peace talks stalled from August to October. Thereafter, Van Fleet was restricted to maintaining frontline defensive positions as the war became largely one of attrition and trench warfare.

Van Fleet, notoriously a fighting general, grew increasingly frustrated when superiors repeatedly turned down his plans for major offensives, although in mid-1952 his forceful protests eventually persuaded them to authorize limited smaller operations against Communist positions, assaults that yielded little advantage. He was known for his use of massive artillery fire. Van Fleet devoted much effort to reforming, rebuilding, and strengthening the demoralized Republic of Korea forces, who by late 1952 comprised almost three quarters of his frontline troops. In 1952, his only son and namesake was lost in air combat.

In February 1953, shortly before the armistice, Van Fleet turned over Eighth Army to Lieutenant General Maxwell D. TAYLOR. He resigned in April 1953. The following month, he published articles echoing MacArthur's asseverations that, had vacillating and indecisive political leaders uncompromisingly exercised unrestrained American power, they could have achieved total victory in 1951, charges that delighted Republican critics but infuriated Ridgway, Taylor, and army chief of staff General J. Lawton COLLINS.

In 1954 Van Fleet served as President Dwight D. EISENHOWER's special envoy to the Far East, and as a Defense Department consultant in the early 1960s suggested that Adlai Stevenson's failure to defend the botched BAY OF PIGS invasion required his dismissal as his country's United Nations representative. Van Fleet died in Washington, D.C., on 23 September 1992. An inspiring battlefield commander, he was somewhat deficient in broader diplomatic skills.

See also BLOODY RIDGE, BATTLE OF; COLD WAR; CONTAINMENT; HEARTBREAK RIDGE, BATTLE OF.

Further reading: Braim, Paul F. *The Will to Win: The Life of Gen. James A. Van Fleet.* Annapolis, Md.: Naval Institute Press, 2001; Cole, Hugh M. *The United States Army in World War II: The Lorraine Campaign.* Washington, D.C.: Government Printing Office, 1950; Hermes, Walter G. *The United States Army in the Korean War: Truce Tent and Fighting Front.* Washington, D.C.: Government Printing Office, 1966; MacDonald, Charles B. *The United States Army in World War II: The Last Offensive.* Washington, D.C.: Government Printing Office, 1973.

— Priscilla Roberts

Van Rensselaer, Stephen (1764–1839) *U.S. militia general*

Born on 1 November 1794 in New York City into a prominent Dutch-American family, Stephen Van Rensselaer lost his father at age five and was reared by his grandfather, Philip Livingston. Graduating from Harvard in 1782, the following year he married Margaret Schuyler, the daughter of Major General Philip SCHUYLER, and began to exercise control over a vast fortune.

Van Rensselaer entered politics in 1789, when he was elected to the New York Assembly. He served in the New York Senate from 1791 to 1795 and was lieutenant governor from 1795 to 1801. After an unsuccessful bid for the governorship of New York in 1801, he returned to the state

assembly. A man of means, he was also active in the state militia, rising to the rank of major general in 1812.

Although he had no actual military experience at the beginning of the War of 1812, Van Rensselaer was given charge of defending northern New York against British attack. He set up his headquarters at Lewiston and by October 1812 had put together a force of 6,000 men. His troops lacked discipline, training, equipment, and experienced leadership, and did not comprise a force capable of offensive action. To make matters worse, Van Rensselaer was unable to obtain the support of Brigadier General Alexander Smyth, who commanded 1,600 regulars at nearby Buffalo and refused his requests for assistance. Only Lieutenant Colonel Winfield SCOTT, commanding one of the regular regiments, answered his appeals.

Under pressure from his superiors in Albany and convinced that his own force would evaporate with the onset of winter, Van Rensselaer decided to undertake an invasion of Upper Canada, ordering his men across the Niagara to attack Queenstown on 13 October 1812. The initial force of 600 men was led by Colonel Solomon Van Rensselaer, a kinsman, and Captain John E. WOOL, the HEIGHTS senior regular army officer present. As the Battle of Queenstown developed, more troops were committed, and Winfield Scott assumed command. However, when the fighting became more intense and casualties mounted, the remaining militia troops refused to cross the river, and American forces in Canada (almost 900 men) were forced to surrender.

After the defeat at Queenstown, Van Rensselaer resigned from the service and returned to his political career. He again ran unsuccessfully for governor in 1813, then served in the House of Representatives from 1822 to 1829 and cast the deciding vote in the New York delegation for John Quincy Adams in the disputed election of 1824. He served on the Erie Canal Commission and founded Rensselaer Polytechnic Institute. Van Rensselaer died in Albany, New York, on 26 January 1839.

See also WAR OF 1812: LAND OVERVIEW.

Further reading: Adams, Henry. *History of the United States During the Administration of James Madison.* Vol. 6. New York: Albert & Charles Boni, 1930; Berton, Pierre. *The Invasion of Canada, 1812–1813.* Boston: Little, Brown, 1980; Hickey, Donald R. *The War of the 1812: A Forgotten Conflict.* Urbana: University of Illinois Press, 1985; Mahon, John K. *The War of 1812.* Gainesville: University Press of Florida, 1972.

— J. W. Thacker

Vaught, Wilma (1930–) *U.S. Air Force general*

Born on 15 March 1930 in Pontiac, Michigan, Wilma Vaught earned a B.S. degree in business from the University of

Illinois. She joined the air force in 1957 and advanced rapidly as a comptroller, distinguishing herself at various posts. In 1966 she was the first woman to deploy operationally with a STRATEGIC AIR COMMAND bombardment wing, and in 1972 she became the first female air force officer to attend the Industrial College of the Armed Forces. In 1980 she was promoted to brigadier general. She retired from the air force in 1985.

In 1986, President Ronald Reagan signed legislation creating the Women in Military Service for America (WIMSA) Memorial Foundation; the foundation was charged with designing, raising funds for, and building a memorial honoring WOMEN IN THE MILITARY. A few months later Vaught was elected its president. The memorial, located at the main gate at Arlington National Cemetery, was dedicated in October 1997. It includes a museum and theater. Also located there is the computerized registry being compiled by the foundation of the nearly 2 million women who have served in the nation's armed forces.

Further reading: Vaught, Wilma. *The Day the Nation Said Thanks.* Washington, D.C.: Military Women's Press, 1999.

— Jean Ebbert

Vaux, Battle of (1 July 1918) *World War I*
engagement in the Château Thierry/Belleau Wood series of battles

A German offensive launched on 27 May 1918 had broken the Allied lines and advanced to Château Thierry, 60 miles from Paris. The Allies committed their reserves, including American units, and by 3 June had brought the German attack to a halt. Counterattacks by the U.S. 2d Division, which consisted of the 4th Marine Brigade and 3d Army Brigade, began on 6 June. By the 25th, the marines had driven the Germans from Belleau Wood, while the 3d Brigade, under Brigadier General Edward Lewis, had advanced toward the village of Vaux, about two miles to the southeast. Lewis's troops entrenched west of the village and carried out patrol actions. During the night of 23–24 June, the brigade suffered more than 400 casualties in a gas shell bombardment.

The German lines around Vaux formed a wedge protruding into the 3d Brigade's front. On 25 June, the French III Corps, under which 2d Division was operating, ordered the capture of Vaux to straighten the lines and acquire stronger defensive positions on the high ground east of the town.

Vaux, consisting of 82 stone buildings, had been abandoned by its 250 inhabitants. Through ground and aerial observation, prisoner interrogations, and reports from refugees, U.S. officers were able to plot the village and its

defenses in detail, which greatly aided the attack. Vaux and the surrounding area were held by the German 402d Regiment, supported by machine guns, mortars, and artillery. The defenders were partially entrenched but had not completed work on their positions. The plan of attack called for 2d Battalion of 9th Infantry Regiment to advance on Vaux from the southwest while 3d Battalion, 23d Infantry Regiment, moved from the east.

At 5:00 A.M. on 1 July, artillery preparation began. It continued throughout the day; by afternoon, Vaux had been reduced to rubble. The bombardment peaked at 5:00 P.M. as the infantry moved into attack position. German artillery fire, which had been sporadic during most of the day, became heavy from 4:00 to 5:30 P.M., especially in the 9th Infantry sector.

Just before 6:00 P.M., Allied artillery opened a rolling barrage, and moments later the American infantry advanced behind the wave of shellfire with drill-ground precision. Some Germans fought from Vaux's cellars, and machine gun fire slowed the Americans on the right, but the bombardment had broken the defenders into isolated groups, and resistance was quickly overcome. Within one hour the town had been cleared of Germans and the important high ground beyond it was taken in what AMERICAN EXPEDITIONARY FORCE (AEF) commander General John PERSHING termed "a brilliantly executed operation." A supporting French attack on the American right, however, had been halted after a short advance. In the predawn hours of 2 July, German reserves counterattacked but were easily repulsed.

German casualties in the battle were approximately 300 killed and more than 600 captured; American casualties were fewer than 200. Over the next several days, the 2d Division consolidated its position, but made no further advance. On 9 July it was relieved by the U.S. 26th Division.

See also CHÂTEAU THIERRY/BELLEAU WOOD, BATTLES OF; WORLD WAR I, COURSE OF U.S. INVOLVEMENT.

Further reading: Coffman, Edward M. *The War to End All Wars: The American Military Experience in World War I.* Lexington: University Press of Kentucky, 1998; Spaulding, Oliver L., and John W. Wright. *The Second Division, American Expeditionary Force in France, 1917–1919.* New York: Hillman Press for the Second Division Association, 1937.

— Jim Piecuch

Veracruz, landing at and siege of (9–27 March 1847) *Amphibious landing by U.S. forces at Veracruz, Mexico, during the MEXICAN-AMERICAN WAR*

Although early American successes in New Mexico and California were important for the United States in the conflict, the two primary campaigns of the war were Major General Zachary TAYLOR's effort in northern Mexico and Major General Winfield SCOTT's campaign in central Mexico from Veracruz to Mexico City. Taylor's victories in the north, including the Battle of BUENA VISTA in February 1847, proved of little strategic importance, since they failed to induce Mexico to talk peace.

Scott, meanwhile, wrote a strategic plan to end the war, and he persuaded President James K. POLK to let him command the army that would carry it out. This plan, developed in cooperation with U.S. Gulf of Mexico commander Commodore David Conner, called for opening a second front by an amphibious invasion of Mexico's largest port, Veracruz, followed by an overland campaign to take Mexico City. Scott then drew off troops from Taylor's forces in the north and from units in the United States to form a new army. He gathered this force from the mouth of the Rio Grande south to Tampico, and he used Lobos Island, between Veracruz and Tampico, as the final staging base for the Veracruz invasion.

Veracruz was a formidable objective. A wall with nine strong points for cannon surrounded the city. Stretched out for a mile along the coast in front of the city, another thick wall was anchored on each end by a large fort. Commodore Conner's reports convinced Scott that Veracruz was well defended and that the Mexicans would vigorously resist an invasion. The city of 15,000 inhabitants also housed 3,000 well-supplied Mexican troops. The defenders had set thick clusters of prickly pear in front of the city wall and had dug a line of *trous de loup*, conical holes with sharpened stakes, to impale soldiers landing on the beach. Besides the defensive forces within the city walls, on the seaward side of Veracruz loomed a colonial-era fort, San Juan de Ulúa, with its 100 guns manned by 1,000 defenders. Scott noted that the fort "had the capacity to sink the entire American navy."

Rather than risk a costly assault on the Mexicans' main defensive positions, Scott planned to land his army several miles below Veracruz on Collado Beach. For the largest U.S. amphibious landing prior to the North African invasion in World War II, Scott ordered specially built boats to move his assault force from the large naval ships to the beach. A total of 141 of these flat-bottomed, double-ended, broad-beamed rowboats (called "surfboats" at the time) were built for the assault; each could load approximately 40 soldiers and would have a crew of eight sailors with a naval officer in charge.

On 9 March 1847, the U.S. Navy, supporting the operation with gunfire, landed more than 10,000 troops at Collado, without a single casualty. The Mexican defenders decided to remain within their fortified positions and await an assault.

After the landing, Scott opted for a siege of Veracruz. His staff argued against it, fearful that the longer the troops stayed in the lowlands around Veracruz, the greater the chances would be for them to contract yellow fever. But Scott held firm. He feared that an assault would be a bloodbath for both sides and result in the loss of anywhere from 2,000 to 3,000 attackers.

Supported by heavy naval guns brought ashore by Commodore Matthew C. PERRY, who had replaced Conner on the day of the invasion, and by gunfire from the ship of the line *Ohio*, Scott's force encircled Veracruz and began the siege. On 25 March, Mexican division general Juan Morales slipped out of Veracruz by sea, turning over his command to Brigade General Juan José Landero.

On 27 March, Landero surrendered the city; the Americans occupied Veracruz the next day. Mexican casualties were somewhere between 200 and 1,000. Scott lost 13 killed and 55 wounded. The city of Veracruz then served as a vital resupply port and base for U.S. forces throughout the remainder of the war. U.S. forces finally evacuated Veracruz on 1 August 1848, several months after the Treaty of GUADALUPE HIDALGO ended the war.

See also MEXICAN-AMERICAN WAR, COURSE OF.

Further reading: Bauer, K. Jack. *Surfboats and Horse Marines: U.S. Naval Operations in the Mexican War, 1846–48.* Annapolis, Md.: Naval Institute Press, 1969; Eisenhower, John S. D. *Agent of Destiny: The Life and Times of General Winfield Scott.* New York: Free Press, 1997.

— Paul Coe Clark, Jr.

Veracruz, occupation of (21 April–23 November 1914)   *U.S. military seizure of Mexico's principal port* The administration of President Woodrow WILSON, in an attempt to promote democracy in Mexico, developed a policy of coercion to remove General Victoriano Huerta from the presidency. Huerta had come to power in February 1913 through the overthrow and assassination of President Francisco Madero. The Wilson administration was considering military intervention when an incident at the Mexican oil center of Tampico in April 1914—the brief detention of a small group of U.S. sailors—led Wilson to ask Congress for permission to use military force to obtain redress. Before Congress responded, the administration learned that a German ship bearing military supplies for Huerta was about to land at Veracruz. The president ordered U.S. forces to seize the customs house and dock facilities to prevent its arrival. Wilson believed that there would not be any substantial opposition to the landing and that many Mexicans actually would welcome intervention as a way of getting rid of Huerta.

With only three hours to plan and launch the intervention, on 21 April 1914, the initial U.S. landing party of

787 officers and men came ashore and quickly gained control of the customs house and docks. Most of Huerta's troops had been withdrawn from Veracruz, leaving the city defended primarily by the municipal militia and some local citizens using army weapons. Fighting soon began, with U.S. forces suffering four killed and 20 wounded on the first day. The unexpected resistance by Mexican forces and the absence of any Mexican officials with whom to deal led to a major change in U.S. plans. The original goal of confining the intervention to dock area was expanded to include occupation of the entire city. More troops came ashore, bringing the total to 6,000 by the end of the second day. In fewer than 48 hours, the occupation of Veracruz was complete.

Total U.S. losses in the invasion and occupation were 19 killed and 71 wounded. There was never an accurate count of Mexican casualties, primarily because the tropical climate required that the bodies be rapidly burned. There were probably at least 200 Mexicans killed and another 300 wounded; most of the Mexican casualties were noncombatant civilians, accidentally killed in the house-to-house fighting.

Given Mexico's experience with foreign invasions in the 19th century, Mexican federal law provided for harsh punishment for any official cooperating with a foreign invader. As a result, Mexican officials refused to cooperate in the administration of the city, and Rear Admiral Frank F. Fletcher had to declare martial law, with U.S. officers assuming all government functions. To support the occupation, Washington sent an infantry brigade under Brigadier General Frederick FUNSTON, who assumed overall command of operations at Veracruz.

President Wilson had earlier linked the end of the occupation with the removal of Huerta, but the occupation continued after Huerta resigned on 15 July 1914. With Huerta out, various revolutionary factions contended for power. Wilson still wanted to influence the course of political events in Mexico. In addition, American forces controlled a large supply of seized military supplies in Veracruz, so the decision to relinquish control of the city would have an important effect on who would rule the country. In September, the Wilson administration indicated to the government of Venustiano Carranza in Mexico City that U.S. forces would be withdrawn, but this plan stalled over U.S. concerns about what would happen to the few local citizens who had cooperated with the occupation. Under growing political and military pressure himself, Carranza on 9 November issued a blanket amnesty for all Mexicans who had served the occupation government. The entire American force of some 7,000 troops was evacuated on 23 November 1914.

See also PUNITIVE EXPEDITION INTO MEXICO; ZIMMERMANN TELEGRAM.

Further reading: Eisenhower, John S. D. *Intervention: The United States and the Mexican Revolution, 1913–1917.* New York: W. W. Norton, 1993; Quirk, Robert E. *An Affair of Honor: Woodrow Wilson and the Occupation of Veracruz.* New York: W. W. Norton, 1967; Sweetman, Jack. *The Landing at Veracruz: 1914.* Annapolis, Md.: Naval Institute Press, 1987.

— Don M. Coerver

Vicksburg, campaign and siege of (19 May–4 July 1863) *Decisive Civil War campaign that gave the Union control of the Mississippi River*

Union successes in early 1862 gave the North control of the entire length of the Mississippi River except for the fortified hilltop town of Vicksburg, Mississippi. Confederate resurgence in late summer and fall 1862 bolstered the town and added a bastion downstream at PORT HUDSON, Louisiana, giving the South control of the intervening stretch of river. Major General Ulysses S. GRANT's late fall campaign foundered on the twin facts that it was impossible to take Vicksburg from the north and that it seemed equally impossible to get at Vicksburg from any other direction. In January 1863, Grant encamped his Army of the Tennessee on the Louisiana shore just upstream from Vicksburg and began a series of unsuccessful schemes to get around Vicksburg with the aid of Rear Admiral David Dixon PORTER's naval flotilla, using various networks of creeks and bayous.

Undaunted, Grant and Porter adopted an audacious scheme. The naval flotilla ran the Vicksburg batteries with minimal damage on 16 April 1863. Grant's army marched down the Louisiana shore, and the navy ferried it to the east bank below Vicksburg on 30 April. While Grant used a daring cavalry raid to keep Confederate Lieutenant General John C. PEMBERTON confused, the bulk of Grant's army marched boldly northeastward toward Jackson, Mississippi, living partially off the land while swatting aside feeble Confederate resistance in the Battles of Grand Gulf and Raymond.

Jackson fell on 14 May. Grant's men destroyed whatever facilities the town offered as a Confederate base, then turned westward to face the still befuddled Pemberton. The latter's superior, Confederate theater commander General Joseph E. JOHNSTON, ordered Pemberton to advance from fortress Vicksburg and cut Grant's tenuous supply line. Grant, however, was privy to Confederate counsels thanks to a Union spy, and moved to thwart Pemberton's hesitant sortie. The armies collided on 16 May in the Battle of CHAMPION'S HILL, in which Grant was triumphant.

The following day, Pemberton attempted to hold the east bank of the crossing of Big Black River midway

The capture of Vicksburg, Mississippi, 4 July 1863. Lithograph, Currier & Ives   *(Library of Congress)*

between Jackson and Vicksburg in hopes that one of his divisions severed in the previous day's rout might rejoin him there. In fact, the division had slunk off to join a force under Johnston lurking east of Jackson. Grant's army arrived at Big Black Bridge and pitched into Pemberton without ceremony, routing him again. The Confederates fled all the way to the Vicksburg defenses.

Grant followed the next day and, eager to maintain momentum, assaulted the city on 19 May. With insufficient reconnaissance and preparation, the attack failed. On 22 May, Grant tried again; once again, the Confederates stopped him, this time inflicting high casualties.

Grant now settled in for a siege. Union skirmishers constantly sniped the Confederate lines, keeping the defenders' heads down, while heavy siege guns and mortars, including those of the fleet in the river, pounded the town and Rebel lines day after day. Night after night, Union troops pressed their saps and trenches closer to the Confederates, until by the beginning of July only a dozen yards or fewer separated the foes in many places. The Confederates responded as their dwindling stock of ammunition allowed. Food also became scarce in Vicksburg. The garrison was soon reduced to a diet of mule meat and other unsavory dishes, while the citizens lived in caves they had dug in the hard clay hillsides to escape the constant bombardment.

Two days' march to the east, Johnston hovered with an army of reinforcements sent by Richmond to lift the siege of Vicksburg; but Grant, also reinforced, countered with a heavily manned line of eastward-facing defenses, and Johnston, despite the desperate urging of Confederate authorities, never attempted to relieve the beleaguered garrison.

On 3 July Pemberton requested terms. After negotiations, he succeeded in getting something better than the unconditional surrender terms that had been Grant's trademark since FORT DONELSON. At 10:00 A.M. on 4 July, Vicksburg formally surrendered. Although the Confederacy lost no time in violating the parole Grant allowed the garrison—many of the 20,000 men who surrendered would later oppose him at CHATTANOOGA—the impact was nevertheless enormous. The first consequence was the surrender, five days later, of Port Hudson to other Union forces. The Mississippi was now entirely in Union hands and open to the commerce of the Midwest. The Confederacy was cut off from the produce and troops (if any could be had) of Louisiana, Arkansas, and Texas. Above all,

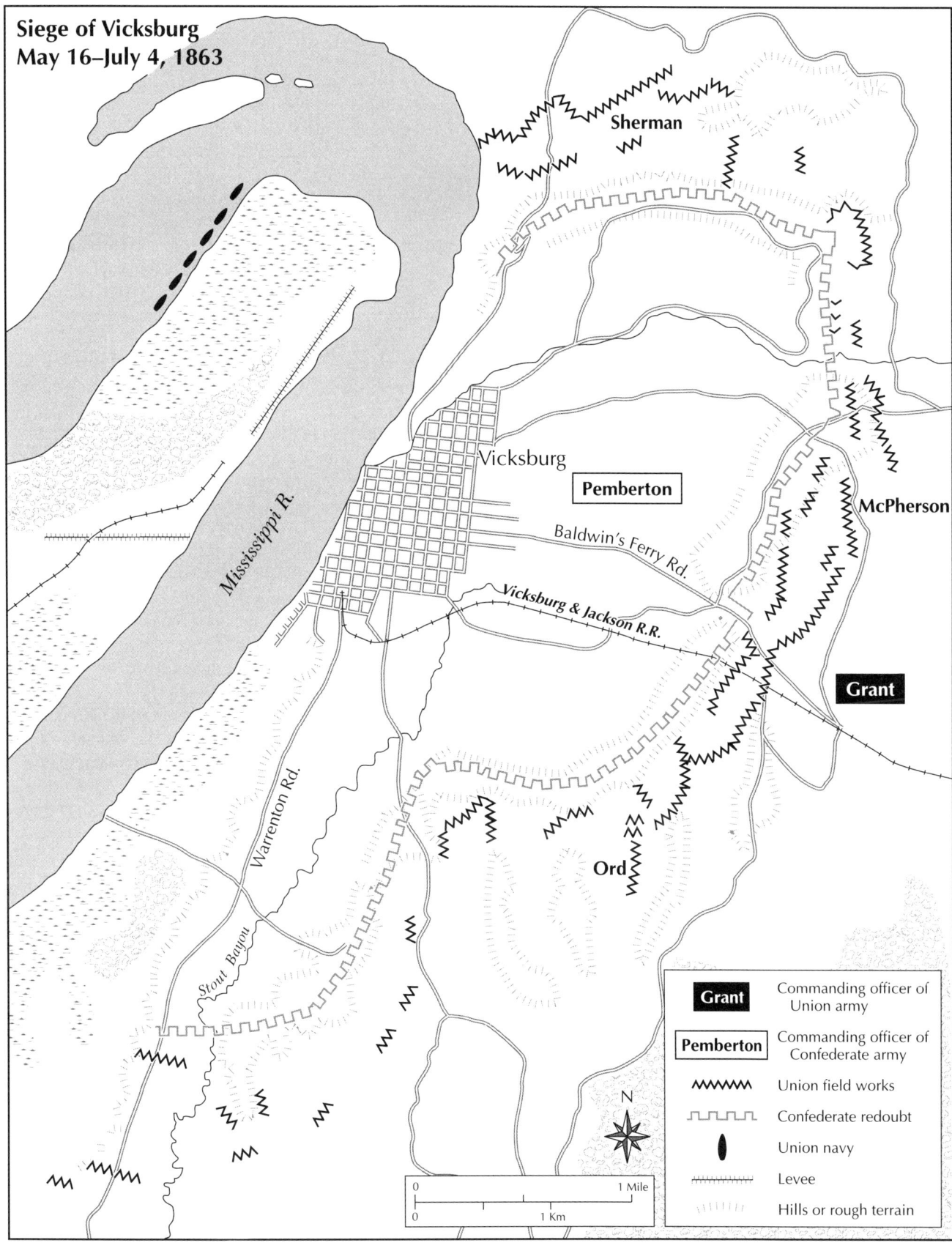

Siege of Vicksburg
May 16–July 4, 1863

Sherman

Mississippi R.

Vicksburg

Pemberton

Baldwin's Ferry Rd.

McPherson

Vicksburg & Jackson R.R.

Grant

Warrenton Rd.

Ord

Stout Bayou

N

Grant	Commanding officer of Union army
Pemberton	Commanding officer of Confederate army
⋀⋀⋀⋀⋀	Union field works
⊓⊓⊓⊓⊓	Confederate redoubt
●	Union navy
┼┼┼┼┼	Levee
⋮⋮⋮⋮⋮	Hills or rough terrain

0   1 Mile
0   1 Km

Northern morale was greatly strengthened and that of the South correspondingly depressed, especially as the loss of Vicksburg came in the wake of Union victory and Confederate defeat at GETTYSBURG. The Union now held a major advantage in the war.

See also CIVIL WAR: LAND OVERVIEW; GRIERSON, BENJAMIN H.

Further reading: Arnold, James R. *Grant Wins the War: Decision at Vicksburg.* New York: Wiley, 1997; Ballard, Michael B. *Pemberton: A Biography.* Jackson: University Press of Mississippi, 1991; Bearss, Edwin C. *The Vicksburg Campaign.* 3 vols. Dayton, Ohio: Morningside, 1995; Winschel, Terrence J., ed. *Triumph and Defeat: The Vicksburg Campaign.* Campbell, Calif.: Savas, 1998; Winschel, Terrence J. *Vicksburg: Fall of the Confederate Gibraltar.* Abilene, Tex.: McWhiney Foundation, 1999.

— Steven E. Woodworth

Vietnam War, causes of

The United States first became interested in Vietnam in the mid-19th century, when Washington became wary of French threats to U.S. interests in China. Later, President Woodrow WILSON's World War I call for the "self-determination of peoples" resonated strongly in Vietnam, and the failure of France to grant meaningful concessions there led to a rebellion, easily crushed by the colonial administration. Removal of the moderates, however, opened the door to the more radical Indochinese Communist Party (ICP) led by Ho Chi Minh, which then assumed the role of chief opponent to the French. Many Vietnamese supported the Communists because they were first and foremost anti-French.

Ironically, the United States got into World War II in December 1941 partly because of Vietnam. In 1940 the Japanese established bases in northern Indochina to halt aid to China. In early 1941 they moved into southern Indochina, which put them within bomber range of the Philippines. President Franklin D. ROOSEVELT responded by freezing Japanese assets and placing an embargo on oil and scrap metal to Japan. Tokyo's response was the Attack on PEARL HARBOR.

In May 1941, meanwhile, Ho Chi Minh had formed an umbrella resistance group, the Vietminh, to fight both the Japanese and French, whom the Japanese left in nominal control. With U.S. entry into the war, the OFFICE OF STRATEGIC SERVICES (OSS), forerunner of the CENTRAL INTELLIGENCE AGENCY (CIA), sent agents into Vietnam. These men helped to train the Vietminh, which cooperated with the Allies, and they assured Ho that the United States would support him in the quest for independence.

In March 1945, the French planned a coup against the Japanese in Vietnam. The Japanese moved first, arresting the French. Thus, there was a power vacuum in Vietnam when, at the end of the war, Japan declared its former colonies independent. In Vietnam, Tokyo recognized a government under Emperor Bao Dai. Meanwhile, acting under provisions of the Potsdam Conference, the British took the Japanese surrender south of the 17th parallel; the Chinese accepted the Japanese surrender north of it.

In this power vacuum, Ho proclaimed the independence of the Democratic Republic of Vietnam (DRV). In a bid for U.S. support, the declaration of independence began with the words of the American Declaration of Independence. Meanwhile, the British commander in southern Vietnam, on his own authority, released the French from Japanese prison camps and allowed them to take control there.

In March 1946, the French and Ho concluded an agreement, in which Paris recognized the DRV as independent and agreed to a future plebiscite to determine whether Vietnam would be one state. In return, Ho allowed some French troops back into the north to protect European lives and property there. This arrangement might have worked but for the incredibly poor foresight of the French governor-general of Indochina, Thierry d'Argenlieu. He proclaimed the independence of the south and in November 1946 ordered military action in the northern port city of Haiphong. This touched off the so-called 1946–54 Indochina War.

In the war the United States supported the French, at first haltingly and then enthusiastically. The Asian desk of the State Department strongly supported Vietnamese independence, but the European desk pointed out the critical importance of France. With the onset of the COLD WAR, Washington believed that the Soviet Union was poised to take over Europe, and France was the only continental European military power of any weight. The price of French support in Europe was U.S. support for the French in Vietnam.

In September 1949, the Communists come to power in China. In June 1950, war began in Korea, and China entered that conflict in October. Paris then convinced Washington that Indochina and Korea were interdependent fronts in the struggle against communism. Yet, once the Communists had come to power in China, the war in Indochina was for all intents and purposes lost to the French as the Chinese offered equipment and base areas for the Vietminh along their long common border.

To win popular support in Washington and in France for an increasingly unpopular war, Paris responded with the fiction that it had created an independent state in Vietnam under Bao Dai and that it was a matter of democracy versus communism. Washington chose to believe this lie. Vietnamese nationalists did not, and they joined the Vietminh.

By the early 1950s, the United States was paying 80 percent of the cost of the war. In May 1954, France lost the great Battle of Dien Bien Phu. There was talk at the time of U.S. military intervention—among its most ardent advocates was Vice President Richard NIXON—but President Dwight D. EISENHOWER rejected the French pleas.

The scene then switched to discussions already planned for Geneva to discuss a range of colonial issues. In July 1954 the conferees, with the United States an observer, agreed that Vietnam was one independent state, temporarily divided at the 17th parallel. Vietminh armed forces would be regrouped into the North and French forces into the South. Elections were to be held in 1956 throughout Vietnam.

In 1954 Emperor Bao Dai, then living in France, selected Ngo Dinh Diem, a Catholic nationalist, as premier in the South. In 1955, when the two men quarreled, Diem staged a plebiscite, which he won handily and used as justification to become president of a new Republic of Vietnam. Washington backed Diem and supplied him massive economic assistance. Secure in U.S. support, Diem refused to enter into talks with the DRV concerning the elections, which Washington believed the Communists would win. The refusal to hold these elections was a direct violation of the Geneva Convention and the reason for the renewal of the war, initiated by Vietminh political cadres in the South, by 1959.

Initially the U.S. military was active in an advisory capacity only. Under President John F. KENNEDY at the end of 1961, however, Washington sharply escalated the number of advisers and increased military aid for several reasons: the CONTAINMENT doctrine; the domino theory, the belief that all South Asia would be threatened if communism triumphed in Vietnam; U.S. national prestige; and domestic U.S. political considerations, including recent foreign policy setbacks for the Kennedy administration.

After the assassinations of both Diem and Kennedy in late 1963, the conflict continued to escalate. Kennedy's successor, Lyndon B. JOHNSON, was determined not to be the first U.S. president to lose a major war. The irony here is that Johnson wanted to end U.S. involvement, and in fact tried to fight the war on the cheap in order to save his cherished Great Society domestic programs. In 1965, sensing victory, Hanoi sent native northerners south, introduced new weapons, and attacked American facilities directly. Johnson responded by sending the marines and then army combat troops, and he authorized air strikes against the North. The war had escalated in a way neither side anticipated, let alone wanted.

See also VIETNAM WAR, COURSE OF.

Further reading: Mann, Robert. *A Grand Delusion: America's Descent into Vietnam.* New York: Basic Books, 2000; Spector, Ronald H. *The U.S. Army in Vietnam. Advice and Support: The Early Years, 1941–1960.* Washington, D.C.: Center of Military History, U.S. Army, 1985; Tucker, Spencer C. *Vietnam.* Lexington: University Press of Kentucky, 1999.

— Spencer C. Tucker

Vietnam War, course of (1955–1975)

The American war in Vietnam is best understood by dividing it into three phases: the advisory phase, 1955–64; the Americanization phase, 1965–68; and the Vietnamization phase, 1969–75.

The Vietnam War grew out of the COLD WAR, Asian nationalism, and U.S. domestic politics. Vietnam's geography and terrain influenced the application of military strategy and the conduct of operations. To the north, Vietnam shares a border with the People's Republic of China, which made possible direct Chinese intervention in the war. In geopolitical terms, this was the same situation that caused a stalemate in the 1950–53 KOREAN WAR. Without a much larger war it would be impossible to stop the flow of military equipment and supplies into North Vietnam. To the west, Vietnam shared extensive borders with Laos and Cambodia. The length of these made them almost impossible to close. Cambodia and Laos also provided Communist insurgents with sanctuaries. U.S. forces could not enter these states without expanding the war. Geographic circumstances and the desire of American presidents to fight a limited war confined to the borders of South Vietnam eliminated exhaustion and annihilation strategies, leaving only attrition strategy.

The Advisory Phase

In 1955, Ngo Dinh Diem became president of South Vietnam. He rejected the Geneva agreement and refused to allow the nationwide election it required. Fearful that North Vietnamese leader Ho Chi Minh would win the elections and that all Vietnam would become Communist, President Dwight D. EISENHOWER supported this stance. His administration now provided direct aid and military assistance to the RVN. In 1956, the U.S. formed the Military Assistance and Advisory Group (MAAG) in the RVN. Then, in the late 1950s, a Communist insurgency began in the South. The insurgency was designed to undermine and eventually overthrow the government of the RVN, reunifying the country. Its weapons were politicalization, persuasion, intimidation, threats, terrorism, and murder. The insurgents came to be known by the pejorative "Vietcong" (Vietnamese Communists, VC). In 1959 the DRV began development of the Ho Chi Minh Trail. Operating from North Vietnam through eastern Laos into South Vietnam, it provided direct support to the insurgency in the South.

Vietnam War, 1965–1972

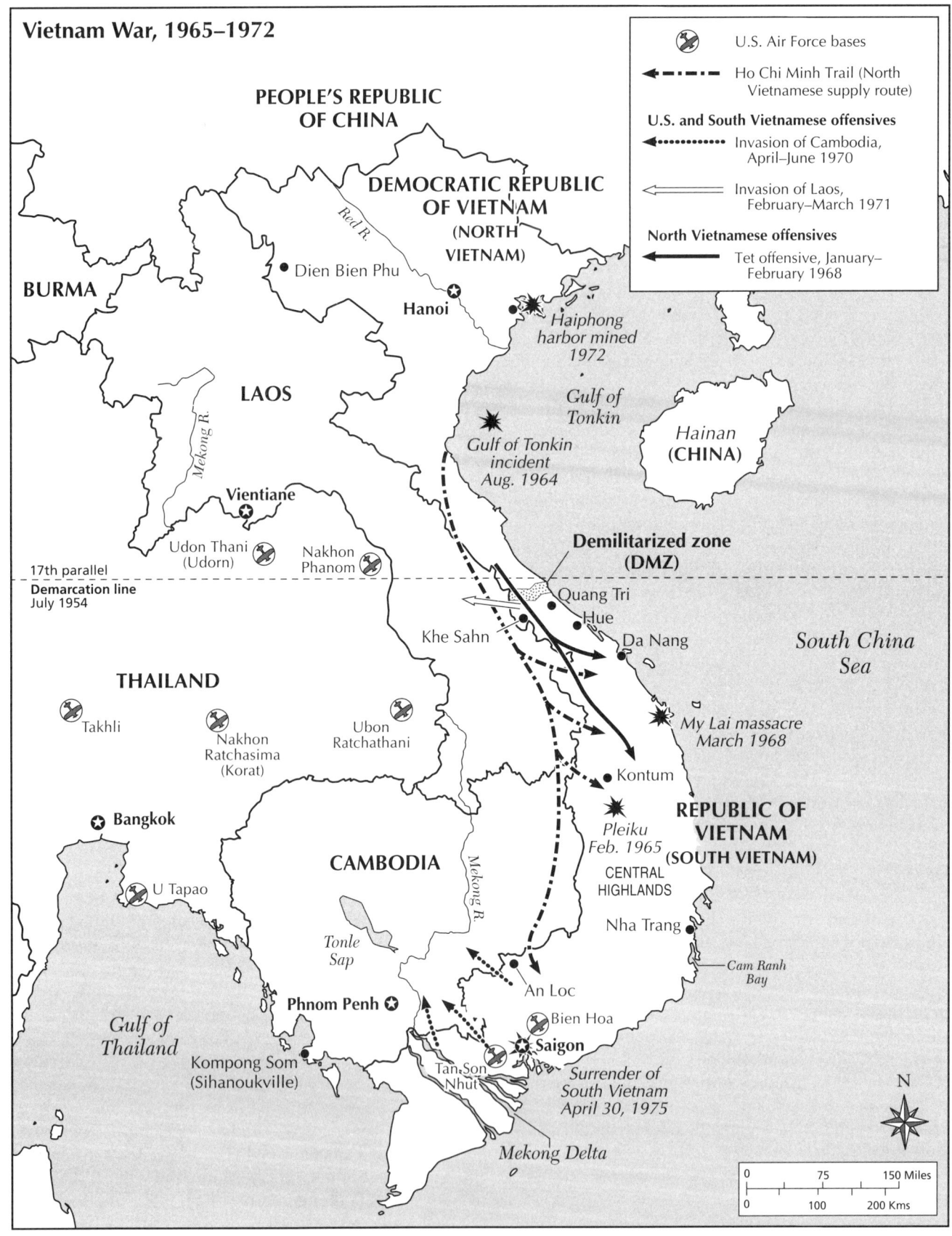

U.S. Air Force bases

Ho Chi Minh Trail (North Vietnamese supply route)

U.S. and South Vietnamese offensives

Invasion of Cambodia, April–June 1970

Invasion of Laos, February–March 1971

North Vietnamese offensives

Tet offensive, January–February 1968

PEOPLE'S REPUBLIC OF CHINA

DEMOCRATIC REPUBLIC OF VIETNAM (NORTH VIETNAM)

Red R.

Dien Bien Phu

BURMA

Hanoi

Haiphong harbor mined 1972

LAOS

Gulf of Tonkin

Hainan (CHINA)

Mekong R.

Gulf of Tonkin incident Aug. 1964

Vientiane

Udon Thani (Udorn)

Nakhon Phanom

17th parallel

Demarcation line July 1954

Demilitarized zone (DMZ)

Quang Tri

Hue

THAILAND

Khe Sahn

Da Nang

South China Sea

Takhli

Nakhon Ratchasima (Korat)

Ubon Ratchathani

My Lai massacre March 1968

Bangkok

CAMBODIA

Kontum

REPUBLIC OF VIETNAM (SOUTH VIETNAM)

Pleiku Feb. 1965

CENTRAL HIGHLANDS

Mekong R.

Nha Trang

U Tapao

Tonle Sap

Cam Ranh Bay

Gulf of Thailand

Phnom Penh

An Loc

Bien Hoa

Kompong Som (Sihanoukville)

Tan Son Nhut

Saigon

Surrender of South Vietnam April 30, 1975

Mekong Delta

N

| 0 | 75 | 150 Miles |

| 0 | 100 | 200 Kms |

Bell UH-1B Iroquois (Huey) gunship flying with Navy Light Attack Helicopter Squadron 4 (HAL-4) in support of Navy riverine operations in South Vietnam.   *(San Diego Aerospace Museum)*

The National Liberation Front (NLF) came into being in 1960. Completely dominated by the DRV, it led, organized, and coordinated the insurgency.

In 1960 John F. KENNEDY was elected president of the United States. He appointed Robert McNAMARA secretary of defense and Dean Rusk secretary of state. The Kennedy administration, like those of Harry S. TRUMAN and Eisenhower before it, continued the CONTAINMENT policy and committed the United States to support the war in Vietnam. It, however, adopted a new strategic military doctrine known as FLEXIBLE RESPONSE, under which the United States developed and expanded its ability to conduct limited wars. The size of the army was increased; new technologies, such as the helicopter, were advanced; and counterinsurgency doctrine was developed.

In 1961, Kennedy sent two advisers, General Maxwell TAYLOR and Walt Rostow, to Vietnam to assess the situation. They concluded that the situation was deteriorating and recommended a large increase in American advisers and an expanded role for the U.S. military in combating the insurgency. In 1962, U.S. advisers increased from 700 to 1,200, and the Military Assistance Command, Vietnam (MACV) was established.

Increasing tension between the United States and the USSR precluded Kennedy from deescalating in Vietnam. Soviet leader Nikita Khrushchev committed the USSR to support communist insurgencies in developing countries and created a crisis over Berlin that threatened to erupt into war. And, for political reasons, Kennedy could not appear "soft" on communism.

Elements of the 3d Brigade, 82d Airborne Division on a search-and-destroy mission in the village of Thon Vuong Pham, south of Hue   *(U.S. Army Military History Institute)*

In November 1963, disloyal South Vietnamese generals who had the approval of the Kennedy administration assassinated President Diem. Twenty days later, Kennedy was assassinated and Lyndon B. JOHNSON became president. He retained Kennedy's cabinet and foreign policy. By the end of 1963, the United States had more than 15,000 servicemen in Vietnam and had expended some $500 million in aid.

In 1964 the situation continued to deteriorate. Communist control in South Vietnam was expanding. Then, on 2 August, North Vietnamese torpedo boats attacked the U.S. destroyer *Maddox*, which was involved in intelligence-gathering activities in the Gulf of Tonkin. In an alleged second incident, on 4 August, the torpedo boats were thought to have attacked the *Maddox* and another destroyer, the *Turner Joy*. The second incident probably never took place. Nevertheless, these TONKIN GULF INCIDENTS caused

Johnson to retaliate with bombing and seek congressional approval for military operations in Vietnam. The resulting TONKIN GULF RESOLUTION passed Congress with overwhelming support, empowering the president to "take all necessary measures to repel an armed attack against the forces of the United States and prevent further aggression." In November Johnson easily won reelection.

The Americanization Phase

Late in 1964 and early in 1965, the VC initiated a series of attacks against U.S. installations and personnel. Johnson's advisers recommended retaliation. In March, Operation ROLLING THUNDER, an air campaign against North Vietnam, commenced. It sought to halt the infiltration of men and material into South Vietnam and to convince Hanoi that it could not win. McNamara and his advisers believed that by "graduated pressure" the DRV could be convinced of American resolve and superiority and that some breaking point would be reached whereby the North would seek a negotiated settlement favorable to Washington and Saigon. To protect American air bases, marine combat units were deployed to Vietnam.

Hanoi also sent regular Peoples Army of Vietnam (PAVN, North Vietnamese Army, NVA) units south; by early 1965, three PAVN regiments were operating in the RVN. As the tempo of the war increased, so did the number of American combat forces. U.S. Army divisions followed the marines. In October 1965, the 1st Cavalry Division, an air mobile division that rode into battle in helicopters, fought regular regiments of the PAVN in the Battle of the IA DRANG VALLEY. Although both sides sustained heavy losses, the kill ratio was 10 to 1 in the U.S. favor. MACV commander General William C. WESTMORELAND reasoned that such battles would bleed the Communist side to death. His operational approach was the "search and

destroy" mission, in which large units would search out enemy forces and engage them in battle, resulting in a "protracted war of attrition."

PAVN leader General Vo Nguyen Giap learned from the Ia Drang battle. He recognized that he lacked the firepower to engage the U.S. forces in head-to-head contests and that other tactics had to be developed. The PAVN was lighter and faster than U.S. forces, and it was usually able to avoid battles on American terms. Nonetheless, by the end of 1967 the United States had 485,000 military personnel in Vietnam, and Westmoreland was predicting victory. Westmoreland was not much interested in the "other war," the pacification program designed to win the loyal support of the people of the RVN, the battle for the "hearts and minds" of the Vietnamese people. He emphasized ground combat operations.

In 1967, the Communist leadership again decided to escalate. It planned a major offensive designed to bring the war to a decisive end. Its January 1968 TET OFFENSIVE

Lieutenant Colonel John Paul Vann reviews an operational plan with Republic of Vietnam (ARVN) officers.   *(Department of Defense)*

The Vietnam War was sometimes called the first helicopter war. Here a Bell CH-47A Chinook transports a badly damaged UH-1 over South Vietnam. Note the gunner manning an M-60 machine gun on the Chinook's tail ramp.

was the turning point of the war. Tactically and operationally it was a major victory for the United States and RVN, in which half the Communist fighters involved were casualties. The Communists had also failed in their major objective: winning the South Vietnamese people to their side. However, politically and strategically, it proved a major defeat for the United States. Although the U.S. Army and the Army of the RVN (ARVN) fought well and quickly restored the situation, the early Communist victories, including fighting in Saigon and bloody battles for Hue, belied Westmoreland's earlier optimistic reports. Many Americans concluded that the government was lying to them and that the war could not be won. Opposition to the draft fueled the antiwar mood in the United States.

Vietnamization Phase

The final phase of the war began in 1968. Clark Clifford replaced McNamara as secretary of defense. Tasked by Johnson to study options and consider the Pentagon's request for additional troops to Vietnam, he concluded that the war could not be won and undertook a campaign to convince the president of this. The Tet Offensive, in con-

cert with domestic fallout over the assassinations of Dr. Martin Luther King, Jr., and Senator Robert Kennedy, the Civil Rights movement, and the antiwar/antidraft protests, shook Johnson's confidence, and he decided not to run for a second term. Belatedly, during the fall presidential campaign he announced a halt to the bombing of North Vietnam. General Creighton ABRAMS replaced Westmoreland as MACV commander in July, and in November, Republican Richard M. NIXON was elected president. At the end of the year, U.S. troop strength in South Vietnam stood at 536,100 personnel.

Taking office in January 1969, President Nixon appointed Melvin LAIRD as secretary of defense, William Rogers as secretary of state, and Henry KISSINGER as National Security Advisor. Nixon expanded the policy adopted at the end of the Johnson administration of turning more of the fighting over to the South Vietnamese. Known as "Vietnamization," it increased the size and capabilities of the ARVN and gradually withdrew U.S. ground forces. Nixon intensified the bombing campaign and entered into secret negotiations with the North Vietnamese. He also ordered secret B-52 bombing of Cambodia and later sent U.S. ground troops into that country, all to buy time for Vietnamization. But these actions intensified the antiwar movement in the United States. By December 1970, U.S. troop strength had declined to 334,600. In January 1973, following an intense bombing campaign of North Vietnam (LINEBACKER II), the United States, RVN, NLF, and DRV signed the PARIS PEACE ACCORDS and American prisoners of war started coming home. U.S. casualties amounted to 47,244 killed in action, and 10,446 deaths from other causes. Another 153,329 received serious wounds. During the same period, 15.4 million middle- and upper-class American men successfully evaded the draft. The burden of fighting the war fell disproportionately on lower-class Americans. Early in 1973, Nixon also ended the military draft.

The war continued in South Vietnam, and the RVN government requested the military assistance promised by Nixon and Kissinger during the peace negotiations. But the Watergate scandal paralyzed the administration and Nixon resigned. His successor, Gerald R. Ford, was unable to secure congressional assistance for America's ally. In April 1975, the RVN fell to PAVN forces. During the Vietnam War, RVN armed forces lost at least 110,357 killed in action and 400,026 wounded. Hanoi has announced that 1,100,000 Communist fighters lost their lives and another 600,000 were wounded during the period 1954–75. It has given civilian deaths at more than 2,000,000 over the same time period.

See also AIR FORCE, U.S.; ARMY, U.S.; CASUALTIES IN U.S. WARS; KHE SANH, BATTLE OF; LINEBACKER I; NAVY, U.S.; MARINES, U.S.; VIETNAM WAR, CAUSES OF U.S. INVOLVEMENT.

Further reading: Andrade, Dale. *America's Last Vietnam Battle: Halting Hanoi's 1972 Easter Offensive.* Lawrence: University Press of Kansas, 2001; Clarke, Jeffrey J. *Advice and Support: The Final Years, 1965–1973. The U.S. Army in Vietnam.* Washington, D.C.: Center of Military History, 1988; Davidson, Philip B. *Vietnam at War: The History, 1946–1975.* New York: Oxford University Press, 1988; Herring, George C. *America's Longest War: The United States and Vietnam, 1950–1975.* 3d ed. New York: McGraw-Hill, 1996; Karnow, Stanley. *Vietnam: A History.* New York: Penguin Books, 1984; Spector, Ronald H. *After Tet: The Bloodiest Year in Vietnam.* New York: Free Press, 1993; Tucker, Spencer C. *Vietnam.* Lexington: University Press of Kentucky, 1999.

— Adrian R. Lewis

Vincennes, Battle of (23–25 February 1779)
American Revolutionary War battle

In 1778, Lieutenant Colonel George Rogers CLARK led a small force of Virginians into Illinois Territory, capturing several British posts and French settlements and swaying French settlers to the American cause. Clark also met with Native-American leaders and gained pledges of peace from many of them, thus upsetting Britain's war strategy. British Lieutenant Governor Henry "Hair Buyer" Hamilton, so named for his rumored offer of bounties for rebel scalps, now feared a threat to the tenuous link between Detroit and Quebec and sought to reestablish British hegemony in the West.

Leading a force of British regulars, Canadian militia, and northern Indians, Hamilton moved into the Illinois country in late 1778, captured Fort Sackville at Vincennes, and laid plans for a spring offensive against Clark and the American settlements in the West.

Realizing his likely fate should he delay, Clark resolved to take Vincennes while much of Hamilton's force was away preparing for spring planting. Vincennes, a French-settled town and fort on the Wabash River in present Indiana, was held by only 33 British regulars and 50 militiamen. Clark sent an armed row galley with some 40 or 50 men and artillery by water, while he and the bulk of his men marched overland. The two forces would then rendezvous near Vincennes before attacking.

On 5 February 1779, Clark departed Kaskaskia, near Saint Louis, with 172 Virginians and French volunteers to march the 180 miles to Vincennes. The difficult winter march was compounded by flooded rivers, which left broad plains of chest-deep water. Clark's overland force reached Vincennes on the 23rd. Although the galley and its artillery had not arrived, Clark resolved to attack before Hamilton discovered his presence.

Invading Vincennes at dark, Clark's force immediately invested the fort and brought it under a withering fire.

Hamilton initially believed the firing to be the drunken carousal of locals, but soon realized his mistake. Despite their superiority in artillery, the British defenders were driven from loopholes and cannon ports by furious American fire, which continued late into the night, wounding seven of Hamilton's men.

At dawn on the 24th, Clark demanded the unconditional surrender of Fort Sackville. Hamilton refused and vowed to fight to the last. However, his French militiamen lost heart as they witnessed local French inhabitants join the American attackers. Hamilton weakened further as the Americans coldly executed four pro-British Indians in view of the defenders. Fearing such an end for himself, Hamilton negotiated further and surrendered on 25 February.

Suffering only a single casualty, Clark had achieved a significant coup. While the capture of Vincennes did not secure the West for the Americans, the capture of Hamilton and the apparent British inability to protect their Indian allies prompted many Indians to desert the British, even if temporarily. This delayed British strategic plans for more than a year. Clark's victory also bolstered the morale of American settlers and encouraged others to move west, increasing the American presence there sufficiently to withstand the fighting to come.

See also AMERICAN REVOLUTIONARY WAR: LAND OVERVIEW.

Further reading: Rankine, Hugh F. *George Rogers Clark and the Winning of the West.* Richmond: Virginia Independence Bicentennial Commission, 1976; Skaggs, David Curtis, ed. *The Old Northwest in the American Revolution: An Anthology.* Madison: State Historical Society of Wisconsin, 1977.

— David M. Carload

Virginia, CSS   *Confederate navy ironclad that engaged USS MONITOR in the first battle between ironclad ships in history*

Constructed at the dry dock at the Norfolk (Gosport) Naval Yard, Virginia, on the hull of the scuttled and burned U.S. Navy steam frigate *Merrimack,* the *Virginia* measured $263' \times 51' \times 22'$ (draft). The *Virginia's* 195'-long casemate was built of 20 inches of pine and four inches of oak, then covered with two layers of two-inch-thick iron plate fashioned from railroad track hammered at the Tredegar Iron Works of Richmond. The casemate's sides and ends were angled at 35 degrees to deflect projectiles. The *Virginia's* design was the collaborative effort of Lieutenant John M. BROOKE, Chief Engineer William P. Williamson, and Naval Constructor John L. Porter.

The *Virginia's* two engines delivered a total of 1,200 horsepower through one propeller. Its maximum speed was

CSS *Virginia* fitting out in the drydock at the Norfolk Navy Yard, early 1862.   *(Naval Historical Foundation).*

nine knots. The crew complement was 320 men, and it mounted six nine-inch Dahlgren smoothbore guns and two 6.4-inch Brooke rifles in broadsides and a seven-inch Brooke rifle on a pivot mount at each end, for a total of 10 guns. The *Virginia* also mounted an underwater four-foot ram at its bow.

Commissioned on 17 February 1862, the *Virginia* was captained by Flag Officer Franklin BUCHANAN, who was determined to attack the Union blockading fleet at Hampton Roads. The *Virginia* sortied on 8 March and sank the Union sloop *Cumberland* and the frigate *Congress*. The next day it sortied again, under Lieutenant Catesby ap Roger JONES, and fought an inconclusive duel with the *Monitor*. Too deep in draft to be gotten up the James, the *Virginia* was subsequently scuttled near Craney Island on 11 May 1862 to prevent capture.

See also CIVIL WAR, NAVAL OVERVIEW; IRONCLADS, CONFEDERATE IN CIVIL WAR; MALLORY, STEPHEN; *MONITOR V. VIRGINIA*.

Further reading: Flanders, Alan B. *The Merrimac: The Story of the Conversion of the USS Merrimac into the Con-* *federate Ironclad Warship, CSS Virginia*. Portsmouth, Va.: A. B. Flanders, 1982; Stern, Philip Van Doren. *Confederate Navy: A Pictorial History*. New York: Da Capo Press, 1992; Tucker, Spencer C. *A Short History of the Civil War at Sea*. Wilmington, Del.: Scholarly Resources, 2001.

— A. J. L. Waskey

Voorhees, Tracy S. (1890–1974) *Undersecretary of the army*

Born on 30 June 1890 at New Brunswick, New Jersey, Tracy Stebbins Voorhees earned degrees from Rutgers University and Columbia Law School. During World War I he served as assistant to the director of the War Trade Board's Bureau of Imports. From 1919 until 1942 Voorhees practiced law in New York.

In 1942, after the United States entered World War II, Voorhees joined the army with the rank of colonel. Throughout the war he was assigned to the Surgeon General's Office, as director of its legal and control divisions. In 1947 Voorhees became administrator of food relief for occupied areas, Germany, Japan, and Korea.

In June 1948 Voorhees was appointed assistant secretary of the army, serving on a committee that determined overall American policy toward Germany. (It was increasingly clear that Germany would remain divided indefinitely.) In August 1949 he rose to undersecretary. Voorhees's staunch support for the massive increases in defense spending recommended in the 1950 policy planning paper NSC-68 put him at odds with his superior, Secretary of Defense Louis JOHNSON, and he resigned in 1950.

As a private citizen, Voorhees continued to campaign publicly for enhanced defense spending. In 1950 he joined former Secretary of War Robert P. PATTERSON and Harvard president James B. Conant in establishing the Committee on the Present Danger (to lobby for the implementation of major increases in defense spending). From 1951 to 1953 Voorhees was vice chairman of the CPD. The KOREAN WAR, which began in June 1950, greatly facilitated its efforts.

An unwavering anticommunist, who as a Rutgers University trustee defended the institution's decision to fire several faculty members suspected of Communist affiliations, in the mid-1950s Voorhees served as the president's personal representative for Hungarian Refugee Affairs and as chairman of the President's Committee for Hungarian Refugee Relief. In the late 1950s Voorhees helped to found the Committee to Strengthen the Frontiers of Freedom, which demanded implementation of the 1958 Gaither Report's recommendations for greatly enhanced American defense budgets. Voorhees died at Sugar Hill, New Hampshire, on 25 September 1974.

See also COLD WAR; CONTAINMENT, DOCTRINE AND COURSE OF; MILITARY-INDUSTRIAL COMPLEX.

Further reading: Rearden, Steven L. *History of the Office of the Secretary of Defense.* Vol. 1. *The Formative Years, 1947–1950.* Washington, D.C.: Historical Office, Office of the Secretary of Defense, 1984; Sanders, Gerry W. *Peddlers of Crisis: The Committee on the Present Danger and the Politics of Containment.* Boston: South End Press, 1983.

— Priscilla Roberts

Vought, Chance M. (1890–1930) *U.S. aviation pioneer and aircraft designer*

Born on 26 February 1888 on Long Island, New York, Chance Milton Vought attended public schools and then studied engineering at both the Pratt Institute and New York University, although he did not receive a degree from either school.

Vought studied aeronautical engineering with Orville and Wilbur WRIGHT and then worked with Harold F. McCormick as a consulting engineer and pilot in 1910. In 1912 he attended the U.S. Army training school at Fort Sam Houston, Texas, and received his pilot's license. That same year he became consulting engineer for the Aero Club of Illinois. In 1913, Vought was aeronautical engineer and pilot at the Lille School of Aviation. In August 1914, he became the editor of *Aero and Hydro*, an aviation trade journal.

During the initial stages of World War I, Vought worked for the Mayo Company, building and designing a military aircraft. He was chief engineer of the Wright Company and eventually became chief engineer for the Wright-Martin Aircraft Company. While in this position, he designed and constructed the PLV biplane, the Simplex flying boat, the Wright Model V military plane, and the Wright-Hispano flying boat.

With U.S. entry into the war in April 1917, Vought worked as a consulting engineer for the government's Bureau of Aircraft Production. After the war, he founded the Lewis & Vought Corporation. Vought's company eventually developed for the navy the F4U Corsair, one of the finest fighters and ground support aircraft ever built. Vought was the director and vice president of the United Aircraft and Transport Corporation, which was a merger of his company along with Pratt & Whitney, Boeing Company, and Boeing Airlines. Vought died on Long Island on 25 July 1930.

See also AIRCRAFT, FIXED WING.

Further reading: Fredriksen, John C. *Warbirds: An Illustrated Guide to U.S. Military Aircraft, 1915–2001.* Santa Barbara: ABC-Clio, 1999; Moran, Gerard P. *Aeroplanes Vought, 1917–1977.* Temple City, Calif.: Historical Aviation Album, 1978.

— Joseph M. Williams

W

Wabash, Battle of   See ST. CLAIR'S EXPEDITION.

Waesche, Russell R. (1886–1946) *U.S. Coast Guard officer and commandant*

Born on 6 January 1886 in Thurmont, Maryland, Russell Randolph Waesche attended Purdue University in 1903 for one year to study Electrical Engineering, then attended the U.S. Revenue Cutter Service School of Instruction. On graduation in 1906 he was commissioned an ensign. Over the next decade Waesche was stationed in the North Atlantic, on the Great Lakes, and in the Pacific Northwest.

In 1915 the Revenue Cutter Service merged with the Life Saving Service to form the U.S. COAST GUARD. The following year, Waesche became the first head of its Division of Communications, holding this post during World War I. He was responsible for organization, modernization, and extension of the coastal land lines network, as well as for the completion of a radio communications system.

In 1923, Waesche was promoted to lieutenant commander, and, in 1926, to commander. He held a variety of ship commands, then in 1928 became chief ordnance officer of the Coast Guard. In 1932 he was appointed aide to the Coast Guard commandant. In June 1936 President Roosevelt passed over more senior officers to appoint Waesche commandant of the Coast Guard, with the rank of rear admiral. He won promotion to vice admiral in 1942 and to admiral in 1945, becoming the first Coast Guard officer to hold these ranks.

As commandant, Waesche implemented new gunnery practices, reorganized administration, and founded the Coast Guard Institute and Correspondence School for warrant officers and enlisted men. Per his request, the U.S. Lighthouse Service and the Bureau of Marine Inspection were both reassigned to the Coast Guard, in 1939 and 1942, respectively.

The Coast Guard under Waesche played a key role during World War II. It escorted convoys and conducted anti-submarine warfare, sinking 12 U-boats. It also supervised ocean weather stations, conducted air patrol and rescue operations, and set up a coastal communications network. U.S. Coast Guardsmen saw combat in numerous small vessels and took part in every major naval landing operation in the Atlantic and Pacific theaters. The number of Coast Guard personnel rose from 10,000 before the war to some 171,000 by 1945. In addition to its own vessels, the Coast Guard manned more than 500 army and navy vessels.

Waesche retired in January 1946 for reasons of health. He died in Bethesda, Maryland, on 17 October 1946.

See also ATLANTIC, BATTLE OF THE (WORLD WAR II).

Further reading: Bloomfield, Howard V. L. *The Compact History of the United States Coast Guard.* New York: Hawthorn Books, 1966; Johnson, Robert Erwin. *Guardians of the Sea: History of the United States Coast Guard, 1915 to the Present.* Annapolis, Md.: Naval Institute Press, 1987; Willoughby, Malcolm F. *The U.S. Coast Guard in World War II.* Annapolis, Md.: Naval Institute Press, 1957.

— David R. Tavenner

Wainwright, Jonathan M. ("Skinny") (1883–1953) *U.S. Army general*

Born on 23 August 1883 in Walla Walla, Washington, Jonathan Mayhew Wainwright graduated from the U.S. Military Academy, WEST POINT, where he was first captain, in 1906. Commissioned in the cavalry, in 1916 he served along the Texas-Mexican border. He then trained infantry troops for World War I service. In July 1918 the 27th Infantry, to which Wainwright was temporarily attached, joined the AMERICAN EXPEDITIONARY FORCE in France, and he served first in the British sector and then in the SAINT MIHIEL and MEUSE-ARGONNE offensives, winning several decorations for gallantry, before rejoining the cavalry in late 1918 for occupation duty in Germany. Between the wars Wainwright alternated between troop duty and staff assignments. He commanded the 3d Cavalry Regiment in 1936, winning promotion to temporary brigadier general and command of the 1st Cavalry Brigade at Fort Bliss, Texas, in 1938.

In September 1940, Wainwright, now temporary major general, assumed command of the Manila-based Philippine Division, the largest U.S. unit in the archipelago, working under General Douglas MACARTHUR to ready the islands to defend themselves against an anticipated Japanese assault. Shortly after the Japanese attack on PEARL HARBOR, on 10 December the Japanese invaded Luzon in the Philippines. The North Luzon Force, a poorly equipped and poorly trained grouping of Filipino and American troops placed under Wainwright's command in late November, failed to repel the invasion. On MacArthur's orders, Wainwright redeployed his forces to the BATAAN Peninsula and then to CORREGIDOR, successfully withstanding Japanese attacks in January and February 1942, efforts in which Wainwright's leadership and personal courage were crucial.

On President Franklin D. ROOSEVELT's orders, on 11 March 1942 MacArthur left Bataan for Australia, and Wainwright, promoted to lieutenant general, assumed command of American and Philippine forces, authority ultimately clarified to include those in Mindanao, Panay, and northern Luzon. Lacking reinforcements or extensive resupply, he held out valiantly on Bataan until 9 April 1942, retreating forthwith to the Corregidor island fortress. Fearing a massacre of sick and wounded, on 6 May Wainwright surrendered Corregidor to the Japanese, three days later ordering all other Philippine defenders to follow suit. MacArthur criticized Wainwright's decision; but Chief of Staff General George C. MARSHALL respected it, commending Wainwright's last-ditch defense efforts as warranting the Medal of Honor.

Wainwright spent three years, sometimes beaten and humiliated, in Japanese prison camps in the Philippines, Taiwan, and Manchuria. The emaciated general was liberated in time to witness Japan's formal September 1945 surrender in Tokyo Bay. Returning to the United States, he received a hero's welcome, addressed a joint session of Congress, and commanded the Texas-based Fourth Army before retiring in August 1947. He died at Fort Sam Houston, Texas, on 2 September 1953.

See also KING, EDWARD P.; PHILIPPINES, LOSS OF THE; WORLD WAR II, CAUSES OF U.S. ENTRY; WORLD WAR II, COURSE OF U.S. INVOLVEMENT: PACIFIC THEATER.

Further reading: Ancheta, Celedonio A. *The Wainwright Papers: With Notes and Comments.* 4 vols. Quezon City, Philippines: New Day Publishers, 1980–1982; Beck, John Jacob. *MacArthur and Wainwright: Sacrifice of the Philippines.* Albuquerque: University of New Mexico Press, 1974; Schultz, Duane P. *Hero of Bataan: The Story of General Jonathan M. Wainwright.* New York: St. Martin's Press, 1981; Wainwright, Jonathan M. *General Wainwright's Story.* Edited by Robert Considine. Garden City, N.Y.: Doubleday, 1946.

— Priscilla Roberts

Wake Island (8–23 December 1941) *An isolated island outpost, the short-lived defense of which lifted American morale in the dark days immediately after the Pearl Harbor disaster during World War II*

Located 2,000 miles west of PEARL HARBOR, Wake Island became an American possession in 1899. In 1935, Pan American Airways turned it into a stop for a flying clipper route across the Pacific. Six years later, the U.S. Navy began to convert the atoll into a seaplane and submarine base. These facilities were still incomplete when the United States entered World War II.

Shortly before the outbreak of hostilities, Wake received a token garrison, consisting of 387 marines from the 1st Defense Battalion, 62 additional marines, and 12 Grumman F4F-3 Wildcat fighters from Marine Fighter Squadron (VMF) 211, along with 69 sailors and six U.S. Army radiomen. The atoll's population also included 72 Pan American employees and 1,146 construction workers.

With the start of the Pacific War on 8 December 1941 (7 December, Pearl Harbor time), Japanese medium bombers and flying boats from the MARSHALL ISLANDS subjected Wake to almost daily bombings. In their first strike against the atoll, Japanese airmen destroyed seven marine fighters on the ground and killed or wounded half of VMF 211's personnel. The marines subsequently received considerable aid from the atoll's construction workers, with more than 300 joining marine gun crews or providing other essential services.

On the morning of 11 December, Rear Admiral Sadamichi Kajioka tried to capture Wake with a small Japanese flotilla and 450 Special Naval Landing Force (SNLF) troops. Commanding the American ground defenses, Major James P. S. Devereux waited until the attackers closed to 4,500 yards before opening fire with six five-inch guns. Marine gunners sank the destroyer *Hayate* and hit several other ships. VMF 211 pursued the fleeing invaders with its four remaining Wildcats and sank the destroyer *Kisaragi*.

Humiliated by this surprising tactical reverse, the Japanese navy reinforced Kajioka's Wake invasion force with the aircraft carriers *Soryu* and *Hiryu* plus more cruisers, destroyers, and landing troops. Kajioka returned to Wake on the night of 22–23 December and landed 900 SNLF men on the atoll's south shore before dawn without subjecting American defenses to a preparatory bombardment.

Commander Winfield Scott Cunningham, senior officer in the Wake garrison, informed his superiors at Pearl

Harbor of the Japanese arrival and learned he could expect no relief. Although marine counterattacks wiped out one Japanese beachhead and reduced the size of a second, Cunningham ordered the atoll surrendered after 11 hours of confused and bloody close infantry combat.

The Japanese navy sacrificed two destroyers, one submarine, 21 aircraft, and lost 900 to 1,000 dead to gain possession of Wake Island. American deaths totaled 124: 46 Marines, three sailors, and 75 civilians.

Instead of mourning Wake's fall, the American public celebrated the garrison's 16-day stand against superior odds and the disproportionate Japanese losses as a latter-day Alamo. Wake Island would remain an American rallying point until the end of the war. Wake Island, bypassed when the United States began its Pacific advance, remained in Japanese hands for the remainder of the war.

See also WORLD WAR II, COURSE OF U.S. INVOLVEMENT: PACIFIC THEATER.

Further reading: Cressman, Robert J. *"A Magnificent Fight": The Battle for Wake Island.* Annapolis, Md.: Naval Institute Press, 1995; Kinney, John F., and James M. McCaffrey. *Wake Island Pilot: A World War II Memoir.* Washington, D.C.: Brassey's, 1995; Urwin, Gregory J. W. *Facing Fearful Odds: The Siege of Wake Island.* Lincoln: University of Nebraska Press, 1997; ———. *Wake Island in World War II: An Annotated Bibliography.* Huntsville, Ala.: U.S. Army Space and Strategic Defense Command, 1996.

— Gregory J. W. Urwin

Walker, Mary E. (1832–1919) *First woman doctor to serve with the Army Medical Corps, and Medal of Honor recipient*

Born on 26 November 1832 in or near Oswego, New York, Mary Edwards Walker received her early education at home. She taught briefly, then entered Syracuse Medical College in 1853. Graduating in 1855, she married fellow physician Albert Miller, but she retained her maiden name. The marriage lasted only four years.

When the Civil War began, Walker closed her practice in Rome, New York, anticipating that the U.S. Army would need skilled surgeons. She traveled to Washington, D.C., but was unable to obtain an appointment as a physician. Walker remained in Washington to lobby for such a post. In the meantime she worked as a hospital volunteer and helped organize the Women's Relief Association.

Walker's search for a way to join the war as a surgeon led her in 1862 to the Virginia battlefields. She aided surgeons at tent hospitals in Warrenton and Fredericksburg, although evidently in a nursing capacity rather than as a physician. She continued to lobby for a surgeon's position,

and in 1863 her persistence paid off when she received appointment as an assistant surgeon with the Army of the Cumberland.

Confederate troops captured Walker in April 1864 and imprisoned her in Richmond. Freed in August in a prisoner exchange, Walker did not return to the tent hospitals but served in administrative positions, first at a hospital and then at an orphanage, until she resigned in June 1865. That same year, Walker was awarded the Medal of Honor for meritorious service.

Walker then set up a medical practice in Washington, D.C., where she became an outspoken advocate for feminist causes. Her practice of wearing men's clothing, a habit since childhood, caused men and women alike to mock her; she once was arrested for masquerading as a man. In 1917 her Medal of Honor was revoked by the Board of Medal Awards, which judged that it had been unwarranted;

Mary E. Walker *(Library of Congress)*

evidently it had not been recorded in War Department records. Hers was only one of several hundred others revoked by the board. She refused to return the award and wore it until her death. Walker died in Oswego on 21 February 1919. Congress restored the Medal of Honor to her in 1977.

See also AMERICAN RED CROSS; MEDICINE, MILITARY; WOMEN IN THE MILITARY.

Further reading: Filler, Louis. "Walker, Mary Edward," *Notable American Women, 1607–1950.* Edited by Edward T. James. Cambridge, Mass.: Belknap Press of Harvard University Press, 1971: 532–33; Snyder, Charles McCool. *Dr. Mary Walker: The Little Lady in Pants.* Salem, N.H.: Ayer, 1962.

— Tracy M. Shilcutt

Walker, Walton H. ("Johnny") (1889–1950) *U.S. Army general*

Born on 3 December 1889 at Belton, Texas, Walton Harris Walker attended the Virginia Military Institute during 1907–08, then transferred to the U.S. Military Academy, WEST POINT, graduating in 1912. Commissioned in the infantry, he participated in the 1914 U.S. occupation of VERACRUZ.

After U.S. entry into World War I, Walker commanded the 13th Machine Gun Battalion in France and participated in both the SAINT MIHIEL and MEUSE-ARGONNE offensives. Twice cited for gallantry, he was awarded two Silver Stars and attained the rank of major.

After the war, Walker was on occupation duty in Germany, reverting to his permanent rank of captain on his return home. Walker graduated from the Field Artillery School in 1920, the advanced course at Fort Benning in 1923, the Command and General Staff School in 1926, and the Army War College in 1936. He taught at the Infantry School (1920–22), the Coast Artillery School, and at West Point (1923–25). He served in Tientsin (Tianjin), China, with the 15th Infantry Regiment (1930–33). He also served in the War Plans Division of the Army General Staff, 1937–40. Walker won promotion to lieutenant colonel in 1935 and temporary colonel in 1941, commanding the 36th Infantry Regiment. Promoted brigadier general in July 1941, he commanded the 3d Armored Brigade.

Walker took command of the 3d Armored Division in January 1942, after the U.S. entry into World War II, and was promoted major general the next month. In September he established the Desert Training Center to train units for service in North Africa. In April 1943 he took command of IV Armored Corps, Camp Campbell, Kentucky. Redesignated XX Corps, it was sent to Britain in February 1944 and committed to France that July as part of Lieutenant General George S. PATTON's Third Army. Known as the "Ghost Corps" for its speed, it spearheaded Patton's advance across Europe, reducing Metz in November 1944, and reaching Linz, Austria in May 1945. Promoted lieutenant general in May, Walker then headed 8th Service Command, Dallas, Texas.

After briefly heading Fifth Army in Chicago in 1948, Walker took command of Eighth Army of four infantry divisions on occupation duty in Japan. Walker began a training program in the summer of 1949, but the outbreak of the KOREAN WAR in June 1950 found the divisions still undertrained, at about two-thirds strength with much of their weaponry and equipment unserviceable, and led by commanders who had never directed a division in combat. Walker led three of these divisions in Korea, along with five Republic of Korea (ROK) divisions that were combat-battered; short on large-caliber weapons, equipment, and ammunition; and led by inexperienced commanders. Walker also had to contend with United Nations commander General of the Army Douglas MACARTHUR's chief of staff, Major General Edward M. ALMOND, who consistently undermined him.

Walker established his reputation in the defense of the PUSAN PERIMETER. He ably defeated every Korean People's Army (KPA, North Korean) thrust, spending much of each day traveling from one threatened spot to another, cajoling or threatening his division commanders. His leadership and determination were vital in holding the perimeter.

Walker's men broke out of the Pusan Perimeter after the INCHON LANDING, and by late October they were deep into North Korea. Following the Chinese Communist intervention that same month, Walker extricated his army, halting along the Chongchon River.

Logistical shortfalls prevented Eighth Army from resuming its attack until 24 November. The Chinese struck the next day, crushing the ROK II Corps, threatening Eighth Army's right flank. Walker ordered a general withdrawal, during which a scorched earth policy deprived Communist forces of winter shelter and food.

Walker habitually sped from one spot to another in his jeep. On 23 December 1950, while traveling to visit a front-line command, his jeep was struck head-on by a South Korean truck, and Walker was killed. In January 1951 he was posthumously promoted to full general.

Further reading: Appleman, Roy E. *U.S. Army in Korea: South to the Naktong, North to the Yalu.* Washington, D.C.: Office of the Chief of Military History, 1961; Hoyt, Edwin P. *The Pusan Perimeter.* New York: Stein & Day, 1984; Mossman, Billy C. *U.S. Army in the Korean War: Ebb and Flow, November 1950–July 1951.* Washington, D.C.: Center of Military History, United States Army, 1990.

— Uzel W. Ent

Walker, William (1824–1860) *The most successful and controversial of 19th-century American filibusters*
Born on 5 May 1824 in Nashville, Tennessee, William Walker was precocious. A doctor by age 20, he then practiced law in New Orleans and became the editor of the *New Orleans Crescent* in 1848. The next year, he traveled to San Francisco, working first for the *San Francisco Herald* and then a law firm in Marysville.

It was in California that Walker became intrigued by the idea of filibustering—the unofficial intrusion of Americans into the affairs of neighboring nations. In 1853, Walker led an expedition into the Mexican state of Sonora. Arriving at La Paz, he imprisoned the governor and created the so-called Republic of Lower California. After much of his army deserted, Walker was forced to return to the United States, and he surrendered to the army at San Diego. The U.S. government arraigned Walker before a federal court for violation of American neutrality laws, but he was acquitted the next year.

In 1855, Walker carried out a filibustering expedition into Nicaragua in order to help the Liberal government, based in Leon, to wrest control from the Conservative government in Granada. With a mercenary army of some 60 men, he seized control and became Nicaragua's strongman by November. However, in 1856 Great Britain, which had interests along Nicaragua's Mosquito Coast, supplied Costa Rica with arms and encouraged an attack on Walker. The Costa Rican army soon occupied Rivas and the Virgin Bay. Walker attempted to defend Rivas, but retreated after taking heavy losses. He retook the city only after the opposing force left it because of a cholera epidemic and potential revolt among the soldiers.

Walker's activities in Nicaragua soon gained him more enemies. He was elected president in 1856 by a suspiciously large margin, which cost him allies among the propertied elite. He also brought in a number of questionable soldiers, including Texans who called themselves Walker's Rangers, but who became infamous for plundering the Nicaraguan countryside rather than defending it. That same year, the Costa Rican army returned to Nicaragua in an attempt to take Granada and Leon. Rather than see Granada fall to his enemies, Walker evacuated the city and burned it to the ground.

Walker managed to hold off the Costa Ricans until 1857, when he surrendered to the U.S. Navy and returned to the United States. He attempted to return to Nicaragua later that year, but he was captured by Commodore Hiram Paulding and put on trial for yet another violation of neutrality law. This did not stop him from planning yet another expedition to Nicaragua, and Walker again was acquitted.

In 1860, English colonists on the Honduran island of Ruatan asked Walker's help in preventing the turnover of the island from British control to the Hondurans. After a short struggle, he surrendered to the British authorities, who turned him over to the Hondurans. Walker was summarily executed by firing squad on 12 September 1860 at Truxillo, Honduras.

Further reading: Carr, Albert Z. *The World and William Walker.* New York: Harper & Row, 1963; Rosengarten, Frederic, Jr. *Freebooters Must Die! The Life and Death of William Walker, the Most Notorious Filibuster of the Nineteenth Century.* Wayne, Pa.: Haverford House, 1976; Scroggs, William O. *Filibusters and Financiers: The Story of William Walker and His Associates.* New York: Russell & Russell, 1944.

— Adrienne Caughfield

war crimes *Violations by nations or individuals of the commonly accepted laws of war*
Conventions, treaties, and other international agreements regulate the laws of war. Despite the uncivilized nature of warfare, laws of war help to keep warring armies under control, prevent reprisals, and ease the prospects of postconflict reconciliation. Historically, the concept of war crimes is quite recent. For most of human history, only the vaguest of rules governed warfare, and what few rules existed were generally ignored. There were exceptions, including the sanctity of religious sites, exchanges, safe-conduct, and cease-fires for burying dead and tending to wounded. The concept of rules governing war developed slowly over several centuries.

Laws of war also protect noncombatants. Thus, populations are not to be subject to starvation as a war tactic; civilians should not be attacked; and hospitals, religious sites, and historic monuments are to be protected. Carpet bombing and the use of land mines in populated areas, as well as the employment of chemical and biological weapons, are illegal. Prisoners of war are to be treated humanely and not tortured or killed.

Internationally, these concepts are outlined by various conventions, mainly the Geneva Conventions and agreements concluded at The Hague in the Netherlands. These date back to the 1860s. The current conventions include the Geneva Convention of 1949, created in response to atrocities committed during World War II, as well as two 1977 Geneva Protocols. The 1949 Geneva Convention extended the jurisdiction of the laws of war to include noninternational conflicts, in addition to war between nations.

War crimes tribunals have followed major modern conflicts. The most famous of the 20th century are the Nuremberg and Tokyo trials after World War II. These brought out the controversial defense for committing war crimes—that of following orders.

The American experience with war crimes is sporadic. After the Civil War, Confederate major Henry Wirz was convicted of violating the laws of war in the only major war crimes trial of the conflict. Wirz commanded the ANDERSONVILLE, Georgia, prison camp, where as many as 13,700 Union POWs died of neglect and maltreatment out of 50,000 detained there between February 1864 and April 1865. In his defense, Wirz maintained that he followed orders under duress. The court found, however, that he had willingly neglected the prisoners, and it sentenced him to death.

The United States led the prosecution of Nazi and Japanese war criminals after World War II. At Nuremberg, 182 Nazi leaders were tried by Allied tribunals for war crimes, mostly in relation to the Holocaust, the mass killing of Jews by the Germans during the conflict. Eighty-nine were convicted. The United States was the most active of the Allied powers in prosecuting German war criminals. It indicted more individuals than the other three occupying powers combined. Curiously, the Soviet Union was the least interested in the process.

War crimes trials were also held in Japan after the war. General Douglas MACARTHUR opened the Tokyo tribunal in January 1946. There judges from the Allied countries that fought in the Pacific presided over 28 trials dealing with crimes against humanity, mistreatment of prisoners of war, and other war crimes. Seven received the death sentence, and the remainder were sentenced to prison terms. In both tribunals, the accused often used the excuse of having been "following orders" as their chief defense. Some attempted to challenge the jurisdiction of the tribunals, but without success. It is certainly true that prosecution in war crimes had largely been the province of the victor.

The most famous war crime involving American forces occurred during the VIETNAM WAR on 16 March 1968, when troops of Company C, 1st Battalion of the 20th Infantry, under command of Captain Ernest Medina and 2nd Lieutenant William CALLEY, killed approximately 400 Vietnamese civilians in what came to be known as the MY LAI MASSACRE. Despite obvious evidence that the operation had gone terribly wrong, Medina and Calley's superiors did nothing to investigate it. Only in early 1969, when a letter describing the event reached Congress and *Life* magazine published an article on the incident, was there a call for an investigation. Army Chief of Staff General William WESTMORELAND, who had commanded in Vietnam, appointed Lieutenant General William Peers to investigate the incident. This led to the indictment of 25 individuals charged either in the massacre or in the subsequent cover-up. Calley and 12 others were charged with war crimes. Calley's defense was that he was following orders and that he and his men treated all Vietnamese in the area of Son My as the enemy. All of the others either had charges dropped or received minor administrative punishments. Ultimately, only Calley was convicted, and in the end he served only three days behind bars. Many saw him as a scapegoat in the army's attempt to avoid further bad publicity and scandal.

As a result of the My Lai incident, all branches of the U.S. armed forces increased their training in the laws of war and war crimes. The Uniform Code of Military Justice also includes provisions for prosecuting violations of the laws of war.

Today the International War Crimes Tribunal at The Hague investigates and prosecutes war crimes, including those associated with the war in the former Yugoslavia and the atrocities in Rwanda. Although President Bill Clinton signed the 1998 International Criminal Court Treaty (the Rome Treaty), which was intended to create a permanent war crimes court, the U.S. government has yet to sign the treaty because of concerns over sovereignty, jurisdiction, and other possible conflicts with U.S. interests.

Further reading: Bilton, Michael, and Kevin Sim. *Four Hours at My Lai.* New York: Penguin, 1993; Conot, Robert E. *Justice at Nuremberg.* New York: Harper & Row, 1983; Maga, Timothy P. *Judgment at Tokyo: The Japanese War Crimes Trials.* Lexington: University Press of Kentucky, 2001; Hersh, Seymour M. *Cover-Up: The Army's Secret Investigation of the Massacre at My Lai 4.* New York: Random House, 1972; ———. *My Lai 4: A Report on the Massacre and Its Aftermath.* New York: Random House, 1970; Osiel, Mark J. *Obeying Orders: Atrocity, Military Discipline, and the Law of War.* New Brunswick, N.J.: Transaction Publishers, 1999.

— William Thomas Allison

War of 1812: causes

The War of 1812 was one of the strangest in American history. Most citizens of the United States did not wish it, and the British government, at war with Napoléon, certainly did not want it. The country was goaded into war by a small number of influential advocates, dubbed the "war hawks."

The causes of the war were largely maritime in nature. When France and Great Britain went to war in 1793, the United States, while neutral, became embroiled when merchant vessels trading with Europe became targets for seizure by both France and Great Britain. Following Napoléon's declaration of the Continental System, barring British goods from French-controlled Europe, Britain retaliated with the Orders in Council of 1806 that forbade neutrals from trading with France and states allied with it. In November 1807, London declared that all neutral vessels bound for the Continent must first stop at a British port. While Napoléon's Berlin Decree of 1806 and Milan Decree of 1807 also imposed unacceptable conditions on American shipping interests, Great Britain's actions were generally regarded as more controversial.

In order to enforce the Orders in Council, British vessels would monitor American harbors, stopping and searching ships just as they cleared ports. Both Thomas JEFFERSON's and James Madison's administrations introduced measures to curb British and French abuses, including the Embargo Act of 1807, the Non-Intercourse Act of 1809, and Macon's Bill Number Two of 1810. However, these were not initially successful.

Impressment was the other major maritime cause of the war. Britain was strapped for seamen in its wars against France, and Royal Navy warships were soon halting American ships and taking off those seamen it judged to be British citizens. Britain did not recognize expatriation, so naturalization was no protection for the seamen. Because so many seamen on British warships had been pressed, and with punishment brutal and pay abysmal, many sailors deserted, and a great many of these found their way into U.S. merchant ships and even warships. In 1807, in the CHESAPEAKE–LEOPARD AFFAIR, the British ship of the line *Leopard* stopped the American frigate *Chesapeake* off Chesapeake Bay and fired into it when Captain James BARRON refused to allow his ship to be searched. Barron then lowered his flag, and the British mustered the American crew and took off four of them. There was an outburst of national outrage over this incident. Thomas Jefferson would have had a more popular and successful war than that of 1812, but he did not want war and worked to resolve the crisis peacefully.

Clearly the British government regarded the United States with disdain. If Britain, fighting for its survival against Napoléon, had to trample on American rights in the process, it mattered little. In this sense, the War of 1812 is sometimes referred to as the Second War for Independence.

Another major cause of the war was the belief in the United States that the British were abetting Native-American unrest in the Old Northwest. This ignored the fact that U.S. land grabs and violations of treaties drove the Indians to the side of the British. After the November 1811 Battle of TIPPECANOE, British arms were found in the deserted Indian village of Prophetstown, confirming American suspicions.

Other causes of the war were an economic downturn, especially in the West, blamed not without reason on the inability to export tobacco and cotton. Ironically, the northeastern part of the country, the area most susceptible to the maritime disruptions, opposed war.

Finally, and not least, there was the lure of Canada. Expansionists, primarily a small but vocal minority from western states, pointed to the large number of U.S. citizens who had settled in Upper Canada. They hoped to annex Upper Canada, perhaps all Canada, to the United States.

Ultimately the Madison administration gave in to the demands of war hawks such as Henry Clay of Kentucky, Felix Grundy of Tennessee, and John C. CALHOUN of South Carolina. Congress declared war on 18 June 1812. Ironically, had there been a transatlantic cable there would have been no war. London, hard-pressed for American wheat, announced the suspension of the Orders in Council two days before.

See also TECUMSEH; WAR OF 1812: LAND OVERVIEW; WAR OF 1812: NAVAL OVERVIEW.

Further reading: Brown, Roger H. *Republic in Peril: 1812.* New York: W. W. Norton, 1971; Hickey, Donald R. *The War of 1812: A Forgotten Conflict.* Urbana: University of Illinois Press, 1990; Horsman, Reginald. *The Causes of the War of 1812.* Philadelphia: University of Pennsylvania Press, 1962.

— Spencer C. Tucker

War of 1812: land overview

In 1812 war erupted between the United States and Great Britain. Given the two nations' disparity in naval strength, the bulk of the fighting would be on land. President James Madison was determined to seize Upper Canada, which had a large immigrant population from the United States.

On paper the odds heavily favored the United States. The entire population of British North America was only 300,000 people, and Canada could raise only 86,000 militia to supplement 10,000 British regulars, with little hope of reinforcement because of the war with Napoléon in Europe. In contrast, the United States had a population of 8,000,000. The U.S. Army had only about 7,000 men actually in service. However, the United States could call upon more than 700,000 militia.

The British had two chief advantages. British troops in Canada, while small in number, were well-trained regulars with a commander of genius in Major General Isaac Brock. By contrast, at the outset the Americans were poorly trained and poorly supplied, and they were ineptly led. Finally, there were the Indians. Goaded by the 1811 Battle of TIPPECANOE, most Northwest Indians allied with the British, who promised them an Indian state following a British victory. The western Indians, led by TECUMSEH, often tipped the scale in favor of the British in the early battles.

Madison wanted to concentrate all available resources for an attack against Montreal, but U.S. Army major general Henry DEARBORN persuaded Madison that decentralized offensives aimed at Montreal, the Niagara region, and the Detroit frontier would disperse British military

War of 1812, 1812–1815

resources defending against invasion. This strategy required a degree of coordination and expertise beyond the capability of the U.S. military leaders in 1812. The land campaigns would naturally devolve into four distinct theaters of operation rather than reflect a unified national effort.

The northwest theater of operations included the states and territories northwest of the Ohio River and Upper Canada that bordered the Great Lakes. In July 1812 Governor William HULL, who had been granted a commission as a brigadier general, invaded Upper Canada from Detroit with a poorly disciplined army of 1,500 men. British interdiction of his supply line and the surrender of FORT MACKINAC led him to abandon the invasion. A British-Indian counteroffensive, led by General Brock and Tecumseh, soon cleared Upper Canada and forced Hull to surrender DETROIT on 16 August. Adding to these disasters was the ambush and massacre by the Indians of American troops and their families who attempted to evacuate FORT DEARBORN the following day.

Major General William Henry HARRISON replaced Hull, but he faced severe manpower and logistical challenges. In January 1813 a portion of his army was defeated and the wounded slain by the Indians in the battle and massacre of the RIVER RAISIN. Harrison then established bases at FORT MEIGS and FORT STEPHENSON, where he withstood attacks by the British during the spring and summer. Oliver Hazard PERRY's victory in the September 1813 Battle of LAKE ERIE collapsed the British logistics network and forced the British to abandon Detroit. On 5 October at Moraviantown on the Thames River, Harrison's mounted troops attacked the British-Indian force and killed Tecumseh. This Battle of the THAMES ended both British influence and organized Indian opposition to U.S. expansion in the Northwest. However, expiring enlistments caused Harrison's army to unravel, and he abandoned most of western Ontario.

The Central theater saw operations along the Saint Lawrence River and in the Niagara region. Major General Stephen VAN RENSSELAER led a small force of regulars across the Niagara River to attack the British in the 13 October 1812 Battle of QUEENSTON HEIGHTS. The assault failed, and militia reinforcements refused to cross into Canada to support the attack. Dearborn's operation directed at Montreal also failed, ending his plans for conquering Canada in 1812.

In 1813 both belligerents conducted major raids against the other. In April Dearborn attacked YORK (Toronto), where his army met disaster when a powder magazine exploded and killed Brigadier General Zebulon PIKE. In May the British raided the U.S. naval base at SACKETT'S HARBOR but were defeated there by Brigadier General Jacob BROWN after several determined assaults. On the Niagara front the Americans captured FORT GEORGE but

were defeated in June during engagements at STONEY CREEK and Beaver Dams. The American destruction of Newark in December prompted British retaliation against FORT NIAGARA, Black Rock, and BUFFALO, where they burned public buildings.

Major General James WILKINSON, who replaced Dearborn, planned to attack Montreal from the Saint Lawrence while Major General Wade Hampton led an army from Plattsburg. Sharp disagreements between Hampton and Wilkinson hindered operations and led to defeats at CHATEAUGUAY and CHRYSLER'S FARM.

As Napoléon neared defeat in Europe, Britain could release thousands of experienced veterans to Canada. This development influenced Madison to appoint more energetic officers such as Jacob Brown, Alexander MACOMB, Edmund GAINES, and Winfield SCOTT. These leaders applied training and discipline that significantly improved army performance. In July 1814 Brown crossed the Niagara River and captured FORT ERIE. He met strong British resistance on 5 July at CHIPPEWA, where Scott's well-disciplined troops traded volleys with the enemy and then executed a bayonet charge. On 25 July Brown met the British at LUNDY'S LANE and there fought a violent but indecisive five-hour battle that demonstrated the ability of well-trained U.S. soldiers.

The British then attempted a siege at Fort Erie but failed when an American sortie destroyed their siege guns. The final British operation in the north consisted of an offensive mounted by more than 11,000 veteran troops and naval forces along the LAKE CHAMPLAIN corridor south from Montreal. Brigadier General Alexander Macomb had only 4,500 largely untrained regulars and militia to defend at PLATTSBURG; however, Master Commandant Thomas MACDONOUGH's decisive defeat of the British fleet on 11 September 1814 halted the offensive.

The Atlantic theater included British amphibious raids in the Chesapeake Bay and along coastal waterways to induce Americans to withdraw their support for the war. Throughout 1813, towns such as Havre de Grace, Maryland, and Hampton, Virginia, suffered pillage. In August 1814 Britain conducted a more significant operation to attack the U.S. capital of WASHINGTON with more than 4,000 veteran troops supported by a large naval force. Brigadier General William Winder commanded American forces defending the capital. Although U.S. militia forces greatly outnumbered the British, during the 24 August Battle of BLADENSBURG they quickly broke and ran. The British then took Washington and burned a number of public buildings, including the White House and the Capitol. The next day the British returned to their transports to sail farther up the Chesapeake and attack BALTIMORE.

At Baltimore Brigadier General Samuel Smith positioned some 13,000 troops to defend the town and strengthened FORT McHENRY to defend Baltimore Harbor. On 12 September, the British troops engaged a strong American force near North Point but were halted. During the night of 13–14 September the British fleet bombarded Fort McHenry with rockets and gunfire to force entry into the harbor. The Americans withstood the bombardment and the British then departed.

The southern theater of operations included the sparsely settled hinterland and the Gulf region to the Mississippi River. Campaigns there reflected an internal war against the Creek Indians, who had been encouraged by the British, and British raids against strategic points such as Mobile and New Orleans. The CREEK WAR began in August 1813, when a faction known as the Red Sticks attacked and massacred over 250 Americans at Fort Mims on the Alabama River. American militia rallied under Major General Andrew JACKSON, who took the offensive and won a decisive victory in the Battle of HORSESHOE BEND in March 1814. The Creek War ended with a treaty that ceded almost all Creek lands to the United States.

As commander of the military district that included New Orleans, Jackson strengthened key sites, such as Fort Bowyer at the entrance to Mobile Bay. He also attacked the Spanish at PENSACOLA to capture the town and deny the British use of its harbor. The main British blow fell at New Orleans. Jackson established defensive positions near the Rodriguez Canal, where the Mississippi River protected his right flank and the Cypress Swamps protected his left, and he fortified his front with a large parapet to provide protection for a unique assembly of regulars, militia, freemen, volunteers, Indians, and Baratarian pirates led by Jean LAFFITE. Jackson had 3,500 men and artillery in a strong defensive position. In the 8 January 1815 Battle of NEW ORLEANS Major General Edward Pakenham launched a frontal attack with some 5,300 men against the Americans. Ground fog lifted just as the British closed on the American position. The Americans devastated the British ranks with artillery and musket fire. The British suffered 2,600 casualties, including Pakenham and his two senior subordinates, all killed. Jackson lost only 13 killed and 58 wounded. Ironically, the Treaty of GHENT had ended the war a month before the battle.

The war's land campaigns had little influence on the conflict's final outcome. At least it was a cheap war in terms of casualties. Only 1,877 American soldiers and sailors were killed in action; another 4,000 were wounded. The war led to increased respect by the British for the United States; in this sense it is sometimes known as the Second War for Independence. The war also fostered Canadian nationalism and insured that Canada would not become part of the United States. And it offered valuable lessons on the need for military preparedness. Few of these lessons were heeded. In the United States the myth of "citizen soldiers"

and self-taught generals persisted, but the postwar army made impressive strides in professionalism, administration, and efficiency. In the end the War of 1812 prompted the rapid rise of manufacturing in the United States and an increase in American patriotism that helped to bring the country together as one nation.

See also WAR OF 1812: CAUSES; WAR OF 1812: NAVAL OVERVIEW.

Further reading: Barbuto, Richard V. *Niagara 1814: America Invades Canada.* Lawrence: University Press of Kansas, 2000; Hitsman, J. Mackay. *The Incredible War of 1812.* Rev. ed. Toronto: Robin Brass Studio, 1999; Mahon, John K. *The War of 1812.* Gainesville: University Presses of Florida, 1972; Quimby, Robert S. *The U.S. Army in the War of 1812: An Operational and Command Study.* East Lansing: Michigan State University Press, 1997.

— Steven J. Rauch

War of 1812: naval overview

During the Anglo-French war that began in 1793, both belligerents violated U.S. neutral rights, and America's maritime trade suffered. In addition, British ships hovered about and practically blockaded American ports, seized American ships at sea, and on occasion impressed American seamen from merchant ships and even naval vessels, the CHESAPEAKE–LEOPARD AFFAIR of 1807 being a case in point. Simultaneously, French decrees barred neutral ships from visiting England or from entering Continental ports on penalty of seizure.

When the War of 1812 began, Secretary of the Navy Paul Hamilton wanted to use the navy to defend trade, but Congress restricted cruiser operations to American waters and, despite a war being fought for "Free Trade and Sailors' Rights," adjourned without funding new ships. The result was that 10 of the 18 seagoing ships available for war in 1812 had been built before 1801. Moreover, the navy was short of guns, ammunition, and personnel.

With respect to building up the navy, representatives of the coast and commerce favored doing so but were opposed by those representing inland areas and agrarian interests. A majority favored the use of the 250 or so gunboats built during Thomas JEFFERSON's presidency and opposed the use of either cruisers or privateers. The special session of Congress held in July 1811 to consider relations with Britain merely authorized timber purchases, although during three years of war the navy nearly doubled in size. Because of its weak navy, once at war the United States relied upon commerce raiding and privateering, the latter emanating particularly from Baltimore and being largely responsible for forcing Britain to provide escorts for its merchant ships and transports.

American naval captains who favored squadron operations were opposed by those who reasoned that Britain would retaliate and seize American merchant ships. When John RODGERS, Stephen DECATUR, and William BAINBRIDGE took squadrons into the Atlantic, Britain sent the crack ordnance expert Philip Broke in the frigate *Shannon* to cruise off American ports. Nevertheless, the winning of 12 out of 16 ship encounters proved the quality of American vessels and their crews. The most exciting meetings occurred on 19 August 1812, when the *Constitution*, under Captain Isaac HULL, captured the frigate *Guerriere;* 18 October 1812, when the U.S. sloop of war *Wasp*, under Captain Jacob Jones, took the sloop of war *Frolic;* on 25 October 1812, when the frigate *United States*, under Decatur, captured the frigate *Macedonian;* and on 29 December 1812, when the frigate *Constitution* under Captain Bainbridge, captured the frigate *Java* off the Brazil coast and destroyed it. On the other hand, on 1 June 1813, the U.S. frigate *Chesapeake* was captured by the British frigate *Shannon;* on 28 March 1814, the U.S. frigate *Essex* under Captain David PORTER was taken by two English vessels in the harbor of Valparaiso, Chile; and on 15 January 1815, the U.S. frigate *President*, under Decatur, was taken by a British squadron, although not before the Americans had completely disabled one of the British vessels.

Meanwhile, Britain so increased the number of ships capable of opposing frigates that they virtually blockaded the United States and shut down its trade. While almost 900 American ships and 6,000 men fell prey to the British between 1806 and 1812, the loss of more than 1,000 British ships during the war was a major reason for Britain's desire for peace.

Nonmaritime causes of the War of 1812 included the war hawks' calls for expansion into Canada and British-fostered Indian unrest. Correct American strategy would have been to cut British communications westward to the Great Lakes by seizing Montreal. Instead, the American and British naval commanders on Lake Ontario built fleets that never fought but served as deterrents. On LAKE ERIE, however, on 10 September 1813 Commodore Oliver Hazard PERRY defeated Captain John Heriot Barclay and saved the Northwest Territory for the United States. On LAKE CHAMPLAIN, Master Commandant Thomas MACDONOUGH defeated a British squadron commanded by Captain George Downey, with the result that British soldiers retreated from New York State. In retaliation for an American raid on YORK, Canada, however, Britain sent 5,000 troops escorted by Vice Admiral Sir Alexander Cochrane to raid Washington and the Chesapeake. Captain Joshua BARNEY's flotillamen fought well against British troops at BLADENSBURG, Maryland, but provided only some extra minutes for the American government to evacuate the capital, which the British partially burned.

The issue of impressment died with the defeat of Napoléon at Waterloo because Britain no longer needed American seamen in the struggle against France. Neither impressment nor neutral rights were mentioned in the Treaty of GHENT, and no change in territory occurred.

After the war, Jefferson's gunboats were sold and Congress provided funds for substantially strengthening the navy. In 1815, the Board of Navy Commissioners was created to advise the secretary of the navy on nautical matters. A naval race on the Great Lakes was averted by an Anglo-American agreement of 1817 to keep the lakes free of arms. In the war the small U.S. Navy had acquired a fighting reputation second to none.

See also NAVY, U.S.; PRIVATEERING IN THE WAR OF 1812; WAR OF 1812: CAUSES; WAR OF 1812: LAND OVERVIEW.

Further reading: Barnes, James. *Naval Actions During the War of 1812.* New York: Harper & Brothers, 1896; Bird, Harrison. *Navies in the Mountains: The Battles on Water of Lake Champlain and Lake George, 1609–1814.* New York: Oxford University Press, 1962; Tucker, Spencer C. *The Jeffersonian Gunboat Navy.* Columbia: University of South Carolina Press, 1993.

— Paolo E. Coletta

War Plan Orange *U.S. strategic plan to defeat Japan*
In the summer of 1903, the U.S. Army and U.S. Navy formed the Joint Army and Navy Board to develop war plans to deal with potential adversaries. It assigned colors to represent specific countries. Orange represented Japan.

As a consequence of the SPANISH-AMERICAN WAR, the United States acquired the Philippines and Guam, extending its territory and influence in the Pacific and opening the possibility of a future conflict with Japan. A rising power in the Pacific, Japan had defeated Russia in war in 1905. War Plan Orange first began in 1906 as a strategy for a primarily naval war. It evolved over time and, after World War I, anticipated that in the event of war between the two countries, Japan would seize the lightly defended American outposts in the Pacific. Superior U.S. naval and air power would then push westward, conquering the Japanese islands in the central Pacific. U.S. planners predicted that Japan would favor a campaign of attrition, hoping to wear down the U.S. fleet. Finally, both sides foresaw a climactic naval battle to decide mastery of the western Pacific. Once the U.S. fleet was victorious, it would impose a naval blockade of the Japanese home islands. This and air strikes would bring about the ultimate goal of Japanese surrender.

After World War I, the Joint Board gained a permanent staff in the form of the Joint Planning Committee, comprised of officers from both the Army and Navy War Plans Divisions. In addition, officers at the Naval War College refined Orange through chart maneuvers and war games.

Army and navy planners disagreed over where to establish the principal U.S. Pacific naval base. Discussions centered on both Guam and the Philippines. The issue became moot, thanks to the 1922 Washington Naval Treaty, which prohibited the building of new fortifications. Pearl Harbor would be the closest American naval base to the Philippines.

Other differences surfaced. The army wanted to defend the Philippines until reinforcements arrived. The navy thought that the islands would be lost at the opening of the war. Planners agreed the central Pacific was the most viable route to the Philippines. This would mean securing the islands Japan took from Germany after World War I: the MARIANA ISLANDS, the MARSHALL ISLANDS, and the Carolines. Two schools of thought emerged. One, dubbed the "through ticket to Manila," favored a quick thrust across the central Pacific. The other preferred a more cautious strategy. The latter position ultimately prevailed.

See also ATOMIC BOMB, DECISION TO EMPLOY; LEAPFROGGING; WORLD WAR II, COURSE OF U.S. INVOLVEMENT: PACIFIC THEATER.

Further reading: Linn, Brian McAllister. *Guardians of Empire: The U.S. Army and the Pacific, 1902–1940.* Chapel Hill: University of North Carolina Press, 1997; Miller, Edward S. *War Plan Orange: The U.S. Strategy to Defeat Japan, 1897–1945.* Annapolis, Md.: Naval Institute Press, 1991; Spector, Ronald H. *Eagle Against the Sun.* New York: Free Press, 1985.

— Trevor K. Plante

Warren, Gouverneur K. (1830–1882) *U.S. Army general*

Born on 8 January 1830 in Cold Spring, New York, Gouverneur Kemble Warren graduated from the U.S. Military Academy, WEST POINT, in 1850. Commissioned a brevet second lieutenant in the Topographical Engineers, he was promoted to full second lieutenant in 1854 and first lieutenant in 1856. As an engineer, Warren worked on river and canal projects, surveyed potential railroad routes, and generated maps of western territories. He also taught mathematics at West Point.

With the outbreak of the Civil War, Warren entered the Volunteer organization as lieutenant colonel of the 5th New York Infantry and saw action at Big Bethel. In September 1861 he was promoted to captain in the regular army and colonel of the 5th New York Regiment.

In 1862 Warren commanded a brigade in V Corps, Army of the Potomac, participating in the Peninsular campaign and the SEVEN DAYS' BATTLES. Wounded at Gaines' Mill and brevetted lieutenant colonel, U.S. Army, he returned to duty, leading his brigade in the Battles of Second BULL RUN/MANASSAS, ANTIETAM/SHARPSBURG, and FREDERICKSBURG. Promoted to brigadier general, U.S. Volunteers, in September 1862, in March 1863 Warren joined the staff of Major General Joseph HOOKER as chief engineer, Army of the Potomac. He remained in that position when Major General George G. MEADE replaced Hooker after the debacle at CHANCELLORSVILLE.

On the second day at GETTYSBURG (2 July), Warren found the left flank of the army unprotected and rushed troops to Little Round Top, where determined resistance broke the Confederate attack and likely saved the Army of the Potomac. It was the turning point of the battle and in the war in the East. Wounded in the fight for Little Round Top, Warren was brevetted to colonel in the regular army and in August he was promoted to major general of Volunteers (to rank from May). From August 1863 to March 1864, he directed the II Corps in place of the wounded Major General Winfield Scott HANCOCK and participated in a number of engagements, including Bristoe Station, for which he was brevetted brigadier general in the U.S. Army.

In March 1864, Warren assumed command of V Corps, Army of the Potomac, and led it throughout the OVERLAND CAMPAIGN and at PETERSBURG. During the final days on the Petersburg front, he and his corps fell under the command of Major General Philip SHERIDAN, who summarily relieved Warren for perceived failings in the Battle of FIVE FORKS. In May 1865, after briefly commanding the District of Vicksburg, Warren resigned his Volunteer commission and reverted to his regular rank of major of engineers.

Brevetted to major general for war service, Warren continued as one of the army's top engineers while laboring to clear his name. Promoted to lieutenant colonel in 1879, he finally received justice. After repeated requests, Warren was granted a court of inquiry that not only exonerated him of Sheridan's charges but also found fault in his dismissal. Shortly after this verdict, which did little to assuage his broken spirit, Warren died at his Newport, Rhode Island, home on 8 August 1882.

See also CIVIL WAR, LAND OVERVIEW.

Further reading: Taylor, Emerson G. *Gouverneur Kemble Warren: The Life and Letters of an American Soldier, 1830–1882.* Boston: Houghton Mifflin, 1932; Pfanz, Harry W. *Gettysburg: The Second Day.* Chapel Hill: University of North Carolina Press, 1987.

— David Coffey

war reporting

Reporting of war news has a long history, with early accounts of battles being written by Xenophon, Homer, and Julius Caesar. The period from the end of the Roman Empire to the 17th century lacks any authoritative accounts of military engagements; but the rise of global powers and the resulting wars for empire, combined with the invention of the printing press and a literate society, produced the need for war correspondents. Henry Crabb Robinson of the London *Times*, Charles Lewis Gruneison of the London *Morning Post*, John Bell of the London *Oracle*, and George Wilkins Kendall of the New Orleans *Picayune* are examples of early war correspondents.

Although editors printed accounts of battles during the FRENCH AND INDIAN WAR, the AMERICAN REVOLUTIONARY WAR, and the WAR OF 1812, American war correspondence truly began with the Civil War. Prior to the Civil War, most newspaper editors printed battle accounts based on information supplied by witnesses or participants, not by professional correspondents. Brief descriptions with sketchy details reprinted from one newspaper to another provided only the barest of facts.

The Civil War saw the introduction of photography on the battlefield. Individuals such as Matthew Brady recorded images of famous generals and soldiers, and of the carnage of war. Photos revealed more about the war, but photographers sometimes rearranged the scenes for effect.

Journalists, such as Sylvanus Cadwallader, who accompanied General Ulysses S. GRANT, recorded events, although much of the information was still secondhand and less reliable.

During the 1898 SPANISH-AMERICAN WAR a different type of reporting began to develop. The so-called Yellow Press, led by Joseph Pulitzer and William Randolph Hearst, placed emphasis on selling newspapers. Before the war they sensationalized atrocities and inflamed American sentiment against the Spanish. Bold headlines reporting the sinking of the USS *MAINE*, and the publication of a letter from a Spanish official insulting President William McKinley led the public to cry for war.

When war came, attempts at censorship failed to prevent wildly exaggerated stories from being printed. The speed of communication also altered the manner in which war reporting occurred, with military officials seeking to restrict the access of reporters to information considered vital to the war effort.

During WORLD WAR I, reporters allowed to write about the war posted a $10,000 bond that would be forfeited if they did not print the truth or if they revealed important military information. Critical comments about the war effort could result in a reporter being sent back to the United States, as was the case with Westbrook Pegler, who broke General John J. PERSHING's censorship rules by reporting the increase in deaths from the lack of dry clothing and warm shelters for American soldiers returning from the front. Women reporters such as Henrietta Hull experienced additional prohibitions on their reporting, as they were restricted to Paris. Even male reporters could not spend time with soldiers in the trenches.

During WORLD WAR II strict censorship was imposed. As soon as the United States entered the war, the government created the Office of Censorship and the Office of War Information. The patriotic atmosphere prevalent throughout the country, however, resulted in a generally favorable treatment of the U.S. war effort, so censorship was limited.

During the war many journalists followed soldiers into the front lines to obtain firsthand knowledge of their experiences. The best known of these was Ernie PYLE. His account of the beach after the NORMANDY INVASION brought the reality of war back home to the American public. His description of destroyed tanks and trucks on the beaches and in the water, the German-emplaced obstacles, the piles of discarded life jackets and shells, soldiers' packs and rations floating on the water, all gave an effective image of the chaos and destruction of the battle. Pyle convinced his readers that despite all of this, the battle was worth the cost because the Allies had gained a foothold in France. Pyle later transferred to the Pacific theater, where he continued to write about the war until he was killed by Japanese fire in April 1945 on OKINAWA. His frank and honest portrayal of combat made him very popular with the troops.

During the KOREAN WAR reports from many correspondents, especially Marguerite Higgins and Homer Bigart, openly described the chaos and disorganization of the U.S. military. This led General Douglas MACARTHUR to impose severe restrictions on press access. While Higgins and Bigart believed that the reality of the situation would inspire the American public to increase their support of the war efforts, MacArthur feared that negative reporting would result in the North Koreans winning the psychological war. Although the military failed to issue guidelines for self-censorship until MacArthur's decision to restrict the press, war correspondents and commanders afterward reached an understanding on the sort of information that should be revealed.

The VIETNAM WAR brought a tremendous change in the way war was reported. For one thing, it was covered so extensively on television that it was known as "the first television war." Images were relayed by satellite and available almost immediately in living rooms across America. During the early years correspondents traveled with the troops when space was available. In the field they witnessed events that often contradicted the official press releases. With no official censorship in place, journalists such as

Morley Safer and Malcom Browne questioned whether the United States could actually win the war. Most reporting was favorable and supportive of the U.S. war effort, although this support diminished after the 1968 TET OFFENSIVE, when many Americans turned against the war. A major turning point occurred when Walter Cronkite, the highly respected CBS anchorman, voiced his concerns about the veracity of military claims that the war was being won. Anxious for scapegoats following the war, many in the U.S. military came to believe, falsely, that antiwar reporting had cost America the war. As a consequence of the Vietnam experience, during the administrations of Ronald Reagan and George H. W. BUSH, reporters were often excluded from military operations. When the U.S. forces invaded GRENADA in 1983, the press obtained its information from secondhand sources or by hiring vessels to gain access to the island. After this exclusion of the press, an agreement with military officials resulted in the creation of the "journalist pool." This system was utilized during Operations DESERT SHIELD and DESERT STORM, but dissatisfaction among the media led to a revised agreement by which reporters would enjoy access to the troops unless it was militarily not feasible.

Currently the Department of Defense National Media Pool coordinates short-notice departures from Andrews Air Force Base, with media representatives invited on board when troops are deployed in combat situations. Attempts to achieve a balance between mission safety and the right of the American public to know about U.S. military operations continue.

See also PROPAGANDA.

Further reading: Emery, Michael C. *On the Front Lines: Following America's Foreign Correspondents Across the Twentieth Century.* Washington, D.C.: American University Press, 1995; Mathews, Joseph James. *Reporting the War.* Minneapolis: University of Minnesota Press, 1957; May, Antoinette. *Witness to War: A Biography of Marguerite Higgins.* New York: Beaufort Books, 1983; Tobin, James. *Ernie Pyle's War: America's Eyewitness to World War II.* New York: Free Press, 1997.

— Cynthia Clark Northrup

Warrington, Lewis (1782–1851) *U.S. Navy officer*
Born on 3 November 1782 in Williamsburg, Virginia, Lewis Warrington attended William and Mary College and joined the navy as a midshipman in 1800. Throughout the QUASI-WAR WITH FRANCE, Warrington served aboard the frigate *Chesapeake* during several sweeps of the West Indies and later served in the TRIPOLITAN WAR on the schooner *Vixen.* He advanced to lieutenant in 1805, before returning to the United States to command a gunboat at Norfolk. Warrington next transferred as executive officer of the brig *Siren* and spent several years conveying diplomatic dispatches between France and the United States.

When the War of 1812 commenced, Warrington sailed with Commodore John RODGERS's squadron aboard the frigate *United States.* He rose to master commandant in 1813 before taking command of the sloop of war *Peacock.* While cruising off Cape Canaveral on 29 April 1813, Warrington encountered the British brig *Epervier* and gave battle. The two ships were evenly matched but, after a battle of 45 minutes, the British vessel struck its flag with losses 10 times greater than its opponent. Congress awarded Warrington a gold medal, and he received an elegant sword from his native state. The *Peacock* went on to conduct cruises along the Irish and Portuguese coasts, netting an additional 14 prizes. Warrington then rounded the Cape of Good Hope into the Indian Ocean and further harassed British shipping. Unaware that the Treaty of GHENT had been signed six months previously, on 30 June 1815 Warrington engaged and defeated the brig *Nautilus.* This was the last naval action of the War of 1812, but Warrington relinquished his prize when informed of the situation.

Warrington returned to the Mediterranean in 1815, commanding the frigate *Macedonian.* He returned home in 1820 to assume control of navy yards at Norfolk and Pensacola, having selected the location of the latter with Captain James BIDDLE. He also led the East India Squadron between 1824 and 1826. Warrington subsequently served many years on the Navy Board and, when that office was abolished in 1841, became chief of the Bureau of Docks and Yards. His final assignment was as head of the Bureau of Ordnance from 1847 to 1851. Warrington died in Washington, D.C., on 12 October 1851.

See also WAR OF 1812: NAVAL OVERVIEW.

Further reading: McKee, Christopher. *A Gentlemanly and Honorable Profession: The Creation of the U.S. Naval Officer Corps, 1794–1815.* Annapolis, Md.: Naval Institute Press, 1991; Pratt, Fletcher. *Preble's Boys: Commodore Preble and the Birth of American Seapower.* New York: Sloan, 1950.

— John C. Fredriksen

Washington, burning of (24–26 August 1814) *Major event during the War of 1812*
During 1813 and 1814 the British navy, supported by the Royal Marines and British army, controlled the waters of the Chesapeake Bay, conducting a series of waterborne raids against coastal towns along the Chesapeake and its tributaries.

In early August 1814, although American commanders were forewarned that a British raid was imminent, they did not know the precise location. British Rear Admiral Sir George Cockburn wanted to strike at Washington, D.C., believing that the capture of a capital was "always so great a blow to the government of a country," and the British sought revenge for the burning of YORK (Toronto) by the Americans. British commanders also anticipated that attacks on Annapolis and Baltimore would be easier from the land than by sea. British ground forces under Major General Robert Ross landed at Benedict, Maryland, during 19–20 August, forcing the self-destruction of Commodore Joshua BARNEY's small Chesapeake Flotilla.

U.S. Army brigadier general William Winder correctly believed that the cities of Baltimore, Washington, and Annapolis were possible targets, but neither he nor Secretary of War John ARMSTRONG made any concerted attempt to defend the capital. Winder was also handicapped by the apathy of Secretary Armstrong when confronted with the danger to Washington. Although overall the American force was numerically superior to the British invasion force, Winder spread his 6,000 militiamen and 500 regulars to try to defend all three cities. In addition, the Americans were no match for the 4,500 well-trained British veterans of the Napoleonic Wars.

The British skillfully masked their actual objective. Winder realized that Washington was the true target only on 24 August, after learning that the British were already marching on BLADENSBURG. He gathered his forces opposite Bladensburg, but, after feeble resistance, the American forces fled the field in a rout that became known as "the Bladensburg Races." Only Barney's sailors and marines managed a serious effort.

President James Madison was caught up in the retreat as citizens and government officials abandoned Washington. As many of the government documents as could be carried were evacuated, but many were left behind because of a shortage of wagons. First Lady Dolley Madison evacuated the White House bringing what papers and valuables she could. U.S. Navy captain Thomas Tingey, following standing orders, fired the Washington Navy Yard, along with new frigate *Columbia,* sloop of war *Argus,* and several gunboats.

The British army entered Washington on the evening of the 24th. Ross intended to ransom the city, but was unable to find anyone who was authorized to do so. His troops then began to set fire to the government buildings. The Capitol, White House, Treasury, War Office, Arsenal, and various smaller buildings were all put to the torch. After a particularly severe storm (which may have included a tornado) struck Washington on the 25th, Ross retraced his steps to join the fleet at Benedict. Although the storm helped to put out the fires, many government documents were destroyed. The chief military consequence was the destruction of the navy yard.

The British raid was a major embarrassment to the Madison administration, but at the time Washington possessed little strategic or military value. The raid did stimulate a major review of U.S. defense policies. The British moved on to Baltimore, but there they were turned back by a determined defense.

See also WAR OF 1812: LAND OVERVIEW OF.

Further reading: Lord, Walter. *The Dawn's Early Light.* New York: W. W. Norton, 1972; Pitch, Anthony S. *The Burning of Washington: The British Invasion of 1814.* Annapolis, Md.: Naval Institute Press, 1998.

— Michael J. Manning

Washington, George (1732–1799) *Commander in chief of the Continental Army during the American Revolutionary War and first president of the United States*

Born on 22 February 1732 in Westmoreland County, Virginia, George Washington had little formal education but learned to write well. He had sufficient facility in mathematics to master surveying and secure an appointment as surveyor of Culpepper County in 1749. Washington received his first military appointment at age 20 as a major in the Virginia militia.

Beginning in 1753, Washington was involved in the struggle between Britain and France for North America. His actions on behalf of the Crown as a colonel in the Virginia militia to maintain British control of the Ohio country led to the first shots fired in the 1754–63 FRENCH AND INDIAN WAR. In 1755, Washington volunteered to accompany British Major General Edward BRADDOCK as his aide-de-camp on his ill-fated attack against FORT DUQUESNE, and in 1758 he commanded Virginia troops as part of

George Washington is named commander in chief of the Continental army, 15 June 1775.   *(Library of Congress)*

Brigadier General John FORBES's successful expedition to capture that French fort.

From 1759 to 1775, Washington lived as a modestly prosperous planter at his home, Mount Vernon. He represented his state as a delegate to both the First and Second Continental Congresses in Philadelphia in 1774 and 1775. On 15 June 1775, during the Second Continental Congress, Washington was named commander in chief of the newly created CONTINENTAL ARMY. Despite his lack of significant military experience, Washington possessed a reputation for honesty and judgment, and his quiet, dignified manner earned respect.

As commander in chief, Washington never exercised the full authority granted to him, partly because of the chaotic nature of the American war effort, but primarily because he was careful not to appear to be a rival to the authority of Congress. While this deference to political authorities at times hindered his ability to carry out his duties, it established a precedent that American military professionals still follow today.

Throughout the American Revolutionary War, Washington sought to improve the discipline and training of his volunteer army. Poorly armed, lacking gunpowder and clothing, prone to short enlistments, and led by officers who had little knowledge of their duties, the Continental army struggled. With limited resources and faced with the superiority of the British army's training and discipline and British dominance at sea, Washington could fight only a defensive war. Washington would attack when British forces were vulnerable, but not in such a way as to expose his own army to total defeat.

Washington's initial efforts resulted in near disasters. In the summer of 1776, he nearly lost his entire force during early fighting in New York, and the remnants of his army were driven into Pennsylvania by the end of the year. That the army survived at all is a testimony to Washington's personal leadership, personal courage, and strength of will.

Although he sought the advice of his subordinates, Washington was a bold and aggressive commander when opportunities arose. Using deception and spies, Washington availed himself of enemy weaknesses. At TRENTON and PRINCETON in 1776, at GERMANTOWN in 1777, and MONMOUTH COURTHOUSE in 1778, Washington struck British detachments with skill and determination. In the latter encounter, the American Continentals finally displayed improved combat skills, a product of Major General Friedrich von STEUBEN's emphasis on drill and discipline.

The alliance with France in 1778 provided Washington with the means to achieve victory. With augmentation from a professional field force, money to pay soldiers and buy supplies, and, most importantly, with the French navy, Washington could now strike a decisive blow. In 1781, coordinating a combined land and sea effort, Washington rapidly moved the Franco-American army from New York to Virginia to meet with a French fleet and trap a British force under Lieutenant General Charles Lord Cornwallis at YORKTOWN, Virginia. Although an American army would be in the field for two more years, Yorktown was the decisive victory that finally forced the British government to abandon its efforts to quell the rebellion.

In 1787, Washington became president of the convention that produced the United States Constitution. In 1789, he became the first president of the new government formed under the Constitution. He established the two-term precedent and set the tone and protocol for the new republic. Granted the rank of lieutenant general by Congress, Washington took field command of 15,000 militia during the WHISKEY REBELLION in 1794. He retired to Mount Vernon in 1797 and died there on 14 December 1799, revered as the father of his country.

See also BOSTON, SIEGE OF; CONWAY CABAL; FORT NECESSITY CAMPAIGN; FORT WASHINGTON; FRANCE AND THE AMERICAN REVOLUTION; LAFAYETTE, MARIE-JOSEPH P. Y. R. G. DU MOTIER; MILITIA, ORGANIZATION AND ROLE OF; MORRISTOWN, BATTLE OF; VALLEY FORGE.

Further reading: Brookhiser, Richard. *Founding Father: Rediscovering George Washington.* New York: Free Press, 1996; Flexner, James T. *George Washington in the American Revolution, 1775–1783.* Boston: Little, Brown, 1968; Freeman, Douglas Southall. *George Washington.* 7 vols. New York: Scribner's, 1949–1957; Frothingham, Thomas G. *Washington, Commander in Chief.* Boston: Houghton Mifflin, 1930.

— Keith D. Dickson

Washington and London naval agreements (1922, 1930) *Arms control agreements reached between the two world wars*

The end of World War I and the establishment of the League of Nations served as foundations for broader international efforts to reduce the arms race. Such efforts also were sparked by financial considerations. A number of arms limitations conferences were held, attended by Britain, France, Italy, Japan, the United States, and other powers. In the naval sphere, two important meetings occurred—in Washington, during 1921–22, and in London in 1930. Treaties and agreements negotiated in these conferences had a dramatic impact on naval strategy and war planning, overseas basing, shipbuilding, and international diplomacy, especially in the Pacific.

On taking office in 1921, President Warren G. Harding followed up on a British suggestion to hold talks on the limitation of naval construction. The United States was then building ships at a rate that would have made it the premier naval power in the world. The Naval Arms Limitation Conference began on 21 November 1920, with U.S. Secretary of State Charles Evans Hughes announcing that not only was his government prepared to build fewer ships, but also that it was willing to reduce the number of major combatants in its fleet. Following heated negotiations, on 6 February 1922 a series of treaties and resolutions were signed.

The first of the seven treaties provided for limits in tonnage of battleships and aircraft carriers. The United States and Britain each were allowed 525,000 tons; Japan, 315,000; and France and Italy, 175,000 tons each. Britain had to scrap 1,500,000 tons of warships. The United States also scrapped four dreadnought battleships and others under construction.

In addition, major capital ships were limited to 35,000 tons displacement and could not mount guns greater than 16-inch caliber. Although the Japanese were unhappy with the limitation on their capital ship construction, they secured a pledge from the United States and Britain not to fortify their Pacific bases within striking range of Japan. There was no limit on the construction of submarines and smaller warships.

The lack of progress in additional naval reductions at the failed 1927 Geneva Conference was a further indication of continued problems between the major powers in the Pacific. Nevertheless, attempts at further reductions continued to be a significant issue in the United States for a variety of reasons. For internal military, political, and economic reasons (a recession in the early 1920s and the Great Depression that began in 1929), the United States did not build up to the tonnage allowed by the Washington treaty as Congress refused to appropriate adequate funding.

The London Naval Conference of 1930 proposed, in the opening lines of the treaty, "to carry forward the work begun by the Washington Naval Conference." In reality, this conference was an attempt to at least slow the rearmament of key powers in both Europe and Asia. France and Italy were excused from certain provisions and the United States, Britain, and Japan negotiated separately for reductions in naval tonnage in the Pacific.

The system devised under the Washington treaty came apart in the politically charged environment of German, French, and Italian rearmament and Japanese aggression in China. While the London treaty attempted to expand limitations on naval forces by including submarines and smaller combatants, the very foundations of peace and the naval arms control effort were crumbling. Although Japan signed the treaty, internal dissension in that country between the weak civilian leadership and the increasingly politically powerful Imperial Japanese Navy and Army made these additional arms control agreements untenable in terms of verification, compliance, and long-term success.

By 1935, Japan refused to follow the provisions of the Washington treaty and withdrew from the second London Conference of 1936. War with China began in July 1937 and the naval forces necessary to conduct and support the 1941 offensives against British and U.S. bases in the Pacific were being built, crewed, and trained virtually unfettered by international naval arms limitation agreements.

See also NAVY, U.S.

Further reading: Evans, David C., and Mark R. Peattie. *Kaigun: Strategy, Tactics, and Technology in the Imperial Japanese Navy, 1887–1941.* Annapolis, Md.: Naval Institute Press, 1997; Goldman, Emily O. *Sunken Treaties: Naval Arms Control Between the Wars.* University Park: Pennsylvania State University Press, 1994; Petz, Stephen E. *Race to Pearl Harbor: The Failure of the Second London Naval Conference and the Onset of World War II.* Cambridge, Mass.: Harvard University Press, 1974.

— J. G. D. Babb

Washita River, Battle of the (27 November 1868)

The U.S. Army's first major victory over the Southern Plains tribes in fighting following the Civil War

In the summer of 1868, Cheyenne warriors slipped from their reservation in Indian Territory to raid western Kansas. These violations of the Medicine Lodge treaties infuriated Commander of the Department of the Missouri major general Philip H. SHERIDAN, who organized a punitive campaign.

Recognizing the difficulty of catching mounted Indians in warm weather, Sheridan decided to strike in the winter, when they were more vulnerable. With the onset of freezing temperatures, the Southern Plains bands came together in large villages, which made tempting targets. Decreased hunting limited the Indians' food supply, and lack of grass weakened their ponies. Because U.S. soldiers rarely took the field in wintertime, Indians exercised less vigilance.

To improve the army's prospects for success, Sheridan directed three columns to converge on the native villages clustered in the Canadian and Washita Valleys. Major Andrew W. Evans was to march eastward from Fort Bascom, New Mexico, with 563 cavalry, infantry, and four mountain howitzers. Major Eugene A. Carr was to sweep to the southeast from Fort Lyon, Colorado, with 650 troopers drawn from three cavalry regiments. Sheridan's strongest column was to consist of 11 companies of the 7th U.S. Cavalry and the newly raised 19th Kansas Cavalry, based at Camp Supply in northern Indian Territory. Command of this force fell to Lieutenant Colonel George A. CUSTER, one of Sheridan's favorite officers.

When heavy snows delayed the arrival of the 19th Kansas, the indefatigable Custer commenced operations on 23 November with his 800 7th Cavalrymen. Custer attempted to follow the back trail of an outbound Cheyenne war party but lost it in the deepening snow. Pushing on, the soldiers discovered the trail of returning Kiowa braves on 26 November, which led them to a small Cheyenne village of 51 lodges on the south bank of the Washita River shortly after midnight. Unknown to Custer, several larger villages containing 6,000 Arapaho, Kiowa, Cheyenne, and Comanche stretched for 10 miles downstream.

Utilizing the remaining hours of darkness, Custer divided the 7th Cavalry into four battalions. At dawn on 27 November, the troopers slashed into the village from all sides and quickly overwhelmed their surprised opponents. Custer captured 53 women and children and claimed that his men killed 103 warriors, but the dead included many women and children. The Cheyenne would insist that they lost only about a dozen fighting men. Among them lay village chief Black Kettle, a longtime peace advocate. The 7th Cavalry's dead included two officers and 20 enlisted men. Most of these fell with Major Joel H. Elliott, who rode downstream to round up fleeing noncombatants, only to be cut off by hundreds of aroused warriors from neighboring villages.

Confronted by this formidable threat, Custer destroyed the property of Black Kettle's people, slaughtered their pony herd, and successfully withdrew the 7th Cavalry to Camp Supply.

Although tarnished by controversy, Custer's victory vindicated Sheridan's winter strategy and had an intimidating effect on the Southern Plains tribes. Those bands would return to their reservations in the coming months, but most would resume hostile activities in the future.

See also AMERICAN INDIAN WARS; MACKENZIE, RANALD S.; RED RIVER WAR; SALT CREEK PRAIRIE RAID; SAND CREEK MASSACRE; SIOUX WARS.

Further reading: Hoig, Stan. *The Battle of the Washita: The Sheridan-Custer Indian Campaign of 1867–69.* Garden City, N.Y.: Doubleday, 1976; Kraft, Louis. *Custer and the Cheyenne: George Armstrong Custer's Winter Campaign on the Southern Plains.* El Segundo, Calif.: Upton & Sons, 1995; Utley, Robert M. *Cavalier in Buckskin: George Armstrong Custer and the Western Military Frontier.* Norman: University of Oklahoma Press, 1988; Utley, Robert M. *Frontier Regulars: The United States Army and the Indian, 1866–1890.* New York: Macmillan, 1973.

— Gregory J. W. Urwin

Watchtower, Operation (7 August 1942– 9 February 1943) *Code name for the Allied Solomon Islands Campaign against Japan in the Pacific theater during World War II*

After the American naval victories in the Battles of the CORAL SEA and MIDWAY earlier in 1942, Allied (primarily American but also Australian) forces adopted an island-hopping strategy in NEW GUINEA and the Solomons from late 1942 into 1943. These islands were in close proximity to one another and thus easily lent themselves to such a strategy. U.S. amphibious and naval forces would attack and subdue a Japanese island base, then use it as a staging point for an assault on the next Japanese-held island.

The Allies targeted GUADALCANAL, an island located near the southeastern tip of the Solomon islands, as their primary strategic objective in Operation Watchtower because the Japanese were constructing an air base there. This operation was planned as the first phase in an effort to subdue the powerful Japanese base at Rabaul on New Britain. From Guadalcanal, land-based aircraft could strike at Japanese forces in the region and support the island-hopping strategy.

Major General Alexander A. VANDEGRIFT's 1st Marine Division landed on the nearby island of Tulagi as well as on Guadalcanal on 7 August 1942. The marines managed to take the Japanese airfield, which they renamed Henderson Field. Then, on the night of 9 August, the Allies suffered a major defeat when, in the Battle of SAVO ISLAND, the Americans lost three cruisers and a destroyer and the Australians one cruiser, while the Japanese lost no ships.

Rear Admiral Richmond K. TURNER, who had tactical command of operations on Guadalcanal, then ordered the transport vessels to retire beyond range of Japanese attack. This decision left 11,000 marines on the island and another 7,000 marines on Tulagi. The situation was precarious, as the marines ashore had rations for only one month and ammunition for only four days. But the United States managed to keep them supplied. Henderson Field was essential to winning the battle, and the Japanese made repeated efforts to take it. For six months, fighting on Guadalcanal raged as both America and Japan reinforced their troops ashore.

Meanwhile, ongoing battles occurred in the air above and seas around Guadalcanal as the Japanese endeavored to run supplies at night from Rabaul down the "Slot" to the island. Gradually, Allied air and sea power prevailed. Guadalcanal was secured in early February 1943, when Japanese destroyers evacuated the last remaining Japanese soldiers.

Allied forces then progressed in a northwestern direction through the Solomons chain. To the southwest, General Douglas MACARTHUR's troops simultaneously assaulted New Guinea. Both were regarded as essential preludes to the planned attack on Rabaul. This attack never occurred because the Japanese stronghold was bypassed when LEAPFROGGING replaced island-hopping.

See also SOLOMON ISLANDS CAMPAIGN; WORLD WAR II, U.S. INVOLVEMENT: PACIFIC THEATER.

Further reading: Coggins, Jack. *The Campaign for Guadalcanal.* New York: Doubleday, 1972; Frank, Richard B. *Guadalcanal: The Definitive Account of the Landmark Battle.* New York: Random House, 1990; Hough, Frank O., et al. *Victory and Occupation: History of U. S. Marine Corps Operations in World War II. Vol. 1, Pearl Harbor to Guadalcanal.* Washington, D.C.: Government Printing Office, 1968; Spector, Ronald H. *Eagle Against the Sun: The American War with Japan.* New York: Free Press, 1985.

— David J. Ulbrich

Watie, Stand (1806–1871) *Confederate general and principal chief of the Confederate Cherokee*
Born on 12 December 1806 near present-day Calhoun, Georgia, Stand Watie in the early 1830s became a member of a Cherokee faction that believed removal to the West was inevitable. This faction favored cooperation with U.S. government officials and voluntary relocation. The faction was opposed by a group led by principal chief John Ross, who had the support of the majority of Cherokees.

In 1837 Watie and other pro-removal Cherokees signed the Treaty of New Echota, Georgia, and relocated to what is now Oklahoma. The majority of the Cherokees, led by Ross, rejected the Treaty of New Echota and refused to leave Georgia. They were forcibly removed over the "Trail of Tears" during 1838 and 1839.

On 22 June 1839 many of the treaty signers were assassinated, including Watie's brother, uncle, and cousin. Watie barely escaped. A deadly feud broke out between the two factions, with Watie the acknowledged leader of the pro-removal Cherokees. In 1846 the two sides signed a treaty, whereby they ended internal fighting.

When the CIVIL WAR began in 1861, Watie joined the Confederate cause in order to protect the Cherokees' right to own slaves. Commissioned a colonel, he recruited a regiment of Cherokee to serve in the Confederate army. It was later known as the 2d Cherokee Regiment of Mounted Rifles.

Watie's regiment participated in several battles, including WILSON's creek (10 August 1861), PEA RIDGE (6–8 March 1862), and the First Battle of Cabin Creek (1 July 1863). The 2d Cherokee became famous for guerrilla warfare against much larger numbers of Union troops. Watie's two greatest victories came in 1864, when he captured the Union steamboat *J. R. Williams,* and in the Second Battle

of Cabin Creek (19 September 1864), during which his troops seized some $1.5 million of Union supplies.

Watie became the only Native-American general during the Civil War when he was promoted to brigadier general in May 1864. He was also the last Confederate commander to surrender to the Union, on 23 June 1865, more than two months after General Robert E. LEE's surrender at APPOMATTOX.

After the Civil War Watie continued his involvement in Cherokee Nation politics. He died at Honey Springs, Indian Territory, on 9 September 1871.

Further reading: Cunningham, Frank. *General Stand Watie's Confederate Indians.* Norman: University of Oklahoma Press, 1998; Dale, E. E., and Gaston Litton. *Cherokee Cavaliers: Forty Years of Cherokee History as Told in the Correspondence of the Ridge-Watie-Boudinot Family.* Norman: University of Oklahoma Press, 1939; Knight, Wilfred. *Red Fox: Stand Watie and the Confederate Indian Nations During the Civil War Years in Indian Territory.* Glendale, Calif.: Arthur H. Clark, 1988.

— Mary S. Rausch

Waxhaws Creek, Battle of (29 May 1780) *American Revolutionary War battle*
In the course of the 1780 siege of CHARLESTON by British forces under Lieutenant General Sir Henry Clinton, Colonel Abraham Buford and his 350-man 3d Virginia Continentals and some 50 North Carolina militia were sent to reinforce the beleaguered city. They had reached Lenud's Ferry on the Santee River when they learned that Major General Benjamin LINCOLN had surrendered Charleston on 11 May. Buford then ordered his men to withdraw to Salisbury, North Carolina.

News of Buford's force reached British Lieutenant General Charles Lord Cornwallis at Nelson's Ferry up the Santee. Buford's withdrawal toward the Cape Fear River was slowed by his large supply train. Since the rebels were beyond the reach of his own slow-moving force, Cornwallis dispatched Lieutenant Colonel Banastre Tarleton's 170-man legion. It consisted of the British 17th Dragoon Regiment and Loyalist infantry from New York.

In an effort to catch Buford, Tarleton's command rode some 105 miles in just 54 hours. On 29 May they were within striking distance of the Patriot force. In order to slow his adversary, Tarleton sent Buford a summons to surrender, exaggerating the size of his force as 700 men. While the two sides discussed terms, Tarleton sent men through the woods to cut off an American retreat.

According to Patriot troops who were passing through an open wood near the town of Waxhaws, the truce had not ended when a British bugle call initiated an attack on their rear. Although Buford was taken completely by surprise, he refused to surrender and hurriedly formed a battle line. He ordered the men not to fire until the British force was close upon them. Although the Patriots felled a few British troops and shot Tarleton's horse from under him, the British cavalry quickly closed upon the Americans and broke Buford's line.

Buford then raised a white flag and tried to surrender, but the legion ignored Patriot pleas for quarter. The British officers lost control of their men, who believed their leader had been slain. The British then cut down the unresisting colonists. Seeing that surrender was hopeless, the remaining Americans picked up their weapons to fight, but in vain.

At Waxhaws Tarleton's force suffered but five killed and 15 wounded. A total of 113 Americans were killed and another 150 seriously wounded, only 53 of whom survived. Tarleton left the wounded on the field and paroled them where they fell.

The Americans claimed that Tarleton's men bayoneted the wounded. Whatever the actual facts of the matter, the expression "Tarleton's quarter" became synonymous with British brutality in the war, and Tarleton earned the nickname of "Bloody Ban." The remainder of Buford's force escaped into North Carolina.

See also AMERICAN REVOLUTIONARY WAR: LAND OVERVIEW.

Further reading: Bass, Robert D. *The Green Dragon: The Lives of Banastre Tarleton and Mary Robinson.* New York: Holt, 1973; Edgar, Walter B. *Partisans and Redcoats: The American Revolution in the South Carolina Backcountry.* New York: Morrow, 2001; Pancake, John S. *The Destructive War: The British Campaign in the Carolinas, 1780–1782.* Tuscaloosa: University of Alabama Press, 1985; Scheer, George F., and Hugh F. Rankin. *Rebels and Redcoats: The Living Story of the American Revolution.* Cleveland: World, 1957.

— Brian D. Frank

Wayne, Anthony ("Mad Anthony") (1745–1796)
Continental army general and commander of the Legion of the United States

Born on 1 January 1745 at Waynesboro, Pennsylvania, Wayne was educated at the Academy in Philadelphia but quit school to become a surveyor. Later elected to the Pennsylvania colonial assembly, he was soon identified with the Patriot cause.

Commissioned a colonel of the 4th Pennsylvania Regiment in January 1776, Wayne had no formal military training. He first distinguished himself during the American Revolutionary War in covering the retreat of forces under Brigadier General John SULLIVAN from Canada in 1776.

This brought Wayne promotion to brigadier general in February 1777.

Wayne fought well in the September Battle of the BRANDYWINE but was subsequently surprised in the action at PAOLI. Wayne demanded a court-martial, which exonerated him. He then fought with distinction in the October Battle of GERMANTOWN and spent the winter at VALLEY FORGE. The next summer he led the van in the Battle of MONMOUTH COURT HOUSE, holding off a British attack and allowing the Continental forces time to regroup. His best-known action of the war, however, came in the July 1779 Battle of STONY POINT, New York, when, in a night attack, his troops captured a fortified British position using only the bayonet. The action brought him the Thanks of Congress and a gold medal.

In September 1780, Wayne helped to prevent the British capture of WEST POINT, and in 1781 he quelled a mutiny of the Pennsylvania line. Transferring to the south, Wayne fought in the YORKTOWN CAMPAIGN, then joined Major General Nathanael GREENE and took the surrender of Savannah in July 1782 and of Charleston that December. He then pacified the Creek and Cherokee Indians. Wayne won a brevet promotion to major general before leaving the army in December 1782. His audacity as a battlefield general led to the nickname from his colleagues of "Mad Anthony."

Wayne then farmed in Pennsylvania and was a member of the state assembly in 1785 and a delegate to the Constitutional Convention. He subsequently moved to Georgia to manage land holdings there. Although unsuccessful in a bid for the U.S. Senate from that state in 1788, Wayne won election to the U.S. House of Representatives in 1791, but was expelled from that body in March 1792 for corrupt election practices.

That year, with Wayne's fortunes at low ebb and following the disastrous HARMAR and ST. CLAIR EXPEDITIONS, President George WASHINGTON recalled Wayne as a major general to command the 5,000-man LEGION OF THE UNITED STATES. Wayne took advantage of prolonged negotiations with the Indians to train his force, emphasizing close-order drill, field fortification, marksmanship, proper sanitation, and esprit de corps.

In the summer of 1794, Wayne led this force, supported by Kentucky militia, in an invasion of the Ohio Territory. In August he won the decisive Battle of FALLEN TIMBERS, breaking forever the power of the Native Americas in the eastern region of the Old Northwest. The battle also did much to restore the prestige of the army, and Wayne richly deserves to be called the father of the new U.S. Regular Army. Wayne became ill and died at Presque Isle (now Erie), Pennsylvania, on 15 December 1796.

See also AMERICAN REVOLUTIONARY WAR: LAND OVERVIEW; ARMY, U.S.

Further reading: Fox, Joseph L. *Anthony Wayne: Washington's Reliable General.* Chicago: Adams Press, 1988; Kohn, Richard. *Eagle and Sword: The Federalists and the Creation of the Military Establishment in America, 1783–1802.* New York: Free Press, 1975; Palmer, Dave R. *1794: America, Its Army, and the Birth of the Nation.* Novato, Calif.: Presidio Press, 1994.

— Spencer C. Tucker

Welles, Gideon (1802–1878) *Secretary of the navy during the Civil War*

Born on 1 July 1802 in Glastonbury, Connecticut, Gideon Welles was educated in private schools, studied law, and later became the editor of the *Hartford Times* and took a leading role in organizing the Democratic Party in Connecticut. He served in the Connecticut legislature from 1827 to 1835. In addition, Welles served as state controller of public accounts and postmaster of Hartford until the Whigs took power in 1841. Thereafter, he served as chief of the navy's Bureau of Provisions and Clothing. Switching to the new Republican Party in 1856, Welles founded the *Hartford Evening Press*, which supported the Republicans.

Following Abraham LINCOLN's election to the presidency, the new president appointed Welles secretary of the navy. Although the U.S. Navy had few ships available for immediate service, Welles and Gustavus V. FOX, later assistant secretary of the navy, immediately chartered and purchased civilian vessels for conversion into warships. They also initiated construction of new vessels. Under Welles's able leadership, the Navy's 42 warships in 1861 grew to approximately 670 ships by the end of the war. The secretary resisted Northern pleas to provide ships to defend the Federal coastline; rather, he used the ships to blockade the Confederacy, isolating the South, and to operate on the great rivers of the West. Welles also ordered construction of ironclad warships in response to Southern ironclad production.

Welles overhauled and reorganized Navy Department administration. He established the post of assistant secretary, increased the number of staff bureaus, forced into retirement officers no longer physically able to perform active duty, supported the promotion of officers based on merit rather than seniority, standardized ranks for line officers, and kept his department free of corruption and graft. Most of Welles's administrative changes remained in place long after his departure.

Welles continued to serve as naval secretary after the war under President Andrew Johnson. He resigned in 1869 when President Ulysses S. GRANT assumed office. Welles returned to Hartford to write newspaper and magazine articles on the war. In 1874, Welles published *Lincoln and Seward.* He died at Hartford, Connecticut, on 10 February 1878. His wartime diary was published in 1911.

See also CIVIL WAR, NAVAL OVERVIEW; IRONCLADS, U.S. IN CIVIL WAR.

Further reading: Beale, Howard K., ed. *The Diary of Gideon Welles.* 3 vols. New York: W. W. Norton, 1960; Niven, John. *Gideon Welles: Lincoln's Secretary of War.* Baton Rouge: Louisiana State University Press, 1994.

— Alexander Mendoza

Wells, William (1770–1812) *Indian agent and fighter*

Born in 1770 near Jacob's Creek, Pennsylvania, William Wells moved with his family to Kentucky in 1779. In 1784, at age 14, he was captured by the Miami Indians and taken to present Indiana. There he was adopted by a Wea chief and took up life as a "white Indian." Named Apekonit ("wild carrot") for his red hair, Wells participated in raids against white settlements along the Ohio River Valley. He met Miami war chief LITTLE TURTLE, who became his lifelong friend and father-in-law.

On the initiation of fighting between the tribes in the Northwest Territory and the United States in 1790, Wells took a leading role, most notably in the utter defeat of ST. CLAIR'S EXPEDITION in November 1791. Wells played a key role in taking eight cannon. Shortly thereafter, however, Wells was reunited with his white family and for a brief time reentered white society in order to secure the release of his wife, who had been taken prisoner. Wells then acted as a scout for Major General Anthony WAYNE, playing an important role in the latter's victory in the August 1794 Battle of FALLEN TIMBERS. Among other things, he located cannon that he had helped to capture from St. Clair, turning them over to Wayne. He was largely responsible for getting Little Turtle to agree to the August 1795 Treaty of Greenville.

In 1797, Wells accompanied Little Turtle to a meeting in Washington with President John Adams. That same year, he secured the post of deputy Indian agent at Fort Wayne, which he held until 1800 and then again from 1802 to 1809 until forced out by partisan politics. In vain, Wells warned U.S. authorities that only fair treatment would keep the Indians of the Northwest friendly to the United States.

Reappointed in 1811, Wells was at FORT DEARBORN (Chicago) at the beginning of the WAR OF 1812. The commander there, Captain Nathan Heald, delayed orders from Brigadier General William HULL quickly to evacuate, and hostile Potawatomi Indians soon surrounded the fort. Although they promised safe passage to the fort's inhabitants, news of Hull's withdrawal from Canada led the Potawatomi to ambush the 96 whites, soldiers and dependents, and their Miami Indian escorts once they had left the fort's safety.

Wells, marching at the head of the column, and most of the party were killed on August 15; some survivors were ultimately ransomed. Wells died dressed in Indian regalia, his face painted black, an Indian sign of certain impending death.

See also ST. CLAIR, ARTHUR.

Further reading: Carter, Harvey Lewis. *The Life and Times of Little Turtle: First Sagamore of the Wabash.* Urbana: University of Illinois Press, 1987; Edmonds, David. *The Potawatomis: Keepers of the Fire.* Norman: University of Oklahoma Press, 1978; Hutton, Paul A. "William Wells: Frontier Scout and Indian Agent," *Indiana Magazine of History* 74 (1978): 183–222.

— Spencer C. Tucker

western North Carolina, uprising in (1771) *Revolt by inhabitants of western North Carolina against local and colonial government officials*

As the Piedmont area of the colony was settled, its people, mostly Scots-Irish and German, developed deep grievances over the manner in which they were taxed, forced to pay legal fees, and in many ways exploited by the colonial government, which was then dominated by the people of the tidewater, populated mostly by settlers of English and Scottish Highlands descent. Both sectional and ethnic differences added to the basic sense of injustice.

The first mass meeting of discontented westerners was held in October 1766 at Sandy Creek in Orange County. The meeting issued "Regulator Advertisement Number I," which appealed to the people of North Carolina to resist local oppression. Over the next several years, other "Regulator" documents would cite specific injustices.

In 1767, royal governor William Tryon admitted in private correspondence that many of the grievances were justified, including the embezzlement of public funds by local sheriffs. While he did not deal directly with the injustices, Tryon did issue warnings to public officials to not abuse the privilege of their offices. In 1768, the term "Regulator" came to be applied to the protestors. When the Regulators petitioned Tryon to redress their grievances, however, he denounced them.

More disturbances occurred, notably at Hillsborough court in September 1770. Meanwhile, efforts to gain redress through the colonial assembly not only failed, but the dominant eastern faction in the assembly pushed through the Johnson Riot Act, specifically directed at the Regulators. It made rioting an act of treason.

In 1771, Tryon issued orders for a special court to be held at Hillsborough in March. On 19 March, he called out militia to protect the judicial proceeding. On 3 May, at Smith's Ferry near Johnston Court House, Tryon reviewed this force of 1,068 officers and men, most from the eastern part of the colony. Another militia force of 284 officers and men, under Brigadier General Hugh Waddell, was to approach from the Cape Fear River.

On May 9, Tryon arrived with his force at Hillsborough. That same day, Waddell left Salisbury; but, after crossing the Yadkin River, he was halted by a much larger body of armed Regulators. Waddell then called a council of war and decided to withdraw to Salisbury.

Tryon left Hillsborough on 11 May to go to the relief of Waddell. His route of advance would take him through the heart of Regulator country. On the 14th, the militia reached Great Alamance Creek, where they rested. Two days later they resumed their march and had gone about five miles when they encountered a force of about 2,000 Regulators blocking the road. Tryon refused to hear a petition from the Regulators and instead demanded that they lay down their arms. When the Regulators refused, Tryon ordered his militia to open fire.

During the ensuing Battle of ALAMANCE the better-disciplined militia defeated the Regulators. The militia lost nine killed and 61 wounded. Regulator losses may have been nine dead, but the number of wounded were more difficult to assess as casualties were carried off. Of 14 Regulators captured, one was executed on the spot and six were subsequently tried and hanged for treason. Subsequent to the battle, Tryon issued a proclamation of amnesty, with a few exceptions, to any Regulators who would take an oath of allegiance to the government. Many Regulators, however, left North Carolina with their families. Some 200 former Regulators took part in the Loyalist uprising at MOORE'S CREEK BRIDGE in February 1776.

See also MILITIA, ORGANIZATION AND ROLE OF.

Further reading: Powell, William S. *North Carolina: Through Four Centuries.* Chapel Hill: University of North Carolina Press, 1989; ———. *The War of the Regulation and the Battle of Alamance, May 16, 1771.* Raleigh, N.C.: State Department of Archives and History, 1949.

— A. J. L. Waskey

West Florida, annexation of (1810) *Action that added the coastal plain on the Gulf of Mexico between the Perdidio and Iberville Rivers to the United States*

The territory had been claimed by Spain in 1492, explored by Hernando Desoto in the 1540s, occupied by France in 1695, and transferred to the British under the Treaty of PARIS of 1763, which ended the FRENCH AND INDIAN WAR. The Treaty of PARIS of 1783, ending the American Revolutionary War, returned the area to Spain.

In 1808, Emperor Napoléon installed his brother Joseph Bonaparte as king of Spain, and rumors of a possible seizure of West Florida by Spain led to calls in West Florida for a convention. With the consent of Governor Don Carlos Debault Delassus, delegates from the districts of San Feliciana, Baton Rouge, Saint Helena, and Tauchipaho assembled in convention at Saint John's Plains in July. Revolutionary factions then seized control. Declaring independence, they produced a constitution, organized a government, and chose John Rhae as president. A standing army of 104 men led by Philemon Thomas assembled and was ordered to take the Spanish fort at Baton Rouge.

Under a lone-star flag, Thomas stormed the fort, which was garrisoned by about 20 men under Louis Grandpré. Thomas's men next captured Baton Rouge and Governor Delassus. Declaring West Florida a free and independent republic, the revolutionaries then sought annexation by the United States. Simultaneously, they requested money and land for those who had planned and carried out the revolution.

On 27 October President James Madison, ignoring the West Florida Republic, claimed West Florida for the United States. He acted on the legal theory that it belonged to the United States because it had been part of the Louisiana Purchase. Madison ordered Governor William C. C. Claiborne in New Orleans to occupy West Florida and govern it as part of the Orleans Territory.

Token opposition arose in several places, especially at the Baton Rouge fort, but this evaporated following the appearance of U.S. troops. By the end of 1810 American forces had occupied West Florida from the Perdido River to the Mississippi, except for Mobile, which was occupied on 15 April 1813.

See also PATRIOT WAR.

Further reading: Fuller, Hubert Bruce. *The Purchase of Florida: Its History and Diplomacy.* 1906. Gainesville: University Presses of Florida, 1964.

— A. J. L. Waskey

Westmoreland, William Childs (1914–) *U.S. Army general, commander of U.S. forces in Vietnam, and chief of staff of the army*

Born on 26 March 1914 in Spartanburg County, South Carolina, William Westmoreland studied for a year at the Citadel. He then entered the U.S. Military Academy, WEST POINT, where he became first captain, the ranking cadet militarily, in the class of 1936.

Commissioned in the field artillery, early in World War II Westmoreland commanded a battalion in Tunisia and SICILY, then served successively as executive officer of division artillery and division chief of staff of the 9th Infantry Division, attaining the rank of colonel. Qualifying as a parachutist after the war, Westmoreland commanded the 504th Parachute Infantry Regiment, then was chief of staff of the 82d Airborne Division. Next came faculty assignments at the Command and General Staff College and the Army War College.

During the KOREAN WAR Westmoreland commanded the 187th Airborne Regimental Combat Team and advanced to brigadier general. Following Pentagon staff duty and studies in management at Harvard University, he returned to Washington as a major general and secretary of the General Staff. From 1958 to 1960 he commanded the 101st Airborne Division at Fort Campbell, Kentucky, then served as superintendent of the U.S. Military Academy (1960–63) and as commanding general of the XVIII Airborne Corps (1963–64), advancing to lieutenant general.

In January 1964, Westmoreland was sent to Vietnam as deputy to General Paul HARKINS; in June 1964, he succeeded Harkins as commander, U.S. Military Assistance Command, Vietnam (MACV), with promotion to full general. During the next four years, Westmoreland presided over the development of an extensive infrastructure of ports, airfields, depots, and base camps, and an accompanying massive buildup of American forces in Vietnam, with those forces taking over the dominant role in the fighting.

Left to devise his own approach to the conduct of the war, Westmoreland determined on a war of attrition. Thus "body count" became the measure of merit, and Westmoreland sought to inflict punishing losses on the Communist forces by conducting large sweeps, multibattalion and sometimes multidivision, primarily in the deep jungle. Newly developed airmobile forces played a prominent role in these operations. Using search and destroy tactics, these forces did inflict severe losses, but the desired effect was not achieved. Rather than cease its aggression against the South, North Vietnam simply absorbed its losses and continued pouring men and matériel into the conflict.

After the surprising and widespread coordinated Communist attacks all across South Vietnam in the 1968 TET OFFENSIVE, Westmoreland, encouraged by Chairman of the Joint Chiefs of Staff Earle WHEELER, sought additional troops. This precipitated a wide-ranging reexamination of the war in Washington, resulting in denial of the request and Westmoreland's replacement by Creighton ABRAMS. Westmoreland then was installed as army chief of staff.

During his 1968–72 tenure as chief of staff, Westmoreland traveled widely as a speaker. Planning for the army's transition to an all-volunteer force was a key issue during these years. Following retirement Westmoreland continued to speak widely and published his memoirs. In

1982, the Columbia Broadcasting System aired a television documentary accusing Westmoreland of deceiving his superiors about the true strength of Communist forces during his service in Vietnam. Westmoreland sued for libel and then, as the trial neared its conclusion, settled out of court. Westmoreland ran unsuccessfully for governor of South Carolina and has been in demand as a speaker at patriotic events.

See also JOHNSON, LYNDON B.; VIETNAM WAR.

Further reading: Furgurson, Ernest B. *Westmoreland: The Inevitable General.* Boston: Little, Brown, 1968; Westmoreland, William C. *A Soldier Reports.* Garden City, N.Y.: Doubleday, 1976; Zaffiri, Samuel. *Westmoreland: A Biography of General William C. Westmoreland.* New York: William Morrow, 1994.

— Lewis Sorley

West Point *Name given to a location—famous as the site of the U.S. Military Academy—on the Hudson River about 50 miles north of New York City*

Here there is a promontory and plateau on the west bank of the river where it makes a double-angle turn. Henry Hudson anchored his ship, the *Half Moon*, there in September 1609.

During the American Revolutionary War, Continental army commander General George WASHINGTON recognized the strategic importance of this point in controlling navigation on the Hudson and urged that strong fortifications be built there. A massive chain also was placed across the river at West Point as part of the defensive system. In 1780, the British arranged for the traitorous Major General Benedict ARNOLD, commanding the garrison, to surrender West Point to them for $30,000 and a major generalcy in the British army. The plot was discovered and thwarted.

In 1790, the U.S. government purchased 1,795 acres at West Point from Stephen Moore, and on 16 March 1802, Congress authorized establishment of the U.S. Military Academy and a Corps of Engineers, consisting of five officers and 10 cadets, to be located at West Point. The academy evolved and was placed on firm footing by Sylvanus THAYER, superintendent from 1817 to 1833. From its modest beginnings evolved a corps that today numbers some 4,000 cadets on a campus many times larger than the original. For many years, the name West Point has been synonymous with the academy.

See also EDUCATION: HIGHER MILITARY SCHOOLS; MILITARY ACADEMIES.

Further reading: Ambrose, Stephen E. *Duty, Honor, Country: A History of West Point.* Baltimore, Md.: Johns Hopkins University Press, 1999; Atkinson, Rick. *The Long Gray Line.* New York: Henry Holt, 1999.

— Uzal W. Ent

Weyand, Frederick C. (1916–   ) *U.S. Army general*
Born on 15 September 1916 in Arbuckle, California, Frederick Carlton Weyand graduated from the University of California at Berkeley in 1939. Commissioned a 2d lieutenant in the reserves in 1938, he was called to active duty and served with the 6th Artillery Regiment between 1940 and 1942. Promoted to major by November 1942, he then graduated from the Command and General Staff College at Fort Leavenworth, Kansas.

Following service with the Office of the Chief of Intelligence, War Department General Staff, Weyand became assistant chief of staff for intelligence (S-2) in the CHINA-BURMA-INDIA theater in 1944–45. Following World War II, he served on staff duty in both Washington and Hawaii.

After graduating from the Infantry School at Fort Benning, Georgia, in 1950, Weyand, by then a lieutenant colonel, commanded a battalion of the 7th Infantry Regiment and then served as assistant chief of staff for operations (G-3) of the 3d Infantry Division during the KOREAN WAR. After several years of staff duty and following graduation from the Army War College in 1958, Weyand commanded, as a full colonel, the 6th Infantry Regiment in Germany. Promoted to brigadier general in July 1960, Weyand served in the Pentagon until he was promoted to major general and given command of the 25th Infantry Division at Schofield Barracks, Hawaii, in 1964.

From 1966 into 1968, Weyand served in the VIETNAM WAR as commander of first the 25th Infantry and then II Field Force. Promoted in quick succession to lieutenant general (August 1968) and full general (October 1970), he served as the military adviser during the Paris Peace Talks. Returning to Vietnam, Weyand was deputy commander under General Creighton ABRAMS and then commander of the United States Military Assistance Command, Vietnam (MACV), between 1970 and 1973.

After serving briefly as the commander of the U.S. Army, Pacific, Weyand became vice chief of staff of the army in 1973. After a year in that position, he served as the chief of staff of the army from October 1974 to September 1976. Weyand retired from active service in October 1976.

See also TET OFFENSIVE.

Further reading: Bell, William G. *Commanding Generals and Chiefs of Staff, 1775–1995: Portraits and Biographical Sketches of the United States Army's Senior Officer.* Washington, D.C.: U.S. Army Center of Military History, 1997; Sorley, Lewis. *A Better War: The Unexamined Victories and*

Final Tragedy of America's Last Years in Vietnam. New York: Harcourt, Brace, 1999.

— Alexander M. Bielakowski

Wheeler, Earle G. (1908–1975) *U.S. Army general, army chief of staff, and chairman of the Joint Chiefs of Staff*

Born on 13 January 1908 in Washington, D.C., Earle Gilmore Wheeler graduated from the U.S. Military Academy, WEST POINT, in 1932 and was commissioned in the infantry. Following early service with the 15th Infantry Regiment in Tientsin, China, he taught mathematics at West Point and, on U.S. entry into World War II, trained troops in the United States. Late in the war, in December 1944, he went to Europe as chief of staff of the 63d Infantry Division.

Subsequently Colonel Wheeler commanded the 351st Infantry in Trieste (1951–52), served three years in a NATO staff assignment, and commanded the 2d Armored Division (1958–60). From that point forward, his career was exclusively concerned with Pentagon duty at the highest levels, beginning with two years as director of the Joint Staff. In 1962 he was promoted to full general and appointed army chief of staff and then, two years later, chairman of the Joint Chiefs of Staff (JC), a post he held for six years.

As chairman of the JCS, General Wheeler was deeply involved in VIETNAM WAR deliberations under three presidents—John F. KENNEDY, Lyndon B. JOHNSON, and Richard M. NIXON. His influence, and that of the Joint Chiefs, was often minimal, especially in a Pentagon dominated by Secretary of Defense Robert MCNAMARA. Wheeler sought to achieve unanimity of views among the chiefs on all controversial issues, arguing that to do otherwise would only give the civilians greater leverage; but this approach was largely unavailing, especially in attempting to dissuade the Johnson administration from a policy of "gradualism" with respect to conduct of the war. Wheeler was also frustrated by inability to get the president to call up reserve forces to help meet escalating requirements for troops in Vietnam and maintain effective troop levels elsewhere.

Wheeler consistently supported General William WESTMORELAND's recurring requests for deployment of additional forces to fight the Vietnam War. Following the Communist 1968 TET OFFENSIVE, Wheeler urged Westmoreland to request some 206,000 additional troops, apparently hoping that this would at long last precipitate a reserve call-up and provide forces to reconstitute the strategic reserve. Although the ploy backfired, instead leading to reversal of the American buildup in Vietnam, Wheeler was continued as chairman for an additional two years. He retired in July 1970 and died in Frederick, Maryland, on 18 December 1975.

Further reading: Clarke, Jeffrey J. *United States Army in Vietnam. Advice and Support: The Final Years, 1965–1973.* Washington, D.C.: Center of Military History, United States Army, 1988; Palmer, Bruce, Jr. *The 25-Year War: America's Military Role in Vietnam.* Lexington: University Press of Kentucky, 1984; Perry, Mark. *Four Stars.* Boston: Houghton Mifflin, 1989.

— Lewis Sorley

Wheeler, Joseph (1836–1906) *Confederate and U.S. Army general*

Born on 10 September 1836 near Augusta, Georgia, Joseph Wheeler graduated from the U.S. Military Academy, WEST POINT, in 1859. Commissioned a second lieutenant in the 1st Dragoons, he was transferred to the Mounted Rifles in the New Mexico Territory in 1860.

With the outbreak of the Civil War, Wheeler entered Confederate service as a first lieutenant of artillery at Pensacola, Florida. In September 1861, Wheeler was named colonel of the 19th Alabama Infantry, which he led during the Battle of SHILOH. In July 1862 Wheeler became chief of cavalry, Army of Mississippi (later the Army of Tennessee). He fought numerous engagements during General Braxton BRAGG's 1862 Kentucky campaign, earning promotion to brigadier general in October. In January 1863, following his performance in the Battle of STONES RIVER/MURFREESBORO, Wheeler was promoted to major general. That year he led numerous raids and participated in the Battle of CHICKAMAUGA. After serving at CHATTANOOGA, Wheeler joined Lieutenant General James LONGSTREET's advance on Knoxville.

At the beginning of the 1864 ATLANTA CAMPAIGN Wheeler assisted in the defense of Ringgold Gap, which saved the Army of Tennessee from destruction. Wheeler and his troopers performed spectacularly during the fighting around Atlanta, routing two major Federal raids and supporting General John Bell HOOD's infantry. But in August he launched a fruitless raid into eastern Tennessee that almost destroyed his corps and left Hood without much-needed cavalry support. After the fall of Atlanta, Wheeler and most of his command remained in Georgia to oppose Union Major General William T. SHERMAN's MARCH TO THE SEA, but his troopers' poor behavior drew much criticism.

In 1865, Wheeler and his cavalry fought well during the Carolina campaign. He and a portion of his command managed to avoid surrender by fleeing to Georgia, where later he was captured. Released in June, he settled eventually in Alabama. In 1881 he entered politics, serving eight terms in the U.S. House of Representatives.

In 1898, with the outbreak of the SPANISH-AMERICAN WAR, Wheeler offered his services to the United States and was commissioned a major general of Volunteers. He led a division in Cuba and was present during the attack on SAN JUAN HEIGHTS. Later he served in the Philippines. Commissioned a full brigadier general in the U.S. Army in June 1900, Wheeler retired in September. He died on 25 January 1906 in Brooklyn, New York.

See also CIVIL WAR, LAND OVERVIEW; FORREST NATHAN BEDFORD; HAMPTON, WADE; STUART, JAMES EWELL BROWN.

Further reading: Coffey, David. *John Bell Hood and the Struggle for Atlanta.* Abilene, Tex.: McWhiney Foundation Press, 1998; Dyer, John P. *"Fightin' Joe" Wheeler.* Baton Rouge: Louisiana State University Press, 1941.

— Toby Thompson

Whiskey Rebellion (July–November 1794)
Insurrection of farmers in western Pennsylvania against the whiskey excise tax

As part of Secretary of the Treasury Alexander HAMILTON's plan to fund the national debt, in 1791 Congress approved a 25 percent excise tax on distilled spirits.

Because whiskey was produced primarily on the western frontier, where it often served as a medium of exchange and could be more easily transported than bulk corn, the tax fell disproportionately hard on small farmers. Federal attempts to collect the tax in the four westernmost counties of Pennsylvania were met with resistance as angry farmers terrorized revenue collectors, disrupted the mail, and stopped judicial proceedings.

In July 1794, an angry mob forced federal troops guarding the home of John Neville, a revenue collector, to surrender. This event, combined with earlier provocations, led Associate Supreme Court Justice James Wilson to certify on 4 August 1794 that the courts could not function. A few days later, on 12 August, insurgents gathered at Braddock's Field, threatening to burn down Pittsburgh unless the whiskey tax was repealed. In the meanwhile, Wilson's certification allowed President George WASHINGTON to invoke a 1792 statute that permitted the president to summon troops in time of emergency. On 7 August, Washington issued a proclamation ordering the insurgents to disperse and calling upon Virginia, Maryland, New Jersey, and Pennsylvania to furnish troops.

Although Republicans such as Thomas JEFFERSON and James MADISON sympathized with the farmers' complaints against the tax (albeit not necessarily approving of their actions), Washington, along with Hamilton and other Federalists, saw the issue more as a question of maintaining the lawful authority of the new federal government than the collection of the tax itself. Federalists also saw the Whiskey Rebellion as a sign that the mob mentality of the French Revolution might have arrived in America.

If Washington had hoped that the proclamation alone would end the rebellion, the threats against Pittsburgh forced him to act. Washington and Hamilton traveled to Harrisburg to await the arrival of militia from Pennsylvania, New Jersey, Maryland, and Virginia. Approximately 15,000 militia answered the call. Granted the rank of lieutenant general by Congress, Washington stayed with the troops for approximately two weeks before leaving Hamilton and Henry LEE in charge with instructions to march into western Pennsylvania and crush the rebellion. When Hamilton and Lee set the "Army of the Constitution" in motion toward Pittsburgh, the Whiskey Rebellion quickly collapsed. Some 20 insurgents were captured. The two chief leaders, David Bradford and James Marshel, fled to Ohio. Although two of the insurgents were convicted of treason, both received presidential pardons.

This was the first exercise of presidential authority to call out the militia to suppress insurrection, and it had far-reaching repercussions. First, it demonstrated that the federal government would enforce its laws. Second, it led Washington to condemn "popular societies" for inciting the rebellion. This veiled reference to Republicans served only to increase the political divide between Republicans and Federalists. Third, it led to a subtle shift in public opinion against the Federalists. Although Federalists retained their majority in Congress in the congressional elections of 1794, Republicans gained seats. Once Republicans captured control of the White House and both houses of Congress in the election of 1800, one of their first acts was to repeal the whiskey tax.

See also CONSTITUTION OF 1789; SHAYS'S REBELLION.

Further reading: Boyd, Steven R., ed. *The Whiskey Rebellion: Past and Present Perspectives.* Westport, Conn.: Greenwood Press, 1985; Palmer, Dave R. *1794: America, Its Army, and the Birth of the Nation.* Novato, Calif.: Presidio Press, 1994; Slaughter, Thomas P. *The Whiskey Rebellion: Frontier Epilogue to the American Revolution.* New York: Oxford University Press, 1988.

— Justin D. Murphy

White Bird Canyon, Battle of (17 June 1877) *First battle of the 1877 Nez Perce War*

White encroachment into Oregon's rich Wallowa Valley in the 1870s fractured the tenuous peace that existed between aggressive settlers and Chief JOSEPH's Nez Perce band. Since 1863, Nez Perce bands had remained on their homelands in the Snake River region of Oregon and Idaho in generally peaceful defiance of a treaty that removed most of the Nez Perce people to a reservation. But growing pressure from settlers prompted the government finally to order the removal of the "non-treaty" Nez Perces.

In May 1877, after several meetings with Brigadier General Oliver O. HOWARD, commander of the Department of the Columbia, Joseph and his people were given 30 days to abandon their homes. While they reluctantly prepared to comply, Joseph and other leaders continued to consider other options, including armed resistance, which Joseph hoped to avoid.

Further negotiations were rendered useless when, in June, three drunken men from White Bird's band killed four white settlers, initiating a campaign that would last almost four months, cover hundreds of miles, and engage thousands of U.S. soldiers. On 15 June, news of the killings reached Howard at Fort Lapwai. He quickly dispatched Captain David Perry and two troops of cavalry (105 officers and men) plus 10 Nez Perce INDIAN SCOUTS to protect settlers along the Salmon River. At Grangeville, Perry learned that vengeful Nez Perce warriors had killed another 15 settlers. Perry's command, supported by 11 Idaho volunteers, moved to catch the Indians before they could reach the fastness of the Idaho mountains.

On 17 June, Perry's exhausted troopers approached the Nez Perce camp near the Salmon River at the mouth of White Bird Canyon. The previous night, Nez Perce leaders had decided to attempt peace negotiations; but, should that fail, they would fight. As half of the 135 Nez Perce fighting force slept off the effects of drunkeness, some 70 warriors took up excellent positions about the canyon. As a small detail led by the Idaho volunteers advanced, a Nez Perce delegation appeared under a white flag of truce. The volunteers opened fire.

Perry tried to organize a charge, but his position deteriorated quickly. Nez Perce warriors proved determined fighters and gifted marksmen as they assailed the soldiers on both flanks. Inexperienced troopers broke and ran while others fought a desperate, losing battle. Perry managed to rally a portion of his command and fought off numerous attacks as he withdrew to Mount Idaho.

Captain Perry's casualties told of a decisive defeat. One officer and 33 troopers were killed and two soldiers and two Idaho volunteers were wounded in the action at White Bird Canyon. The Nez Perce counted only three wounded. The Nez Perce victory signaled the beginning of one of the most remarkable campaigns in American history.

See also BEAR PAW MOUNTAIN, BATTLE OF; BIG HOLE RIVER, BATTLE OF; CANYON CREEK, BATTLE OF; CLEARWATER RIVER, BATTLE OF; NEZ PERCE WAR.

Further reading: Lavender, David. *Let Me Be Free: The Nez Perce Tragedy.* New York: HarperCollins, 1992; Utley, Robert M. *Frontier Regulars: The United States Army and the Indian, 1866–1891.* Lincoln: University of Nebraska Press, 1973.

— Toby Thompson

White Plains, Battle of (27 October–4 November 1776) *Important battle of the American Revolutionary War*

For Continental army commander General George WASHINGTON, British army North American commander Major General Sir William Howe must have seemed a gift from King George III. Thanks to Howe's strategy, American forces had escaped near destruction twice in the early fall of 1776. At White Plains, which followed, Howe could have ended the war but failed to administer the coup de grace, permitting the American commander to save his demoralized men.

The sequence began on 27 August 1776, when Howe landed his force of redcoats and Hessians on LONG ISLAND. Washington rushed to the scene and saw American officers and men running in all directions, unable to cope with the British regulars. But Howe ordered his men to stand fast, possibly because he believed the American cause near its end.

Washington's successful withdrawal of survivors to Manhattan can be accounted a miracle. When the British landed at KIP'S BAY on 15 September, Washington heard heavy artillery fire. Arriving at the scene, he found Patriot soldiers being bayoneted in the back as they ran from the field. Yet again, however, Howe ordered his men to stand fast. And in another demonstration of control and calm, Washington kept open escape routes from Manhattan to the county of Westchester, to the north.

Moving up the East River, Howe landed with 13,000 men at Throg's Neck, where a rearguard American action held him for 10 days, sufficient time for Washington to dig in on three hills around Westchester's county seat of White Plains. Washington had 14,000 men, one of the largest forces he would ever command. On 27 October, with the full force of his Royal Artillery, redcoats, and Hessians, Howe struck at Continental army Brigadier General Alexander McDougall's 1,600-man brigade positioned on Chatterton Hill.

The New Yorkers held briefly, during which time they received a severe cannonade and the first formal cavalry charge of the war by a crack British dragoons unit. Chatterton Hill was lost and McDougall's brigade put to flight. Maryland and Delaware units, stationed behind the New Yorkers, continued the fight, which surprised the British and gave Washington breathing time.

Instead of rapidly crushing a disintegrating enemy army, Howe again called a halt, and during the evening of 4 November he ordered his men to strike their tents for winter quarters in Manhattan and encampments across New Jersey. Washington was left to face defections by his troops and to learn of colonists eager to join the king's forces. What White Plains proved, however, was that a great commander, such as Washington, does not think in terms of battles but rather options. Howe would learn that in December, when Washington attacked TRENTON, and in January 1777, when the American general took PRINCETON.

See also AMERICAN REVOLUTIONARY WAR: LAND OVERVIEW.

Further reading: Freeman, Douglas Southall. *George Washington.* vol. 4, *Leader of the Revolution.* New York: Scribner, 1951; Hoffman, Renoda. *Yesterday in White Plains.* White Plains, N.Y.: Renoda Hoffman, 1989; Scheer, George F., and Hugh F. Rankin. *Rebels and Red-coats: The American Revolution Through the Eyes of Those Who Fought and Lived It.* New York: Da Capo, 1957.

— Milton Goldin

Whitney, Eli (1765–1825) *American inventor*

Born on 8 December 1765 in Westboro, Massachusetts, Eli Whitney attended Yale College. In 1792, while visiting Catharine Greene, the widow of American Revolutionary War Major General Nathaniel GREENE, near Savannah, Georgia, Whitney designed a machine that separated the cotton seeds from the fibers, a task that had previously required hours of manual labor to perform. The first cotton gin, operational in 1793, sparked an agricultural revolution that vastly increased cotton production and reinforced the institution of slavery in the South.

Whitney then focused his energy on a new venture. In 1798 he developed a system for the large-scale production of firearms and received a contract from the federal government to manufacture 10,000 muskets at $13.40 each. By creating a pattern, similar to one used by dressmakers, Whitney could hire unskilled mechanics to produce the firearms and at the same time achieve a standardization that allowed parts from any weapon to be used on another. He thus introduced the principle of interchangeable parts. Integral to this system was Whitney's development of a milling machine that allowed a worker to cut metal in a specific pattern.

Whitney established a factory in New Haven, Connecticut, and created the American system of manufacture. Although the initial deadline for the delivery of the muskets was scheduled for two years, difficulties and refinements in the system resulted in production taking eight years. In 1811 Whitney received a second contract for 15,000 firearms that he managed to produce in just two years. Whitney died in New Haven, Connecticut, on 8 January 1825.

See also COLT, SAMUEL; SMALL ARMS: RIFLES.

Further reading: Latham, Jean Lee. *Eli Whitney, Great Inventor.* Champaign, Ill.: Garrard Publishing, 1963;

Fuller, Claud E. *The Whitney Firearms.* Huntington, W.Va.: Standard Publishing, 1946.

— Cynthia Clark Northrup

Whitney, William C. (1841–1904) *U.S. secretary of the navy*

Born on 5 July 1841 in Conway, Masasachusetts, William Collins Whitney practiced law and made a fortune in the 1880s by obtaining the Metropolitan Street Railway franchise for New York City. Active in Democratic politics, in 1884 he effectively functioned as a campaign manager in Grover Cleveland's successful presidential bid. Cleveland rewarded him with an appointment as secretary of the navy in 1885.

Despite initial protests over his business connections, Whitney energetically built up the United States fleet, which since the CIVIL WAR had fallen far behind its European and even some Latin American counterparts. Whitney persuaded Congress to appropriate $80 million to construct 93,000 tons of technologically advanced new iron and steel vessels, including five steam-powered cruisers and two battleships, the MAINE among them, equipped with heavy guns and armor. He waged war on waste and corruption, decommissioned decrepit vessels, and refused to accept ships built by contractors who employed obsolete standards.

Whitney encouraged industry to develop innovative gun foundries, steel mills, and shipbuilding plants, technically sophisticated enough to produce and finish the ships and ordnance he required. In addition, he supported reorganization of the Navy Department and the establishment of a departmental planning bureau. Rather less logically, Whitney's personal distaste for Captain Alfred T. MAHAN, the second president of the new Naval War, College, led him to initiate ultimately unsuccessful attempts to downgrade that institution. Even so, Whitney helped lay the early foundations of the modern U.S. Navy, preparing it for the SPANISH-AMERICAN WAR and moving it along a trajectory that President Theodore ROOSEVELT and other American internationalists would pursue enthusiastically throughout the 20th century.

Whitney held no other public position after leaving office in 1889, but throughout the 1890s he remained active in business and Democratic politics. He died in New York City on 2 February 1904.

See also EDUCATION: HIGHER MILITARY SCHOOLS; NAVY, U.S.

Further reading: Herrick, Walter R. "William C. Whitney, 7 March 1885–5 March 1889," in *American Secretaries of the Navy,* edited by Paolo E. Coletta. Vol. 1. Annapolis, Md.: Naval Institute Press, 1982: 405–412; Hirsch, Mark D.

William C. Whitney: Modern Warwick. New York: Dodd Mead, 1948; Swanberg, W. A. *Whitney Father, Whitney Heiress.* New York: Scribner's, 1980.

— Priscilla Roberts

Wilderness, Battle of the (5–6 May 1864) *Civil War battle, part of the Overland Campaign, between Union forces under Lieutenant General Ulysses S. Grant and General Robert E. Lee's Confederate Army of Northern Virginia*

GRANT, general in chief of Union forces, chose to travel with Major General George G. MEADE's Army of the Potomac in the eastern theater of the war. Grant and Meade planned to move through the tangled undergrowth known as the Wilderness before bringing Lee to battle in more open terrain farther south. Grant made it clear that the destruction of LEE's army, not the capture of the Confederate capital of Richmond, was the main goal. Lee hoped to detect any Union move and strike the Federals in the Wilderness. The Confederate commander believed that the wooded terrain would make it difficult for the Union leaders to use their considerable advantages in numbers—about 120,000 men to his 70,000—and artillery.

The Union move began on 4 May, and initially all went well. The Federals crossed the Rapidan River and were halfway through the Wilderness by the afternoon. However, the Union artillery and long supply train were falling behind the infantry, and the Federal command decided to halt. Meanwhile, Lee was working hard to assemble his army and strike the Federals. He ordered his II Corps commander, Lieutenant General Richard S. EWELL, to probe the Union forces on 5 May, but Lee wanted Lieutenant General James LONGSTREET's I Corps to arrive before starting a major engagement.

On 5 May, Ewell's Southerners made contact with Major General Gouverneur K. WARREN's V Corps along Orange Turnpike. Grant and Meade decided to attack the Confederates, hoping to destroy Lee's army, in spite of the difficult terrain. Warren's troops launched several attacks near Sanders's Field. After a back and forth struggle, the lines stabilized, and both sides began to entrench.

Farther south, on the Orange Plank Road, a separate battle raged throughout 5 May. Lee's III Corps, under Lieutenant General Ambrose P. HILL, almost seized the key intersection of the Plank and Brock Roads. A Union division from the VI Corps held the position long enough to allow Major General Winfield S. HANCOCK's II Corps to rejoin the rest of the Union army. By the end of the day, the Union troops were poised to launch a major attack the next day.

Early on the morning of 6 May, Hancock began the Union assault along the Plank Road. Acting as a wing commander, Hancock had almost half of Meade's army under his control, and he drove Hill's corps back. Just as the Union troops neared a decisive victory, Longstreet's corps arrived and blunted the offensive.

Later in the morning, the Southerners found a path around the Union left flank, and Longstreet launched an attack that threw Hancock's troops back to the Brock Road. Longstreet was seriously wounded in the attack, and when the Confederates tried to renew the offensive later in the afternoon, they were repulsed by Hancock's strongly entrenched men.

As the battle died down on the southern flank, the Confederates mounted an attack on the other end of the Union line. Major General John B. GORDON's division spearheaded an assault that routed a portion of the Union right flank. However, increasing darkness and Union reinforcements enabled the Federals to establish a new position.

The Battle of the Wilderness was a tactical draw that was costly to both sides. The Confederates suffered about 11,000 casualties, while the Federals lost more than 17,000 men. Strategically, neither side had gained a decisive advantage; but Grant retained the initiative, and he was determined to keep the pressure on Lee.

See also CIVIL WAR, LAND OVERVIEW; OVERLAND CAMPAIGN.

Further reading: Rhea, Gordon C. *The Battle of the Wilderness, May 5–6, 1864.* Baton Rouge: University of Louisiana Press, 1994; Steere, Edward. *The Wilderness Campaign. The Meeting of Grant and Lee.* Reprint. Mechanicsville, Pa.: Stackpole Books, 1994.

— Curtis S. King

Wilkes, Charles (1798–1877) *U.S. Navy officer and explorer*

Born on 3 April 1798 in New York City, Charles Wilkes was appointed a midshipman in 1818. With a lively interest in science and exploration, Lieutenant Wilkes in 1833 headed the navy's Depot of Charts and Instruments and then led an expedition to the South Seas.

Leaving Hampton Roads, Virginia, in August 1838, Wilkes charted the waters around Tahiti and Samoa before sailing south to Antarctica. As he coasted the ice shelf, his findings proved the existence of a continent. Wilkes next visited New Zealand, Tonga, and Fiji. Important were Wilkes's subsequent observations of Hawaii, where he recognized the potential of Pearl Harbor as an anchorage; of Oregon, where he bolstered American claims to that territory; and of California, where he noted the feeble Mexican official presence at San Francisco. Rounding South Africa, Wilkes reached home in June 1842 and was promoted to commander.

Wilkes had accomplished much; his expedition had surveyed 280 islands in the Pacific, in addition to mapping 800 miles of the Oregon country and more than 1,500 miles of Antarctica. Specimens from his expedition formed the core collection of the Smithsonian Institution.

Wilkes blemished these successes by quarreling with subordinates, officers and men alike. A storm of accusations soon appeared in the press, and Wilkes was publicly reprimanded for meting out illegal punishments to his crew. This unseemly bickering cost Wilkes dearly. When he began in 1844 to publish the findings of the expedition, Congress made miserly appropriations. Compiling the 19-volume report of the expedition would drag on for 30 years.

Early in the Civil War, Wilkes, now a captain, was assigned to command the screw frigate *San Jacinto.* Acting on his own initiative, he seized Confederate diplomats James Mason and John Slidell aboard the British steamer *Trent* on 8 November 1861. While his action was lauded by much of the Northern press, the TRENT AFFAIR brought a confrontation with Great Britain. In July 1862, Wilkes took command of the James River flotilla that shelled Richmond. Promoted to commodore in August, he moved to the West India Squadron and again overstepped his authority, causing further problems with Britain. Relieved in June 1863, Wilkes quarreled publicly with Secretary of the Navy Gideon WELLES and was court-martialed. Found guilty of insubordination, he was suspended from command.

Following the war, Wilkes returned to publishing the findings of his expedition, but Congress remained unsupportive. Wilkes died at Washington, D.C., on 8 February 1877.

See also CIVIL WAR, NAVAL OVERVIEW.

Further reading: Stanton, William. *The Great United States Exploring Expedition of 1838–1842.* Berkeley: University of California Press, 1975; Viola, Herman, and Carolyn Margolis. *Magnificent Voyagers: The U.S. Exploring Expedition, 1838–1842.* Washington, D.C.: Smithsonian Press, 1985; Wilkes, Charles. *The Narratives of the U.S. Exploring Expedition.* Brookfield, Vt.: Gregg Press, 1970.
— Malcolm Muir, Jr.

Wilkinson, James (1757–1825) *U.S. Army general, inveterate plotter, and spy*
Born on 1 January 1757 in Calvert County, Maryland, James Wilkinson interrupted his medical studies in September 1775 to accept a captain's commission during the American Revolutionary War. He served briefly in the siege of BOSTON and then was part of Colonel Benedict ARNOLD's attack on Quebec, rising to the rank of captain. By December 1776 he was a major and aide-de-camp to Major General Horatio GATES. He won promotion to

lieutenant colonel in 1777 for his services with Continental army commander General George WASHINGTON at TRENTON and PRINCETON. Rejoining Gates's command, he was deputy adjutant general for the Northern Department. Gates selected him to report to Congress the news of victory in the Battle of SARATOGA.

Brevetted brigadier general in November 1777 at age 20, Wilkinson soon after became secretary of the newly created Board of War. Involved in the CONWAY CABAL against Washington, he was forced to resign. Wilkinson then secured the position of clothier general, an office he was also forced to resign in March 1781 when his accounts were audited.

After the war, Wilkinson became a farmer in Bucks County, Pennsylvania, where he was a brigadier general in the militia and a member of the state legislature. In 1784 he moved to Kentucky and became the leading advocate for its separation from Virginia. Gaining a trading monopoly in New Orleans and a $2,000 yearly pension from the Spanish government, Wilkinson was involved in a variety of political and business schemes. After repeated business failures, he rejoined the Army in October 1791 as a lieutenant colonel but was promoted to brigadier general in March 1792 when he joined Major General Anthony WAYNE's newly formed LEGION OF THE UNITED STATES. Plotting against and openly quarreling with Wayne, Wilkinson nonetheless became the ranking general in the army on Wayne's death in 1797.

In 1798, Wilkinson returned to the southern frontier and resumed his secret dealings with the Spanish. By 1805, he was the governor of the Louisiana Territory, engaged in numerous business ventures and still receiving payments from the Spanish government. In 1806 he was ordered to take command of the southern frontier and became part of the Burr conspiracy. As the chief witness against Aaron BURR, Wilkinson himself barely escaped indictment. He subsequently returned to his old command.

During the War of 1812 Wilkinson was promoted to major general and led a disastrous expedition against Montreal in 1813, ending in defeat in the Battle of CRYSLER'S FARM. Relieved of his command, he became embroiled in a quarrel with Secretary of War John ARMSTRONG and was court-martialed but found not guilty. After the war he returned to his plantation near New Orleans, where he wrote *Memoirs of My Own Times.* In 1821 Wilkinson journeyed to Mexico to obtain a land grant in Texas. He died in Mexico City on 28 December 1825, having never won a battle nor lost a court-martial.

See also AMERICAN REVOLUTIONARY WAR: LAND OVERVIEW; TERRE AUX BOEUFS AFFAIR.

Further reading: Jacobs, James Ripley. *Tarnished Warrior: Major General James Wilkinson.* New York: Macmillan,

1938; Kohn, Richard H. *Eagle and Sword: The Federalists and the Creation of the Military Establishment in America, 1783–1812.* New York: Free Press, 1975; Mahon, John K. *The War of 1812.* Gainesville: University of Florida Press, 1972; Schreve, Royal Ornan. *The Finished Scoundrel: General James Wilkinson, Sometime Commander in Chief of the Army of the United States, Who Made Intrigue a Trade and Treason a Profession.* Indianapolis: Bobbs-Merrill, 1933.

— Jack W. Thacker

Williams, Jonathan (1750–1815) *U.S. Army officer and educator*
Born on 26 May 1750 in Boston, Massachusetts, Jonathan Williams was educated at Harvard College. He then visited London to conduct family business and there came under the sway of his famous uncle, Benjamin Franklin. It was through this productive association that Williams became acutely interested in, and adept at, science. He subsequently spent the American Revolutionary War years in Europe as an agent, helping to secure arms in France.

Williams returned to the United States in 1785, studied science at Harvard, and relocated to Philadelphia as a member of the prestigious American Philosophical Society. In 1799 he published a noted tract, *Thermometric Navigation,* and the following year he gained appointment as a major in the 2d Regiment of Artillery and Engineers. In this capacity he translated several French military manuals. Williams proved instrumental in founding the U.S. Military Philosophical Society, intended as a conduit for all the latest European military literature and practices. By 1800 his publishing activities had brought him to the attention of the newly elected president, Thomas JEFFERSON, himself a lay scientist.

In 1802 Jefferson authorized creation of the U.S. Military Academy, WEST POINT, as the nation's first school for officers. He tapped Williams to serve as its first superintendent based upon his solid credentials as an engineer and scientist. Williams faced extreme difficulties in administering his charge; the academy was small, underfunded, and initially consisted of only 10 cadets. Moreover, he grew incensed over the fact that he, as an engineering officer, could not command line troops of the local garrison. When Jefferson failed to rectify this dispute for him, Williams resigned from West Point in 1803.

In April 1805, Jefferson finally authorized Williams to command all military personnel garrisoned at West Point, and he was reinstated as a lieutenant colonel. Williams continued to enhance West Point by imposing a rigorous curriculum that stressed scientific methodology and mathematics. In his spare time he lent his talents to designing and constructing numerous fortifications in and around New York City.

When the War of 1812 commenced, Williams requested command of Castle Williams on Governor's Island, but he was refused on account of his engineer status. This prompted him to resign a second time, to serve in the militia. Williams was elected to Congress in 1814 from Philadelphia, but he died there on 16 May 1815, before taking his seat.

See also MILITARY ACADEMIES.

Further reading: Crackel, Theodore J. *Mr. Jefferson's Army: Political and Social Reform of the Military Establishment, 1801–1807.* New York: New York University Press, 1987.

— John C. Fredriksen

Williamsburg, Battle of (5 May 1862) *First major engagement of the Civil War Peninsular campaign*
The battle involved approximately 41,000 Union and 32,000 Confederate troops. Pressured by Union Major General George B. McCLELLAN's Army of the Potomac, on 2 May 1862 Confederate general Joseph E. JOHNSTON ordered his forces to evacuate their defensive positions near the Warwick River between the James and York Rivers and retreat toward the Confederate capital.

Pursued by two Federal divisions under Brigadier Generals Joseph E. HOOKER and William F. Smith, Johnston ordered Major General James LONGSTREET to block the Union advance. Hooker's division encountered the Confederate rear guard near Williamsburg on 5 May. Hooker ordered his troops to assault the Confederate position at Fort Magruder. The sound of battle drew Johnston back to oversee the fighting, but he left Longstreet in command.

As Confederate troops repulsed the initial Federal attacks on Fort Magruder, Longstreet brought more brigades into action and launched a counterattack against the Union forces. The Confederates threatened the Union left flank until reinforcements from Brigadier General Phillip KEARNY's command came up and stabilized the Federal line. Subsequently, William F. Smith ordered Brigadier General Winfield Scott HANCOCK to advance on the Confederate left flank, where he succeeded in capturing two abandoned redoubts. A Confederate counterattack led by Brigadier Generals Jubal A. EARLY and Daniel Harvey HILL met heavy resistance. Hancock's forces then contained the Confederate attack and forced Hill to break off the assault. However, the Federals failed to capitalize on Hancock's localized success, allowing the Confederates to continue their withdrawal toward Richmond.

The results of the battle were inconclusive. The Federals suffered 2,283 casualties, while the Confederates sustained about 1,575. Johnston's army was able to continue unmolested toward Richmond until the next test of strength at SEVEN PINES/FAIR OAKS.

See also CIVIL WAR, LAND OVERVIEW; SEVEN DAYS, BATTLES OF THE.

Further reading: Newton, Steven H. *Joseph E. Johnston and the Defense of Richmond.* Lawrence: University Press of Kansas, 1998; Sears, Steven. *To the Gates of Richmond: The Peninsula Campaign.* New York: Ticknor & Fields, 1998; Hastings, Earl C., and David Hastings. *A Pitiless Rain: The Battle of Williamsburg, 1862.* Shippensburg, Pa.: White Mane, 1997.

— Alexander Mendoza

Willing expedition (1778–1779) *American Revolutionary War raid down the lower Mississippi River*

Apparently unsuccessful in business in Natchez, Mississippi, before the war, James Willing traveled to Philadelphia in 1777 and met with the Commerce Committee of the Continental Congress, warning of a threat by the British to close the Mississippi River above New Orleans. The committee arranged a commission for Willing as a navy captain.

There is no record of Willing's exact orders, but letters suggest that he was supposed to carry dispatches and then return with stores back up the Mississippi and Ohio to Fort Pitt. Willing claimed—and it seems likely—that he was also instructed to seize British property along the way.

In any case, Willing obtained supplies at Fort Pitt and fitted out an armed boat, the *Rattletrap,* a galley with 10 oars and a stern sweep, and enlisted some 30 volunteers. The expedition departed Fort Pitt on 10 January 1778, headed down the Ohio River and into the Mississippi.

By the time Willing and his men arrived in Natchez on 19 February, they had already established a name for themselves. On the way they seized goods, captured several boats, gained 10 new recruits, and harassed settlers at the Spanish post near the mouth of the Arkansas River to the point that the latter petitioned the British for protection. Willing's crew also seized the plantation and property of Loyalist Anthony Hutchins, a Willing nemesis, just above Natchez. Two days after the arrival of the *Rattletrap* in Natchez, the settlers there promised neutrality in the war in return for Willing's protection. Several even volunteered to join Willing and his men.

Willing's guarantee did not extend beyond Natchez, and he and his men wreaked havoc on British planters to the south while en route to New Orleans. They destroyed crops, killed stock, burned homes, and kidnapped slaves. Many of the plantation owners believed that the destruction was a matter of Willing exacting revenge for his business failures in the area. Not everything was destroyed, however. The property of those supporting the American cause was untouched.

On 23 February the Americans captured the British sloop *Rebecca,* with 14 6-pounders and two swivels. For a time, this ended British control of the river. Later the *Rebecca* was refitted at New Orleans as the cruiser *Morris.*

The arrival of Willing and his men in New Orleans caused an uproar. As early as 16 May, Governor Don Bernardo de Gálvez and even Oliver Pollock, one of the original supporters of the expedition, urged Willing to depart. Both were anxious to maintain the uneasy peace then existing. Willing subsequently returned to Philadelphia. He was later captured by the British and held in New York.

See also AMERICAN REVOLUTIONARY WAR: LAND OVERVIEW.

Further reading: Haynes, Robert V. "James Willing and the Planters of the Natchez: The American Revolution Comes to the Southwest," *Journal of Mississippi History* 37, no. 1 (1975): 1–40; Smith, Charles R. "Willing's Marine Expedition," *By Valor and Arms* 2, no. 3 (1976): 47–52.

— Luke Charles Wullenwaber

Wilson, James Harrison (1837–1925) *U.S. Army general*

Born on 2 September 1837 near Shawneetown, Illinois, James Harrison Wilson attended McKendree College for one year, then in 1855 enrolled at the U.S. Military Academy, WEST POINT, where he graduated in 1860. Commissioned a brevet second lieutenant in the Topographical Engineers, Wilson served at Fort Vancouver until the outbreak of the Civil War.

Promoted to full-rank second lieutenant in June 1861 and first lieutenant that September, Wilson served as chief topographical engineer during the Port Royal expedition and in the reduction of FORT PULASKI. As a volunteer aide to Major General George B. MCCLELLAN, he participated in the Maryland campaign of September 1862. With the staff rank of lieutenant colonel, he served as chief topographical engineer and inspector general on Major General Ulysses S. GRANT's staff during the VICKSBURG and CHATTANOOGA campaigns.

Named a brigadier general of U.S. Volunteers in October 1863, Wilson served briefly as chief of the Cavalry Bureau in Washington, proving himself a gifted organizer. In April 1864, he assumed command of a cavalry division in the Army of the Potomac, with which he participated in the OVERLAND CAMPAIGN, in actions around PETERSBURG, and in the SHENANDOAH VALLEY CAMPAIGN. In October, Wilson went west to command the Cavalry Corps of the Military Division of the Mississippi. His cavalry played a leading role in the fall campaign that ended in the destruction of the Confederate Army of Tennessee after the Battle of NASHVILLE.

Brevetted through brigadier general in the regular army and to major general of Volunteers, Wilson mounted a devastating raid through Alabama and Georgia in 1865 that included the defeat of Confederate cavalry commander Lieutenant General Nathan Bedford FORREST at Selma. In May, elements of Wilson's command captured Confederate president Jefferson DAVIS at Irwinsville, Georgia. Brevetted to major general in the regular army, Wilson was promoted to major general of Volunteers to rank from May 1865.

Mustered out of the Volunteer organization in January 1866, Wilson remained with the army as lieutenant colonel of the new 35th Infantry Regiment but continued to pursue engineering duties until honorably discharged at his own request in 1870. Wilson then became a railroad executive and wrote prolifically. In 1898, he returned to duty as a major general of Volunteers during the SPANISH-AMERICAN WAR, seeing action in Puerto Rico and Cuba. Later he participated in the suppression of the 1900 BOXER UPRISING in China. In 1901, he was retired with the regular rank of brigadier general. Wilson died at Wilmington, Delaware, on 23 February 1925.

See also CAVALRY; CIVIL WAR, LAND OVERVIEW; MACKENZIE, RANALD S.; MERRITT, WESLEY; MILES, NELSON; SHERIDAN, PHILIP H.

Further reading: Longacre, Edward G. *From Union Stars to Top Hat: A Biography of the Extraordinary General James Harrison Wilson.* Harrisburg, Pa.: Stackpole Books, 1972; Starr, Stephen Z. *The Union Cavalry in the Civil War.* 3 vols. Baton Rouge: Louisiana State University Press, 1979–85.

— Shane Nall

Wilson, Woodrow (1856–1924) *President of the United States during World War I*

Born on 28 December 1856 at Staunton, Virginia, and reared in Augusta, Georgia, Thomas Woodrow Wilson would be forever shaped by his memories of the horrors of the Civil War and difficulties of Reconstruction. As the son of a Presbyterian minister and seminary professor, Wilson was also the product of a strict religious and strong academic upbringing. After graduating from Princeton University in 1879 and studying law at the University of Virginia for a year, Wilson attempted a legal practice in Atlanta and obtained his Ph.D. in political science and history at Johns Hopkins University in 1886. By then he had joined the faculty at Bryn Mawr College. In 1890 Wilson returned to Princeton, serving first as professor of jurisprudence and political economy before becoming president of the university in 1902. Wilson won national acclaim for his academic reforms and in November 1910 was elected governor of New Jersey. His success in pushing through reform legislation caught the attention of progressive-minded Democrats, who supported his candidacy for president in 1912. The Republican Party split and Wilson won the presidential election.

As president, Wilson was chiefly interested in domestic policy. He pushed through the Underwood tariff, the Federal Reserve Act, the Federal Trade Commission Act, and the Clayton Antitrust Act. He also sought to implement a diplomacy based on morality. Wilson vowed that the United States would forgo territorial conquests, and he and his first secretary of state, William Jennings Bryan, negotiated a series of "cooling off" agreements with Latin American countries. Indeed, in the fall of 1914 Wilson outlined a proposal by which nations in the Western Hemisphere would guarantee each others' territorial integrity and political independence. This later become the cornerstone for his League of Nations covenant. This notwithstanding, Wilson became a major interventionist.

Despite Wilson's best intentions to avoid conflict with U.S. neighbors, the political upheaval of the Mexican Revolution led Wilson to send marines to seize VERACRUZ in April 1914 and then to dispatch Brigadier General John J. PERSHING and 11,000 troops in the PUNITIVE EXPEDITION INTO MEXICO (March 1916–January 1917) to pursue Pancho Villa.

Wilson proclaimed U.S. neutrality when World War I began in August 1914, but his sympathies lay with the Allied side. Germany's sinking of the passenger liner *LUSITANIA* (7 May 1915), which claimed 128 American lives, led Wilson to issue a series of threatening notes that compelled Germany to halt unrestricted submarine warfare.

Although Wilson won reelection in 1916 primarily because he had kept the United States out of the war, he had pushed through a national preparedness policy, including the NATIONAL DEFENSE ACT of 1916, which more than tripled the size of the peacetime army. After Germany resumed unrestricted submarine warfare in February 1917 and attempted to induce Mexico into declaring war on the United States in the ZIMMERMANN TELEGRAM, Wilson addressed Congress on 2 April 1917, asking for a declaration of war, which was passed on 6 April.

Wilson set idealistic goals of making the world safe for democracy and ending all wars; however, America's allies did not share all of the idealist principles that Wilson established in his Fourteen Points of 8 January 1918. After the ARMISTICE of 11 November 1918 ended the war, Wilson traveled to Europe as the head of the U.S. delegation to the peace conference. The resulting PARIS PEACE SETTLEMENT of 1919 was essentially his work and included his proposal for a League of Nations.

By the time Wilson returned to the United States on 8 July 1919, the popular mood had shifted toward isolationism, and Senator Henry Cabot Lodge insisted upon restricting the League's power. Wilson embarked upon a cross-country speaking tour to sway public opinion, but on 2 October 1919 he suffered a stroke that left him virtually incapacitated for the remainder of his administration. When he rejected any compromises in the agreements, the Senate ultimately refused to ratify the Treaty of Versailles or enter the League of Nations. Wilson died in Washington on 3 February 1924.

See also LATIN AMERICAN INTERVENTIONS, EARLY 20TH CENTURY; WORLD WAR I, COURSE OF U.S. INVOLVEMENT.

Further reading: Ferrell, Robert H. *Woodrow Wilson and World War I, 1917–1921.* New York: Harper & Row, 1985; Link, Arthur S. *Woodrow Wilson and the Progressive Era, 1910–1917.* New York: Harper & Row, 1954.

— Justin D. Murphy

Wilson's Creek, Battle of (Oak Hills or Springfield)

(10 August 1861) *Civil War battle*
Wilson's Creek is located about 10 miles southwest of Springfield, Missouri. The battle there, also known as Oak Hills or Springfield, was the culmination of the fighting that had occurred in Missouri since mid-June 1861. U.S. Army brigadier general Nathaniel Lyon had driven Missouri's pro-Confederate militia forces under Major General Sterling Price from central Missouri into the southwest corner of the state. Lyon now hoped to drive the Confederates out of Missouri altogether.

By late July 1861 Price had retreated to Cowskin Prairie, Missouri. Price then marched to Cassville, Arkansas, where he united with forces under Brigadier General Benjamin McCulloch. In early August this combined force of approximately 10,000 men moved toward Springfield to do battle with the smaller Union force. Lyon, outnumbered almost two to one, was unable to secure reinforcements from departmental commander Major General John C. FRÉMONT, who claimed that a Confederate force at New Madrid, Missouri, made it impossible for him to spare additional troops.

Lyon, who had established his reputation for boldness and vigor, refused to withdraw without a fight. When he discovered the combined Confederates near the intersection of Wilson's Creek and the Fayette-Springfield road, he decided to attack before retreating toward Springfield. Colonel Franz Sigel persuaded Lyon to allow him to take 1,200 men and swing around the Confederates to attack them from the south, while Lyon's remaining 4,200 men would hit the Confederates head on.

Lyon's attack began at dawn on 10 August, his troops enjoying early success. Price was eventually able to regroup and form a battle line of about 3,000 men at Oak Hill. Here the fighting stabilized, with neither side able to gain the advantage.

Sigel's attack was even more successful, with the surprised Confederates fleeing in panic. McCulloch tried to stabilize the situation, sending forward Missouri cavalry and part of Colonel Louis Hebert's 3d Louisiana Regiment. The Louisianans wore gray uniforms, the exact color worn by an Iowa regiment under Sigel. For this reason the Union troops held their fire, allowing Hebert's men to deliver a deadly volley into the advancing Union column. The Union line fell apart and retreated in panic. Sigel made little effort to rally his troops or communicate his situation to Lyon.

With Sigel no longer a threat, Price and McCulloch concentrated on bringing their superior resources to bear in the Oak Hill area. They then launched two attacks on Union forces, but the Union troops held their positions. Lyon, conversely, tried to carry the Rebel line on Oak Hill, during which effort he was killed. Command of Union forces then fell to Major Samuel D. Sturgis. Knowing that his troops were outnumbered, that they were exhausted, and that ammunition was low, Sturgis decided to retreat back to Springfield.

Although Price wanted to follow and destroy the Federals, McCulloch demurred because many of his regiments were out of ammunition. In the battle the Union forces lost about 1,300 men and the Confederates about 1,200.

The Battle of Wilson's Creek left the fate of Missouri again in question. Price followed it by a campaign into western Missouri that captured the Union garrison at Lexington in mid-September 1861.

See also CIVIL WAR, LAND OVERVIEW; PEA RIDGE, BATTLE OF.

Further reading: Castel, Albert. *Sterling Price and the Civil War in the West.* Baton Rouge: Louisiana State University Press, 1968; Piston, William Garrett, and Richard W. Hatcher. *Wilson's Creek: The Second Battle of the Civil War and the Men Who Fought It.* Chapel Hill: University of North Carolina Press, 2000.

— Bruce Tap

Women Accepted for Volunteer Emergency Service (WAVES) (1942–1948) *U.S. Navy Women's Reserve*

WAVES stood for "Women Accepted for Volunteer Emergency Service." More than 85,000 women served in the navy's Women's Reserve during World War II. On 30 July 1942, President Franklin D. ROOSEVELT signed Public Law 689, which established the WAVES. The navy immediately commissioned about 150 women to set up recruiting and training programs and to provide administrative leadership.

Anticipating the WAVES's creation, the navy appointed an advisory council composed of deans and presidents of women's colleges. The council recommended that Mildred MCAFEE, president of Wellesley College, head the Women's Reserve. The navy commissioned McAfee as a lieutenant commander, its first woman officer. About 20 of the first commissioned women joined her in Washington, D.C., and another 11 were sent to naval district headquarters throughout the country to recruit other women.

By the fall of 1942, the navy had established training units for women officers at Smith College and nearby Mount Holyoke College. A 16-week training program, similar to that for male reserve officers, consisted of rigorous physical conditioning and instruction in military drill, plus classroom instruction in naval organization, history, protocol, ships and aircraft, correspondence, communications, and law. More than 10,500 women officers were trained on the two campuses. Of that total, nearly 3,200 went on to further, specialized training in such fields as aeronautical engineering, air navigation, ship design, inventory management, and intelligence.

In February 1943, the navy opened its training facility for enlisted women at Hunter College in New York City. When it closed in October 1945, the Hunter College unit had trained nearly 81,000 enlisted WAVES, and more than 5,000 enlisted women in the U.S. Coast Guard and Marine Corps. Large numbers of women went on to advanced, specialized training. Approximately 13,000 women served in the navy's Hospital Corps as technicians and therapists, or as pharmacist's mates. More than 20,000 enlisted WAVES served in aviation specialties such as air traffic control, gunnery, and parachute rigging.

By war's end, women constituted roughly 2 percent of the navy, but in some of its critical areas—mail service, personnel administration, communications, and ordnance calculations, for example—they comprised 50 to 80 percent of the work force. McAfee estimated that the women had freed a sufficient number of men to crew 10 battleships, 10 aircraft carriers, 28 cruisers, and 50 destroyers.

Following the war, several hundred commissioned and enlisted navy women personnel were still in the service when, in July 1948 President Harry S. TRUMAN signed into law the Women's Armed Services Integration Act that abolished the Women's Reserve. The name WAVES was no longer accurate, but it remained in popular and quasi-official use until the early 1970s. The act allowed the army, navy, Marine Corps, and newly established air force to accept women as members of regular and reserve forces.

See also WOMEN IN THE MILITARY.

Further reading: Ebbert, Jean, and Marie-Beth Hall. *Crossed Currents: Navy Women in a Century of Change.* 3d ed. Washington, D.C.: Batsford Brassey's, Inc., 1999; Holm, Jeanne. *Women in the Military.* 2d ed. San Francisco: Presidio Press, 1992.

— Jean Ebbert and Marie-Beth Hall

Women Airforce Service Pilots (WASPs)

(1943–1944) *The first women to fly for the U.S. military*

At the outbreak of World War II, Nancy Harkness Love and Jacqueline COCHRAN were determined to use their aviation expertise for the war effort. Both women had many flight hours and saw no reason why women aviators should not fly for their country. The Army Air Force initially rejected the idea. But with an alarming shortage of pilots, the Air Transport Command hired 25 women as civilians to ferry aircraft from factories to bases or embarkation ports. These women had at least 500 hours of flying time (the average was more than 1,000 hours) and commercial licenses. The group—the Women's Auxiliary Ferry Squadron (WAFS), with Love as its leader—began ferrying aircraft on 21 October 1942.

Meanwhile, Jacqueline Cochran had plans of her own. With the most experienced women aviators flying with the WAFS, she founded the Women's Flying Training Detachment (WFTD), supported by Army Air Forces commanding general Henry H. ARNOLD.

The women in this new group were licensed pilots but had fewer hours of flying time and lacked commercial licenses. They went into training and, if successful, joined the WAFS ferrying aircraft. The first class graduated in April 1943.

On 5 August 1943, the two groups united to become the Women Airforce Service Pilots (WASP), with Cochran in charge. The planes they flew ranged from trainers to medium bombers and included many types of fighters. As more pilots became available, they were assigned to different types of flying jobs. They instructed students, towed gliders and targets, delivered weapons and cargo, and tested aircraft after maintenance or repair. The jobs were not without risk. The planes of some women pilots towing targets were hit by bullets, while other planes were forced down for mechanical reasons—some having been sabotaged with sugar in the gas tanks.

In all, more than 25,000 women applied to fly; 1,830 were accepted, and 1,074 made it through training. Of these, 38 WASPs lost their lives. During the war, WASPs flew more than 60 million miles. With the war winding down, and more male pilots available, the WASP was disbanded on 20 December 1944.

In 1949, the air force and the army offered reserve commissions to former WASPs. Of the 300 who accepted, 100 were recalled to active duty during the KOREAN WAR in a nonflying status. Nine of these women continued on active duty until they retired; five even served in Southeast Asia during the VIETNAM WAR.

As civilian pilots, the WASPs had few benefits. There was no death benefit for those who died in service; their families did not even rate a memorial gold star. After the war, the women were not eligible for care in veterans' hospitals if needed. Not until 1977 were the WASPs belatedly recognized as military personnel and granted veterans status, when President Jimmy Carter signed Public Law 95-292.

See also AIR FORCE, U.S.

Further reading: Keil, Sally Van Wagenen. *Those Wonderful Women in Their Flying Machines: The Unknown Heroines of World War II.* New York: Four Directions, 1990; Verges, Marianne. *On Silver Wings: The Women Airforce Service Pilots of World War II, 1942–1944.* New York: Ballantine, 1991; Williams, Vera S. *WASPs: Women Airforce Service Pilots of World War II.* Osceola, Wis.: Motorbooks International, 1994.

— Marie-Beth Hall

women in the military (1948 to present)

Women have served in the military throughout America's history. Until the 20th century, their service was usually adjunct, except for those who posed as men. Some of these were eventually discovered or later revealed their disguises, while an unknown number successfully kept their secrets.

The first women officially to join the U.S. military served in the ARMY NURSE CORPS, established in 1901, and in the NAVY NURSE CORPS, established in 1908. The first women other than nurses to serve officially were the women enlisted during World War I: nearly 12,000 in the Naval Reserve and more than 300 in the Marine Corps Reserve. All were discharged by 1920.

Women have made important contributions in America's wars, not necessarily as members of the armed forces. This photograph shows 13 women shipyard workers during World War I. They worked as "rivet heaters" and "rivet passers-on" at the Puget Sound Naval Shipyard, Bremerton, Washington.   *(National Archives)*

During World War II the army, navy, Marine Corps, and Coast Guard (under the Department of the Navy during wartime) established women's reserve programs. Almost 400,000 women served, and about 10 percent of them held commissions as officers. Their widely acknowledged contributions to victory led the services to conclude that women could serve in the regular military forces in peacetime as well as in wartime emergencies.

Thus, in 1948, Congress passed the Women's Armed Services Integration Act, signed by President Harry S. TRUMAN in July. This landmark legislation opened a new era. The act did not cover the Coast Guard, but the history of Coast Guard servicewomen has been closely connected to that of women in other armed services.

While the 1948 act allowed women to plan careers in the military profession, it heavily restricted both their presence and progress. Their numbers, for example, could not exceed 2 percent of the regular forces, nor could a woman officer gain permanent rank higher than lieutenant colonel or commander.

Promotion opportunities for women were considerably fewer than for men; women could not become commanding officers, nor could they enter many professional specialties, particularly those closely related to combat. A servicewoman would be discharged if and when she became pregnant. Marriage was not grounds for discharge, but it could lower already slender promotion chances. Her husband did not receive the benefits and privileges long accorded to servicemen's wives. Despite these restrictions, the services managed to attract and retain a viable cadre of women.

During the KOREAN WAR in 1951, the military failed to recruit as many women as it needed. One consequence was the formation of the Defense Advisory Committee for Women in the Armed Services (DACOWITS), its members drawn from women distinguished in business, professional, or public life. DACOWITS remains a leading advocate for equity and fairness—in law, policy, and practice—for servicewomen.

Several forces converged in the mid-1960s to increase the percentages of women in the armed forces and to widen their opportunities. One was the VIETNAM WAR, requiring more and more women to fill jobs vacated by men sent to combat. Increasing public resistance to the war led President Richard NIXON to end the draft in 1973; henceforth the military would be an all-volunteer force. Concurrently, the feminist and equal rights movements prompted closer public scrutiny of military women's circumstances.

This convergence has brought servicewomen much closer to full equity with servicemen. Since 1967, they have been eligible for promotion to the highest military ranks, and in 2000 almost 3 percent of all admirals and generals were female. Women have held significant command positions. In the 1970s they entered the service academies and RESERVE OFFICER TRAINING CORPS (ROTC) programs. Most service training and assignment is gender-integrated, although women still cannot serve in a few specialized units and they are restricted from ground combat.

By the early 1970s, the military had to dismantle its long-standing opposition to allowing its women to combine motherhood with active service. Servicewomen's husbands gained the same benefits and privileges accorded to servicemen's wives. The military continues to adjust its policies to the fact that its ranks include numerous couples who both have military careers, and many service members are parents.

In the 1980s and 1990s, women edged closer to the heart of the military profession. They served together with men in armed conflicts in the Middle East, Bosnia, PANAMA, Kosovo, Haiti, and GRENADA. During the 1986 attack on Libya, six air force women flew in the refueling planes involved. In Panama, a female military police officer led her troops in what became a three-hour infantry firefight. In the 1991 Gulf War, army women piloted assault helicopters into Iraq on the war's second day and continued to serve throughout the entire operation. Navy women have commanded air squadrons and combatant ships. In 2001, 12 military women were astronauts, serving as shuttle pilots and mission specialists, and others had trained for duty on the space station.

Some military women have been prisoners of war, and some have come home in body bags. High-ranking officers have stated that the armed forces could not fully mobilize for war without its women members.

As of 31 May 1999, nearly 191,000 women were serving in the army, navy, Marine Corps, and air force, with another nearly 3,500 in the Coast Guard, constituting roughly 15 percent of active-duty forces. American servicewomen, all but fully integrated into the nation's military, are a modern reality. Yet some people continue to oppose their presence, claiming that it impairs military readiness, and they blame women for many of the military's shortcomings. The events at and following the TAILHOOK CONVENTION of 1991 revealed how deeply some servicemen oppose women joining them in combat units. A small, vehement minority of civilians, including some military veterans, supports that opposition.

Yet one truth remains today unchanged from the exigencies of a century ago: the military needs women. To obtain and retain them, it must treat them equitably. When it has treated them as the skilled, loyal members they are, it has found them eager to accept their share of military service as part and parcel of their citizenship.

See also DESERT SHIELD; DESERT STORM.

Further reading: Ebbert, Jean, and Marie-Beth Hall. *Crossed Currents: Navy Women in a Century of Change.*

3d ed. Washington, D.C.: Brassey's, 1999; Holm, Jeanne. *Women in the Military.* 2d ed. San Francisco: Presidio Press, 1992; Stiehm, Judith Hicks. *Arms and the Enlisted Women.* Philadelphia: Temple University Press, 1989.

— Jean Ebbert and Marie-Beth Hall

Women's Army Corps (WAC) *The World War II women's army reserves*

On 14 May 1942 Congress passed legislation to establish the Women's Army Auxiliary Corps (WAAC). President Franklin D. ROOSEVELT signed the bill the next day. Members of the WAAC were to serve "with" the army, but not "in" it. While Oveta Culp HOBBY, chosen as the director of the WAAC, was assigned the rank of major, the other women officers were appointed as first, second, and third officers. The enlisted women were junior leaders, leaders, staff leaders, technical leaders, first leaders, and chief leaders. These titles were the equivalent of private, corporal, sergeant, staff sergeant, technical sergeant, and master sergeant. The women received less pay than men with the equivalent rank or rate. The WAAC bill also failed to provide the women with government life insurance, death benefits, or veteran's medical benefits.

An initial 3,340 officer candidates arrived at Fort Des Moines, Iowa, the first WAAC training center, in July 1942. This group included 40 black women candidates, who would go on to serve in segregated units. The first enlisted auxiliaries began training a month later. Many of these early enlistees had joined with the understanding that they would be given assignments close to home. However, army needs soon dictated that WAACs be sent far away, some even overseas. As early as November 1942, Lieutenant General Dwight D. EISENHOWER requested five WAAC officers for service in North Africa. Their ship was torpedoed, but the women were rescued and went on to serve on Eisenhower's staff until the end of the war.

With the expanding need for WAACs overseas, army leaders requested that the auxiliary be converted to the Women's Army Corps, by which the women would serve "in" the army, not just "with" it. Thus they would be entitled to the same pay, ranks, protections, and benefits as the men. On 3 July 1943, the WAC bill became law; some 75 percent of the WAAC decided to remain in the service and join the WAC.

Originally, the army expected the women to fill clerical billets, but the women soon proved they could cope with many different jobs. The Army Air Force, to which 40 percent of all women were assigned, used half of its women in nontraditional jobs. Women served as weather observers, cryptographers, radio operators, parachute riggers, bombsight maintenance specialists, and sheet metal workers. A few were even assigned flying duties as radio operators, mechanics, and aerial photographers.

The top-secret project of building an atomic bomb also employed army women. More than 400 were assigned to the MANHATTAN PROJECT, mostly in Oak Ridge, Tennessee, or Los Alamos, New Mexico. While many were assigned to clerical or administrative duties, one army woman ran the cyclotron and another was an electronics construction technician. The WAC unit at Los Alamos received the Meritorious Unit Award and one woman was awarded the Legion of Merit.

Ultimately, more than 150,000 women served in the army during World War II, many of them overseas. Before the end of the war, more than 8,300 army women served in England, France, Italy, and Germany. They followed the men up the boot of Italy, and went into France only a month after the NORMANDY INVASION. Many of the women chosen for overseas duty were bilingual or specialists in communications. The Army Air Force in Europe even used women mechanics, control tower operators, and weather forecasters.

The African-American WACs, like black army men, served in segregated units. One of these units, with 800 enlisted women and 30 women officers, was assigned to the 6888th Central Postal Directory Battalion in England and later in France.

Overseas service was not without danger. WACs in England suffered through incendiary bombs early in the war and V-1 buzz bombs and V-2 rockets later. Both headquarters and living areas were hit. More than 5,000 WACs also served under primitive living conditions in the Southwest Pacific and the CHINA-INDIA-BURMA theater of war. Many in these areas suffered from malaria and other tropical illnesses.

WAC members earned eight Legion of Merits, three Air Medals, 10 Soldier's Medals, 16 Purple Hearts, and five Bronze Stars. Their successful service in World War II paved the way for the passage of the Women's Armed Service Integration Act of 1948, which permitted women to serve as career members of the armed forces.

See also ARMY, U.S.; WOMEN IN THE MILITARY.

Further reading: Bellafaire, Judith. *The Women's Army Corps: A Commemoration of World War II Service.* Washington, D.C.: U.S. Army Center of Military History, 1993; Bell, Iris Y. *Los Alamos WPACs/WACs: World War II, 1943–1946.* Sarasota, Fla.: Coastal Printing, 1993; Treadwell. Mattie. *The Women's Army Corps.* Washington, D.C.: U.S. Army Center of Military History, 1954.

— Marie-Beth Hall

Wood, Leonard (1860–1927) *U.S. Army general and chief of staff of the army*

Born on 9 October 1860 in Winchester, New Hampshire, Leonard Wood trained as a physician. He joined the Army

Major General Leonard Wood   *(Library of Congress)*

Medical Department in 1885 and was assigned to Arizona. Shortly afterward, he featured prominently in the expedition that Brigadier General Nelson A. MILES mounted to capture the Apache Indian chieftain GERONIMO, receiving the Medal of Honor for his efforts. After assignments in California and Georgia, in 1895 Wood became attending surgeon to the War Department in Washington, D.C., making several influential political friends, including Assistant Secretary of the Navy Theodore ROOSEVELT, who cherished an expansive vision of his country's future international role. During the SPANISH-AMERICAN WAR, the two served together in Cuba in the 1st Volunteer Cavalry Regiment (the "Rough Riders"), and their well-publicized exploits greatly boosted both their subsequent careers.

Appointed military governor of Cuba and holding the rank of brigadier general of Volunteers (captain in regular army Medical Corps), Wood promptly instituted wide-ranging and controversial economic, municipal, medical, sanitary, educational, and administrative reforms. In 1903 Roosevelt, now president, advanced Wood to major general over many more senior officers and appointed him military

governor of the Philippine Moro province, charged with suppressing the ruling insurgent radical Islamic Malay regime. This Wood did. His campaign culminated in the bloody 1906 Mount Dajo battle, in which American troops killed or wounded over 600 Moro men, women, and children, efforts Roosevelt firmly supported despite ensuing public criticism.

In 1910, Wood became army chief of staff, a position Congress had created in 1903. After a lengthy battle with Adjutant General Frederick C. AINSWORTH, and with backing from Secretary of War Henry L. STIMSON, Wood successfully established his office's dominance within the army hierarchy, a victory that ensured consolidated U.S. military leadership through a strengthened general staff system. He and Stimson also introduced assorted significant administrative reforms, although when his term ended in 1914 Wood still considered the army deficient as a modern professional force. As commander of the Department of the East, headquartered in New York, Wood therefore campaigned incessantly, forcefully, and publicly for greater military preparedness, including not just increased defense spending on equipment and facilities but also universal military training for all American male citizens to provide a reservoir of readily available manpower in wartime.

The outbreak of World War I in Europe in August 1914 and the possibility of American intervention gave Wood's efforts added topicality. He joined Roosevelt and other pro-Allied upper-class Easterners in sponsoring the PLATTSBURG MOVEMENT to establish military training camps for college students, businessmen, and other potential wartime officer candidates. Wood's bellicose efforts (which clearly sought American intervention in the war), his association with prominent Republicans, and his effectively insubordinate criticisms of government policy distanced him from the decidedly more moderate preparedness efforts of President Woodrow WILSON's Democratic administration.

To Wood's dismay, when the United States went to war in April 1917, Wilson appointed Wood's former subordinate, Brigadier General John J. PERSHING, as commander in chief of the AMERICAN EXPEDITIONARY FORCES (AEF) and refused Wood a combat command, assigning him to unspectacular training duties in the Midwest.

In 1920 Wood ran unsuccessfully for the Republican presidential nomination, losing to Warren G. Harding, who subsequently appointed him civil governor of the Philippines. Wood instituted substantial reforms, but clashed repeatedly with Philippine leaders who demanded greater influence within his administration and favored Philippine independence, which Wood opposed for commercial and strategic reasons. Following surgery for a brain tumor, Wood died in Boston, Massachusetts, on 7 August 1927.

See also ROOT, ELIHU.

Further reading: Hagedorn, Hermann. *Leonard Wood: A Biography.* New York: Harper & Brothers, 1931; Hitchman, James H. *Leonard Wood and Cuban Independence, 1898–1902.* The Hague: Nijhoff, 1971; Lane, Jack C. *Armed Progressive: A Study of the Military and Public Career of Leonard Wood.* San Rafael, Calif.: Presidio Press, 1978; Linn, Brian McAllister. *Guardians of Empire: The U.S. Army and the Pacific, 1902–1940.* Chapel Hill: University of North Carolina Press, 1997.

— Priscilla Roberts

Woodring, Harry H. (1887–1967) *Assistant secretary of war and secretary of war*
Born on 31 May 1887 in Elk City, Kansas, Harry Hines Woodring embarked on a career in banking, briefly interrupted when he joined the U.S. Army during World War I. He completed officer training but did not see active service. In the 1920s he became active in the American Legion and Democratic politics, running successfully for governor of Kansas in 1930. Two years later, Woodring was narrowly defeated when he sought reelection, but in April 1933 his early support for Franklin D. ROOSEVELT's successful presidential bid was rewarded when he was appointed assistant secretary of war.

Woodring energetically supported military reforms, including the institution of competitive bidding for contracts for army equipment and supplies, a change tight interwar defense budgets made particularly critical. A champion of air power, he urged development of the B-17 bomber and pushed to enhance Army Air Corps autonomy by establishing the General Headquarters, Air Force. When Secretary of War George Dern died in 1936, Woodring succeeded him. As international crises intensified in Europe and Asia, Woodring, ably assisted by Army Chief of Staff General Malin CRAIG, moved to repair the damage two decades of neglect had inflicted on the military and prepare the United States for potential war. They completely revised overambitious existing American mobilization schemes, introducing the smaller but more workable Protective Mobilization Plan, which envisaged the raising of a 400,000-man army within three months, rising to one million men five months later, a blueprint closely followed in the pre–PEARL HARBOR period. Woodring likewise overhauled plans for industrial mobilization, which when implemented in the 1939–41 period proved crucial to American defense efforts. He also won congressional approval for increasing authorized Air Corps strength from 2,320 to 6,000 aircraft.

Woodring was bedeviled by constant intrigues by Louis A. JOHNSON, his assistant secretary, who coveted Woodring's position. More significantly, in late 1939 and early 1940, Woodring, arguing that the president was denuding the United States of supplies vital to its own defense, doggedly opposed Roosevelt's decision to transfer scarce surplus military equipment and aircraft to Britain to assist that nation's war effort against Germany. Woodring feared that a British defeat, which he thought only too probable, would leave the United States dangerously vulnerable to a victorious Germany. In June 1940 an exasperated Roosevelt finally replaced him with the eminent Republican statesman Henry L. STIMSON, who shared the president's own pro-Allied outlook. Woodring returned to Kansas, twice more running unsuccessfully for governor. He died in Topeka, Kansas, on 9 September 1967.

See also LEND-LEASE; MILITARY-INDUSTRIAL COMPLEX.

Further reading: Bell, William Gardner. *Secretaries of War and Secretaries of the Army: Portraits and Biographical Sketches.* Washington, D.C.: Center of Military History, United States Army, 1981; Kreidberg, Marvin A., and Merton G. Henry. *History of Mobilization in the United States Army, 1775–1945.* Washington, D.C.: Department of the Army, 1955; McFarland, Keith D. *Harry H. Woodring: A Political Biography of FDR's Controversial Secretary of War.* Lawrence: University Press of Kansas, 1975; Watson, Mark Skinner. *Chief of Staff: Prewar Plans and Preparations.* Washington, D.C.: Historical Division, Department of the Army, 1950.

— Priscilla Roberts

Wool, John E. (1784–1869) *U.S. Army general*
Born on 29 February 1784 in Newburgh, New York, John Ellis Wool lived there until the death of his father, when he moved to his grandfather's farm near Troy, New York. He then apprenticed to an innkeeper, worked in a store in Troy, and joined the militia in 1807.

At the beginning of the War of 1812, Wool accepted a commission as captain in the 13th Infantry Regiment after he raised a company of volunteers for military service. He gained distinction during the October 1812 Battle of QUEENSTON HEIGHTS, in which he was wounded and captured. Released, he became a major in the 29th Infantry Regiment. In September 1814, Wool and his men helped delay the advance of 10,000 British regulars marching toward PLATTSBURG, earning him a brevet promotion to lieutenant colonel.

Wool remained in the army after the war, transferring to the 6th Infantry in 1815 as a major. In April 1816 he won promotion to colonel and became inspector general of the Northern Division. In 1821 he became one of the army inspectors general. He held the post for more than two decades and used it to push for the creation of an ordnance department and the acquisition of modern artillery.

Wool was brevetted brigadier general in 1826. In 1832 he went on a fact-finding trip to Europe to observe the

French siege of Antwerp. In 1836 he assisted Brigadier General Winfield SCOTT in the removal of the Cherokees over the "Trail of Tears" from Georgia and North Carolina to the Indian Territory. Wool complained to his superiors about the treatment of the Indians.

Promoted to brigadier general in June 1841, at the start of the MEXICAN-AMERICAN WAR in May 1846 Wool supervised the training of volunteer troops throughout the Ohio Valley. In July he provided Major General Zachary TAYLOR with 12,000 trained volunteers. In August, Wool led a force of 3,400 regulars and volunteers from Camp Crockett, San Antonio, to Chihuahua, Mexico, but then moved east to Saltillo to link up with Taylor's troops who were threatened by a much larger Mexican army under General Antonio López de Santa Anna at Buena Vista. In all, Wool's men marched 900 miles. Wool arrived in time to help secure victory in the 22–23 February 1847 Battle of BUENA VISTA with Santa Anna's troops. For his role in the battle, Wool received a brevet promotion to major general. Beginning in November, following Taylor's transfer, Wool commanded all occupation forces in northern Mexico until the end of the war.

Wool then commanded the Division of the East at Troy, New York, until 1853, when he took command of the Department of the East at Baltimore. In 1854 he took command of the Department of the Pacific, a post he held until 1857, when he again commanded the Department of the East.

At the beginning of the Civil War, Wool, at age 77, was determined to participate. He quickly reinforced Fort Monroe, Virginia, holding it for the Union. He then commanded the Department of Virginia and led the May 1862 combined operation that took Portsmouth and Norfolk, Virginia. Promoted major general, he assumed command of the Middle Department at Baltimore. In January 1863 he took command of the Department of the East at New York City, where he helped to quell the July 1863 draft riots. Wool retired from the army the next month, concluding 51 years of service. He died in Troy, New York, on 10 November 1869.

See also WAR OF 1812: LAND OVERVIEW.

Further reading: Bauer, K. Jack. *The Mexican War: 1846–1848.* New York: Macmillan, 1974; Cook, Adrian. *The Armies of the Streets: The New York City Draft Riots of 1863.* Lexington: University Press of Kentucky, 1974; Lavender, David. *Climax at Buena Vista: The American Campaigns in Northeastern Mexico.* New York: J. B. Lippincott, 1966.

— Matthew Meyers

World War I, causes of U.S. involvement

(1914–1917) *American intervention in World War I arguably ensured Allied victory*

U.S. involvement was not what the American public had sought. In August 1914, general war broke out in Europe, ranging Britain, France, Russia, Belgium, and Japan (the Allies) against Germany, Austria-Hungary, and the Ottoman Empire (the Central Powers). U.S. President Woodrow WILSON called on American citizens to remain neutral both in thought and action. Most Americans sympathized with the Allied side, but only a small East Coast elite of pro-Allied partisans, its most prominent spokesman being former president Theodore ROOSEVELT, favored American intervention.

Existing international law permitted Americans to trade freely with all belligerents, subject to blockades, and to travel on belligerent merchant vessels even inside war zones. American insistence on maintaining these rights soon precipitated crises with both warring camps. For the Allies, their ability to purchase massive quantities of war supplies in North America and increasingly to obtain U.S. financing for these was crucial to winning the war, while, for Germany, cutting this vital lifeline was equally critical. While clashing sporadically with Britain over orders-in-council that restricted American trade with Germany, the Wilson administration effectively acquiesced to the British blockade, simultaneously sanctioning enormous British purchases of American matériel, from spring 1915 ever more substantially funded by private American loans and credits.

In early 1915, German strategists began to use SUBMARINES, a novel technology, to destroy Allied shipping, sinking merchant vessels without warning. On 7 May 1915, a submarine torpedoed the British passenger liner *LUSITANIA* off the coast of Ireland, killing 1,198 people, including 124 Americans. After a sharp exchange of notes, German officials temporarily acquiesced to American demands to respect passenger ships, pledges renewed after a similar incident in March 1916. Pro-German, anti-British, and neutral forces in Congress repeatedly introduced—but the administration blocked—resolutions forbidding Americans to trade with belligerents or travel on their ships.

Wilson repeatedly offered to mediate in the conflict, but intransigence on both sides and the pro-Allied leanings of his close adviser, Colonel Edward M. House, and his secretary of state, Robert Lansing, undercut his endeavors. Although in 1916 he approved moderate increases in American defense budgets, in November 1916 the president won reelection on a fundamentally antiwar platform. Almost immediately he backed a Federal Reserve Board initiative to discourage further American funding of the Allies, a move that by December had precipitated a British foreign exchange (currency) crisis and drastically reduced British orders in the United States. Wilson then called on both belligerents to state the terms on which they would negotiate peace, and on 9 January 1917 he publicly advocated a "peace without victory."

Ironically, later that month the apparently oblivious German High Command chose to resume unlimited submarine warfare, intending to destroy Allied shipping, cut off American supplies, and achieve victory before the still unprepared United States could mobilize effectively against Germany. Wilson immediately broke diplomatic relations with Germany. That same month, German foreign minister Arthur Zimmermann indiscreetly dispatched a telegram with a proposal for the Mexican government. This stated that if the United States and Germany were at war and Mexico, with whom American relations had been strained since 1914, was to range itself on the German side, a German victory would restore to Mexico its territories seized by the United States in the 19th century. On 1 March, Wilson published this ZIMMERMANN TELEGRAM, which Zimmermann foolishly acknowledged to be genuine.

Later that month, German submarines sank several American merchant ships. This was the primary reason behind the U.S. decision to go to war; but the Zimmermann Telegram and revelations of sabotage by German agents in the United States were also factors, and a democratic revolution in Russia in March simultaneously freed the Allies from the authoritarian czarist taint. On 2 April Wilson asked Congress formally to declare war on Germany, which it did four days later, although not until 7 December 1917 did the United States go to war with Austria-Hungary.

American reluctance to intervene notwithstanding, World War I demonstrated that in any major war all United States decisions on trade, finance, and neutral rights were liable significantly to affect that conflict's outcome, and hence no warring power could afford to ignore the United States.

See also WORLD WAR I: COURSE OF U.S. INVOLVEMENT.

Further reading: Calhoun, Frederick S. *Power and Principle: Armed Intervention in Wilsonian Foreign Policy.* Kent, Ohio: Kent State University Press, 1986; Devlin, Patrick. *Too Proud to Fight: Woodrow Wilson's Neutrality.* New York: Oxford University Press, 1973; Keene, Jennifer D. *The United States and the First World War.* New York: Longman, 2000; Knock, Thomas J. *To End All Wars: Woodrow Wilson and the Quest for a New World Order.* New York: Oxford University Press, 1992; Link, Arthur S. *Wilson.* 5 vols. Princeton, N.J.: Princeton University Press, 1947–65; May, Ernest R. *The World War and American Isolation, 1914–1917.* Cambridge: Harvard University Press, 1959.

— Priscilla Roberts

World War I, course of U.S. involvement (6 April 1917–11 November 1918)

The United States entered World War I almost three years after the start of the conflict. During the period of U.S.

neutrality, Americans generally favored the Allies against the Central Powers, but the prevailing sentiment was a desire to stay out of the war. Events in 1917, especially the German decision to resume unrestricted submarine warfare, led to a U.S. declaration of war against Germany on 6 April 1917.

The American entry into the war was a tremendous morale boost for the Allies and a corresponding blow for the Central Powers. It also meant an immediate financial lift to the hard-pressed Allies. However, it would be months before the United States was able to do anything militarily. In fact, it took the country well over a year to train and transport sufficient troops to Europe to have a significant influence on the war. Preparing the U.S. military to fight on a European battlefield was quite another thing from issuing a declaration of war.

Although Congress had passed the NATIONAL DEFENSE ACT in 1916 and then authorized the expansion of the military to 235,000 men in the regular army and almost 460,000 in the National Guard, by April 1917 these goals had not been met. When the United States declared war, the regular army numbered only 127,000 men. An additional 66,000 National Guardsmen were in federal service along the border with Mexico, and another 100,000 were under state control. The navy was in better shape, but many of its 360 ships, including 151 warships, were undermanned, and the ships themselves were in need of repair.

The first task at hand was to raise a sufficiently large military establishment to influence the course of the war. In May 1917 Congress passed the Selective Service Act. It required all men between the ages of 21 and 30 to register for the draft. In 1918 this was extended to ages 18 to 45. Ultimately 24 million men were registered. Between April 1917 and November 1918, the army grew from just slightly more than 200,000 men, including federalized National Guardsmen, to 3,685,458 men. Of this total, almost 2.2 million were

A Curtiss H-12 "Large America" flying boat taking off in 1918 *(San Diego Aerospace Museum)*

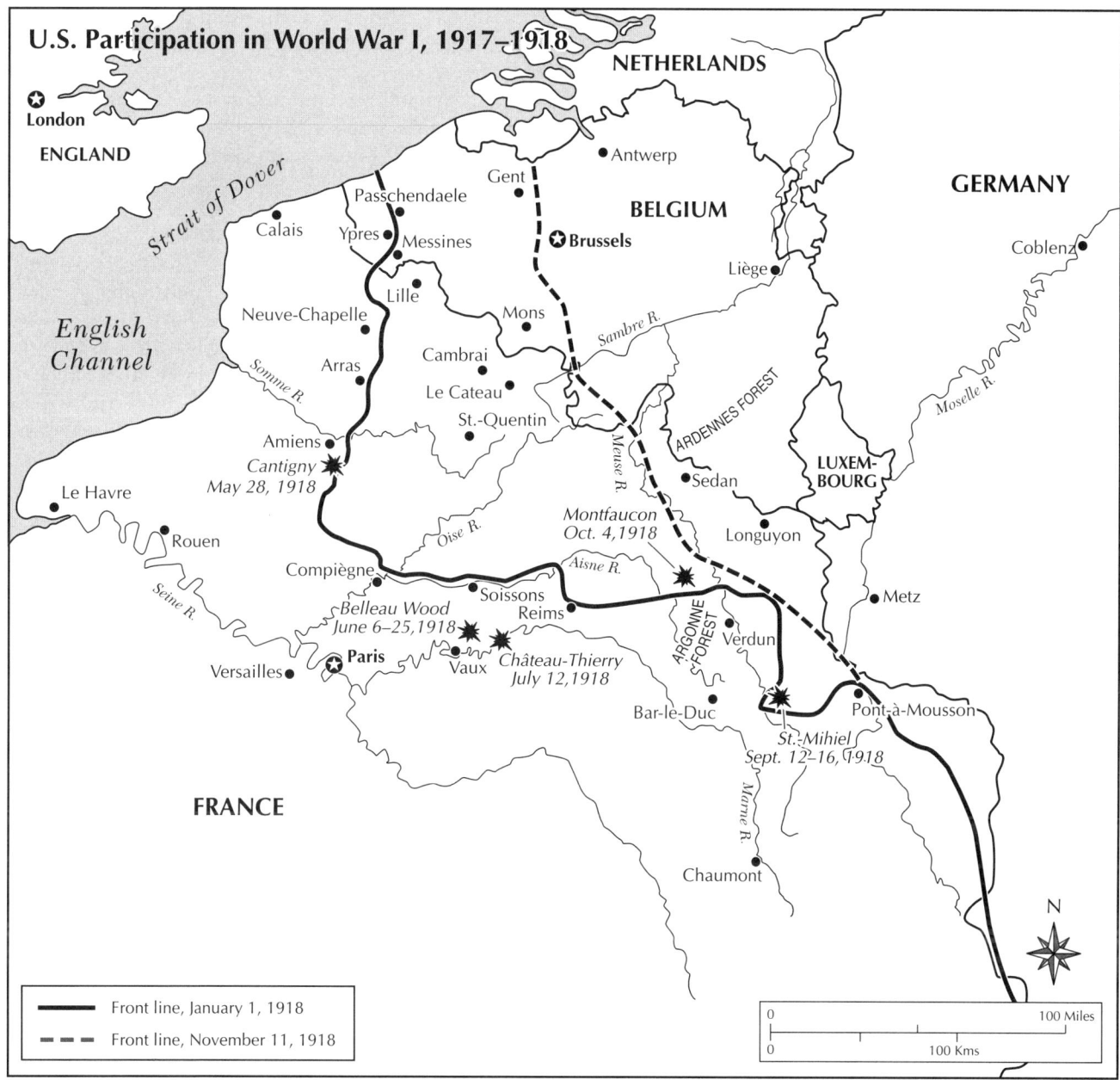

U.S. Participation in World War I, 1917–1918

Front line, January 1, 1918
Front line, November 11, 1918

conscripts. But of the 29 divisions (1,000 officers and 27,000 men each) that saw action in France, only 11 were draftee divisions; the remainder consisted of seven regular and 11 National Guard divisions, all volunteer. To command the army and U.S. Marine Corps contingents that made up the AMERICAN EXPEDITIONARY FORCES (AEF), Congress appointed army brigadier general John J. "Black Jack" PERSHING, who most recently had led the PUNITIVE EXPEDITION IN MEXICO.

The navy, while not completely ready for war, was at least better prepared than the army. Rear Admiral William SIMS immediately assumed command of U.S. naval forces

in European waters. In April 1917, on an urgent appeal from London, U.S. destroyers were sent to Queenstown (now Cobh), Ireland, to be employed as convoy escorts and take part in antisubmarine patrols under British command. By July there were 34 destroyers in Queenstown. This was the first time that American warships had operated under foreign command. A U.S. destroyer flotilla also went to Brest, France, to escort troop-laden transports.

Expanding the army was relatively easy when compared to the logistical nightmare of training and equipping such a large force. Trained officers to administer the transition from a peacetime to a wartime military were in short supply. Altogether, the army, navy, and marines only had 11,000 officers in April 1917. At least 200,000 were needed in the expanded military. In many cases, new officers learned drills the night before a training session. Training facilities were inadequate. The army had to build more than 30 temporary camps in the United States to train the men before they were shipped to France. In the first year alone, the army ordered some 80 million undershirts and underwear. Despite the laudable efforts of Secretary of War Newton BAKER and others, serious shortcomings lasted to the end of the war.

Naval operations were geared to support the army. Transporting American soldiers, their equipment, and supplies to France proved its most important assignment. The government requisitioned and purchased ships to build "a bridge to France." It also began an expanded shipbuilding program, and some 109 interned German vessels, including the 54,000-ton passenger ship *Vaterland* (renamed the *Leviathan*), were pressed into service. Still, almost half the ships used in this work were British. While many soldiers remembered the trip over as a miserable time of overcrowded conditions and seasickness, they arrived in Europe unscathed. Only six transports were sunk by U-boats, all in European waters, and four of these were on the return voyage. Sims had insisted on the imposition of a CONVOY SYSTEM, which the British instituted in May 1917. More than any other single factor, the convoy insured the safe passage of American troops and supplies. In the desperate conditions of the summer of 1918 the United States was transporting more than 300,000 men a month to France.

The 1st Infantry Division arrived in France in time to parade down the Champs Elysée on 4 July 1917, but it was soon broken up for training. Other units followed, but the great rush to France occurred beginning in June 1918 under the pressure of the Ludendorff offensives, when manpower became critical to the Allies. In July more than 300,000 U.S. troops were sent to France. Because manpower was the key, the U.S. troops used mostly French and British equipment. Few American-made artillery pieces saw action in France, and no U.S.-made tank or aircraft went into combat on the western front.

Both the army and navy provided an air arm in the war. When the war began, the Army Air Service had only 65 officers, of whom only 35 could fly. They were amalgamated with American volunteers of the LAFAYETTE ESCADRILLE in the French army. They began combat duty in March 1918 under Colonel William MITCHELL. Soon the Americans had three air squadrons. The army had only 55 planes when the war began. When the war ended, the United States had 3,227 de Haviland-4 aircraft, a British design. The navy employed Curtiss float planes to assist in locating submarines.

The navy also sent a battleship division to join the British Grand Fleet at Scapa Flow, in the Orkney Islands. It did not see action, as the German High Seas Fleet prudently stayed in port. Of much more use were some 120 subchasers that were sent to France and provided useful training for junior officers destined for higher command in World War II.

Before the spring of 1918, most U.S. troops in France were in training. Until May 1918, American casualties were slight, and only 163 soldiers had been killed in action. From the end of May to November, these numbers changed drastically as the AEF entered the battle in full strength. The big question for Pershing in the spring of 1918 was how the AEF would be used on the Western Front. To avoid being bound to the many Allied agreements on territory to be taken from the Central Powers, President Woodrow WILSON held that the United States was merely an associated rather than allied power. Wilson instructed Pershing that in military operations he was to "cooperate" with other forces fighting the Central Powers but to keep in mind that U.S. forces were a separate and distinct component of the combined forces, and that their identity was to be preserved. To Pershing, this meant that the Americans should fight in a distinct U.S. army, holding its own section of the front, not amalgamated in, or assigned to, British and French units. Under the pressure of the March 1918 German offensive, the British and the French pleaded for American troops as fillers, stiffened by their own tried-and-tested units. Pershing sought an independent American force, holding a portion of the front. But under the pressure of the German offensive and President Wilson's new orders, he gave way, although U.S. troops were committed as entire divisions.

On 28 May, American forces, spearheaded by the 28th Infantry regiment of the 1st Division, launched the first truly American action of the war against the German-held village of CANTIGNY, wrestling control of it from the Germans. While minuscule in comparison to other battles on the western front, the Battle of Cantigny was significant for American morale and in showing that U.S. forces could defeat German soldiers on the battlefield.

A marine brigade of the 2d Division and elements of the 3d and 28th Divisions helped the French to stem another German offensive at CHÂTEAU-THIERRY. On 6 June, the marines, along with elements of two infantry divisions, took the offensive at Belleau Wood, a square mile held by seasoned German troops. It took the Americans a week to capture it; their losses were heavy, but their effort surprised the Germans.

U.S. forces also played a key role in the last major German offensive of the war, the Second Battle of the MARNE, at Reims, on 15 July 1918. By the 18th the German attack had failed, and Allied forces went on the offensive at Soissons.

The allied supreme commander, the French marshal Ferdinand Foch, now reluctantly agreed to Pershing's demand for an American attack in the SAINT MIHIEL salient. It began on 15 September 1918 with an artillery bombardment of 1.1 million shells in only four hours. In addition, the Allies massed 1,500 aircraft. The attack caught the Germans at a most inopportune time, as they were withdrawing. Nevertheless, the attack was a success. During the period 12–16 September, American and French forces liberated 200 square miles of French territory that had been held by the Germans for four years, killed or wounded 2,300 enemy soldiers, and captured another 13,000. The American First Army suffered 7,000 casualties. Pershing wanted to continue the drive to Metz but, in a stormy session, Foch refused.

Pershing then had to shift his forces in short order to participate in the MEUSE-ARGONNE OFFENSIVE that began on 26 September and lasted the remainder of the war. To achieve their objectives, American forces had to break through the heavily fortified Hindenburg line, 10 miles in depth. It was the greatest battle in which American troops had ever fought. Not until 1944 were the numbers involved—1,031,000, of whom 135,000 were French and 896,000 American—surpassed. At the cost of more than 26,000 dead and 95,000 wounded, American troops finally broke through the Hindenburg line and forced the Germans to retreat. In the process, they captured more than 25,000 prisoners and inflicted almost 100,000 casualties. The combination of American efforts in the Meuse-Argonne and Allied attacks along the Western Front forced Germany to seek peace.

The fighting ended with an ARMISTICE on 11 November 1918. Pershing had opposed an armistice and wanted to continue the war until the Germans surrendered, but the pressure was great to end the fighting. Winning the peace would turn out to be more difficult. American forces had turned the tide of the war. The United States did not win the war, but it is hard to see how the Allies could have won without American help. U.S. losses were small in percentage compared to the casualties suffered by the other powers; out of some 1,390,000 American troops and seamen who saw active combat duty, 49,000 were killed in action or died of wounds; 230,000 more were wounded. Another 57,000 died from disease, largely the result of an influenza-pneumonia pandemic that swept through the camps in America and France in the fall of 1918.

See also AISNE-MARNE COUNTEROFFENSIVE; ATLANTIC, BATTLE OF (WORLD WAR I); PARIS PEACE SETTLEMENT; SELECTIVE SERVICE; SIMS, WILLIAM S.; VAUX, BATTLE OF; WORLD WAR I, CAUSES OF U.S. INVOLVEMENT.

Further reading: Coffman, Edward M. *The War to End All Wars: The American Military Experience in World War I.*

Madison: University of Wisconsin Press, 1986; Farwell, Byron. *Over There: The United States in the Great War, 1917–1918.* New York: W. W. Norton, 1999; Hallas, James H. *Doughboy War: The American Expeditionary Force in World War II.* Boulder, Colo.: Lynne Rienner Publishers, 2000; Keene, Jennifer D. *Doughboys: The Great War and the Remaking of America.* Baltimore: Johns Hopkins University Press, 2001; Stallings, Laurence. *The Doughboys: The Story of the AEF, 1917–1918.* New York: Harper & Row, 1963.

— David L. Snead and Spencer C. Tucker

World War II, causes of U.S. entry

In the late 1930s U.S. politicians and the public alike feared American involvement in the intensifying international crises in Europe and Asia. Many Americans believed that the aftermath of World War I and the failure of the League of Nations to preserve peace proved that their country's intervention in the previous war had been mistaken, and they strenuously attempted to avoid entanglement in further overseas conflicts. In 1935 Congress passed the first Neutrality Act, renewed with slight modifications every year until 1939, which endeavored to distance the United States from war by forbidding or severely restricting American trade with or travel on the vessels of any belligerent nation.

Opposition to Roosevelt's policies was spearheaded by the America First Committee. Founded in July 1940 by a group of conservative midwestern Republican businessmen, this organization supported a strong defense but opposed many of Roosevelt's measures as liable to drag the United States into a war in which no major American interests were threatened. Its efforts were countered by the Committee to Defend America by Aiding the Allies, headed by William Allen White, a Kansas newspaper editor. The committee argued that assistance to the Allies to enable them to keep fighting represented the best means to keep the United States out of war. More openly interventionist was the Fight for Freedom or Century Group. Both these groups worked closely with the Roosevelt administration.

Unlike many Americans, President Franklin D. ROOSEVELT, a fervent interventionist at the time of World War I, was eager to check the growing influence and territorial designs of expansionist fascist dictatorships in Europe and Asia, which he and his close advisers believed ultimately menaced U.S. strategic, economic, and ideological interests. In October 1937, shortly after Japan invaded China, he rather vaguely suggested that peace-loving nations might "quarantine" aggressor nations, but obvious public misgivings dissuaded him from following up this proposal. In September 1938, Roosevelt even congratulated British prime minister Neville Chamberlain on the Munich

Agreement, by which Germany obtained the Sudetenland from Czechoslovakia. Despite gradually tightening embargoes, U.S. businessmen also continued to provide considerable quantities of war supplies to Japan until late 1940, substantially facilitating Japan's ongoing war against China.

When general European war began in September 1939, Roosevelt unequivocally and immediately ranged the United States in the broad Allied, antifascist camp. In October 1939, Roosevelt won revision of the Neutrality Act to permit the Allies to purchase war supplies on a cash-and-carry basis. After France's June 1940 defeat by Germany, and despite fears that Britain might not continue the battle alone, Roosevelt ordered the War and Navy Departments to resupply Britain's military, exchanged 50 obsolescent destroyers for long leases on eight British Caribbean naval bases, instituted a massive American rearmament program to upgrade the depression-era skeleton United States armed forces, and obtained SELECTIVE SERVICE legislation to draft young Americans into the military. He appointed two prominent Republican interventionists, Henry L. STIMSON and Frank KNOX, to head the War and Navy Departments, respectively.

After winning an unprecedented third term in 1940, Roosevelt proceeded even more aggressively. In March 1941 he obtained LEND-LEASE legislation, authorizing the government to furnish war supplies on credit to a near-bankrupt Britain and other nations, notably China and the Soviet Union. From early 1941 onward, Britain and the United States privately coordinated their wartime strategies. Moving ever closer to outright war with Germany, in April 1941 Roosevelt excluded German warships, which were inflicting severe depredations on merchant ships bound for Britain, from the Western Hemisphere and a zone extending halfway across the Atlantic, including Greenland. In July, U.S. Marines occupied Iceland; on several occasions in late 1941, American warships escorting Allied convoys engaged German vessels in direct conflict; and in November, Congress permitted the arming of American merchantmen in the war zone, although American public and congressional support for a declaration of war remained problematic.

War, however, eventually resulted from the concurrent Pacific crisis. The Tripartite Pact that Japan, Germany, and Italy signed in September 1940 obliged each nation to assist the others should one be attacked by an opponent other than the existing belligerents. The Japanese believed that the world's preoccupation with the European war provided an ideal opportunity for them to annex Southeast Asian territories. U.S. officials hoped to defer tackling the Pacific situation until the Atlantic war was resolved, but in the summer of 1941, following the establishment by Japan of bases in Indochina, the United States imposed a near-complete embargo on sales of oil and scrap metal to Japan, whose military possessed fuel sufficient for only two years. Despite continuing Japanese-American negotiations, neither side would compromise over their diametrically opposed views on Japan's position in China.

On 7 December 1941, Japanese aircraft and submarines unexpectedly attacked the United States Pacific Fleet in its Hawaiian PEARL HARBOR base, inflicting heavy casualties and outraging Americans. The following day, Congress declared war on Japan, and three days later Germany and Italy declared war on the United States, breaking the impasse that previously had prevented Roosevelt taking the final step to forthright intervention. Each Axis power mistakenly assumed that an irresolute United States would ultimately accept a negotiated peace—a miscalculation that effectively ensured that all three Axis powers ended the war defeated.

See also ATLANTIC, BATTLE OF THE (WORLD WAR II); LINDBERGH, CHARLES; *REUBEN JAMES*.

Further reading: Dallek, Robert. *Franklin D. Roosevelt and American Foreign Policy, 1932–1945.* New York: Oxford University Press, 1979; Heinrich, Waldo H. *Diplomacy and Force: America's Road to War, 1931–1941.* Edited by Marc Gallicchio and Jonathan Utley. Chicago: Imprint Publications, 1996; Herzstein, Robert Edwin. *Roosevelt and Hitler: Prelude to War.* New York: Paragon House, 1989; Reynolds, David. *The Creation of the Anglo-American Alliance, 1937–1941: A Study in Competitive Cooperation.* Chapel Hill: University of North Carolina Press, 1982; Thompson, Robert Smith. *A Time for War: Franklin Delano Roosevelt and the Path to Pearl Harbor.* New York: Prentice-Hall, 1991.

— Priscilla Roberts

World War II, course of U.S. involvement: Europe
Most extensive and complex military operations in American history

The Japanese attack on the American fleet at Pearl Harbor on 7 December 1941 and the subsequent declaration of war on the United States by Germany thrust the United States into a global and total war. At the hurriedly called Arcadia Conference in Washington two weeks later, President Franklin D. ROOSEVELT, British prime minister Winston S. Churchill, and their military chiefs of staff reaffirmed the strategic decision to defeat Germany first (previously agreed upon during the so-called ABC-1 Conversations of January–March 1941) and agreed upon the general strategic concept for victory in Europe. The five-phased Arcadia Strategy involved the mobilization and buildup of Allied forces and resources; the maintenance and extension of Allied lines of communications; the erosion of Axis strength through a strategic air campaign; the

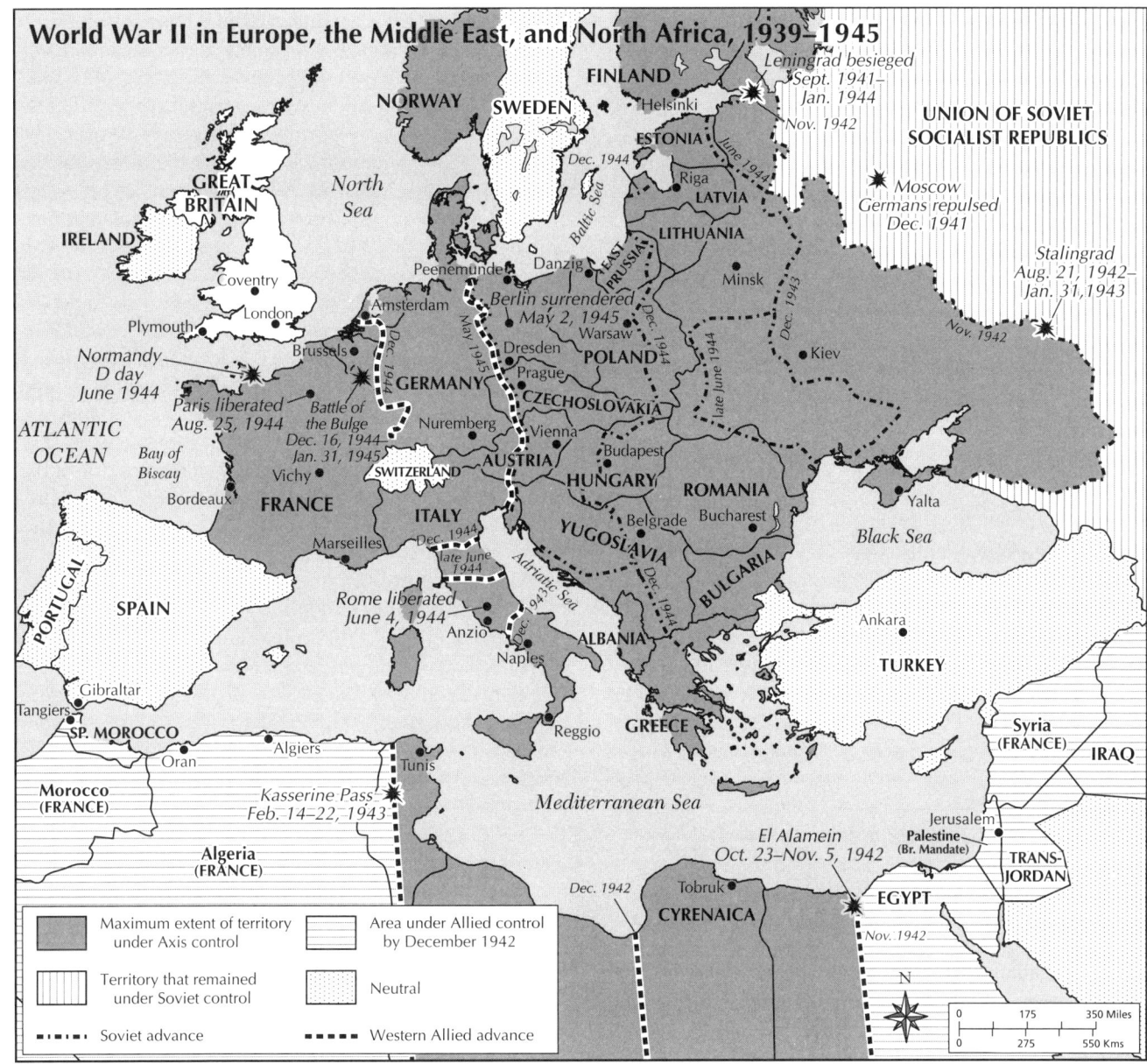

World War II in Europe, the Middle East, and North Africa, 1939–1945

isolation of Axis powers by "closing the ring" around Germany; and the eventual invasion of the European continent and the final destruction of Germany. This strategic framework largely describes the course of American military involvement in the European theater of World War II.

American mobilization began about eight months before Pearl Harbor, spurred by Roosevelt's conception of America as the "great arsenal of democracy." FDR's LEND-LEASE policy in March 1941 proved a catalyst for American industrial mobilization, and the U.S. production effort proved to be a success by any measure, as American factories, shipyards, and farms produced prodigiously. American industry produced almost two-thirds of all military equip-

ment during the war. By the end of 1942, the United States had out-produced the Axis powers altogether: 47,000 aircraft to 27,000, 24,000 tanks to 11,000, and six times as many heavy artillery pieces. The Ford Motor Company alone eclipsed Italian war production. In 1944, the United States aircraft industry produced 73,876 combat aircraft; by contrast, Germany manufactured only 86,311 during the entire war. American shipbuilding productivity increased by 25 percent a year, creating a vast maritime arm that projected U.S. power and transported American production and food to overseas theaters of operation.

Serving as the arsenal of democracy drained huge American manpower sources and forced U.S. military

Some 240 U.S. volunteer pilots flew with the Royal Air Force from September 1940 to September 1942. Seen here are two Eagle Squadron's Spitfires landing.   *(Hulton-Getty Picture Collection)*

leaders to make difficult choices about how to allocate manpower. The service support forces required to fight a global war further limited the men available for combat units. The prewar army estimate that 200 army divisions would be required to prosecute the war had to be reduced by more than half by army chief of staff General George C. MARSHALL. His "90-division gamble" forced American commanders in Europe to commit their divisions to sustained combat, with little time to retrain and refit. Eighty-nine of the 90 divisions were committed to combat by the end of the war and American forces were absent a strategic reserve for most of the last year of the war. Still, a 90-division force was a realistic meeting ground of American strategy, production, and manpower.

In order for American economic might to tip the European military balance, the Allies had to secure Atlantic and Mediterranean lines of communication from U-boat wolf packs. After December 1941 the German submarine war spread to American shores, and the initial advantage in the Battle of the ATLANTIC swung toward the submarines. Throughout 1942 and 1943, Anglo-American naval forces desperately sought to wrest the initiative from the U-Boats. In 1942 Germany sank 8 million tons of shipping; the 2.6 million alone between January and April exceeded that lost in all of 1941. In all, 1,662 Allied ships were lost. German successes continued into 1943, sinking almost 800,000 tons in February and March. Despite the great increase in American industrial production, British imports sank to one-third of their 1939 level. The U-boat appeared to have the upper hand.

New radio intelligence technology and improved tactics by Anglo-American forces, buttressed by burgeoning American shipping and aircraft production, which by October 1943 had replaced all losses since 1939 and which

added escort aircraft carriers to Allied convoys and long-range B-24 Liberator bombers for antisubmarine duty, swung the war to a grim battle of attrition. By May 1943 German U-boat monthly losses were more than double their production and outstripped cargo ship sinkings. The German High Command withdrew its U-boats from the Atlantic, signaling a decisive shift in the war.

Although a new snorkel-equipped U-boat made an appearance in mid-1944, the security of the Atlantic sea-lanes, prerequisite to the success of the Arcadia strategy, had allowed the American air and ground forces to deploy to Europe in the decisive numbers required to execute the remaining phases of the strategy. The U.S. Army's seizure of France's Atlantic ports in August 1944 brought an end to Germany's ability to reopen the Battle of the Atlantic on any scale.

Equally important to securing the Atlantic shipping lanes was the Allied campaign to destroy Axis infrastructure. When the U.S. Army Air Force joined the STRATEGIC BOMBING campaign in 1942, it brought a doctrinal outlook different from that of the Royal Air Force. The RAF favored area bombing at night to strike at German morale; American doctrine favored precision daylight bombing of specific "bottleneck" targets, which, if destroyed, would bring the German economy to collapse. The U.S. Eighth Air Force under Major General Ira C. EAKER had the principal strategic bombing mission, and undertook it beginning in late 1942 from bases in North Africa against Italy and the Balkans, and later from southern Italy against Austria and the PLOESTI oilfields in Romania, and from Britain against the industrial heart of Germany.

Eaker's airmen had confidence that their superior Norden bombsight, heavily armed B-17 Flying Fortresses, and superior formation defensive tactics would validate their precision-bombing doctrine and drive Germany to its knees. Their combat experience in 1943 dampened their enthusiasm, however. In the summer and fall of 1943 the Eighth Air Force suffered disastrous losses from savage German fighter attacks while attacking bottleneck German ball bearing and aircraft factories at SCHWEINFURT AND REGENSBERG. In one week in October the Eighth Air Force lost 148 bombers and crews on four missions, 60 of them in another attack on Schweinfurt. The conclusion was clear: Unescorted daylight bombing was impossible. Had the war ended in 1943, the American strategic bombing campaign would have been a failure.

But like their ground counterparts, American airmen also learned from their experience and improved their operational effectiveness. The key to their success proved to be the drop-tank modifications that extended the range of the fighter escorts. The long-range escort fighter transformed the air war. Standard American fighter aircraft such as the P-38 Lightning and the P-47 Thunderbolt were fitted with drop-tanks, but it was the remarkable P-51 Mustang that best combined aerial combat capabilities with extended range. By March 1944 P-51s were escorting Allied bombers all the way to Berlin and back. The result was catastrophic for the Luftwaffe, which found itself engaged in a massive battle of attrition it could not withstand. By the spring of 1944 the Allies had command of the air.

Delayed by its support of the NORMANDY LANDINGS (Operation Overlord), the strategic bombing campaign exploited its new advantage in earnest beginning in the late summer of 1944. The U.S. Fifteenth Air Force, flying out of the Mediterranean theater, supported the Eighth Air Force. During the last year of the war the bombing of Germany was relentless. Seventy-two percent of all the bombs dropped on Germany fell after 1 July 1944. German oil, chemical, transportation, and railway targets were ravaged. By March 1945, approximately 7,000 American bombers and fighters were attacking Germany.

While the contributions of the American strategic bombing campaign to victory were enormous, the costs of the effort should also be considered. At least 25 percent of the total American industrial effort went into aviation. The Army Air Force (AAF) grew to 2.4 million personnel, 31 percent of the army's strength, and personnel policies dictated that the AAF got the best men. Moreover, 40 percent of all U.S. aircraft procurement costs went into heavy bombers. Operational costs were even starker. The Eighth and Fifteenth Air Forces lost 29,000 aircrew in the war in Europe—more than the U.S. Army's losses in the Normandy or Ardennes campaigns or the U.S. Navy's or U.S. Marine Corps' losses in the Pacific theater.

Although Roosevelt, Churchill, and their military chiefs agreed on the broad strokes of the Arcadia strategy, they disagreed fundamentally on the key issue of the timing and nature of the Allied return to the Continent. In this debate, the British and the Americans were influenced by their respective experiences in World War I. Dominated by the shadows of the Somme and Passchendaele, Churchill and the British Chiefs of Staff were wary of a premature return to the Continent and instead favored operations in the Mediterranean to close the ring around Germany. The

North American P-51D Mustangs of the 4th Fighter Squadron, 52d Fighter Group, of the Fifteenth Air Force based in Madma, Italy, 1944. The P-51 was one of the best fighters of World War II.   *(San Diego Aerospace Museum)*

Men of the 370th Infantry Regiment moving forward at Prato, Italy, 1945. The Abruzzi mountain range looms in the background. *(National Archives)*

U.S. Joint Chiefs of Staff (JCS), led by Marshall, had drawn a different conclusion from World War I, deducing that only when the large AMERICAN EXPEDITIONARY FORCES (AEF) arrived in France had the war been won. To the JCS, a large-scale, direct cross-Channel attack at the earliest opportunity was the strategic key to victory. An early second front in Europe promised the best aid to the Soviet Union, which had been carrying the brunt of the war against the Wehrmacht; the earliest defeat of Germany; and the speediest way to get on with the next great task, that of defeating Japan.

The disparity between German and Allied strength in France, British reluctance, and Roosevelt's ambivalence (shaped greatly by Churchill's arguments) precluded a cross-Channel attack in 1942. Marshall's plan to concentrate forces in Britain for a 1943 invasion was foiled by FDR's insistence on a major initiative against Germany in 1942 in order to sustain American public support for his "Germany First" strategy. The result was Operation TORCH, the Anglo-American invasion of North Africa in November 1942.

Lieutenant General Dwight D. EISENHOWER commanded the Torch operation, and successfully landed task forces—some embarking from as far away as the United States—at Casablanca, Oran, and Algiers, overcoming initial resistance by Vichy French forces and advancing on Tunisia. By February 1943 German forces in Tunisia, commanded by Field Marshal Erwin Rommel and Lieutenant General Jürgen von Arnim, had stabilized the front along the western border of Tunisia. Rommel then badly mauled the poorly dispersed American II Corps in the battle of the KASSERINE PASS. It was a disappointing performance for the U.S. Army in its first important combat operations against the Wehrmacht.

German command problems and British pressure from General Sir Bernard Law Montgomery's Eighth Army arriving from Egypt prevented German exploitation of the Kasserine victory and drew the Germans east and away from the Americans to their ultimate defeat in May at Montgomery's hands at the Battle of Mareth. Given this respite, Eisenhower reorganized. Lieutenant General George S. PATTON took command of II Corps in March and immediately began to revitalize it. Its successes over the subsequent six weeks demonstrated the determination that American commanders showed throughout the war to learn from their experiences and to demonstrate steady and consistent improvement in combat operations.

Forces in being have a way of creating their own strategy, and the presence of a large Anglo-American force in North Africa created enormous pressure for the continuation of a Mediterranean strategy. Marshall's call for a 1943 cross-Channel attack, presented during the Casablanca Conference in January 1943, fell prey to Churchill's persuasive arguments to Roosevelt that Sicily should be the "great prize" for 1943. Knocking Italy from the Axis ranks, opening the Mediterranean to Allied shipping, and better positioning Allied air forces for the combined bomber offensive against Germany were gains too lucrative to resist. Moreover, the redeployment of forces to Britain for a cross-Channel attack could cost the Allies the initiative that had so recently been wrestled from the Nazis.

On 9–10 July 1943, the U.S. Seventh Army, commanded by Patton, and the British Eighth Army, under Montgomery, invaded Sicily with eight seaborne and two airborne divisions. It was the largest amphibious operation of World War II. Operation Husky went less smoothly than planned, with the airborne operations especially rocky. Allied forces landed from the sea largely unscathed, however, and Husky provided the first large-scale test of the new LST (Landing Ship Tank), LCI (Landing Craft Infantry), and LCT (Landing Craft Tank) beaching craft. It was a resounding success.

Sicily's broken terrain, especially in Montgomery's eastern sector, and stiff German resistance slowed the Allied advance until August, when a series of amphibious hooks along Sicily's north coast by Patton's forces turned German defenses. German forces skillfully withdrew at night across the Strait of Messina, and Patton triumphantly (and flamboyantly) entered Messina on 17 August. The three German divisions that escaped would make their presence painfully felt in the ensuing Italian campaign.

Victory in Sicily exacerbated American concerns that they were being drawn into a Mediterranean sideshow. The Americans saw the Mediterranean theater (and especially Italy) in terms of its contribution to the cross-Channel attack; they saw no decisive results springing from a campaign in Italy. Still, the Italian ouster of Mussolini following the invasion of Sicily and the cumulative losses in German equipment and manpower resulting from the campaigns were strong magnets that attracted the Allies to the Italian mainland.

In early September, Anglo-American forces invaded the Italian boot. A plan by the new Italian government secretly to surrender and assist the 82d Airborne Division to land in Rome was aborted and the Wehrmacht disarmed the Italian army, quickly reestablished control, and launched strong counterattacks against Lieutenant General Mark CLARK's Fifth Army in the vicinity of SALERNO. Although overwhelming Allied air support and naval gunfire forced the Germans to shift to the defensive, ceding Naples to the Allies and establishing the Gustav line across the peninsula 75 miles north of Naples, neither Clark's Fifth Army nor Montgomery's Eighth Army could breach the Gustav line in five costly offensives attempted between October and mid-January 1944. The last of these, the U.S.

36th (Texas) Division's bloody and abortive attempt to cross the Rapido River on 20 January, resulted in more than 1,000 American dead.

An American amphibious landing behind the Gustav line at ANZIO (Operation Shingle) on 22 January positioned the U.S. VI Corps 30 miles south of Rome in an attempt to break the deadlock. Although the landing surprised the Germans, it floundered when its commander, Major General John P. Lucas, failed speedily to expand his bridgehead and German forces concentrated to contain the landing. VI Corps spent the next three months defending against German offensives and the Allies were forced to intensify their pressure against the Gustav line in an effort to relieve the beleaguered VI Corps. The resulting battles of attrition included particularly bloody fighting around the abbey of MONTE CASSINO and served neither the Germans nor the Allies well, although German losses in men and matériel were irreplaceable and most likely created the conditions for the success of Operation Diadem in May, which cracked the Gustav line and opened Rome to the Allies. Although Clark entered Rome on 4 June 1944, German forces established the so-called Gothic line 150 miles to the north. Germany would remain in control of northern Italy for most of the remainder of the war. It is questionable whether the 26 German divisions drawn to oppose the 17 Allied divisions in Italy justified the campaign's strategic rationale.

While the Italian campaign was underway, the Anglo-American dispute over the timing and nature of the return to France was resolved at the Teheran Conference in November 1943 when Roosevelt and Stalin overruled Churchill's objections and committed the alliance to a major cross-Channel attack in the spring of 1944. Eisenhower commanded the Supreme Headquarters Allied Expeditionary Force (SHAEF), responsible for planning and executing Overlord, the operation to open the long-awaited second front. Montgomery, responsible for the landing forces, commanded 21st Army Group, composed of British First Army, under Lieutenant General Sir Miles C. Dempsey, and U.S. First Army, under Lieutenant General Omar N. BRADLEY.

Although the shortest and most obvious invasion route led to Pas de Calais, Allied planners chose Normandy, because it was comfortably within Allied air support range, more distant from German reserves, and in the lee of the sheltering Cotentin Peninsula. Operation Fortitude, an elaborate Allied deception plan involving a fictitious army group commanded by Patton, successfully persuaded Hitler to maintain significant forces in the Pas de Calais area for weeks after the invasion. A massive Allied aerial interdiction campaign, carefully coordinated with Fortitude, attacked the transportation network that served Normandy and effectively isolated the battlefield.

On D day, 6 June 1944, three airborne divisions and five ground divisions landed on five heavily obstacled and defended beaches code-named Gold, Juno, Sword, Utah, and Omaha. Two British divisions and one Canadian division landed to the east on Gold, Juno, and Sword; the U.S. 4th Division landed on Utah; and the U.S. 1st Division landed on Omaha. The British 6th Airborne seized the Orne River bridges to seal the eastern flank; the 82d and 101st Airborne Divisions jumped in to shield the western beaches. Opposing the Allies were three German divisions, with most of the German panzer units held in reserve and not to be committed until the Allied main attack was clearly identified.

The British and Canadian landings went as planned for the most part, with the hardest fighting faced by the British 50th Division on Gold. However, British advances stalled on the open terrain before Caen, and that key city would not be in British hands until 8 July—and then at heavy cost.

The American airborne forces were badly scattered in their night drops and suffered heavy casualties while accomplishing their assigned missions. Their dispersion confused the Germans about their size and objectives, however, and thus mitigated some of the bad effects. The Utah landings went smoothly. But at Omaha, the U.S. 1st Division, reinforced by the U.S. 29th Division, encountered a formidable combination of obstacles, terrain, and heavy enemy opposition that pinned the initial forces on the beach for a substantial period. For a time, Bradley considered diverting follow-on forces to other beaches; by mid-morning, however, small groups of soldiers had made their way up the bluffs and began to clear the heights. By the end of the day, all the beaches were securely in Allied hands, although the Omaha beachhead was in some places less than a mile deep. Most of the 4,649 American casualties were suffered on "bloody Omaha."

While the British concentrated on seizing Caen, American forces turned up the Cotentin Peninsula to seize the port of Cherbourg. After heavy fighting, Cherbourg fell into American hands on 27 June, although surrendering German forces so damaged the port facilities that the port was not operational until 7 August. Following the capture of Cherbourg, Bradley's forces turned south toward St. Lô into the *bocage* of western Normandy. The Norman hedgerows provided ideal defensive positions for the Germans and negated American mobility. In July, the U.S. First Army suffered 40,000 casualties, while pressing the Germans hard with the fresh divisions accumulating in the postinvasion buildup.

On 25 July, Bradley's Operation COBRA opened with a massive and concentrated bombardment by 1,800 bombers from the Eighth Air Force that shattered the German Panzer Lehr Division and opened the way for an American breakout. Bradley's forces poured through the Avranches gap. Eisenhower quickly activated 12th Army Group under Bradley, giving command of U.S. First Army to Lieutenant General Courtney Hodges and activating Patton's Third Army.

In Patton, the Americans had the ideal commander to exploit the breakout and pursuit of the German army in France. His army spilled into Brittany, one corps turning to secure the port of Brest and the others racing 90 miles west toward LeMans and Paris. By 13 August, two American corps were at Argentan and the Canadians were a mere 20 miles away at Falaise. West of them, inside a large pocket, were the largest part of three German armies. Poor coordination between Bradley and Montgomery wasted an opportunity to trap the Germans, and large numbers of Germany's best troops escaped through the FALAISE-ARGENTAN Gap. The Germans did lose more than 60,000 soldiers killed or captured, and vast quantities of equipment. Organized resistance in Normandy was shattered as German units fled for the Seine River.

The American pursuit was relentless, with German forces in disarray and suffering great losses in men and equipment. On 15 August, in Operation DRAGOON, Allied forces composed of the U.S. Seventh Army under Lieutenant General Alexander Patch landed in southern France, swept aside German resistance, captured Marseilles, and advanced rapidly up the Rhône valley. Paris was liberated on 25 August and within a week German forces had been cleared from the rest of France. On 4 September British forces captured the port of Antwerp intact. Eisenhower, overextended logistically, ordered a pause along the Belgian-German border. The Germans had lost 60 divisions in Normandy, along with most of their equipment; 265,000 men had been killed or wounded, and 350,000 taken prisoner. It was a spectacular victory. Just 90 days after D day, the defeat of Germany seemed at hand.

The Wehrmacht's talent for reconstitution and reorganization was never better illustrated than in its efforts to patch together a new front along the Schelde, Meuse, and Rhine tributaries of the Dutch-German border area during the first weeks of September. The Western Allies, at their logistical limits, faced a continuous battlefront from Dutch Zealand to Basel and were unable to maintain operations on a broad front. Given this situation (and the fact that Eisenhower's strategic reserve was limited to the newly constituted First Allied Airborne Army), Eisenhower approved Montgomery's ambitious proposal to use airborne forces to leap the Meuse and Neder Rhine Rivers onto the North German Plain and the Ruhr heartland.

Operation MARKET GARDEN, the most daring and famous airborne operation of the war, began on 17 September 1944 and had the U.S. 101st and 82d Airborne Divisions seizing bridges at Eindhoven and Nijmegen, respectively, and the British 1st Airborne Division (supported by the 1st Polish Airborne Brigade) seizing the bridges over the Rhine at Arnhem, Netherlands. The airborne forces were to hold the bridges until the British XXX Corps advanced 60 miles across the Netherlands along a single macadam roadway to the Rhine. Plagued by bad luck (elements of the 9th and 10th SS Panzer Divisions were refitting in Arnhem) and an overly ambitious concept, Market Garden failed short of the Rhine. Although the airborne divisions successfully secured the bridges, XXX Corps was unable to force its way to Arnhem before the 1st Airborne Division had to withdraw with the loss of more than 7,000 men. Allied forces held a salient deep into Holland but had failed to force a Rhine crossing. As winter approached, Allied armies ground to a halt in heavy fighting before the formidable German Siegfried line (West Wall), particularly in the HÜRTGEN FOREST and on the Roer, and all hope for an end of the war in 1944 evaporated.

Optimistic that he retained the strategic initiative and that the Germans would remain on the defensive, Eisenhower planned to resume the offensive in January with the main attack being led by Montgomery in the north, where the North German Plain favored operations. A surprise German offensive by two new Panzer armies in the Ardennes against Hodges's First U.S. Army on 16 December therefore dramatically caught the Allies off guard. The opening attack of the Battle of the BULGE shattered two American divisions and weakened two others in heavy fighting, although the U.S. 99th and 2d Divisions stubbornly held on to the northern shoulder of the salient on the Elsenborn Ridge, thereby limiting the width of the penetration. The German spearheads pushed on, their ultimate objective being the great port of Antwerp and Allied logistical paralysis. Strong resistance by the 7th Armored Division at St-Vith and the 101st Airborne Division at Bastogne denied the use of key road junctions and further disrupted the Nazi timetable. Surrounded at Bastogne by vastly superior forces, the 101st Airborne refused to surrender.

Although surprised, Eisenhower reacted swiftly, directing Montgomery to assume control of the fight on the northern shoulder and committing Patton's Third Army to the counterattack. Responding brilliantly, Patton wheeled his army 90 degrees and drove toward Bastogne. His 4th Armored Division broke through to Bastogne on 26 December. The weather also cleared, allowing Allied aircraft an opportunity to strike the Germans on the ground. By mid-January Allied counterattacks had eliminated the bulge. U.S. losses were the greatest of the war: 100,000 casualties. The Germans lost perhaps 120,000 personnel casualties, 800 tanks, and 1,000 aircraft. Hitler's desperate gamble had squandered the last remaining German reserves. By March 1945, Eisenhower's armies would systematically eliminate all German resistance west of the Rhine, killing or capturing 225,000 Germans while clearing the Rhineland. These losses were all the more staggering in light of Germany's limited manpower commitment in western Europe. Never did the Americans and the British face more than a quarter of the German army, the vast majority of which opposed the Soviets on the Eastern Front.

Eisenhower's strategic plan for the invasion of Germany envisioned an encirclement of the Ruhr with the main attack conducted by Montgomery in the north and secondary attacks by Bradley's 12th Army Group in the south. But 9th Armored Division's opportunistic seizure of a bridge across the Rhine at Remagen on 7 March persuaded Eisenhower to shift the main effort to Bradley, who promptly pushed strong forces across the river. Patton followed suit to the south at Oppenheim on 22 March and Montgomery finally crossed north at Wesel on the 23rd. German Army Group B, 318,000 strong, was encircled on 3 April and surrendered on 18 April, effectively ending organized Wehrmacht resistance in western Germany. Consistent with his political guidance, Eisenhower halted his forces on the Elbe River in the north and on the Mulde River inside the Czechoslovakian frontier in the south. To Churchill's great displeasure, this decision allowed Soviet forces to take Berlin and liberate Prague. In the absence of a political directive to race the Soviets to Berlin and Prague, Eisenhower's decision was appropriate.

Hitler committed suicide on 30 April, Berlin fell to the Soviets on 2 May, and on 7 May German General Alfred Jodl signed a general surrender of German forces at Eisenhower's headquarters in Reims, France; 8 May was officially proclaimed V-E Day. The great American "Crusade in Europe" was complete.

See also CONVOY SYSTEM; OFFICE OF STRATEGIC SERVICES; RHINE CROSSING; SELECTIVE SERVICE; TAYLOR, MAXWELL D.; ULTRA SECRET AND CODEBREAKING; WORLD WAR II, CAUSES OF U.S. ENTRY; WORLD WAR II, U.S. INVOLVEMENT: PACIFIC THEATER.

Further reading: Eisenhower, Dwight D. *Crusade in Europe.* Garden City, N.Y.: Doubleday, 1948; Esposito, Vincent J. *The West Point Atlas of American Wars.* Vol. 2: 1900–1953. New York: Frederick Praeger, 1953; Keegan, John. *The Second World War.* New York: Viking Press, 1989; MacDonald, Charles B. *The Mighty Endeavor: American Armed Forces in the European Theater in World War II.* New York: Oxford University Press, 1969; Weigley, Russell F. *Eisenhower's Lieutenants: The Campaign in France and Germany, 1944–1945.* Bloomington: Indiana University Press, 1981; Willmott, H. P. *The Great Crusade: A New Complete History of the Second World War.* New York: Free Press, 1989.

— Charles F. Brower

World War II, course of U.S. involvement: Pacific theater

The United States entered World War II as a consequence of the 7 December 1941 Japanese surprise attack on PEARL HARBOR, in the Hawaiian Islands. The leaders of Japan's military government hoped they could cripple U.S. naval power sufficiently to purchase enough time to conquer and fortify a defensive ring that would include much of the natural resources of Asia. In the Japanese military scenario, the United States would dash its forces against this defensive shield, finally giving up and recognizing Japanese hegemony in East Asia.

The Pearl Harbor attack wiped out much of the firepower of the U.S. Pacific Fleet, especially the battleships, but it missed its primary target—the aircraft carriers, then at sea on maneuvers. The attack also unified a divided United States behind the war effort.

During December 1941, the Japanese invaded the PHILIPPINES and they struck at British possessions, including Malaya. The Japanese also captured Guam and WAKE ISLAND, cutting U.S. lines of supply and communication to the Philippines. On 22 December, Japanese troops began an invasion of Luzon, the largest island in the Philippine archipelago. General Douglas MACARTHUR, commander of U.S. and Filipino forces, had hoped to defend the islands at the beaches but was forced to fall back on the original plan of retreating into the BATAAN Peninsula and CORREGIDOR Island. Trapped there without adequate supplies of food and ammunition, the defenders fought stoutly but could not withstand Japanese pressure. Bataan fell in April 1942 and Corregidor in May. By then, President Franklin D. ROOSEVELT had ordered MacArthur to Australia.

Japan also struck at the British possessions of Hong Kong, Malaya, and Singapore. To cut off the overland supply route to China, the Japanese invaded Burma and pressed to the borders of India. The resource-rich Dutch East Indies also fell to the Japanese. In just six months, Japan had occupied states with a total of 100 million people and captured 250,000 enemy soldiers. All this was at a cost to themselves of only 15,000 casualties (including wounded), 380 aircraft, and 4 destroyers.

Following Pearl Harbor, however, the United States mounted a series of successful carrier raids against the Japanese, including Lieutenant Colonel James DOOLITTLE's 18 April 1942 strike at TOKYO itself. These raids encouraged the Japanese leaders, who were in any case reluctant to go over to defensive warfare, to extend their conquests. In mid-1942, however, U.S. naval forces were able to stem the Japanese advance in two key battles. In May, the Japanese attempted to land forces at Port Moresby on the south coast of New Guinea in an effort to isolate Australia. Thanks to code-breaking, essential in both battles, the United States was aware of the broad

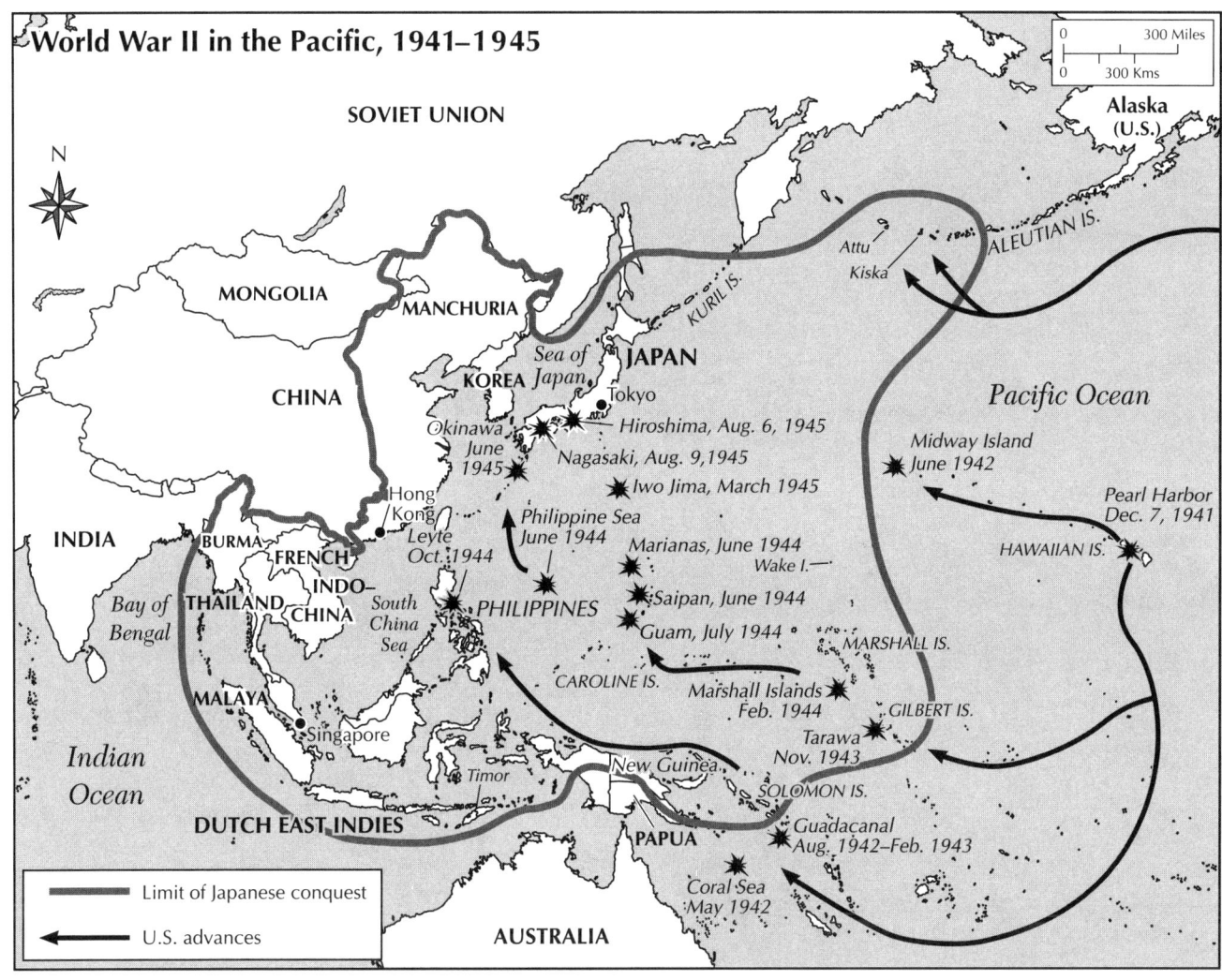

World War II in the Pacific, 1941–1945

outlines of the Japanese plan. In the resulting Battle of the CORAL SEA, the U.S. Navy fought the Japanese to a draw in the first major sea battle between fleets that never came within sight of one another, being fought by naval aircraft. Although tactically the battle was a victory for Japan, the invasion force bound for Port Moresby turned back.

In June, the commander of the Japanese Combined Fleet, Admiral Isoroku Yamamoto, planned an elaborate effort to secure Midway Island and draw out the U.S. Fleet so that he might destroy it. The resulting Battle of MIDWAY saw the Japanese lose four fleet carriers and a considerable number of planes and trained pilots to only one carrier lost for the United States. It was a crushing defeat for Japan. Midway bought the time that Admiral Chester NIMITZ needed to bring new naval construction on line and take the offensive. As a part of their Midway operation, the Japanese occupied the Aleutian islands of Attu and Kiska (which, however, the Americans retook in 1943).

Despite the early activity in the Pacific, the United States and Britain had agreed to concentrate first on Germany, which they considered the more dangerous military opponent. As it worked out, however, the buildup in Britain and campaigns in North Africa allowed additional resources beyond those originally planned to be sent to the Pacific, and the United States and its allies were able to go over on the offensive. The British assumed overall direction of the CHINA-BURMA-INDIA theater (CBI), while the United States had responsibility for the Pacific Ocean area.

This vast area gave scope for two separate commands: MacArthur in the Southwest Pacific, which included Australia, New Guinea, the Solomon and Philippine Islands, and most of the Indonesian archipelago; and Nimitz in the central Pacific area. Although the two were loosely coordinated through the Joint Chiefs of Staff, in essence they conducted separate campaigns.

Safeguarding Australia was critical to the Allied effort against Japan. Late in 1942, the United States began an

Grumman F6F-3 Hellcat. This F6F-3 of VF-1 is pushed aside after returning to the carrier USS *Yorktown* with combat damage, 19 June 1944.   *(San Diego Aerospace Museum)*

offensive in the SOLOMON ISLANDS to the northeast. In August 1942 the 1st Marine Division landed at GUADAL-CANAL. Fighting raged on Guadalcanal and offshore in a series of costly naval contests. In the Battle of SAVO ISLAND, the U.S. Navy absorbed its biggest defeat ever in a fair fight. Gradually the Americans, thanks to superior resupply capabilities, secured the upper hand. In January 1943, the Japanese evacuated by sea their remaining troops on the island. It was the first major defeat on land for Japanese forces.

U.S. and Australian forces also gained a victory on the island of New Guinea. Then, in Operation Cartwheel, MacArthur's troops seized Japanese installations on Bougainville, New Georgia, Vella Lavella, and Cape Gloucester. The Joint Chiefs of Staff ordered MacArthur to change his slow "island-hopping" strategy to one of

"LEAPFROGGING," bypassing Japanese strongholds such as the island of Truk and Rabaul on New Britain Island, cutting them off from resupply and allowing them simply to "wither on the vine." MacArthur continued his drive to the Admiralty Islands and along the north coast of western New Guinea, capturing Japanese bases at Aitape, Hollandia, and Biak. By September 1944, his forces had reached Morotai in the Mollucas, continually driving closer to the Philippines.

While MacArthur's forces pushed through the Southwest Pacific, U.S. Navy and Marine Corps forces began a campaign in the central Pacific. By 1943, Nimitz had eight *Essex*-class carriers and new fast battleships. WAR PLAN ORANGE, the prewar U.S. strategic plan for fighting Japan, envisioned a drive through the central Pacific to take the Japanese-held islands there as stepping-stones toward Japan itself. The offensive began in the Gilbert Islands with the seizure of TARAWA AND MAKIN in November 1943. The MARSHALL ISLANDS, northeast of the Gilberts, were the next target. Beginning in January 1944, U.S. forces took Eniwetok and Kwajelin. Then in June 1944, the United States launched a particularly important campaign against the MARIANA ISLANDS. Saipan, Guam, and Tinian were taken to provide bases for long-range B-29 bombers to strike the Japanese home islands.

The Japanese could not allow this to go unchallenged, and they launched a naval effort that culminated in the Battle of the PHILIPPINE SEA. This first fleet action between the Japanese and U.S. naval forces in two years in effect destroyed the Japanese fleet as a credible fighting force. Most Japanese losses were from U.S. naval aircraft. At the same time, U.S., British, and Chinese forces were pushing back the Japanese in Southeast Asia in the CBI, in the process reopening land routes to China.

As B-29 bombers from the Marianas began to strike Japan, U.S. submarines were strangling Japan's war economy. The U.S. Navy in the Pacific theater became the greatest practitioner of submarine warfare in history, succeeding where Germany had failed in World Wars I and II. The United States built long-range SUBMARINES, with a deep-dive capability, one of the best-kept secrets of the war. The usual diving depth was 300 feet, but U.S. boats could dive to 400 feet without stressing the hull and deeper if necessary. Often enemy depth charges exploded harmlessly above them. In the first two years of the war, U.S. submarines suffered because of the very poor quality of their torpedoes. This problem was overcome by 1944.

Consolidated B-24 Liberators flying in formation. The Liberator was one of the primary U.S. strategic bombers of World War II, and more than 6,000 served in the Pacific theater. *(San Diego Aerospace Museum)*

At the beginning of the war, Japan had 6 million tons of merchant shipping, only a marginal capability. The Japanese built another 2 million tons during the war, but U.S. submarines sank a total of 4.8 million of the 8 million tons. The Japanese suffered greatly from a shortage of oil. They were so short of aviation fuel by 1944 that they could scarcely train pilots. U.S. submarines also took a heavy toll in Japanese navy ships—sinking 200 in all, including a battleship and eight carriers. In American submarine successes, code-breaking played a major role. Still, 51 U.S. subs were lost, the highest casualty rate within the U.S. Navy, but far fewer than the number lost by either Japan or Germany.

During the summer and early autumn of 1944, American planners considered their next move. Chief of Naval Operations Admiral Ernest KING and Nimitz both advocated bypassing the Philippines and striking at Formosa off the coast of China. General MacArthur objected strenuously, noting the proximity of the Philippines to existing American bases and the political connection to the United States. In the end, Roosevelt decided that MacArthur could retake the Philippines, while Nimitz would head for Okinawa.

U.S. troops invaded the island of Leyte on 20 October 1944. The Japanese then launched a last-ditch fleet effort, culminating in the Battle of LEYTE GULF, the largest naval battle ever fought. In the end, the Japanese navy was dealt a crushing blow at sea.

Japan's setbacks in battle in 1943 and 1944 were in large part the result of the nation's increasingly precarious economic condition. Japan had only a small fraction as much industrial capacity as the United States, and much of this was dependent on raw materials and oil from overseas. Japan had also lost its most experienced pilots in the great sea fights of 1942–44. Both the quantity and quality of Japanese troops and equipment decreased as the war dragged on.

Although Japan was clearly losing the war, its soldiers and sailors nevertheless fought fiercely. The war between the United States and Japan was one of remarkable ferocity, with little quarter given on either side. The Japanese warrior code regarded surrender as dishonorable, and the Japanese often fought to the last. Late in the war, the Japanese utilized suicide pilots, known as Kamikazes, who attempted to crash their explosives-laden aircraft into U.S. ships.

The Japanese attitude toward war was also reflected in their treatment of Allied prisoners of war, who fared far worse at the hands of the Japanese than did those captured by the Germans and Italians in the European theater. Roughly 40 percent of Allied prisoners taken by the Japanese died in captivity. Individual GIs understood this and reacted accordingly. The Japanese gained a reputation

for brutality in most of the territory they occupied during the war, a fact to which few Japanese have yet faced up in their histories of the war.

As American forces approached the Japanese home islands in 1945, Japanese resistance stiffened. That year saw continuous fighting in the Philippines. Manila was recaptured in February, but only after heavy fighting devastated the Philippine capital. Two island battles that year further highlighted the Japanese willingness to fight on. In February, more than 6,000 Americans perished in the battle to take IWO JIMA, a small volcanic island in the Bonin Islands between the Marianas and the Japan. Almost all of the 22,000 Japanese defenders of Iwo Jima died. The Battle for OKINAWA, April–June 1945, was even more costly, claiming 12,000 American lives, along with 70,000 Japanese soldiers and 80,000 Okinawan civilians. Fighting here saw the Japanese for the first time systematically employ Kamikaze pilots. Indeed, in the fighting for Okinawa, the U.S. Navy sustained more casualties than in all of its previous wars combined.

Meanwhile, the B-29s intensified a strategic bombing campaign against the Japanese homeland. Conducted by Lieutenant General Curtis E. LeMAY's Twentieth Air Force, based in the Marianas, it shifted to the firebombing of Japanese cities by massed bombers flying at relatively low altitude at night. The most destructive single air raid in history was the massive firebomb raid on TOKYO during the night of 9–10 March 1945. The bombing burned out 15 square miles of the city and killed at least 83,000 people and injured another 100,000.

By mid-1945 Washington had begun preparations for an invasion of the Japanese home islands. The plan, code-named Downfall, was to consist of two stages: Operation Olympic would be the invasion of Kyushu (the southernmost island) in November 1945. It would be followed by Operation Coronet, the invasion of the main island of Honshu, in March 1946. Based on the demonstrated record of Japanese fanaticism, U.S. planners anticipated casualties in the hundreds of thousands. Little wonder that the United States was prepared to make Pacific concessions to the Soviet Union to bring it into the war and to employ the ATOMIC BOMB.

On August 6 an American B-29 dropped an atomic bomb on Hiroshima, killing about 80,000 outright or from the effects of radiation. Three days later the United States dropped another bomb on Nagasaki, killing at least 40,000 there. The day before the Nagasaki bombing, the Soviet Union, in accordance with pledges extended during the wartime conferences, entered the war against Japan. On 10 August, Emperor Hirohito, speaking directly to the Japanese people for the first time, announced his decision to capitulate. The formal surrender occurred on 2 September on board the battleship *Missouri* in Tokyo Bay. World War II, the costliest conflict in human history, was over.

See also PHILIPPINES, RETAKING OF; SUBMARINE WAR-
FARE AGAINST JAPAN (WORLD WAR II); WORLD WAR II,
CAUSES OF U.S. ENTRY.

Further reading: Bergerud, Eric. *Touched with Fire: The
Land War in the South Pacific.* New York: Viking, 1996;
Chappell, John D. *Before the Bomb: How America
Approached the End of the Pacific War.* Lexington: Uni-
versity Press of Kentucky, 1996; Dower, John. *War Without
Mercy: Race and Power in the Pacific War.* New York: Pan-
theon, 1996; Spector, Ronald. *Eagle Against the Sun: The
American War with Japan.* New York: Free Press, 1984.

— Mark D. Van Ells

Worth, William J. (1794–1849) *U.S. Army general
and hero of the Mexican-American War*
Born on 1 March 1794 in Hudson, New York, William
Jenkins Worth briefly worked as a clerk for an Albany
merchant before the WAR OF 1812 prompted him to join
the army. Worth quickly rose from private to commissioned staff officer, assigned to young Brigadier General
Winfield SCOTT, the beginning of a personal and professional association that foundered during the MEXICAN-
AMERICAN WAR.

During the War of 1812, Worth distinguished himself
in the Battle of CHIPPEWA, and he was grievously wounded
in the Battle of LUNDY'S LANE, winning promotion to
brevet major. His leg wound plagued him for the remainder of his life.

After recovering, Worth remained in the army and was
appointed commandant of cadets at the U.S. Military
Academy, WEST POINT, in 1820. Although something of a
martinet, Worth insisted on discipline and military bearing
that set the standard at the academy. Considered the finest
horseman in the army, Worth later won renown in command of troops in Florida during the Second SEMINOLE
WAR, in which his insistence on campaigning in the summer
months crushed Seminole resistance and ended that
bloody conflict. President John Tyler recognized his
achievement by advancing him to brevet brigadier general.

Worth demonstrated both his best and worst personal
traits during the Mexican-American War. He resigned his
commission on the eve of hostilities while attached to
Major General Zachary TAYLOR's command after a feud
with Brigadier General David Twiggs over senority of rank.
Returning to the army after fighting began, he skillfully
led troops in the Battle of MONTERREY, boring through
house walls in street fighting to flank Mexican strongpoints.
Lionized in dispatches that George Kendall published in
the New Orleans *Picayune,* Worth became a national hero
and was promoted to brevet major general. Transferred to
Major General Winfield Scott's command for the campaign

on Mexico City, he publicly feuded with his one-time
patron, severing a friendship of more than 30 years.

After the war, Worth was assigned command of the
Departments of Texas and New Mexico. He died at San
Antonio on 7 May 1849. Fort Worth, Texas, is named in his
honor.

Further reading: Bauer, K. Jack. *The Mexican War,
1846–1848.* Reprint. Lincoln: University of Nebraska
Press, 1992; Wallace, Edward S. *General William Jenkins
Worth: Monterrey's Forgotten Hero.* Dallas: Southern
Methodist University Press, 1953.

— Dan Monroe

Wounded Knee, incident at (29 December 1890)
Last major confrontation of the American Indian Wars
Many events combined to incite the showdown at
Wounded Knee: Indians had been stripped of their traditional ways of life; the great bison herds were gone; disease devastated entire tribes; and the reservation system
made Indians dependent on government handouts, but
promised goods often fell short of needs. Corrupt or inept
agents and government officials profited at Indian expense.
The Indian Bureau persistently insisted on converting
Indians to the white man's way of life. Even the reservations had been broken up, tribes scattered, and surplus
lands sold to white settlers. While most Indians had little
choice but to accept their fate, others such as Hunkpapa
Sioux chief SITTING BULL and Miniconjou Sioux chief Big
Foot remained defiant. Increasingly, frustrated Indians
rejected reservation life in an attempt to rekindle their traditional ways. Many embraced the hope offered by the
Ghost Dance.

The Ghost Dance movement spread among tribes of
the West in 1889 and 1890. Popularized by Pauite shaman
Wovoka, who claimed to be a messiah, the Ghost Dance
promised a time when Indian dead would rejoin the living
in a utopian existence unencumbered by the white man.
Wovoka's message included a strong moral code and the
admonishment to live in peace until the new day arrived.
But among the Sioux of the northern plains, the Ghost
Dance became a last means of resistance. To the elaborate
dances and chants they added ghost shirts, which promised
to protect the wearer from harm (namely, soldiers' bullets).

Alarmed by the Ghost Dance influence on Sioux reservations, Indian Bureau agents requested military assistance. A crackdown followed. On 15 December 1890,
Sitting Bull was killed by Indian police, who had come to
arrest him, when Ghost Dance warriors attempted to rescue the defiant chief. As news of Sitting Bull's death circu-
lated among other camps, fear and anger mounted. Big
Foot was next on the list to be apprehended; he and his

people headed for Chief RED CLOUD's Pine Ridge reservation. Big Foot believed that Red Cloud's camp would offer the best protection. Unfortunately, he and his people never made it to Pine Ridge.

On 28 December, Major Samuel Whitside's squadron of the 7th Cavalry caught up with Big Foot's band. Whitside informed the chief that he had orders to take him to the cavalry camp at Wounded Knee. Big Foot, ill with pneumonia, understood and cooperated, and Whitside allowed him to ride in the army ambulance for the remainder of the journey. When they arrived at the camp, the Indians were halted and carefully counted. Whitside assigned them a camp, issued rations, and furnished several tents. Additionally, he sent a regimental surgeon and a stove to Big Foot's tent.

During the night, the remainder of the regiment arrived, and Colonel James Forsyth assumed command. Significantly, this was the regiment that Lieutenant Colonel George A. CUSTER had led to destruction at the hands of Sioux and Cheyenne warriors in the Battle of the LITTLE BIGHORN in 1876.

The following morning, Indians were issued hardtack for breakfast and then ordered to hand over their arms. Closely surrounded by 500 cavalrymen and covered by four rapid-firing Hotchkiss guns, the warriors complied. When the soldiers failed to recover weapons known to be among the Sioux—specifically Winchester repeating rifles—groups of them began to search the lodges. Still not satisfied, the officers ordered the Indians to lower their blankets and submit to individual searches.

As the search progressed, a medicine man began the Ghost Dance, encouraging warriors to resist. He reminded them that their ghost shirts would protect them from bullets. The warriors continued to cooperate until one refused to surrender his Winchester. When a soldier attempted to disarm him, the rifle went off. Several warriors dropped their blankets, leveled their rifles, and fired on the soldiers. The soldiers returned fire instantaneously and a bloody close-in fight that both sides wanted to avoid ensued. More than 150 Indians, including Big Foot, women, and children, lost their lives at Wounded Knee; at least 50 others were wounded. Army losses totaled 25 dead and 39 wounded, many of these from friendly fire.

Colonel Forsyth, never expecting an altercation, had failed to arrange his units to avoid firing on each other. When the Hotchkiss guns raked the camp, exploding shells sent flying shrapnel everywhere, striking Indians and soldiers alike. At the insistence of an outraged Major General Nelson MILES, a military court investigated the disaster. Miles also relieved Forsyth, who was later reinstated.

In 1973, members of the American Indian Movement seized control of Wounded Knee, South Dakota, to protest the reservation administration. Two people were killed during the 71-day occupation; 12 were wounded, including two U.S. marshals; and nearly 1,200 were arrested.

See also AMERICAN INDIAN WARS; SIOUX WARS.

Further reading: Utley, Robert M. *The Indian Frontier of the American West 1846–1890.* Albuquerque: University of New Mexico Press, 1984; Brown, Dee. *Bury My Heart at Wounded Knee.* New York: Holt, Rinehart & Winston, 1970.

— Mark N. Calandra

Wright, Wilbur and Orville (1867–1912; 1871–1948)
American inventors who developed the first powered airplane

Wilbur Wright was born on 16 April 1867 near Millville, Indiana, and his brother Orville on 19 August 1871 at Dayton, Ohio. Neither attended college, but they established a print shop and a bicycle manufacturing and repair business. Lifelong bachelors, in the late 1890s they became absorbed in the challenge of constructing a mechanically powered flying machine that a human pilot could direct and control. Early experiments at Kitty Hawk, North Carolina, with large kite-gliders proved disappointing, and in 1901 the brothers constructed a homemade wind tunnel of bicycle spoke wire and hacksaw blades to measure the aerodynamic forces operating on flying-machine wings, data they used to modify and improve their wing design. They also devised a suitable steering rudder. With their machinist's assistance, they then turned to developing a four-cylinder engine to power and steer an aircraft, incorporating mechanisms to direct it through all three axes—namely, vertical and horizontal rudders and a control to warp the wings sideways.

Over several hours on 17 December 1903, five spectators watched the Wrights' first powered flights. The initial flight covered 120 feet in 12 seconds; the last, 856 feet in 59 seconds. Within two years, the brothers greatly improved their designs, remaining aloft for up to 39 minutes, at which point, fearing others might pirate their idea, they decided to cease flying while they patented their invention and found suitable customers for it.

In February 1908, the Wrights negotiated a $25,000 contract with the U.S. Army, promising to manufacture an aircraft that could carry a pilot and passenger for an hour or more at a speed no less than 40 miles per hour; they delivered this machine to the army in September. The Wrights also signed an agreement with an interested French group. After demonstrating their new machines in Europe, the brothers became celebrities, establishing the Wright Company in 1909, with New York offices and a Dayton factory, flying field, and training school, where army and navy aviators trained.

Wilbur, who took the lead in prosecuting rival aircraft builders for patent infringement, died of typhoid fever on 1 May 1912. Orville designed several new types of aircraft before selling his Wright Company shares in 1915. During World War I he remained active as an airplane and pilotless bomb designer. Shy and retiring, he spent much time in laboratory work, but remained a prominent figure in the American aviation world. Orville Wright died in Dayton, Ohio, on 30 January 1948, having watched the powered aircraft he and his brother pioneered become a major instrument of victory in World War II.

See also AIRCRAFT, FIXED WING; CURTISS, GLENN H.; STRATEGIC BOMBING.

Further reading: Crouch, Tom D. *The Bishop's Boys: A Life of Wilbur and Orville Wright.* New York: Norton, 1989; Howard, Fred. *Wilbur and Orville: A Biography of the Wright Brothers.* New York: Knopf, 1987; Jakab, Peter L. *Visions of a Flying Machine: The Wright Brothers and the Process of Invention.* Washington, D.C.: Smithsonian Institution Press, 1990; Wright, Wilbur, and Orville Wright. *The Papers of Wilbur and Orville Wright.* 2 vols. Edited by Marvin W. Farland. New York: McGraw-Hill, 1953; ————. *The Published Writings of Wilbur and Orville Wright.* Edited by Peter L. Jakab and Rick Young. Washington, D.C.: Smithsonian Institution Press, 2000.

— Priscilla Roberts

Yamassee War (1715–1718) *War between southern colonists and many southeastern Indian tribes, particularly the Yamassee and Creek*

For the first 40 years of South Carolina's existence as a British colony, its economy was based on the Indian deerskin trade. Indians as well as colonists quickly became dependent on the trade that supplied pelts in exchange for European goods. Many of the southeastern tribes jockeyed for a favored position with the Carolinians; some, such as the Yamassee, even relocated closer to Charleston to facilitate their involvement in the trade. The system, however, was open to severe abuses. Many Indians lodged complaints against colonial traders, charging them with such action as falsifying weights and measures and even with debauching the Indians' wives. Over time the credit-based trade also led to the Indians becoming increasingly in debt to the traders. By 1711, the average adult male Indian was in debt for about two years of labor.

Historically, Carolinians enslaved enemy Indians; however, by the 1700s traders were selling friendly Indian women and children into slavery to compensate for Indian debts. The colonial government attempted to regulate the traders but had little control on the frontier. By 1715, many Indians had reached the limit of their endurance.

On 15 April, the Yamassee initiated the attack, killing almost every trader in their midst. In the following days, most of the other southern Indian tribes followed suit. If the Cherokee had joined the attack, it is possible that the entire colony of South Carolina could have fallen to the Indians.

For months, South Carolina refugees flooded into Charleston as attacks along the frontier continued. By July Indian raids had pushed back white settlers to within a 30-mile radius of Charleston. By August, military aid from neighboring colonies had arrived, and a successful militia counterattack resulted in many Yamassee being captured and sold into slavery. But other Indian groups continued their devastating warfare, and South Carolina's best hope rested with a Cherokee alliance.

By August 1715 Carolinians were campaigning vigorously to secure Cherokee support. At the same time Creek headmen attempted to curry Cherokee favor as well. In January 1716, the Cherokee made their choice and murdered the Creek emissaries, securing their alliance with the English. By March, most of the fighting was over; the Creek had migrated closer to their French allies, and the Yamassee had fled to Florida. Sporadic raids continued for years, and the English did not conclude peace officially with the Creek until November 1717.

South Carolina began rebuilding that year, but the war had been costly. Close to one-third of the cultivated land had been abandoned, with the subsequent loss of crops and livestock. The Indian trade (and thus South Carolina's economy) suffered severely in the wake of the war, although the number of deerskins exported had recovered by 1722. In addition, the English lost international prestige as many southern Indians found favor with the French and Spanish. Finally, the Lord Proprietors' unresponsiveness to the needs of the colony in the wake of the Yamassee War directly led to the overthrow of South Carolina's proprietary government in 1719.

See also AMERICAN INDIAN WARS; TUSCARORA WAR.

Further reading: Crane, Verner W. *The Southern Frontier, 1670–1732.* Ann Arbor: University of Michigan Press, 1929; Corkran, David. H. *The Creek Frontier, 1540–1783.* Norman: University of Oklahoma Press, 1967.

— Lisa L. Crutchfield

Yangtze River (Chang Jiang) Patrol ("YangPat")

From 1853 to 1941, U.S. Navy gunboats patrolled the waters of China's great central watershed to protect U.S. commercial, military, and missionary interests. YangPat began in 1853 with the deployment to Shanghai of the U.S. Navy steamer *Susquehanna* and its subsequent patrol along the 3,500-mile-long Yangtze. This first patrol in the midst of the great Taiping Rebellion began more than 90 years of direct U.S. military intervention in China. This era of U.S. naval activity in support of Western imperialism in China ended in late 1941, just before the Japanese attack on PEARL HARBOR.

The United States, along with six other major Western powers and Japan, provided land and naval contingents in China to protect foreign-controlled outposts, known as concessions, and treaty ports, and to patrol the internal waterways of China during this period. The United States was, in fact, a relative latecomer to the process of dividing China into "spheres of influence," and adopted an "open door" policy for trade and commerce without actual occupation. U.S. gunboats protected shipping, escorted diplomats and emissaries, and provided security for American citizens along the Yangtze and its major tributaries from Shanghai to Chungking (Chongjing).

There were numerous incidents of combat and minor skirmishes among U.S. Navy vessels and Chinese rebels, warlords, and bandits. The ships of YangPat operated from the Taiping Rebellion (1854–65), through the conflicts that ended the Ch'ing (Qing) dynasty (1911–12), and into the confusing warlord period (1912–27). In the confrontation between the Nationalists (Guomindang, or Kuomintang) and Japan, the United States openly sided with the Nationalists. Perhaps the most famous incident involving YangPat was the *Panay* incident in December 1937, when Japanese forces attacked the USS *PANAY* on Yangtze patrol. The next four years on the Yangtze continued to be tense and dangerous for U.S. ships on patrol. The *Luzon* and the *Oahu*, the last ships of the U.S. Yangtze Patrol, left Chinese waters in December 1941. These two vessels were later lost in battles against the Japanese, and the surviving crew members fought in the final defense at CORREGIDOR in the Philippines.

See also BOXER UPRISING.

Further reading: Tolley, Kemp. *Yangtze River Patrol: The U.S. Navy in China.* Annapolis, Md.: Naval Institute Press, 1971.

— J. G. D. Babb

Yankee-Pennamite Wars (1769–1807) *Wars fought over conflicting claims to the Wyoming Valley in Pennsylvania*

The Susquehanna River flows through the fertile Wyoming Valley in northeastern Pennsylvania. The Wyoming is about 25 miles long by three to four miles wide. In 1662 King Charles II, with poor maps and little knowledge of the New World, granted the Wyoming Valley for settlement to Connecticut. Then in 1681 he unknowingly granted the same land to William Penn.

In 1768 the Susquehanna Company was formed to settle the Connecticut land grant. When the Connecticut settlers (Yankees) arrived, they found Pennsylvanians (Pennamites) already occupying much of the land.

The issue of ownership soon led to fighting. The Yankees built a number of blockhouses as well as Fort Durkee and Forty Fort. The Pennamites also built forts, including Fort Wyoming (present-day Wilkes-Barre). In 1775 the Yankees prevailed over the Pennamites in the Battle of Nanticoke.

The American Revolutionary War complicated the issue. The Susquehanna Company employed propaganda to brand the Pennamites as Loyalists. Charged with treason, many Pennamites were sent to Connecticut for trial. The Yankee pressure on the Pennamites indeed drove some of them into supporting the British cause. Fighting between the two groups distracted both the Continental Congress and the Continental army commander, General George WASHINGTON.

In 1778 Major John Butler, a Loyalist officer at FORT NIAGARA, marched an army of 400 Loyalists and some 450 Seneca and Cayuga Indians to the Wyoming Valley. Colonel Zebulon Butler, a Yankee and a Continental officer on leave, then moved north with a force of 80 regulars and some 400 militia to stop the Loyalists.

The resulting Battle of the Wyoming Valley, 3 July 1778, was brief. The Indians surprised the Patriots with a flanking attack, causing the militia to give way. Nearly 300 Americans were massacred, while the Loyalists reported only 3 killed and 8 wounded. Following his victory, Major Butler then burned much of the valley.

After the American Revolutionary War, the settlers returned; both Connecticut and Pennsylvania still claimed the valley. In 1782, the Continental Congress authorized a court of arbitration to settle the issue. Meeting at Trenton, New Jersey, the court issued the Trenton Decree, awarding the disputed land to Pennsylvania.

In 1784, the Second Pennamite War began. It was prompted by a land commission set up by Pennsylvania. Supposedly formed to arbitrate claims, the commission operated simply as a device for removing the Yankees. Alexander Patterson, commanding a group of Pennsylvania rangers, seized Yankee property and drove Yankees from the valley, arresting those who refused to leave. John Franklin, a veteran of the war, organized the Yankees into an army, which drove Patterson's rangers from the valley. By 1794, the fighting ceased.

In 1787, the Confirming Act recognized the claims of Yankees who had settled before the Trenton Decree. The Compromise Act of 1799 offered Pennsylvania claimants compensation through lands in Luzerne County, Pennsylvania. The Act of 1807 recognized Yankee claims without regard to the Trenton Decree.

Further reading: Gray, Ernest. *The Sesqui-Centennial of the Battle of Wyoming, July 2–3–4, 1778–1928.* Wilkes-Barre, Pa.: Wyoming Historical and Genealogical Society, 1928; Stefon, Frederick J. "The Wyoming Valley." *Beyond Philadelphia: The American Revolution in the Pennsylvania Hinterland.* Edited by John B. Frantz and William Pencak. University Park: Pennsylvania State University Press, 1998.

— A. J. L. Waskey

Yeager, Charles E. ("Chuck") (1923–) *U.S. Air Force general and test pilot, the first person to break the sound barrier*

Born on 13 February 1923 in Myra, West Virginia, Charles "Chuck" Elwood Yeager enlisted in the U.S. Army Air Forces as a private in September 1941. Accepted into pilot training, he earned his wings and a commission at Luke Field, Arizona, in March 1943.

Yeager's first assignment was as pilot of a P-39 Aircobra with the 363d Fighter Squadron at Tonopah, Nevada. Deployed with his squadron to Great Britain in November 1943, Yeager flew P-51 Mustangs over France. Shot down in March 1944, he was assisted by the French resistance to Spain and returned to his squadron in July. He was credited with 11.5 kills, including a Me-262 jet.

Captain Yeager returned to the United States in early 1945 as a flight instructor. In July he was assigned to Wright Field, Ohio, to test the P-80 Shooting Star and P-84 Thunderjet, America's first jet fighter aircraft. Yeager was then selected to pilot the Bell XS-1 rocket. In August 1947 he went to Muroc Field, California, as the XS-1 project officer.

On 14 October 1947, the XS-1, attached to the belly of a B-29, was carried to 21,000 feet and released. Yeager became the first person to break the sound barrier—that is, go faster than the speed of sound (Mach 1)—when he piloted his craft to an altitude of 43,000 feet at a speed of more than 700 mph, or Mach 1.06. He proved that while the aircraft vibrated on approaching the sound barrier, it flew smoothly once it had broken through the "barrier."

During the next two years, Colonel Yeager flew the X-1 40 times, exceeding 1,000 mph and reaching more than 70,000 feet altitude, and he became the first pilot to make a ground takeoff in a rocket aircraft. In 1952, Yeager attended Air Command and Staff College but the next year was back to flying the X-1A. In December 1953, he became the first person ever to fly more than twice the speed of sound when he pushed the X-1A to Mach 2.44 (1,650 mph).

Yeager next commanded the 417th Fighter Squadron in Europe. In 1957, he joined the 413th Fighter Wing at George AFB, California, and in 1958 became commander of the 1st Fighter Squadron, flying new F-100 Super Sabres. In June 1961, Yeager graduated from the Air War College, and the following year he became commandant of the Aerospace Research Pilot School (the air force test pilots school), which trained military pilots to be astronauts.

In July 1966, Yeager took command of the 405th Fighter Wing in the Philippines. He flew 127 combat missions during the VIETNAM WAR. Upon his return to the United States in February 1968, he assumed command of the 4th Fighter Wing at Seymour Johnson AFB, North Carolina. In July 1969, Yeager was assigned to the Seventh Air Force at Ramstein AFB, Germany, as vice commander. In August he was promoted to brigadier general. In 1971, he served as U.S. defense representative to Pakistan, and in March 1973 he was sent to the Air Force Inspection and Safety Center, Norton AFB, California, becoming its director in June. Yeager retired from active duty in March 1975.

In addition to his military awards, Yeager won the MacKay Trophy, the Collier Trophy, the Harmon Trophy, and the Gold Medal of the Fédération Aéronautique Internationale. In 1973 he was inducted into the National Aviation Hall of Fame. In 1976 President Gerald Ford and Congress awarded him a peacetime Medal of Honor. In 1985 President Ronald Reagan presented him with the Presidential Medal of Freedom.

Yeager wrote two autobiographies and acted in, or was technical adviser for, a number of movies, television shows, documentaries, and commercials. He served on the National Commission on Space and on the commission that investigated the 1986 *Challenger* space shuttle disaster. At the beginning of the 21st century, he was still active as a consultant test pilot for the Air Force Flight Test Center at Edwards AFB, California.

See also AIR FORCE, U.S.

Further reading: Hallion, Richard P. *Test Pilots: The Frontiersmen of Flight.* Garden City, N.Y.: Doubleday, 1981; Wolfe, Tom. *The Right Stuff.* New York: Farrar, Strauss & Giroux, 1979; Yeager, Chuck, and Leo Janos. *Yeager: An Autobiography.* New York: Bantam Books, 1985; Yeager, Chuck, and Charles Leerhsen. *Press On: Further Adventures in the Good Life.* New York: Bantam Books, 1988; Young, James O. *Meeting the Challenge of Supersonic Flight.* Edwards AFB, Calif.: Air Force Flight Test Center History Office, 1997.

— William Head

York, Alvin C. (1887–1964) *U.S. Army sergeant and World War I hero*

Born on 13 December 1887 in Pall Mall, Tennessee, the third of 11 children, Alvin York took over the family farm after his father's death, supplementing his income by working as a laborer for the Federal Highway Commission.

In June 1917, following the U.S. declaration of war against Germany, York was ordered to report for military service. York's appeal for conscientious objector status was rejected. This created a dilemma for York, who was an elder in the Church of Christ in Christian Union. His battalion commander, Major George E. Buxton, himself a Bible scholar, convinced York that men of religious conviction could fight.

Assigned to G Company, 328th Battalion, 82d Division, York arrived in France in May 1918. In late June he and his company took up position outside Rambucourt. In late September the 328th left SAINT-MIHIEL for the Argonne Forest.

On 8 October 1918 in the Argonne, Corporal York led 17 men into action against the Germans. His force was soon cut off and under fire. With half of his men dead or wounded, York almost single-handedly killed more than 20 German soldiers, knocked out several machine gun emplacements, withstood a seven-man German bayonet charge, and took 132 prisoners, four of whom were officers.

The modest York, the epitome of the "citizen soldier," found himself acclaimed a hero. In November York was promoted to sergeant for his actions, and in February 1919, he was awarded the Distinguished Service Cross by AMERICAN EXPEDITIONARY FORCES (AEF) Commander General John J. PERSHING. During the ceremony, Pershing called York "the greatest civilian soldier of the war." On 18 April 1919 York received the Medal of Honor. He was also awarded the French croix de guerre. Supreme Allied Commander Marshal Ferdinand Foch described York's deed as "the great accomplishment by any private soldier of all the armies of Europe."

York returned to the United States in May 1919. After a tumultuous reception in New York City, he returned home to Pall Mall. Apart from speaking trips, he remained there until his death on 6 September 1964. York founded the York Institute, a center for Christian learning, and donated most of the money he derived from his notoriety to it and to other charities.

See also WORLD WAR I, COURSE OF U.S. INVOLVEMENT.

Further reading: Lee, David D. *Sergeant York: An American Hero.* Lexington: University Press of Kentucky, 1985; Perry, John. *Sgt. York: His Life, Legend, and Legacy.* Nashville, Tenn.: Broadman & Holman, 1997; York, Alvin C. *Sergeant York: His Own Life Story and War Diary.* Garden City, N.Y.: Doubleday, Doran, 1928.

— Joshua Lee Bandy

York/Toronto, attack on (27 April 1813)

Amphibious operation during the War of 1812

In the spring of 1813, the newly installed U.S. secretary of war, John ARMSTRONG, promulgated a strategy for the capture of Montreal. Ancillary to this was the reduction of the port of Kingston, Ontario, at the eastern end of Lake Ontario, which served as a British naval base. Armstrong anticipated that it could be stormed by a surprise over-the-ice assault, but regional American commanders Major General Henry DEARBORN and Commodore Isaac CHAUNCEY demurred. They believed that Kingston was too heavily fortified to attack and suggested instead an amphibious descent upon York (Toronto), the provincial capital of Upper Canada, for the purpose of seizing a large warship under construction there. Surprisingly, Armstrong agreed to this major alteration in his strategy, and throughout the spring of 1813 troops and boats for the expedition assembled at SACKETT'S HARBOR, New York.

On 24 April 1813 Chauncey's fleet of 14 vessels embarked 1,700 of Dearborn's soldiers, although adverse weather delayed their departure until the following day. Actual command of the landing had been entrusted to Brigadier General Zebulon M. PIKE, the noted explorer. Two days later the fleet appeared off York harbor, much to the alarm of garrison commander Major General Sir Roger Hale Sheaffe. Sheaffe had at his disposal only 700 militia, Indians, and soldiers of the 8th Regiment to oppose the landing. His men were dispersed over a wide area.

On 26 April, Pike directed his first wave to land under the cover of an intense naval bombardment, but strong winds carried the boats to a point west of the town. First ashore was a body of the U.S. Regiment of RIFLEMEN, under Lieutenant Colonel Benjamin FORSYTH, who scoured the woods for the enemy. Pike then personally took charge of the second wave, consisting of the 6th, 15th, and 16th U.S. Infantry, and led it against the British batteries. The British resisted stoutly; but, following an accidental explosion at one battery, Sheaffe commenced an orderly withdrawal. Pike pushed ahead in pursuit and occupied the town of York without further resistance. However, while he was interrogating several prisoners, a gunpowder magazine exploded, mortally wounding Pike and inflicting heavy losses on the Americans.

In the confusion that followed, Sheaffe's men escaped capture. British losses amounted to 62 killed, 34 wounded, and 50 missing; the American losses totaled 54 killed and more than 200 wounded, principally by the explosion. Order was finally restored by Colonel Cromwell Pearce, who then drew up articles of capitulation. The Americans promised to respect private property, but when a human scalp allegedly was found dangling in the government building, widespread looting resulted. Much destruction ensued before order could be restored.

The capture of York was a significant action in that it denied badly needed supplies to the British fleet on LAKE ERIE, thereby contributing greatly to the ultimate American victory there. However, the destruction of the capital engendered lingering resentment thoughout Canada. This resentment found expression the following year with the burning of goverment buildings in Washington, D.C.

See also WAR OF 1812: LAND OVERVIEW; WAR OF 1812: NAVAL OVERVIEW.

Further reading: Benn, Carl. *The Battle of York.* Belleville, Ontario, Canada: Mika Publishing, 1984; Malcomson, Robert. *Lords of the Lake: The Naval War on Lake Ontario, 1812–1814.* Annapolis, Md.: Naval Institute Press, 1998.

— Jonh C. Fredriksen

Yorktown campaign (1 August–19 October 1781)
Final decisive campaign of the American Revolutionary War

By early 1781, the American Revolutionary War was at stalemate. British lieutenant general Charles, Lord Cornwallis, had waged an aggressive campaign in the South against Continental army forces led by Major General Nathanael GREENE, but following his pyrrhic victory over Greene in the March 1781 Battle of GUILFORD COURT HOUSE, Cornwallis moved his depleted and exhausted troops north into Virginia, ending up at the little tobacco port of Yorktown on Chesapeake Bay.

At the same time, British troops under Brigadier General Benedict ARNOLD, the American turncoat, had been conducting raids into the Chesapeake Bay, and Continental army commander General George WASHINGTON dispatched 1,200 men to the area under Major General Marie Joseph Paul Gilbert du Motier, Marquis de LAFAYETTE, in an unsuccessful effort to trap Arnold.

Washington still hoped to drive the British from New York City. Toward that end, he had positioned the bulk of his army at White Plains, New York. In mid-July, 4,000 French troops arrived at Newport, Rhode Island, under Lieutenant General Jean Baptiste Donatien de Vimeur, Comte de Rochambeau. The French general marched his men to White Plains and placed them under Washington's command. Washington was also heartened to learn from Admiral Jacques, Comte de Barras, who had sailed into Newport with a small squadron, that Admiral François Joseph, Comte de Grasse, was sailing from France with a major fleet. De Grasse was bound for the West Indies, where the war at sea between Britain and France was being waged, but he would come north during hurricane season.

On 14 August, Washington received word that de Grasse would sail not for New York but for Chesapeake Bay, where he would remain until the end of October. Washington immediately saw the possibility of a strategic concentration of land forces against Cornwallis at Yorktown, supported by French control of the bay. On 21 August he ordered 2,000 Continental army troops and the 4,000 French troops south, leaving only 2,000 Continentals to monitor the enemy forces under Lieutenant General Sir Henry Clinton, the British commander in North America, in New York. Not until 2 September did Clinton realize what had happened.

On 5 September, Washington learned of the safe arrival in the Chesapeake of de Grasse with 28 ships of the line and 3,000 land troops. Soon de Grasse had put the troops ashore, and French ships were ferrying the allied troops down the bay. The land forces assembled at Williamsburg, Virginia, on 26 September. Washington had 9,000 American soldiers (3,000 of them militia, who did not take part in the fighting) and 6,000 French. The allies outnumbered Cornwallis, who had 7,000 men, two to one.

Three weeks before, on 5 September, a naval engagement had been fought between 19 British ships of the line under Admirals Thomas Graves and Alexander Hood and the 28 ships of the line under de Grasse. While this Second Battle of the CHESAPEAKE was indecisive from a tactical point of view, strategically it was one of the most important battles in naval history, for it left the French in control of the bay. Indeed, the French position was strengthened because, during the battle, Barras had slipped into the bay with his eight ships of the line and siege artillery. With the French advantage now 36 ships of the line to 19 for the British, Graves and Hood sailed for New York, leaving Cornwallis to his fate.

On 28 September, the American and French ground forces invested Yorktown. Under the supervision of French military engineers, the allies dug a series of zigzag trenches and lines toward the British positions. On 6 October, the parallels were within 800 yards of the British lines. The next day the allies begin a massive artillery bombardment. Then, on the night of 14–15 October, American and French infantry stormed two key positions on the British left, redoubts 9 and 10, forcing a further constriction in the British lines.

Too late Cornwallis decided on an escape attempt across the York River to Gloucester Point. A storm on the night of 16–17 October frustrated his plan. That same night, 350 British light infantry mounted a diversionary attack at the juncture between the American and French positions, causing only minor casualties and spiking four guns. French infantry and American artillerymen drove off the raiders, and within hours the guns were back in action.

On 17 October, more than 100 allied guns and mortars began a massive bombardment of the British positions. Running out of ammunition, short of supplies, and with no hope of immediate relief, Cornwallis decided to surrender. At 10:00 A.M. on 17 October a British drummer mounted a parapet and beat the signal to parley. Cornwallis sought a parole for his men but Washington refused, remembering

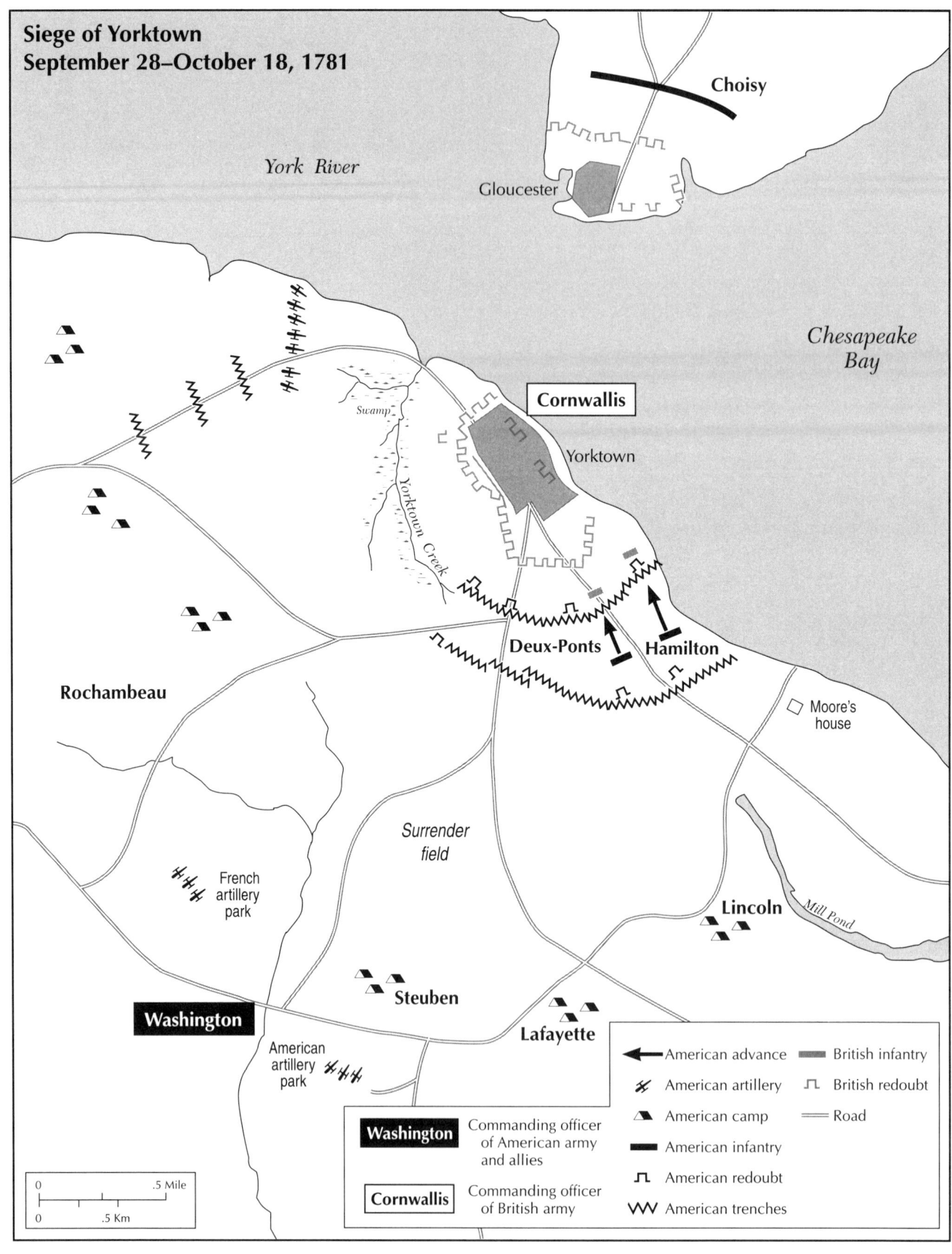

**Siege of Yorktown
September 28–October 18, 1781**

Choisy

York River

Gloucester

Chesapeake Bay

Swamp

Cornwallis

Yorktown

Yorktown Creek

Deux-Ponts

Hamilton

Rochambeau

Moore's house

French artillery park

Surrender field

Lincoln

Mill Pond

Steuben

Washington

Lafayette

American artillery park

0   .5 Mile
0   .5 Km

→ American advance
✗ American artillery
▲ American camp
▬ American infantry
⊓ American redoubt
⋁⋁⋀ American trenches

▬ British infantry
⊓ British redoubt
═ Road

Washington Commanding officer of American army and allies

Cornwallis Commanding officer of British army

the storm of controversy over paroles that had ensued after the Battle of SARATOGA. Cornwallis then agreed to surrender his men as prisoners of war.

On 19 October, the formal surrender occurred. Cornwallis claimed illness, and Brigadier General Charles O'Hara represented the British. O'Hara attempted to surrender to Rochambeau, who insisted that it should be to Washington, but O'Hara declined this request and designated Major General Benjamin LINCOLN instead. The British troops marched out to stack arms between rows of French and American troops to the tune of "The World Turned Upside Down."

A total of 8,077 British surrendered: 840 seamen, 80 camp followers, and 7,157 soldiers. During the siege, the British lost 156 killed and 326 wounded. The allies sustained but 75 killed and 199 wounded, two-thirds of these French.

The British defeat at Yorktown brought down the British government and led to a change of policy in London in favor of cutting British losses and seeking to drive a wedge between the United States and its French ally. Although two more years of war lay ahead, the Battle of Yorktown ensured that the United States would win its independence.

See also AMERICAN REVOLUTIONARY WAR: LAND OVERVIEW; CONTINENTAL ARMY; FRANCE AND THE AMERICAN REVOLUTION.

Further reading: Davis, Burke. *The Campaign That Won America: The Story of Yorktown.* New York: Dial Press, 1970; Hibbert, Christopher. *Redcoats and Rebels: The American Revolution through British Eyes.* New York: W. W. Norton, 1990; Lumpkin, Henry. *From Savannah to Yorktown: The American Revolution in the South.* Columbia: University of South Carolina Press, 1981; Morrissey, Brenden. *Yorktown, 1781: The World Turned Upside Down.* London: Osprey Publishing, 1997.

— J. A. Menzoff

Z

Zimmermann Telegram (16–17 January 1917)
Telegram from Germany's foreign minister to his ambassadors in Mexico and Washington, proposing that Mexico go to war against the United States

Shortly after Germany announced its resumption of unlimited submarine warfare in January 1917—an action likely to provoke war with the United States—German foreign minister Arthur Zimmermann used a Scandinavian transatlantic cable supposedly reserved for peace negotiations to dispatch telegrams to his ambassadors in Mexico City and the United States.

Mexican relations with the United States had been in a state of intermittent crisis since 1914, leading President Woodrow WILSON in 1916 to dispatch the PUNITIVE EXPEDITION INTO MEXICO under Brigadier General John J. PERSHING to hunt down the bandit revolutionary Pancho Villa. Zimmermann proposed that if Germany and the United States went to war, and Mexico were to join Germany, upon a German victory Mexico would regain the territories of Texas, New Mexico, Arizona, and California, annexed by the United States in the 1840s. He also suggested that Japan might be induced to join such an anti-American alliance.

Both the U.S. Department of State and British naval intelligence intercepted these and several later messages. On 24 February, these were passed to President Wilson, who made them public on 1 March. Mexico and Japan both hastily denied any complicity in the scheme, but on 3 March Zimmermann, although complaining vehemently about Allied interception of his communications, admitted them to be genuine. Wilson unavailingly hoped that publication of these messages would break a congressional filibuster against the arming of American merchant ships, a measure considered likely to precipitate open war with Germany.

For several more weeks German agents continued their attempts to persuade Mexico to conclude an anti-American alliance; but on 14 April, immediately after the United States Congress finally declared war against Germany, Mexico announced that it would remain neutral. Although the Zimmermann Telegram was not a major cause of American intervention against Germany, the intrigues its publication revealed helped to convince both Wilson and the broad American public of Germany's deep-rooted hostility and antagonism, reinforcing their faith that their country was amply justified in entering the war.

See also LUSITANIA; WORLD WAR I, CAUSES OF U.S. ENTRY.

Further reading: Beesly, Patrick. *Room 40: British Naval Intelligence 1914–18.* San Diego: Harcourt Brace Jovanovich, 1982; Doerries, Reinhard R. *Imperial Challenge: Ambassador Count Bernstorff and German-American Relations, 1908–1917.* Chapel Hill: University of North Carolina Press, 1989; Spencer, Samuel R. *Decision for War, 1917: The Laconia Sinking and the Zimmermann Telegram as Key Factors in the Public Reaction Against Germany.* Rindge, N.H.: R. R. Smith, 1953; Tuchman, Barbara. *The Zimmerman Telegram.* New York: Viking Press; 1958.

— Priscilla Roberts

Zouaves *Distinctive Union and Confederate units during the Civil War*

Zouaves were semisocial, semimilitary companies in the United States prior to the war, so named because they adopted uniforms that resembled those worn by Muslim auxiliaries to the French army in North Africa. This uniform consisted of a short dark blue or gray jacket (generally trimmed in red, yellow, or light blue), baggy red or blue pants (also usually trimmed in red, yellow, or light blue), and white leggings. The headgear consisted of a fez or kepi of either red or dark blue, which was then generally trimmed in red, yellow, or light blue. A great number of volunteer regiments were mustered in wearing these colorful uniforms.

During the war, most regiments ultimately decided to abandon the uniform. In the Union army, this decision was based primarily on its cumbersome nature in combat. In addition, by 1863, the Union army was attempting to standardize uniforms for ease in supply. In the Confederate army, the decision to abandon the uniform was primarily the result of limited supplies and the inability often to supply even the most basic clothing necessities. Although a few militia units did retain the uniform after the war, by the end of the 19th century it had completely disappeared from use.

See also CIVIL WAR: LAND OVERVIEW.

Further reading: Lloyd, Mark. *Combat Uniforms of the Civil War.* New York: Mallard Press, 1990; Troiani, Don, and Brian C. Pohanka. *Don Troiani's Civil War.* Mechanicsburg, Pa.: Stackpole Books, 1995.

— Alexander M. Bielakowski

Zumwalt, Elmo R., Jr. (1920–2000) *U.S. Navy admiral and chief of naval operations*
Born on 20 November 1920 in San Francisco, Elmo Russell Zumwalt graduated from the U.S. Naval Academy, Annapolis, in 1942. His wartime service included combat assignments off GUADALCANAL and the PHILIPPINES. During the KOREAN WAR, he served on a battleship. During the 1950s, he spent time at the Naval War Colleges and as special assistant to the secretary of the navy. In 1959 he commanded the frigate *Dewey,* the first U.S. Navy ship specifically designed to carry guided missiles.

While attending the National War College in 1962, Zumwalt delivered a lecture titled "The Problem of Succession in the Kremlin," which attracted much attention—among others, from Assistant Secretary of Defense for International Affairs Paul NITZE, who consequently made Zumwalt his aide. In 1963, Nitze became secretary of the navy and Zumwalt his senior aide. Promoted in 1965 to rear admiral, Zumwalt was the youngest American to gain that rank. He imbibed both Nitze's suspicions of the Soviet Union and détente and his belief that involvement in the VIETNAM WAR misguidedly diverted U.S. energies from the overshadowing Soviet threat.

These views came into play when, in 1968, after the presidential decision to withdraw gradually from Vietnam, Zumwalt became commander of U.S. naval forces in Vietnam, where he supervised the gradual "Vietnamization" of operations as the United States relinquished many combat functions to South Vietnamese forces. Zumwalt authorized extensive use of the herbicide Agent Orange to protect his largely riverine forces by destroying foliage that could give cover to enemy troops. Even after his son and namesake, who served under him, developed fatal cancer, possibly due to such exposure, Zunwalt defended this decision as having saved more lives than it took.

Appointed chief of naval operations in 1970, Zumwalt served a controversial four years. Attempting to restore naval morale by modernizing the service, he moved aggressively to recruit minorities and women, combat racism, and eradicate outmoded traditions. Convinced that a serious Soviet threat existed, he decommissioned older ships and instituted a building program designed to produce a mixture of large, sophisticated, nuclear-fueled ships and numerous smaller, relatively low-cost specialized vessels. Even so, Zumwalt argued that President Richard M. NIXON's reluctance to demand increased defense expenditures had caused American naval capabilities to decline vis-à-vis the Soviets. Two years after retiring in 1974, Zumwalt publicized these criticisms in his memoir *On Watch.* In 1979 he, like Nitze, opposed ratification of the SALT II disarmament treaty, which they claimed jeopardized American security. He also campaigned for compensation for war veterans exposed to Agent Orange. Zumwalt died of cancer in Durham, North Carolina, on 2 January 2000.

See also AFRICAN-AMERICANS IN THE MILITARY; NAVY, U.S.; WOMEN IN THE MILITARY.

Further reading: Love, Robert W., Jr., ed. *The Chiefs of Naval Operations.* Annapolis, Md.: Naval Institute Press, 1980; Reynolds, Clark G. *Famous American Admirals.* New York: Van Nostrand Reinhold, 1980; Zumwalt, Elmo R., Jr. *On Watch: A Memoir.* New York: Quadrangle Books, 1976; Zumwalt, Elmo R., Jr., Elmo Zumwalt III, and John Pekkanen. *My Father, My Son.* New York: Macmillan, 1986.

— Priscilla Roberts

Glossary

★ —————————————————————————————————————

The purpose of this glossary is to provide a listing of acronyms, abbreviations, and specialized terms and phrases used throughout the history of American land, sea, and air military forces.

AA antiaircraft

AAA antiaircraft artillery

AB Air Base

abatis X-shaped field obstructions, with sharpened edges facing the attacker

ABM antiballistic missile

ADC Air Defense Command

AEF American Expeditionary Forces (U.S. forces in France during World War I)

AFB Air Force Base

AGM air-to-ground missile

Air America U.S. clandestine airline established by George Doole in 1959 to carry soldiers and matériel in support of fighting against Communist forces in Southeast Asia.

ALLB AirLand Battle (USA); post-Vietnam army combat doctrine emphasizing main-force unit engagements

Alligator First-generation Landing Vehicle, Tracked (LVT-1), developed by Donald A. Roebling and first integrated in the Fleet Marine Force in 1941.

AMC Air Mobility Command (USAF)

ANZUS defense agreement signed by the United States, Australia, and New Zealand in 1951

AP armor-piercing (ammunition category)

APC armored personnel carrier

army military formation comprising at least two corps or many divisions and usually commanded by a full general

army group military formation originating in World War I comprising at least two armies

AT antitank

ATC Air Transport Command

ATGM antitank guided missile

AWACS Airborne Warning and Control System

BAR Browning Automatic Rifle

barbette a mound of earth or a protected platform, from which guns may fire over the crest of a parapet; also, a cylinder of armor protecting a gun on a warship

bastion a defensive structure consisting of two faces and two flanks

battalion Military unit. Of infantry it is approximately 600–1,000 strong and several companies; it is usually commanded by a lieutenant colonel.

battery Basic artillery unit, usually composed of 4–8 guns; in a fort, in the field, or on ship, it also refers to the place from which guns are fired.

battlecruiser Warship. Capital ship involving battleship armament on a cruiser hull. It is designed for speed and hitting power, but sacrifices armor.

battleship Warship. Capital ship and heaviest gunned warship. Term derived from line-of-battle ship or ship of the line.

BLT Battalion Landing Team (U.S. Marine Corps)

BMEWS Ballistic Missile Early Warning System

brig Warship. In the Age of Fighting Sail, the smallest square-rigged seagoing warship.

brigade a group of several or more regiments of infantry or cavalry, usually put together for limited duration or a particular task. Usually commanded by a brigadier general.

C2 command and control

C3 command, control, and communications

C3I command, control, communications, and intelligence

CAS close air support

casemate a fortified position or chamber or an armored enclosure on a warship with embrasures through which guns may fire

CBI China-Burma-India theater, World War II

CCC Civilian Conservation Corps

CAT Civil Air Transport, U.S.-sponsored organization that provided support to the French in the first Indochina War

CFV cavalry fighting vehicle

CI Counterintelligence

CIC Combat Information Center (control center on a naval ship)

CinC Commander in chief

CO Commanding Officer

column Military or naval formation of greater length than breadth

company A unit of infantry, usually of 100–250 men, usually of three platoons, traditionally commanded by a captain.

corporal military enlisted rank above private first class

corvette Small warship. In the Age of Fighting Sail it referred to a sailing ship with a flush deck and single tier of guns. Current usage refers to a warship smaller than a destroyer employed on escort and patrol duties.

CP command post

cruiser Warship smaller than a battleship, of moderate armament and high speed; successor to the frigate. Its roles include reconaissance for the battle fleet and independent action such as commerce raiding. It also conducts shore bombardment missions.

CSA Confederate States of America

D day decision day; day on which an operation commences

destroyer Warship. Small, lightly armed and armored, and of high speed, destroyers were first developed to deal with the threat to battleships posed by small, fast torpedo boats. The ship type's original name was Torpedo Boat Destroyer. Destroyers came to fulfill a variety of roles, including protecting convoys against submarines and serving as pickets for the battle fleet. Today's destroyers are larger vessels, capable of performing a multitude of roles.

division Principal army formation, whether infantry, cavalry, or armor, along with supporting elements such as artillery and engineers. Traditionally commanded by a major general, U.S. divisions in World War I were quite large, consisting of 27,000 men; now they consist of 10,000–15,000 men.

DMZ Demilitarized Zone

DOW Died of Wounds

DPICM Dual-purpose improved conventional munitions

dragoons Mounted infantry. Dragoons traditionally used horses for transportation and then fought on foot.

dreadnought super battleships, beginning with the British ship of that name in 1906, the first all big-gunned battleship, faster and more powerful than any other capital ship

DUKW two-and-one-half-ton amphibious truck, known as "Duck"

dustoff Vietnam-era nickname for medical evacuation by helicopter of dead and wounded, originally taken from the radio call sign of Army helicopter pilot Major Charles L. Kelly

E+E escape and evasion

ECCM electronic counter-countermeasures

ECM electronic countermeasures

ELINT electronic intelligence

embrasure An opening through which a weapon may be fired.

enfilade Hitting an enemy line from an angle, as opposed to straight on. An attacking and enfilading force could concentrate its entire fire on a portion of the enemy line, while the enemy would have available only a portion of its firepower.

envelopment Attack to the side of an enemy force. A single envelopment means fixing an enemy force in front and on one side; a double envelopment means an attack on both sides of the enemy force.

ETO European Theater of Operations

EW electronic warfare

FA field artillery

FAC forward air controller

FB firebase

flag officer commodore or admiral, so designated usually only when in command

flank attack Action in which an attacking force strikes from the side an enemy force deployed in line. This allows the attacking force to deploy maximum firepower against minimum enemy firepower and also the opportunity of rolling up the entire enemy battle line.

fleet Largest naval formation, commanded by an admiral

flotilla A formation of small warships

formation A body of units, usually involving combined arms and supporting units, capable of operating independently from the main body; also, a pattern or method of drawing up and deploying army, air force, or naval units for battle, an example of which would be the column or line for ground troops.

frigate Warship of the Age of Fighting Sail. Ship-rigged, three-masted warship. Not large enough to stand in the main battle line, frigates were employed for reconnaissance and on detached service, including commerce raiding. In today's navies they are ships just smaller than destroyers.

FSB fire support base

galley Oared fighting warships; in U.S. history, these were small vessels, used on interior waterways or along the coasts.

gendarme originally a mounted man-at-arms, later a policeman

G1 U.S. administrative staff section (division or higher), Personnel

G2 U.S. administrative staff section (division or higher), Intelligence

G3 U.S. administrative staff section (division or higher), Training

G4 U.S. administrative staff section (division or higher), Supply

G5 U.S. administrative staff section (division or higher), Civil Affairs

GI Government Issue; slang term used to refer to U.S. infantrymen during World War II

GO General Order

GOC Ground Observer Corps

grenadier infantry trained to throw hand grenades; also, elite infantry

gunboat small warship

gunny Marine Corps slang for gunnery sergeant

HE high explosive

HEAT High-explosive antitank ammunition

Hessians Term applied to German mercenaries, many of whom were from Hesse, who served in the British army during the American Revolutionary War

Higgins Boat Shallow-draft, bow-ramped, troop landing craft of World War II, designed by Andrew Jackson Higgins

HE High-explosive (ammunition category)

howitzer Artillery piece popularized in the mid-18th century. The short-barreled howitzer was originally designed to hurl explosive shells at high angle.

Hump, the nickname for the high-altitude and hazardous air route across the Himalayas used to fly lend-lease supplies to China via India in World War II

ICBM intercontinental ballistic missile

ICM Improved conventional munitions

IFV infantry fighting vehicle

IO information operations

IRBM intermediate range ballistic missile

Jäger Term given to riflemen in pre-20th century armies; it means "hunter."

JCS Joint Chiefs of Staff

jeep Corruption of GP (general purpose), a quarter-ton truck

Jolly Green Giant Vietnam-era search-and-rescue helicopter (HH-53)

KIA killed in action

LCM Landing Craft, Mechanized

LCVP Landing Craft, Vehicle, and Personnel

line Military or naval formation of greater breadth than length.

Loach Vietnam-era observation helicopter (OH-6A)

LST Landing Ship, Tank

LVT Landing Vehicle, Tracked

M-1 Model 1, designation for both a rifle and a carbine of World War II. See SMALL ARMS: RIFLES.

M-14 assault rifle of the Vietnam War era. See SMALL ARMS: RIFLES.

M-16 Assault rifle of the Vietnam War era. See SMALL ARMS: RIFLES.

MAC Military Airlift Command (USAF)

MACV Military Assistance Command, Vietnam

MATS Military Air Transport Service (USAF)

medevac medical evacuation by helicopter of dead and wounded

MIA missing in action

MIRV Multiple Independently Targeted Reentry Vehicle

MLRS Multiple-Launch Rocket System

mm milimeter

monitor Warship type. A coastal vessel, armed with the heaviest guns for shore bombardment.

mortar A smoothbore artillery piece, firing an explosive shell at high angles. The largest mortars are of fixed elevation, with the range being determined by the amount of the charge.

MSgt master sergeant (rank)

MP Military Police

NAS Naval Air Station

NATO North Atlantic Treaty Organization

NBC nuclear, biological, chemical

NCO noncommissioned officer

NORAD North American Aerospace Defense Command

oblique order Method of moving troops on the battlefield to mass on an enemy flank

OSS Office of Strategic Services, World War II-era U.S. intelligence organization

Panzer "Armor" or tank in German. Applied to formations of tanks and loosely to the tanks themselves.

parapet An earthen embankment or masonry barrier along the forward edge of a rampart providing protection for troops and guns positioned behind it

PBR Patrol Boat, River

Pfc. private first class (rank)

PGM Precision-guided munitions

PJ pararescueman (USAF)

platoon Unit of infantry, up to about 40 men in three squads; usually, three platoons make up a company. Traditionally commanded by a lieutenant.

private postinduction enlisted rank

private first class enlisted rank above private

PME   professional military education

Pvt.   private (rank)

POW   prisoner of war

R and D   research and development

RADAR   Radio Direction and Ranging

RCT   Regimental Combat Team

redan   field fortification

redoubt   a small enclosed earthwork in land defense

regiment   Basic infantry and cavalry unit, numbering up to about 1,000 men, today made up of three battalions. Traditionally commanded by a colonel.

rifleman   Originally, a soldier equipped with a rifle instead of a smoothbore musket; riflemen were originally employed as skirmishers and to pick off enemy officers.

SAC   Strategic Air Command

SAGE   Semiautomatic Ground Environment air defense system

sally port   A gate or passage used by troops to make a sortie.

SAM   surface-to-air missile

scarp   A retaining wall made of masonry in permanent defenses

SEAL   sea-air-land, specifically referring to elite U.S. Navy Commandos

SEATO   Southeast Asia Treaty Organization

section   usually, two guns of a battery

sergeant   Noncommissioned officer ranking above a corporal. Grades of sergeant carry progressively more leadership and management duties.

ship of the line   Warship, the largest of the Age of Fighting Sail. The term derived from line-of-battleship, the largest ships that were capable of standing in the main battle line. The largest U.S. Navy ship of the line was the 120-gun *Pennsylvania*.

Sgt.   sergeant (rank)

SHAEF   Supreme Headquarters, Allied Expeditionary Force (World War II)

sitrep   situation report

sloop   Warship. Smaller than the frigate, the term referred to a warship with all its guns on one deck. Sloops were fore-and-aft rigged on a single mast. Sloops of war were employed on a variety of assignments. Merchant sloops were the most popular trading vessels in the American colonies.

SSgt.   staff sergeant (rank)

TSgt.   technical sergeant (rank)

SOG   Studies and Observation Group

SOS   Services of Supply

specialist   Noncommissioned rank awarded for vocational competence

spotter   An observer stationed for the purpose of identifying and observing targets, reporting results of gunfire to the firing agency (e.g., artillery, naval ships)

squad   Infantry unit, the smallest army formation. Three squads make up a platoon. Traditionally commanded by a sergeant.

squadron   In the army, it refers to a unit of cavalry, usually about 100 strong, commanded by a captain. In the navy and air force, it refers to a group of warships or planes on detached service or forming a division within a fleet.

staff college   school for training officers, usually at the rank of major, for higher command

TACAIR   Tactical Air Command

tank   Armored, tracked combat vehicle; term derived from 1916 British name to disguise the contents of the crates in which the vehicles were shipped to France

TF   Task Force

TG   Task Group

TFX   Tactical Fighter, Experimental (prototype designation for F-111)

TNT   Trinitrotoluene (explosive)

TOC   tactical operations center

Tory   English sympathizer during the American Revolutionary War

TRADOC   Training and Doctrine Command (USA)

troop   a company of cavalry

UDT   underwater demolition team

Unit   body of soldiers all of the same arm, such as infantry or artillery

UNREP   Underway Replenishment

USA   United States Army

USAAF   United States Army Air Forces

USAF   United States Air Force

USAR   United States Army Reserve

USCG   United States Coast Guard

USMC   United States Marine Corps

USN   United States Navy

USO   United Service Organization

USS   United States Ship

V-E   Victory in Europe, World War II

V-J   Victory in Japan, World War II

van   the head of a column of ships or troops

V/STOL   Vertical/Short Takeoff and Landing

WAC   Women's Army Corps

WAAF   Women's Auxiliary Air Force

WAFS   Women's Auxiliary Ferrying Service

warrant officer   Military officer ranking below commissioned officer and above noncommissioned officer; rank designates a high degree of competence in a technical or occupational specialty

WASPS   Women's Air Force Service Pilots

water battery   a defensive work lacking embrasures with its guns en barbette, usually located close to the water

Water Buffaloes Second-generation Landing Vehicle, Tracked (LVT-2) initially produced in 1942–43 and used during amphibious operations

WAVES Women Accepted for Voluntary Emergency Service (U.S. Navy)

WIA Wounded in Action

WO Warrant Officer (see above)

WP white phosphorus, a type of ammunition

XO executive officer

A Selective Bibliography of U.S. Military History

General Works

Hogan, David W. *225 Years of Service: The U.S. Army, 1775–2000.* Washington, D.C.: Center of Military History, United States Army, 2000.

Howarth, Stephen. *To Shining Sea: A History of the United States Navy, 1775–1998.* Norman: University of Oklahoma Press, 1999.

Krulak, Victor H. *First to Fight: An Inside View of the U.S. Marine Corps.* Annapolis, Md.: Naval Institute Press, 1999.

Leckie, Robert. *The Wars of America.* Updated edition. New York: HarperCollins, 1992.

Lehman, John F. *On Sea of Glory: Heroic Men, Great Ships, and Epic Battles of the American Navy.* New York: Free Press, 2001.

Millett, Allan R., and Peter Maslowski. *For the Common Defense: A Military History of the United States of America.* New York: Free Press, 1994.

Snow, Donald M. *From Lexington to Desert Storm and Beyond: War and Politics in the American Experience.* Armonk, N.Y.: M. E. Sharpe, 2000.

Weigley, Russell F. *The American Way of War: A History of United States Military Strategy and Policy.* New York: Macmillan, 1973.

———. *History of the United States Army.* Bloomington: Indiana University Press, 1984.

Colonial Period to 1763

Anderson, Fred. *Crucible of War: The Seven Years' War and the Fate of British North America, 1754–1766.* New York: Knopf, 2000.

Downey, Fairfax. *Louisbourg: Key to a Continent.* Englewood Cliffs, N.J.: Prentice-Hall, 1965.

Drake, Samuel Adams. *The Border Wars of New England Commonly Called King William and Queen Anne's War.* New York: Scribner, 1897.

Flexner, James Thomas. *Mohawk Baronet: A Biography of Sir William Johnson.* Syracuse, N.Y.: Syracuse University Press, 1989.

Jennings, Francis. *Empire of Fortune: Crowns, Colonies, and Tribes in the Seven Years' War in America.* New York: W. W. Norton, 1990.

Leach, Douglas Edward. *Flintlock and Tomahawk: New England in King Philip's War.* New York: W. W. Norton, 1966.

Leckie, Robert. *A Few Acres of Snow: The Saga of the French and Indian Wars.* New York: Wiley, 1999.

Lee, E. Lawrence. *Indian Wars in North Carolina, 1663–1763.* Raleigh: North Carolina Division of Archives and History, 1997.

Peckham, Howard H. *The Colonial Wars, 1689–1762.* Chicago: University of Chicago Press, 1990.

Schultz, Eric B., and Michael Tougias. *King Philip's War: The History and Legacy of America's Forgotten Conflict.* Woodstock, Vt.: Countryman Press, 1999.

Schwartz, Seymour. *French and Indian War: The Imperial Struggle of North America.* New York: Simon & Schuster, 1995.

American Revolutionary War Era, 1763–1789

Alden, John R. *The American Revolution 1775–1783.* New York: Harper & Row, 1954.

Black, Jeremy. *War for America: The Fight for Independence, 1775–1783*. Stroud, England: Alan Sutton Publishing, 1991.

Brooks, Victor. *The Boston Campaign: April 1775–March 1776*. Conshohocken, Pa.: Combined Publishing, 1999.

Buckman, John. *The Road to Guilford Courthouse: The American Revolution in the Carolinas*. New York: Wiley, 1997.

Conway, Stephen. *The British Isles and the War of American Independence*. New York: Oxford University Press, 2000.

Ellis, Joseph J. *Founding Brothers: The Revolutionary Generation*. New York: Knopf, 2000.

Flexner, James Thomas. *Washington: The Indispensable Man*. Boston, Mass.: Little, Brown, 1969.

Freeman, Douglas S. *George Washington*. 5 vols. New York: Charles Scribner's Sons, 1947–1958.

Gould, Dudley C. *Times of Brother Jonathan: What He Ate, Wore, Believed & Used for Medicine During the War of Independence*. Middletown, Conn.: Southfarm Press, 2001.

Hibbert, Christopher. *Redcoats and Rebels: The American Revolution Through British Eyes*. New York: W. W. Norton, 1990.

Higginbotham, Don. *The War for American Independence*. New York: Macmillan, 1971.

Ketchum, Richard M. *Saratoga: Turning Point of America's Revolutionary War*. New York: Henry Holt, 1997.

———. *The Winter Soldiers*. Garden City, N.Y.: Doubleday, 1973.

Lefkowitz, Arthur S. *The Long Retreat: The Calamitous American Defense of New Jersey, 1776*. New Brunswick, N.J.: Rutgers University Press, 1999.

Mackay, James A. *I Have Not Yet Begun to Fight: A Life of John Paul Jones*. New York: Atlantic Monthly Press, 1999.

Martin, James Kirby. *Benedict Arnold, Revolutionary Hero: An American Warrior Reconsidered*. New York: New York University Press, 1997.

Middlekauff, Robert. *The Glorious Cause: The American Revolution, 1763–1789*. New York: Oxford University Press, 1982.

Miller, Nathan. *Sea of Glory. The Continental Navy Fights for Independence, 1775–1783*. New York: David McKay, 1974.

Royster, Charles. *A Revolutionary People at War: The Continental Army and the American Character, 1775–1783*. Chapel Hill: University of North Carolina Press, 1979.

Ward, Christopher. *The War of the Revolution*. 2 vols. New York: Macmillan, 1952.

Yesenko, Michael R. *General George Washington's Campaigns of 1775, 1776, and 1777*. Union, N.J.: MRY, 1999.

The Early Republic, 1789–1861

Ambrose, Stephen E. *Undaunted Courage: Meriwether Lewis, Thomas Jefferson, and the Opening of the American West*. New York: Simon & Schuster, 1996.

Ball, Durwood. *Army Regulars on the Western Frontier, 1848–1861*. Norman: University of Oklahoma Press, 2001.

Barbuto, Richard V. *Niagara, 1814: America Invades Canada*. Lawrence: University Press of Kansas, 2000.

Bauer, K. Jack. *The Mexican War*. New York: Macmillan, 1974.

———. *Surfboats and Horse Marines: U.S. Naval Operations in the Mexican War, 1846–1848*. Annapolis, Md.: Naval Institute Press, 1969.

———. *Zachary Taylor: Soldier, Planter, Statesman of the Old Southwest*. Baton Rouge: Louisiana State University Press, 1985.

Coles, Harry L. *The War of 1812*. Chicago: University of Chicago Press, 1965.

Crackel, Theodore J. *Mr. Jefferson's Army: Political and Social Reform of the Military Establishment, 1801–1809*. New York: New York University Press, 1987.

DeKay, James T. *Chronicles of the Frigate Macedonian, 1809–1822*. New York: W. W. Norton, 2000.

Eisenhower, John S. D. *Agent of Destiny. The Life and Times of General Winfield Scott*. Norman: University of Oklahoma Press, 1999.

———. *So Far From God: The U.S. War with Mexico, 1846–1848*. New York: Random House, 1989.

Fitz-Enz, David G. *Plattsburg, The Final Invasion: The Decisive Battle of the War of 1812*. New York: Cooper Square Press, 2001.

George, Christopher T. *Terror on the Chesapeake: The War of 1812 on the Bay*. Shippensburg, Penn.: White Mane Books, 2000.

Hardin, Stephen L. *Texian Iliad: A Military History of the Texas Revolution*. Austin: University of Texas Press, 1994.

Hickey, Donald R. *The War of 1812: A Forgotten Conflict*. Urbana: University of Illinois Press, 1989.

Horsman, Reginald. *The Causes of the War of 1812*. Philadelphia: University of Pennsylvania Press, 1962.

Leiner, Frederick C. *Millions for Defense: the Subscription Warships of 1798*. Annapolis, Md.: Naval Institute Press, 2000.

Mahon, John K. *The War of 1812*. Gainesville: University Presses of Florida, 1972.

Malcomson, Robert. *Lords of the Lake: The Naval War on Lake Ontario, 1812–1814.* Annapolis, Md.: Naval Institute Press, 1998.

Morris, John D. *Sword of the Border: Major General Jacob Jennings Brown, 1775–1828.* Kent, Ohio: Kent State University Press, 2000.

Norton, Louis A. *Joshua Barney: Hero of the Revolution and 1812.* Annapolis, Md.: Naval Institute Press, 2000.

Owsley, Frank L. *Struggle for the Gulf Borderlands: The Creek War and the Battle of New Orleans, 1812–1815.* Reprint. Tuscaloosa: University of Alabama Press, 2000.

———, and Gene A. Smith. *Filibusters and Expansionists: Jeffersonian Manifest Destiny, 1800–1821.* Tuscaloosa: University of Alabama Press, 1997.

Palmer, Michael A. *Stoddert's War: Naval Operations During the Quasi-War with France, 1798–1801.* Annapolis, Md.: Naval Institute Press, 2000.

Prucha, Francis Paul. *The Sword of the Republic: The United States Army on the Frontier, 1783–1846.* Bloomington: Indiana University Press, 1977.

Remick, Norman T. *Mr. Jefferson's West Point.* Warren Grove, N.J.: N. T. Remick, 2001.

Remini, Robert V. *Andrew Jackson and the Course of American Empire.* New York: Harper & Row, 1981.

Resch, John P. *Suffering Soldiers: Revolutionary War Veterans, Moral Sentiment, and Political Culture in the Early Republic.* Amherst: University of Massachusetts Press, 1999.

Robotti, France D. *The USS Essex: and the Birth of the American Navy.* Holbrook, Mass.: Hadleigh, 2000.

Schroeder, John H. *Matthew Calbraith Perry: Antebellum Sailor and Diplomat.* Annapolis, Md.: Naval Institute Press, 2001.

Skaggs, David Curtis, and Gerard T. Altoff. *A Signal Victory: The Lake Erie Campaign, 1812–1814.* Annapolis, Md.: Naval Institute Press, 1997.

Skaggs, David C., and Larry L. Nelson, eds. *The Sixty Years' War for the Great Lakes, 1754–1814.* East Lansing: Michigan State University Press, 2001.

Skeen, Carl E. *Citizen Soldiers in the War of 1812.* Lexington: University Press of Lexington, 1999.

Smith, Gene A. *"For the Purposes of Defense": The Politics of the Jeffersonian Gunboat Program.* Newark: University of Delaware Press, 1995.

Tucker, Spencer C., and Frank T. Reuter. *Injured Honor: The Chesapeake-Leopard Affair, June 22, 1807.* Annapolis, Md.: Naval Institute Press, 1996.

———. *The Jeffersonian Gunboat Navy.* Columbia: University of South Carolina Press, 1993.

Utley, Robert M. *Frontiersmen in Blue: The U.S. Army and the Indian, 1848–1865.* Reprint. Lincoln: University of Nebraska Press, 1981.

Whipple, A.B.C. *To the Shores of Tripoli: The Birth of the U.S. Navy and Marines.* Annapolis, Md.: Naval Institute Press, 2001.

Winders, Richard Bruce. *Mr. Polk's Army: The American Military Experience in the Mexican War.* College Station: Texas A&M University Press, 1997.

The Civil War, 1861–1865

Bailey, Anne J. *The Chessboard of War: Sherman and Hood in the Autumn Campaigns of 1864.* Lincoln: University of Nebraska Press, 2000.

Bak, Richard. *The CSS Hunley: The Greatest Undersea Adventure of the Civil War.* Dallas: Taylor, 1999.

Beringer, Richard E., et al. *Why the South Lost the Civil War.* Athens: University of Georgia Press, 1986.

Borit, G. S. *Jefferson Davis's Generals.* New York: Oxford University Press, 2000.

Bradley, Michael R. *Tullahoma: The 1863 Campaign for the Control of Middle Tennessee.* Shippensburg, Pa.: Burd Street Press, 2000.

Burne, Alfred H. *Lee, Grant, and Sherman: A Study in Leadership in the 1864–1865 Campaign.* Lawrence: University Press of Kansas, 2000.

Castel, Albert. *Decision in the West: The Atlanta Campaign of 1864.* Lawrence: University Press of Kansas, 1992.

Catton, Bruce. *The Army of the Potomac.* 3 vols. Garden City, N.Y.: Doubleday, 1951–53.

Coffey, David. *John Bell Hood and the Struggle for Atlanta.* Abilene, Tex.: McWhiney Foundation Press, 1998.

Connelly, Thomas L. *Army of the Heartland: The Army of Tennessee, 1861–1862.* Baton Rouge: Louisiana State University Press, 1967.

———. *Autumn of Glory: The Army of Tennessee, 1862–1865.* Baton Rouge: Louisiana State University Press, 1971.

Cozzens, Peter. *The Terrible Sound: The Battle of Chickamauga.* Urbana: University of Illinois Press, 1992.

———. *The Shipwreck of Their Hopes: The Battles for Chattanooga.* Urbana: University of Illinois Press, 1994.

Coski, John M. *Capital Navy: The Men, Ships, and Operations of the James River Squadron.* Mason City, Iowa: Savas, 1996.

Davis, William C. *Jefferson Davis: The Man and His Hour.* New York: HarperCollins, 1991.

———. *Duel Between the First Ironclads.* Mechanicsburg, Pa.: Stackpole Books, 1994.

Donald, David Herbert. *Lincoln.* New York: Simon & Schuster, 1995.

DeKay, James T. *Monitor: The Story of the Legendary Civil War Ironclad.* London: Pimlico, 1999.

Fishel, Edwin C. *The Secret War for the Union: The Untold Story of Military Intelligence in the Civil War.* New York: Houghton Mifflin, 1996.

Foote, Shelby. *The Civil War, A Narrative*. 3 vols. New York: Random House, 1958–1974.

Frazier, Donald S. *Blood and Treasure: Confederate Empire in the Southwest*. College Station: Texas A&M University Press, 1995.

Freeman, Douglas Southall. *R. E. Lee*. 4 vols. New York: Scribner's, 1934–36.

———. *Lee's Lieutenants: A Study in Command*. 3 vols. New York: Scribner, 1942–44.

Gallagher, Gary W. *Lee and His Army in Confederate History*. Chapel Hill: University of North Carolina Press, 2001.

Glatthaar, Joseph T. *The March to the Sea and Beyond: Sherman's Troops in the Savannah and Carolinas Campaigns*. New York: New York University Press, 1985.

Grant, Ulysses S. *Personal Memoirs of U.S. Grant*. 2 vols. Reprint. New York: Library of America, 1990.

Griffiths, Paddy. *Battle Tactics of the American Civil War*. Marlborough, U.K.: Crowood, 2001.

Hattaway, Herman, and Archer Jones. *How the North Won*. Urbana: University of Illinois Press, 1983.

Haughton, Andrew. *Training, Tactics, and Leadership in the Confederate Army of Tennessee: Seeds of Failure*. Portland, Oreg.: Frank Cass, 2000.

Hearn, Chester G. *Naval Battles of the Civil War*. San Diego: Thunder Bay Press, 2000.

Hendrickson, Robert. *The Road to Appomattox*. New York: Wiley, 1998.

Kaltman, Al. *The Genius Robert E. Lee: Leadership Lessons for the Outgunned, Outmanned, and Underfinanced*. Paramus, N.J.: Prentice-Hall, 2000.

McFeely, William S. *Grant: A Biography*. New York: W. W. Norton, 1981.

McMurry, Richard. *Atlanta 1864: Last Chance for the Confederacy*. Lincoln: University of Nebraska Press, 2000.

McPherson, James M. *Battle Cry of Freedom: The Civil War Era*. New York: Oxford University Press, 1988.

McWhiney, Grady, and Perry D. Jamieson. *Attack and Die: Civil War Military Tactics and the Southern Heritage*. Tuscaloosa: University of Alabama Press, 1982.

Madden, David. *Beyond the Battlefield: The Ordinary Life and Extraordinary Times of the Civil War Soldier*. New York: Simon & Schuster, 2000.

Marszalek, John F. *Sherman: A Soldier's Passion for Order*. New York: Free Press, 1993.

Mindell, David A. *War, Technology, and Experience Aboard the USS Monitor*. Baltimore: Johns Hopkins University Press, 2000.

Morris, Roy, Jr. *Sheridan: The Life and Wars of General Phil Sheridan*. New York: Crown, 1992.

O'Brien, Sean M. *Mountain Partisans: Guerilla Warfare in the Southern Appalachians, 1861–1865*. Westport, Conn.: Praeger, 1999.

Olmstead, Edwin, Wayne Stark, and Spencer C. Tucker. *The Big Guns. Civil War Siege, Seacoast and Naval Cannon*. Alexandria Bay, N.Y.: Museum Restoration Service, 1997.

Perret, Geoffrey. *Ulysses S. Grant: Soldier and President*. New York: Random House, 1997.

Pfanz, Harry L. *Gettysburg: The Second Day*. Chapel Hill: University of North Carolina Press, 1987.

Power, J. Tracy. *Lee's Miserables: Life in the Army of Northern Virginia from the Wilderness to Appomattox*. Chapel Hill: University of North Carolina Press, 1998.

Ragan, Mark K. *Union and Confederate Submarine Warfare in the Civil War*. Mason, Iowa: Savas Publishing, 1999.

Reid, Brian H., and John Keegan. *The American Civil War and the Wars of the Industrial Revolution*. London: Cassell, 1999.

Robertson, James I., Jr. *Stonewall Jackson: The Man, the Soldier, the Legend*. New York: Macmillan, 1997.

Sears, Stephen W. *Chancellorsville*. Boston: Houghton Mifflin, 1996.

———. *George B. McClellan: The Young Napoleon*. New York: Ticknor & Fields, 1988.

———. *Landscape Turned Red: The Battle of Antietam*. New York: Ticknor & Fields, 1983.

———. *To The Gates of Richmond: The Peninsula Campaign*. New York: Ticknor & Fields, 1992.

Sherman, William T. *Memoirs of General William T. Sherman*. Reprint. New York: Penguin Books, 2000.

Silverstone, Paul H. *Civil War Navies, 1854–1883*. Annapolis, Md.: Naval Institute Press, 2001.

Simson, Jay W. *Naval Strategies of the Civil War: Confederate Innovations and Federal Opportunism*. Nashville: Cumberland House, 2001.

Starr, Stephen Z. *The Union Cavalry in the Civil War*. 3 vols. Baton Rouge: Louisiana State University Press, 1979–85.

Still, Wiulliam N. *The Confederate Navy: The Ships, Men, and Organization, 1861–1865*. Annapolis, Md.: Naval Institute Press, 1999.

———., John M. Taylor, and Norman C. Delaney. *Raiders & Blockaders: The American Civil War Afloat*. Dulles, Va.: Brasseys's, 2000.

Swanson, Clifford L. *The Sixth United States Infantry Regiment, 1855 to Reconstruction*. Jefferson, N.C.: McFarland, 2001.

Sword, Wiley. *Embrace an Angry Wind: The Confederacy's Last Hurrah, Spring Hill, Franklin, and Nashville*. New York: HarperCollins, 1992.

Symonds, Craig L. *Confederate Admiral: The Life and Wars of Franklin Buchanan*. Annapolis, Md.: Naval Institute Press, 1999.

Tanner, Robert G. *Retreat to Victory? Confederate Strategy Reconsidered*. Wilmington, Del.: Scholarly Resources, 2001.

Trudeau, Noah Andre. *Like Men of War: Black Troops in the Civil War, 1862–1865.* Boston: Little, Brown, 1998.

———. *Bloody Roads South: The Wilderness to Cold Harbor, May–June 1864.* Boston: Little, Brown, 1989.

———. *The Last Citadel: Petersburg, Virginia, June 1864–April 1865.* Boston: Little, Brown, 1991.

———. *Out of the Storm: The End of the Civil War, April–June 1865.* Boston: Little, Brown, 1994.

Tucker, Spencer C. *Andrew Foote: Civil War Admiral on Western Waters.* Annapolis, Md.: Naval Institute Press, 2000.

———. *A Short History of the Civil War at Sea.* Wilmington, Del.: Scholarly Resources, 2001.

———. *Raphael Semmes and the Alabama.* Abilene, Tex.: McWhiney Foundation Press, 1996.

Warner, Ezra J. *Generals in Gray: Lives of the Confederate Commanders.* Baton Rouge: Louisiana State University Press, 1959.

———. *Generals in Blue: Lives of the Union Commanders.* Baton Rouge: Louisiana State University Press, 1964.

Waugh, John C. *The Class of 1846: From West Point to Appomattox: Stonewall Jackson, George McClellan, and Their Brothers.* New York: Warner Books, 1994.

Weigley, Russell F. *A Great Civil War: A Military and Political History, 1861–65.* Bloomington: Indiana University Press, 2000.

Williams, David. *Johnny Reb's War: Battlefield and Homefront.* Abilene, Tex.: McWhiney Foundation Press, 2000.

Williams, Kenneth P. *Lincoln Finds a General: A Military Study of the Civil War.* New York: Macmillan, 1949–1959.

Wise, Stephen R. *Gate of Hell: Campaign for Charleston Harbor, 1863.* Columbia: University of South Carolina Press, 1994.

Wood, W. J. *Civil War Generalship: The Art of Command.* New York: Da Capo Press, 2000.

Woodworth, Steven E. *Civil War Generals in Defeat.* Lawrence: University Press of Kansas, 1999.

———. *Jefferson Davis and His Generals: The Failure of Confederate Command in the West.* Lawrence: University Press of Kansas, 1991.

Early Modern America, 1865–1914

Alshire, Peter. *The Fox and the Whirlwind: General George Crook and Geronimo.* New York: Wiley, 2001.

Ambrose, Stephen E. *Upton and the Army.* Baton Rouge: Louisiana State University Press, 1964.

Brereton, T. R. *Educating the U.S. Army: Arthur L. Wagner and Reform, 1875–1905.* Lincoln: University of Nebraska Press, 2000.

Clendenen, Clarence. *Blood on the Border: The United States Army and the Mexican Irregulars.* New York: Macmillan, 1969.

Cosmas, Graham H. *An Army for Empire: The United States Army in the Spanish-American War.* Reprint. College Station: Texas A&M University Press, 1998.

Eisenhower, John S. D. *Intervention: The United States and the Mexican Revolution, 1913–1917.* New York: W. W. Norton, 1993.

Haley, James L. *The Buffalo War: The History of the Red River Indian Uprising of 1874.* Garden City, N.Y.: Doubleday, 1976.

Hall, Linda B., and Don M. Coerver. *Revolution on the Border: The United States and Mexico, 1910–1920.* Albuquerque: University of New Mexico Press, 1988

Hutton, Paul Andrew. *Phil Sheridan and His Army.* Lincoln: University of Nebraska Press, 1985.

Jamieson, Perry D. *Crossing the Deadly Ground: United States Army Tactics, 1865–1899.* Tuscaloosa: University of Alabama Press, 1994.

Leckie, William H. *The Buffalo Soldiers: A Narrative of the Negro Cavalry in the West.* Norman: University of Oklahoma Press, 1967.

Linn, Brian M. *The Philippine War, 1899–1902.* Lawrence: University Press of Kansas, 2000.

Marolda, Edward J., ed. *Theodore Roosevelt, the U.S. Navy, and the Spanish-American War.* New York: St. Martin's Press, 2001.

O'Toole, G. J. A. *The Spanish War: An America Epic, 1898.* New York W. W. Norton, 1984.

Reckner, James R. *Teddy Roosevelt's Great White Fleet.* Annapolis, Md.: Naval Institute Press, 2001.

Smith, Angel, Davila Cox, and Emma Aurora. *The Crisis of 1898: Colonial Redistribution and Nationalist Mobilization.* New York: St. Martin's Press, 1999.

Tate, Michael L. *The Frontier Army in the Settlement of the West.* Norman: University of Oklahoma Press, 1999.

Utley, Robert M. *Cavalier in Buckskin: George Armstrong Custer and the Western Military Tradition.* Norman: University of Oklahoma Press, 1988.

———. *Frontier Regulars: The United States Army and the Indian, 1866–1891.* Reprint. Lincoln: University of Nebraska Press, 1989.

———. *The Indian Frontier of the American West, 1846–1890.* Albuquerque: University of New Mexico Press, 1984.

Wallace, Edward, and E. Adamson Hoebel. *The Comanches: Lords of the South Plains.* Norman: University of Oklahoma Press, 1952.

Wooster, Robert. *Nelson A. Miles and the Twilight of the Frontier Army.* Lincoln: University of Nebraska Press, 1995.

———. *The Military and United States Indian Policy, 1865–1903.* New Haven: Yale University Press, 1988.

Worcester, Donald E. *The Apaches: Eagles of the Southwest.* Norman: University of Oklahoma Press, 1979.

World War I, 1914–1918

Coffman, Edward M. *The War to End All Wars: The American Military Experience in World War I.* Madison: University of Wisconsin Press, 1986.

Freidel, Frank. *Over There: The Story of America's First Great Overseas Crusade.* Revised edition. New York: McGraw-Hill, 1990.

Feuer, A. B. *The U.S. Navy in World War I: Combat at Sea and in the Air.* Westport, Conn.: Praeger, 1999.

Grotelueschen, Mark E. *Doctrine Under Trial: American Artillery Employment in World War I.* Westport, Conn.: Greenwood Press, 2001.

Johnson, Douglas V., and Rolfe L. Hillman. *Soissons, 1918.* College Station: Texas A&M University Press, 1999.

Johnson, Herbert A. *Wingless Eagles: U.S. Army Aviation Through World War I.* Chapel Hill: University of North Carolina Press, 2001.

Suskind, Richard. *The Battle of Belleau Wood: The Marines Stand Fast.* London: Macmillan, 1969.

Tuchman, Barbara W. *The Zimmerman Telegram.* New York: Viking, 1965.

Tucker, Spencer C. *The Great War, 1914–18.* Bloomington: Indiana University Press, 1998.

Vandiver, Frank E. *Black Jack: The Life and Times of John J. Pershing.* 2 vols. College Station: Texas A&M University Press, 1977.

Weintraub, Stanley. *A Stillness Heard Round the World: The End of the Great War: November 1918.* New York: E. P. Dutton, 1985.

Interwar Years and World War II, 1918–1945

Ambrose, Stephen E. *D-Day, June 6, 1944: The Climactic Battle of World War II.* New York: Simon & Schuster, 1994.

———. *Eisenhower: Soldier, General of the Army, President-Elect, 1890–1952.* New York: Simon & Schuster, 1983.

Balkoski, Joseph. *Beyond the Beachhead: The 29th Infantry Division in Normandy.* Mechanicsburg, Pa.: Stackpole Books, 1999.

Beloote, James H., and William M. Belotte. *Titans of the Seas: The Development and Operations of Japanese and American Carrier Task Forces during World War II.* New York: Harper & Row, 1975.

Bergerud, Eric M. *Fire in the Sky: The Air War in the South Pacific.* Boulder, Colo.: Western Press, 2000.

Bickel, Keith B. *Mars Learning: The Marine Corps Development of Small Wars Doctrine, 1915–1940.* Boulder, Colo.: Westview Press, 2001.

Blair, Clay. *Ridgway's Paratroopers: The American Airborne in World War II.* New York: Dial Press, 1985.

———. *Silent Victory: U.S. Submarine War Against Japan.* 2 vols. New York: Lippincott, 1975.

Blumenson, Martin. *Kasserine Pass: Rommel's Bloody Climactic Battle for Tunisia.* New York: Cooper Square Press, 2000.

———, ed. *The Patton Papers: 1940–1945.* Revised edition. Boston: Houghton Mifflin, 1974.

Bradley, Omar N. *A Soldier's Story.* New York: Holt, 1951.

Chamberlain, Peter, and Chris Ellis. *British and American Tanks of World War Two: The Complete Illustrated History of British, American, and Commonwealth Tanks, 1939–45.* London: Cassell, 2000.

Clausen, Henry C. *Pearl Harbor: Final Judgement.* New York: Da Capo Press, 2001.

Connaughton, Richard M. *MacArthur and Defeat in the Philippines.* New York: Overlook Press, 2001.

Cooper, Belton Y. *Death Traps: The Survival of an American Armored Division in World War II.* Novato, Calif.: Presidio Press, 1998.

Crave, Wesley F., and James L. Cate. *Army Air Forces in World War II.* Chicago: University of Chicago Press, 1948.

Cressman, Robert. *The Official Chronology of the U.S. Navy in World War II.* Annapolis, Md.: Naval Institute Press, 2000.

Cutler, Thomas J. *The Battle of Leyte Gulf, 23–26 October 1944.* New York: HarperCollins Publishers, 1994.

D'Este, Carlo. *Fatal Decision: Anzio and the Battle for Rome.* New York: HarperCollins, 1991.

———. *Patton: A Genius for War.* New York: HarperCollins, 1995.

Donald, David. *American Warplanes of World War II.* New York: Barnes & Noble, 1995.

Eisenhower, Dwight D. *Crusade in Europe.* Garden City, N.Y.: Doubleday, 1948.

Finlayson, Kenneth. *An Uncertain Trumpet: The Evolution of U.S. Army Infantry Doctrine, 1919–1941.* Westport, Conn.: Greenwood Press, 2001.

Ford, Daniel. *Flying Tigers: Claire Chennault and the American Volunteer Group.* Washington, D.C.: Smithsonian Institution Press, 1991.

Horman, Lynn M., and Thomas Reilly. *Black Knights: The Story of the Tuskegee Airmen.* Gretna, La.: Pelican, 2001.

Huie, William B. *From Omaha to Okinawa: The Story of the Seabees.* Annapolis, Md.: Naval Institute Press, 1999.

Jackson, Kathi. *They Called Them Angels: American Military Nurses of World War II.* Westport, Conn.: Praeger, 2000.

Jones, Ken. *Admiral Arleigh (31-Knot) Burke: The Story of a Fighting Sailor.* Annapolis, Md.: Naval Institute Press, 2001.

Kilvert-Jones, Tim. *Omaha Beach: V Corps Battle for the Beachhead.* Conshohocken, Pa.: Combined Publishing, 1999.

Knox, Donald. *Death March: The Survivors of Bataan.* New York: Harcourt Brace Jovanovich, 1981.

Komatsu, Keiichiro. *Origins of the Pacific War and the Importance of "Magic."* New York: St. Martin's Press, 1999.

Linn, Brian M. *Guardians of Empire: The U.S. Army and the Pacific, 1902–1940.* Chapel Hill: University of North Carolina Press, 1997.

Lisio, Donald J. *The President and Protest: Hoover, MacArthur, and the Bonus Riot.* 2d ed. New York: Fordham University Press, 1994.

Loxton, Bruce, with Chris Coulthard-Clark. *The Shame of Savo: Anatomy of a Naval Disaster.* Annapolis, Md.: Naval Institute Press, 1994.

MacDonald, Charles B. *A Time for Trumpets: The Untold Story of the Battle of the Bulge.* New York: William Morrow, 1985.

———. *The Mighty Endeavor: American Armed Forces in the European Theater in World War II.* New York: Oxford University Press, 1969.

Monahan, Evelyn. *All This Hell: U.S. Nurses Imprisoned by the Japanese.* Lexington: University Press of Kentucky, 2000.

Morison, Samuel Eliot. *History of United States Naval Operations in World War II.* 15 vols. Boston: Little, Brown, 1947–60.

Moy, Timothy. *War Machines: Transforming Technologies in the U.S. Military, 1920–1940.* College Station: Texas A&M University Press, 2001.

Odom, William O. *After the Trenches: The Transformation of U.S. Army Doctrine, 1918–1939.* College Station: Texas A&M University Press, 1999.

Perret, Geoffrey. *There's a War to Be Won: The United States Army in World War II.* New York: Random House, 1991.

Pogue, Forrest C. *George C. Marshall.* 4 vols. New York: Viking, 1963–87.

Prange, Gordon W. *At Dawn We Slept: The Untold Story of Pearl Harbor.* New York: McGraw Hill, 1981.

Price, Christopher. *Britain, America, and Rearmament in the 1930s.* New York: Palgrave, 2001.

Raines, Edgar. *Eyes of Artillery: The Origins of Modern U.S. Army Aviation in World War II.* Washington, D.C.: Center of Military History, 2000.

Rickard, John N. *Patton at Bay: The Lorraine Campaign, September to December, 1944.* Westport, Conn.: Praeger, 1999.

Ross, Steven T. *U.S. War Plans, 1938–1945.* Boulder, Colo.: Lynne Rienner Publishers, 2001.

Sides, Hampton. *Ghost Soldiers: The Forgotten Epic Story of World War II's Most Dramatic Mission.* New York: Random House, 2001.

Spector, Ronald H. *Eagle Against the Sun: The American War with Japan.* New York: Free Press, 1985.

Stoler, Mark A. *Allies and Adversaries. The Joint Chiefs of Staff, the Grand Alliance, and U.S. Strategy in World War II.* Chapel Hill: University of North Carolina Press, 2000.

Tuchman, Barbara W. *Stilwell and the American Experience in China: 1911–45.* New York: Macmillan, 1970.

Walker, J. Samuel. *Prompt & Utter Destruction: Truman and the Use of Atomic Bombs Against Japan.* Chapel Hill: University of North Carolina Press, 1997.

Weigley, Russell F. *Eisenhower's Lieutenants: The Campaign in France and Germany, 1944–1945.* Bloomington: Indiana University Press, 1981.

Willmott, H. P. *The Barrier and the Javelin: Japanese and Allied Pacific Strategies, February to June 1942.* Annapolis, Md.: Naval Institute Press, 1983.

Wilt, Alan F. *The French Riviera Campaign of August 1944.* Carbondale: Southern Illinois University Press, 1981.

Modern America, 1945–present

Bacevich, A. J., and Eliot A. Cohen. *War Over Kosovo: Politics and Strategy in a Global Age.* New York: Columbia University Press, 2001.

Blair, Clay. *The Forgotten War: America in Korea, 1950–1953.* New York: Times Books, 1987.

Blight, James, and Peter Kornbluh, eds. *Politics of Illusion: The Bay of Pigs Invasion Reexamined.* Boulder, Colo.: Lynne Rienner Publishers, 1998.

Borowski, Harry R. *A Hollow Threat: Strategic Air Power and Containment Before Korea.* Westport, Conn.: Greenwood Press, 1982.

Bowie, Robert R. *Waging Peace: How Eisenhower Shaped an Enduring Cold War Strategy.* New York: Oxford University Press, 2000.

Bowman, Martin W. *U.S. Naval Aviation: 1946–1999.* Stroud, England: Sutton, 1999.

———. *Shades of Blue: U.S. Naval Air Power Since 1941.* Shrewsbury, England: Airlife, 1999.

Burrows, William E. *By Any Means Necessary: America's Secret Air War in the Cold War.* New York: Farrar, Straus & Giroux, 2001.

Caspar, Lawrence E. *Falcon Brigade: Combat and Command in Somalia and Haiti.* Boulder, Colo.: Lynne Rienner Publishers, 2001.

Catchpole, Brian. *The Korean War.* New York: Carroll & Graff, 2000.

Cowart, Glen C. *Miracle in Korea: The Evacuation of X Corps from the Hungnam Beachhead.* Columbia: University of South Carolina Press, 1992.

Crane, Conrad C. *American Air Power Strategy in Korea, 1950–1953.* Lawrence: University Press of Kansas, 2000.

Craven, John P. *The Silent War: The Cold War Beneath the Sea.* New York: Simon & Schuster, 2001.

Cutler, Thomas J. *Brown Water, Black Berets: Coastal and Riverine Warfare in Vietnam.* Annapolis, Md.: Naval Institute Press, 2000.

Dunstan, Simon. *Vietnam Tracks: Armor in Battle, 1945–1975.* Novato, Calif.: Presidio Press, 1982.

Freedman, Lawrence. *Kennedy's Wars: Berlin, Cuba, Laos, and Vietnam.* New York: Oxford University Press, 2000.

Friedman, Norman. *The Fifty-Year War: Conflict and Strategy in the Cold War.* Annapolis, Md.: Naval Institute Press, 1999.

Grathwol, Robert P. *Berlin and the American Military: A Cold War Chronicle.* New York: New York University Press, 1999.

Haydock, Michael D. *City Under Siege: The Berlin Blockade and Airlift, 1948–1949.* New York: Brassey's, 1999.

Heefner, Wilson A. *Patton's Bulldog: The Life and Service of General Walton H. Walker.* Shippensburg, Pa.: White Mane, 2001.

Hess, Gary R. *Presidential Decisions for War: Korea, Vietnam, and the Persian Gulf.* Baltimore: Johns Hopkins University Press, 2001.

Hofmann, George F., and Donn A. Starry. *Camp Colt to Desert Storm: The History of U.S. Armored Forces.* Lexington: University Press of Kentucky, 1999.

Hogan, David W. *Rangers or Elite Infantry? The Changing Role of U.S. Army Rangers from Dieppe to Grenada.* Wesport, Conn.: Greenwood Press, 1992.

Hoopes, Townsend. *Driven Patriot: The Life and Times of James Forrestal.* Annapolis, Md.: Naval Institute Press, 2000.

Joes, Anthony J. *The War for South Vietnam, 1954–1973.* Westport, Conn.: Greenwood Press, 2001.

Larzelere, Alex. *The Coast Guard at War: Vietnam 1965–1975.* Annapolis, Md.: Naval Institute Press, 1997.

Mardola, Edward J., and Robert J. Schneller. *Shield and Sword: The United States Navy and the Persian Gulf War.* Annapolis, Md.: Naval Institute Press, 2001.

Mitchell, George C. *Matthew B. Ridgway: Soldier, Statesman, Scholar, Citizen.* Pittsburgh: Cathedral, 1999.

Moore, Harold G., and Joseph L. Galloway. *We Were Soldiers Once . . . and Young: Ia Drang—The Battle That Changed the War in Vietnam.* New York: Random House, 1992.

Muir, Malcolm, Jr. *Black Shoes and Blue Water: Surface Warfare in the United States Navy, 1945–1975.* Washington, D.C.: Department of the Navy, Naval Historical Center, 1996.

Neufeld, Jacob. *The Development of Ballistic Missiles in the United States Air Force, 1945–1960.* Washington, D.C.: Office of Air Force History, 1990.

Norris, John, and William Fowler. *NBC: Nuclear, Biological and Chemical Warfare on the Modern Battlefield.* New York: Brassey's, 1998.

Parrish, Thomas. *Berlin in the Balance, 1945–1949: The Blockade, the Airlift, the First Major Battle of the Cold War.* Reading, Mass.: Perseus Books, 1999.

Peebles, Curtis. *Shadow Flights: America's Secret Air War Against the Soviet Union.* Novato, Calif.: Presidio Press, 2000.

Pokrant, Martin. *Desert Storm at Sea: What the Navy Really Did.* Westport, Conn.: Greenwood Press, 1999.

———. *Desert Shield at Sea: What the Navy Really Did.* Westport, Conn.: Greenwood Press, 1999.

Pry, Peter V. *War Scare: Russia and America on the Nuclear Brink.* Westport, Conn.: Praeger, 1999.

Sandars, C. T. *America's Overseas Garrisons: The Leasehold Empire.* New York: Oxford University Press, 2000.

Sandler, Stanley. *The Korean War: No Victors, No Vanquished.* Lexington: University Press of Kentucky, 1999.

Sherwood, John D. *Fast Movers: America's Jet Pilots and the Vietnam Experience.* New York: Free Press, 2000.

Snead, David L. *The Gaither Committee, Eisenhower, and the Cold War.* Columbus: Ohio State University Press, 1999.

Sorley, Lewis. *A Better War: The Unexamined Victories and Final Tragedy of America's Last Years in Vietnam.* New York: Harcourt Brace, 1999.

Spector, Ronald H. *The U.S. Army in Vietnam: Advice and Support, The Early Years, 1941–1960.* Washington, D.C.: U.S. Army Center of Military History, 1983.

Stanton, Shelby L. *America's Tenth Legion: X Corps in Korea, 1950.* Novato, Calif.: Presidio Press, 1989.

Tucker, Spencer C. *Vietnam.* Lexington: University Press of Kentucky, 1999.

Westmoreland, William. *A Soldier Reports.* Graden City, N.Y.: Doubleday, 1976.

Miscellaneous

Alexander, Joseph H. *The Battle History of the U.S. Marines: A Fellowship of Valor.* New York: HarperPerennial, 1999.

Ambrose, Stephen E. *Duty, Honor, Country: A History of West Point.* Reprint. Baltimore: Johns Hopkins University Press, 1999.

Baer, George W. *One Hundred Years of Sea Power: The U.S. Navy, 1890–1990.* Stanford, Calif.: Stanford University Press, 1994.

Bell, William G. *Commanding Generals and Chiefs of Staff, 1775–1995: Portraits and Biographical Sketches of the United States Army's Senior Officer.* Washington, D.C.: Center of Military History, U.S. Army, 1999.

Birkheimer, William E. *Historical Sketch of the Organization, Administration, Matériel, and Tactics of The Artillery, United States Army.* Washington, D.C.: Chapman, 1884.

Brooks, Victor. *How America Fought Its Wars: Military Strategy from the American Revolution to the Civil War.* Conshohocken, Pa.: Combined Publishing, 1999.

Brown, Charles H. *Dark Sky, Black Sea: Aircraft Carrier Night and All-Weather Operations.* Annapolis, Md.: Naval Institute Press, 1999.

Browning, Robert S. III. *Two If by Sea: The Development of American Coastal Defense Policy.* Westport, Conn.: Greenwood Press, 1983.

Buckley, Gail L. *American Patriots: The Story of Blacks in the Military from the Revolution to Desert Storm.* New York: Random House, 2001.

Budd, Richard M. *Serving Two Masters: The Development of American Military Chaplaincy, 1860–1920.* Lincoln: University of Nebraska Press, 2001.

Chapelle, Howard I. *The History of the American Sailing Navy. The Ships and Their Development.* New York: W. W. Norton, 1949.

Clancy, Tom. *Special Forces: A Guided Tour of U.S. Army Special Forces.* New York: Berkeley Books, 2001.

Clark, George B. *Treading Softly: U.S. Marines in China, 1819–1949.* Westport, Conn.: Praeger, 2001.

Dastrup, Boyd L. *The Field Artillery: History and Sourcebook.* Westport, Conn.: Greenwood, 1994.

Dean, Francis H. *America's Navy and Marine Corps Airplanes, 1918 to the Present.* Atglen, Pa.: Schiffer, 1999.

Ebbert, Jean, and Marie-Beth Hall. *Crossed Currents: Navy Women in a Century of Change.* 3d ed. Washington, D.C.: Brassey's, 1999.

Edgerton, Robert B. *Hidden Heroism: Black Soldiers in America's Wars.* Boulder, Colo.: Westview Press, 2001.

Ellis, John. *The Social History of the Machine Gun.* New York: Pantheon, 1975.

Estes, Kenneth W. *Marines Under Armor: The Marine Corps and the Armored Fighting Vehicle, 1916–2000.* Annapolis, Md.: Naval Institute Press, 2000.

Firebaugh, Millard S. *Naval Engineering and American Sea Power.* Dubuque, Iowa: Kendall/Hunt, 2000.

Futrell, Robert Frank. *Ideas, Concepts, Doctrine: Basic Thinking in the United States Air Force, 1907–1984.* 2 vols. Maxwell AFB, Ala.: Air University Press, 1989.

Garnett, Griffin T. *The Sandscrapers: A Forgotten Navy.* Bryn Mawr, Pa.: Buy Books, 1999.

Goodpseed, Michael. *When Reason Fails: Portraits of Armies at War: America, Britain, Israel, and the Future.* Westport, Conn.: Praeger, 2001.

Hackemer, Kurt. *The U.S. Navy and the Origins of the Military-Industrial Complex, 1847–1883.* Annapolis, Md.: Naval Institute Press, 2001.

Holm, Jeanne. *Women in the Military.* 2d ed. Novato, Calif.: Presidio Press, 1992.

Joes, Anthony J. *America and Guerilla War.* Lexington: University Press of Kentucky, 2000.

Johnson, Robert Erwin. *Guardians of the Sea: History of the United States Coast Guard 1915 to the Present.* Annapolis, Md.: Naval Institute Press, 1987.

La Feber, Walter. *Inevitable Revolutions: The United States in Central America.* 2d ed. New York: W. W. Norton, 1993.

Lambeth, Benjamin S. *The Transformation of American Air Power.* Ithaca, N.Y.: Cornell University Press, 2000.

Landau, Alan M., and Terry Griswold. *U.S. Special Forces.* Ann Arbor, Mich.: Lowe & B. Hould, 1999.

Lanning, Michael L. *The African-American Soldier: From Crispus Attucks to Colin Powell.* Secaucus, N.J.: Carol Publishing, 1999.

Lewis, Emanuel Raymond. *Seacoast Fortifications of the United States: An Introductory History.* Washington, D.C.: Smithsonian Institution Press, 1970.

Lurie, Jonathan. *Military Justice in America: The U.S. Court of Appeals for the Armed Forces, 1775–1980.* Lawrence: University Press of Kansas, 2001.

Maihafer, Harry J. *Brave Decisions: Fifteen Profiles in Courage and Character from American Military History.* Dulles, Va.: Brassey's, 1999.

Millett, Allan R. *Semper Fidelis: The History of the United States Marine Corps.* New York: Free Press, 1980.

Musicant, Ivan. *The Banana Wars: A History of United States Military Intervention in Latin America from the Spanish-American War to the Invasion of Panama.* New York: Macmillan, 1990.

Neiberg, Michael S. *Making Citizen Soldiers: ROTC and the Ideology of American Military Service.* Boston: Harvard University Press, 1999.

Packard, Wyman H. *A Century of U.S. Naval Intelligence.* Washington, D.C.: Department of the Navy, 1996.

Peebles, Curtis. *Dark Eagles: A History of U.S. "Black" Aircraft Programs.* Novato, Calif.: Presidio, 1999.

Polmar, Norman. *The Naval Institute Guide to the Ships and Aircraft of the U.S. Fleet.* Annapolis, Md.: Naval Institute Press, 2001.

Roscoe, Theodore. *On the Seas and in the Skies: A History of the U.S. Navy's Air Power.* New York: Hawthorn Books, 1970.

Sarnecky, Mary T. *A History of the U.S. Army Nurse Corps.* Philadelphia: University of Pennsylvania Press, 1999.

Schroder, Walter K. *Davisville and the Seabees.* Charleston, S.C.: Arcadia, 1999.

Stiehm, Judith Hicks. *Arms and the Enlisted Women.* Philadelphia: Temple University Press, 1989.

Stone, John. *The Tank Debate: Armour and the Anglo-American Military Tradition.* Abington, England: Marston, 2000.

Reference Works and Atlases

Beede, Benjamin R. *The War of 1898 and U.S. Interventions, 1898–1934: An Encyclopedia.* New York: Garland, 1994.

Blanco, Richard L., ed. *The American Revolution, 1775–1783: An Encyclopedia.* 2 vols. New York: Garland, 1993.

Boatner, Mark M. III. *The Civil War Dictionary.* Revised edition. New York: David McKay, 1988.

———. *The Biographical Dictionary of World War II.* Novato, Calif.: Presidio Press, 1996.

Chambers, John W., and Fred Anderson, eds. *The Oxford Companion to American Military History.* New York: Oxford University Press, 1999.

Davis, William C. *The Illustrated Directory of the Civil War: The Soldiers, Generals, Weapons, and Battles of the Civil War.* London: Salamander, 2001.

DeRouen, Karl R. *Historical Encyclopedia of U.S. Presidential Use of Force, 1789–2000.* Westport, Conn.: Greenwood Press, 2001.

Frazier, Donald S., ed. *The United States and Mexico at War: Nineteenth-Century Expansionism and Conflict.* New York: Macmillan Reference, 1998.

Fredriksen, John C. *Warbirds: An Illustrated Guide to U.S. Military Aircraft, 1915–2001.* Santa Barbara, Calif.: ABC-Clio, 1999.

———. *American Military Leaders: From Colonial Times to the Present.* 2 vols. Santa Barbara, Calif.: ABC-Clio, 1999.

———. *America's Military Adversaries: From Colonial Times to the Present.* Santa Barbara, Calif.: ABC-Clio, 2001.

Gallay, Alan, ed. *Colonial Wars of North America, 1512–1763: An Encyclopedia.* New York: Garland, 1996.

Heidler, David S., and Jeanne T. Heidler, eds. *Encyclopedia of the War of 1812.* Santa Barbara, Calif.: ABC-Clio, 1997.

———., eds. *Encyclopedia of the Civil War.* 5 vols. Santa Barbara, Calif.: ABC-Clio, 2000.

Holsinger, M. Paul. *War and American Popular Culture: A Historical Encyclopedia.* Westport, Conn.: Greenwood Press, 1999.

Silverstone, Paul H. *The Sailing Navy, 1775–1854.* Annapolis, Md.: Naval Institute Press, 2001.

Symonds, Craig L. *A Battlefield Atlas of the American Revolution.* Annapolis, Md.: Nautical and Aviation Publishing, 1986.

———. *A Battlefield Atlas of the Civil War.* Annapolis, Md.: Nautical and Aviation Publishing, 1983.

———. *Historical Atlas of the U.S. Navy.* Annapolis, Md.: Naval Institute Press, 1995.

Tucker, Spencer C., ed. *Encyclopedia of the Korean War.* 3 vols. Denver: ABC-Clio, 2000.

———., ed. *Encyclopedia of the Vietnam War.* 3 vols. Santa Barbara, Calif.: ABC-Clio, 1998.

United States Military Academy, Department of Military Art and Engineering. *The West Point Atlas of American Wars.* 2 vols. New York: Holt, 1995.

Vinson, Anne Cipriano, ed. *The United States in the First World War: An Encyclopedia.* New York: Garland, 1995.

Index

★ ————————————————————————————

Note: Page numbers in **boldface** indicate main topics; *italic* page numbers denote illustrations.